CliffsNotes®
ASVAB with CD-ROM

CliffsNotes®

ASVAB with CD-ROM

by
Fred N. Grayson, M.A., 1ˢᵗ Lt., USAF (Ret'd)

Contributing Authors

M. Mazen Al-khatib, Ph.D.

Christopher Bender, Ph.D.

Elaine Bender, M.A.

Gordon Chenery, M.A.

Ransford Clarke, M.S.

Kevin DiBitetto

Lisa Gay, M.A.

William Gilmore

Gordon Gonyea, M.A.

Tracy Halward, Ph.D.

Michael Hamid, Ph.D.

Sasheena Kurfman

Christi Heuer, M.S.

Seema Kurup, M.A.

David Levy, M.A.

Gabriel Lombardi, Ph.D.

Rob Mohr, Ph.D.

Sulev Oun

Jo Palmore, M.S.

Jerry Truglia

Christopher A. Taylor, M.A.T.

Mark Weinfeld, M.S.

Douglas Weisman, M.Ed.

WILEY

Wiley Publishing, Inc.

About the Author

As an independent book developer and publisher, Fred N. Grayson has published hundreds of books in conjunction with many major publishers. In addition, he has also written and/or coauthored dozens of books in the test preparation field.

Editorial

Acquisitions Editor: Greg Tubach

Project Editor: Suzanne Snyder

Copy Editor: Mike Thomas

Technical Editors: Karl Huehne, SFC Thomas Johnson, Loren Luedemann, Steve Math, Tom Page, Barbara Swovelin

Composition

Proofreader: Melissa D. Buddendeck

Wiley Publishing, Inc. Composition Services

CliffsNotes® ASVAB with CD-ROM

Published by:
Wiley Publishing, Inc.
111 River Street
Hoboken, NJ 07030-5774
www.wiley.com

Copyright © 2010 Wiley Publishing, Inc.

Published by Wiley, Hoboken, NJ
Published simultaneously in Canada

Library of Congress Cataloging-in-Publication data is available from the publisher upon request.

ISBN: 978-0-470-56683-1 (pbk)
ISBN: 978-0-470-63870-5 (ebk)

Printed in the United States of America
10 9 8 7 6 5 4 3 2 1

Table of Contents

PART II: SUBJECT AREA REVIEW

PART III: FOUR FULL-LENGTH PRACTICE TESTS

PART IV: MILITARY CAREER OPPORTUNITIES

Study Guide Checklist

❏ 1. Read "Introduction to the ASVAB," starting on page 1.

❏ 2. Pay particular attention to the format of the test, starting on page 1.

❏ 3. Take the Diagnostic Test, pages 13–32. Follow the time limits, and attempt to simulate actual test-taking conditions.

❏ 4. Check your answers, using the Diagnostic Test answer key, pages 33–34.

❏ 5. Examine the explanation for any questions that you missed or that you were unsure of.

❏ 6. Carefully read Part II, Subject Area Review, pages 45–262. Make sure to do the Practice Questions that end each review section.

❏ 7. Take the first full-length practice test, pages 265–294. Follow the time limits, and attempt to simulate actual test-taking conditions.

❏ 8. Check your answers, using the answer key, pages 295–297.

❏ 9. Examine the explanations for any questions that you missed or that you were unsure of.

❏ 10. Either reread the review sections for any areas where you are struggling or proceed to take the other three practice tests.

Introduction to the ASVAB

If you're reading this book, it means that you've already decided to consider taking the ASVAB (Armed Services Vocational Aptitude Battery) to qualify for the military. The ASVAB is an exam that presents a series of individual tests to measure various academic and vocational skills.

Forms and Format of the ASVAB

ASVAB Subtests

There are three major versions of the test. Two of them are "pencil-and-paper" tests and the third is the Computer Adaptive Test (CAT). Briefly, the pencil-and-paper tests have nine components and the CAT has ten. These will be covered later in this section.

The first version is the *student version,* and is given once or twice a year to high school students who are planning to take the exam sometime in their junior or senior year. It may also be known as the *institutional version*. This test can be used to determine your aptitude for both military and civilian jobs, and your guidance counselor can help you evaluate the results.

A second form, known as the *production version,* is for those enlisting directly into the service. This is normally administered by the military, and is used to determine which jobs would be best for you. It is given at a Military Entrance Processing Station (MEPS). You may take either the pencil-and-paper version, or the computerized version (CAT ASVAB). All branches of the military use this exam.

About the CAT ASVAB

CAT stands for *computer adaptive test* and means that the computer adapts its questions based on your answers. The first question you will get will be of medium difficulty. If you answer it correctly, the next question you get will be slightly more difficult. If you answer it incorrectly, the next question will be somewhat easier, and so on. The key to scoring well on the CAT ASVAB is to *focus your efforts on the earlier questions*. The better you do in the beginning, the better you will do overall because the final score is normally based on both the number of correct answers and the level of difficulty.

About the AFQT

There is a shortened version of the ASVAB, known as the AFQT, or Armed Forces Qualifying Test. This is not a separate test, but rather a score based on a combination of both your verbal and your mathematics scores (Arithmetic Reasoning, Word Knowledge, Paragraph Comprehension, and Mathematics Knowledge). Its purpose is to determine whether you can qualify to enlist in any of the different branches of the military. The score for this section is a percentile. Thus, if you get an 85 on this part of the test, it means you've scored higher than 85 percent of the applicants who have taken this test.

Although the AFQT is based on four subjects, the two Verbal subtest scores are counted twice—a combination of your Word Knowledge and Paragraph Comprehension scores—and then added to the Arithmetic and Mathematics scores. This results in your *raw* score for the test. The computers then convert this raw score into your percentile score.

Why is the AFQT so important? You must score at least 31 to be eligible to enlist in the Army, and achieve higher scores for enlistment in the other branches. The chart below shows what scores you need.

Service Branch	Required AFQT Score (with H.S. Diploma)	Required AFQT Score (without H.S. Diploma)
Army	31	31
Navy	35	50
Marines	32	50
Air Force	35	65
Coast Guard	35	50

Specifics Regarding the Test Versions

Most people entering the military take the CAT ASVAB, rather than the Production version. Below is the breakdown of the exam. There are ten subtests, because on this version of the exam, Auto Information and Shop Information are broken into two separate subtests.

Subtests	# Questions	Minutes	Description
General Science	16	8	Measures your knowledge of Life Science, Earth and Space Science, and Physical Science.
Arithmetic Reasoning	16	39	Measures your ability to solve basic mathematics.
Word Knowledge	16	8	Measures your ability to understand the meaning of words through synonyms.
Paragraph Comprehension	11	22	Measures your ability to obtain information from written materials.
Mathematics Knowledge	16	18	Measures your knowledge of mathematics concepts and applications.
Electronics Information	16	8	Measures your knowledge of electrical current, circuits, devices, and electronic systems.
Auto Information	11	6	Measures your knowledge of automotive maintenance and repair.
Shop Information	11	5	Measures your knowledge of tools as well as wood and metal shop practices.
Mechanical Comprehension	16	20	Measures your knowledge of the principles of mechanical devices, structural support, and properties of materials.
Assembling Objects	16	12	Measures your spatial and problem-solving abilities.
TOTAL	145	146	

The second version of the military-administered test is the *production test*—the pencil-and-paper exam. It takes about 3½ hours and contains nine subtests (combining Auto Information and Shop Information). The advantage of this version is that you can change your answers. Merely erase what you've indicated on the answer sheet, and make the change. Your score is based on the number of *correct* answers, so it pays to guess if you don't know the answer.

Subtests	# Questions	Minutes
General Science	25	11
Arithmetic Reasoning	30	36
Word Knowledge	35	11
Paragraph Comprehension	15	13
Mathematics Knowledge	25	24
Electronics Information	20	9
Auto & Shop Information	25	11
Mechanical Comprehension	25	19
Assembling Objects	25	15
TOTAL	225	149

The *student version* is also a paper-and-pencil test and is approximately three hours long. It consists of eight subtests. Assembling Objects is *not* in this version. It also combines both Auto and Shop Information.

Subtests	# Questions	Minutes
General Science	25	11
Arithmetic Reasoning	30	36
Word Knowledge	35	11
Paragraph Comprehension	15	13
Mathematics Knowledge	25	24
Electronics Information	20	9
Auto & Shop Information	25	11
Mechanical Comprehension	25	19
TOTAL	200	134

Finally, the AFQT consists of the four subtests discussed earlier. Remember that on this version, both the Word Knowledge and Paragraph Comprehension scores are counted twice. It pays to spend a little extra time reviewing these topics.

Subtests	# Questions	Minutes
Arithmetic Reasoning	30	36
Word Knowledge	35	11
Paragraph Comprehension	15	13
Mathematics Knowledge	25	24
TOTAL	105	84

Taking the Test

In this book, you will be able to practice with questions that replicate the types of questions that you will find on the exam. There are several test-taking techniques that are important if you are to score as high as possible on this test.

Guess the Correct Answer

Should you guess? Absolutely! The ASVAB is a multiple-choice test, and each section presents four answer choices. Because there is no penalty for incorrect answers on this test, it is to your advantage to guess if you don't know the answer.

Understand Multiple-Choice Questions

Because the ASVAB is made up of multiple-choice questions and each question has four choices, you must understand that to begin with you have a 25 percent chance of guessing correctly, merely by closing your eyes and selecting an answer. However, if you understand how multiple-choice questions are constructed, it will be somewhat easier to approach these questions. For each question, *there is only one correct answer.* The other three choices are incorrect.

There are levels of incorrectness. Some choices are more wrong than others. In test-development language, these incorrect answers are called *distractors* because they distract you from the correct answer. You may find one choice that is almost correct, but not quite right. Another choice may be completely incorrect. And the third choice may be almost right, almost wrong, or totally incorrect.

If you think you know the correct answer without even looking at the other choices, you're probably right. Most studies have shown that your first instinct is usually correct. Those who do poorly on multiple-choice tests are those who overanalyze the question. They think they know the answer, but then start to question their choice.

For example, if you were asked the following question, what would you select?

The Washington Monument is located in

- **A.** the state of Washington.
- **B.** New York City.
- **C.** Washington, D.C.
- **D.** Chicago.

The correct choice would be **C**, Washington, D.C. However, the overthinker starts to get concerned and thinks, "This question is too easy. I wonder if it's asking about some other Washington Monument—maybe there's another one in Washington state."

Now, this is a very simplistic example, but it is actually what happens to you if you analyze a question too much. Read the question for what it is. The questions are not tricky. The trick is in choosing the answers.

Because you don't lose any points for guessing, understanding how to guess and improve your odds is helpful. The multiple-choice questions on this test have four choices, so your odds are 1 out of 4 that you can pick correctly. To put it another way, you have a 25 percent chance of guessing correctly.

These aren't great odds, so you have to find a way to increase them. To do so, you use the process of elimination. Start by eliminating any answers that you know are completely incorrect. In the earlier question, you might be reasonably sure that the Washington Monument isn't located in Chicago, so you can eliminate choice **D**. Now you have to select the correct answer out of only three choices—1 out of 3, or 33 percent. You've just increased your odds from 25 percent to 33 percent.

How do you get to the next level? Suppose that you know that the Washington Monument is on the East Coast. You can eliminate Washington state. You only have two choices—1 out of 2, 50 percent. The odds are getting better. You may be confused as to whether the Washington Monument is in New York City or Washington, D.C., but you can take a guess, and you have a reasonable chance of guessing correctly. Of course, if you knew the answer immediately, you got it right—and that's 100 percent.

How can you use this technique to increase your score on the entire test? For example, there are 225 questions on the pencil/paper ASVAB. If you know the answers to 150 questions, you've already reached a score of 66 percent. That leaves only 100 questions for which you don't know the answers immediately. It is important, however, that you answer all of the questions on the test, and now you can make educated guesses. If you can increase your odds to 50 percent on each of the questions you're not sure about, you've now answered another 50 questions correctly—a total of 185 out of 225 questions—a score of 82 percent. Not bad.

Therefore, it makes sense to guess. Whether it's an educated guess or just a blind guess, you increase your odds of improving your score on every question.

Examples of Questions

This book goes into detail in other sections, but here are the types of questions you will encounter on the actual exam. See how you do on them.

Circle the letter of the answer choice that best answers the question.

General Science

1. An eclipse of the sun throws the shadow of the

   A. moon on the sun.
   B. moon on the Earth.
   C. Earth on the sun.
   D. Earth on the moon.

Arithmetic Reasoning

2. How many 36-passenger buses will it take to carry 144 people?

   A. 3
   B. 4
   C. 5
   D. 6

Word Knowledge

3. The wind is **variable** today.

   A. mild
   B. steady
   C. shifting
   D. chilling

Paragraph Comprehension

4. In certain areas, water is so scarce that every attempt is made to conserve it. For instance, on one oasis in the Sahara Desert, the amount of water necessary for each date palm tree has been carefully determined.

   How much water should each tree be given?

   A. no water at all
   B. exactly the amount required
   C. water on alternate days
   D. water only if it is healthy

Auto and Shop Information

5. A car uses too much oil when which of the following parts are worn?

   A. pistons
   B. piston rings
   C. main bearings
   D. connecting rods

Mathematics Knowledge

6. If $x + 6 = 7$, then x is equal to

   A. -1.
   B. 0.
   C. 1.
   D. 8.

Mechanical Comprehension

7. In the figure below, which post holds up the greater part of the load?

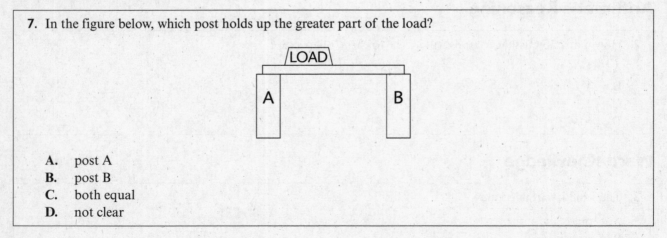

   A. post A
   B. post B
   C. both equal
   D. not clear

Electronics Information

8. In the following circuit diagram, the resistance is 100 ohms, and the current is 0.1 amperes. The voltage is

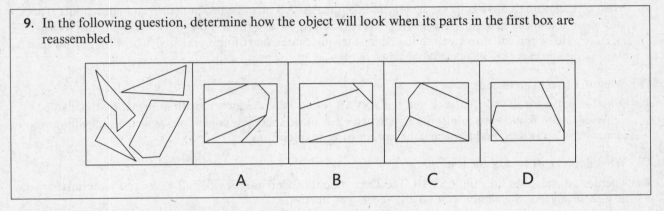

    A.   5 volts.
    B.   10 volts.
    C.   100 volts.
    D.   1,000 volts.

Assembling Objects

9. In the following question, determine how the object will look when its parts in the first box are reassembled.

The correct answers are: 1. **B**, 2. **B**, 3. **C**, 4. **B**, 5. **B**, 6. **C**, 7. **A**, 8. **B**, 9. **C**.

Scoring

Your ASVAB scores are compiled into various subsets to help measure your potential for various activities. The scores from the ASVAB can be used for both civilian and military careers. These scores are valid predictors of success in training programs and on-the-job performance for enlisted military occupations, 80 percent of which are applicable in civilian life. That means that even if you don't join the military, you can still use your scores to help you choose a career path.

The subsets are as follows:

- **Verbal Ability Composite:** Word Knowledge plus Paragraph Comprehension; measures your potential for verbal activities.
- **Math Ability Composite:** Arithmetic Reasoning plus Mathematics Knowledge; measures your potential for mathematical activities.
- **Academic Ability Composite:** Verbal Ability plus Math Ability composites; measures your potential for further formal education.

Questions Commonly Asked about the ASVAB

Q. Who can take the ASVAB?

A. This test is primarily designed for students in the 10th through 12th grades, as well as those in two-year postsecondary schools.

Q. What is my aptitude?

A. Your aptitude is your readiness to become proficient in a specific type of activity. The test measures this aptitude, and offers you an indication of where your strengths lie.

Q. Do I need parental consent to take the test?

A. No, there is no requirement to obtain parental consent in order to take this exam. The scores generated on the test become records of the school.

Q. Where do I take the ASVAB?

A. Most of the more than 900,000 students who take the ASVAB take the test in their own high schools. Check with your guidance counselor. If, however, you're planning to take the test on your own, visit your local recruiter. He or she will direct you to the nearest testing center, one of approximately 65 Military Entrance Processing Stations (MEPS) throughout the country.

Q. What if I plan to go to college?

A. Whether college is in your plans or not, the ASVAB results will provide you with information that can be extremely helpful in determining your capacity for advanced academic education, as well as in helping you identify the areas that might be ideal for further career exploration.

Q. What does it cost to take the test?

A. There is no charge to take the ASVAB. The Department of Defense provides all of the test materials for you, as well as pays for the administration and scoring of the test.

Q. Once I've taken the test, what is my obligation to the military?

A. You have no obligation to join the military. However, you will be required to sign an authorization that permits the release of your scores to all of the military services. Then, you will undoubtedly be called by recruiters from the Army, Navy, Air Force, and Marine Corps, as well as the U.S. Coast Guard, so they can try to convince you to join their branch of the service.

Q. What about recruiters?

A. If a recruiter contacts you, make the time to talk to him or her. A recruiter can answer a lot of your questions about the benefits available to you in the military, including salaries, jobs, training, and travel.

Q. Is there a relationship between the ASVAB and Selective Service registration?

A. No, there is no relationship between them. Your ASVAB scores are not available to the Selective Service.

Q. What if I'm planning to become a commissioned officer?

A. Most branches of the service require you to have a college degree in order to become a commissioned officer, and you need the degree if you are applying for Officer Training Schools or Officer Candidate Schools. However, despite the fact that the ASVAB is not required for these schools, the results can still assist you in career planning.

Q. Are my scores going to be released?

A. No. The scores are only for use by the Armed Services and your guidance counselor, and are good for enlistment purposes for up to two years after taking the ASVAB. After that, your personal information and scores are retained by the Department of Defense only for research purposes.

Q. How are my ASVAB scores used?

A. If you are planning to enter the military, your scores are used to help determine which military specialties would be right for you. If you have no intention of enlisting, you can still use the scores as an aptitude test that can help guide you in future career choices.

You will receive your scores on a report called the *ASVAB Student Results Sheet.* This is not a pass/fail test. Instead, your grade will be a percentile score, indicating how you compare to others who have taken the test. For example, if you receive a percentile score of 75 percent, it means you have scored as well as, if not better than, 75 percent of the other people taking the test when you did.

Q. Can you actually study for this test?

A. Absolutely! Studies show that the more you read the material and the more sample questions and tests you work on, the more familiar the material will become to you. Therefore, you will encounter far fewer "surprises" on the actual test. To that aim, we have provided hundreds of pages of review material to help you understand the basics of what will appear on the test, as well as hundreds of questions for practice. In addition, there are three full-length sample ASVABs as well as a practice AFQT (later in this book). Be diligent with your studying and try to take the tests under simulated conditions—find a quiet room and time yourself. After all, if you're serious about joining the military, it makes sense to apply yourself to the fullest.

Q. How can I prepare for the ASVAB?

A. Reviewing the content and concepts of these various subtests will be invaluable in helping you understand the material that you will encounter on the test. In addition, familiarity with directions and question types is a major step toward scoring high on the actual ASVAB.

Furthermore, it is always extremely helpful to go back to some of your textbooks to review the material you may already have learned. Once you've read through this book and taken the practice tests, you will have a better idea of what you need to focus on to improve your scores. Reread the book. Reread your old textbooks. Talk to your teachers if you are having specific problems in some of the ASVAB test subjects.

Q. How can I find out more about careers?

A. You can consult *ASVAB 18/19 Career Exploration Program,* usually available in your guidance office. The book includes an Interest Finder, which is a self-administered interest inventory.

A Final Word about Careers

One of the major purposes of this exam is to help you and the military find a career choice that will be suitable for your level of knowledge and skill levels. But first you should determine which branch of the service is for you. Take the time to visit your local recruiters from each of the four branches of the military—Army, Navy, Air Force, and Marines, as well as the U.S. Coast Guard. Even though they may be similar in a lot of ways, each branch of the service will offer you different opportunities, both educationally and toward your future career path.

PART I

DIAGNOSTIC TEST

The following test is half the length of the official ASVAB. Use this test to get an idea of your strengths and weaknesses.

Give yourself the following time limits for the various problem types:

- General Science: 5.5 minutes
- Arithmetic Reasoning: 18 minutes
- Word Knowledge: 5.5 minutes
- Paragraph Comprehension: 6.5 minutes
- Auto and Shop Information: 5.5 minutes
- Mathematics Knowledge: 12 minutes
- Mechanical Comprehension: 9.5 minutes
- Electronics Information: 4.5 minutes
- Assembling Objects: 4.5 minutes

Answer Sheet for Diagnostic Test

(Remove this sheet and use it to mark your answers.)

General Science

1 Ⓐ Ⓑ Ⓒ Ⓓ
2 Ⓐ Ⓑ Ⓒ Ⓓ
3 Ⓐ Ⓑ Ⓒ Ⓓ
4 Ⓐ Ⓑ Ⓒ Ⓓ
5 Ⓐ Ⓑ Ⓒ Ⓓ
6 Ⓐ Ⓑ Ⓒ Ⓓ
7 Ⓐ Ⓑ Ⓒ Ⓓ
8 Ⓐ Ⓑ Ⓒ Ⓓ
9 Ⓐ Ⓑ Ⓒ Ⓓ
10 Ⓐ Ⓑ Ⓒ Ⓓ
11 Ⓐ Ⓑ Ⓒ Ⓓ
12 Ⓐ Ⓑ Ⓒ Ⓓ

Arithmetic Reasoning

1 Ⓐ Ⓑ Ⓒ Ⓓ
2 Ⓐ Ⓑ Ⓒ Ⓓ
3 Ⓐ Ⓑ Ⓒ Ⓓ
4 Ⓐ Ⓑ Ⓒ Ⓓ
5 Ⓐ Ⓑ Ⓒ Ⓓ
6 Ⓐ Ⓑ Ⓒ Ⓓ
7 Ⓐ Ⓑ Ⓒ Ⓓ
8 Ⓐ Ⓑ Ⓒ Ⓓ
9 Ⓐ Ⓑ Ⓒ Ⓓ
10 Ⓐ Ⓑ Ⓒ Ⓓ
11 Ⓐ Ⓑ Ⓒ Ⓓ
12 Ⓐ Ⓑ Ⓒ Ⓓ
13 Ⓐ Ⓑ Ⓒ Ⓓ
14 Ⓐ Ⓑ Ⓒ Ⓓ
15 Ⓐ Ⓑ Ⓒ Ⓓ

Word Knowledge

1 Ⓐ Ⓑ Ⓒ Ⓓ
2 Ⓐ Ⓑ Ⓒ Ⓓ
3 Ⓐ Ⓑ Ⓒ Ⓓ
4 Ⓐ Ⓑ Ⓒ Ⓓ
5 Ⓐ Ⓑ Ⓒ Ⓓ
6 Ⓐ Ⓑ Ⓒ Ⓓ
7 Ⓐ Ⓑ Ⓒ Ⓓ
8 Ⓐ Ⓑ Ⓒ Ⓓ
9 Ⓐ Ⓑ Ⓒ Ⓓ
10 Ⓐ Ⓑ Ⓒ Ⓓ
11 Ⓐ Ⓑ Ⓒ Ⓓ
12 Ⓐ Ⓑ Ⓒ Ⓓ
13 Ⓐ Ⓑ Ⓒ Ⓓ
14 Ⓐ Ⓑ Ⓒ Ⓓ
15 Ⓐ Ⓑ Ⓒ Ⓓ

Paragraph Comprehension

1 Ⓐ Ⓑ Ⓒ Ⓓ
2 Ⓐ Ⓑ Ⓒ Ⓓ
3 Ⓐ Ⓑ Ⓒ Ⓓ
4 Ⓐ Ⓑ Ⓒ Ⓓ
5 Ⓐ Ⓑ Ⓒ Ⓓ
6 Ⓐ Ⓑ Ⓒ Ⓓ
7 Ⓐ Ⓑ Ⓒ Ⓓ
8 Ⓐ Ⓑ Ⓒ Ⓓ

Auto and Shop Information

1 Ⓐ Ⓑ Ⓒ Ⓓ
2 Ⓐ Ⓑ Ⓒ Ⓓ
3 Ⓐ Ⓑ Ⓒ Ⓓ
4 Ⓐ Ⓑ Ⓒ Ⓓ
5 Ⓐ Ⓑ Ⓒ Ⓓ
6 Ⓐ Ⓑ Ⓒ Ⓓ
7 Ⓐ Ⓑ Ⓒ Ⓓ
8 Ⓐ Ⓑ Ⓒ Ⓓ
9 Ⓐ Ⓑ Ⓒ Ⓓ
10 Ⓐ Ⓑ Ⓒ Ⓓ
11 Ⓐ Ⓑ Ⓒ Ⓓ
12 Ⓐ Ⓑ Ⓒ Ⓓ
13 Ⓐ Ⓑ Ⓒ Ⓓ

Mathematics Knowledge

1 Ⓐ Ⓑ Ⓒ Ⓓ
2 Ⓐ Ⓑ Ⓒ Ⓓ
3 Ⓐ Ⓑ Ⓒ Ⓓ
4 Ⓐ Ⓑ Ⓒ Ⓓ
5 Ⓐ Ⓑ Ⓒ Ⓓ
6 Ⓐ Ⓑ Ⓒ Ⓓ
7 Ⓐ Ⓑ Ⓒ Ⓓ
8 Ⓐ Ⓑ Ⓒ Ⓓ
9 Ⓐ Ⓑ Ⓒ Ⓓ
10 Ⓐ Ⓑ Ⓒ Ⓓ
11 Ⓐ Ⓑ Ⓒ Ⓓ
12 Ⓐ Ⓑ Ⓒ Ⓓ

Mechanical Comprehension

1 Ⓐ Ⓑ Ⓒ Ⓓ
2 Ⓐ Ⓑ Ⓒ Ⓓ
3 Ⓐ Ⓑ Ⓒ Ⓓ
4 Ⓐ Ⓑ Ⓒ Ⓓ
5 Ⓐ Ⓑ Ⓒ Ⓓ
6 Ⓐ Ⓑ Ⓒ Ⓓ
7 Ⓐ Ⓑ Ⓒ Ⓓ
8 Ⓐ Ⓑ Ⓒ Ⓓ
9 Ⓐ Ⓑ Ⓒ Ⓓ
10 Ⓐ Ⓑ Ⓒ Ⓓ
11 Ⓐ Ⓑ Ⓒ Ⓓ
12 Ⓐ Ⓑ Ⓒ Ⓓ

Electronics Information

1 Ⓐ Ⓑ Ⓒ Ⓓ
2 Ⓐ Ⓑ Ⓒ Ⓓ
3 Ⓐ Ⓑ Ⓒ Ⓓ
4 Ⓐ Ⓑ Ⓒ Ⓓ
5 Ⓐ Ⓑ Ⓒ Ⓓ
6 Ⓐ Ⓑ Ⓒ Ⓓ
7 Ⓐ Ⓑ Ⓒ Ⓓ
8 Ⓐ Ⓑ Ⓒ Ⓓ
9 Ⓐ Ⓑ Ⓒ Ⓓ
10 Ⓐ Ⓑ Ⓒ Ⓓ

Assembling Objects

1 Ⓐ Ⓑ Ⓒ Ⓓ
2 Ⓐ Ⓑ Ⓒ Ⓓ
3 Ⓐ Ⓑ Ⓒ Ⓓ
4 Ⓐ Ⓑ Ⓒ Ⓓ
5 Ⓐ Ⓑ Ⓒ Ⓓ
6 Ⓐ Ⓑ Ⓒ Ⓓ
7 Ⓐ Ⓑ Ⓒ Ⓓ
8 Ⓐ Ⓑ Ⓒ Ⓓ

CUT HERE

The following is like the ASVAB test that you will take, only half-length.

General Science

Directions: The following questions will test your knowledge of general science principles. Read the question and select the choice that best answers the question. Indicate that letter on your answer sheet.

1. Which sequence correctly lists the relative sizes from smallest to largest?

    A. DNA, nucleus, cell
    B. DNA, cell, nucleus
    C. cell, nucleus, DNA
    D. nucleus, DNA, cell

2. Which of the following are not correctly paired?

    A. proteins: amino acids
    B. lipids: fatty acids and glycerol
    C. nucleic acids: ribose
    D. carbohydrates: monosaccharide

3. Given the reaction $2 CO (g) + O_2 (g) \rightarrow 2CO_2 (g)$, how many oxygen atoms are represented to the right of the arrow?

    A. 1
    B. 2
    C. 3
    D. 4

4. The correct formula for carbon tetrachloride is

    A. C_4C_4.
    B. C_4Cl.
    C. CCl_4.
    D. CCl.

5. In a plant, pollen is produced in the

    A. anther.
    B. pistil.
    C. xylem.
    D. phloem.

6. Isotopes of the same element differ in the number of

    A. electrons.
    B. protons.
    C. neutrons.
    D. neurons.

7. In a typical food chain, a hawk feeds on snakes that in turn feed on mice, which in turn feed on grass. The producer in this food chain is the

    A. grass.
    B. mice.
    C. snake.
    D. hawk.

8. The pH of a 0.001 NaOH solution is

    A. –3.
    B. 3.
    C. 4.
    D. 11.

9. Which of the following diagrams best represents a sample of the igneous rock granite?

A

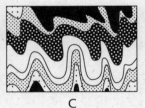

C

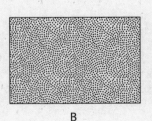

B

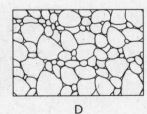

D

    A. Illustration A
    B. Illustration B
    C. Illustration C
    D. Illustration D

10. As you hike along a trail, you encounter the remains of an old volcano. Which group of rocks listed below would you expect to find?

    A. sandstone, cobblestone, limestone
    B. pumice, obsidian, scoria
    C. marble, schist, slate
    D. all of the above

11. The plant hormone most closely associated with stress is

    A. auxin.
    B. cytokinin.
    C. ethylene gas.
    D. abscisic acid.

12. What numbers should be placed in front of magnesium (Mg) and gold (Au), respectively, in order to balance the following equation?

    $Mg + AuCl_3 \rightarrow MgCl_2 + Au$

    A. 1, 2
    B. 2, 2
    C. 2, 3
    D. 3, 2

IF YOU FINISH BEFORE TIME IS CALLED, CHECK YOUR WORK ON THIS SECTION ONLY. DO NOT WORK ON ANY OTHER SECTION IN THE TEST.

Arithmetic Reasoning

Directions: Each of the following questions will test your knowledge about basic arithmetic. Read the question and select the choice that best answers the question. Indicate that letter on your answer sheet.

1. Mary has an appointment in 50 minutes. It is now 3:50 p.m. When is Mary's appointment?

    A. 3:00 p.m.
    B. 4:00 p.m.
    C. 4:40 p.m.
    D. 4:45 p.m.

2. Siri earned $520 last week. Her pay is based on a 6% commission of all sales. What were Siri's total sales last week?

    A. $31.20
    B. $86.67
    C. $3,120.00
    D. $8,666.67

3. Marty has 16 pencils and 4 times as many erasers. How many more erasers than pencils does Marty have?

    A. 4
    B. 32
    C. 48
    D. 64

4. Last week, Craig ran the race in $13\frac{2}{3}$ minutes. This week, he ran it in $12\frac{5}{12}$ minutes. By how many seconds did his time improve?

    A. 15
    B. 75
    C. 120
    D. 150

5. Trey can tie 45 knots in 8 minutes. At this rate, how long will it take him to tie 60 knots?

    A. 10 minutes
    B. $10\frac{2}{3}$ minutes
    C. 12 minutes
    D. $12\frac{1}{2}$ minutes

6. Security answered five calls between 5:00 and 6:00 p.m., three calls between 6:00 and 7:00 p.m., no calls between 7:00 and 8:00 p.m., and eight calls between 8:00 and 9:00 p.m. What was the average number of calls per hour answered between 5:00 and 9:00 p.m.?

    A. 4
    B. $5\frac{1}{3}$
    C. 6
    D. 16

7. A recliner originally priced at $900 was discounted 30%. Because it didn't sell, it was reduced another 20%. What is the total percent of discount?

    A. 56%
    B. 50%
    C. 48%
    D. 44%

8. A circular swimming pool 5 feet high has a volume of 125π cubic feet. What is the distance across the widest part of the pool?

    A. 5 feet
    B. 10 feet
    C. 20 feet
    D. 25 feet

9. Mrs. Lanis plans to put flowers in her yard except in each corner, as shown. What area of her yard remains for the flowers?

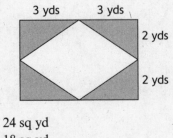

    A. 24 sq yd
    B. 18 sq yd
    C. 12 sq yd
    D. 6 sq yd

10. A check register shows a $512.33 beginning balance, a deposit of $120.30, withdrawals of $35 and $60, another deposit of $21.84, and a withdrawal of $36.89. What is the ending balance?

    A. $238.30
    B. $522.58
    C. $596.36
    D. $786.36

11. Carlo takes out a loan of $600 that charges an annual interest rate of 15%. If he repays the loan in monthly installments over a one-year period, what will his payments be?

    A. $690.00
    B. $90.00
    C. $57.50
    D. $7.50

12. Danielle is decorating a package with ribbons. If she cut a 5-foot piece of ribbon into 4-inch pieces, how many smaller ribbons are there?

    A. 12
    B. 15
    C. 18
    D. 24

13. Admission to a museum costs $15.50 per adult and $8.75 per child. What is the cost for a family of two adults and four children to see the museum?

    A. $52.50
    B. $66.00
    C. $79.50
    D. $93.00

14. You have seven quarters. How many more quarters are needed to fill a $10.00 quarter wrapper?

    A. 3
    B. 13
    C. 28
    D. 33

15. A cardboard square measuring 10 inches on each side is to be cut from a sheet of cardboard. If 2-inch squares are cut from each corner and the sides are then folded upward, what is the volume of the resulting box?

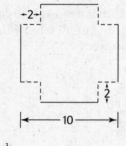

    A. 40 in³
    B. 72 in³
    C. 80 in³
    D. 100 in³

IF YOU FINISH BEFORE TIME IS CALLED, CHECK YOUR WORK ON THIS SECTION ONLY. DO NOT WORK ON ANY OTHER SECTION IN THE TEST.

Word Knowledge

Directions: This portion of the exam will test your knowledge of the meaning of words. Each question has an underlined word. Decide which of the four choices most nearly means the same as the underlined word; then indicate that letter on your answer sheet.

1. Finagle most nearly means

    A. fly.
    B. trick.
    C. turn a corner.
    D. sell out.

2. Impair most nearly means

    A. weaken.
    B. help.
    C. encourage.
    D. double.

3. His play on the court was pivotal.

    A. laughable
    B. crucial
    C. helpful
    D. blameless

4. The sound was amplified throughout the ship.

    A. filtered
    B. dampened
    C. heard
    D. expanded

5. They were engaged in a very tenuous negotiation.

    A. strong
    B. faulty
    C. insignificant
    D. important

6. Mature most nearly means

    A. full grown.
    B. inedible.
    C. overweight.
    D. concise.

7. Stalwart most nearly means

    A. unmoving.
    B. brave.
    C. fearful.
    D. timid.

8. They had rudimentary plans for the building.

    A. mature
    B. elementary
    C. final
    D. complete

9. She was unable to placate her child.

    A. encourage
    B. pacify
    C. argue with
    D. forget

10. Provincial most nearly means

    A. metropolitan.
    B. unhelpful.
    C. thoughtful.
    D. unsophisticated.

11. Terminate most nearly means

    A. start.
    B. stop.
    C. endure.
    D. devour.

12. They thought that he was imprudent.

    A. tactful
    B. careful
    C. careless
    D. willing

13. He was unable to find his <u>quarry.</u>

    A. lake

    B. prey

    C. home

    D. demolition site

14. <u>Ruse</u> most nearly means

    A. a trick.

    B. a track.

    C. cake icing.

    D. a collar.

15. <u>Torpid</u> most nearly means

    A. hot.

    B. excitable.

    C. sluggish.

    D. compassionate.

IF YOU FINISH BEFORE TIME IS CALLED, CHECK YOUR WORK ON THIS SECTION ONLY. DO NOT WORK ON ANY OTHER SECTION IN THE TEST.

Paragraph Comprehension

Directions: This is a test of reading comprehension. Read each paragraph and then select the choice below that best answers that question. Indicate that letter on your answer sheet.

1. In the early 1900s, horticulturist George Washington Carver developed more than 325 products from the peanut. Peanut meatloaf and chocolate-covered peanuts were just two of the food items that Carver developed. However, most interestingly, Carver also engineered many unusual peanut products. For example, he formulated beauty products from the peanut such as hand lotion, shaving cream, and shampoo.

   The best title for this selection is

   A. Carver and Peanut Food Products.
   B. Carver's Many Peanut Products.
   C. Carver's Beauty Products from the Peanut.
   D. The Life of George Washington Carver.

2. College professors often present pedantic lectures. This fact is emphasized by yawning, sleepy students in many classrooms.

   In this context, the word *pedantic* means

   A. dull.
   B. exciting.
   C. childish.
   D. inspiring.

3. To the untrained eye, differentiating between an alligator and a crocodile is a difficult task. However, there is one main difference between these two reptiles. Alligators tend to have wide, rounded snouts, while crocodiles have longer, more pointed noses.

   Which of the following is implied by the above passage?

   A. You can never tell the difference between a crocodile and an alligator.
   B. There are no discernible physical differences between crocodiles and alligators.
   C. Most people can differentiate between crocodiles and alligators if they know about the reptiles' differing snout structures.
   D. Only experts can distinguish between crocodiles and alligators.

4. Mineral forms of carbon vary greatly. For example, both diamonds and graphite are forms of carbon. However, graphite is very weak and soft while diamonds are the hardest gemstones known to man.

   This passage is mainly about

   A. diamonds.
   B. graphite.
   C. the likenesses between diamonds and graphite.
   D. the varying mineral forms of carbon.

Questions 5 and 6 relate to the following passage.

   Many environmentalists believe natural gas to be the answer to decreasing pollution produced by other traditional forms of energy. Although, like oil, natural gas comes from the Earth's crust, it burns cleaner than oil does.

   As a result, there is great emphasis from environmentalists and manufacturers on developing more vehicles that operate on natural gas rather than regular fuel. Proponents of natural-gas vehicles state that such vehicles emit up to 95% less pollution than standard gasoline or diesel vehicles.

5. The principal reason for using natural gas vehicles is

   A. they are more attractive than their gasoline and diesel counterparts.
   B. they emit less pollution and are safer for the environment.
   C. they are less expensive to operate than traditional vehicles.
   D. they are mandated by law.

6. You may conclude from the passage selection that

   A. there is great emphasis on producing natural gas vehicles to reduce pollution.

   B. traditional vehicles that operate on gasoline or diesel fuel produce very little pollution.

   C. the difference in emissions between regular vehicles and natural-gas vehicles is unimportant.

   D. natural gas is a pollutant and should not be used to fuel vehicles.

Questions 7 and 8 relate to the following passage.

Because of their reputation from myth and legend of sucking blood from animals and humans, vampire bats are viewed as heinous creatures. However, someday these greatly feared but little-known animals might save lives.

Scientists have discovered that vampire bats do not suck blood from other animals. Rather, they make tiny cuts in the skin of such animals as cows. Interestingly, the bats' saliva contains a substance that aids in blood clotting. Thus, this substance might eventually be used to prevent heart attacks and strokes.

7. In this context, the word *heinous* means

   A. playful.

   B. friendly.

   C. busy.

   D. monstrous.

8. The author apparently feels that

   A. vampire bats are dangerous to humans.

   B. vampire bats are harmful to cows.

   C. vampire bats have potential in the medical field.

   D. vampire bats are friendly creatures.

IF YOU FINISH BEFORE TIME IS CALLED, CHECK YOUR WORK ON THIS SECTION ONLY. DO NOT WORK ON ANY OTHER SECTION IN THE TEST.

Auto and Shop Information

Directions: There are two parts to this test. The first will test your basic knowledge of automobiles. The second will test your knowledge of basic shop practices and the use of tools. Read each question carefully and select the choice that best answers the question. Indicate that letter on your answer sheet.

1. A vehicle's check engine light becomes illuminated on the dashboard. The first step in diagnosing the problem would be to

   A. disconnect and reconnect the battery's negative terminal.
   B. leave the vehicle running for at least 30 minutes.
   C. drive the vehicle 50 miles or until the light turns off.
   D. connect a diagnostic tool to the OBD (on-board diagnostic) system.

2. An engine is using too much oil. Which one of the following is the most likely cause?

   A. vacuum leak
   B. tapered cylinder walls
   C. stuck thermostat
   D. worn valve guide

3. An engine overheating usually means a failure in the

   A. lubrication system.
   B. cooling system.
   C. anti-lock brake system.
   D. on-board diagnostic system.

4. Looking at the following figure, what is being illustrated?

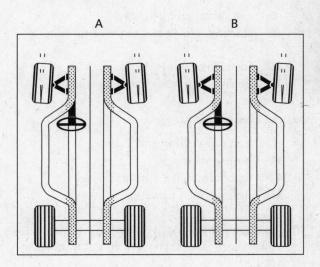

   A. caster angles
   B. camber angles
   C. toe-in and toe-out configurations
   D. thrust angle

5. To tighten any critical bolts

   A. use a proper bar.
   B. use a breaker bar.
   C. use an impact wrench.
   D. use a torque wrench.

6. Which of the following measurements is the dial caliper NOT used for?

   A. inside measurement
   B. outside measurement
   C. depth measurement
   D. pressure measurement

7. A camber measurement can tell us which of the following about a tire problem?

   A. The top of the tire is leaning toward the car.
   B. The top of the tire is leaning away from the car.
   C. The tire is straight up.
   D. All of the above.

8. You would use a Forstner bit if you were

   A. installing ceiling lighting.
   B. starting screw holes to avoid splitting wood.
   C. installing cabinet doors.
   D. drilling thin holes in sheet metal.

9. A chisel is used for

   A. accurate cutting and shaping.
   B. pulling nails.
   C. determining if a surface is level.
   D. drilling holes in wood.

10. The hammer illustrated below has one magnetized end and one non-magnetized end. It is primarily used

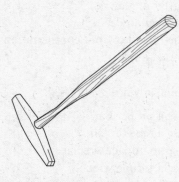

   A. to hang picture frames.
   B. for upholstery work.
   C. for working in tight places.
   D. to remove old glass shards.

11. The tool below is a

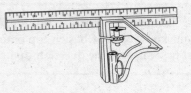

   A. contractor's square.
   B. sliding T-bevel.
   C. try square.
   D. combination square.

12. One of the advantages of box-end wrenches is that they have _____ or _____ points within an enclosed circle.

   A. 1, 4
   B. 8, 10
   C. 6, 12
   D. 3, 5

13. If you're pouring concrete for a walk, you should dig down at least

   A. 2 inches.
   B. 4 inches.
   C. 6 inches.
   D. 8 inches.

IF YOU FINISH BEFORE TIME IS CALLED, CHECK YOUR WORK ON THIS SECTION ONLY. DO NOT WORK ON ANY OTHER SECTION IN THE TEST.

Mathematics Knowledge

Directions: This section will test your knowledge of basic mathematics. Read each question carefully and select the choice that best answers the question. Indicate that letter on your answer sheet.

1. $\left(\sqrt{2}\right)^4 =$

   A. 2
   B. 4
   C. 8
   D. 16

2. Simplify $\dfrac{9x^2}{y} \div \dfrac{3y^2}{x^3}$.

   A. $\dfrac{27y}{x}$

   B. $\dfrac{3x^5}{y^3}$

   C. $\dfrac{3x^6}{y^2}$

   D. $\dfrac{27x^2y^2}{x^3y}$

3. The probability of rolling an even number on a set of two dice is

   A. $\dfrac{1}{2}$.

   B. $\dfrac{5}{9}$.

   C. $\dfrac{15}{36}$.

   D. $\dfrac{17}{36}$.

4. In circle O, the radius is 6 units long. Find the diagonal of square $QRST$.

   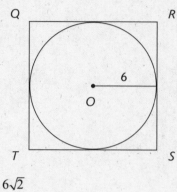

   A. $6\sqrt{2}$
   B. 12
   C. $12\sqrt{2}$
   D. 18

5. If 6 less than twice a number is added to 10, the result is 2. An equation that represents this is

   A. $6 - 2x = 10 + 2$.
   B. $6 - 2x + 10 = 2$.
   C. $2x - 6 = 10 + 2$.
   D. $2x - 6 + 10 = 2$.

6. Rounded to the nearest tenth, $826 \div 12$ is

   A. 68.8.
   B. 68.9.
   C. 69.0.
   D. 70.0.

7. If $x = -1$, then $-2x^2 - 3x + 4 =$

   A. -1.
   B. 1.
   C. 5.
   D. 9.

8. 9 is what percent of 60?

   A. 5.4%
   B. 15%
   C. 18%
   D. 54%

9. If a rectangle has a length of 18 inches and a width of 6 inches, what is the perimeter of the rectangle in feet?

   A. 4
   B. 24
   C. 48
   D. 108

10. Solve for b: $\dfrac{b}{5} + \dfrac{b}{3} = 1$

    A. $\dfrac{1}{8}$

    B. $\dfrac{1}{15}$

    C. $\dfrac{8}{15}$

    D. $\dfrac{15}{8}$

11. In triangle ABC, if the measure of $\angle A$ is half the measure of $\angle B$, what is the measure of $\angle C$?

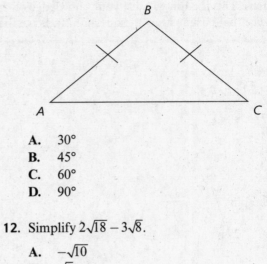

    A. 30°
    B. 45°
    C. 60°
    D. 90°

12. Simplify $2\sqrt{18} - 3\sqrt{8}$.

    A. $-\sqrt{10}$
    B. $\sqrt{2}$
    C. $-\sqrt{2}$
    D. 0

IF YOU FINISH BEFORE TIME IS CALLED, CHECK YOUR WORK ON THIS SECTION ONLY. DO NOT WORK ON ANY OTHER SECTION IN THE TEST.

Mechanical Comprehension

Directions: This section will test your knowledge of mechanical principles. Read each question carefully and then select the choice that best answers the question. Indicate that letter on your answer sheet.

1. A body resists motion because of its

    A. mass.
    B. weight.
    C. volume.
    D. All the above.

2. Block A has the same volume as block B but twice the mass. Hence

    A. A has twice the density of B.
    B. B has twice the density of A.
    C. A and B have the same mass agreement.
    D. A and B have the same density.

3. A Volvo moving in a straight line with an initial velocity of 15.6 m/s accelerates at a rate of 1.24 m/s^2 for 8 seconds. The displacement during this time is

    A. 425 meters.
    B. 850 meters.
    C. 164 meters.
    D. 400 meters.

4. A ball thrown vertically upward with an initial speed v reaches a maximum height h. If the initial speed of the object is doubled, then the maximum height will increase by a factor of

    A. 8.
    B. 6.
    C. 4.
    D. 2.

5. An object is dropped from a building. If the speed of impact is to be tripled, from how much higher should the object be dropped?

    A. 3 times higher
    B. 4 times higher
    C. 6 times higher
    D. 9 times higher

6. In the screw jack shown in the figure, if the ratio $R/p = 7$, the mechanical advantage (Fo/Fi) is most approximately

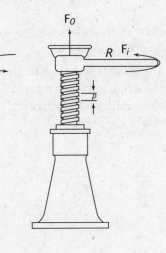

    A. 14.
    B. 21.
    C. 22.
    D. 44.

7. The mass of an element is determined mainly by its

    A. atomic number.
    B. number of protons and neutrons.
    C. electron arrangement.
    D. atomic size.

8. The weight of a 70-kilogram astronaut on the surface of a planet with a mass of 3×10^{24} kilograms and radius of 5×10^6 m is nearly

    A. 686 N.
    B. 586 N.
    C. 560 N.
    D. 70 N.

9. Two spheres of 3-kilogram mass each are joined by a 2-meter rod of negligible weight. If the system rotates at 5 rad/s around the center point of the rod, the rotational kinetic energy of the system (considering the spheres to be point masses) is

   A.   7.50 joules.
   B.   75.0 joules.
   C.   3.00 joules.
   D.   30.0 joules.

10. The amount of work needed to stop a moving object depends most on

    A.   the velocity and mass of the object.
    B.   the mass and acceleration of the object.
    C.   the weight and momentum of the object.
    D.   All of the above.

11. A truck pulls a crate at a constant speed with a 1,500 N force. The frictional force on the crate equals

    A.   more than 1,500 N.
    B.   less than 1,500 N.
    C.   1,500 N.
    D.   Impossible to figure out.

12. A stone thrown straight up takes 4 seconds to reach its maximum height. The maximum height is nearly

    A.   39 meters.
    B.   78 meters.
    C.   157 meters.
    D.   None of the above.

IF YOU FINISH BEFORE TIME IS CALLED, CHECK YOUR WORK ON THIS SECTION ONLY. DO NOT WORK ON ANY OTHER SECTION IN THE TEST.

Electronics Information

Directions: The following portion of the exam will test your knowledge of electronics, electrical, and radio information. Read each question carefully and select the choice that best answers the question. Indicate that letter on your answer sheet.

1. The signal S(t) shown in the figure below has an amplitude of

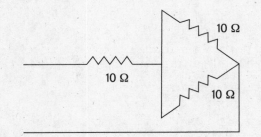

A. 10 volts.
B. 2.5 volts.
C. 15 volts.
D. 5 volts.

2. The total resistance for the circuit shown in the figure below is

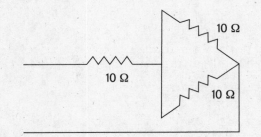

A. 20 ohms.
B. 15 ohms.
C. 30 ohms.
D. 25 ohms.

3. Which of the following components has an identification number only?

A. capacitor
B. coil
C. resistor
D. diode

4. Changing the amplitude of a high frequency signal in correspondence with the amplitude of a low frequency signal is called

A. frequency multiplication.
B. frequency filtration.
C. amplitude modulation.
D. DC shifting.

5. The total capacitance of the circuit shown in the figure below is

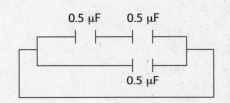

A. 0.75 µF.
B. 1 µF.
C. 0.5 µF.
D. 1.5 µF.

6. If the power dissipated in the circuit shown in the figure below is 1 watt, then the value of the unknown resistors R =

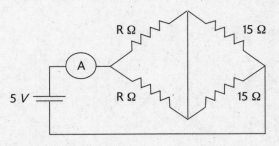

A. 25 ohms.
B. 10 ohms.
C. 15 ohms.
D. 35 ohms.

Questions 7 and 8 are based on the following figure.

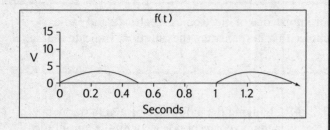

7. The signal f(t) shown in the figure above is a

   A. triangular signal.
   B. square wave.
   C. half-wave rectified sinusoidal signal.
   D. DC shifted wave.

8. What electronic component can be used to generate the signal f(t) shown in the figure above?

   A. a diode
   B. a resistor
   C. a transistor
   D. a capacitor

9. The resistance of a copper wire is proportional to its

   A. diameter.
   B. length.
   C. radiance.
   D. cross-section area.

10. In a semiconductor device, the current is conducted by

    A. electrons only.
    B. holes only.
    C. electrons and holes.
    D. photons.

IF YOU FINISH BEFORE TIME IS CALLED, CHECK YOUR WORK ON THIS SECTION ONLY. DO NOT WORK ON ANY OTHER SECTION IN THE TEST.

Assembling Objects

Directions: In the Assembling Objects portion of the ASVAB there are two types of questions. One type is very similar to solving a jigsaw puzzle. The other is a matter of making appropriate connections given a diagram and instructions. In each of the questions, the first drawing is the problem, and the remaining four drawings offer possible solutions. Look at each of the four illustrations, and then select the choice that best solves that particular problem. Indicate that letter on your answer sheet.

1.

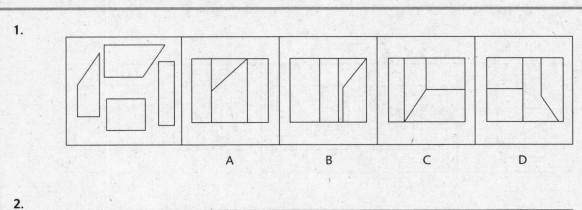

A B C D

2.

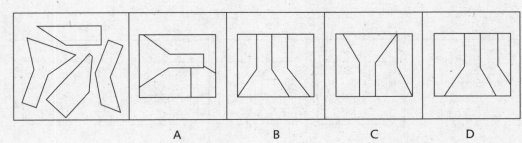

A B C D

3.

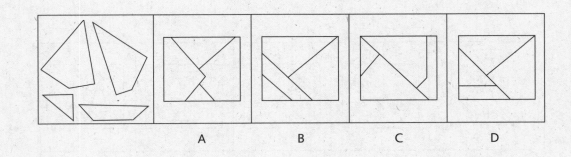

A B C D

4.

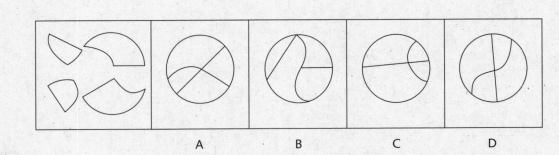

A B C D

5.

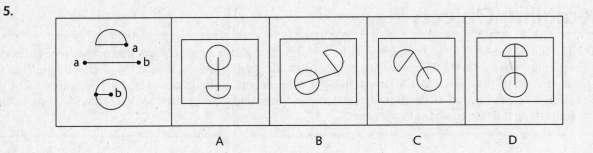

A   B   C   D

6.

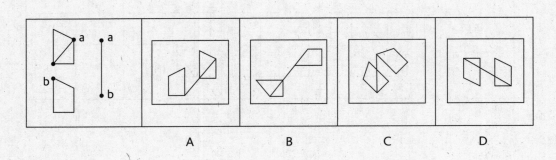

A   B   C   D

7.

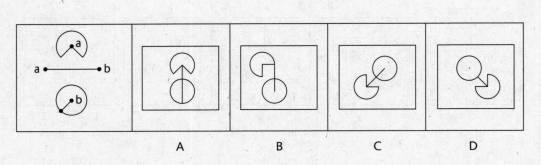

A   B   C   D

8.

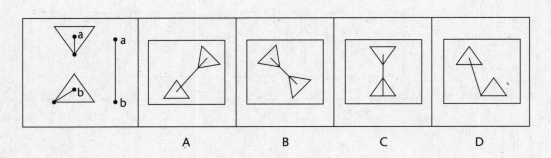

A   B   C   D

IF YOU FINISH BEFORE TIME IS CALLED, CHECK YOUR WORK ON THIS SECTION ONLY. DO NOT WORK ON ANY OTHER SECTION IN THE TEST.

Answer Key for Diagnostic Test

General Science

1. A	5. A	9. A
2. C	6. C	10. D
3. D	7. A	11. D
4. C	8. D	12. D

Arithmetic Reasoning

1. C	6. A	11. C
2. D	7. D	12. B
3. C	8. B	13. B
4. B	9. C	14. D
5. B	10. B	15. B

Word Knowledge

1. B	6. A	11. B
2. A	7. B	12. C
3. B	8. B	13. B
4. D	9. B	14. A
5. C	10. D	15. C

Paragraph Comprehension

1. B	4. D	7. D
2. A	5. B	8. C
3. C	6. A	

Auto and Shop Information

1.	D	6.	D	11.	D
2.	D	7.	D	12.	C
3.	B	8.	C	13.	C
4.	C	9.	A		
5.	D	10.	B		

Mathematics Knowledge

1.	B	5.	D	9.	A
2.	B	6.	A	10.	D
3.	A	7.	C	11.	B
4.	C	8.	B	12.	D

Mechanical Comprehension

1.	A	5.	D	9.	B
2.	A	6.	D	10.	A
3.	C	7.	B	11.	C
4.	C	8.	C	12.	B

Electronics Information

1.	D	5.	A	9.	B
2.	B	6.	D	10.	C
3.	D	7.	C		
4.	C	8.	A		

Assembling Objects

1.	C	4.	D	7.	C
2.	B	5.	C	8.	B
3.	B	6.	B		

Diagnostic Test Answers and Explanations

General Science

1. **A.** DNA is found in the nucleus, an organelle located inside of most cells.

2. **C.** The building blocks of nucleic acids are nucleotides.

3. **D.** There are two molecules with two atoms each.

4. **C.** Carbon is +4 and fluorine –1. A neutral atom will equal 0.

5. **A.** The anther produces pollen, the male gamete, while the pistil or carpel produces the female gamete.

6. **C.** All isotopes of any element have the same number of electrons and protons, only differing in the number of neutrons in the nucleus. A neuron is a nerve cell, having nothing to do with isotopes.

7. **A.** In this food chain, the producer is the grass. Mice are the primary consumers, the snake is the secondary consumer, and the hawk is the tertiary consumer.

8. **D.** NaOH is a strong base. pH + pOH = 11.

9. **A.** This diagram shows a clear crystalline structure. Diagrams B and D represent sedimentary rock structures and diagram C represents the banding pattern common in some metamorphic rocks.

10. **D.** The old volcano would lead you to expect igneous rocks of assorted types (Choice B) for sure, but the question mentions no other geologic processes that may have occurred at the site. It would be possible to find sedimentary rocks, Choice A, and metamorphic rocks, Choice C, in the region as well, depending on other geologic factors.

11. **D.** Abscisic acid is responsible for the closing of stomatal opening by the guard cells.

12. **D.** Make sure the number of specific atoms on each side is the same, and that the lowest-possible whole number ratio is achieved.

Arithmetic Reasoning

1. **C.** If it is 3:50 p.m. now, there are 10 minutes until 4:00 p.m. and then an additional 40 minutes until the appointment, so Mary's appointment is at 4:40 p.m.

2. **D.** Earnings = sales × commission rate. So $520 = sales × 6%. Therefore, sales = $\frac{\$520}{6\%} = \frac{\$520}{.06} = \$8666.67$.

3. **C.** There are 4 × 16, or 64 erasers. So there are 64 – 16, or 48 more erasers.

4. **B.** Convert minutes to seconds. $13\frac{2}{3}$ minutes = $13\frac{2}{3} \times 60 = 820$ seconds. $12\frac{5}{12}$ minutes = $12\frac{5}{12} \times 60 = 745$ seconds. The overall improvement is 820 – 745 = 75 seconds.

5. **B.** The proportion $\frac{45 \text{ knots}}{8 \text{ minutes}} = \frac{60 \text{ knots}}{x \text{ minutes}}$ can be used to find the number of minutes to tie 60 knots. Cross multiply. $45x = 8 \times 60$ so $45x = 480$ and $x = \frac{480}{45} = 10\frac{2}{3}$ minutes.

6. **A.** The average is found by adding the total number of calls answered and dividing by the number of hours. The total number of calls is 5 + 3 + 0 + 8 = 16. The number of hours between 5:00 and 9:00 p.m. is 4. So the average is $\frac{16}{4} = 4$ per hour.

7. **D.** The total percent discounted is the total dollar amount discounted divided by the original price. The first discounted amount is $900 × 30% = $270. The second discounted amount is 20% of the reduced price. So $900 – $270 = $630 × 20% = $126. The total dollar amount discounted is $270 + $126 = $396. The percent discounted is $\frac{396}{900} = 0.44 = 44\%$.

8. **B.** The distance around the widest part of the pool is equivalent to the pool's diameter. The diameter is twice the radius. The volume of a circular pool is $\pi r^2 h$.

   So $125\pi = \pi r^2 5$. $r^2 = \frac{125\pi}{5\pi}$ and $r = \sqrt{25} = 5$.

   Therefore, the diameter of the pool is 5 × 2 = 10 feet.

9. **C.** Find the total area of the figure and subtract each shaded region. The dimensions of the figure are 6 yards by 4 yards so the area of the total figure is 6 × 4 = 24 square yards. Each shaded region is a triangle with a base of 2 yards and height of 3 yards. The area of each triangle is $\frac{1}{2}bh = \frac{1}{2} \cdot 2 \cdot 3 = 3$. Because there are 4 triangles, the area of the shaded region is 4 × 3 = 12 square yards. The area remaining for the flowers is 24 – 12 = 12 square yards.

10. **B.** Deposits are added to the balance while withdrawals are subtracted.
    $512.33 + $120.30 = $632.63 – $35 = $597.63 – $60 = $537.63 + $21.84 = $559.47 – $36.89 = $522.58.

11. **C.** The interest on the loan is $600 × 15% = $90. The total amount to be repaid is $600 + $90 = $690. If this is paid in monthly installments, the amount paid each month is $\frac{690}{12} = \$57.50$.

12. **B.** There are 12 × 5 = 60 inches in a 5-foot piece of ribbon. If this is divided into 4-inch pieces, there are $\frac{60}{4} = 15$ pieces.

13. **B.** The cost for two adults is 2 × $15.50 = $31.00. The cost for four children is 4 × $8.75 = $35.00. The total cost for the family is $31.00 + $35.00 = $66.00.

14. **D.** There are four quarters in $1.00. So 40 quarters are needed to fill a $10.00 quarter wrapper. If there are seven quarters, then 40 – 7 = 33 quarters are still needed.

15. **B.** The volume of a box = length × width × height. The length and width are both equal to 10 – 2 – 2 = 6 inches. The height = 2 inches, so the volume is 6 × 6 × 2 = 72 in³.

Word Knowledge

1. **B.** *Trick.* <u>Finagle</u> means connive or scheme.

2. **A.** *Weaken.* <u>Impair</u> means diminish or undermine.

3. **B.** *Crucial.* <u>Pivotal</u> means important or critical.

4. **D.** *Expanded.* <u>Amplified</u> means increased or boosted.

5. **C.** *Insignificant.* <u>Tenuous</u> means unsubstantial or trivial.

6. **A.** *Full grown.* <u>Mature</u> means developed or ripened.

7. **B.** *Brave.* <u>Stalwart</u> means resolute or valiant.

8. **B.** *Elementary.* <u>Rudimentary</u> means primary or basic.

9. **B.** *Pacify.* <u>Placate</u> means calm or soothe.

10. **D.** *Unsophisticated.* <u>Provincial</u> means rural or unpolished.

11. **B.** *Stop.* <u>Terminate</u> means cease or halt.

12. **C.** *Careless.* <u>Imprudent</u> means heedless or reckless.

13. **B.** *Prey.* <u>Quarry</u> means the hunted or victim.

14. **A.** *A trick.* A <u>ruse</u> is a ploy, subterfuge, or scheme.

15. **C.** *Sluggish.* <u>Torpid</u> means inactive or lethargic.

Paragraph Comprehension

1. **B.** Because both food products and beauty products are mentioned, this title best describes the paragraph as a whole.

2. **A.** The second sentence states that students in college classrooms are often yawning and sleepy. Thus, many college lectures might be described as dull.

3. **C.** The third sentence explains that snout structure is different in crocodiles and alligators.

4. **D.** The first sentence of the selection states that carbon has varying forms and the paragraph develops this topic sentence further.

5. **B.** The selection states that environmentalists believe natural gas to be a way to decrease pollution. The next paragraph states that natural gas vehicles emit up to 95% less pollution than their gasoline and diesel counterparts.

6. **A.** The first sentence of the second paragraph states that there is great emphasis on producing such vehicles.

7. **D.** Because vampire bats are thought to be ruthless bloodsuckers, many perceive them to be evil creatures.

8. **C.** The selection states that vampire bats' saliva might be useful in blood clotting, thus preventing heart attacks and strokes.

Auto and Shop Information

1. **D.** Connecting a diagnostic tool to the vehicle will enable you to immediately read the code pertaining to the vehicle's problem in order to maintain proper maintenance.

2. **D.** Worn valve guides allow oil to seep into the combustion chamber, where it becomes part of the combustion process and winds up emitted from the tailpipe.

3. **B.** Engines run at extremely hot temperatures, which is why it is important that the cooling system pumps water or coolant throughout the engine's chambers, maintaining proper temperatures.

4. **C.** In the illustration, Part A is a toe-in configuration and Part B is a toe-out configuration. Toe settings are designed to compensate for the amount the tire will turn away from straight ahead. A correct setting allows the tires to go straight down the road without scraping against the road surface.

5. **D.** To ensure proper clamping, a torque wrench must be used to tighten any critical bolts to specific torque values.

6. **D.** The dial caliper is a multifunctioning measuring instrument capable of inside, outside, depth, and step measurements.

7. **D.** Leaning toward the car is considered a negative camber, leaning away from the car is considered a positive camber, and straight up is considered a zero camber.

8. **C.** A Forstner bit is used to drill holes that extend nearly all the way through a piece of wood. It is often used to insert cabinet hinges. The bits range from $\frac{1}{4}$ inch to 1 inch or larger.

9. **A.** The chisel is a precision instrument that is carefully sharpened in order to remove material from wood.

10. **B.** This is a tack hammer, used primarily for upholstery work. The magnetic end picks up and starts a tack into the upholstery. The non-magnetic side is then used to finish driving in the tack the rest of the way.

11. **D.** The combination square is a multifunctional tool. It can mark 90° and 45° angles. It can be used as a try square, depth gauge, and marking gauge. It is an extremely precise instrument.

12. **C.** Box-end wrenches have either 6 or 12 points, which enables the wrench to fit snugly over the nut or bolt, which also has 6 or 12 points.

13. **C.** You should dig down at least 6 inches, cover and level the bottom with 2 inches of sand and/or gravel, and pour the concrete to a depth of 4 inches.

Mathematics Knowledge

1. **B.** $\left(\sqrt{2}\right)^4 = \sqrt{2} \cdot \sqrt{2} \cdot \sqrt{2} \cdot \sqrt{2} = \sqrt{16} = 4$

2. **B.** $\dfrac{9x^2}{y} \div \dfrac{3y^2}{x^3} = \dfrac{9x^2}{y} \times \dfrac{x^3}{3y^2} = \dfrac{9x^5}{3y^3} = \dfrac{3x^5}{y^3}$

3. **A.** There are 6^2, or 36 total, possible outcomes when rolling two dice. There is one way to roll 2, three ways to roll 4, five ways to roll 6, five ways to roll 8, three ways to roll 10, and one way to roll 12. So there are $1 + 3 + 5 + 5 + 3 + 1$, or 18 ways, to roll an even number. Therefore, the probability of rolling an even number is $\dfrac{18 \text{ even rolls}}{36 \text{ total rolls}} = \dfrac{1}{2}$.

4. **C.** If the radius is 6, the diameter is 12, so the square has a side length of 12. The diagonal of the square is the hypotenuse of a right triangle with sides equal in length to the square. The diagonal, d, is found by using the Pythagorean theorem. $d^2 = 12^2 + 12^2 = 144 + 144 = 288$, so $d = \sqrt{288} = \sqrt{2 \times 144} = 12\sqrt{2}$.

5. **D.** Six less than twice a number is represented by $2x - 6$. If 10 is added to that, the expression is $2x - 6 + 10$, so the equation is $2x - 6 + 10 = 2$.

6. **A.** $826 \div 12 = 68.83$. Rounded to the nearest tenth, it's 68.8.

7. **C.** Substitute -1 for x. So $-2x^2 - 3x + 4 = -2(-1)^2 - 3(-1) + 4 = -2 + 3 + 4 = 5$.

8. **B.** $9 = p \times 60$ so $p = \dfrac{9}{60} = 0.15 = 15\%$

9. **A.** Convert inches to feet. 12 inches = 1 foot, so 18 inches = 1.5 feet and 6 inches = 0.5 feet. The perimeter, in feet, is $1.5 + 0.5 + 1.5 + 0.5 = 4$.

10. **D.** Eliminate the fractions by multiplying the entire equation by the least common multiple (LCM) of 5 and 3. The LCM is 15, so $15 \cdot \dfrac{b}{5} + 15 \cdot \dfrac{b}{3} = 15 \cdot 1$ and $3b + 5b = 15$. $8b = 15$, therefore $b = \dfrac{15}{8}$.

11. **B.** All angles in a triangle add to $180°$, so $\angle A + \angle B + \angle C = 180°$. Triangle ABC is isosceles, so $\angle A = \angle C$ and if $\angle A$ is half $\angle B$, then $\angle B = 2\angle A$.

    Using substitution, $\angle A + 2\angle A + \angle A = 180°$.

    $4\angle A = 180°$, so $\angle A = \dfrac{180}{4} = 45°$.

    Therefore, $\angle C$ also $= 45°$.

12. **D.** $2\sqrt{18} - 3\sqrt{8} = 2\sqrt{2 \times 9} - 3\sqrt{2 \times 4} = 2 \cdot 3\sqrt{2} - 3 \cdot 2\sqrt{2} = 6\sqrt{2} - 6\sqrt{2} = 0$.

Mechanical Comprehension

1. **A.** Newton's first law states that a body remains in its present condition until acted on by external forces. Newton's second law states that force is proportional to mass.

2. **A.** Because density is the ratio of mass to volume, and because mass is proportional to weight, doubling the weight doubles the mass and hence doubles the density.

3. **C.** $s = v_o t + 0.5at^2 = 15.6 \times 8 + 0.5(1.24)(8^2) =$ approximately 165. Working from the inside parentheses: $(1.24 \times 64) = 79.36 \times 0.5 = 39.68$. $15.6 \times 8 = 124.8 + 39.68 = 164.48$. Rounded, it would be 164.

4. **C.** Because $s = v_o t + \frac{1}{2} gt^2$ and $v_f = v_o + gt$, where s = distance of travel, v_o = initial velocity, g = acceleration, and t = time, we see that t changes from v/g to $2\,v/g$ and s changes from $1.5\,v^2/g$ to $6v^2/g$, i.e., it increases by a factor of 4.

5. **D.** The new height should be 9 times greater because the speed of impact is proportional to the square root of the height.

6. **D.** The mechanical advantage equals 2π times the ratio R/p, which is approximately 44.

7. **B.** The majority of the mass of an atom is located in the nucleus. The nucleus is comprised of protons and neutrons, thus accounting for the mass of the element.

8. **C.** $F = \dfrac{6.67 \times 10^{-11} \times 3 \times 10^{24} \times 70}{\left(5 \times 10^6\right)^2} = 560.28$ N

9. **B.** The rotational kinetic energy $E_k = 0.5\,I\omega^2$ where I = moment of inertia $= (2)(3)(1) = 6$ kg $\cdot$ m^2 and $\omega = 5$ rad/s. Thus $E_k = 75$ joules.

10. **A.** Mass and speed are the most determining factors.

11. **C.** This is a consequence of Newton's first and second laws of motion.

12. **B.** Because the stone reaches its maximum height in 4 seconds, that maximum height equals $\frac{1}{2} gt^2 = \frac{1}{2}(9.8)\left(4^2\right) = 78.4$ m.

Electronics Information

1. **D.** The shown signal has an amplitude of 5 volts. Its frequency is 1 Hz, and its DC shift is 5 volts.

2. **B.** The total resistance in the circuit can be calculated as follows:

$$\frac{1}{\frac{1}{10} + \frac{1}{10}} + 10 = 15 \ \Omega$$

3. **D.** Diodes have identification numbers to identify them. Capacitance is measured in farads. Inductance of a coil is measured in henries. Resistance is measured in ohms.

4. **C.** Changing the amplitude of a high frequency signal in correspondence with the amplitude of a low frequency signal is called amplitude modulation.

5. **A.** Total capacitance of the circuit is calculated as follows:

$$\frac{1}{\frac{1}{0.5} + \frac{1}{0.5}} + 0.5 = 0.75 \ \mu F$$

6. **D.** The unknown resistors values (R) can be calculated as follows:

$$P = \frac{V^2}{R_{total}} = \frac{5^2}{\frac{1}{\frac{1}{R} + \frac{1}{R}} + \frac{1}{\frac{1}{15} + \frac{1}{15}}} = 1 \ watt$$

$$\therefore = \frac{25}{\frac{R}{2} + \frac{15}{2}} = 1 \rightarrow R = 2 \times \left(25 - \frac{15}{2}\right) = 35 \ \Omega$$

7. **C.** f(t) is a half-wave rectified sinusoidal signal.

8. **A.** A diode can be used to generate the signal f(t).

9. **B.** The resistance of a wire conductor is proportional to its length.

10. **C.** The current in a semiconductor device is conducted by electrons and holes.

Assembling Objects

For answers, see the answer key, earlier in this section.

PART II

SUBJECT AREA REVIEW

The following subject areas are reviewed in this part:

- General Science
- Arithmetic Reasoning
- Word Knowledge
- Paragraph Comprehension
- Auto and Shop Information
- Mathematics Knowledge
- Mechanical Comprehension
- Electronics Information
- Assembling Objects

The General Science section of the ASVAB is designed to evaluate your understanding of the basic concepts that you studied in the life sciences, the physical sciences, and earth/space sciences. This section reviews the concepts that you covered in your high school general sciences courses. This section also includes review questions and answers with explanations. Please note that on the ASVAB exam, the General Science questions are not broken down by branch. The questions are mixed together.

The ASVAB contains 25 General Science questions. You will have 11 minutes to answer these questions.

Life Sciences

The Cellular Basis of Life

Cells make up all living organisms. Some organisms consist of a single cell, while others are composed of multiple cells organized into tissues and organs.

All cells share two basic features:

- **A plasma membrane** (the outer boundary of the cell)
- **Cytoplasm** (a semi-liquid substance that composes the foundation of the cell)

Cells can be classified as either prokaryotic or eukaryotic:

- **Prokaryotic cells** are relatively simple cells, such as those of bacteria.
- **Eukaryotic cells** are more complex and contain many internal bodies (*organelles*) that carry out specialized functions.

The main components of eukaryotic cells include the following:

- **The nucleus** contains *DNA*. (Deoxyribonucleic acid is the hereditary material in humans and almost all other organisms. It is the building block of our genetic makeup.)
- **Mitochondria** is where the cell produces energy and the site of cellular respiration.
- **Chloroplasts** are where plant cells make food (sugar); animal cells do not contain chloroplasts.
- **Ribosomes** are where the cell makes proteins.

Movement Through the Plasma Membrane

For cells to exchange materials with the external environment, substances must be able to move through the plasma membrane (the "skin" of a cell). Materials pass through the plasma membrane in one of the following four ways:

- **Diffusion:** The passive movement of molecules from a region of higher concentration to a region of lower concentration.
- **Osmosis:** A special type of diffusion that involves the movement of water into and out of the cell.
- **Facilitated diffusion:** Diffusion of molecules across the cell membrane with the help of special proteins in the cell membrane.
- **Active transport:** Movement of molecules across the cell membrane from a region of lower concentration to a region of higher concentration with the help of special proteins in the cell membrane. Active transport requires the cell to expend energy.

Photosynthesis

Plants make their own food from simple molecules such as carbon dioxide and water in a process known as *photosynthesis*. This process requires energy, which the plant obtains from sunlight and captures by way of specialized pigments (*chlorophyll*) in the chloroplasts of its cells. As a byproduct of photosynthesis, oxygen is released into the atmosphere. This process can be summarized with the following equation:

$$\text{carbon dioxide} + \text{water} \rightarrow \text{glucose (sugar)} + \text{oxygen} + \text{water}$$

Plants absorb light in the red and blue wavelengths for use in photosynthesis. Chlorophyll molecules reflect green light, which is why most plants' leaves appear green.

Cellular Respiration and Fermentation

Animals, plants, and microorganisms obtain the energy they need through the process of *cellular respiration*. In cellular respiration, the cell breaks down carbohydrates (such as glucose) to produce water and carbon dioxide. Energy is released during this process and is stored in the form of *adenosine triphosphate* (ATP). When a cell needs energy, the bonds in ATP molecules are broken down and the cell uses the stored energy in metabolism. This process of cellular respiration, which requires the presence of oxygen, can be summarized by the following equation:

$$\text{glucose} + \text{oxygen} \rightarrow \text{water} + \text{carbon dioxide} + \text{energy (ATP)}$$

When no oxygen is present, the cells of some organisms (for example, yeast) carry out a form of *anaerobic respiration* (respiration without oxygen) known as fermentation. The products of fermentation are carbon dioxide and ethanol.

Cell Division

One distinguishing feature of living organisms is that their cells can divide and reproduce exact copies of themselves. Cell division, combined with cell expansion, allows for the growth and development of organisms. The two types of cell division are mitosis and meiosis.

Mitosis

Most of the cells in the body of an organism undergo *mitosis*. When a cell undergoes mitosis, it produces two exact copies of itself. Before the cell divides, it goes through a synthesis phase during which the DNA (genetic information of a cell) molecules duplicate in each chromosome. Because the DNA duplicates before cell division, the two cells produced during mitosis (*daughter cells*) each have a complete set of chromosomes containing all of the necessary DNA that was present in the original cell (*parent cell*). After the chromosomes divide, the cytoplasm of the cell divides into two new cells. Thus, the end result of mitosis is an equal separation and distribution of the chromosomes from one parent cell into two new daughter cells.

Meiosis

Specialized cells in the body of an organism (*germ cells* or *sex cells*) undergo a unique type of cell division called *meiosis* that produces four daughter cells from each parent cell. These daughter cells, each containing half the number of chromosomes as the parent cell, function as gametes (eggs and sperm). Most plant and animal cells contain two sets of chromosomes. Human cells contain 46 chromosomes organized into 23 pairs. For sexual reproduction to occur, gametes from two individuals must unite to form a new individual (*embryo*). For unification to occur successfully, while maintaining the normal number of chromosomes in each individual, the germ cells giving rise to the gametes must undergo meiosis. In humans, meiosis produces egg cells and sperm cells that contain 23 chromosomes each—one member of each chromosome pair. When the gametes unite at fertilization, the normal chromosome number (46 in humans) is reestablished in the resulting *zygote*. The end result of meiosis is the production of four genetically distinct daughter cells from each parent cell.

Genetics

Genetics is the study of how genes control characteristics or traits in living organisms. Genes are portions of DNA molecules that determine the characteristics of an individual. Through the processes of meiosis (which produces eggs and sperm) and *reproduction* (when eggs and sperm unite to form a zygote), genes are transmitted from parents to offspring.

Genes can take on various forms called *alleles*. For example, in humans there are two alleles controlling earlobe type. One allele codes for earlobes that are attached, while the other allele codes for earlobes that hang free. The alleles inherited from each parent determine the type of earlobes a person has.

The following terms summarize the most important genetic concepts:

- **Genotype:** All of the genes present in an individual.
- **Phenotype:** The expression of the genes in an individual.
- **Homozygote:** An individual in which both alleles for a given gene are the same.
- **Heterozygote:** An individual in which the two alleles for a given gene are different.
- **Dominant allele:** An allele that is expressed in an individual when present with either another dominant allele or a recessive allele; usually represented by a capital letter.
- **Recessive allele:** An allele that is masked (not expressed) in an individual when present with a dominant allele; usually represented by a lowercase letter.

Example: In humans, the free-earlobes allele is dominant over the attached-earlobes allele. An individual may possess three possible genotypes for earlobe structure:

- Two alleles for free earlobes (EE)
- Two alleles for attached earlobes (ee)
- One allele for free earlobes and one allele for attached earlobes (Ee)

Because the free-earlobes allele is dominant and the attached-earlobes allele is recessive, the homozygous dominant individual (EE) and the heterozygous individual (Ee) both develop free earlobes, while only the homozygous recessive individual develops attached earlobes.

For some characteristics, one allele does not display dominance over another allele. Instead, the two characters blend to create an intermediate phenotype in the heterozygote. For example, in snapdragons, two alleles code for flower color: one red (R) and one white (r). Heterozygous snapdragons (Rr), which contain one red allele and one white allele, are pink. When neither allele shows dominance over the other, the alleles are said to display *incomplete dominance*.

If both alleles are equally shown, this is known as *codominance*. A popular example of this is hair color in short-horn cattle. The animals have two alleles for hair color—red and white. These alleles are codominant so cattle with both alleles have red and white hairs on their bodies, creating a new phenotype called *roan*.

Multiple genes on one or more chromosomes control many traits. This condition is known as *polygenic inheritance*.

DNA is packaged into chromosomes inside the nucleus of cells. For the DNA of an individual (*genotype*) to be expressed (as a *phenotype*), the cell must process the DNA into proteins. To convert the message encoded in the DNA molecule into the appropriate protein(s), two basic processes must occur:

- **Transcription:** The message encoded on the DNA molecule inside the nucleus is copied onto another molecule called *messenger RNA* (mRNA).
- **Translation:** The mRNA molecule moves out of the nucleus into the cytoplasm of the cell and attaches to a *ribosome* (the part of a cell that manufactures protein). *Transfer RNA* (tRNA) molecules pick up amino acids (the building blocks of proteins) in the cytoplasm, bring them to the ribosome, and link them in the order of the code that the mRNA molecule contains. Strings of amino acids make up proteins.

The flow of information from DNA → mRNA → protein is known as the *central dogma* of molecular biology.

Principles of Evolution

Evolution is defined as the change in one or more characteristics of a population of organisms over time. The process of evolution can be summarized by the following principles:

- A large amount of genetic variation is present among living organisms.
- Organisms must compete with each other for a limited supply of natural resources.
- Those individuals that are best able to survive and reproduce are selected through a process called *natural selection*.

Two essential points underlie natural selection:

- The genetic variation that occurs among individuals is random.
- Traits that allow an individual to survive and reproduce are passed on to the individual's offspring.

Therefore, individuals that are better adapted to their environment are more likely to reproduce and pass on their genes to the next generation. The ability of some individuals to survive and reproduce to a greater degree than other individuals is known as *differential reproductive fitness* or "survival of the fittest."

As the most reproductively fit individuals contribute a higher percentage of alleles to the next generation, the population gradually evolves.

Other factors that contribute to evolution include:

- **Mutations:** Mutations give rise to new alleles that didn't previously exist in the population. Mutations may be harmful and selected against, or they may be beneficial and selected for.
- **Migration:** Migration is the movement of individuals into or out of a population, which results in gene flow between two or more populations.
- **Random genetic drift:** Random genetic drift occurs when a small group of individuals leaves a population and establishes a new population in a geographically isolated region. These individuals may become reproductively isolated from the original population and develop into a separate species.

Several pieces of evidence strongly support evolution:

- **The fossil record** illustrates evidence of a descent of modern organisms from common ancestors.
- **Comparative anatomy** has shown similar structures on many organisms. For example, the forelimbs of such diverse animals as humans, porpoises, cats, birds, and bats are strikingly similar, even though the forelimbs are used for different purposes (lifting, swimming, flying, and so on). Also, many organisms have structures that they don't use. In humans, these vestigial structures include the appendix, the fused tail vertebrae, and wisdom teeth. The figure on page 51 illustrates the forelimbs of a human and two other animals showing the similarities in construction. These anatomical similarities are considered evidence for evolution.
- **Embryology** offers additional evidence for evolution. The embryos of fish, reptiles, chickens, rabbits, and humans share many similarities. For example, all have gill slits, a two-chambered heart, and a tail with muscles. In the later stages of embryo development, the organisms appear less and less similar.
- **Biochemical studies** have shown there are similarities among all living organisms. For example, DNA and RNA serve as the basis for inheritance in all living organisms, and the structure of the genetic code is virtually identical in all living organisms.

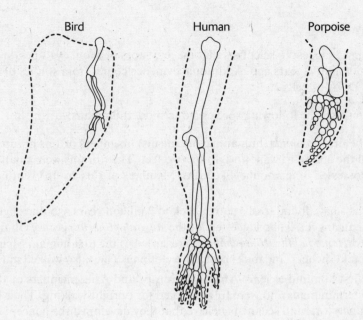

Bird   Human   Porpoise

The Origin and Evolution of Life

Scientists believe that the universe originated about 15 billion years ago with a huge explosion known as the Big Bang. The gases and dust from the explosion produced the earliest stars, and over a period of years, the stars exploded and their debris formed other stars and planets. The solar system is thought to have formed this way 4 to 5 billion years ago. During the next billion years, the Earth cooled, forming a hardened outer crust, and the first living organisms appeared approximately 3.5 billion years ago.

Scientists believe that the first cells lived within the organic environment of the Earth and used organic compounds to obtain energy. However, the organisms would soon use up the organic materials if they were the only source of nutrition and energy. The evolution of a pigment system that could capture energy from the sun and store it in chemical bonds was essential for the evolution of living things. The first organisms to possess these pigments were photosynthetic bacteria, ancestors of modern cyanobacteria. Oxygen, which is produced as a byproduct of photosynthesis, enriched the atmosphere.

Similar to photosynthesis is *chemosynthesis,* a process used by certain organisms to produce energy—but without sunlight. This energy comes from the oxidation of chemicals that ooze up from the earth's crust. These organisms, possibly descended from the earliest life on Earth, are normally found on the ocean floor.

Approximately 1.5 billion years ago, in an oxygen-rich environment, the first eukaryotic cells came into being. One theory explaining the development of eukaryotic cells suggests that bacteria were engulfed by larger cells. The bacteria remained in the larger cells and performed specific functions, such as energy production or photosynthesis, which could explain the origin of *mitochondria* (energy-producing organelle of a cell) and *chloroplasts* (sites of photosynthesis in plant cells). The cells were then able to carry out more complex metabolic functions, and eventually came to be the dominant life forms.

For billions of years, the only life on Earth existed in the nutrient-rich environments of oceans, lakes, and rivers. About 600 million years ago, as the atmosphere became rich in oxygen, living organisms began to colonize land. The first multicellular organisms were probably marine *invertebrates* (animals that lack a spine), followed by wormlike animals with stiff rods in their backs. These organisms, now called *chordates,* were the ancestors of amphibians, reptiles, birds, and mammals.

Human Evolution

Fossils and fragments of jaws suggest to scientists that the ancestors of monkeys, apes, and humans began their evolution approximately 50 million years ago. Additional evidence comes from studies of biochemistry and changes that occur in the DNA of cells.

Scientific evidence indicates that the following species led to modern humans:

- *Australopithecus:* The first *hominids* (humanlike organisms), members of this group displayed a critical step in human evolution: the ability to walk upright on two feet. Their brains were small in comparison with humans, and they possessed long, monkeylike arms. Members of this group eventually died out about 1 million years ago.

- *Homo habilis:* Scientists have found fossils dating back to 2 million years ago that suggest greater brain capacities for this species than any fossil has suggested for the *Australopithecus* species. On the basis of brain size, these fossils are called *Homo habilis*. *Homo habilis* is regarded as the first human. Members of this species were able to make tools, build shelters, and make protective clothing. They also walked upright on two feet.

- *Homo erectus:* The first hominid to leave Africa for Europe and Asia, members of this species were about the same size as modern humans and were fully adapted for upright walking. Their brains were much larger than those of their ancestors, and scientists believe that they developed the concept of language.

The earliest fossils of *Homo sapiens* date to about 200,000 years ago. Scientists classify modern humans in this species. The evolution from *Homo erectus* to *Homo sapiens* is thought to have taken place in Africa. Fossil evidence shows a gradual change over the span of 200,000 years, but no new species have emerged.

Classification of Life (Taxonomy)

The Earth is home to more than 300,000 species of plants and 1 million species of animals. Taxonomists classify organisms in a way that reflects their relationships with each other. All living organisms are named according to an international system in which the organism is given a two-part name. The first name reflects the *genus* (plural *genera*) in which the organism is classified, while the second name is the *species*. For example, humans are assigned the name *Homo sapiens*.

A group of organisms that can mate with each other under natural conditions and produce fertile offspring is known as a species. Individuals of different species usually do not mate. If they are forced to mate, their offspring are usually sterile and cannot produce offspring of their own. For example, a horse (*Equus caballus*) can mate with a donkey (*Equus assinus*); however, the offspring (a mule) is sterile and cannot reproduce.

The standard classification scheme provides a mechanism for bringing together various species into progressively larger groups, as follows:

- **Genus:** Consists of one or more related species
- **Family:** Consists of similar genera
- **Order:** Consists of families with similar characteristics
- **Class:** Consists of orders with similar characteristics
- **Phylum (or Division):** Consists of related classes (the term *division* is used for classifying plants and fungi, while *phylum* is used for classifying animals and animallike organisms)
- **Kingdom:** Consists of related divisions or phyla
- **Domain:** Consists of related kingdoms; the broadest level of classification

The classification scheme that is currently most widely accepted recognizes three domains:

- **Archaea**
- **Eubacteria**
- **Eukarya**

Domain Eukarya is subdivided into four kingdoms: Protista (now often called Protoctista), Fungi, Plantae, and Animalia.

The following illustration shows hypothetical relationships among organisms.

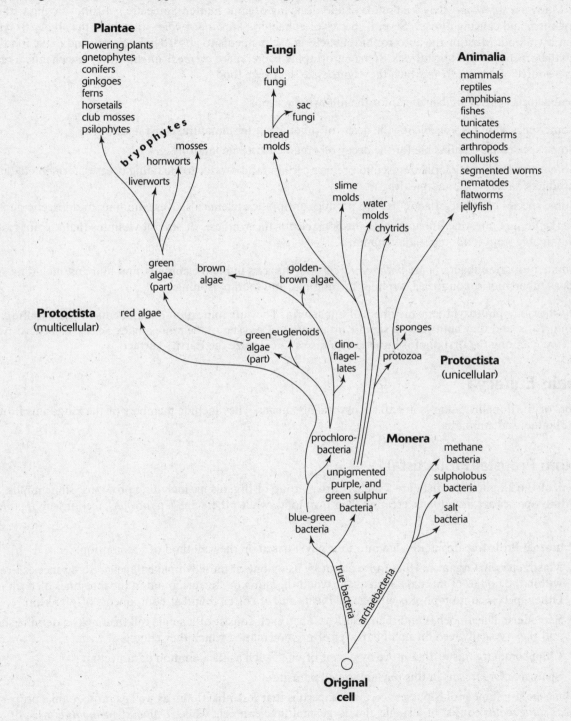

Domain Archaea

Members of the domain Archaea are primitive bacteria, most of which are prokaryotic anaerobic organisms that use methane production in their energy metabolism. They are primarily found in marshes and swamps.

Domain Eubacteria

Members of the eubacteria are prokaryotic organisms. You can find them in nearly all environments on Earth, including soil, water, and air. Most species of eubacteria are *heterotrophic*—they acquire their food from organic matter. Many are *saprobic*—they feed on dead and decaying organic matter. Some are *parasitic*—living within a host organism and causing disease. Several species of eubacteria are *autotrophic*—they have the ability to synthesize their own food. Most of the autotrophic eubacteria use pigments to absorb light energy and make food through the process of photosynthesis. Some autotrophic bacteria are *chemosynthetic*—they use chemical reactions as a source of energy from which they synthesize their own food.

Many eubacteria species are beneficial for the following reasons:

- Some species are responsible for the decay of organic matter in natural ecosystems.
- Some species are responsible for the decay of organic matter in landfills.
- Some species of eubacteria are used to prepare certain food products, including cheeses, fermented dairy products, sauerkraut, and pickles.
- Some species of eubacteria are used to produce antibiotics, chemicals, dyes, vitamins, and insecticides.
- In the human intestine, eubacteria are responsible for the synthesis of several vitamins that are not readily obtainable from food, especially vitamin K.

Unfortunately, many eubacteria are *pathogenic,* causing diseases in plants, animals, and humans, including such diseases as tuberculosis, gonorrhea, syphilis, pneumonia, and food poisoning.

Cyanobacteria are photosynthetic members of eubacteria. They are important components of the plankton found in oceans, and they contribute a significant amount of oxygen to the atmosphere. Scientists believe cyanobacteria were among the first photosynthetic organisms to colonize the Earth's surface.

Domain Eukarya

Members of the domain Eukarya are all eukaryotic organisms. They include members of the kingdoms Protista, Fungi, Plantae, and Animalia.

Kingdom Protista (Protoctista)

Members of the kingdom Protista are a highly varied group of organisms, including protozoa, slime molds, and algae. Many species are *autotrophs*, creating their own food, while others are *heterotrophs*, feeding on organic matter.

- **Protozoa:** Protozoa are subdivided into four phyla based on their method of locomotion:
  - **Mastigophora:** Organisms that move about by using one or more whiplike flagella. Some species live within the bodies of animals, such as the wood-digesting organisms found in the intestines of termites. Other species contain photosynthetic pigments and are often found as components of plankton.
  - **Sarcodina:** The amoebas and their relatives. They each consist of a single cell that lacks a definite shape, and they typically feed on small particles of organic matter, which they engulf.
  - **Ciliophora:** Organisms that move by means of cilia, such as the common paramecium.
  - **Sporozoa:** Organisms in this phylum are all parasites.
- **Slime molds:** Slime molds possess certain properties that resemble fungi, as well as protozoalike properties. *True slime molds* consist of a single, flat, large, multinucleate cell, while *cellular slime molds* consist of amoebalike cells that live independently but unite with other cellular slime mold cells to form a single, large, flat, multinucleate organism.

- **Algae:** The term *algae* refers to a large number of photosynthetic organisms that range from single-celled forms to complex, multicellular organisms that resemble plants. Algal species occur in bodies of both fresh and saltwater. Algae are subdivided into several divisions, based in part on the pigments they possess:

  - **Red algae:** Almost exclusively marine organisms (seaweeds) and include both single-celled and multicellular species.

  - **Golden-brown algae (dinoflagellates):** Single-celled organisms that are surrounded by thick plates that give them an armored appearance.

  - **Golden algae (diatoms):** Single-celled organisms with cell walls containing *silica* (glass). In the ocean, diatoms carry out photosynthesis and serve as an important food source at the base of food chains.

  - **Brown algae:** Primarily multicellular marine organisms (seaweeds); include the rockweeds and kelps.

  - **Green algae:** Include both single-celled forms and complex, multicellular organisms. They share many characteristics with plants and are thought to be the ancestors of higher plants.

Kingdom Fungi

Fungi, together with eubacteria and some protists, are the major decomposers of organic matter on Earth. Most fungi digest nonliving organic matter such as wood, leaves, and dead animals. However, some fungi are parasitic, living off other living organisms. Parasitic fungi cause many diseases affecting plants, animals, and humans. Other fungi are economically important, including species used to flavor cheeses. One species, *Penicillium notatum,* is the original source of the antibiotic penicillin.

The method by which they obtain nutrients distinguishes fungi from the other kingdoms. Fungi secrete enzymes into the environment that break down organic matter, and then they absorb the nutrients through their cell membranes. This process is referred to as *extracellular digestion.*

Kingdom Plantae

Plants are multicellular eukaryotic organisms with the ability to produce their own food through the process of photosynthesis. They are divided into two main groups:

- **Nonvascular plants:** Plants that do not have specialized tissues for transporting water and nutrients. Nonvascular plants include the mosses, liverworts, and hornworts. Because these plants lack conducting tissues, they cannot grow very large and cannot retain water for extended periods of time, which is why they are typically found only in moist areas. They also must rely on the presence of water for fertilization to occur.

- **Vascular plants:** Plants that contain specialized structures for transporting water and nutrients. The vascular plants encompass several divisions of plants. They are characterized by the presence of two types of specialized tissue, the xylem and the phloem. *Xylem* conducts water and minerals upward through the plant, while *phloem* transports sugars from the leaves, where they are made during photosynthesis, to other parts of the plant body. The vascular tissue also serves as a means of support in the plant, so vascular plants are capable of maintaining a much larger size than nonvascular plants.

The different types of vascular plants include:

- **Seedless vascular plants:** Among the seedless vascular plants are the ferns and fern allies (whisk ferns, club mosses, spike mosses, and horsetails). These plants reproduce by producing spores on the surfaces of their leaves or in specialized cone-shaped structures.

- **Vascular plants with unprotected seeds:** The vascular plants that produce unprotected (naked) seeds are known as gymnosperms. Their seeds are not enclosed within tissues of the female parent. Included in the gymnosperms are pines, firs, spruces, redwoods, cypresses, yews, cycads, ginkgoes, and ephedra.

  Mature trees produce male and female cones. The male cones produce pollen grains, which contain sperm, while the female cones produce two or three egg cells that develop within ovules located on the surfaces of the cone scales.

- **Vascular plants with protected seeds:** The *angiosperms* are the most highly developed and complex of the vascular plants. They are the flowering plants, of which more than a quarter of a million species have been identified. The seeds of angiosperms develop within protective tissues of the female parent.

Angiosperms deserve more discussion. The flower of the angiosperm consists of four rings of modified leaves:

- **Sepals:** Sepals comprise the outer ring of modified leaves that enclose and protect the developing flower bud. In some species the sepals are small and green, while in others they become colored and resemble petals.
- **Petals:** Petals comprise the next ring of modified leaves found in the flower. Flower petals are usually colorful and serve to attract pollinators.
- **Stamens (male reproductive structures):** These structures comprise the third ring of modified leaves. Each stamen consists of a stalk called the *filament* with a bulbous structure at the end called the *anther,* in which pollen grains are produced.
- **Pistil (female reproductive structure):** This structure consists of a tubular structure called the *style,* with a sticky surface at the top for catching pollen called the *stigma,* and an enlarged region (*ovary*) at the base. Within the ovary, an embryo sac develops that consists of eight nuclei.

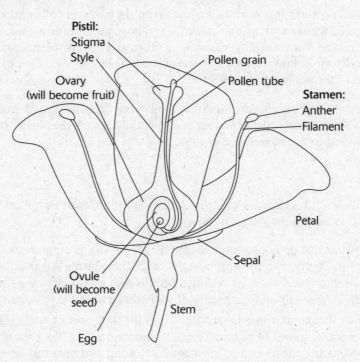

During pollination, pollen grains land on the stigma of a female flower where they germinate and form a pollen tube. The pollen tube grows down the style and into an opening in the ovary. When the pollen tube reaches the ovary, two sperm cells are released. One sperm cell unites with the egg cell in the embryo sac to form a diploid zygote, while the second sperm unites with two other nuclei to form a triploid endosperm. The remaining nuclei in the embryo sac degenerate.

The zygote develops into an embryo surrounded by the endosperm, which serves as nutritive tissue for the developing embryo. The ovary tissue expands, forming a fruit, which serves as a protective covering for the developing seed. The protective fruit tissue also serves as an important dispersal mechanism:

- Fleshy fruits are often eaten by animals, and the seeds travel inside the animals to other locations where they are dispersed when the animals defecate.
- Some fruits have barbs or hooks on the outer fruit that attach to the fur of animals and are dispersed in that manner.

- Some fruits become dry when they mature. Some of these split open quite forcefully, ejecting their seeds great distances, while other dry fruits have thin paper tissue attached to the seeds that serve as wings for dispersal by wind.

Structure and Function of Higher Plants

All higher plants have four types of tissues:

- **Vascular tissues:** These tissues include xylem, which conducts water and minerals from the roots upward throughout the plant, and phloem, which transports dissolved foods in all directions throughout the plant.
- **Dermal tissues:** Dermal tissues cover the outside of the plant and consist primarily of *epidermal cells* (equivalent to the skin cells of humans). These tissues protect the plant from injury and water loss.
- **Ground tissues:** These tissues are located between the vascular tissues and dermal tissues and are responsible for storing carbohydrates that the plant produces.
- **Meristematic tissues:** Meristematic tissues are found in regions where the plant is actively growing (where cell division is occurring). *Primary meristematic tissues* are found in the root tips and shoot tips and are responsible for growth in length. *Secondary (lateral) meristematic* tissues are found only in woody plants and are responsible for growth in width.

Plant Organs

The three organs found in plants are the roots, the stems, and the leaves. Flowers are modified leaves.

The main functions of the roots are:

- Anchoring the plant in the soil
- Taking in water and minerals from the soil

The main functions of the stems are:

- Supporting the plant
- Transporting water, minerals, and sugars by the vascular system
- Storing water and food

The main functions of the leaves are:

- Making food for the plant through photosynthesis
- Allowing for evaporation and gas exchange through pores on the surfaces of leaves called *stomata*

Kingdom Animalia

Animals are multicellular eukaryotic organisms. They differ from plants in that they are heterotrophic: They take in food and digest it into smaller components. The primary mode of reproduction in animals is sexual. Two major groups of animals exist: the invertebrates and the vertebrates. *Invertebrates* are animals that do not have a spine, while *vertebrates* are animals with spines.

Invertebrates

The invertebrates are represented by numerous phyla, and comprise approximately 95 percent of all animal species.

- **Phylum Porifera** includes a number of simple animals commonly referred to as sponges.
- **Phylum Cnidaria** includes hydras, jellyfish, sea corals, and sea anemones.
- **Phylum Platyhelminthes** includes the flatworms, such as planaria and tapeworms.
- **Phylum Aschelminthes** (also known as Nematoda) includes the nematodes, or roundworms, many of which are microscopic.

- **Phylum Annelida** includes the segmented worms, such as earthworms and leeches.
- **Phylum Mollusca** includes soft-bodied animals, such as the snail, clam, squid, oyster, and octopus. Some members secrete a hard shell.
- **Phylum Arthropoda** includes spiders, ticks, centipedes, lobsters, and insects.
- **Phylum Echinodermata** includes sea stars, brittle stars, sea urchins, and sea cucumbers. These animals have spiny skin that helps protect them from predators. All echinoderms have an internal support system called an *endoskeleton* and a large body cavity containing a set of canals called a *water vascular system*.
- **Phylum Chordata** includes both invertebrate members and vertebrate members.

Vertebrates

Members of the phylum Chordata that have spines are classified in the subphylum Vertebrata. The more than 40,000 living species of vertebrates are divided into several classes encompassing the fishes, amphibians, reptiles, birds, and mammals.

- **Fishes** are aquatic animals with a streamlined shape and a functional tail that allows them to move rapidly through water. Fishes exchange gases with their environment through gills, although a few species possess lungs that supplement gas exchange.
- **Amphibians** are animals that live both on land and in water. They include the frogs, toads, and salamanders. Amphibians live on land and breathe air; however, they also are able to exchange gases through their skin and the inner lining of their mouth. Amphibians remain in moist environments to avoid dehydration, and lay their eggs in water because the eggs would quickly dry out on land. Young amphibians (for example, tadpoles) live in the water, while the adults live on land.
- **Reptiles** include lizards, snakes, crocodiles, alligators, and turtles. Reptiles possess a dry, scaly skin that retards water loss, and the structure of their limbs provides better support for moving quickly on land. Their lungs have a greater surface area than those of amphibians, allowing them to inhale greater quantities of air. The circulatory system in reptiles includes a three-chambered heart that separates oxygen-rich blood from oxygen-poor blood. Reproduction in reptiles occurs on land.
- **Birds** possess many structures that make them adapted to flight. For example, the body is streamlined to minimize air resistance, they have feathers, and their bones are light and hollow. Feathers also serve to insulate against loss of body heat and water. Birds are *homeothermic*, meaning they are able to maintain a constant body temperature. The rapid pumping of their four-chambered heart and a high blood flow rate contribute to this characteristic.
- **Mammals** are animals that have hair and nourish their young with milk that they produce through mammary glands. The presence of body hair or fur helps maintain a constant body temperature in these homeothermic animals. Several types of mammals exist:
    - **Monotremes** are egg-laying mammals that produce milk. The duck-billed platypus and the spiny anteater are monotremes.
    - **Marsupials** are mammals whose embryos develop within the mother's uterus for a short period of time before birth. After birth, the immature babies crawl into the mother's abdominal pouch, where they complete their development. Kangaroos, opossums, and koala bears are marsupials.
    - **Placental mammals** include rabbits, deer, dogs, cats, whales, monkeys, and humans. These mammals have a placenta—a connection between the embryo and the mother's uterine wall that allows the embryo to obtain nutrients from the mother. Embryos are attached to the placenta and complete their development within their mother's uterus.

All mammals are characterized by a highly developed nervous system, and many have developed acute senses of smell, hearing, sight, taste, or touch. Mammals rely on memory and learning to guide their activities. They are considered the most successful group of animals on Earth today.

Anatomy and Physiology

Nutrition and Digestion

All the elements and compounds that a living organism takes in are considered nutrients. Animals, including humans, are heterotrophic organisms, and their nutrients consist of preformed organic molecules. These organic molecules usually must be processed into simpler forms by digestion before cells can take them in.

The nutrients used by animals include:

- **Carbohydrates:** The basic source of energy for all animals. Glucose is the carbohydrate most often used as an energy source; it is metabolized during cellular respiration to provide energy in the form of adenosine triphosphate (ATP). Other useful carbohydrates include maltose, lactose, sucrose, and starch.
- **Lipids:** Used to form cellular membranes, the sheaths surrounding nerve fibers, and certain hormones. One type of lipid, fat, is a useful energy source made from fatty acids and glycerol.
- **Nucleic acids:** Used to make DNA and RNA. They are obtained from ingesting plant and animal tissues.
- **Proteins:** Form the framework of the animal body and are major components of membranes, muscles, ligaments, tendons, and enzymes. Twenty different amino acids make up proteins. While the body can make some amino acids, others must be supplied by diet.
- **Minerals:** Required by animals in small amounts and include phosphorous, sulfur, potassium, magnesium, and zinc. Animals usually obtain these minerals when they consume plants.
- **Vitamins:** Organic compounds essential in trace amounts for animal health. Some vitamins are *water-soluble* (break down easily in water), while others are *fat-soluble* (break down easily in fats).

The Human Digestive System

Human digestion is a complex process that consists of breaking down large organic masses into smaller particles that the body can use as fuel. The major organs or structures that coordinate digestion in humans include the mouth, esophagus, stomach, small intestine, and large intestine.

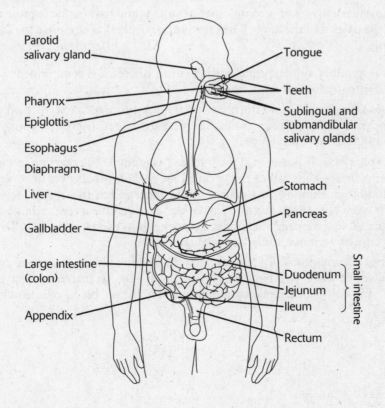

The following list goes into more detail on the major parts of the digestive system:

■ **Mouth:** The mouth is a specialized organ for receiving food and breaking up large organic masses into smaller particles. This process is accomplished through a combination of biting and chewing by the teeth and moistening by saliva. During chewing, the tongue moves food around and manipulates it into a mass called a *bolus*. The bolus is pushed back into the pharynx (throat) and forced through the opening to the esophagus.

■ **Esophagus:** This thick-walled muscular tube located behind the windpipe extends through the neck and chest to the stomach. The bolus of food moves through the esophagus by a series of rhythmic muscular contractions (*peristalsis*). The esophagus joins the stomach at a point just below the diaphragm. A valve-like ring of muscle called the *cardiac sphincter* surrounds the opening to the stomach. The sphincter relaxes as the bolus passes through and then quickly closes.

■ **Stomach:** This expandable pouch is located high in the abdominal cavity. Layers of stomach muscle contract and churn the bolus of food with gastric juices to form a soupy liquid called *chyme*. The stomach stores food and prepares it for further digestion. The chyme spurts from the stomach through a sphincter into the small intestine.

■ **Small intestine:** This structure, which is about 23 feet long in the average human, is divided into three sections:

  ■ **Duodenum:** The first 10 to 12 inches; where most chemical digestion takes place.

  ■ **Jejunum:** The next 10 feet; where most absorption occurs.

  ■ **Ileum:** The final 12 feet; where absorption is completed. Substances that have not been digested or absorbed then pass into the large intestine.

■ **Large intestine:** This structure, also known as the colon, is about 3 feet in length. The colon's chief functions are to absorb water and to store, process, and eliminate the residue following digestion and absorption. The intestinal matter remaining after water has been reclaimed is known as *feces*. Feces consist of nondigested food particles, billions of mostly harmless bacteria, bile pigments, and other materials. The feces are stored in the rectum and passed out through the anus to complete the digestion process.

Human Respiratory System

The human respiratory system consists of a complex set of organs and tissues that capture oxygen from the environment and transport the oxygen to the lungs. The organs and tissues that comprise the human respiratory system include the following:

■ **Nose:** The human respiratory system begins with the nose, where air is conditioned by warming and moistening. Hairs trap dust particles and purify the air.

■ **Pharynx:** Air passes from the nose into the pharynx (throat). From the pharynx, two tubes called *Eustachian tubes* open to the middle ear to equalize pressure. The pharynx also contains tonsils and adenoids, which trap and filter microorganisms.

■ **Trachea:** From the pharynx, air passes into the trachea (windpipe). The opening to the trachea is a slitlike structure called the *glottis*. A thin flap of tissue called the *epiglottis* folds over the opening during swallowing and prevents food from entering the trachea. At the upper end of the trachea, several folds of cartilage form the *larynx,* or voice box. In the larynx, flaplike tissues called *vocal cords* vibrate when a person exhales and produce sounds. At its lower end, the trachea branches into two large *bronchi*. These tubes branch into smaller *bronchioles,* which terminate into sacs called *alveoli*.

■ **Lungs:** Human lungs are composed of approximately 300 million alveoli, which are cup-shaped sacs surrounded by a capillary network. Red blood cells pass through the capillaries, and oxygen enters and binds to the hemoglobin. In addition, carbon dioxide contained in the red blood cells leaves the capillaries and enters the alveoli.

Human Circulatory System

The function of the human circulatory system is to transport blood and oxygen from the lungs to various tissues of the body. The components of the human circulatory system include the following:

- **Heart:** The human heart is about the size of a clenched fist. It contains four chambers: two atria and two ventricles. Oxygen-poor blood enters the right atrium through a major vein called the *vena cava.* The blood passes into the right ventricle and is pumped through the *pulmonary artery* to the lungs for gas exchange. Oxygen-rich blood returns to the left atrium via the *pulmonary vein.* The oxygen-rich blood flows into the left ventricle, from which it is pumped through a major artery, the *aorta. Coronary arteries* supply the heart muscle with blood. The heart is controlled by nerves that originate on the right side in the upper region of the atrium at a node called the *pacemaker.*

- **Blood:** The fluid portion of the blood, the plasma, is a straw-colored liquid composed primarily of water. Nutrients, hormones, clotting proteins, and waste products are transported in the plasma. Red blood cells and white blood cells are also suspended in the plasma.

- **Red blood cells:** Also called erythrocytes, red blood cells are disk-shaped cells produced in the bone marrow. They do not have a nucleus and are filled with hemoglobin. *Hemoglobin* is a red-pigmented protein that binds loosely to oxygen and carbon dioxide and transports these substances throughout the body. Red blood cells usually have immune-stimulating antigens on their surfaces.

- **White blood cells:** Also called *leukocytes,* white blood cells are generally larger than red blood cells and contain nuclei. They are also produced in the bone marrow and have various functions in the body. Certain white blood cells, called *lymphocytes,* are part of the immune system. Other cells, called *neutrophils* and *monocytes,* function primarily as *phagocytes;* they attack and engulf invading microorganisms.

- **Platelets:** Platelets are small, disk-shaped blood fragments produced in the bone marrow. They lack nuclei and are much smaller than red blood cells. They serve as the starting material for blood clotting.

- **Lymphatic system:** The lymphatic system is an extension of the circulatory system and consists of:
  - **Lymph:** A watery fluid derived from plasma that has seeped out of capillaries.
  - **Lymphatic vessels:** Capillaries that return fluids to the circulatory system.
  - **Lymph nodes:** Hundreds of tiny, capsulelike bodies located in the neck, armpits, and groin; the lymph nodes filter the lymph and digest foreign particles.
  - **Spleen:** The site where red blood cells are destroyed; it is composed primarily of lymph node tissue.

Human Excretory System

The human excretory system removes waste from the body through the kidneys. The human kidneys are bean-shaped organs located on either side of the spine at about the level of the stomach and liver. Blood enters the kidneys through renal arteries and leaves through renal veins. Tubes (*ureters*) carry waste products from the kidneys to the urinary bladder for storage or release. The product of the kidneys is *urine,* a watery solution of waste products, salts, organic compounds, uric acid, and urea. *Uric acid* results from the breakdown of nucleic acids and *urea* results from the breakdown of amino acids in the liver. Both of these nitrogen-rich compounds can be poisonous to the body and must be removed in the urine.

Human Endocrine System

The human body has two levels of coordination: nervous coordination and chemical coordination. *Chemical coordination* is centered on a system of glands known as *endocrine glands,* which secrete hormones that help coordinate the major body systems. These glands are situated throughout the body and include the following:

- **Pituitary gland:** The pituitary gland is located at the base of the human brain.
- **Thyroid gland:** The thyroid gland lies against the pharynx at the base of the neck.
- **Adrenal glands:** The adrenal glands are two pyramid-shaped glands lying atop the kidneys.

- **Pancreas:** The pancreas is located just behind the stomach. It produces two hormones: insulin and glucagon.
- **Ovaries:** The ovaries in females function as endocrine glands; they secrete estrogens, which encourage the development of secondary female characteristics.
- **Testes:** The testes in males also function as endocrine glands; they secrete androgens (including testosterone), which promote secondary male characteristics.

Human Nervous System

Nervous coordination enables the body to rapidly respond to external or internal stimuli. The human nervous system is divided into the *central nervous system* (the brain and spinal cord) and the *peripheral nervous system* (the nerves extending to and from the central nervous system).

Central Nervous System

The spinal cord extends from the base of the brain to the end of the spine. Three membranes called *meninges* surround the spinal cord and protect it. The neurons of the spinal cord serve as a coordinating center and a connecting system between the peripheral nervous system and the brain.

The brain is the organizing and processing center of the central nervous system. It is the site of consciousness, sensation, memory, and intelligence. The brain receives impulses from the spinal cord and from 12 pairs of cranial nerves coming from and extending to the other senses and organs. The brain can also initiate activities without external stimuli. Three major regions of the brain are recognized:

- **Hindbrain:** The hindbrain consists of the following three regions:
  - **Medulla:** The swelling at the tip of the brain; serves as a passageway for nerves extending to and from the brain and controls life functions such as breathing, heart rate, circulation, digestion, and other involuntary functions.
  - **Cerebellum:** Lies adjacent to the medulla; coordinates muscle contractions.
  - **Pons:** The swelling between the medulla and the midbrain; acts as a bridge between various regions of the brain.
- **Midbrain:** The midbrain lies between the hindbrain and forebrain. It consists of a collection of crossing nerve tracts and a group of fibers that arouse the forebrain when something unusual happens.
- **Forebrain:** The forebrain consists of the following regions:
  - **Cerebrum:** The site of such activities as speech, vision, movement, hearing, smell, learning, memory, logic, creativity, and emotion.
  - **Thalamus:** Serves as an integration point for sensory impulses.
  - **Hypothalamus:** Synthesizes hormones for storage in the pituitary gland and serves as the control center for hunger, thirst, body temperature, and blood pressure.
  - **Limbic system:** A collection of structures that rings the edge of the brain and serves as centers of emotion.

Peripheral Nervous System

The peripheral nervous system is a collection of nerves that connect the brain and spinal cord to other parts of the body and the external environment. It includes the following:

- **Sensory somatic system:** Carries impulses from the external environment and the senses; it permits humans to be aware of the outside environment and react to it voluntarily.
- **Autonomic nervous system:** Works on an involuntary basis; it is divided into two regions:
  - **Sympathetic nervous system:** Prepares the body for emergencies; impulses propagated by the sympathetic nervous system cause the heartbeat to increase, the arteries to constrict, and the pupils to dilate.
  - **Parasympathetic nervous system:** Allows the body to return to its normal state following an emergency, and is also responsible for helping digestion and preparing the body for sleep.

Human Reproduction

Reproduction is an essential process for the survival of a species. Human reproduction takes place by the coordination of the male and female reproductive systems. In humans, both males and females have evolved specialized organs and tissues that produce haploid cells by meiosis, the sperm and the egg. These cells fuse to form a zygote that eventually develops into a growing fetus. A network of hormones is secreted that controls both the male and female reproductive systems and assists in the growth and development of the fetus, as well as the birthing process.

Male Reproductive System

The male reproductive system is composed of the following structures:

- **Testes (or testicles):** Two egg-shaped organs located in a pouch outside the body called the *scrotum.*
- **Seminiferous tubules:** Coiled passageways within the testes where sperm cells are produced.
- **Penis:** The organ responsible for carrying the sperm cells to the female reproductive tract; within the penis, the sperm are carried in a tube called the *urethra.*
- **Semen:** Fluid composed of secretions from the prostate gland, seminal vesicles, and Cowper's glands, plus the sperm cells.

Female Reproductive System

The organs of the female reproductive system include the following structures:

- **Ovaries:** Two oval organs lying within the pelvic cavity that produce and release eggs for fertilization. They also produce sex hormones.
- **Fallopian tubes:** Tubes leading from the ovaries that the eggs enter after they are released from the ovaries following meiosis; the site of fertilization of the egg by the sperm.
- **Uterus:** A muscular organ in the pelvic cavity to which the eggs travel through the Fallopian tubes.
- **Endrometrium:** The inner lining of the uterus; it thickens with blood and tissue in anticipation of a fertilized egg cell. If fertilization fails to occur, the endometrium degenerates and is shed in the process of *menstruation.*
- **Cervix:** The opening at the lower end of the uterus.
- **Vagina:** The tube leading from the cervix to outside the body; the vagina receives the penis and the semen.

The sperm cells in the semen pass through the cervix and uterus into the Fallopian tubes, where fertilization takes place. Fertilization brings together 23 chromosomes from the male (sperm) and 23 chromosomes from the female (egg), resulting in the formation of a fertilized egg cell (called a zygote) with 46 chromosomes—the number present in normal human cells.

Ecology

Ecology is the discipline of biology concerned primarily with the interaction between organisms and their environments. The many levels of organization among living organisms include the following:

- **Population:** A population is a group of individuals belonging to one species living in a defined area.
- **Community:** A community consists of the various plant and animal species living in a defined area. Within a community, each population of organisms has a *habitat* (the physical location where an organism lives) and a *niche* (the role that organism plays in the community).
- **Ecosystem:** An ecosystem includes all the organisms living together in a community, interacting with each other and with nonliving factors (water, light, soil, and so on).

Organisms living together in an ecosystem interact with each other in various ways, including the following:

- **Mutualism:** The relationship between two organisms is mutually beneficial, such as the relationship between fungi and cyanobacteria in lichens.
- **Commensalism:** The relationship benefits one organism but does not affect the other organism, such as the bacteria living in the intestines of humans.

- **Parasitism:** The relationship benefits one organism, while the other is harmed. The microorganisms that cause human diseases are parasites.
- **Predation:** The relationship benefits one organism and the other is harmed (as in parasitism). Predation occurs when one organism feeds on another organism.

One of the major factors responsible for sustaining an ecosystem is the flow of energy within it. Energy is transferred from one organism to another in an ecosystem through food chains. Food chains are composed of the following:

- **Producers:** Photosynthesizing organisms (plants, algae) that absorb the energy from the sun to make their own food.
- **Primary consumers:** Organisms that feed directly on producers (herbivores).
- **Secondary consumers:** Organisms that feed on primary consumers (carnivores).
- **Decomposers:** Organisms (fungi, slime molds, bacteria) that break down dead organisms and recycle the nutrients back into the environment.

Many food chains interact to form a food web.

The food pyramid illustrates the availability of food in an ecosystem at successive levels (*trophic levels*) of a food chain. The number of producers, which are always at the base of the pyramid, is high, and the number of consumers at the top of the pyramid is always low. The difference in numbers of individuals at each trophic level occurs because only a small percentage of the food energy available at one level can be passed on to the next, because much of the energy is used up during metabolism in the organisms at each level. The following figure shows a hypothetical food pyramid.

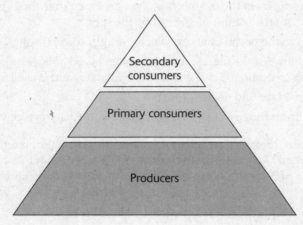

Another mechanism for sustaining an ecosystem is the recycling of nutrients and minerals. Carbon, nitrogen, and phosphorus are examples of substances that are recycled through ecosystems. Much of the carbon is recycled through respiration; however, the majority is recycled through decomposition. Nitrogen, which is vital for the synthesis of proteins and nucleic acids, is released to the atmosphere as waste products by bacteria.

All of life is confined to a five-mile vertical space around the surface of the Earth, called the *biosphere*. The biosphere is composed of the living organisms and the physical environment that blankets the Earth. The physical environment includes the rocky material of the Earth's surface, the water on or near the Earth's surface, and the blanket of gases surrounding the Earth.

The biosphere is divided into subunits called *biomes*. Each biome is characterized by climatic conditions that determine which species will live there. Examples of biomes include deserts, tropical forests, temperate forests, prairies, tundra, and taiga (the southern edge of the tundra).

Chemistry

Matter and Atomic Structure

Matter is defined as anything with a definite mass that takes up volume. The three common states of matter are solids, liquids, and gases. Matter can be made of simple materials such as diamond, water, or neon, or it can be made of very complex materials such as heat-resistant shields on the space shuttle, blood plasma, or anesthesiology gases. The differences between solids, liquids, and gases are numerous, but they can be summarized as follows:

- **Solids** have a defined mass, volume, and shape.
- **Liquids** have a defined mass and volume, but not a defined shape.
- **Gases** have a defined mass, but not a defined volume or shape (they will expand to fill any container).

All of the matter you see and use is made of a few fundamental particles called protons, neutrons, and electrons. These *subatomic particles* make up atoms. *Atoms* are specific collections of protons and neutrons surrounded by electrons. These subatomic particles differ in mass and charge, as seen in the following table:

Subatomic particle	Symbol	Actual mass (grams)	Relative charge
Proton	p or p$^+$	$1.673 \cdot 10^{-24}$	+1
Neutron	*	$1.675 \cdot 10^{-24}$	0
Electron	e or e–	$9.109 \cdot 10^{-28}$	−1

Protons and neutrons are located at the center of the atom and make up a region called the *nucleus*. Outside of the nucleus are the electrons, which make up the electron cloud. The current model of an atom is fairly complex, but the figure below provides a rough representation. The electrons are not randomly arranged in the electron cloud, but occupy locations called *orbitals*. These orbitals can be arranged in shells. The illustration shows how electrons can be arranged in shells around the nucleus of an atom, although the actual picture is much more complex than this "solar system model" of the atom would indicate.

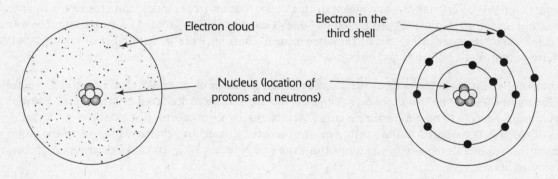

With these three particles, atoms can be made, and from these atoms, every solid, liquid, and gas in the universe is formed. Conceivably, the number of combinations of subatomic particles is infinite, but not all combinations are stable. In fact, only 118 elements have been found or created. An *element* is a material that cannot be chemically broken down into something simpler. Elements are made of atoms and, as noted, atoms are made of electrons, protons, and neutrons.

The Periodic Table

To save time and space, elements have been assigned a one- or two-letter designation called an *atomic* or *elemental symbol*. Always capitalize the first letter and, if there is a second letter, always write it in lowercase. Without this rule, some chemical formulas might be misinterpreted. (Co is the symbol for cobalt, but CO is the symbol for a compound containing one carbon atom and one oxygen atom.) A list of all atomic symbols is given in the periodic table.

PERIODIC TABLE OF THE ELEMENTS

1 **H** 1.0079																	2 **He** 4.0026
3 **Li** 6.941	4 **Be** 9.012											5 **B** 10.811	6 **C** 12.011	7 **N** 14.007	8 **O** 16.00	9 **F** 19.00	10 **Ne** 20.179
11 **Na** 22.99	12 **Mg** 24.30											13 **Al** 26.98	14 **Si** 28.09	15 **P** 30.974	16 **S** 32.06	17 **Cl** 35.453	18 **Ar** 39.948
19 **K** 39.10	20 **Ca** 40.08	21 **Sc** 44.96	22 **Ti** 47.90	23 **V** 50.94	24 **Cr** 51.00	25 **Mn** 54.93	26 **Fe** 55.85	27 **Co** 58.93	28 **Ni** 58.69	29 **Cu** 63.55	30 **Zn** 65.39	31 **Ga** 69.72	32 **Ge** 72.59	33 **As** 74.92	34 **Se** 78.96	35 **Br** 79.90	36 **Kr** 83.80
37 **Rb** 85.47	38 **Sr** 87.62	39 **Y** 88.91	40 **Zr** 91.22	41 **Nb** 92.91	42 **Mo** 95.94	43 **Tc** (98)	44 **Ru** 101.1	45 **Rh** 102.91	46 **Pd** 105.42	47 **Ag** 107.87	48 **Cd** 112.41	49 **In** 114.82	50 **Sn** 118.71	51 **Sb** 121.75	52 **Te** 127.60	53 **I** 126.91	54 **Xe** 131.29
55 **Cs** 132.91	56 **Ba** 137.33	57 **. La** 138.91	72 **Hf** 178.49	73 **Ta** 180.95	74 **W** 183.85	75 **Re** 186.21	76 **Os** 190.2	77 **Ir** 192.22	78 **Pt** 195.08	79 **Au** 196.97	80 **Hg** 200.59	81 **Tl** 204.38	82 **Pb** 207.2	83 **Bi** 208.98	84 **Po** (209)	85 **At** (210)	86 **Rn** (222)
87 **Fr** (223)	88 **Ra** 226.02	89 **†Ac** 227.03	104 **Rf** (261)	105 **Db** (262)	106 **Sg** (263)	107 **Bh** (262)	108 **Hs** (265)	109 **Mt** (266)	110 **§** (269)	111 **§** (272)	112 **§** (277)	§ Not yet named					

	58 **Ce** 140.12	59 **Pr** 140.91	60 **Nd** 144.24	61 **Pm** (145)	62 **Sm** 150.4	63 **Eu** 151.97	64 **Gd** 157.25	65 **Tb** 158.93	66 **Dy** 162.50	67 **Ho** 164.93	68 **Er** 167.26	69 **Tm** 168.93	70 **Yb** 173.04	71 **Lu** 174.97
* Lanthanide Series														
† Actinide Series	90 **Th** 232.04	91 **Pa** 231.04	92 **U** 238.03	93 **Np** 237.05	94 **Pu** (244)	95 **Am** (243)	96 **Cm** (247)	97 **Bk** (247)	98 **Cf** (251)	99 **Es** (252)	100 **Fm** (257)	101 **Md** (258)	102 **No** (259)	103 **Lr** (260)

Although it may appear to have an unusual shape, the periodic table is an incredibly useful document. The elements are arranged from left to right in order of the number of protons in their nucleus (the number of protons in a nucleus is called an element's *atomic number*). Thus, the element hydrogen is listed first because atoms of hydrogen have only one proton in the nucleus. The element helium has two protons in the nucleus, so it is listed second. The atomic number of iron (Fe) is 26, so it has 26 protons in its nucleus and is listed just after manganese (Mn, atomic number 25) and just before cobalt (Co, atomic number 27).

Atomic Number

The atomic number is a very important concept in chemistry. Not only does every iron atom have 26 protons in its nucleus, but any atom that has 26 protons in its nucleus *must be* an iron atom. The atomic number is the defining characteristic of an atom. All atoms of the same element must have the same number of protons, but can have differing numbers of neutrons and electrons.

If the number of electrons is the same as the atomic number (number of protons), then the atom is neutral because the number of negative and positive charges is the same. If there are fewer electrons than protons, a *cation* will result, which will have a positive charge. Metals usually form cations (for example, Ag forms Ag^+). If an excess of electrons compared to the number of protons exists, a negative charge will arise on the atom, resulting in an *anion*. Nonmetals usually form anions (for example, N forms N^{3-}). An atom, or group of atoms, with a charge is called an *ion*.

Isotopes

Elements that have the same number of protons, but different numbers of neutrons, are called *isotopes*. An example of an element with two isotopes is copper. All copper atoms contain 29 protons; however, 69% of copper atoms contain 34 neutrons and 31% contain 36 neutrons. The two types of copper atoms will have different masses because they have a different number of neutrons; however, they are both copper atoms. Magnesium is an element with 3 isotopes; all magnesium atoms have 12 protons, but 79% have 12 neutrons, 10% have 13 neutrons, and 11% have 14 neutrons. To differentiate between these isotopes, a value called the *mass number* is used.

The mass number of an element is the number of protons and neutrons in an atom. Thus, 79% of magnesium atoms have a mass number of 24, 10% have a mass number of 25, and 11% have a mass number of 26.

Atomic Mass

This difference in atomic composition is reflected by the *atomic mass* (or atomic weight) of an element. In the periodic table, the atomic mass is the number found underneath each atomic symbol. By definition, the atomic mass is the average mass of all the naturally occurring isotopes of an element. The atomic mass of magnesium is listed as 24.305 *amu* (*atomic mass units*), although no atom of Mg actually has this mass; it is obtained by averaging the masses of the three Mg isotopes.

Electrons

Another piece of useful information found within the periodic table is the number of electrons found in the outer shell of an atom. These electrons are known as *valence electrons* and are responsible for holding atoms together when making a compound. Each column in the periodic table is called a *group* and each group of atoms has a similar configuration of electrons. Taking a look at the first column of the periodic table (1A), you will find H, Li, Na, K, Rb, Cs, and Fr. Each of these elements has only one electron in its outer shell; group 2A elements have two electrons in their outer shell; group 8A elements have eight electrons in their outer shell.

The periodic table gets its name from the repetitive trends occurring for the elements when the elements are arranged by atomic number (*not* the atomic mass). These trends allow distinctions between the different elements, and a major distinction is that of metals and nonmetals. Notice that in the periodic table there is a dark "stair step" line found on the right-hand side of the periodic table. Elements to the left of the line are *metals,* elements to the right of the line are called *nonmetals,* and elements that straddle the line are called *metalloids* (or *semimetals*). These are elements that have physical and chemical properties of both metals and nonmetals. Silicon (Si) and germanium (Ge) are examples of metalloids — both are used extensively in computer chips and solar cells.

Atoms, Molecules, and Compounds

From the periodic table, you can see that there are many elements. Think for a moment, though, about the matter around you. The number of different materials, colors, odors, tastes, and tactile sensations is almost limitless. How can 112 different elements make up the billions of different materials that we perceive every day?

Most of the materials you see are not made of just one type of element. Most of the materials are made of compounds. *Compounds* are substances with two or more *different* atoms of an element bound together. Examples of compounds are water (H_2O), sulfuric acid (battery acid, H_2SO_4), sodium hydrogen carbonate (baking soda, $NaHCO_3$), sucrose (table sugar, $C_{12}H_{22}O_{11}$), and sodium chloride (table salt, NaCl). Each of these substances is made of more than one kind of element. If those elements are nonmetals (for example, H_2O, H_2SO_4, and $C_{12}H_{22}O_{11}$), they are classified as molecules. *Molecules* are collections of nonmetals that are tightly bound together. When a metal and a nonmetal are bound together (for example, NaCl or Na_2CO_3), they are classified as *formula units*.

Some elements also occur in molecular form, and examples include oxygen (O_2), hydrogen (H_2), nitrogen (N_2), and fluorine (F_2). Thus, when chemists speak of elemental hydrogen, they actually refer to two hydrogen atoms bound together, which is different than just two atoms of hydrogen.

A compound will have different properties than the elements that make it up. Thus, hydrogen is a gas at room temperature and is quite flammable; oxygen is a gas at room temperature that supports combustion, but water (made from hydrogen and oxygen) is a *liquid* at room temperature and doesn't burn or support combustion. Because water has different properties than the elements that comprise it, water is a compound of hydrogen and oxygen and not simply a mixture.

Chemical Equations and Reactions

To describe the chemical changes that occur around and inside of you, chemists have developed a shorthand notation in which the symbols for elements and compounds are written showing the chemical change. An example of a chemical equation is the combustion of propane (C_3H_8) with elemental oxygen (O_2) to form carbon dioxide (CO_2) and water (H_2O):

$$C_3H_8 + O_2 \rightarrow CO_2 + H_2O$$

The equation is written with *reactants* on the left of the reaction and *products* on the right. The arrow shows that a reaction is taking place. While this equation shows the transformation of propane and oxygen into two different compounds, the equation is not quite complete. Because of the *Law of Conservation of Mass,* matter cannot be created or destroyed, and the same kind and number of atoms must appear on each side of the reaction arrow. Thus, to correctly write the equation above, coefficients in front of each chemical species must be added. The coefficient is the number that is added in order to balance both sides of the equation.

$$C_3H_8 + 5\,O_2 \rightarrow 3\,CO_2 + 4\,H_2O$$

Thus, one molecule of propane will react with five molecules of oxygen to form three molecules of carbon dioxide and four molecules of water. Information about the state of the reactant or product is written after each chemical formula to indicate whether that substance is a gas (g or ↑), liquid (l), solid (s or ↓), or dissolved in water (aq):

$$C_3H_8\,(g) + 5\,O_2\,(g) \rightarrow 3\,CO_2\,(g) + 4\,H_2O\,(l)$$

Many different types of chemical reactions are possible; however, you can classify some of them according to one of the four basic reaction types: synthesis, decomposition, single replacement, or double replacement.

Synthesis (or combination) reaction: When two or more different substances react to form one compound.

>   *Examples:* $Mg(s) + F_2\,(g) \rightarrow MgF_2\,(s)$
> $2Mg(s) + O_2\,(g) \rightarrow 2MgO(s)$

Decomposition reaction: When one substance breaks down into two or more different materials.

>   *Examples:* $2NaHCO_3\,(s) \rightarrow Na_2CO_3\,(s) + CO_2\,(g) + H_2O(l)$
> $Cu(OH)_2\,(s) \rightarrow CuO(s) + H_2O(l)$

Single replacement (or single displacement) reaction: When an element reacts with a compound and an exchange takes place.

>   *Examples:* $Zn(s) + CuBr_2\,(aq) \rightarrow Cu(s) + ZnBr_2\,(aq)$
> $3Ag(NO_3)(aq) + Al(s) \rightarrow Al(NO_3)_3\,(aq) + 3Ag(s)$

In the first reaction, zinc (Zn) and copper (Cu) exchange, and in the second reaction, silver (Ag) and aluminum (Al) exchange.

Double replacement (or double displacement or metathesis) reactions: When two compounds react and an exchange occurs.

>   *Examples:* $Ag(NO_3)(aq) + NaCl(aq) \rightarrow Na(NO_3)(aq) + AgCl(s)$
> $FeCl_3\,(aq) + 3Na(OH)(aq) \rightarrow 3NaCl(aq) + Fe(OH)_3\,(s)$

In the first reaction, silver (Ag) and sodium (Na) exchange, and in the second reaction, iron (Fe) and sodium (Na) exchange.

Acids, Bases, and Solutions

An *acid* is a compound that increases the quantity of hydrogen ions (H^+) in an aqueous solution. A *base* is a compound that decreases the H^+ concentration by increasing hydroxide (OH^-) concentration. The *pH scale* is a measure of how much acid is in a solution. Solutions with a low pH (0–7) are considered *acidic;* solutions with a pH of exactly 7 are *neutral* (neither acidic nor basic); and solutions with a high pH (7–14) are considered *basic.*

Because acids and bases are all around you, it is a good idea to know some of the more common compounds that constitute acids and bases. Examples of common acids include the following:

- **Acetic acid** ($HC_2H_3O_2$): Vinegar is a 5% solution of acetic acid.
- **Carbonic acid** (H_2CO_3): This acid is found in carbonated beverages, resulting from CO_2 dissolving in water.
- **Citric acid** ($H_3C_6H_5O_7$): This acid is found in citrus fruits and is responsible for their tangy flavor.
- **Hydrochloric acid** (HCl): This acid is found in gastric juices of humans.
- **Nitric acid** (HNO_3): This acid is used in fertilizer production.
- **Phosphoric acid** (H_3PO_4): This acid is used in colas to prevent bacterial growth, and is also used in fertilizer production.
- **Sulfuric acid** (H_2SO_4): This acid is the most industrially produced compound in the world and is also used in car batteries.

Examples of common bases include the following:

- **Ammonia** (NH_3): This base is used as a general cleanser and in fertilizers.
- **Lime** (CaO): This base is used to raise the pH of soil for farming.
- **Lye** (NaOH): This base is used in the manufacture of soap.
- **Milk of magnesia** ($Mg(OH)_2$): This base is used as an antacid.
- **Sodium carbonate** (Na_2CO_3): This base is used in paper manufacturing and water softening.

Pure water is neutral and therefore is neither acidic nor basic. When acids and bases react, they form water and salt as the products. For example:

$$NaOH(aq) + HCl(aq) \rightarrow H_2O(l) + NaCl(aq)$$

The sodium hydroxide (base) reacts with hydrochloric acid to form water and sodium chloride (salt).

A *solution* is a homogeneous mixture composed of a *solvent* (the material in greater proportion) and a *solute* (the material dissolved in the solvent). Saltwater is an example in which water is the solvent and sodium chloride (NaCl) is the solute.

Important Elements of the Periodic Table

The first 20 elements of the periodic table are among the most abundant on Earth and in the universe. These elements are important in the materials that we use every day and especially in our own metabolic function.

- **Hydrogen (H) (Atomic number: 1):** This clear, colorless, odorless, low-density gas is the most abundant element in the universe (although not on Earth). It occurs as a diatomic molecule in its elemental form (H_2) and was used in balloons and dirigibles until the *Hindenburg* disaster. When hydrogen ions (H^+) are dissolved in water, they cause the solution to be acidic. Water is made of two parts hydrogen to one part oxygen (H_2O).
- **Helium (He) (Atomic number: 2):** This clear, colorless, odorless, low-density gas is the second most abundant element in the universe, although it is only present as a very small fraction of the Earth. Because it is not flammable, it is used as a substitute for hydrogen in balloons and blimps. It is very unreactive and occurs as single atoms in its elemental form.

- **Lithium (Li) (Atomic number: 3):** This low-density metal is very reactive in the elemental state, and easily forms a +1 ion (Li^+). A major use of lithium is to treat bipolar disorders such as manic depression.

- **Beryllium (Be) (Atomic number: 4):** This low-density metal is used in high-tech alloys for its strength, but machinists must be careful as the dust is toxic.

- **Boron (B) (Atomic number: 5):** Boron is a metalloid, but its oxide finds use in heat-resistant glass and in borax, a cleaning agent.

- **Carbon (C) (Atomic number: 6):** Carbon is a solid at room temperature, but is a versatile element. Diamond, one of the hardest substances known, and graphite, a material used as a lubricant and in pencil lead, are both made of pure carbon. Obviously, these two materials are remarkably different and their properties have to do with how the carbon atoms bond. Carbon always forms four bonds and is one of the few elements that can form stable, long chains with itself. Carbon is the basis of organic chemistry. A major environmental concern is the production of carbon dioxide (CO_2) from the burning of fossil fuels. Although CO_2 constitutes only a small percentage of the overall atmosphere (less than 0.1%), it is one of the major contributors to the greenhouse effect.

- **Nitrogen (N) (Atomic number: 7):** This clear, colorless, odorless gas makes up about 78% of the Earth's atmosphere. In its elemental form, it occurs as a diatomic species (N_2) and is a very stable molecule. It is not flammable and reacts with few other elements. Scuba divers have to be careful about not rising to the water's surface too quickly or nitrogen bubbles can form in their blood vessels and cause the bends. A major use of nitrogen is in ammonia (NH_3) and in nitrates (NO_3^-), both of which are used in fertilizers. Nitrogen isn't toxic, but neither plants nor animals can metabolize it. Certain bacteria (*nitrogen-fixing* bacteria) can metabolize nitrogen.

- **Oxygen (O) (Atomic number: 8):** Oxygen is a clear, colorless, odorless gas that supports combustion. It reacts with almost all elements to form stable oxides. In its elemental state, it is a diatomic molecule (O_2) and makes up about 20% of the atmosphere. The ozone layer in the stratosphere is made of a triatomic oxygen molecule (O_3). Hydrogen peroxide (H_2O_2) is a common disinfectant for minor cuts that decomposes into water and molecular oxygen.

- **Fluorine (F) (Atomic number: 9):** Fluorine is a pale yellow gas that is very reactive. Elemental fluorine occurs as a diatomic molecule (F_2) and can etch glass. Compounds containing fluoride (F^-, the anion of fluorine) are used in toothpaste to help make tooth enamel more resistant to decay.

- **Neon (Ne) (Atomic number: 10):** Neon is a clear, colorless, odorless, nonflammable gas that does not support combustion. Neon is quite unreactive. It is used in neon signs, but not exclusively; other gases may be used in signs as well.

- **Sodium (Na) (Atomic number: 11):** Sodium is a shiny, soft, solid, reactive metal in its elemental state. It reacts vigorously with water to liberate elemental hydrogen, and sometimes this reaction is violent enough to ignite the evolving H_2. It readily forms +1 cations (Na^+) and is found only in the cationic state in nature. It makes up a major constituent of ocean brine; table salt is made of one part sodium and one part chlorine (NaCl).

- **Magnesium (Mg) (Atomic number: 12):** Magnesium is a shiny, solid metal that reacts slowly with water at room temperature. Elemental magnesium burns brightly when ignited. Chlorophyll, a chemical responsible for the green color of plants and used by plants to capture the sun's energy, contains a magnesium atom in the center of the molecule.

- **Aluminum (Al) (Atomic number: 13):** Aluminum is a lightweight, shiny, solid metal used in products ranging from soft drink cans to airplane wings. It is a durable metal that forms a thin oxide coating (Al_2O_3) that prevents further reaction. As a result, you often find aluminum used in applications where iron would rust (for example, railings at a beach).

- **Silicon (Si) (Atomic number: 14):** Silicon is a solid, shiny semimetal whose oxide (SiO_2) is a major constituent in glass, sand, and quartz. Silicon is important to computer technology, which requires elemental silicon for computer chips. Many caulking materials contain silicone, a silicon-based polymer.

- **Phosphorus (P) (Atomic number: 15):** Phosphorus is a solid at room temperature, but can occur in white, red, or even black forms. White and red are the most common forms and can be symbolized as P_4. White phosphorus is so reactive it must be stored in distilled water so it will not ignite spontaneously with oxygen in the air. Phosphate salts (PO_4^{3-}) are mined for use in fertilizers, matches, and even soft drinks.

- **Sulfur (S) (Atomic number: 16):** Sulfur is a yellow, brittle solid that is mined in its elemental form (S_8). Sulfur has many industrial uses as sulfuric acid (H_2SO_4), but the common consumer is familiar with its use in car batteries. Sulfur emissions from coal-burning power plants result in the formation of sulfur oxides (SO_2 and SO_3), which ultimately are converted to H_2SO_4, the principal acid in acid rain.

- **Chlorine (Cl) (Atomic number: 17):** Chlorine is a yellow gas with a choking odor. In its elemental form it is diatomic (Cl_2), toxic, and quite reactive. This element readily forms anions with a –1 charge (Cl^-). This ion is a major constituent of ocean brine and when reacted with sodium forms table salt. Bleach consists of a solution of hypochlorite (ClO^-), a chlorine-oxygen anion. Swimming pools are kept relatively free of algae and bacteria by chemicals that contain chlorine. Ozone destruction in the stratosphere is thought to occur when chlorofluorocarbons (CFCs) are subjected to high-intensity ultraviolet radiation, causing chlorine atoms to be torn off CFC molecules and react with O_3.

- **Argon (Ar) (Atomic number: 18):** Argon is a clear, colorless, odorless, nonreactive gas that makes up about 1% of the atmosphere. Its major uses are in light bulbs to blanket tungsten filaments, neon signs, and in welding to prevent more reactive gases (for example, oxygen) from reacting with hot materials.

- **Potassium (K) (Atomic number: 19):** Potassium is a shiny, soft, solid, reactive metal in its elemental state. It reacts with water even more vigorously than sodium to liberate hydrogen. In nature, only the +1 cation (K^+) is found, not the elemental state. Potassium is an important nutrient in muscle contraction and is used in fertilizers.

- **Calcium (Ca) (Atomic number: 20):** Calcium is a shiny metal that reacts with water more vigorously than magnesium, but not enough to ignite the liberated hydrogen as sodium and potassium metals do. Calcium readily forms a +2 cation (Ca^{2+}) and is a major constituent of tooth enamel ($Ca_5(PO_4)_3(OH)$) and bones. Marble is the mineral calcium carbonate ($CaCO_3$), and lime, used to reduce soil acidity, is CaO.

By looking at the various descriptions of the elements, you can note a reoccurrence of properties. This "periodic" nature of the elements is why the periodic table is so useful. The following groups of the periodic table are particularly important:

- **Group 1A, the alkali metals.** This group consists of Li, Na, K, Rb, Cs, and Fr and all react to form +1 ions. These elements form salts that are soluble in water.

- **Group 2A, the alkaline earth metals.** This group consists of Be, Mg, Ca, Sr, Ba, and Ra and all react to form +2 ions.

- **Group 5A, the pnictogens.** This group consists of N, P, As, Bi, and Sb and all react to form –3 ions.

- **Group 6A, the chalcogens.** This group consists of O, S, Se, Te, and Po and all react to form –2 ions.

- **Group 7A, the halogens.** This group consists of F, Cl, Br, I, and At and all react to form –1 ions.

- **Group 8A, the noble gases.** This group consists of He, Ne, Ar, Kr, Xe, and Rn, none of which are very reactive. These elements do not readily form ions, or even compounds.

Measurements

Knowing the chemical properties of various elements and compounds is obviously essential to understanding chemistry, but of nearly equal importance is being able to measure quantities of chemicals. To systematically quantify such properties as mass, length, temperature, and the quantity of material, the *Systeme Internationale d'Unites* (SI units) was developed. The following table lists common SI units.

Common SI Units of Measurement in Chemistry		
Property	**Unit**	**Abbreviation**
Mass	kilogram	kg
Length	meter	m
Temperature	kelvin	K
Amount of material	mole	mol

To express very large or very small numbers, another concept is used, *metric system prefixes*. The following table lists common prefixes encountered in chemistry.

Common Metric Prefixes		
Prefix Name	**Prefix Abbreviation**	**Meaning**
giga-	G	1 billion, 1,000,000,000
mega-	M	1 million, 1,000,000
kilo-	k	1 thousand, 1,000
hecta-	h	100
deka-	da	10
deci-	d	0.1
centi-	c	0.01
milli-	m	1 thousandth, 0.001
micro-	μ	1 millionth, 0.000001
nano-	n	1 billionth, 0.000000001

With these two concepts, it is possible to express very large or very small quantities in a uniform way that other scientists can understand. Thus, if you have 1,000,000 grams, it can be reported as 1 megagram or 1 Mg. If the length of a piece of material is 0.00005 meters, it can be reported as 0.05 millimeters or 0.05 mm.

There is no SI unit for volume. Because volume will have units of length cubed, officially, scientists would use cubic meters (m^3) to express volume. In practice, cubic meters are rarely used and a unit called the *liter* was established. See the following table for common conversions for mass, length, and volume.

Common Conversions for Mass, Length, and Volume		
Mass Conversions	**Length Conversions**	**Volume Conversions**
1 pound = 453.59 g	1 inch = 2.54 cm	$1\ m^3$ = 264.17 gallons
1 kg = 1,000 g	1 km = 0.6214 miles	$1\ dm^3$ = 1 liter (1 L)
1 g = 1,000 mg	1 m = 100 cm	$1\ cm^3$ = 1 mL
	1 m = 1,000 mm	1 L = 1000 mL
	1 km = 1,000 m	

Although the SI unit of temperature is the *kelvin,* it is more common to measure temperature in the *Celsius scale* (formerly called the *centigrade scale*) or in Fahrenheit. The formulas to convert from one scale to another are given below.

To convert from Celsius (°C) to kelvin (K): K = 273 + °C

To convert from Celsius (°C) to Fahrenheit (°F): °F = (1.8 × °C) + 32

To convert from Fahrenheit (°F) to Celsius (°C): °C = (°F – 32) ÷ 1.8

The unit most useful to chemists is the mole because a mole defines how much material is present. By definition, one *mole* of anything is $6.022 \cdot 10^{23}$ of that material. This is an unfathomably large number. (For example, a mole of pennies would stretch to the sun and back 38 billion times stacked side by side!) The mole is a useful unit of measure for chemists because dealing with an individual atom means dealing with a mass so small, no balance in the world could measure it. Because of the way mass and moles are defined, the atomic weight of any atom is equivalent to one mole of that element. Thus, 55.847 grams of element 26 (iron, Fe) is $6.022 \cdot 10^{23}$ Fe atoms. For oxygen (atomic number 8), only 15.9994 grams contains 1 mole ($6.022 \cdot 10^{23}$) of oxygen atoms. This concept can be further extended to compounds, so that one mole of water (H_2O) has a mass of 18.01528 grams (this figure was obtained by adding the atomic mass of two hydrogens and one oxygen). The value 18.01528 g/mol is called the *molar mass* (the mass of one mole of a compound or element).

This concept is directly applicable to chemical reactions because chemical reactions are written in terms of molar ratios. Look at the balanced chemical reaction below:

$$C(s) + O_2\,(g) \rightarrow CO_2\,(g)$$

You can interpret this reaction as one atom of carbon reacting with one molecule of oxygen to form one molecule of carbon dioxide. You can also interpret it as one mole of carbon reacting with one mole of oxygen molecules to form one mole of carbon dioxide. Furthermore, you can now associate masses with this reaction because one mole of carbon is 12 grams, one mole of O_2 is 32 grams, and one mole of CO_2 is 44 grams. In all reactions, the combined masses of the reactants should equal the combined masses of all of the products. This is a result of the Law of Conservation of Mass that was stated earlier.

This concept can be applied to another chemical reaction, $2C(s) + O_2\,(g) \rightarrow 2CO(g)$.

In this reaction, two moles of carbon react with one mole of molecular oxygen to yield two moles of carbon monoxide. In such a case, 24 grams of carbon (2 moles of C $\times$ 12 g/mole) and 32 grams of O_2 will form 56 grams of CO (2 moles of CO $\times$ 28 g/mole).

Energy

In addition to mass conservation, energy is conserved. Energy can be either a reactant or a product of a reaction. The two main types of energy are kinetic and potential. *Kinetic energy* is the energy of motion. The faster something is moving, the higher its kinetic energy. Kinetic energy will often express itself in terms of temperature; the atoms of hot materials generally move more quickly than the atoms of cold materials. *Potential energy* is energy that is stored (it has the potential to do work). This type of energy is dependent on the distance an object is from the ground or, more importantly for chemists, the types of chemical bonds that are present. When bonds form, energy is released; when bonds break, energy is absorbed.

Radioactivity

The energy stored in the nucleus of an atom is also a type of potential energy. This energy is used in nuclear power plants, radiation therapy medical treatments, and even to build powerful bombs. This energy releases when an unstable nucleus decomposes into a more stable nucleus. Oftentimes, this nuclear change results in the emission of a *gamma ray* (a high-energy light particle) or it may even emit a neutron, a *beta particle* (an electron), or an *alpha particle* (two neutrons and two protons).

It is impossible to determine exactly which atom will emit radiation, but scientists can measure an average decay time. The most useful measurement is the half-life. The *half-life* of a material is the time it takes for 50% of it to decay into another species of material. The half-life of the uranium isotope with a mass number of 235 (U-235, the isotope used in building the first nuclear bomb) is 700 million years. If you had 100 grams of U-235, in 700 million years (one half-life) there would only be 50 grams left. After 1.4 billion years (two half-lives), only 25 grams of U-235 would be left. After 2.1 billion years (three half-lives), only 12.5 grams of U-235 would remain. After each half-life period, 50% of the remaining material converts to a new material. In this case, the U-235 decays into Th-231.

Metals

A quick look at the periodic table indicates that the vast majority of elements are metals. Therefore, many elements share common properties. The metals all are

- Solid at room temperature (mercury—Hg—is an exception, as it is a liquid)
- Malleable, which means that you can hammer them into thin sheets
- Ductile, which means that you can draw them into thin wires

- Sectile, which means that you can cut them into thin sheets
- Good conductors of heat and electricity
- Shiny
- Silvery in color (except for copper and gold)

Most metals are found combined with oxygen or sulfur in nature; however, the *coinage metals* (copper, silver, and gold) can occur in their native (that is, elemental) state.

Metals can also form *alloys*, which are solid mixtures of two or more metals. An *amalgam* is a mixture of mercury with some other metal and can be a solid or liquid, depending on the amount of mercury.

Organic Chemistry

Organic chemistry is the study of carbon-based molecules. (There are a few exceptions; materials that contain pure carbon [diamond, graphite, charcoal, anthracite, and so on] and carbon oxides such as CO, CO_2, or carbonates [CO_3^{2-}] are not considered organic molecules.) Because carbon can attach to other carbon atoms and form long chains, the number and variety of organic compounds is vast. Proteins, DNA, cell walls, oils, hair, pharmaceuticals, gasoline, ethanol, herbicides, and plastics are all examples of organic (carbon-based) materials.

As an example of the differences between organic compounds, look at the properties of these various alcohols:

- **Methanol (wood alcohol),** CH_4O, is used as a solvent in chemistry, but can cause blindness if consumed orally by humans.
- **Ethanol (grain alcohol),** C_2H_6O, is the main ingredient in alcoholic beverages for consumption.
- **Propanol (rubbing alcohol),** C_3H_8O, is used topically to disinfect open cuts.

You name simple organic compounds by the number of carbon atoms in a continuous chain, so that the prefix meth- indicates one carbon atom, eth- indicates two carbon atoms, and prop- indicates three carbon atoms. The following table shows common prefixes.

Organic Prefixes			
Number of C Atoms in a Chain	Prefix	Number of C Atoms in a Chain	Prefix
1	meth-	6	hex-
2	eth-	7	hept-
3	prop-	8	oct-
4	but-	9	non-
5	pent-	10	dec-

Physics

Motion

Motion occurs when an object or body is moved from one place to the next. The three types of motion are *translational, rotational,* and *vibrational.* Translational (or linear) motion involves motion in a straight line; rotational motion happens when motion occurs about an axis; and vibrational motion entails motion about a fixed point.

For more on the subject of motion, please see www.cliffsnotes.com/go/ASVAB2E.

Translational Motion

Two factors characterize the motion of an object in a straight line: a change in position or *displacement* of the object over a period of time, and movement with respect to a reference point. The motion of an object can be described quantitatively by making references to its *speed, velocity,* and *acceleration.*

Speed, Velocity, and Acceleration

The *speed* of an object is a measure of how fast it is moving and can be calculated using the following equation:

$$\text{Speed} = \frac{\text{Distance traveled}}{\text{Time taken}}$$

Like speed, *velocity* describes how fast an object is moving. Unlike speed, velocity specifies the direction of motion as well. In this respect, speed is said to be a *scalar quantity* while velocity is described as a *vector quantity.* The mathematical representation of the velocity of an object is given by the following equation:

$$\text{Velocity} = \frac{\text{Displacement}}{\text{Time}}$$

When the velocity of an object changes with time, the object is said to be *accelerating.* In general, an increase in velocity is called *acceleration* and a decrease in velocity is called *deceleration.* Both can be calculated using the following equation:

$$\text{Acceleration} = \frac{\text{Change in velocity}}{\text{Time}}$$

Acceleration, like velocity, is a vector quantity. Acceleration is positive when acceleration occurs in the same direction in which the object is moving (*acceleration*), and negative when acceleration occurs in a direction opposite to that in which the object is moving (*deceleration*).

Graphical Analysis of Motion

You can analyze the motion of an object by using two types of graphs: *position-time graphs* and *velocity-time graphs.*

- **A position-time graph** shows how the displacement or position of a moving object changes with time. As a result, the velocity of such an object is equal to the slope of the graph.
- **A velocity-time graph** illustrates how the velocity of an object changes over time. Hence, you can determine the acceleration of an object from the slope of a velocity-time graph. In addition to acceleration, you can use a velocity-time graph to determine the distance covered by an object that is undergoing acceleration. You can derive the distance traveled by an object in motion from the area under the graph.

Motion in One Dimension

Motion occurs in one dimension when an object or body moves along either the x or y coordinate. Motion along the x coordinate is often referred to as *linear motion,* while motion along the y coordinate is referred to as *motion in a vertical plane* or *free fall.* In many instances, the acceleration of an object along either coordinate is constant or is such that the acceleration can be considered constant. When this constancy occurs, motion can be quantified using a series of equations called the *equations of kinematics.*

Equations of Kinematics

Kinematics is the study of how things move. The equations of kinematics consist of four main equations that are the result of the mathematical manipulation of the equations used to calculate velocity and acceleration. These equations involve five variables:

x = displacement

a = acceleration

v = final velocity

v_o = initial velocity

t = time

The equations are:

$$v = v_o + at$$

$$x = \frac{1}{2}(v_o + v)t$$

$$x = v_o t + \frac{1}{2}at^2$$

$$v^2 = v_o^2 + 2ax$$

Each of the equations of kinematics contains four of these five variables. Therefore, if you know three of them, you can calculate the fourth variable by solving the relevant equation.

Motion in Vertical Plane

All objects above the Earth undergo vertical motion with an acceleration of about 9.8 m/s². This *vertical motion* is called *free fall* and is the result of the force of gravity. Because all objects above the Earth have the same acceleration, the motion of an object undergoing vertical motion can be quantified using the equations of kinematics.

When using the equations of kinematics to describe the motion of an object in free fall, the acceleration due to gravity, g, is substituted for a, and is y substituted for x. In addition, you can consider the vector quantities v and y as positive when they are directed downward and negative when directed upward.

When an object is thrown upward it will undergo uniform deceleration, as a result of gravity, until it comes to rest. The object will then begin to fall, during which time it is uniformly accelerated by the force of gravity. If air resistance is neglected, then the time required for the object to rise is the same as the time required for the object to fall.

Newton's Laws of Motion

A force is defined as a *push* or a *pull*. Force can set in motion an object at rest, or change the velocity of an object in motion. At any particular time, multiple forces can act on an object. How these multiple forces affect the motion of the object is governed by a collection of laws called *Newton's laws of motion*. The laws of motion are as follows:

- **First law of motion:** An object that has no net or unbalanced force acting on it will remain at rest or it will move with a constant velocity in a straight line.
- **Second law of motion:** The acceleration of an object is directly proportional to the net force acting on it and inversely proportional to its mass.
- **Third law of motion:** When one object exerts a force on a second object, the second object will exert a force on the first that is equal in magnitude but opposite in direction.

The first law of motion emphasizes the concept of *inertia,* which is defined as the tendency of an object to resist changes in its motion. Thus, the first law is often called the *law of inertia.*

The second law enables us to calculate the net force acting on an object and is often stated in the form of the following equation:

$$F = ma$$

F is the net force in newtons, *m* is the mass of the object in kilograms,
and *a* is acceleration in meters per second squared (m/s^2).

Like velocity, force is a vector quantity, having both magnitude and direction. Force is positive when it is applied in the same direction as the motion it generates and negative when applied in a direction that is opposite to the motion.

Weight and Mass

The *weight* (*W*) of an object is the force exerted on it by the force of gravity and, like all forces, is measured in newtons. The force of gravity acts on an object whether it is falling, resting on the ground, or being lifted, and results in a downward acceleration of 9.8 m/s^2. The weight of an object can be calculated using the equation:

$$W = mg$$

W is the weight of the object, *m* is the mass of the object, and *g* is the acceleration due to gravity.

From the weight equation, it is obvious that the *mass* of an object is not the same as its weight. The weight of an object depends on the acceleration due to gravity, and, therefore, varies from place to place. On the other hand, *mass* is a measure of the amount of matter contained within an object and is independent of gravity. Hence, an astronaut weighs less on the moon, where the acceleration due to gravity is about 1.6 m/s^2, but his or her mass is the same as it is on Earth.

Momentum

Momentum refers to moving things. It is a product of the mass of an object and its velocity (p = *m*v). An object at rest has no momentum. To stop an object in motion, you have to impart equal and opposite momentum to that object and that depends on the product of the mass and speed of that object. It is easier to stop a bug flying toward you (hold up your hand) than it would be to stop a truck. Both their velocity and mass differ.

Frictional Force

Friction is the force that opposes the motion between two surfaces that are in contact. The two types of friction are static and kinetic. *Static friction* is the force that opposes motion of an object at rest, while *kinetic friction* is the opposing force between surfaces in relative motion. Kinetic friction is always less of a force than static friction.

Energy and Work

The mass of an object not only measures the amount of matter it contains, but also the amount of energy. The energy of an object can be divided into two main types: potential and kinetic. *Potential energy* is the energy possessed by an object because of its position and is often called stored energy. *Kinetic energy* is the energy possessed by an object because of its motion.

Both the kinetic and potential energy of an object change when work is done by or on the object. Therefore, *work* is defined as the transfer of energy to an object when the object moves because of the application of a force. The work done on an object can be calculated using the formula

$$W = F \times d$$

W is work measured in joules, *F* is force measured in newtons, and *d* is distance measured in meters.

Energy is defined as the capacity to do work. When you raise an object, such as a hammer, above the Earth, you do work against gravity. The work that you do against gravity is the *gravitational potential energy,* and you can calculate it by using the following equation:

$$PE = mgh$$

PE is the potential energy in joules, *m* is mass of the object in kilograms, *g* is the acceleration due to gravity, and *h* is the height above the ground.

As the object falls, it is accelerated by the force of gravity and the object loses gravitational potential energy. According to the Law of Conservation of Energy, energy can neither be created nor destroyed but can be converted from one form to another. Thus, any decrease in the gravitational potential energy of the object is accompanied by a corresponding increase in the object's kinetic energy. You can calculate the kinetic energy of a moving body by using the following equation:

$$KE = \frac{1}{2}mv^2$$

KE is the kinetic energy of the object, *m* is its mass, and *v* is its velocity.

The conversion of energy from one form to another is generally carried out by a number of practical devices. Such devices include the following:

- **Generators:** Convert mechanical energy into electrical energy.
- **Motors:** Convert electrical energy into mechanical energy.
- **Batteries:** Used to convert chemical, thermal, nuclear, or solar energy into electrical energy.
- **Photocells or Photovoltaic cells:** Convert light energy into electrical energy.

The rate at which any device converts energy from one form to another is called the *power* and is defined by the following formula:

$$P = \frac{W}{t}$$

P is power in watts, *W* is work in joules, and *t* is time in seconds.

Fluids

A fluid is any substance that offers little resistance to changes in its shape when pressure is applied to it. Of the three states of matter, only gases and liquids are considered fluids. Of all the properties that characterize fluids, one of the most important is their ability to exert pressure.

Pressure

Pressure is defined as the force exerted per unit area and is mathematically represented by the following equation:

$$P = \frac{F}{A}$$

P is pressure in pascals, *F* is force in newtons, and *A* is area in square meters.

You can explain the ability of fluids to exert pressure by the *kinetic molecular theory,* which states that the particles that make up fluids are in continuous, random motion, as illustrated in the following figure. These particles will undergo collisions with the walls of their container or any surface with which they make contact. Each time a particle makes contact, it exerts a force, and it is this force that is referred to as pressure.

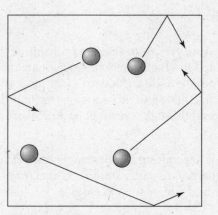

Molecular motion and collisions
of particles in a fluid

Three governing principles are essential when dealing with fluids in motion or at rest: *Archimedes'*, *Pascal's*, and *Bernoulli's* principles.

Archimedes' Principle

According to *Archimedes' principle*, an object immersed in a fluid is buoyed up by a force equal to the weight of the fluid that the object displaces. The magnitude of the buoyant force is given by the following equation:

$$F = \rho V g$$

F is the buoyant force in newtons, ρ is density of the fluid, *V* is volume of the fluid displaced, and *g* is acceleration due to gravity.

It can be proven that the volume of an object immersed in a fluid is the same as the volume of the fluid that it displaces. An object immersed in a fluid will sink or float depending on the relative value of its weight and the buoyant force exerted on it by the fluid. An object will sink if the buoyant force is less than the weight of the object. If the buoyant force equals the weight of the object, the object will float at any depth in the liquid; if the buoyant force is greater than the weight of the object, the object floats with part of its volume above the surface.

Pascal's Principle

Pascal's principle states that any pressure applied to a confined fluid, at any point, is transmitted undiminished throughout the fluid. Pascal's principle led to the development of *hydrostatics*, in which machines, such as the hydraulic lift, use pistons to multiply forces applied to fluids at rest. Pascal's principle is represented by the following equation:

$$\frac{F_1}{A_1} = \frac{F_2}{A_2}$$

F_1 and F_2 are the forces on pistons 1 and 2, respectively and A_1 and A_2 are their respective areas.

Bernoulli's Principle

According to this principle, as the velocity of a fluid increases, the pressure exerted by that fluid decreases. This principle underlies the study of *hydrodynamics*, which is a study of the effects of fluids in motion. Bernoulli's principle offers a partial explanation of how airplanes are able to lift into flight.

For more on the subject of motion, please see www.cliffsnotes.com/go/ASVAB2E.

Sound Waves

Sound waves consist of a series of pressure variations that are transmitted through matter. These pressure variations are of two types: compressions and rarefactions. *Compressions* are areas of high pressure and *rarefactions* are areas of low pressure. The compressions and rarefactions associated with sound waves are produced when a vibrating source causes air molecules to collide and, in so doing, transmit the pressure variations away from the source of the sound. Sound cannot travel through a vacuum because there are no particles present for motion and collision to occur.

The speed at which sound travels in air depends on the air temperature. At sea level and room temperature, the speed of sound is about 343 m/s. In addition to gases, sound can also travel through solids and liquids. In general, the speed of sound is greater in solids and liquids than in gases.

When sound waves encounter hard surfaces, they undergo reflections called *echoes*. The time required for an echo to return to its source can be used to determine the distance between the source and the reflecting surface. Bats use echoes to determine distance while navigating their night flights, as do ships equipped with sonar.

The number of compressions or rarefactions generated in one second by sound waves is called the *frequency* or *pitch* of the sound. However, if the source of the sound is in motion, an observer detecting the sound will perceive sound of higher or lower frequencies. If the source of the sound is moving away from the observer, the observer will detect sound waves of decreasing frequency. Conversely, if the source is moving toward the observer, the observer will detect sound waves of increasing frequency. This apparent change in the frequency of sound because the sound source or observer is in motion is called the *Doppler effect*. The Doppler effect has given rise to many practical applications, including radar detectors and ultrasound.

Electricity

Electricity involves the flow of electrical energy from a source, such as a battery or generator, to a load, such as a lamp or motor. A *load* is any device that transforms electrical energy into other forms of energy. For example, a lamp transforms electrical energy into light and heat energy, while a motor transforms electrical energy into mechanical energy.

Electrical energy is transported in the form of an *electric current,* consisting of the flow of negatively charged *electrons.* This flow of electrons occurs in a closed path, called an *electrical circuit,* in which metal wires conduct the flow of electrons from the source of the electrical energy to the various loads within the circuit. A substance that allows for the flow of an electric current is called a *conductor;* a substance that does not is called an *insulator.*

For an electric current to flow in a conductor, a *potential difference* or *voltage* must exist between its ends. The greater the voltage, the greater the current, and vice versa. All substances, insulators or conductors, offer some form of *resistance* to the flow of an electric current. The amount of resistance depends on the length of the material, the area of the material, and an intrinsic property called *resistivity,* as well as the temperature. The magnitude of the current flowing in a conductor can be calculated using the following equation:

$$I = \frac{V}{R}$$

I is current in amperes, *V* is voltage in volts, and *R* is resistance in ohms.

Earth Science

Geology

The Earth is a relatively solid planet revolving around the sun. The Earth is approximately 8,000 miles in diameter. It is not a uniform sphere but is composed of several layers: core, mantle, asthenosphere (plastic mantle), and crust.

We live on the thinnest layer, the *crust*. The nature of Earth's interior structure has been inferred from seismic (earthquake) activity and studies. The following illustration shows the upper level of the Earth.

The Earth's Crust and Interior

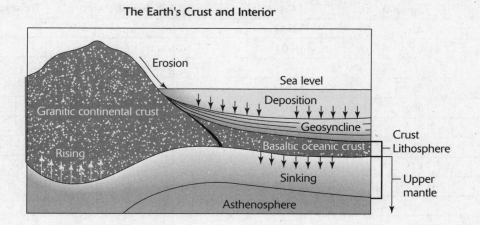

The crust (our home) is, itself, not uniform. The continental portion of the crust is mostly granitic rock. The portions of the crust underlying the oceans are composed mostly of basaltic rock. Both segments of the crust are broken into large tectonic plates that move over the plastic asthenosphere.

This movement is known as *plate tectonics* and helps explain many patterns of major crustal activity, including earthquakes, volcanoes, mountain building, sea-floor spreading, and ocean trenching.

The Earth's crust is stable only over a relatively short period of geologic time. Minor earthquakes occur constantly throughout the crust, volcanoes are active, and the ocean bottoms are constantly in flux.

The rocks of the Earth themselves are constantly changing. Rocks are composed of a mixture of *minerals* (inorganic crystalline substances with definite chemical compositions and unique physical properties). The most common minerals on Earth's crust are feldspar, quartz, mica, pyroxene, and olivine, but many others can be found. These myriad minerals are recombined into various rock types because of crustal activity.

The major rock types—igneous, sedimentary, and metamorphic—are named based on their origin and possess specific structures that allow geologists to identify them. *Igneous rocks* are crystalline; *sedimentary rocks* are composed of cemented rock fragments and may contain fossils; and *metamorphic rocks* are usually foliated (minerals aligned into bands).

The atmosphere and hydrosphere (the watery layer of the earth's suface, including oceans, seas, lakes, ponds, rivers, and streams) interface with the Earth's crust in a vast exchange of energy that causes erosion, weathering, and deposition. The crustal material above sea level is constantly worn down but is constantly replaced as tectonic activity adds new material. Thus the Earth's crust is in a *dynamic equilibrium*.

Meteorology

The Earth's gaseous envelope, our atmosphere, provides a means to absorb, refract, and reflect the energy (solar radiation, or insolation) reaching us from the sun. In the process of these activities the atmosphere maintains a dynamic equilibrium of energy flow that gives us weather and climate. *Weather* is the day-to-day condition of the atmosphere; *climate* is the long-term condition in a given area.

Earth's atmosphere is a layered structure of mainly two gases, nitrogen (78%) and oxygen (21%), with many other gases (1%) mixed in. Although they make up less than 1% of the air, these other gases—which include carbon dioxide, water vapor, sulfur dioxide, argon, and ozone—are important in meteorological events.

The following table shows what elements make up various parts of the Earth and its atmosphere.

Percentage by Volume				
Element	Symbol	Crust	Hydrosphere	Troposphere
Aluminum	Al	0.47	—	—
Calcium	Ca	1.03	—	—
Hydrogen	H	—	66	—
Iron	Fe	0.43	—	—
Magnesium	Mg	0.29	—	—
Nitrogen	*	—	—	78
Oxygen	O	93.77	33	21
Potassium	K	1.83	—	—
Silicon	Si	0.86	—	—
Sodium	Na	1.32	—	—
Others		—	1	1

The layer of the atmosphere we live in is called the *troposphere,* and it is here that the phenomenon called *weather* occurs. Weather variables include air temperature, barometric pressure (air's weight), wind speed and direction, humidity (air's moisture content), cloud cover, and precipitation. The measurement of these weather elements requires the use of specialized instruments such as thermometers, barometers, wind vanes, anemometers, hydrometers, and rain gauges.

Meteorologists use present weather readings from widespread locations to map and delineate large chunks of the troposphere into *air masses* (air parcels with relatively uniform temperature and moisture content). The movement and interaction of these air masses enable scientists to predict or forecast weather changes. For example, when a cold, dry air mass moves into a warm, moist air mass, meteorologists know that the resulting cold front (the interface between the two masses) will trigger thunderstorms as it moves.

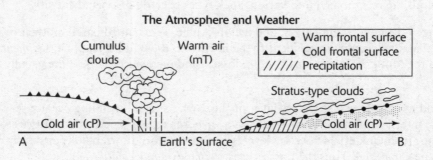

The Atmosphere and Weather

Climate and seasonal variations are caused by the complex interactions of latitude, altitude, water proximity, and change in the Earth's relative axial tilt with respect to the sun. The complexity of these events is one reason climate change and even seasonal changes are not easy to predict.

Much of the energy needed to power Earth's weather and climate is the result of the water cycle that converts insolation into useable force in Earth's transparent air.

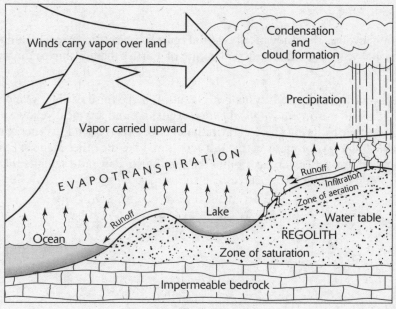

The Water Cycle

Oceanography

Seventy-one percent of the Earth's surface is covered by a relatively thin layer of water. Most of this water contains dissolved salts and resides in four major ocean basins. The rest of the water is found frozen in ice caps at both poles, in seas, lakes, rivers, and in porous rocks in the crust.

The four oceans, from largest to smallest, are the Pacific, Atlantic, Indian, and Arctic. They are largely responsible for the relatively stable environment that has allowed our world to evolve as it has. The tilt of the Earth's axis, its spherical shape, and its rotation create uneven heating of Earth's oceans. This variation in thermal distribution, coupled with the *Coriolis effect* (deflection caused by rotation), gives rise to ocean currents. The ocean waters absorb and release insolation, thus regulating weather and climate. The oceans' currents also influence atmospheric circulation. They are the source of life on Earth. The oceans' currents shape coastlines and constantly resupply fresh water on land.

The ocean basins (the land under the oceans) are mostly stable areas of fine-grained basaltic rock. However, scientists have studied considerable crustal and seismic activity in certain sites on the ocean floor. These locations are responsible for much plate tectonic activity, including sea-floor spreading and trenching, rising midoceanic ridges, and continental plate movement.

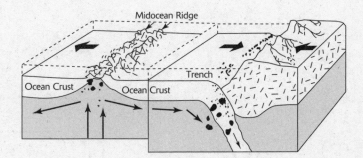

Ocean Basin Reformation

Astronomy

The science of astronomy involves the study of all celestial objects (objects in space) including planet Earth. It was only approximately 400 years ago that the actual nature of Earth's relationship to the vast array of heavenly bodies was observed.

Earth is part of a *heliocentric* (sun-centered) system of planets. It is the third of eight planets (Pluto is no longer considered a planet) that are all moving in *elliptical paths* (orbits) around a typical yellow star, our sun. The sun holds our solar system together by its enormous gravitational effect. Its tremendous energy output of electromagnetic radiation provides energy for many of Earth's activities. Like the other planets, Earth spins (rotates) on its axis as it moves counterclockwise (revolves) around the sun. Earth also has a satellite that orbits Earth, the moon. Earth's axis of rotation is tilted 23 ½ degrees.

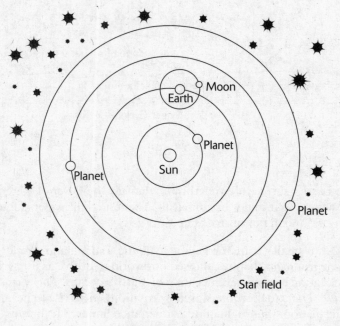

Heliocentric Model

The two major motions of Earth, *rotation* and *revolution,* coupled with Earth's tilt, produce a number of important and familiar effects. Day and night, as well as variations in daylight periods, stem from rotation and the tilt of the Earth's axis. The year and seasons occur because of revolution and axial tilt. Variation in the insolation that powers many of Earth's processes arises from all three factors.

General Science Practice Questions

1. An enzyme converts glucose in the cell into glucose-6-phosphate, ensuring that a gradient usually exists for glucose to enter the cell. Because of its size, glucose usually travels through a protein channel to enter the cell. This type of molecular movement is known as:

    A. osmosis
    B. diffusion
    C. facilitated diffusion
    D. active transport

2. Which sequence correctly lists the terms from largest to smallest?

    A. organ system, organ, tissue, cell
    B. organ system, organ, cell, tissue
    C. cell, tissue, organ, organ system
    D. cell, tissue, organ system, organ

3. The process by which green plants manufacture food in the form of glucose is

    A. photosynthesis.
    B. photorespiration.
    C. cellular respiration.
    D. fermentation.

4. A reproductive cell containing 30 chromosomes will produce _____ cells with _____ chromosomes during meiosis.

    A. 2, 30
    B. 2, 15
    C. 4, 30
    D. 4, 15

5. _____ spend part of their life on land and part of their life in water.

    A. Sponges
    B. Fishes
    C. Amphibians
    D. Reptiles

6. Which two cells would most likely have the same number of chromosomes in their nuclei?

    A. skin cell and fertilized egg cell
    B. sperm cell and liver cell
    C. egg cell and skin cell
    D. sperm cell and fertilized egg cell

7. Which of the following represents the correct order of structures through which food travels in the human digestive system?

    A. mouth → duodenum → esophagus → stomach → large intestine
    B. mouth → pancreas → stomach → small intestine → large intestine
    C. mouth → esophagus → stomach → large intestine → small intestine
    D. mouth → esophagus → stomach → small intestine → large intestine

8. Interactions between the organisms in communities and their physical environment form

    A. food chains.
    B. food webs.
    C. populations.
    D. ecosystems.

9. Which of the following compounds would form a basic solution?

    A. battery acid
    B. water
    C. lye
    D. vinegar

10. The _____ is the genetic makeup of an individual, while the _____ is the physical appearance of the individual.

    A. gene, allele
    B. genotype, phenotype
    C. phenotype, genotype
    D. chromosome, protein

11. What mass of product would you expect given that you started with 17 g of NH_3 and 36.5 g of HCl, using the formula $NH_3 + HCl \rightarrow NH_4Cl$

    A. 17 g
    B. 36.5 g
    C. 53.5 g
    D. 19.5 g

12. Which of the following elements is found in bones?

    A. iron
    B. calcium
    C. fluorine
    D. helium

13. Our Earth is part of a heliocentric system which has at its center the

    A. sun.
    B. Earth.
    C. moon.
    D. None of these.

14. Which statement is true?

    A. Minerals are composed of rocks.
    B. Minerals are formed during erosion.
    C. Rocks are made of minerals.
    D. All minerals have the same chemical makeup.

15. If the temperature is 25°C, what is the temperature in °F?

    A. 25°F
    B. 298°F
    C. 0°F
    D. 77°F

16. Toothpaste contains _____ to prevent tooth decay.

    A. calcium
    B. phosphorous
    C. iron
    D. fluoride

17. A major constituent of seawater is

    A. sodium chloride.
    B. nitrogen.
    C. iron.
    D. aluminum.

18. Oxygen-poor blood enters the human heart through the _____, is pumped to the lungs where it receives oxygen, and returns to the heart through the _____.

    A. right atrium, left atrium
    B. left atrium, right atrium
    C. left ventricle, right ventricle
    D. pulmonary artery, vena cava

19. What element is found in matches, soft drinks, DNA, and fertilizers?

    A. phosphorus
    B. fluorine
    C. iron
    D. silicon

20. Why do constellations appear to change in the night sky throughout the year?

    A. The constellations move through a cyclic path throughout the year.
    B. The Earth rotates on an axis.
    C. The Earth revolves around the sun.
    D. The constellations move in random paths throughout the year.

21. Why do stars appear to move through the night sky?

    A. Stars orbit the Earth.
    B. Stars orbit our solar system.
    C. The Earth rotates on an axis.
    D. The Earth revolves around the sun.

22. Which phrase best describes the environment of Earth?

    A. a steady, unchanging star
    B. a dynamic equilibrium
    C. regular predictable catastrophes
    D. constant energy imbalance

23. Which of the following structure-function pairs is mismatched?

    A. ribosome — protein synthesis
    B. mitochondrion — cellular respiration
    C. chloroplast — photosynthesis
    D. nucleus — ATP production

24. Life on Earth is found on Earth's

    A. core.
    B. mantle.
    C. asthenosphere.
    D. crust.

25. The largest ocean on the planet is the

    A. Antarctic Ocean.
    B. Pacific Ocean.
    C. Indian Ocean.
    D. China Sea.

Answers and Explanations for Practice Questions

1. **C.** In facilitated diffusion, a molecule moves with its concentration gradient into cells that have a protein channel to allow the large or charged molecule to make its way through the plasma membrane. Because of the conversion of glucose to another molecule, there is usually a lower concentration of glucose in the cell, causing it to want to enter the cell. Also, since glucose is a fairly large, polar molecule, it generally requires a protein channel to allow its entrance.

2. **A.** An organ system such as the circulatory system would be very complex, consisting of multiple parts. The specific organ that controls the circulatory system is the heart. The heart is made of muscle tissue composed of specific types of cells designed to make the heart contract.

3. **A.** Choices B, C, and D are all forms of cellular respiration, which is the process by which organisms break down glucose to obtain energy.

4. **D.** Meiosis leads to the production of 4 haploid daughter cells from one diploid parent cell with 15 chromosomes.

5. **C.** Amphibians spend the early part of their life cycle (from the egg stage through the tadpole stage) in water before moving onto land, where they spend their adult stages. Sponges, A, and fishes, B, spend their entire life cycle in the water, whereas reptiles, D, spend their entire life cycle on land.

6. **A.** Human body cells have 46 chromosomes and human sex cells have 23. When a sperm unites with an egg, a new cell will form with a new set of 46 chromosomes. A skin cell is a body cell and a fertilized egg (or zygote) is made through the combination of sperm and egg.

7. **D.** Movement of food in the human digestive system begins in the mouth, where it is chewed and moisturized to form a bolus. It then moves down the esophagus to the stomach, where it is combined with gastric juices and churned into a soupy liquid called chyme. From the stomach, it moves into the small intestine, where much of the digestion and absorption occurs. Any substances that are not digested or absorbed move into the large intestine, which processes the residue into feces for elimination from the body.

8. **D.** An ecosystem is formed through the interaction of the living organisms in communities and their physical environment (rocks, soil, light, air, and water). Food chains, A, and food webs, B, describe the transfer of energy among organisms in an ecosystem. A population, C, is a group of individuals of the same species occupying a defined area.

9. **C.** Lye is sodium hydroxide, and any compound that increases the hydroxide concentration is considered a base. Battery acid (sulfuric acid) and vinegar (acetic acid) are acidic. Water is neutral (neither acidic nor basic).

10. **B.** The genetic makeup of an individual constitutes that individual's genotype, while the appearance of the individual (the expression of the genes in the genotype) constitutes that individual's phenotype. An allele is one version of a gene, A; for example, the red allele is the gene for flower color. The chromosome, D, is the physical structure that contains the DNA of an organism, but does not itself confer the genotype.

11. **C.** The Law of Conservation of Mass must be obeyed, so the mass of products must equal the mass of reactants (17g + 36.5g = 53.5g).

12. **B.** Bones are made mostly of a calcium phosphate mineral. Iron is an important component in red blood cells, fluorine is not biologically important (although it can be used to reduce dental caries), and helium has no known human biological activity.

13. **A.** The sun is the center of our solar system and holds the other members of the system (planets, asteroids, comets, and so on) in orbit with its enormous gravitational pull.

14. **C.** Rocks are made of minerals. All of the other answer choices are false.

15. **D.** Using the formula °F = [1.8 × (°C)] + 32, you can see that the answer will be 77°F. For Choice B, 273 was added to 25, which would give the temperature in kelvin.

16. **D.** Calcium and phosphorus are important nutrients for maintaining teeth and bones, but fluoride is added to react with the surface of the tooth enamel so that it becomes less soluble to the acids secreted by bacteria.

17. **A.** Sodium chloride (NaCl) is table salt and is one of the salts that causes seawater to be salty.

18. **A.** The pathway for blood through the human heart starts when oxygen-poor blood enters the right atrium through a major vein called the vena cava. The blood passes through the tricuspid valve into the right ventricle, and is then pumped through the pulmonary artery to the lungs for gas exchange. Oxygen-rich blood returns to the left atrium of the heart through the pulmonary vein. It then flows through the bicuspid (mitral) valve into the left ventricle, from which it is pumped through a major artery called the aorta.

19. **A.** Phosphorus is found in all of these applications.

20. **C.** Motions of the Earth cause celestial objects to change positions. In June, the Earth is at a completely different position with respect to the sun than it is in December. Because of this revolution, the Earth will face different constellations throughout each month.

21. **C.** Motions of the Earth cause celestial objects to change positions. The Earth rotates on an axis, causing the sun and stars to appear to rise in the east and set in the west each day and night.

22. **B.** Earth's environment is constantly changing, but at any given time the Earth's environment is stable enough to support life and provide changes without major crust, atmospheric, or hydrospheric disruption.

23. **D.** The nucleus contains the genetic information for an organism in the form of DNA. ATP is produced by cellular respiration, which takes place in the mitochondria and the cytoplasm.

24. **D.** Life on Earth requires liquid water, atmospheric gases, and nutrients from the solid Earth. All of these are found on or near the surface of the crust.

25. **B.** The Pacific Ocean has the largest surface area and greatest average depth of the four oceans of the Earth.

Arithmetic Reasoning

None of the questions on the Arithmetic Reasoning section simply ask you to perform a numerical computation; instead, you will need to solve mathematical word problems by performing arithmetic computations.

This section reviews all of the computational skills that you need to do well on this part of the ASVAB, and it includes plenty of examples. This section also provides sample problems for you to try so that you can be certain that you can handle the material on the test.

The ASVAB contains 30 Arithmetic Reasoning questions. You will have 36 minutes to answer these questions.

Using Numbers

Whole Numbers

The numbers 0, 1, 2, 3, 4, and so on are called *whole numbers*. The whole number system is a place value system—that is, the value of each digit in a whole number is determined by the place it occupies. For example, in the number 6,257, the 6 is in the thousands place, the 2 is in the hundreds place, the 5 is in the tens place, and the 7 is in the ones place.

The following table contains a summary of whole number place values:

Ones	1
Tens	10
Hundreds	100
Thousands	1,000
Ten thousands	10,000
Hundred thousands	100,000
Millions	1,000,000
Ten millions	10,000,000
Hundred millions	100,000,000
Billions	1,000,000,000

Therefore, you would read the number 5,124,678 as "five million, one hundred twenty-four thousand, six hundred seventy-eight."

1. Write the number thirty million, five hundred seven thousand, three hundred twelve.

   30,507,312

2. Write in words the number 34,521.

   Thirty-four thousand, five hundred twenty-one.

Rounding Whole Numbers

Rounding whole numbers can often help you determine the correct answer to a multiple-choice question more quickly. When you need only an approximate value of a whole number, you can use the following procedure to round off the number to a particular place.

The procedure for rounding whole numbers is as follows:

1. Underline the digit in the place being rounded off.
2. If the digit to the right of the underlined digit is less than 5, leave the underlined digit as it is. If the digit to the right of the underlined digit is equal to 5 or more, add 1 to the underlined digit.
3. Replace all digits to the right of the underlined digit by 0s.

   Round off the number 34,521 to the nearest hundred.

Because you are rounding to the nearest hundred, begin by underlining the digit in the hundreds place, which is 5.

   34,<u>5</u>21

Now, look to the right of the underlined digit. Because the number to the right of the 5 is 2, leave the 5 as it is, and replace all digits to the right of the 5 with 0s.

   34,500

Fractions

A fraction is made up of two numbers separated by a line that is known as a *fraction bar*. Typically, you use a fraction to represent a part of a whole. For example, in the diagram below, note that five out of eight pieces of the diagram are shaded:

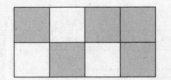

In this case, you could use the fraction $\frac{5}{8}$ to represent the fact that 5 of the 8 equal pieces have been shaded. In the same way, you could use the fraction $\frac{3}{8}$ to represent the fact that 3 of the 8 pieces are unshaded.

Fractions in which the number on the top is *less than* the number on the bottom are said to be *proper fractions*. Thus, the fractions $\frac{2}{9}, \frac{5}{8}$, and $\frac{3}{7}$ are proper fractions. The value of a proper fraction is always less than 1.

Fractions in which the number on the top is either *equal to or greater than* the number on the bottom are called *improper fractions*. For example, the fractions $\frac{5}{2}, \frac{7}{4}$, and $\frac{11}{5}$ are improper. If the number on the top of the fraction is greater than the number on the bottom, the value of the fraction is greater than 1. If the number on the top and the number on the bottom are equal, as in $\frac{8}{8}$, the fraction is equal to 1.

A *mixed number* is a whole number together with a fraction, such as $7\frac{1}{2}$ or $3\frac{5}{8}$. The mixed number $7\frac{1}{2}$ represents the number 7 plus the fraction $\frac{1}{2}$. As you will see later, every improper fraction can be written as a mixed number, and vice versa.

> Classify the following numbers as proper fractions, improper fractions, or mixed numbers: $\frac{8}{9}, \frac{6}{6}, 5\frac{2}{3}, \frac{6}{4}$, and $\frac{112}{113}$.

The numbers $\frac{8}{9}$ and $\frac{112}{113}$ are proper fractions, the numbers $\frac{6}{6}$ and $\frac{6}{4}$ are improper fractions, and $5\frac{2}{3}$ is a mixed number.

Decimals

The numbers 10, 100, 1,000, 10,000, and so on, are called the *powers of 10*. Fractions like $\frac{7}{10}$, $\frac{59}{100}$, and $\frac{323}{1000}$, which have numbers on the bottom that are powers of 10, are called *decimal fractions*.

Decimals are typically written using a shorthand notation in which the number on the top of the fraction is written to the right of a dot, called a *decimal point*. The number on the bottom of the fraction is not written, but is indicated in the following way: If the number to the right of the decimal point contains one digit, the number on the bottom of the fraction is 10; if the number to the right of the decimal point contains two digits, the number on the bottom of the fraction is 100; and so on. Therefore, $\frac{7}{10} = .7$, $\frac{59}{100} = .59$, and $\frac{323}{1000} = .323$. The decimal .7 is read "point seven," or "seven-tenths." In the same way, .59 is read "point fifty-nine," or "fifty-nine hundredths."

---

1. Write the following fractions using decimal notation: $\frac{3}{10}$, $\frac{157}{1000}$, and $\frac{7}{100}$.

$\frac{3}{10} = .3$, $\frac{157}{1000} = .157$, and $\frac{7}{100} = .07$. Note that in the last example, you must place a 0 between the decimal point and the 7 to indicate that the number on the bottom is 100.

---

2. Write the following decimals as fractions: .7, .143, and .079.

$.7 = \frac{7}{10}$, $.143 = \frac{143}{1000}$, and $.079 = \frac{79}{1000}$.

A number that consists of a whole number and a decimal is called a *mixed decimal*. The number 354.56, for example, represents the mixed number $354\frac{56}{100}$.

---

3. Write the following mixed numbers as mixed decimals: 76.3 and 965.053.

$76.3 = 76\frac{3}{10}$ and $965.053 = 965\frac{53}{1000}$.

Percents

A percent is a special decimal fraction whose bottom number is 100 (the word percent means *per hundred*) and is often written using a special symbol: "%." Thus, $\frac{67}{100}$ can be written 67%, and $\frac{3}{100}$ can be written 3%. Note that, just as every percent can be written as a fraction, every percent can also be written as a decimal. For example, $51\% = \frac{51}{100} = .51$ and $7\% = \frac{7}{100} = .07$.

A quick way to rewrite a percent as a decimal is to move the decimal point two places to the left and drop the percent sign. Thus, $35\% = .35$. In a similar way, to write a decimal as a percent, move the decimal point two places to the right and put in a percent sign. Thus, $.23 = 23\%$.

---

1. Write the following decimals as percents: .23, .08, and 1.23.

    $.23 = 23\%$, $.08 = 8\%$, and $1.23 = 123\%$.

---

2. Write the following percents as decimals: 17%, 2%, and 224%.

    $17\% = .17$, $2\% = .02$, and $224\% = 2.24$.

Arithmetic Operations

Addition, subtraction, multiplication, and division are called the *fundamental operations of arithmetic*. To solve the word problems that the ASVAB asks in the Arithmetic Reasoning section, you need to be able to add, subtract, multiply, and divide whole numbers and decimals. This section reviews these mathematical techniques.

Addition

Addition of Whole Numbers

When you add numbers, the result is called the *sum*. The first step in adding whole numbers is to line them up, placing ones under ones, tens under tens, hundreds under hundreds, and so on. Then, add each column of numbers, beginning with the ones, and moving to the tens, hundreds, thousands, and so on. If the sum of the digits in any column is 10 or more, write down the last figure of the sum as a part of the answer, and then carry the other figures into the next column.

For example, suppose you are asked to add 37, 64, and 151. Begin by lining up the numbers in columns as shown below:

$$\begin{array}{r} 37 \\ 64 \\ \underline{151} \end{array}$$

Now, add the digits in the units column: $7 + 4 + 1 = 12$. Because this number is more than 10, write the 2 below the units column in the answer, and carry the 1 over to the tens column:

$$\begin{array}{r} \overset{1}{3}7 \\ 64 \\ \underline{151} \\ 2 \end{array}$$

Now add the 1 that you carried to the other digits in the tens column: $1 + 3 + 6 + 5 = 15$. Put the 5 below the tens column, and carry the remaining 1 to the hundreds column:

$$\begin{array}{r} \overset{1}{3}7 \\ 64 \\ \underline{151} \\ 52 \end{array}$$

Because $1 + 1 = 2$, the final answer would be 252:

$$\begin{array}{r} 37 \\ 64 \\ \underline{151} \\ 252 \end{array}$$

Add 235, 654, and 12.

$$\begin{array}{r} 235 \\ 654 \\ \underline{12} \\ 901 \end{array}$$

Addition of Decimals

Adding decimal numbers is also a very straightforward process. Simply line up the decimal points of the numbers involved, and add as you normally would. Suppose you wish to add 23.31, 19, and 3.125. Begin by writing the numbers in a column, lining up the decimal points:

$$
\begin{array}{r}
23.31 \\
19. \\
\underline{3.125}
\end{array}
$$

Note that the number 19 is a whole number, and, as such, the decimal point is to the right of the number—that is, 19 and 19. mean the same thing. If it helps you when you add these numbers, you can fill in the missing spaces to the right of the decimal points with 0s:

$$
\begin{array}{r}
23.310 \\
19.000 \\
\underline{3.125}
\end{array}
$$

Now, position a decimal point in the answer directly below the decimal points of the numbers in the problem:

$$
\begin{array}{r}
23.310 \\
19.000 \\
\underline{3.125}
\end{array}
$$

Finish by adding as described above:

$$
\begin{array}{r}
23.310 \\
19.000 \\
\underline{3.125} \\
45.435
\end{array}
$$

Some problems on the test will ask you to add monetary amounts. Of course, to add monetary amounts, just line up the decimal points, as above, and add the numbers. Thus, expenses of $32.25, $52.35, and $97.16 would lead to a total expense of

$$
\begin{array}{r}
\$\ 32.25 \\
\$\ 52.35 \\
\underline{\$\ 97.16} \\
\$181.76
\end{array}
$$

> **1.** Add 23.56, 876.01, 34, and .007.

$$
\begin{array}{r}
23.56 \\
876.01 \\
34 \\
\underline{.007}
\end{array}
$$

If you like, before beginning the addition, you can put in some 0s so that all of the numbers have the same number of digits:

$$
\begin{array}{r}
23.560 \\
876.010 \\
34.000 \\
\underline{.007} \\
933.577
\end{array}
$$

2. If Brian buys three items priced at $3.45, $65.21, and $143.50, how much has he spent?

To find the answer to this problem, you need to add the three amounts spent:

$$\begin{array}{r} \$3.45 \\ \$65.21 \\ \underline{\$143.50} \\ \$212.16 \end{array}$$

Subtraction

Subtraction of Whole Numbers

When you subtract two numbers, the result is called the *difference.* The first step in subtracting two whole numbers is to line them up, placing ones under ones, tens under tens, hundreds under hundreds, and so on. Then, subtract each column of numbers, beginning with the ones, and moving to the tens, hundreds, thousands, and so on. If, in any step, the digit on the top is smaller than the digit on the bottom, increase the figure on top by 10 by borrowing 1 from the figure directly to the left.

Let's take the following problem as an example:

$$\begin{array}{r} 567 \\ -382 \\ \hline \end{array}$$

The first step is, of course, to subtract 2 from 7. Because 7 is bigger than 2, no borrowing is necessary, so this step is easy:

$$\begin{array}{r} 567 \\ -382 \\ \hline 5 \end{array}$$

Now, you need to subtract the numbers in the tens column. Note that 6 is smaller than 8, so you need to borrow 1 from the 5 to the left of the 6. This makes the 6 into a 16, and, by borrowing the 1 from the 5, the 5 becomes a 4:

$$\begin{array}{r} \overset{4}{\cancel{5}}67 \\ -382 \\ \hline 5 \end{array}$$

Next, you can subtract the 8 from the 16, which leaves you with 8. Finally, in the hundreds column, subtracting the 3 from the 4 leaves you with 1:

$$\begin{array}{r} \overset{4}{\cancel{5}}67 \\ -382 \\ \hline 185 \end{array}$$

Remember that, if you would like to check the answer to a subtraction problem, you can add the difference (that is, the answer) to the bottom number of the subtraction problem, and see if you get the number on top. In this example, $185 + 382 = 567$, so you know that you have the correct answer.

Subtract 534 from 893.

$$\begin{array}{r} 893 \\ -534 \\ \hline 359 \end{array}$$

Subtraction of Decimals

As with addition of decimals, begin by lining up the decimal points of the two numbers that you are subtracting. Then, place a decimal point for the answer directly below the decimal points of the two amounts. For example

$$\begin{array}{r} 265.01 \\ -127.5 \\ \hline \end{array}$$

When performing a subtraction, it helps to write in extra 0s so that both numbers have the same number of digits to the right of the decimal point:

$$\begin{array}{r} 265.01 \\ -127.50 \\ \hline 137.51 \end{array}$$

Of course, to subtract monetary amounts, line up the decimal points and subtract as usual, as in the following example:

$$\begin{array}{r} \$324.56 \\ -\$34.07 \\ \hline \$290.49 \end{array}$$

Jimmy pays a \$14.51 dinner charge with a \$20 bill. How much change does he receive?

Simply subtract \$14.51 from \$20:

$$\begin{array}{r} \$\ 20.00 \\ -\$14.51 \\ \hline \$\ \ \ 5.49 \end{array}$$

Multiplication

Multiplication of Whole Numbers

When you multiply two numbers, the result is called the *product*. The first step in multiplying whole numbers is to line up the numbers, placing ones under ones, tens under tens, hundreds under hundreds, and so on. Now, consider two possible cases.

Case 1: If the number on the bottom of your multiplication problem contains a single digit, multiply every digit in the number on top by this digit. Start on the right, and move to the left. If, at any time, the result of a multiplication is a number that contains more than one digit, write down the ones digit of the number, and carry the tens digit over to the next column, to be added to the result of the multiplication in that column.

Suppose you need to multiply 542 by 3. Write the problem as follows:

$$\begin{array}{r} 542 \\ \times\ 3 \\ \hline \end{array}$$

Begin by multiplying 3 by 2, and write the result, which is 6, below the 3:

$$\begin{array}{r} 542 \\ \times\ 3 \\ \hline 6 \end{array}$$

Next, multiply the 3 on the bottom by the 4 on the top. The result is 12. Write the ones digit from the 12 below the 4 in the problem, and carry the tens digit, which is 1, over to the next column:

$$
\begin{array}{r}
\overset{1}{542} \\
\times\ 3 \\
\hline
26
\end{array}
$$

Finally, multiply the 3 by 5. You should add the result of 15 to the 1 that you carried from the previous column:

$$
\begin{array}{r}
542 \\
\times\ \ 3 \\
\hline
1,626
\end{array}
$$

Case 2: If the number on the bottom contains more than one digit, begin as you did above and multiply every digit on the top by the ones digit of the number on the bottom. Write the result in the usual spot. Then move over to the tens digit of the number on the bottom, and multiply each number on the top by this number. Write the result below the previous result, but position the ones digit of the result below the number you are multiplying by. Continue to the hundreds digit, multiplying as usual, but positioning the ones digit of the result below the hundreds digit of the number on the bottom. Continue until you have multiplied the number on top by every digit on the bottom. Finish by adding together all of the partial products you have written.

The following example illustrates the process that Case 2 describes. To multiply 542 by 63, set up the problem as follows:

$$
\begin{array}{r}
542 \\
\times\ 63 \\
\hline
\end{array}
$$

Begin exactly as you did in the earlier example and multiply the 542 by 3. After doing this, you should have the following:

$$
\begin{array}{r}
542 \\
\times\ 63 \\
\hline
1626
\end{array}
$$

Now multiply the 542 by the 6 in the tens digit of the number on the bottom. Note that the result of this multiplication is 3,252. Also note where you position this number:

$$
\begin{array}{r}
542 \\
\times\ \ 63 \\
\hline
1626 \\
3252
\end{array}
$$

When multiplying, be careful to line up the numbers correctly. As the last step, add the 1,626 to the 3,252, as the following shows:

$$
\begin{array}{r}
542 \\
\times\ \ 63 \\
\hline
1\ 626 \\
32\ 52 \\
\hline
34,146
\end{array}
$$

> Multiply 234 by 16.

$$
\begin{array}{r}
234 \\
\times\ \ 16 \\
\hline
1404 \\
234 \\
\hline
3,744
\end{array}
$$

Multiplication of Decimals

Earlier in the sections discussing addition and subtraction of decimals, you saw that the first step in finding the answer is to correctly position the decimal point of the answer. When multiplying numbers with decimals, the procedure is almost exactly the opposite. Begin by ignoring the decimal points in the numbers you are multiplying, and work the problem as if the numbers are whole numbers. Then, after you finish multiplying, you can determine where the decimal point in the answer goes.

To determine the placement of the decimal point, you need to do some counting. Begin by counting the total number of digits to the right of the decimal points in the two numbers you are multiplying. However many digits you count should also be the number of digits to the right of the decimal point in the answer.

The following examples help to make this procedure clear. Remember that, earlier, you solved the problem

$$
\begin{array}{r}
542 \\
\times\ 63 \\
\hline
1\ 626 \\
32\ 52 \\
\hline
34{,}146
\end{array}
$$

Now, suppose that instead the problem had been

$$
\begin{array}{r}
5.42 \\
\times\ 6.3
\end{array}
$$

Note that the number on the top contains two digits to the right of the decimal point, and that the number on the bottom contains one digit to the right of the decimal point. To start, multiply as you normally would, ignoring the decimal points:

$$
\begin{array}{r}
5.42 \\
\times\ 6.3 \\
\hline
1626 \\
3252 \\
\hline
34146
\end{array}
$$

Now, because you have a total of $2 + 1 = 3$ digits to the right of the decimal point in the two numbers that you are multiplying, you need to have three digits to the right of the decimal point in the numbers in the product:

$$
\begin{array}{r}
5.42 \\
\times\ 6.3 \\
\hline
1626 \\
3252 \\
\hline
34.146
\end{array}
$$

That's all there is to it!

What if the problem had been instead:

$$
\begin{array}{r}
5.42 \\
\times\ .63
\end{array}
$$

In this case, you have a total of four digits to the right of the decimal point in the two numbers you are multiplying. Thus, the answer is not 34.146, but rather 3.4146.

Note that if you are multiplying an amount of money by a whole number, you can use the same process as earlier. Of course, when you do this, you will have a total of two digits to the right of the decimal point in the two numbers you are multiplying by, so that the answer will end up in "money" format—that is, it will have two digits to the right of the decimal point.

> John buys four calculators, each of which costs $3.51. What is the total cost of the four calculators?

$$\begin{array}{r} \$\ 3.51 \\ \times \quad 4 \\ \hline \$14.04 \end{array}$$

Division

Division of Whole Numbers

When you divide one number into another, the result is the *quotient*. Division is probably the most complicated of the four fundamental arithmetic operations, but it becomes easier after you realize that the procedure for division consists of four steps that you repeat over and over until you finish. The following sample problems illustrate these four steps.

> Divide 7 into 245.

Begin by writing the problem in the usual way:

$$7\overline{)245}$$

Now, for the first step. Obviously 7 does not go into 2, so you need to determine the number of times that 7 goes into 24. Because 7 goes into 24 three times (with something left over), begin by writing a 3 above the 4 in the problem:

$$\begin{array}{r} 3 \\ 7\overline{)245} \end{array}$$

As a second step, multiply the 3 by the 7 to obtain 21 and write this product below the 24:

$$\begin{array}{r} 3 \\ 7\overline{)245} \\ 21 \end{array}$$

The third step is to subtract the 21 from the 24. When you do this, you get 3. This should be written below the 21, as the following shows:

$$\begin{array}{r} 3 \\ 7\overline{)245} \\ -21 \\ \hline 3 \end{array}$$

The final step in the four-step process is to bring down the next digit from the number that you are dividing into. This next (and last) digit is 5, so bring it down next to the 3 as the following shows:

$$\begin{array}{r} 3 \\ 7\overline{)245} \\ -21 \\ \hline 35 \end{array}$$

Now, the entire procedure starts over again. Divide 7 into 35. It goes in 5 times, so put a 5 next to the 3 in the solution:

$$\begin{array}{r} 35 \\ 7\overline{)245} \\ -21 \\ \hline 35 \end{array}$$

When you multiply and subtract, note that you end up with 0. This means that you have finished, and the quotient (answer) is 35:

$$
\begin{array}{r}
35 \\
7\overline{)245} \\
-21 \\
\hline
35 \\
-35 \\
\hline
0
\end{array}
$$

The procedure for dividing by two-digit numbers (or even larger numbers) is essentially the same, but involves a bit more computation. As an example, consider the following problem:

$$23\overline{)11408}$$

Note that 23 will not go into 11, so you have to divide 23 into 114. To determine how many times 23 goes into 114, you must estimate. You might consider that 23 is almost 25, and that it seems as if 25 would go into 114 four times. So, try 4. Write a 4 on top, and multiply, subtract, and bring down in the usual way:

$$
\begin{array}{r}
4 \\
23\overline{)11408} \\
-92 \\
\hline
220
\end{array}
$$

Continue, as before, by trying to estimate the number of times 23 will go into 220. If you try 9, the process will continue rather nicely:

$$
\begin{array}{r}
49 \\
23\overline{)11408} \\
-92 \\
\hline
220 \\
-207 \\
\hline
138
\end{array}
$$

As a final step, estimate that 23 will go into 138 six times.

$$
\begin{array}{r}
496 \\
23\overline{)11408} \\
-92 \\
\hline
220 \\
-207 \\
\hline
138 \\
-138 \\
\hline
0
\end{array}
$$

If, at any point, you make the incorrect estimate, simply modify your estimate and start over. In the last step above, suppose you thought that 23 would go into 138 seven times. Look what would have happened:

$$
\begin{array}{r}
497 \\
23\overline{)11408} \\
-92 \\
\hline
220 \\
-207 \\
\hline
138 \\
-161
\end{array}
$$

Because 161 is larger than 138, your estimate was too high. Try again, with a smaller number. Divide 12 into 540:

$$
\begin{array}{r}
45 \\
12\overline{)540} \\
-48 \\
\hline
60 \\
-60 \\
\hline
0
\end{array}
$$

Remember that you can always check division problems by multiplying. In this case, because $12 \times 45 = 540$, you know that you have the right answer.

Division with Decimals

Recall that when you add and subtract with decimals, you begin by positioning the decimal point for the answer and then add or subtract as usual. When you divide a whole number into a decimal number, the idea is similar. Begin by putting a decimal point for the quotient (answer) directly above the decimal point in the number that you are dividing into. Then divide as normal. For example, if you need to divide 4 into 142.4, begin as the following shows:

Note the decimal point positioned above the decimal point in 142.4:

$$
4\overline{)142.4}
$$

Now, divide in the usual way:

$$
\begin{array}{r}
35.6 \\
4\overline{)142.4} \\
-12 \\
\hline
22 \\
-20 \\
\hline
24 \\
24 \\
\hline
0
\end{array}
$$

That's all there is to it.

> A dinner bill of $92.80 is shared equally among four friends. How much does each friend pay?

To find the answer, you need to divide $92.80 by 4:

$$
\begin{array}{r}
23.20 \\
4\overline{)92.80} \\
-8 \\
\hline
12 \\
-12 \\
\hline
08 \\
-8 \\
\hline
00 \\
-0 \\
\hline
0
\end{array}
$$

Arithmetic Word Problems

As this section previously mentioned, the Arithmetic Reasoning part of the ASVAB contains 30 real-world word problems that involve arithmetic calculations. If you know how to perform the computations that this section discusses, then the hardest part of these word problems is determining which of the arithmetic operations you need to use to solve the problem.

Basic One-Step and Two-Step Problems

Some of the word problems on the test will involve only a single computation. Others may be multiple-step problems in which you need to perform several computations. The following contains examples of problems of both types. Following this section will be some examples of special types of problems that also appear on the test.

1. Brett earned $225.25 during his first week on a new job. During the second week, he earned $325.50, during the third week he earned $275.00, and during the fourth week he earned $285.75. How much did he earn over the course of the four weeks?

In this problem, all you need to do is add the weekly payments to find the total:

$$\begin{array}{r} \$225.25 \\ \$325.50 \\ \$275.00 \\ \underline{\$285.75} \\ \$1,111.50 \end{array}$$

2. Brett's former job paid him $8.25 an hour. If, during the first of his final two weeks, he worked 21 hours, and during the second he worked 19 hours, how much money did he earn over the course of his last two weeks at his former job?

This is an example of a two-step problem. One way to find the answer is to determine how much Brett made each week by multiplying, and then adding the two weekly totals:

$$\begin{array}{r} \$8.25 \\ \underline{\times 21} \\ \$173.25 \end{array} \qquad \begin{array}{r} \$8.25 \\ \underline{\times 19} \\ \$156.75 \end{array}$$

Then, because $173.25 + $156.75 = $330, you find that he earned $330.

Perhaps you notice an easier way to solve the problem. If you begin by adding the number of hours he worked each week, you get 19 + 21 = 40 as a total. Then, you only need to multiply $8.25 by 40 to get the answer.

3. An office building is 540 ft high, including a 23-ft antenna tower on the roof. How tall is the building without the antenna tower?

In this problem, you need to remove the 23-ft tower from the top of the building by subtracting. This is a one-step problem:

$$\begin{array}{r} 540 \\ \underline{-23} \\ 517 \text{ feet} \end{array}$$

4. At a restaurant, the bill for dinner is $137.50. Bill contributes $20 to the bill, and then leaves. The rest of the bill is split evenly among the remaining five people. How much does each person contribute?

This is another two-step word problem. After Bill leaves, there remains $137.50 – $20 = $117.50 to pay. This amount has to be divided by the five people who remain:

$$
\begin{array}{r}
23.50 \\
5)\overline{117.50} \\
-10 \\
\hline
17 \\
-15 \\
\hline
25 \\
25 \\
\hline
00 \\
\end{array}
$$

Therefore, each person needs to pay $23.50.

Percent and Interest Problems

The ASVAB Arithmetic Reasoning section also contains some problems that involve working with percents and interest. Typically, these problems involve finding percents of numbers. You need to remember two things—first, that the way to find a percent of a number is by multiplying; and second, that before multiplying, you should write the percent as a decimal.

Below are several examples of this type of problem.

> **1.** A family spends 26% of its monthly income on its mortgage. If its monthly income is $2,400, how much does it spend on its mortgage each month?

This problem asks you to find 26% of $2,400. To do this, write 26% as .26, and then multiply:

$$
\begin{array}{r}
\$2,400 \\
\times \quad .26 \\
\hline
14400 \\
4800 \\
\hline
624.00 \\
\end{array}
$$

Thus, the monthly expenditure is $624.00.

> **2.** Bob invests $5,500 in an account that pays 9% annual interest. How much interest does he earn in one year?

Another one-step percent word problem. For this problem, you need to find 9% of $5,500. Begin by writing 9% as a decimal, which is .09 (Note carefully—9% is equal to .09, not .9). Then multiply to finish the problem:

$$
\begin{array}{r}
\$\ 5,500 \\
\times \quad .09 \\
\hline
\$495.00 \\
\end{array}
$$

He will earn $495 in interest in one year.

> **3.** Bob invests $5,500 in an account that pays 9% annual interest. How much money will be in the account at the end of one year?

Note that this problem is based on the preceding problem, but includes an extra step. After determining how much interest is in the account at the end of the year, you must add this amount to the $5,500 to obtain $5,500 + $495 = $5,995.

Ratio and Proportion

Another type of word problem that may appear on the test involves ratios and proportions.

A *ratio* is a comparison of two numbers. For example, a school might say that its student-teacher ratio is 8 to 1. This means that, for every 8 students at the school, there is 1 teacher. Another way to look at this ratio is that, for every 1 teacher, there are 8 students.

You may have seen a ratio written with a colon between the two numbers, as in 8:1. A ratio can also be written as a fraction, as in $\frac{8}{1}$. When it comes to solving word problems involving ratios, it is usually best to write the ratios as fractions so that you can perform computations with them.

In the preceding ratio, we compared a number of people (students) to a number of people (teachers). When you use a ratio to compare two different kinds of quantities, the result is called a *rate*. For example, suppose that a car travels 300 miles in 5 hours. Then you can write the rate of the car as $\frac{300 \text{ miles}}{5 \text{ hours}}$. If you divide the number on the bottom into the number on the top, you get 60, and can then say that the rate of the car is $\frac{60 \text{ miles}}{1 \text{ hour}}$ or simply 60 miles per hour (also known as its speed).

When you divide the number on the bottom of a ratio or a rate into the number on the top, the result is known as a *unit ratio* or a *unit rate*. Often, solving ratio problems hinges on computing a unit ratio or rate. The following problems illustrate the techniques of working with ratios and rates.

---

1. A supermarket customer bought a 15-ounce box of oatmeal for $3.45. What was the cost per ounce of oatmeal?

The rate of cost to ounces is given in the problem as $\frac{\$3.45}{15 \text{ oz}}$. To find the unit cost, you divide $3.45 by 15 ounces.

$$
\begin{array}{r}
.23 \\
15\overline{)3.45} \\
-30 \\
\hline
45 \\
-45 \\
\hline
0
\end{array}
$$

Therefore, the cost is 23 cents per ounce.

---

2. A supermarket sells a 15-ounce box of oatmeal for $3.45. At the same rate, what would be the cost of a 26-ounce box of oatmeal?

This type of problem is known as a *proportion* problem. In a proportion problem, you are given the rate at which two quantities vary, and asked to find the value of one of the quantities given the value of the other. A good way to approach a problem of this type is by first finding the unit rate and then multiplying. Note that in the preceding problem, you already found the unit rate of the oatmeal, which was 23 cents per ounce. The cost of 26 ounces, then, will be 23 cents times 26:

$$
\begin{array}{r}
.23 \\
\times 26 \\
\hline
138 \\
46 \\
\hline
5.98
\end{array}
$$

Thus, 26 ounces costs $5.98.

> **3.** A bus travels at a constant rate of 45 miles per hour. How far can the bus go in $5\frac{1}{2}$ hours?

Previously, you saw that the rate of a vehicle is equal to its distance divided by its time. In the same way, the distance that the vehicle travels is equal to its rate multiplied by its time. You may remember from previous math classes that this formula is written $d = r \times t$, meaning distance equals rate times time.

It is easier to solve this problem if you write $5\frac{1}{2}$ as its decimal equivalent, 5.5. Then, you simply need to multiply 45 by 5.5 to find the distance:

$$
\begin{array}{r}
45 \\
\times 5.5 \\
\hline
225 \\
225 \\
\hline
247.5
\end{array}
$$

Thus, the bus will travel 247.5 miles in $5\frac{1}{2}$ hours.

Measurement

Some of the problems on the ASVAB involve working with measurements and geometric shapes. Two concepts that you should be familiar with are perimeter and area.

The *perimeter* of a figure is the distance around it—that is, the sum of the lengths of its sides. You measure perimeter in units of length, such as in, ft, or meters. The *area* of a figure is the amount of surface contained within its boundaries. You measure area in square units, such as sq in, sq ft, or square meters.

Two important geometric figures for which you should know how to find the perimeter and area are the rectangle and the square.

A *rectangle* is a figure with four sides and the corners are 90°. The opposite sides are the same length. For example, the following figure depicts a rectangle with measurements of 4 in by 3 in:

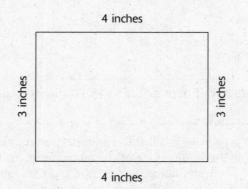

The perimeter of a rectangle is given by the formula $P = 2l + 2w$, which means that, to find the perimeter of a rectangle, you need to add the two lengths plus the two widths. If the rectangle is 4 in by 3 in, then its perimeter is

$P = 2(4) + 2(3)$
$P = 8 + 6 = 14$ in.

The area of a rectangle is given by the formula $A = l \times w$, which means that the area is the length times the width. In this case, the area is 3 in $\times$ 4 in = 12 sq in. By the way, a square inch is simply a square that is an inch long on all four sides. If you look again at the picture of the preceding rectangle, you can see that it can be thought of as consisting of 12 squares that are each an inch on all sides. That is what an area of 12 sq in means.

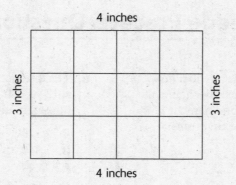

A *square* is a rectangle with four equal sides. In the case of a square, the formulas for the perimeter and the area of a rectangle take a simpler form. The perimeter of a square is $P = 4s$, where s is the length of the side, and the area is $A = s \times s$.

It also helps to know some common measurement conversions, such as the fact that there are 12 inches in a foot, 3 feet in a yard, and 36 inches in a yard.

The following examples review the concepts covered in this section.

1. A small bag of fertilizer covers 20 sq ft of lawn. How many bags do you need to cover a lawn that is 4 yd by 3 yd?

The most direct way to handle this problem is to change the measurements of the lawn to ft because that is how the capacity of the bag of fertilizer is measured. A lawn that is 4 yd by 3 yd is 12 ft by 9 ft. Thus, its area is $12 \times 9 = 108$ sq ft. Now, to determine the number of bags that you need, divide 20 into 108 to get an answer of 5.4 bags. Because, obviously, you cannot purchase 5.4 bags, you would need 6 bags to cover the lawn.

2. A plot of land measures 50 meters by 40 meters. A house 24 meters by 18 meters is built on the land. How much land is left over?

Begin by finding the area of the lot and the house:

$$
\begin{array}{cc}
50 & 24 \\
\times 40 & \times 18 \\
\hline
2000 & 432
\end{array}
$$

Thus, the area of the lot is 2,000 square meters, and the area of the house is 432 square meters. To determine how much area is left, subtract 432 square meters from 2,000 square meters: $2,000 - 432 = 1,568$ square meters that are left over.

Arithmetic Knowledge Practice Questions

1. On opening night, 3,127 people attend a new play. The attendance for the next two nights is 2,944 and 3,009. What is the total number of people who saw the play on the first three nights?

   A. 8,070
   B. 8,080
   C. 9,080
   D. 9,800

2. A truck driver makes $0.10 for every mile he drives. The truck driver is also paid $8.00 per hour. If he drives 200 miles in 4 hours, how much does he earn in total?

   A. $28
   B. $52
   C. $232
   D. $450

3. An employee works 25 hours one week, 32 hours the next week, and 15 hours the week after that. In that three-week period, how many hours did she average each week?

   A. 20
   B. 22
   C. 24
   D. 25

4. A homeowner must pay 2% of the appraised value of the home every year in taxes. If the house is appraised at $256,000, how much will the homeowner pay each year in taxes?

   A. $520
   B. $1,280
   C. $5,120
   D. $51,200

5. A company buys 500 bumper stickers. If the price of bumper stickers is $2 each for the first 200 and $0.50 for each bumper sticker after that, how much does the company pay for the bumper stickers?

   A. $250
   B. $450
   C. $550
   D. $1,050.50

6. The distance from Mark's house to Peter's house is 12 yd, 1 ft, and 17 in. How far apart are the houses, in inches?

   A. 173
   B. 360
   C. 449
   D. 461

7. What is the perimeter, in inches, of a rectangular wall that measures 6 ft 4 in by 8 ft 3 in?

   A. $87\frac{1}{2}$
   B. 164
   C. 175
   D. 350

8. What is the area, in square inches, of a square piece of carpet that measures 6 ft 2 in on a side?

   A. 296
   B. 384
   C. 2,738
   D. 5,476

9. Twenty people each contribute $20 for a party. If 30% of that money is spent on food, how much money was spent on food?

   A. $60
   B. $120
   C. $130
   D. $230

10. Tickets for an amusement park cost $35. When purchased by phone, a 5% service charge applies. What is the total price for four tickets purchased by phone?

    A. $135
    B. $136.75
    C. $145
    D. $147

11. A car is driven 750 miles in 25 hours. What is the rate of the car in miles per hour?

    A. 30
    B. 60
    C. 65
    D. 75

12. A 15-pound roast contains 45 servings. What is its rate in servings per pound?

    A.   2
    B.   3
    C.   4
    D. $6\frac{3}{4}$

13. Light travels 744,000 miles in 4 seconds. What is its speed in miles per second?

    A.   186,000
    B.   187,000
    C.   188,000
    D.   189,000

14. An item is priced at $300. It goes on sale for 25% off. What is the new price?

    A. $225
    B. $250
    C. $275
    D. $325

15. Mark's car mileage in May was 2,374. If 1,752 of those miles were driven for business purposes, how many miles were driven for purposes other than business?

    A.   522
    B.   622
    C.   1,622
    D.   4,126

16. In the election for Union County Comptroller, Mr. Heine got 33,172 votes, and Mr. Palisano got 25,752 votes. By how many votes did Mr. Heine win the election?

    A.   7,420
    B.   8,420
    C.   18,420
    D.   58,924

17. Bob buys 25 pads of paper, each of which contains 70 pieces of paper. What is the total number of pieces of paper that Bob purchases?

    A.   1,750
    B.   1,770
    C.   2,800
    D.   3,571

18. If the average speed of an airplane is 525 miles per hour, how many miles can it travel in 6 hours?

    A.   3,050
    B.   3,120
    C.   3,150
    D.   8,750

19. Jimmy earns an annual salary of $26,124. What is his average monthly salary?

    A. $2,107
    B. $2,177
    C. $2,179
    D. $5,024

20. Mr. Norwalk bought 24 gallons of gasoline, which enabled him to drive 648 miles. On the average, how many miles did he get per gallon of gasoline?

    A.   24
    B.   25
    C.   26
    D.   27

21. Steve played in 14 basketball games. He scored a total of 53 field goals (2 points each), and 20 free throws (1 point each). What was his average number of points per game?

    A.   5
    B.   9
    C.   11
    D.   126

22. How many feet of fencing do you need to enclose a rectangular yard that is 42 ft long and 84 ft wide?

    A.   126
    B.   252
    C.   336
    D.   353

23. How many feet of baseboard do you need to go around a rectangular room if the room has a length of 12 ft and a width of $7\frac{1}{2}$ ft, and you must deduct 4 ft for a doorway?

    A. $15\frac{1}{2}$
    B.   31
    C.   35
    D.   39

24. An equilateral triangle is a triangle whose three sides are of equal length. What is the perimeter of an equilateral triangle whose sides are 5 inches?

   A. 5
   B. 10
   C. 15
   D. 20

25. Fred wishes to enclose with wire a square garden whose sides measure 20 ft. If he decides to wrap the wire around the garden five times, how much will the project cost him if wire costs 40 cents for a spool of 50 ft?

   A. $1.60
   B. $3.20
   C. $6.40
   D. $10.00

26. How much would it cost per month to rent a rectangular office that measures 20 ft by 30 ft if the cost per sq ft per month is $8?

   A. $800
   B. $4,800
   C. $5,600
   D. $7,500

27. What is the cost of sowing grass seed on a 480-square-yd field, if a bag of grass seed covers 60 square yd and costs $7.45?

   A. $44.70
   B. $56.60
   C. $57.20
   D. $59.60

28. Janet wants to carpet a 12-ft by 15-ft rectangular room. If carpet costs $11.50 per sq yd, how much will it cost her to carpet the room?

   A. $230
   B. $690
   C. $1,380
   D. $2,070

29. George bowled three games. His scores were 222, 208, and 197. What was his average score for the three games?

   A. 206
   B. 207
   C. 208
   D. 209

30. A baseball stadium has 1,350 box seats, 3,527 reserve seats, 2,007 general-admission seats, and 4,275 bleacher seats. What is the total number of seats in the stadium?

   A. 10,059
   B. 10,159
   C. 11,149
   D. 11,159

Answers and Explanations for Practice Questions

1. **C.** To find the total number of people who saw the play, add 3,127 and 2,944 and 3,009 to get 9,080.

2. **B.** First, figure out how much the driver makes for his mileage: $0.10 × 200 miles = $20. Then calculate 4 × $8.00 to figure his hourly wages, which equals $32. Then add these two amounts: $20 + $32 = $52.

3. **C.** Add 25 + 32 + 15 and divide by 3 to get 24.

4. **C.** $256,000 × 2% = $256,000 × .02 = $5,120.

5. **C.** The company pays a total of $400 for the first 200 stickers, and then a total of $150 for the next 300 stickers.

6. **D.** Because there are 36 inches in a yard, 12 yd is the same as 12 × 36 = 432 in. In the same way, 1 ft contains 12 in, so the total distance is 432 in + 12 in + 17 in = 461 in.

7. **D.** To begin, find the length of each side in inches. 6 ft 4 in is equal to 72 in + 4 in = 76 in. 8 ft 3 in is the same as 96 in + 3 in = 99 in. The perimeter is (76 × 2) + (99 × 2) = 152 + 198 = 350 in.

8. **D.** Because the problem asks for the area in square inches, you need to express the length of the side in inches. A length of 6 ft 2 in is 6 × 12 + 2 = 72 + 2 = 74 in. The area, then, is 74 × 74 in = 5,476 sq in.

9. **B.** A total of $400 has been contributed ($20 × 20). Multiply this amount by 30% (.30) to get $120.

10. **D.** The four tickets, without the service charge, cost $140. Multiply this amount by 5% (.05) to get the service charge: $7. Add $140 + $7 to get $147.

11. **A.** The rate of the car is $\frac{750 \text{ miles}}{25 \text{ hours}}$. Dividing 25 into 750 gives you 30, so the car is traveling at 30 miles per hour.

12. **B.** The rate is $\frac{45 \text{ servings}}{15 \text{ pounds}}$. Dividing 15 into 45 gives you 3, so there are 3 servings per pound.

13. **A.** The speed (rate) is $\frac{744,000 \text{ miles}}{4 \text{ seconds}}$. Dividing 4 into 744,000 gives you 186,000 miles per second.

14. **A.** $300 × 25% = $300 × 0.25 = $75. Subtract $75 from the original price of $300 to get $225.

15. **B.** To solve this problem, subtract 1,752 from 2,374. This tells you how many miles the car was driven for purposes other than business. Because 2,374 − 1,752 = 622, the car went 622 miles for purposes other than business.

16. **A.** You need to determine how many more votes Mr. Heine got than Mr. Palisano. Because 33,172 − 25,752 = 7,420, Mr. Heine got 7,420 more votes.

17. **A.** To solve this problem, multiply the number of pads times the number of pieces of paper in a pad. Because 25 × 70 = 1,750, this is the total number of sheets of paper that he bought.

18. **C.** Previously, you saw that the formula for distance is $d = r × t$, that is, distance = rate × time. In this case, distance = 525 × 6 = 3,150 miles.

19. **B.** Because there are 12 months in a year, Jimmy's average monthly salary is $26,124 ÷ 12 = $2,177.

20. **D.** He got $\frac{648 \text{ miles}}{24 \text{ hours}}$. Dividing 648 by 24 gives you 27 miles per gallon.

21. **B.** This problem requires several steps. To begin, you need to determine the number of points he scored. The 53 field goals give him 53 × 2 = 106 points. Adding on the 20 free throws gives him 126 points. The average per game is 126 ÷ 14 = 9 points.

22. **B.** You need to find the perimeter of the rectangle. $P = 2 × 42 + 2 × 84 = 84 + 168 = 252$ feet.

23. **C.** The perimeter of the room is 2 × 12 + 2 × 7.5 = 24 + 15 = 39 ft. Subtracting 4 ft for the doorway leaves you needing 35 ft of baseboard.

24. **C.** Three sides of length 5 gives a perimeter of 3 × 5 = 15 in.

25. **B.** The perimeter of the garden is $20 \times 4 = 80$ ft, so you would need $5 \times 80 = 400$ ft to go around it five times. Now, divide 400 ft by 50 ft and you get 8, which means that you need to buy 8 spools. Finally, 8 spools at 40 cents a spool would cost $3.20.

26. **B.** The area of the office is 20 ft $\times$ 30 ft = 600 sq ft. At $8 a sq ft, the total cost would be $600 \times \$8 = \$4,800$ a month.

27. **D.** Because $480 \div 60 = 8$, you need 8 bags to cover the yard. Because each bag costs $7.45, the total cost will be $\$7.45 \times 8 = \$59.60$.

28. **A.** Be careful with this one. Note that the measurement of the room is given in feet, but the cost of the carpet is given in square yards. The easiest way to deal with this problem is to express the measurement of the room in yards; 12 ft by 15 ft is the same as 4 yd by 5 yd, so the room measures 20 square yd. At $11.50 per square yd, the cost to carpet the room would be $20 \times \$11.50 = \$230$.

29. **D.** To find the average of three numbers, begin by adding the numbers, and then divide by 3. Because $222 + 208 + 197 = 627$, and $627 \div 3 = 209$, his average score was 209.

30. **D.** The total number of seats is $1,350 + 3,527 + 2,007 + 4,275 = 11,159$.

Word Knowledge

The ASVAB presents Word Knowledge questions in two formats; both formats test your knowledge of words that have the same or nearly the same meaning. In the first type of question, *synonyms,* the test gives you an underlined word and then asks you to choose the word or phrase that has the same or nearly the same meaning. The second type of question, *words in context,* presents a sentence. You must find the word or phrase that has a nearly identical meaning as the underlined word in the context of the sentence. In short, the Word Knowledge section measures your ability to recognize the meanings of certain words.

> The ASVAB has 35 Word Knowledge questions. There are 22 questions in the synonyms format and 13 in the word-in-context format. You will have 11 minutes to answer these questions.

Improving Your Vocabulary

The ability tested in the Word Knowledge portion is your command of the language—in other words, your vocabulary. By this point in your life, you might think that you know all of the words you will ever need or that it will be impossible to improve your vocabulary. On the contrary! If you are diligent and put your mind to it, there are several ways in which you can improve your vocabulary. Here are two that will definitely help:

- **Read, read, read.** Pick up a newspaper, a magazine, or a novel and make note of words you do not understand. Make a list or put them on note cards. First, try to figure out the meaning of the words by looking at the context in which they are used. Make an educated guess. If you are still not sure, then look up the meaning of the words in a dictionary and write them out in a notebook or on note cards. Then try to make up your own sentences using the words.

- **Learn a new word every day or every other day.** You can get into the habit of looking up a new word in the dictionary every day. Write out the word and its definition on a piece of paper. Then write a sentence using the word. This will help you visualize it. Try using this new word in conversation. Don't pick words that are too technical or specialized (such as medical/scientific terms or proper names).

Unfortunately, neither of the two methods above is going to get you ready for the ASVAB in a short amount of time. The best way to learn a lot of words quickly is to understand prefixes, roots, and suffixes. The "Boosting Your Score with Prefixes, Roots, and Suffixes" section gives you the details.

Boosting Your Score with Prefixes, Roots, and Suffixes

Many words are made up of prefixes, roots, and suffixes.

- **Prefixes:** A prefix goes in front of a root word to change its meaning. For example, *re* is a prefix meaning "again," as in *redo* or *remake.*
- **Roots:** The root is the base of a word. For example, *cred* is the root of *creed* or *credible. Cred* is from the Latin word that means "believe." A *creed* is something you believe, and a person who is *credible* is someone you are willing to believe.
- **Suffixes:** A suffix comes at the end of a word. For example, *ly* means "in a certain fashion." *Slowly* means "in a slow fashion."

If you can familiarize yourself with prefixes, roots, and suffixes, you will find that you can arrive at the meaning of some words by breaking them down. The following sections offer you some common prefixes, roots, and suffixes to help you tackle words that you are unfamiliar with in the Word Knowledge section.

Prefixes

To break down words you do not understand or to help you recognize why a word means what it means, you should become familiar with prefixes. A prefix comes at the beginning of a word.

As an example, look at the word *synonym*. This word is made up of the prefix *syn* plus the root *nym*. If you knew that the prefix *syn* means "with/together" or "same" and the root *nym* means "name" or "word," then you could conclude that the word *synonym* means "same word." And that's what it means!

Here is another example. The word *circumvent* is made up of the prefix *circum* plus the root *vent*. If you knew that the prefix *circum* means "around" and the root *vent* means "go" or "come," then you could conclude that the word *circumvent* means "go around."

What follows is a list of common prefixes that you will often find at the beginnings of certain words. Following the prefix, you will find the meaning of the prefix and a word using the prefix (with a rough definition in parentheses following the word). Try to include a word of your own for each prefix in the space provided. If you want, you can browse through a dictionary to find many examples of words that start with these prefixes.

Prefix	Meaning	Word (Definition)	Your Example
ab-	away from	abnormal (not normal)	
ad-	to, toward	adjoin (join to)	
a-, an-	not, without	apathy (without feeling)	
anti-	against	antiviolence (against violence)	
ambi-	both	ambidextrous (able to use both hands)	
bene-	good	beneficial (good or advantageous)	
circum-	around	circumvent (go around)	
con-	with, together	connect (come together)	
contra-	against	contradict (speak against)	
com-	with, together	communion (coming together)	
de-	down, away	descend (move down)	
dis-	apart, not	discontent (not content)	
e-	out of, from	eject (throw out)	
ex-	out of, from	exclude (leave out)	
hyper-	over	hyperactive (overactive)	
hypo-	under	hypodermic (below the skin)	
inter-	between	interconnected (connected between)	
il-	not	illegal (not legal)	
im-	not	impossible (not possible)	
im-	into	imbibe (drink in)	
in-	not	indiscreet (not discreet)	
in-	into	ingest (take into the body by mouth)	
ir-	not	irrational (not rational)	
mal-	bad, evil	malign (speak badly of)	
ob-	against	obstruct (build against)	
omni-	all	omniscient (knows all)	
peri-	around	periscope (something used to view around)	
post-	after	postgraduate (after graduation)	

Prefix	Meaning	Word (Definition)	Your Example
pre-	before	precede (go before)	
pro-	for, forward	proceed (move forward)	
re-	again, back	reconvene (get together again)	
retro-	back	retrogression (a step back)	
se-	away from	seduce (lead away)	
sub-	under	subhuman (below human)	
sur-, super-	over, above	supersonic (above sound)	
sym-, syn-	together, with	sympathy (feeling with or for)	
trans-	across	transatlantic (across the Atlantic)	

Roots

Roots are central to the meanings of words. If you familiarize yourself with some common roots, then you may be able to better recognize certain words or at least get a general feel for them. By studying the following list of roots, you will be better equipped to break down many words and make sense of them.

Below you will find a root, its meaning, a word using the root (with the definition), and a space in which you can write another word that uses the same root.

Root	Meaning	Word (Definition)	Your Example
ami, amic	love	amicable (friendly)	
anthrop	human, man	anthropology (the study of humanity)	
auto	self	autobiography (a biography of one's self)	
aud	sound	audible (able to be heard)	
brev	short	brevity (shortness of time)	
bio	life	biography (a piece of writing about a life)	
cap	take, seize	capture (take)	
ced	yield, go	intercede (go between)	
corp	body	corporal (having to do with the body)	
cred	believe	credible (able to be believed)	
culp	guilt	culpable (guilty)	
chron	time	synchronize (set to the same time)	
crac, crat	rule, ruler	plutocracy (governance by the wealthy)	
dic	speak, say	malediction (a curse)	
duc, duct	lead	deduct (take away—in other words, lead away)	
demo	people	democracy (governance by the people)	
equ	equal	equidistant (at the same distance)	
grad, gress	step	progression (forward movement)	
graph	writing, printing	autograph (a signature)	
ject	throw	inject (put in)	
luc	light	elucidate (shed light on something)	
log	study of	geology (the study of the Earth)	
mono	one	monochrome (all the same color)	

(continued)

Root	Meaning	Word (Definition)	Your Example
man	hand	manual (something done with the hands)	
min	small	miniscule (very small)	
mit, miss	send	emit (send out)	
mort	death	mortal (able to be killed)	
mut	change	mutate (change)	
nym	word or name	pseudonym (a false name)	
nov	new	renovate (redo, make new)	
pac	peace	pacify (calm down)	
pel, puls	push	compel (make a person do something)	
pot	power	potent (powerful)	
port	carry	portable (able to be carried)	
path	feeling	apathy (a lack of feeling)	
phil	lover of	philosopher (a lover of wisdom)	
quer, quis	ask	query (ask)	
scrib	write	manuscript (something written)	
sed	sit	sedentary (stationary)	
sens	feel	sensory (having to do with the senses)	
sequ	follow	sequel (something that follows another thing)	
son	sound	sonic (having to do with sound)	
tang, tact	touch	tangible (able to be touched)	
vac	empty	vacant (empty)	
ven	come, go	intervene (go between)	
ver	truth	verify (prove true)	
vert	turn	introvert (a person focused inward)	
vit	life	revitalize (fill with energy, life)	
voc	call	convocation (when many people are called together)	

Suffixes

A suffix comes at the end of a word and usually changes the word's function as a part of speech (noun, adjective, adverb, and so on), which also subtly changes the word's meaning. Becoming familiar with suffixes may help you get a sense of the meaning a word is conveying, even if you are not sure what the definition of the word is.

The word *sedate* means "to calm or relax." The following sentences contain words that are made up of the root word *sedate* with different suffixes attached to the end:

The doctor prescribed a *sedative* (something that sedates) to calm her nerves.

The speech was delivered *sedately* (in a sedate manner).

The dog was under *sedation* (in a state of sedation) for the long trip.

Many office workers live a *sedentary* (nonactive) lifestyle.

As you can see, in each of the sentences, the italicized word means generally the same thing, but its function as a part of speech changes. However, you can get a sense of both the word's meaning and its part of speech if you know what the suffix means.

What follows is a list of common suffixes that you may encounter at the ends of certain words. Try applying these suffixes at the ends of words you know (or words from the lists above) to see how the part of speech or the meaning of the word changes.

Suffix	Meaning	Your Example
-able, -ible	capable of or susceptible to	
-ary	of or relating to	
-ate	to make	
-ian	one relating to or belonging to	
-ic	relating to or characterized by	
-ile	relating to or capable of	
-ion	action or condition of	
-ious	having the quality of	
-ism	quality, process, or practice of	
-ist	one who performs	
-ity	state of being	
-ive	performing or tending to	
-ize, ise	to cause to be or become	
-ly	resembling or in the manner of	
-less	without	
-ment	action or process or the result	
-ology	study of	
-y, -ry	state of	

Strategies for Scoring Well

In the ASVAB, you are not penalized for incorrect answers, so it is to your benefit to answer EVERY question, whether you are sure of the answer or not. Do your best to eliminate one or two of the answers and then take your best guess, or take a random guess—just be sure to answer all the questions!

That said, you should also try some of the following test-taking strategies to help you through the Word Knowledge section:

- **Do not panic.** At first, all of the questions and words may seem confusing or overwhelming. But if you relax, take a few deep breaths, and focus, you will be much more mentally equipped to handle the test.

- **Do not look at the answer choices at first.** Try to see if you can come up with your own synonym or definition. You may find that you already know the answer before looking at the choices!

- **Read the word and mentally sound it out.** Are there roots or prefixes you recognize? Does the word seem to have a negative or positive "feel" (sometimes you have to use your instincts!)? Does it sound like any other word you have heard before?

- **Try putting the word in a sentence.** Even if the sentence seems ridiculous, try putting the word in a context you're familiar with—you may recognize the meaning. Have you heard this word before? In what context was it used?

- **Eliminate one or two choices immediately.** It is a general rule of most multiple-choice test-makers to offer one or two choices that are clearly wrong, one choice that seems possible, and one choice that is correct. When it comes to deciding between the two "possible" answers, you must replace the word in the question with both choices. For word-in-context questions, try both possible words in the sentence to see which one "feels" more appropriate.

- **Don't spend too much time on one question.** Every question is worth the same number of points, so move on if you are stuck. You can go back. Go through the section answering the questions that come easily to you and then return to tackle the more difficult questions later.

Word Knowledge Practice Questions

1. Graphic most nearly means

    A.   unclear.
    B.   detailed.
    C.   large.
    D.   childish.

2. Indispensable most nearly means

    A.   trashy.
    B.   ridiculous.
    C.   necessary.
    D.   uninvited.

3. Concoct most nearly means

    A.   make up.
    B.   throw away.
    C.   go through.
    D.   walk around.

4. Degradation most nearly means

    A.   happiness.
    B.   anger.
    C.   celebration.
    D.   poverty.

5. Contradict most nearly means

    A.   talk about.
    B.   see the future.
    C.   fall down.
    D.   be opposed to.

6. The girl emitted a shrill scream at the sight of the realistic Halloween decorations.

    A.   hid
    B.   hoped for
    C.   let out
    D.   kept in

7. The mother could not sleep all night because of her newborn baby's incessant crying.

    A.   loud
    B.   nonstop
    C.   angry
    D.   sorrowful

8. Sequentially most nearly means

    A.   sensibly.
    B.   randomly.
    C.   in order.
    D.   out of order.

9. Culprit most nearly means

    A.   a shy person.
    B.   a shallow waterway.
    C.   the guilty party.
    D.   the most qualified person.

10. Omnipotent most nearly means

    A.   all-knowing.
    B.   all-seeing.
    C.   all-hearing.
    D.   all-powerful.

11. Submissive most nearly means

    A.   meek.
    B.   not intelligent.
    C.   kind.
    D.   strong.

12. The couple held disparate opinions on every topic.

    A.   selfish
    B.   loving
    C.   humorous
    D.   different

13. My boss often speaks to me in a <u>condescending</u> manner.

    A. thoughtful
    B. mysterious
    C. silly
    D. snobbish

14. <u>Demeaning</u> most nearly means

    A. boring.
    B. humiliating.
    C. colorful.
    D. ignorant.

15. <u>Fluctuate</u> most nearly means

    A. remain the same.
    B. follow a downward course.
    C. follow an upward course.
    D. change.

16. <u>Renovate</u> most nearly means

    A. destroy.
    B. restore.
    C. return.
    D. go around.

17. Why do songs <u>evoke</u> such strong emotions in certain people?

    A. hold back
    B. make fun of
    C. call out
    D. change

18. The main challenge of the hike was to <u>circumvent</u> the large mountain.

    A. get over
    B. go under
    C. get through
    D. get around

19. <u>Intercede</u> most nearly means

    A. bring something to an end.
    B. act as a judge.
    C. act as mediator.
    D. laugh at something.

20. <u>Validate</u> most nearly means

    A. make better.
    B. make worse.
    C. make different.
    D. make authentic.

21. <u>Equity</u> most nearly means

    A. injustice.
    B. same distance.
    C. fairness.
    D. different sizes.

22. <u>Culmination</u> most nearly means

    A. the beginning of a project.
    B. the end result.
    C. the process.
    D. the idea behind a project.

23. In <u>hindsight</u>, Mary realized that driving over the drawbridge was a bad idea.

    A. watching from above
    B. seeing through a haze
    C. perceiving after the fact
    D. looking around

24. A mother's love <u>transcends</u> time.

    A. surpasses
    B. stops for
    C. crosses
    D. grows with

25. Hockey games tend to <u>incite</u> violence.

    A. stir up
    B. maintain
    C. discourage
    D. like

26. The mayor will <u>recant</u> his troubling statement.

    A. stood by
    B. take back
    C. was confused by
    D. repeated

27. The dog's <u>fixated</u> gaze was on the hamburger.

    A. unaware
    B. interested
    C. hungry
    D. stuck

28. <u>Sonic</u> most nearly means

    A. relating to the sun.
    B. relating to the moon.
    C. relating to sound.
    D. relating to the earth.

29. <u>Assimilate</u> most nearly means

    A. take in.
    B. make fun of.
    C. rob of.
    D. ignore.

30. The team made a <u>concerted</u> effort to win the baseball game.

    A. separate and disinterested
    B. combined and determined
    C. fast and efficient
    D. slow and painful

31. In many reality-television shows, contestants are encouraged to form <u>alliances</u>.

    A. groups that share the same goals
    B. groups that constantly argue
    C. groups that trick each other
    D. groups that hate each other

32. <u>Ambiguous</u> most nearly means

    A. small.
    B. certain.
    C. bitter.
    D. unclear.

33. <u>Facilitate</u> most nearly means

    A. make easy.
    B. make new.
    C. make difficult.
    D. make different.

34. <u>Tactile</u> most nearly means

    A. airy.
    B. strategic.
    C. concrete.
    D. sweet.

35. <u>Benign</u> most nearly means

    A. behind.
    B. above.
    C. outside.
    D. kind.

Answers and Explanations for Practice Questions

If the underlined word from the question contains a clearly recognizable root or prefix, it is noted in parentheses within the explanation.

1. **B.** Graphic (*graph* = *written* or *drawn*) means "described in vivid detail" or "clearly drawn out," so *detailed* would most closely mean graphic.

2. **C.** Indispensable literally means "not dispensable" (able to be thrown away). So if something is indispensable, it is *necessary;* you cannot do without it.

3. **A.** Concoct means "to create" or *make up,* as in the sentence "The two boys concocted a plan to skip school."

4. **D.** Degradation is a "state of poverty" or "squalor." Using its prefix and root, you can come up with "a step down" (*de* = *down, grad* = *step*).

5. **D.** Contradict means "to go against," as in "Joe's statement that he didn't eat the last slice of pie is contradicted by the empty pie plate." You may have been able to use the roots to help you decipher the meaning (*contra* = *against, dict* = *speak*).

6. **C.** To emit is "to send out" (*e* = *out, mit* = *send*) or *let out.*

7. **B.** Incessant (*in* = *not, cess* = *end*) means "not ceasing," "never ending," "not stopping."

8. **C.** Sequentially means "items are arranged *in order* or in a sequence" (*sequ* = *follow*).

9. **C.** The culprit is "the person who is *guilty*" (*culp* = *guilt*).

10. **D.** Omnipotent means *all-powerful* (*omni* = *all, pot* = *power*).

11. **A.** A submissive (*sub* = *under, miss* = *send*) person is one who is "meek and passive," not aggressive.

12. **D.** Disparate means "opposing" or "different."

13. **D.** Condescend means to "go down to the level of someone inferior" (*con* = *with, descend* = *down*); therefore, a condescending manner can be *snobby.*

14. **B.** Something that is demeaning (*de* = *down*) is something that "puts one down" or "is humiliating."

15. **D.** Fluctuate (*fluc* = *change*) means "to change," "to go up and down," "to not be constant."

16. **B.** Renovate means "to restore" or to "make new again" (*re* = *again, nov* = *new*).

17. **C.** Evoke means "to call out" (*e* = *out, voc* = *call*).

18. **D.** Circumvent means "to go around" (*circum* = *around, vent* = *go*).

19. **C.** Intercede means "to go between" (*inter* = *within, ced* = *go*) or "to mediate."

20. **D.** Validate means "to make authentic or lawful"; in other words, "to show the validity of something."

21. **C.** Equity means "fair and just treatment to something or someone."

22. **B.** Culmination means "the coming together of all parts resulting in the end," thus *the end result.*

23. **C.** Hindsight is "looking back after the fact."

24. **C.** Transcends (*trans* = *across*) means "crosses over."

25. **A.** Incite means "to cause, provoke," or "stir up."

26. **B.** Recant means "to take back."

27. **D.** Fixated means "to be obsessed with" or "stuck on."

28. **C.** Sonic means "relating to sound" (*son* = *sound*).

29. **A.** <u>Assimilate</u> means "to absorb" or "take in." If a group of individuals successfully <u>assimilates</u>, then they have converged and incorporated into one group.

30. **B.** <u>Concerted</u> (*con = with*) means "determined" and "together."

31. **A.** <u>Alliances</u> are "groups that share the same goal"; people in an <u>alliance</u> are "allies."

32. **D.** <u>Ambiguous</u> means "not certain," "something that could go either way," "vague" or "unclear."

33. **A.** <u>Facilitate</u> means "to make able to do" (*fac = do, ate = to make*) or "to make easy."

34. **C.** <u>Tactile</u> means "solid" or "concrete"; something that can be touched.

35. **D.** <u>Benign</u> (*ben = good*) means "kind or good," "not evil."

Paragraph Comprehension

The Paragraph Comprehension section of the ASVAB is designed to measure your ability to understand what you have read and your ability to obtain information from written passages. This section has 15 questions based on 15 or fewer short passages. One or more multiple-choice questions follows each passage. The test asks you to select the best answer that completes a statement or answers a question.

Understanding what you read requires two skills. The first skill is the ability to understand exactly what the passage says. Questions about understanding may ask you to identify facts stated in the passage, or to identify facts from the passage that the question presents in different words. When the same idea or fact is presented in different words, it is known as a paraphrase. You will need to be able to recognize paraphrases. Some of these questions require you to understand the meaning of a word from the passage in which it appears. This skill means you can understand words in context. A third type of literal comprehension question asks you to determine in what order events described in a passage happened.

The second skill for paragraph comprehension requires you to analyze what you have read. One kind of question asks you to identify the main idea of a passage. Another kind asks you to draw a conclusion from the information that the passage presents. This skill requires you to infer something that is not directly stated but that is implied by the content of the passage. Other types of questions ask you to think about how the passage is written. What is the purpose of the passage? What technique of organization or structure did the author use to write the passage? What mood or tone does the passage reflect?

The ASVAB has 15 Paragraph Comprehension questions. You will have 13 minutes to answer these questions.

Test-Taking Strategies

The test requires that you answer 15 questions in a 13-minute period. You should not need to read the directions because you are familiar with them from this chapter. You cannot spend a long time on any single question. If one of the answers immediately appears to you to be correct, quickly check the passage to see if your answer is accurate, and select that answer on the answer sheet. If you are not certain which answer is correct, first eliminate choices that you are sure are not correct. Then glance at the passage and decide which of the remaining possibilities is the best answer. If you find that the question is difficult to understand and do not have any idea about which answer is correct, go on to the next question. Return to the difficult questions after you have completed as many of the other questions as you can.

Be sure that you base your answers **only on the information that is given in the passage.** Sometimes you may have more information about a subject than is given in a passage. You may find a statement in a passage that you do not think is correct. But this section tests your reading ability, not your general knowledge about the subject of the passage. Do not choose an answer that you think is correct based on what you know about the subject of the passage. Only choose answers that are based on information in the passage.

Some test-takers find it helpful to read the question before reading the passage. As you work on the practice questions in this chapter, try that method, as well as the method of reading the passage first and then the question. You should be able to decide which of these two methods makes it easier for you to determine the correct answer.

A sure way to do well on this section is to improve your general reading ability. Reading teachers agree that the best way to improve reading skills is to read as much as possible. The passages on this test use the kind of information that you are likely to find in newspapers and magazines as well as in books. Practice in reading all three kinds of material will be helpful when taking this test.

Kinds of Questions

In this part of this chapter, you can find samples and explanations of each type of question on this test. These are followed by practice questions with the answers explained.

Identifying Stated Facts

These questions require that you read carefully for facts in a passage. Do not choose an answer that adds information not contained in the passage, and be sure that your answer states all the information in the passage about the question. Look for an answer that uses exactly the same wording as a part of the passage.

---

1. A ballad is a type of poem that tells a story. It is written in groups of four lines. The lines rhyme in a set pattern. Often, ballads tell stories about death, or ghosts, or other supernatural beings. Sometimes ballads tell love stories.

   To be a ballad, a poem must

   A. tell a story.
   B. contain a love story.
   C. be only four lines long.
   D. tell stories about death.

The correct answer is **A**. It is stated in the first sentence of the passage. Choices B and D are only sometimes true of ballads. Choice C is not true according to the passage's second sentence.

---

2. The laws of the United States include rules and customs about the display of the United States flag. The flag should be displayed only from sunrise to sunset. It may be displayed at night if it is lighted so that it can be seen. It should be displayed at or near every place where voting is held on election days. It should never touch the ground or the floor. It should never be used for advertising purposes.

   The flag should never be displayed

   A. from sunrise to sunset.
   B. at night.
   C. above the ground or floor.
   D. for advertising purposes.

The correct answer is **D**. It uses the same words that appear in the passage. You probably have seen advertisements that show the American flag. But according to the passage, those advertisements violate rules about the display of the flag. Choices A and C state the opposite of what the paragraph says. The third sentence says the flag *may* be displayed at night, so B is not a correct choice.

Identifying Reworded Facts

When you answer these types of questions, look for information in the answer that states the same facts that the passage states, even though the wording is different. The answer means the same thing as the statement in the passage, even though the words are not exactly the same.

1. In certain areas, water is so scarce that every attempt is made to conserve it. For instance, on an oasis in the Sahara Desert, the amount of water necessary for each date palm has been carefully determined.

   How much water is each tree given?

   A. no water at all
   B. water on alternate days
   C. exactly the amount required
   D. water only if it is healthy

The correct answer is **C**. The passage states "the amount of water necessary for each date palm has been carefully determined." "The amount required" means the same as "necessary."

2. *Liaison* can refer to a person who communicates information between groups. The press secretary to the President of the United States is a *liaison* between the President and journalists. A manufacturing engineer is a *liaison* between a product's designers and the workers involved in making the product.

   The word *liaison* means someone who

   A. argues for a point of view.
   B. analyzes political issues.
   C. helps groups understand each other.
   D. designs products.

The correct answer is **C**. The phrase "communicates information between groups" means a way of helping them understand each other. A is not correct because it states the *liaison* only represents one point of view. Choices B and D are suggested by the examples in the paragraph, but they do not define *liaison*.

Determining Sequence of Events

The sequence of events means the order in which events occur. When a question asks about the order of events, look for key words that tell about time. These are words and phrases that you are familiar with, such as *soon, then, before, after, later, next, previously, lastly, to begin, in a little while, shortly,* and *after an hour.* These key words in the passage point to the answer to the question.

1. To check the engine oil on a car, lift the hood of the car. Be sure it is propped open securely. Locate the dipstick, a rod that goes into the engine. Remove the dipstick to check the oil. Then see if the oil comes up to the line marked on the dipstick. If it does, the engine is full. Next, look at the condition of the oil. It should be light brown and clear, not dark or gritty looking. After replacing the dipstick, add or change oil if necessary. Finally, close the hood, and you're ready to drive.

   After removing the dipstick,

   A. see if the engine is full.
   B. check the condition of the oil.
   C. replace the dipstick.
   D. close the hood.

The correct answer is **A**. According to the passage, this is the first thing to do after removing the dipstick. Choices B, C, and D are introduced by "next," "after," and "finally," words showing that these acts occur later in the order of events.

> 2. Antarctica is now a continent of ice and rocks. It was not always so. Millions of years ago, Antarctica, South America, Australia, and New Zealand formed a supercontinent near the equator. Then moving oceanic plates began to split the supercontinent apart. First, Antarctica, still attached to Australia, drifted south. Later, Antarctica separated from Australia and moved farther south until it rested over the South Pole.
>
> When did Antarctica come to rest over the South Pole?
>
> A. when it was part of a supercontinent
> B. when it was attached to Australia
> C. after it began to drift to the south
> D. after it separated from Australia

The correct answer is **D**. According to the passage, choices A, B, and C list events that occurred before Antarctica came to rest over the South Pole.

Identifying Main Ideas

The main idea of a paragraph is a general statement that tells what the passage says. The main idea is a broad, general statement. The other information in the paragraph is specific, providing support for the main idea by explaining the main idea or giving details and examples to illustrate or prove it. An example of a general statement would be a sentence like "Green vegetables provide nutrients necessary for good health." Specific details supporting this statement could be "spinach contains iron" and "broccoli has large quantities of B vitamins."

Sometimes the main idea of the paragraph is stated. A stated main idea is called the paragraph's topic sentence. This most often is the paragraph's first sentence, but the main idea can also be stated at the end of the paragraph. It is unusual for the main idea to be stated in the middle of a paragraph, but sometimes a paragraph is written that way.

When a question asks you to identify a paragraph's main idea, the correct answer may present the main idea in slightly different words than those used in the paragraph.

Sometimes a writer chooses not to write a sentence stating the main idea. If so, the reader must decide what the main idea is by figuring out what general statement could be made by adding up the specific information in the passage. When you do this, you are inferring the main idea.

> 1. In the 50 years between the end of the Civil War and the beginning of World War I, the United States changed from a rural nation to a power in the modern world. The country expanded to include all the territory between the Atlantic and the Pacific oceans. The population grew, partly as a result of immigration. The economy became increasingly industrial. Increased production of goods led to more trade with other nations.
>
> The main idea of this passage is that
>
> A. immigration increased the country's population.
> B. international trade increased.
> C. the country became a powerful modern nation.
> D. the country's territory expanded.

The correct answer is **C**. It is a general statement. All of the other choices are specific details that demonstrate the growth of the country.

2. Toothpaste can be used to clean chrome faucets and make them shiny. A few tablespoons of white vinegar mixed with water in a spray bottle create an excellent cleaner for windows or mirrors. And wet tea leaves will take the sting out of a burn.

The main idea of this paragraph is

A. some ordinary products have surprising uses.
B. cleaning products don't have to be expensive.
C. vinegar and water mixed create a glass cleaner.
D. tea is a refreshing beverage.

The correct answer is **A.** The three sentences in the paragraph are examples of the general statement that A makes. Choice B describes an idea that the first two sentences of the paragraph imply, but it does not apply to the third sentence. Choices C and D are specific details, not general statements, and while D may be true, the paragraph does not state this idea.

Drawing Conclusions

These questions ask you to decide what you can conclude from information that is in the passage, although the passage does not directly state a conclusion. You can infer the conclusion from the information in the passage. The passage presents separate pieces of information, and drawing a conclusion requires that you see what these pieces of information imply. The passage does not tell you what the answer to the question is. Whatever is directly stated in the passage is not a conclusion. You determine the conclusion based on the logical relationships of information in the passage.

1. Twenty-five percent of all household burglaries can be attributed to unlocked windows or doors. Crime is the result of opportunity plus desire.

To prevent crime, it is each individual's responsibility to

A. provide the desire.
B. provide the opportunity.
C. prevent the desire.
D. prevent the opportunity.

The correct answer is **D.** The first sentence states that twenty-five percent of burglaries result from leaving doors and windows unlocked. This is an opportunity for burglars. The second sentence tells you that crime is made up of not only opportunity but also the criminal's desire to commit a crime. Choice B, providing opportunity, is the opposite of preventing crime. Choices A and B are actions an individual cannot be responsible for in another person. The only logical conclusion, therefore, is that individuals can help to prevent crime by preventing the opportunity.

2. In a survey taken in July of residents of Metropolis, 44% approved of the mayor's job performance, 52% disapproved, and 4% had no opinion. In a similar survey one year ago, 51% approved, 39% disapproved, and 10% had no opinion.

Based on this information, you can conclude

A. the mayor's popularity increased.
B. the mayor's popularity decreased.
C. the mayor took an action the residents did not like.
D. the mayor took an action the residents approved of.

The correct answer is **C.** Choice A contradicts the statistics in the passage. Choice B states in different words facts given in the passage about the change in the mayor's approval rating, but is not a conclusion. You can logically conclude there was a cause for the change. Because the approval rating declined, the cause would have to be an action the residents did not like.

Determining Purpose

Questions about purpose ask you to decide what the passage aims at or intends to do. A paragraph may be written to provide information or explanations. The reader thinks, "Now I know something I didn't know before." The passage may give directions or instructions. The reader learns how to do something. The passage may wish to persuade the reader to agree with what it says. A reader may agree or disagree with the main idea of the passage. This kind of writing is known as an argument.

In determining the purpose of a passage, consider how the sentences relate to each other. If the passage provides reasons for agreeing with a statement, it is probably an argument. If the sentences list a series of steps occurring in a process, the passage usually gives instructions. If the sentences present a series of facts, the passage's purpose is to inform or explain.

---

1. This medicine may be taken on an empty stomach or with food. Do not drive a car or operate heavy machinery after taking this medication because it may make you sleepy. Take one pill each morning until all the pills have been taken. If you forget to take a pill, do not take two pills the following day.

    The purpose of this passage is to

    A. argue against taking two pills in one day.
    B. explain how the medicine may affect you.
    C. give instructions about how to take the medicine.
    D. inform the reader how the medicine will help cure symptoms.

The correct answer is **C**. Choice A is not correct because "do not take two pills" is not an idea you can agree or disagree with. Although the passage says the medication may make you sleepy, the rest of the passage does not explain how the medicine may affect you, so B is not a correct choice. Choice D is incorrect because nothing in the passage discusses how the medicine works.

---

2. As far as genes are concerned, those of chimpanzees and human beings are nearly 99% identical. The bonobo, a species related to chimpanzees, also has this genetic similarity. The genes of monkeys and orangutans are not as similar to human genes. Scientists are trying to find out which genes differ in humans and chimpanzees and how they are different.

    The author of this passage wants to

    A. inform readers about animal and human genes.
    B. explain why chimpanzee and human genes differ.
    C. argue for learning about genes.
    D. argue against experiments using animals.

The correct answer is **A**. Choice B is incorrect because the paragraph does not state the causes for the differences, so it does not explain why the genes differ. The passage does not give reasons for learning about genes. Therefore, C is incorrect. D is incorrect because the passage does not say anything about experiments on animals.

Identifying Technique

Authors can organize a brief passage or paragraph using different techniques. Questions about technique ask you to identify the basis of the passage's structure. Key words connecting sentences in the passage can help you to identify its technique.

If a passage tells a story of events in time order, using words or phrases like *first, soon after, then, next,* or *after a few minutes,* its structure is based on narrative technique. Some paragraphs use description. What is known through the five senses makes up the passage's content. Descriptive paragraphs use the technique of organizing details spatially. Words and phrases like *on, next to, in front of, over, under,* and *to the right (or left)* are what you can expect to see in paragraphs that organize details spatially.

Paragraphs that show how things are similar use comparison as a technique. Paragraphs that show how things are different use contrast as a technique. Some paragraphs use both comparison and contrast. Words and phrases like *similarly, also, likewise,* and *in the same way* show comparison. *But, yet, however,* and *on the other hand* indicate contrasts.

Paragraphs based on cause give information about why things, events, or ideas happen. Paragraphs based on effects give information about the results of events or ideas. Some paragraphs discuss both causes and effects. Words and phrases like *because, for this reason,* and *since* show organization based on cause. *As a result, so, therefore, thus,* and *consequently* indicate effects.

---

1. Today's professional golfers often hit the ball farther than golfers did in the past. One reason is that they spend time physically conditioning themselves. Therefore, they are strong. Golf clubs made of materials developed for modern technology are light, so they are easy to swing. Using computers, engineers design the surface of golf balls to make them travel great distances in the air.

   The organizing technique of this paragraph is best described as

   A. comparison and contrast.
   B. description.
   C. narration.
   D. cause and effect.

The correct answer is **D**. Although the first sentence is a comparison, the rest of the paragraph gives reasons that the ball is hit farther and shows how these causes produce the effect of greater distance.

---

2. The Boston Tea Party was not the first protest against British taxes by the American colonists. A tax had been placed on sugar in 1764. Then, in 1765, the Stamp Act taxed legal documents and newspapers. These taxes were removed after the colonists stopped buying British goods. Two years later, the British put new taxes on lead, paper, glass, and tea. After further protests, all but the tax on tea were removed. Finally, in 1773, the colonists tossed boxes of tea overboard from ships in Boston Harbor to protest this tax.

   The organizing technique of this paragraph is

   A. description.
   B. contrast.
   C. narration.
   D. cause and effect.

The correct answer is **C**. The first date mentioned is 1764, and the last is 1773, so time has passed. Time indicators like "then," "after," and "two years later" confirm that the passage's technique is narration.

Determining Mood and Tone

The mood and tone of a passage consist of the emotions that its content suggests. To answer questions about mood and tone, think about the words in the passage. Are they associated with things that make people feel happy, like a bright sunny day or a special birthday party? Or are they words related to events that usually make people sad, like illness or gloomy weather? Is the language strong and harsh, suggesting that the writer of the passage is angry? Are there exclamation points to indicate excitement? If the passage is a description, think about how you would feel if you were in the place being described or were watching the events described. If the passage describes a person, what facts about that person indicate how the person feels?

1. Through the open window, she saw that the tops of the trees were breaking out in little green buds, which would soon be leaves. The rain had cleaned the air, and she felt a warm breeze signaling the end of winter. Patches of blue sky showed through the clouds, and she heard birds singing.

   The mood of this passage could best be described as

   A. fearful.
   B. hopeful.
   C. disgusted.
   D. comical.

The correct answer is **B.** The clean air, the green buds, the blue sky, the warm breeze, and the singing birds are all descriptive details connected to springtime. Spring is the season when things that have stopped growing during the winter begin to grow again, so it is associated with life and hope. While the passage is happy, it is not funny, so D would not be a good answer.

2. It was a dark and stormy night. The rain rattling on the roof sounded like skeletons dancing. Then I heard a strange sound outside the front door. What could it be? Who would go out in such a storm? I approached the door slowly, and opened it just a crack. I could see nothing. Cautiously, I opened the door another inch or two. But still I saw nothing. A gust of wind—or something—I don't know what—caught the door and opened it fully. With trembling hands, I slammed the door shut to keep out the wind.

   The tone of this passage is

   A. angry.
   B. frightened.
   C. thoughtful.
   D. unhappy.

The correct answer is **B.** Storms often create a spooky mood. Words like "slowly" and "cautiously" as well as the description of the sound of the rain and being unable to see anything when the door is opened add to the tone of fright. The speaker's trembling hands in the last sentence also indicate fear.

Paragraph Comprehension Practice Questions

1. In January 2002, a person buys a car that comes with a three-year or 36,000-mile free replacement guarantee on the engine and transmission. In June 2005, the car has 34,300 miles on it. The transmission fails.

    According to the situation described in the paragraph, the car dealer will

    A. put in a new transmission.
    B. give the person a new car.
    C. not fix the transmission at no cost.
    D. not replace the car's engine.

2. A sonnet is a specific type of poem. It has 14 lines. The lines must rhyme in a set pattern. Sometimes, the last six lines of a sonnet contrast with the first eight lines. Many sonnets are love poems.

    To be a sonnet, a poem must

    A. be a love poem.
    B. present a contrast.
    C. have fewer than 14 lines.
    D. rhyme in a specific way.

3. When many people want to buy a product, the price will probably go up. In the summer, Americans travel more than they do at other times of year. They may take planes or trains, and many families drive to their vacation spots.

    From the information in the paragraph, you can conclude that

    A. gasoline prices will rise in the summer.
    B. gasoline prices will rise in the winter.
    C. gasoline prices will go down in the summer.
    D. gasoline prices will not change in any season.

4. When you send a document to someone by electronic means, you are faxing it. The word "fax" comes from the word "facsimile." Earlier ways of making facsimiles included photocopying and photographing. The oldest facsimiles were handwritten versions of original texts.

    The word "facsimile" means

    A. an electronic copy.
    B. an exact copy.
    C. any document.
    D. a photocopy.

5. The United States Supreme Court is the highest court in the nation. Its nine judges review cases from other courts. They decide if these courts have ruled in a way that agrees with the United States Constitution. But they cannot make new laws. Their decisions are based on a majority vote of the nine judges.

    The main idea of this paragraph is that

    A. the Supreme Court has nine judges.
    B. the Supreme Court is the highest court in the United States.
    C. the Supreme Court cannot make new laws.
    D. the Supreme Court's decisions are based on a majority vote.

6. Most cars today have automatic transmissions. But it is useful to know how to shift gears in a car with a standard transmission. Press the clutch pedal in with your left foot. Then use the shift lever to choose the proper gear. Release the clutch pedal while gently applying pressure to the gas pedal.

    The last thing to do when shifting gears is to

    A. step on the gas.
    B. release the clutch.
    C. use the shift lever.
    D. press down on the clutch.

7. Recycling household waste is very important. Space for landfills where garbage is dumped is becoming scarce. Putting waste in the oceans causes pollution. Recycling is a way for cities to make money by selling recyclable items. And recycling items helps to save natural resources.

The author's purpose in this passage is to

A. explain what recycling is.
B. tell a story.
C. show a contrast.
D. argue for recycling.

8. Jackrabbits are not rabbits but members of the hare family. Hares are larger than rabbits, and they have longer ears. Newborn rabbits are naked and helpless, but infant hares are covered with fur and are aware of their surroundings.

Hares and rabbits are contrasted by describing all of the following except

A. their size.
B. the length of their ears.
C. what color they are.
D. newborn rabbits and hares.

9. Superman originated as a character in a comic book in the 1930s. Then a radio program called *The Adventures of Superman* was created. Later, Superman became part of going to the movies. Short episodes were shown each week in theaters in addition to a feature film. When television became part of American life, it, too, had a weekly program about Superman. In the 1980s several full-length films about Superman appeared.

From this passage, you can conclude

A. Superman is a great hero.
B. Superman has been popular for a long time.
C. Superman has often appeared in films.
D. Superman began in comic books.

10. People may think of pizza as a snack food. But it is nutritious. The crust, made of a kind of bread, provides carbohydrates. The tomatoes contain Vitamin C and provide fiber. The cheese is a good source of calcium that is needed for healthy bones.

Pizza is healthful because it

A. includes a good source of calcium.
B. tastes good.
C. is a snack food.
D. can be ordered in a restaurant or bought frozen to bake at home.

11. The space shuttle is coming in for a landing. Over a loudspeaker, the waiting spectators hear, "STS 42 is now over Brandenburg, making its turn for the coast." They quickly stand, look up, turn their eyes skyward. They hear the sonic boom and stare at the sky even more closely. There it is! First it is only a speck. Then the crowd applauds and cheers as they see it approaching earth.

The spectators who watch the shuttle land feel

A. fear.
B. anger.
C. happiness.
D. excitement.

12. When people are in a group, they may not react to an emergency the same way they would if they were alone. One reason may be that each person thinks someone else has already done something. Or, seeing no one else speak, a person may feel nothing needs to be done. A third possibility is that the person does not want to draw attention to himself or herself.

This passage explains

A. differences between individuals and people in groups.
B. effects of being part of a group.
C. causes for behavior in a group.
D. how people react to an emergency.

13. In 1963, Martin Luther King, Jr. led a protest march in Birmingham, Alabama. Because he did not have a permit to hold the march, he was arrested. Then eight clergymen wrote a letter that was published in the local newspaper. The letter opposed protest marches as a way to end racial problems. While King was in jail, he wrote a reply to that letter. It has been reprinted many times since then under the title "Letter from Birmingham Jail."

King wrote the letter

A. before the protest march.
B. when he was arrested.
C. while he was thinking about racial problems.
D. after he read the clergymen's letter.

14. King was arrested because

A. The clergymen wrote a letter.
B. He did not have a permit to hold the march.
C. There were racial problems in Birmingham.
D. He was put in jail.

15. People sometimes say they will *return back* to a place they have visited. But because "return" means the same thing as "go back to," the expression "return back" is redundant.

The word *redundant* could be used to describe which one of the following phrases?

A. cooperate together
B. walk slowly
C. review again
D. add information

Answers to Practice Questions

1. **C.** Because the car is more than three years old, the free replacement guarantee will not apply. A is not correct because it does not tell whether the customer will have to pay for the work. No information in the paragraph suggests that B would be what would happen. While D may be a true statement, the situation in the paragraph does not describe any problem with the engine.

2. **D.** Choices A and B are statements that describe some but not all sonnets according to the paragraph. C is incorrect because the paragraph states a sonnet has 14 lines.

3. **A.** The paragraph states that Americans travel more in the summer. You can conclude that if they travel more, more gasoline will be used, and the paragraph states that when people want to buy more of a product, the price goes up.

4. **B.** Answers A and D are examples of facsimiles; they do not define the word. C is incorrect because the paragraph indicates that ways of making facsimiles are ways of making copies.

5. **B.** A main idea is a general statement. The other choices are specific facts.

6. **A.** The paragraph is written in the order of things to do, and this is the last action mentioned in the paragraph.

7. **D.** The paragraph explains why recycling is a good idea. The paragraph is not a story (Choice B), and does not have a contrast (Choice C). It does not tell what recycling is, so A is incorrect.

8. **C.** The paragraph discusses all of the other choices.

9. **B.** The paragraph discusses Superman from the 1930s to the 1980s, so one can conclude he has been popular for a long time. Choices C and D are facts stated in the paragraph. Most people would agree with choice A, but it is not part of the information in the paragraph.

10. **A.** It is the only choice that states a fact about why pizza is a nutritious food.

11. **D.** The details in the paragraph about standing up, staring at the sky, the exclamation, "There it is!" and the applause and cheering show that the spectators are excited.

12. **C.** Because the paragraph gives reasons, it is explaining causes. Although the first sentence of the paragraph is a contrast, the paragraph does not explain the contrast, so A is an incorrect choice.

13. **D.** Because King's letter was a reply to the clergymen, he had to have written it after he read their letter.

14. **B.** This fact is stated in the second sentence of the paragraph.

15. **A.** From the paragraph, you can infer that a *redundant* expression is one in which both words have the same meaning. "Cooperate" means "work together," so A is an example of a redundant expression. Choice C may look appropriate because "review" means "look at again." But something can be reviewed more than once.

Auto and Shop Information

The ASVAB includes a section that tests your automobile and shop knowledge. To do well on the Auto questions, you need to understand how automobiles work, and how to fix and repair them. To do well on the Shop section, you need to know what sorts of tools are used for what purposes.

This section starts with an explanation of how automobiles work, and then goes into shop-related content.

The ASVAB contains 25 Auto and Shop Information questions. You will have 11 minutes to answer these questions.

Automobile Knowledge

Engine Basics

The vast majority of vehicles are powered by gasoline-burning engines. Gasoline is mixed with air and burned in cylinders in an *engine block.* The engine block is generally cast of iron or aluminum. Casting is the foundry process of forming a part by pouring molten metal into a mold. All other engine parts are connected to the block.

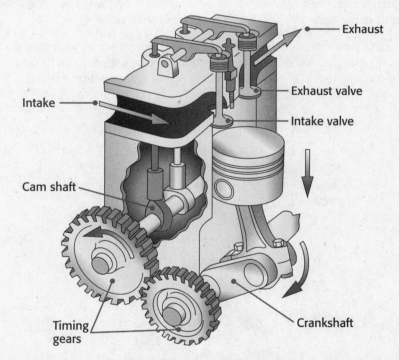

The engine block cylinders are closed at the top by a *cylinder head.* The head is bolted to the block, forming a combustion chamber. In the *combustion chamber,* the air-fuel mixture is burned to power the engine. The combustion process is initiated by an electric spark. To a large extent, the combustion chamber's shape determines how efficiently combustion occurs. Burning the air-fuel mixture progressively and quickly makes an engine more efficient and responsive.

The cylinder head also contains passages that let the unburned air-fuel mixture into the combustion chamber, and send the burnt gases back out. Cylinder heads are usually cast of iron or aluminum. Aluminum has become popular because it's lighter and dissipates heat better. Burning fuel generates immense pressure and heat.

No matter how well the surfaces between the engine block and cylinder head fit together, a cylinder head gasket is needed to keep hot gases from escaping during combustion. *Gaskets* are used to seal joints between many parts of an engine against oil, water, or vapor leaks. Feeding the air-fuel mixture into the cylinder head is the job of the *intake manifold.* The *exhaust manifold* expels the burnt gases.

At the bottom of the engine block is an *oil pan.* The oil pan holds a gallon or more of oil that is needed to lubricate the engine's moving parts. The oil pan and the bottom of the engine block house the crankshaft. The base of the block and the oil pan form an area called the *crankcase.*

Inside each cylinder of the engine block is a lightweight aluminum alloy *piston.* A piston fits in the cylinder that is closed off at the top by the cylinder head. A piston operates similarly to a cannon. In a cannon, the combustion pressures created by a chemical explosion of gunpowder push the cannonball out at great speed. In an engine, the air-fuel mixture acts as the gunpowder, pushing the piston down. While the cannonball flies out of the cannon, the piston can't escape from the cylinder because the crankshaft pushes it back up to burn a fresh charge of air-fuel mixture. Up and down, over and over—this process is called *reciprocating motion.*

The pistons must fit tightly in the cylinders to keep the air-fuel mixture and burnt gases in the combustion chambers, but not so tightly that they can't move up and down smoothly and rapidly with minimal friction. However, no piston can fit tightly enough in the cylinder bore without help. A tight seal and free movement are made possible by the use of *piston rings* that surround the pistons and seal them against the cylinder walls.

Pistons go up and down, but cars move on rotating tires. Reciprocating motion within the engine must be turned into *rotary motion.* Think of riding a bicycle: Your legs push up and down (reciprocating motion) on pedals attached to a crank, which is attached to the bicycle sprocket (rotary motion). The up-and-down motion of the pistons turns a crankshaft in the same way that a bicyclist's legs turn a pedal sprocket.

In an engine, the pistons are attached to connecting rods that take the place of your legs. A crank pin for each connecting rod replaces the bicycle's pedals and is connected to a crank on each end. A series of crank pins, one for each piston, forms the crankshaft. The *crankshaft* is the engine's power output shaft.

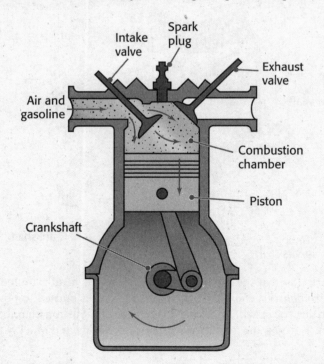

The violent back-and-forth motion of the connecting rods and the friction from rapid rotation of the crankshaft require *bearings* between the connecting rods and the crankshaft, and between the crankshaft and the surfaces of the engine block. These bearings are made of softer metal than other parts and are lubricated with oil to help them move freely.

The crankshaft turns rapidly under normal engine operation, at times at more than 6,000 revolutions per minute (rpm). Each combustion chamber has an explosion every other rotation of the crankshaft. For a four-cylinder engine, that means as many as 12,000 explosions occur every minute of operation (and as few as 1,200 while the engine is idling).

The explosions in the combustion chambers are evenly spaced so that power output from the crankshaft is fairly even and continuous. But smoothing out these power impulses is a major engineering concern. A heavy *flywheel* attached to the end of the crankshaft helps a lot. Because of its weight, it resists changes in speed. (The fewer the cylinders, the fewer the power impulses, and—the more important (and usually the larger)—the flywheel.)

Car engines generally use four, six, or eight cylinders. One convenient way to categorize engines is by the number and arrangement of cylinders. The two most common arrangements are *in-line* and *V* configurations.

Valve Operation

Air-fuel mixture enters the combustion chamber through round holes in the cylinder head called *intake ports.* Burnt gases escape through other round holes called *exhaust ports.* The intake and exhaust ports are opened and closed by precisely machined parts called *valves.* Most engines use one intake and one exhaust valve per cylinder.

A valve spring keeps the valve closed except when the action of a *cam* forces it open. A cam is like a wheel with a bulge on it called a *lobe.* The camshaft carries one cam lobe for each valve and is turned by the crankshaft. The cam may operate the valve directly by pushing on the stem, or use a rocker arm to do the actual pushing. The rocker arm may be operated either directly by the cam or by a push rod between the cam and the rocker arm.

Between the end of the push rod and the cam is a *valve lifter.* The valve lifter is what is actually pushed by the cam lobe. The valve lifter is kept in contact with the push rod by hydraulic action. It is usually designed so that the end that rides on the cam is spherical.

Auto Measurements

Many technical terms relate to engine performance: bore and stroke, displacement, and others. Here's a brief review of what some of them mean and how they apply to an engine.

Bore and Stroke

Bore is the diameter of a cylinder, and *stroke* is how far a piston moves from its highest to lowest point. The top position of a piston is called *top dead center* (TDC), while the lowest position is *bottom dead center* (BDC). *Clearance volume* is the volume in a cylinder with a piston at top dead center. The movement of a piston from TDC to BDC, or from BDC to TDC, is the stroke. When a bore and stroke are of equal length, an engine is said to be *square. Under square* and *over square* mean the bore is smaller or larger than the stroke, respectively.

Displacement

Piston displacement is the volume covered as a piston moves from BDC to TDC. *Engine displacement* is the displacement of one cylinder multiplied by the number of cylinders in the engine. Bore, stroke, and displacement can be measured in imperial or metric units, but it has become customary to state total engine displacement in metric liters.

To convert liters to cubic inches, multiply the number of liters by 61.4 to get the engine's cubic inch displacement (CID).

Torque, Work, and Power

Torque is a turning or twisting force that may or may not result in motion. Torque is applied to the lid of a jar when someone tries to open it, whether the lid comes off or not. The engine applies torque to turn the wheels of the car. Torque is measured in *foot-pounds* (ft-lb). If 50 pounds of force are applied to a crank with a 2-foot handle, then 100 ft-lb of torque will be applied to the crank (50 lb × 2 ft = 100 ft-lb).

In an engine, ideally a lot of torque is produced at low engine speeds to help the car move smoothly without racing the engine. For more information on torque, see the "Transmissions and Axles" section later in this chapter.

Work is the movement of an object against a force. That force can be gravity, friction, or other resistance. Work is measured in terms of force and distance. If a 5-pound weight is lifted 5 feet, the work done is 25 foot-pounds (5 lb × 5 ft = 25 ft-lb).

Power is a measure of how fast work is done. A 5-pound weight can be lifted in 2 seconds or in 30 seconds. The faster the work is accomplished, the greater the power:

$$\text{Power} = \text{Torque} \times \text{Speed}$$

The power of an engine is measured in *horsepower*, a unit supposedly equivalent to the power of one horse, or 33,000 foot-pounds of work per minute. If a horse, or a machine, lifts a 330-pound weight 100 feet in 1 minute, its power will equal 1 horsepower (330 lb × 100 ft = 33,000 ft-lb).

If torque gets a car going, horsepower keeps it going. The power output of an engine is measured in *brake horsepower* (bhp).

Engine Lubrication

If an engine is run without oil, even for a few seconds, severe damage can result because metal should never touch metal in an engine. All moving metal parts actually ride on a thin film of oil. That film of oil is about as thick as the paper of this page.

Oil does more than reduce friction. Oil acts as a coolant, absorbs shocks between bearings and other engine parts, reduces noise, and extends engine life. Oil also helps form a good seal between piston rings and cylinder walls and acts as a cleaning agent.

Viscosity

To do all these jobs, oil must possess a variety of qualities. The most important one is *viscosity*, or the tendency to resist flowing. Because viscosity decreases as oil's temperature increases, oil must not be too thick to properly coat parts at cold temperatures or too thin to maintain an adequate film when warm.

Viscosity of an oil is rated according to standards set by the Society of Automotive Engineers (SAE). A higher viscosity number means the oil is more viscous than oil with a lower number. A "W" after the number means the oil has been formulated for use in cold weather. Some oils have a rating such as 10W-30. The first number is the viscosity of the oil when cold. The second number is the *viscosity index,* an indication of how the oil will flow when hot.

Oil Circulation

Oil under pressure must circulate through an engine to lubricate all moving parts. An oil pump driven by the crankshaft picks up oil from the oil pan. From the oil pump, the oil first goes through a filter, and then into an oil line or gallery that distributes oil to the main bearings and camshaft bearings.

The following illustration shows oil moving through an engine.

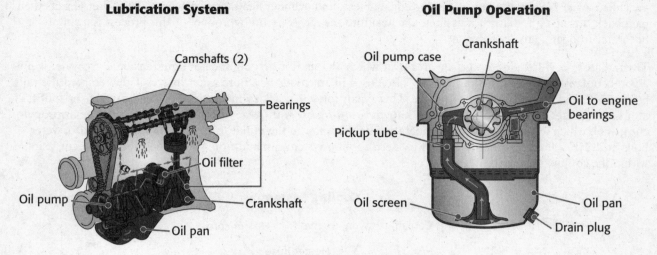

The oil flows through oil passages to all moving parts inside the block and cylinder head.

Oil-feed holes and grooves in the main bearings allow oil to flow around the crankshaft and connecting rod bearings. Some engines contain a passage for oil to flow up the connecting rods to the piston connecting pins. Cylinder walls are lubricated by oil thrown off by the connecting rod bearings.

The valve train needs lubrication also. In some engines, oil flows up the hollow push rods to the rocker arms and valve stems. In overhead cam engines, an oil gallery runs the length of the cylinder head to lubricate camshaft bearings.

Oil Light or Gauge

A constant flow of oil at a steady pressure is necessary for an engine to operate without severe damage. That's why the instrument panel of a car includes either a warning light or a gauge that registers oil pressure. If the light comes on or if the needle falls below an indicated level during normal operation, the engine should be turned off immediately.

It is normal for the oil light to turn on for a second or two when the engine is first started because it takes a moment for oil to begin to circulate and for the system to build up pressure. Until then, only a thin film of oil that didn't drain off from the previous operation coats the parts.

The greatest wear on engine parts takes place during the first few seconds after starting. The system hasn't yet delivered a full supply of oil to all the parts. It is best to allow an engine to idle for 10 or 15 seconds before putting it in gear. Wait at least 30 seconds to put a car in gear during cold winter weather because cold, thick oil takes longer to circulate.

Engine Cooling

Thousands of individual explosions, each one producing temperatures up to 6,000°F, means an engine has a lot of heat to dissipate. Some of the combustion heat escapes with the hot exhaust gases. The rest is absorbed by engine components. Petroleum-based engine oil loses most of its lubricating properties above 400 or 500 °F, so cylinder-wall temperatures must stay below that level.

Small, single-cylinder engines like a lawn mower can easily be cooled by air. Most automobile engines are liquid-cooled. A water mixture called *coolant* circulates through passages throughout the engine. These passages are called *water jackets* and are cast in the engine block and cylinder head to absorb heat. The water jackets then pass back through a radiator to dissipate the heat into the air. A useful byproduct of this process is a supply of hot water to operate the car's heater.

The radiator provides a lot of surface area over which air can flow to cool the hot liquid inside. Pure water is not a good coolant in a radiator, although it is often used in an emergency. Pure water freezes if the temperature falls below 32°F, and expands as it becomes ice. This expansion will crack cylinder block or head castings or split radiator seams. Thus, coolant is added, better known as *antifreeze*. Antifreeze normally contains ethylene or propylene glycol, which lowers the heating temperature of the water in the radiator in order to protect it. Also, water boils at 212°F, a temperature too low for modern cooling systems. In addition, water does not inhibit corrosion within the cooling system itself.

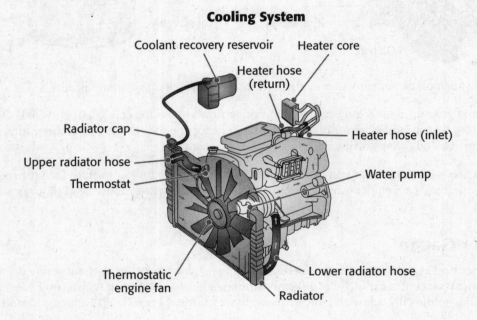

Cooling System

Coolant recovery reservoir Heater core

Heater hose (return)

Radiator cap

Upper radiator hose Heater hose (inlet)

Thermostat Water pump

Thermostatic engine fan Lower radiator hose

Radiator

Four-Stroke Cycle

The opening and closing of the valves by the camshaft must exactly correspond to the up-and-down movement of the piston. As mentioned earlier in the "Bore and Stroke" section of this chapter, the top position of a piston is called *top dead center* (TDC), while the lowest position is *bottom dead center* (BDC). Movement of a piston from TDC to BDC, or from BDC to TDC, is called a *stroke*.

Nearly all modern car engines work on a *four-stroke cycle*. The four-stroke cycle simply means that each cycle is made up of four strokes. The strokes are called the *intake stroke, compression stroke, power stroke,* and *exhaust stroke.* A running engine repeats that cycle over and over in each cylinder.

Fuel Supply

Gasoline-Powered Vehicles

The majority of automotive engines run on gasoline, which is a compound of the elements carbon and hydrogen. Liquid gasoline does not burn. To be used as a fuel in an engine, gasoline must be vaporized and mixed with air. Breaking down gasoline into tiny droplets to be vaporized is called *atomization,* even though the gasoline is not actually broken down into atoms, as the name might imply.

Gasoline may be vaporized by either a carburetor or a fuel injection system. Carburetors are not often used on modern engines. A *carburetor* is a completely mechanical and somewhat crude device that uses flowing air to create a partial vacuum that draws gasoline in a fine spray from a fuel nozzle. A carburetor does not alter fuel flow very rapidly when the throttle is open or shut quickly. Also, because of its positioning on top of the intake manifold, it cannot provide an optimum fuel mixture to each cylinder. The performance and economy of a carbureted engine are lacking when compared to an otherwise similar fuel-injected engine.

Fuel injection systems are different than carburetors because fuel injection systems use specialized nozzles to inject atomized fuel directly into the engine. The fuel injectors, however, are only the nozzle and the valve, which are located along the side of the cylinders. A fuel pump, located further back in the vehicle, sends high-pressured fuel through the fuel lines into the fuel injectors.

Fuel Additives

To maintain gasoline's liquid state in the fuel tank as well as its capability to vaporize in the engine, refineries blend it with additives. The following is a list of a few of the additives commonly blended with gasoline:

- Alcohols as an octane enhancer
- Anti-icers to prevent freeze-up
- Anti-oxidants to minimize gum formation in storage
- Corrosion inhibitors to reduce corrosion in the fuel system

The *octane rating* of gasoline refers to the mixture's capability to resist spontaneous detonation. Oftentimes, with enough compression, gasoline will combust without the use of a spark plug (see more about detonation in the "Ignition" section that follows). *Predetonation* (which is caused when the auto-ignition temperature of the gas mixture lights off due to the temperature of compression) is often referred to as "knocking" and can harm the engine of a vehicle over long periods of time. On the other hand, higher-performance engines generally have higher compression ratios in the cylinders and are more prone to detonation, and therefore require higher octane ratings.

Ignition

Lighting the air-fuel mixture with an electrical spark from a spark plug causes an explosion of gases and heat. In a high-speed V8 engine, more than 20,000 explosions can occur every minute of operation. In order to achieve this spark, you need both an ignition coil and a distributor.

- **Ignition coil:** A spark plug requires a lot of volts, about 10,000, for the current to jump across the gap between the electrodes like a bolt of lightning. The volts are boosted from the battery by a coil. A coil increases the volts (like increasing the pressure on a hose) but reduces the amps (like decreasing the amount of water flowing through a hose).
- **Distributor:** Each spark plug must fire at precisely the proper instant in the piston cycle. In many gasoline engines, the timing is controlled by the *distributor*. The distributor shaft is driven by the engine camshaft at the same speed. The outside terminals on the distributor cap are connected by wires to the spark plugs, while the central terminal is connected to the secondary circuit of the coil. The *rotor* is attached to the distributor shaft and sends current to each spark plug in turn as it lines up with the outside terminals. One end of the rotor is in constant contact with the central terminal. The other end lines up with each of the side terminals in succession. As the rotor spins with the shaft, it sends high-voltage surges from the secondary circuit to the spark plugs. The rotor does not actually touch the outside terminals; the voltage jumps from the rotor as it does at the spark plug electrodes.

  Breaking the primary circuit, so that the high-voltage burst from the secondary circuit occurs just as the rotor meets each side terminal, can be accomplished several ways. Old-fashioned ignition systems relied on breaker points that physically opened and closed. These breaker points wore out, causing inaccurate spark timing and requiring regular maintenance and frequent replacement. Virtually all cars nowadays use electronic switching systems.

If the spark plug fires too soon, detonation can occur. *Detonation* (mentioned previously in the "Fuel Additives" section above) is the spontaneous explosion of some of the unburned air-fuel mixture in the combustion chamber, set off by the heat and pressure of the air-fuel mixture that has already been ignited. This detonation, or knock, greatly increases the stresses on an engine and may cause piston failure, as well as an objectionable noise, much like that which occurs during predetonation (also mentioned earlier in the "Fuel Additives" section).

Many vehicle engines now have Distributorless Ignition Systems (DIS). The engine control unit (ECU) controls the transistors that break the ground side of the circuit, which generates the spark. This gives the ECU total control over spark timing. This type of system has some major advantages—there is no distributor or high-voltage spark-plug wires to wear out. For this reason, DIS are more efficient and can increase the power of the car.

Hybrid Vehicles

Hybrid vehicles refer to automobiles that are powered by two or more power sources. Today, the most common type of hybrid vehicle is the *HEV*, or hybrid electric vehicle. HEVs are powered by both an internal combustion engine and an electric motor. Depending on the driving circumstances, the vehicle can be powered by the engine only, the electric motor only, or by both the engine and the motor. When HEVs are maintaining cruising speed, the wheels are powered by the engine, allowing the batteries for the electric motor to charge. Likewise, if the vehicle is stopped or being driven short distances, the engine shuts off to cut down on emissions and fuel, and the electric motor is used to power the vehicle's drivetrain.

Fuel Cell Vehicles

Fuel cell vehicles are powered by electric motors; however, they have no internal combustion engine to charge the battery system. Instead, the fuel cell device located in the vehicle itself combines hydrogen and oxygen to form water. This process gives off electrons that are used to create the electricity needed to power the electric motor. Fuel cell vehicles must be refueled with hydrogen just as vehicles with combustion engines must be refueled with gasoline.

Electrical System

In addition to the high-voltage ignition system, all of the lights, fans, electric motors, sound systems, and control modules of a vehicle require electric power. Modern automobiles use 12-volt systems to power all of their components and accessories.

Electricity can be generated by moving a magnet within or around a coil of wire. This movement generates a flow of electricity in the wire. The amount of electricity can be increased by using a more powerful magnet, by moving the magnet faster, or by putting more windings in the coil.

Electricity can also be generated by a chemical reaction. As chemicals react with each other, they can cause electrons to flow between them. This electron flow is the principle behind the battery. Electrons flow through a wire in almost the same way that water flows through a hose. However, there are two major differences between the flow of electricity and the flow of water. Electricity always moves at almost the same speed as light (186,000 miles per second), while water can move at any speed; and, except at very high voltages, electrons need a continuous path or they won't move at all, while water will flow from an open hose. Electrons almost always return to where they started, so the flow is circular. If the circuit is broken anywhere, the electrical flow stops. Switches operate by physically connecting and disconnecting a circuit.

Battery

A car's battery produces electrical current through a chemical reaction between sulfuric acid and lead. Grid plates of lead alternate with grid plates of lead oxide in a solution of sulfuric acid and water. The lead plates are linked by a wire or other conductor, as are the lead oxide plates. Separators prevent the grids from touching each other. A group of plates arranged this way is called a *cell*. When a wire connects the two sets of plates, chemical reactions take place and electrons flow through the wire from one set of plates to the other. A cell generates about 2 volts of electrical pressure. Modern car batteries link six cells to generate 12 volts. Adding more plates, or making them larger, increases the amount of electricity a battery can produce.

Batteries are rated in either amp-hours or cold-cranking amps. An *amp-hour rating* tells you how much electricity can be generated before all the chemicals are used up. A 60 amp-hour battery can deliver 3 amps of current per hour for 20 hours (3 amps × 20 hours = 60 amp-hours). A *cold-cranking amp rating* tells you how much current a battery can generate for 30 seconds at 0°F without dropping below 7.2 volts. That's a useful measure for cold-weather starting capability. In cold weather, the chemical reactions in a battery slow down, so the battery provides fewer amps than when it's warm.

Cars that have many electrical accessories, such as power windows and air conditioning, need powerful batteries, particularly in cold weather.

Starting System

To start an engine, the crankshaft must be turned by an external force so the pistons and valves can begin drawing in the air-fuel mixture. A powerful electric *starter* engages the flywheel when the ignition switch is turned to the start position. The starter motor rotates the crankshaft at about 200 rpm. The starter is the largest single user of electrical energy in the car, requiring about 200 amps to crank.

After the engine is started, the starter must disengage. Otherwise, the high rotating speeds of the gasoline engine will destroy the motor in the starter. A *solenoid* usually pulls the gear on the end of the starter into engagement with the flywheel as the starter is energized. When the ignition key returns to the on position, the current to the starter and solenoid is shut off. A spring pushes the starter gear out of engagement. Hybrid vehicles start the same as gasoline vehicles; however, fuel cell vehicles, which run specifically on electricity, do not contain a starter. Instead, the ignition of the vehicle turns on the vehicle's electronic control module, which allows electricity to flow from the power source to the motor.

Electrical System

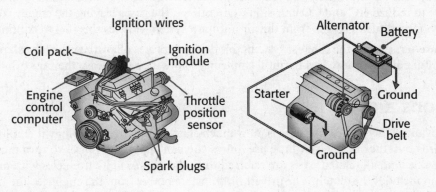

Charging System

Chemical reactions inside a battery cause electricity to flow out of it. But if an electrical current is introduced into a battery, the reactions will reverse and the chemicals will return to their original states. In an automobile, an *alternator* produces electricity to recharge the battery. An alternator works by spinning a rotor inside a stator and produces AC voltage. Diodes and a rectifier change the AC to DC voltage. The faster the engine runs, the more electricity it makes. A battery can be damaged if too much current is put back into it at once or if current is put into it when it is fully charged. A regulator, built into the alternator, prevents this overcharging.

If the alternator doesn't produce enough electrical current to recharge the battery, the battery will eventually use up all its stored electricity. Starting the engine takes a lot of electricity, but as soon as the engine is running, the alternator should provide more than enough power to recharge the battery. Automobiles with lots of electrical equipment need powerful generators as well as powerful batteries.

On-Board Diagnostics

Currently, all modern vehicles are equipped with *on-board diagnostic systems* (OBD), which enable the vehicle to monitor its own diagnostics and report back to the vehicle's computer. Should an input device begin to detect improper operation of the vehicle, malfunction, or disconnection, the vehicle's computer will store a diagnostic trouble code. In the presence of a trouble code, the vehicle's "check engine" light will activate and the problem must be fixed in order to clear the code. All 1996 or newer vehicles are equipped with the OBD II system, which detects potential problems before they affect emissions. Vehicles with OBD II systems are equipped with diagnostic connectors that enable mechanics and state vehicle inspectors to aid in reading and diagnosing trouble codes.

Oxygen sensors, also known as O2 sensors, help make modern electronic fuel injection possible by monitoring the air-to-fuel ratio in the exhaust of a vehicle's engine. In the event that the vehicle begins to run rich (burn too much fuel) or lean (burn not enough fuel), O2 sensors provide feedback that enables the engine to adjust its air-to-fuel ratio for optimal performance. O2 sensors also help the vehicle cut back on emission pollutants by enabling the engine to reduce its unburned fuel, thereby reducing the emission of hydrocarbons.

Emission Control System

A vehicle's emission control system is designed to reduce its three main pollutants: carbon monoxide (CO), unburned hydrocarbons (HC), and oxides of nitrogen (NO_x).

Because of their role in protecting the environment, many emissions control devices are inspected as part of a state's mandatory inspection process. Most of the emission control system's elements are part of the engine's overall control system, and their failure can affect a vehicle's drivability. Some examples of emissions systems are as follows:

- **Exhaust gas recirculation valve:** The EGR valve helps your car run more efficiently and burn all of its fuel by recirculating some of the exhaust and running it through the combustion process again.
- **Air injection systems:** The primary and secondary air injection systems force fresh air into the exhaust ports of the engine to reduce HC and CO emissions. Oftentimes, the gases leaving the engine contain unburned and partially burned fuel. Oxygen from the air injection system enables this fuel to continue to burn.
- **Catalytic converter:** Part of the exhaust system, this device captures all of the vehicle's exhaust gases and helps convert harmful pollutants into less-harmful emissions before they even leave the car's exhaust system.

Transmissions and Axles

No matter how advanced any vehicle's engine is, how much state-of-the-art technology it employs, or how much horsepower it churns out, the vehicle is of little use unless you can apply that power to turn the vehicle's wheels. The transmission, axle, and all related parts are referred to as the *drivetrain*. On vehicles with manual transmissions, the drivetrain includes the clutch. The drivetrain transfers power from the engine to the front wheels, the rear wheels, or all four wheels.

On rear-wheel drive vehicles, the drivetrain usually consists of a *transmission, drive shaft,* and *rear drive axle.* On front-wheel drive vehicles, the drivetrain consists of a *transaxle* that is a combination of transmission and drive axle. All-wheel drive or four-wheel drive vehicles send power to both front and rear axles. For more information on the differences among rear-wheel drive, all-wheel drive, and four-wheel drive vehicles, see "Drivetrain Configurations" and "Drivetrain Advantages" later in this chapter.

The key internal components in any transmission are the gears. It takes a powerful turning force to move a vehicle. Such turning force is known as *torque* (see the "Torque" section earlier in this chapter). Internal combustion engines develop very low torque at low engine speeds, far too low to supply the force needed to move a vehicle's wheels.

Torque Multiplication

You probably know the principle of leverage—how to use a long lever to lift a heavy weight. The ratio of the length between the long end of the lever and the pivot point and the short end and the pivot point indicates how much your strength will effectively multiply. Take the simple example of a child's teeter-totter. It has levers of equal length at each end, so two children must be about the same weight to move the opposite ends of the teeter-totter up and down. The ratio of lever lengths in this case is 1 to 1, usually expressed as 1:1; consequentially, the downward force and the upward force are roughly equal.

Gears are really a series of levers joined to a shaft. While a lever can move only a limited distance, a gear can turn continuously about its shaft. It can also be turned by another gear. In this case, the gear doing the turning is called the *driving gear,* while the one being turned is called the *driven gear.*

If each gear is the same diameter, each gear turns at the same speed, producing no change in torque. If a driven gear is made three times larger than a driving gear, then the driving gear would have to rotate three times to turn the driven gear once, and the work for the engine would be three times easier. This change in gear ratio is called *gear reduction,* because the driven gear turns more slowly than the driving one. A transmission—manual or automatic— uses gear reduction to increase the torque of the engine so the automobile's wheels can be turned. A 3:1 gear reduction, or gear ratio, is about average for the transmission gears that provide the torque to set a vehicle in motion.

Gear Ratio

As the vehicle goes faster, it requires less turning force, or torque, to keep it moving. To make the most efficient use of an engine, a transmission uses other gear combinations, with lower gear ratios, as the vehicle's speed increases. For example, a 3:1 gear ratio may be used to get the vehicle going, then a 2:1 gear ratio may be used to help it gain speed, and finally a 1:1 ratio helps the vehicle reach highway speeds. A transmission with three gears is called a *three-speed transmission.* Transmissions generally offer three-, four-, or five-gear combinations, in addition to reverse. Some high-performance vehicles have as many as six speeds.

A manual transmission is a very simple and extremely reliable mechanical unit. For various forward gear positions, the gearshift lever acts to slide a gear or gears on the main shaft into engagement with a countershaft gear or gears.

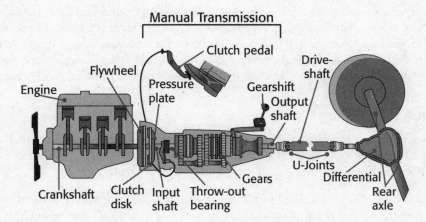

Most automatic transmissions come with a drive gear called the *overdrive gear.* The overdrive gear has a gear ratio of less than 1:1—for example, 0.7:1. For each 0.7 turns of the transmission input shaft, the output shaft turns once. At highway speeds, the engine revolutions per minute (rpm) are lowered. The overdrive gear thus reduces engine wear while improving fuel economy.

Clutch

With a manual transmission, the *clutch* connects and disconnects the engine crankshaft to the transmission. The main components of a clutch are the *flywheel, friction disc,* and *pressure plate.* The cover and pressure plate are bolted to the flywheel, while the friction disc positioned between them is connected by an internal spline to the transmission shaft.

The clutch is disengaged when the flywheel, friction disc, and pressure plate are not contacting each other. When these components are not in contact, the engine and transmission do not transfer power to the drive wheels. When the three parts are in contact, power from the engine is delivered to the transmission, which in turn delivers power to the drive shaft, which in turn transmits power to the drive wheels.

Torque Converter

Virtually every automatic-transmission vehicle today is equipped with a *torque converter*. The torque converter works as an automatic transmission's clutch. One side of the torque converter is attached to the crankshaft and is called the *pump* or *driving member*. The other side is linked to the transmission shaft and is called the *turbine* or *driven member*. The two sides don't touch each other. Transmission fluid, which is just a special type of oil, fills the assembly.

Since the early to mid-1980s, overdrive transmissions are equipped with lock-up torque converters that, inside, have a clutch that separates the load from the power source and is applied and released by a solenoid and fluid pressure. Basically it's a type of a hydrodynamic device that transfers mechanical power from the motor to a load driven by the rotation of a machine. This system increases fuel mileage by the mechanical coupling instead of just the fluid.

Drivetrain Configurations

Rear-Wheel Drive

For years, most engines and transmissions were positioned at the front of the car, yet used to drive the rear wheels. Rear-wheel drive requires a drive shaft to transfer power from the transmission (see the following diagram). The drive shaft has to move up and down at the axle end as the axle goes over bumps, even though the engine and transmission are bolted firmly to the frame. *Universal joints* at each end of the drive shaft allow rotary motion to be transferred between two shafts through varying angles.

Front-Wheel Drive

Most small to mid-size vehicles today have front-wheel drive designs. In front-wheel drive vehicles, the engine is mounted transversely or sideways in the engine compartment. The drive shaft is eliminated and the transmission and drive axle are combined into a single unit called a *transaxle*. Like a transmission, a transaxle may be either manually or automatically shifted. While the clutch, gearing, differential, and other drivetrain components are arranged differently in a front-wheel drive vehicle, they operate in a manner similar to those in a rear-wheel drive vehicle.

Turning the Drive Wheels

When a vehicle goes around a corner, its inside wheels travel a shorter distance than its outside wheels. If the drive axle is geared so that both rear wheels always turn at the same speed, one of the wheels will skid during cornering, making the vehicle difficult to handle and increasing tire wear greatly.

The design of the gears inside the rear axle allows the rear wheels to rotate at different speeds while going around corners. As the inner wheels slow down during a turn, the axles' differential allows the outer wheels to speed up.

Axle Ratio

In the rear differential of a vehicle, the area where the drive shaft meets the rear axles, there are gears that allow the rotational force of the driveshaft to change direction and rotate the rear axles. Manufacturers have designed the rear differential so that there is a final gear reduction that takes place inside of it. This reduction is called the *axle ratio* and the reduction is generally between 2:1 and 4:1. The transmission ratio multiplied by the rear-axle ratio gives the final-drive ratio.

The important thing to keep in mind with the final-drive ratio is to pick the right combination when several are available. A higher final-drive ratio provides high torque and quick acceleration. A lower ratio provides lower torque and better fuel economy.

Drivetrain Advantages

Each type of drivetrain offers distinct advantages:

- **Rear-wheel drive:** Conventional front-engine/rear-wheel drive often offers design and handling advantages in large vehicles and vehicles with very high towing capacity. It's also frequently preferred for high-performance applications.

- **Front-wheel drive:** Front-wheel drive vehicles with transverse engines have become almost as common as rear-wheel drive vehicles used to be. With small and mid-size vehicles, front-wheel drive offers a number of advantages. No drive shaft or heavy rear axle and support components means less weight. The transverse engine shortens the engine compartment, leaving more room for passengers. Traction on slippery roads is improved because the weight of the engine is positioned over the drive wheels, and the vehicle is pulled instead of pushed.

- **Four-wheel drive:** Four-wheel drive enthusiasts have known for years that when road conditions vary, there are real advantages to having all the wheels drive the vehicle. Four-wheel drive vehicles generally operate in two-wheel drive except when four-wheel drive is specifically selected.

- **All-wheel drive:** A useful hybrid of the four-wheel drive system is called all-wheel drive. All-wheel drive is designed for full-time use; engine power is sent to both the front and rear wheels. All-wheel drive vehicles can offer superior traction in the worst driving situations, but the systems are more expensive to engineer, produce, and operate.

The Chassis

Traditionally, the chassis of an automobile included everything bolted to the frame except the body. With today's unibody vehicles, however, the chassis includes so much more hardware that discussions of the chassis are now usually limited to the mechanical parts that locate, isolate, support, direct, or redirect the dynamic activity of the vehicle. The front and rear suspensions and the steering and braking systems are the most important elements of the chassis. Put simply

- **Suspensions** cushion a car's ride and ensure that the wheels maintain contact with the road surface when the car turns, accelerates, and brakes.

- **The steering system** moves the front wheels left or right, controlling the vehicle's direction.

- **Brakes** slow down and/or stop the vehicle by applying frictional pressure to assemblies in contact with the wheels.

Suspension Systems

The heart of a modern vehicle's suspension is a system of springs and shock absorbers. Springs hold the vehicle up, while shock absorbers control or dampen the action of the springs. Three different types of springs (depicted in the following diagram) are used in current car models: the *coil spring,* the *leaf spring,* and the *torsion bar.*

Springs

- **Coil spring:** A coil spring is constructed from a wire or metal bar wound into a coil. A coil spring will return to its original shape after it is stretched or compressed. The coil spring is the most common type of spring used in today's cars.

- **Leaf spring:** A leaf spring is made of layered metal or fiber-reinforced plastic strips. When the two ends of the leaf spring are fastened down, the center springs up and down. Like a coil spring, a leaf spring will return to its natural position when forces acting upon the spring stop. Leaf springs are primarily used on rear-wheel drive vehicles.

- **Torsion bar:** A torsion bar is simply a coil spring that has been straightened out. The spring action comes from twisting the bar torsionally. Torsion bars are widely utilized on four-wheel drive vehicles.

Shock Absorbers

If you've ever ridden in a car with worn-out shocks, you know that the car rolled and pitched long after passing over a bump. Good shocks, on the other hand, make for a smooth ride and good handling.

Shock absorbers return the suspension to its natural position quickly and smoothly. Not only do shock absorbers control the compression of the spring, they control the expansion (or rebound) as well by using fluid or gas forced through holes in the shock absorbers' pistons. The sizes of the holes determine the damping effect of the shock. As a shock absorber compresses or expands, a piston inside moves through oil or hydraulic fluid. The piston's movement is resisted by the fluid, which must pass through small holes in it. If the holes are made smaller, the shock absorber becomes stiffer, and delivers what's commonly known as a sportier ride with firmer handling characteristics.

Springs and shocks are matched with vehicle weight (referred to as *computer-selected springs*). Sometimes they are chosen to correspond with the weight of optional equipment added to individual vehicles as they are built (referred to as a *tuned suspension*).

Front Suspension

The front suspension of any car is a critical subsystem because it performs so many vital functions. In addition to suspending the front-wheel assemblies from the frame, isolating road harshness, and handling braking and steering functions, front-wheel drive front suspensions must control front wheels powered by the drivetrain. The two most commont front-wheel drive front suspensions are the coil spring front suspension and the MacPherson struts.

Coil spring front suspension: In rear-wheel drive vehicles, a coil spring front suspension is the most widely used design. The coil springs are mounted on upper and lower control arms to support the vehicle's suspension.

MacPherson struts: The MacPherson strut design has become popular because it takes up very little space. A MacPherson strut front suspension is a combination strut and shock absorber that's mounted inside a coil spring. The MacPherson strut replaces an upper control arm and is used in most front-wheel drive cars as well as on some rear-wheel drive vehicles. MacPherson struts are also used on the rear suspensions of many vehicles.

Rear Suspension

Even though the rear suspension does not have to contend with steering functions, it still comprises a significant part of a vehicle's suspension system. Generally, rear suspensions fall into one of three types: *solid axle rear suspension, independent rear suspension,* and *semi-independent rear suspension.*

- **Solid axle rear suspension:** In a solid axle rear suspension, a solid axle is suspended and located with leaf springs. The axle can move up and down with road inconsistencies. This durable design is found on most rear-wheel drive cars and trucks. However, as the rear wheel on one side of the axle rolls over a bump, the axle's reaction to the bump affects the wheel at the other side of the axle. The result is that vehicles with solid rear axles cannot achieve as smooth a ride as those with independent rear suspension designs.

- **Independent rear suspension:** On a front-wheel drive vehicle, an independent rear suspension is much simpler to design because there are no drivetrain components to deal with. This type of system requires no physical connection between the rear wheels. Each rear wheel is mounted on a trailing arm and a short swing axle that swings down from the car body. Generally, an independent rear suspension uses a coil spring and shock absorber or MacPherson strut design. Some vehicles use transversely mounted leaf springs instead of coil springs. The independent rear suspension design (see the figure that follows) provides the smoothest ride available because each wheel's action is isolated from the actions of the other wheel.

- **Semi-independent rear suspension:** Sometimes the two wheels use a cross member linking the two trailing arms for greater stability. This design is called a semi-independent suspension. To control sideways movements, a semi-independent rear suspension often uses a track bar.

Steering Systems

The basic operation of a steering system is really quite simple. As you turn the steering wheel, it rotates a shaft connected to a steering gear. The gear moves the tie rods that are connected to the steering arms and steering knuckles. The following diagram depicts the elements of a basic steering system.

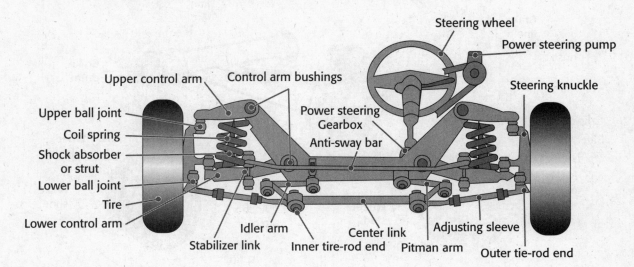

A gear reduction in the steering gear makes turning the wheels easier.

A *rack-and-pinion steering gear* (shown in the figure that follows) is light and compact, and it offers good steering feel. The steering wheel is attached to a pinion gear. The pinion gear interacts with a rack, and the ends of the rack are connected directly to the tie rods that turn the front wheels.

Another common type of steering gear is the *recirculating ball*. In this system a worm gear converts steering-wheel movement to sector-shaft movement. A pitman arm attached to the bottom of the sector shaft moves one tie rod, and an intermediate rod moves the other.

Both rack-and-pinion and recirculating ball systems offer a power-assist feature. In power-steering systems, a pump is driven by a belt connected to the engine crankshaft by a pulley. The pump circulates hydraulic fluid through the steering gear. The pump does most of the work once the driver turns the steering wheel.

Brakes

The brake system applies friction material to parts that revolve with the wheels. The friction material slows the speed of the rotating components. Brake linings provide the friction by pressing on the drums or discs. The brake drums or discs must dissipate the heat that the friction creates, so drums are often finned or discs are vented to provide extra cooling surface.

Brake fluid supplies the necessary force to activate the brake system. This fluid circulates through a series of metal lines and tubes, and is pressurized whenever the brake pedal is pushed. This fluid squeezes the brake shoes against the inside of the tires to slow down the car and eventually stop it.

Brake System

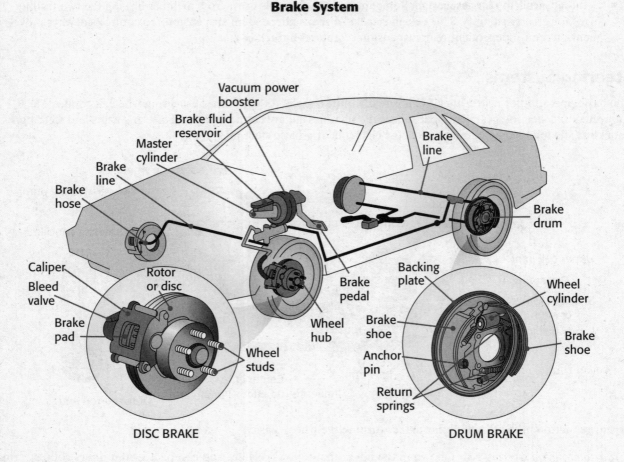

Drum Brakes

In a *drum brake system* (see the following diagram), an aluminum or cast iron drum is bolted to the inside of the wheel mounting surface. Two metal brake linings (*shoes*) are covered with a high-friction/heat-resistant material and positioned inside the drum. It is important that the linings do not touch the drum unless the brakes are applied. A wheel cylinder contains two pistons that push on the brake linings.

When you push the brake pedal, pistons inside the wheel cylinder push on the brake linings and the brake linings push into the sides of the drum, slowing the turning of the wheels.

Disc Brakes

On *disc brakes* (see the following diagram), the disc revolves with the wheel. The linings (pads) are mounted in a caliper assembly that forces the linings into contact with the disc. The linings create friction the same way drum brake shoes do. A wear sensor contacts the disc when the brake linings are worn. The sensor rubbing the disc vibrates at a high pitch to warn the driver that the linings require service.

Anti-Lock Braking System

The *anti-lock braking system* (ABS) is an electronic braking system used on newer vehicles. This system automatically pumps the brake pedal to prevent the wheels from locking up during hard braking. The ABS system consists of three main components:

- The **hydraulic control unit** controls the pressure to the brake calipers.
- The **electronic control module** processes the inputs and sends data to the hydraulic unit.
- The **wheel-speed sensors** tell the electronic control module which wheels are beginning to lock up.

When the vehicle is braking under normal driving circumstances, the ABS system does not operate; however, under extreme braking situations, such as icy conditions or panic stops, the ABS system will take over to prevent the wheels from locking up.

Brake System Wear

Friction means wear. All brake shoes or brake pads wear each time they are used. Virtually all braking systems are self-adjusting; they compensate for loss of lining and constantly reposition themselves to maintain the slight clearance between linings and drums or discs. Excessive clearance in the system will result in excessive brake-pedal travel. Short of actual inspection, drivers have always depended on their ears to tell them when the brake linings need replacement. By the time the sound of metal-on-metal can be heard, however, the discs or drums have probably been damaged.

Except for the mechanical parking brake, braking systems use hydraulic pressure from the master cylinder. The brake pedal forces brake fluid from the master cylinder through the brake lines to push on the pistons in the brake wheel cylinders or calipers.

Brake System Flushing

The entire brake hydraulic system should be flushed thoroughly with clean brake fluid whenever new parts are installed, if there is any doubt about the grade of the fluid in the system, if a fluid has been used that contains the slightest trace of mineral oil, or if any moisture has entered the system. Approximately 1 quart of fluid is required to flush the brake hydraulic system.

Brake Power-Assist Systems

Virtually all current brake systems use a power booster to increase braking effectiveness and reduce pedal effort. Power-assist systems can use either hydraulic or vacuum assist to provide the additional boost. On a hydraulic boost system, the pressure for braking assist is generated by a hydraulic pump. The pump can be driven by the engine or a remotely mounted motor. Most vacuum-assist systems use engine vacuum to boost brake performance. Note: Most diesel engines have hydraulic-assist brakes and do not create vacuums like gas motors do.

Shop Information

Throughout history, tools have been humans' pathway to success. In the earliest times, prehistoric people figured out how to create and use tools to make their lives easier. They used rocks as hammers. They sharpened stones to make axes to chop down trees. And now, in the twenty-first century, we have tools for every conceivable need, including specialized tools for use in outer space.

The material in this section covers the basics of shop tools—both hand and motor tools. In the military, you may be called upon to demonstrate your knowledge of these items, and certainly, on the ASVAB, you will be tested on much of this material.

Measuring Tools

It is important to have the proper tools for measuring and marking as well as skill and accuracy in their use. The foot (') and the inch (") are the measurements used most frequently. Most measuring tools used in woodworking are divided into inches marked in halves, quarters, eighths, and sixteenths. Metric measuring devices may be found, but devices with customary units of measure are more common.

> **For a finished product to turn out as planned, measurements must be made accurately. Remember the adage, "Measure twice, cut once."**

The following illustration shows some common measuring tools, and the list that follows gives a brief explanation of how to use them.

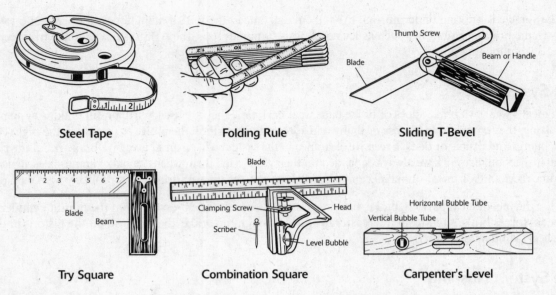

Steel Tape **Folding Rule** **Sliding T-Bevel**

Try Square **Combination Square** **Carpenter's Level**

- **Rulers:** The ordinary 12-, 18-, and 24-inch rulers are used for measuring small projects, as they are more manageable than the larger rulers. They may be made of wood, plastic, or steel.

- **Folding or zigzag rule:** This rule, made of wood or lightweight metal, unfolds to 6 feet in length. It is used to measure distances where slight variations in measurement are not important. This rule is easily bent or broken, particularly when it is not opened properly; more people, therefore, have begun to use steel tape.

- **Steel tape:** The steel tape is a ribbon of steel $\frac{3}{8}$-inch wide and graduated in feet, inches, and fractions of an inch. Available in lengths of 6, 8, 12, 50, and 100 feet, it is ordinarily used to measure distances too long to be measured conveniently with a folding rule. This tape is fixed to a reel housed in a case. After the tape is used, it retracts onto the reel either automatically by a spring or manually by means of a small handle on the case.

- **Steel or carpenter's square:** A carpenter's square is an all-steel, L-shaped or two-arm tool. The long arm is called the blade, and the short arm is called the tongue. These arms meet at right angles; this part of the tool is called the heel. The blade and tongue are marked in inches and fractions. The carpenter's square can be used to measure a board, test it for squareness, or check it for warping. The blade is held along the edge of the board with the tongue across the face of the board; then a line is made along the tongue. If this procedure is done correctly, the line will be at a right angle to the edge of the board.

- **Try square:** The try square is composed of a steel-graduated blade set at a right angle to a thicker beam of steel, plastic, or wood. The beam butts against the stock that is being squared. The try square may be used to mark lines at right angles to an edge or surface, to determine whether a board is the same thickness throughout its length, and to test an edge or surface for squareness.

- **Sliding T-bevel:** The sliding T-bevel is sometimes called a bevel square. At one end is a steel blade ranging from 6 to 12 inches in length, along with a 45° bevel point. The other, slotted end is fitted into a slotted wooden or metal beam or handle and held in place with a thumbscrew. The sliding T-bevel can be set at any desired angle. It can be used to transfer angles from one piece of lumber to another and to test bevels.

- **Combination square:** The combination square is a steel-graduated blade ranging from 6 to 24 inches long. It is grooved along the entire length of one side. The blade is fitted to a metal head, which can be clamped at any distance along the blade. This head has machined edges that are at 90° and 45° angles to the blade. The head is fitted with a level vial, and a steel scriber is set into the end of the head opposite the blade. The head is clamped securely in any position along the blade with the clamping screw. It can be used as a try square, a depth gauge, or a marking gauge. It can also be used to check 45° angles and to test for levelness.

- **Marking gauge:** The marking gauge is used to mark a line parallel to the edge or end of a piece of wood. (A light line is preferable to a deep one. If the line is not plain, a light pencil mark is put on the gauge line.) The marking gauge is made of wood or metal.

- **Divider:** A divider is a pair of pointed metal legs joined together at or near the top. The wing in a wing divider is an arc used to hold the legs apart at the desired distance by means of a setscrew. At one end of the wing is an adjusting screw with a spring that permits fine setting of the legs. A divider is used to describe circles or arcs, to transfer measurements from the work to the rule or from the rule to the work, and to mark lengths into equal parts.

- **Carpenter's level:** The carpenter's level is a 24-inch woodblock (some longer ones are aluminum or plastic) with true surface edges. It is used to determine whether a surface is level or an upright is plumb. It usually has two bubble tubes. The bubble tube in the middle of one of the long edges indicates levelness of a surface. If the bubble comes to rest exactly between the two scratch marks on the bubble tube, the surface is level. The other bubble tube is at a right angle to the first one and indicates vertical level or "plumb." A carpenter's level should be handled with care, as the bubble tubes break easily.

- **Contour gauge:** A contour gauge is used to form an outline of a particular shape. This device is made of many steel teeth that slide backward when they are pressed against a surface. Therefore, when this device is pressed against a surface with an irregular contour, each steel tooth slides backward to the extent necessary, forming an outline or template of the irregular shape. The opposite end of the steel teeth automatically forms a template of the same shape in reverse. The outline desired can then be traced onto wood, paper, tile, linoleum, or any surface. A contour gauge is only 6 inches long; however, two or three of them can be joined together to make templates of wider areas (see three different types of contour gauges in the following figure).

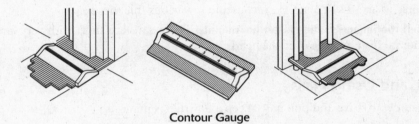

Contour Gauge

Fasteners

Innumerable types of wood fasteners are on the market. To get the desired results in a finished product, the woodworker must use the most suitable size and type of fastener. Selecting the proper fastener requires an understanding of fasteners and their uses.

Nails

Nails provide the simplest and quickest way to fasten two pieces of wood together. They are used primarily on rough or inexpensive work such as house framing, packing boxes, and crates, for which a well-finished surface is of minor importance.

Because nails may be used for numerous purposes, they are manufactured in many different sizes and different materials. The following figure shows some examples.

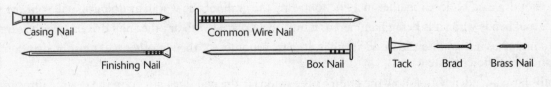

Nails

- **Common wire nails:** Common wire nails are made with large flat heads and come in different lengths, with each length being heavier than a finishing or box nail of the same length. Common wire nails are available in more sizes than any other nail. They are sized by the old English penny system. "Penny" as applied to nail stands for "pound" and refers to the weight of 1,000 nails. For example, nails weighing 6 pounds per 1,000 are six-penny (6d) nails. The letter "d" following the numeral is an abbreviation of *denarius,* which is the Latin word for penny. The largest sizes of these common nails are called spikes.

- **Finishing nails:** These small-headed nails have the same diameters and lengths as penny nails. They are used for medium-fine work in which nail heads should not show. They are sized by the penny and purchased in the same way as common nails.

- **Box nails:** These nails have heavy heads but are made in smaller gauges than common nails. They are used when nails of a larger gauge might split the wood. They are made plain, barbed, coated with resin, or coated with cement. The plain ones are easier to remove from wood, but the others hold better.

- **Casing nails:** Casing nails, which are the same gauges as box nails, have small heads. They are used for such work as blindnailing flooring, as their small heads can be countersunk into the wood.

- **Brads:** Brads are used for fine work such as interior trim and small projects. They are made in lengths ranging from ³⁄₈ to 3 inches in various gauges and are usually sold in 1-pound cardboard boxes labeled with length and gauge. The higher the number, the smaller the diameter of the wire. One of the most commonly used brads is the 1-inch-long, 18-gauge size. Brads should be countersunk into the wood with a nail set; in finer work, the hole should be covered with plastic wood or putty.

- **Tacks:** Carpet or upholstery tacks are made of iron and have sharp points and large heads. They are made in lengths ranging from ³⁄₁₆ to 1¹⁄₈ inches and are sold in ¹⁄₄- to 1-pound cardboard boxes.

- **Brass nails or escutcheon pins:** These nails are made of either brass or copper and have small, round heads. They are available in lengths of ¹⁄₄ to 1¹⁄₂ inches and in various thicknesses.

- **Shingle nails, felt roofing nails, and plaster board nails:** These nails are short with very large heads to prevent the secured material from pulling over the heads.

Driving, Pulling, and Using Nails

While it's relatively simple to drive and pull nails, keep a few things in mind.

- **Driving:** To drive a nail with the claw hammer (carpenter's hammer), grip the handle firmly with one hand near the end of the handle; hold the nail near the point with the thumb and forefinger of the other hand. Place the point of the nail on the wood at the exact spot in which it is to be driven and tap it squarely but lightly until it penetrates the wood to a depth sufficient to hold it securely (this is called "setting" the nail). Remove the fingers and drive the nail into the wood. The face of the hammer should hit flat against the head of the nail. It is helpful to first rest the hammer on the exact spot in which the nail is to be driven to obtain the "feel" or "aim" and ensure a more accurate blow on the nail. (For more information about the claw or carpenter's hammer, see the "Carpenter's Hammer" section later in this chapter.)

- **Pulling:** To pull a nail, slide the claw of the hammer under the head, making certain that the head is caught securely in the slot of the claw. Pull back until the handle of the hammer is nearly vertical; then slip a block of wood under the head of the hammer and pull the nail completely free. The block of wood will prevent the hammer from marring the wood, will increase leverage, and will prevent the nail from pulling out sideways and making a large hole.

Here are the basics on how to use nails:

- Do not drive nails close together in a line following the grain of the wood, as doing so will split the wood.

- If a nail bends while it is being hammered, it must be replaced with another nail driven into the same hole.

- If a nail does not go into the wood straight, it must be removed; then another nail must be driven into the wood at a different place.

- Nails have a tendency to follow the grain of the wood. If the nail does not go in the desired direction because of the grain, blunt the point slightly with a hammer.

- When inserting nails into hardwoods, it is helpful to bore holes for the nails, using an awl or a hand drill. Instead of using the twist drill, cut off the head of the nail and use the nail in the chuck.

A nail gun, which drives a nail pneumatically by the use of a spring powered by air from a compressor, is a fast and efficient way of driving nails, especially for large construction jobs. Some nail guns require electricity to power the compressor; others, however, are battery-powered. There are nail guns for specific purposes: framing, roofing, finishing, and trim work. Guns come in two basic styles: stick and coil, determined by how the nails are loaded.

Screws

Screws offer several advantages over nails. Screws hold wood more securely and are neater in appearance; they can be tightened as necessary and can be removed without damaging the wood. They are, however, more expensive and require more care, time, and effort to insert. Screws are made of steel, copper, bronze, brass, or metal-plated with nickel or brass. Steel screws (bright) are the strongest and the least expensive, but they rust when they become damp. Rust can be prevented by bluing them with a material available commercially.

Classification and Sizes of Screws

Screws are mainly classified according to the shape of the head. The illustration shows some screws, and the list provides some details.

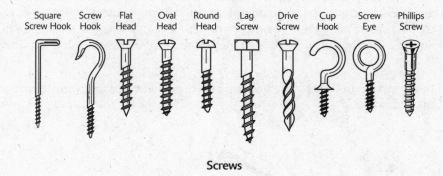

Screws

- **Flathead:** These screws are used where the head is not supposed to show. They should be countersunk and may be covered with plastic wood or doweling. They usually have a bright, blued, or brass finish.
- **Oval head:** These screws are designed primarily for fastening hinges and other hardware to wood. They should be countersunk to the oval part of the head. They usually come in a blued or brass finish.
- **Roundhead:** These screws should not be countersunk. They are for use in places where the head is supposed to show. They are commonly made of brass, although they may be blued or plated.
- **Lag:** These screws have a square bolt-type head and are used in heavy timber construction. They are driven into place with a wrench, and come in diameters of $\frac{1}{4}$ to 1 inch and lengths of 1 to 16 inches.
- **Drive:** Drive screws, which are half nail and half screw, are driven into wood like nails. The partial threading gives them better holding power than nails.
- **Phillips:** Instead of the usual groove in the head, these screws have cross-shaped recesses. They are easier to start than standard screws because the driver point centers itself and the screwdriver is less likely to slip. A Phillips screwdriver is used to insert these screws.
- **Screw hooks, cup hooks, and screw eyes:** These screws, available in various sizes, are made of steel, brass, and galvanized iron. In an occupational therapy clinic, their many uses include hanging tools, paint brushes, belts, and pictures.

Numerous other specialized screws exist, including sheet rock screws, decking screws, screws with square-drive heads and star-bit heads, and so on.

Wood screws are made in lengths ranging from $\frac{1}{4}$ to 5 inches. The diameter or gauge is indicated by numbers running from 0 to 24. The higher the gauge number, the greater the diameter of the screw. The size numbers of the most commonly used screws range from 5 to 12; their lengths range from $\frac{1}{8}$ inch to nearly $\frac{1}{4}$ inch.

> **The types and sizes of screws selected for use depend upon the item being made. About two-thirds of the screw should enter the wood. If the wood is thin, use a thin screw, one with a small gauge number. If a strong, long screw is required, select one with a high gauge number.**

Application of Screws

Two holes of different diameters must be bored in the wood when screws are to be used. The first hole should equal the diameter of the shank, and the second or pilot hole should equal the diameter of the root. In hardwoods, the second hole should be bored as deeply as the screw enters the wood; in softwoods it should be bored about half this distance. When flathead or oval head screws are used, the upper end of the first hole is widened with a countersink bit. The correct size and type of screwdriver must be used for ease in driving and protection of the screw. If the screw is difficult to insert, rubbing it across a piece of dry soap sometimes makes it go into the wood more easily. The screw should be turned so that the screwhead is parallel to the grain of the wood.

Bolts

Bolts differ from screws in that they are not tapered but are the same diameter from end to end. The bolt projects through the pieces being held together, and a square or hexagonal piece of metal, called a *nut,* is screwed onto the projected threaded end. When the piece must be easily removable or adjustable, use a wing nut instead of the regular kind of nut. Bolts are used when great holding strength is required and when wood must be fastened to metal or masonry.

The most common woodworking bolts are stove bolts and carriage bolts. The following illustration shows various kinds of common nuts and bolts.

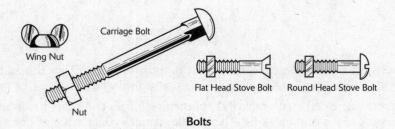

Bolts

When bolts are used, a hole of the same diameter as the bolt is drilled through both of the pieces that are to be held together. A metal washer is always placed between the nut and the wood and usually between the head and the wood. These washers distribute the pressure of the bolt over a larger area, thus preventing the head and nut from digging into the wood. A washer is sized by the hole in its center.

Miscellaneous Hardware

In addition to nails, screws, and bolts, other types of hardware are used in woodworking.

Braces

Braces are used to reinforce joints or cracks and to hold two or more pieces of wood together. The more commonly used braces are the corner brace, the flat corner iron, the mending plate, and the T-plate.

Hinges

A hinge is used to make a joint movable between two pieces of wood. Hinges are made in many different forms and of materials such as brass, iron, galvanized iron, brass-plated iron, and nickel. Hinges are sized according to the length and width of each leaf.

The different types of hinges include the butt hinge, which is used for many items, ranging from doors to jewel boxes; the continuous hinge, which can be obtained in any length and is used for pianos, boxes, and cabinet doors; and the strap and T-hinge, which are used on garage and cellar doors, gates, and toolboxes. The illustration shows these and other types of hinges.

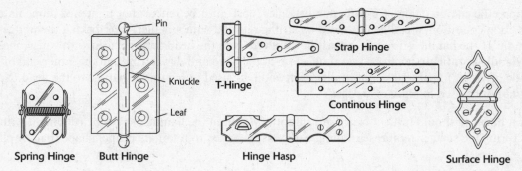

Spring Hinge   Butt Hinge   T-Hinge   Hinge Hasp   Strap Hinge   Continous Hinge   Surface Hinge

Hinges may be set flush or a little below the surface of the wood in a groove called a *gain*. Strap, surface, spring, hasp, and T-hinges are screwed to the surface of the wood without cutting any recess, whereas butt and continuous hinges are recessed. For greater security, hasps should be attached in such a way that the screws are hidden or covered so that they cannot be removed. When hinges are used for the lid of a box or chest, they should be placed so that the distance from each of the end hinges to the edge of the box is equal to the length of the hinge.

Corrugated Fasteners

A corrugated fastener is one of several means by which joints and splices in small timbers and boards may be fastened. They do not provide a secure joint; however, in places that will receive only slight strain, such as the corners of a mitered picture frame, they are a satisfactory means of quickly joining two pieces of wood.

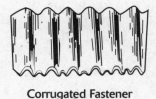

Corrugated Fastener

Hand Tools

Despite modern power equipment, hand tools remain the fundamental tools of woodworking. Even in this age of machines, a great deal of personal satisfaction can be derived from making a project entirely by hand. It is important, however, to know the possibilities and limitations of each hand tool, the means of keeping the tools in good working order, and the methods for developing skills in their use.

Hammer and Nail Sets

Hammers are some of the most used and misused of all hand tools. An understanding of hammer types and their proper uses will increase the user's efficiency.

Carpenter's Hammer

Hammers are sized by the weight of the head: The most common heads weigh 12, 16, and 20 ounces. The 16-ounce head is the best for general use. The *carpenter's hammer*, or *claw hammer*, which has a steel head and a wooden handle, is the most commonly used tool for driving nails. The face of the head is used to drive nails, and the claw is used to pull nails out of the wood. The two types of carpenter's hammers are the plain-faced claw hammer and the ball-faced hammer. The plain-faced claw hammer has a flat face. With this hammer it is easier for the beginner to learn to drive nails, but it is more difficult to drive the heads of the nails flush with the surface of the wood without leaving hammer marks. The face of the ball-faced hammer is slightly rounded or convex. It is generally used in rough work. An expert can use it to drive a nail flush with the surface of the work without damaging the wood.

For safety and efficiency, a hammer handle that becomes loose must be replaced or tightened immediately. If the handle is in good condition, it can be tightened by striking its end with a mallet, thus driving the wedges back into the handle. If the handle is broken, it must be removed from the head and replaced with a new one. If removing the old handle is difficult, it can be sawed off close to the head and driven through the larger end of the eye. Wedges made of either metal or straight-grained softwood are used to secure the handle to the head. Nails or screws should not be used in place of wedges.

The face of a hammer should be kept clean and smooth. Maintain the hammer's face by rubbing it with an emery cloth. If restoring the surface requires grinding, care must be taken to retain its proper shape (ball or plain).

Tack Hammer

The tack hammer is available in 5- and 7-ounce sizes. The 7-ounce double-faced hammer, with one face magnetic, is preferred for upholstery work. The head of a tack can be picked up with the magnetic face of the hammer; then the tack can be tapped into the wood far enough to hold it. The hammer is then turned over, and the nonmagnetic side is used to pound the tack into place. Tack hammers are recommended for light work (Note: Many heavy-duty staplers can do the same work). Care and safety precautions are the same as for the carpenter's hammer.

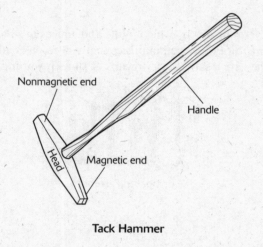

Tack Hammer

Nail Set

In finer work, it is often desirable to sink the nailheads below the wood surface. Sink a finishing nail or brad with a nail set. A nail set is a round, knurled steel shaft 4 to 5 inches long and about $\frac{1}{4}$ inch in diameter with a tapered point. The point is cup shaped to keep it from slipping off the nailhead. The point is available in various sizes ranging from $\frac{1}{32}$ to $\frac{1}{8}$ inch across the cup; it should not be larger than the diameter of the nail being set. The nail set is placed on the nailhead, held in line with the nail, and hit with a hammer until the nail is the desired distance below the surface of the wood.

Drills and Bits

Frequently, it is necessary to drill holes in wood, such as pilot holes for screws, and holes for insertion of saw blades or as part of making a joint. Several kinds of drills and bits, each designed for a certain purpose, are used.

Hand Drill

A hand drill is a relatively small drill used to bore holes with a diameter of $\frac{1}{4}$ inch or less in either wood or metal. Hand drills are normally used for fine cabinetry or other work for which an electric drill may not be appropriate. A hand drill consists of a shaft with a handle at one end and a chuck for holding twist drills at the other. Near the middle of the shaft is a ratchet wheel with a crank handle. Turning this handle causes the shaft and the chuck to turn. Straight shank twist bits ranging from $\frac{1}{32}$ to $\frac{1}{4}$ inch may be used in this drill.

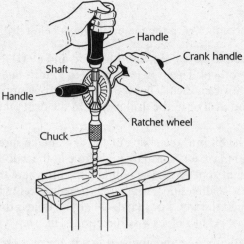

Hand Drill

The chuck for a drill has several V-grooved jaws that hold the tang of the bit. The jaws of the chuck are opened to receive the bit by grasping the shell and turning it to the left. The jaws are closed to secure the bit in place by turning the shell to the right.

A hole can be drilled to a specific depth or several holes can be drilled to the same depth by placing a depth gauge (wooden dowel) over the twist bit. This wood gauge cut to the proper length and slipped over the bit prevents the drill from cutting a hole deeper than desired.

When boring a hole, care must be taken to avoid putting too much force on the head of the drill. The bit may break or unexpectedly go completely through the lumber, throwing the operator off balance and causing an injury.

Brace

A brace is used to drill holes larger than can be drilled with the hand drill. It is made to take bits with round or square shanks as large as $\frac{1}{2}$ inch in diameter, including the screwdriver bit, twist drill, expansive bit, auger bit, and countersink bit. A brace has a head fastened to the crank by a bearing that permits the crank to turn. The crank, which is a steel shaft, provides leverage. The ratchet mechanism on the ratchet brace controls whether or not the chuck turns when the crank is turned. It may be set to permit the chuck to run either forward or backward while remaining stationary as the crank is turned in the other direction. This makes it possible to bore holes and drive screws in places where complete turns of the crank cannot be made.

Breast Drill

The breast drill is used to drill holes in either metal or wood. It will take bits with square or round shanks as large as $\frac{1}{2}$ inch. This drill has a lever for changing the speed of the drill or bit at any time from high (a 3-to-1 ratio) for small holes to low (a 1-to-1 ratio) for large holes. The center position of this lever locks the gears so that the chuck can be opened or closed. The breast plate is adjustable for the operator's comfort. As the operator leans against this plate, more pressure can be applied as the drill is turned. This drill can be used in any position.

Automatic or Yankee Drill

The automatic drill provides an easy and quick way to drill small holes. The drill can be used with one hand. It requires special bits that are inserted in the chuck. These bits range in size from $\frac{1}{16}$ to $1\frac{1}{64}$ inch. Usually, these special bits are stored in the handle of the drill.

Types of Drill Bits

A drill bit is what actually comes in contact with the material that is being drilled. Various types of bits exist:

- **Twist bits:** Twist bits can be used to bore holes in both wood and metal. Smaller holes can be made with these bits than with any of the others. They range from $\frac{1}{32}$ to $\frac{1}{2}$ inch in diameter; they are sized by thirty-seconds and sixty-fourths of an inch. The size of each bit is stamped on its shank. A twist bit with a round shank is used in the hand drill or in the drill press. (In the drill press, it is advisable to use high-speed bits rather than carbon bits.)

  When inserting the shank of the bit into the chuck of the drill, make sure the shank is straight. Before starting to drill, it may be helpful to make a very small guide hole in the wood or metal with an awl or center punch to keep the bit on the right spot. With the point of the bit where the hole is to be drilled, turn the crank of the ratchet in a clockwise direction. Apply light pressure to the handle of the drill, as this pressure keeps the bit progressing through the wood or metal. When the hole is deep enough, pull the bit from the hole while turning the ratchet wheel in a clockwise direction. This step will clear the hole of shavings.

- **Auger bits:** Auger bits have a square tang and are used in a brace or a breast drill. These bits are used exclusively for boring holes in wood. They vary in length from 7 to 10 inches and graduate from $\frac{1}{8}$ to $1\frac{1}{8}$ inches in diameter by $\frac{1}{16}$ inch.

  Insert the tang of the bit into the chuck of the brace as far as possible. Put the point of the spur at the exact center of the spot where the hole is to be bored. Turn the crank of the brace or the handle of the breast drill and apply only enough pressure to assist the spur in drawing the bit into the wood. (As the spur draws the bit down, first the nibs cut the fibers of wood at the edges of the hole, and then the lips chip out the wood to make a hole.) When the hole is the desired depth, back the bit out by turning the crank or handle in the opposite direction until the spur is free from the bottom of the hole. Withdraw the bit the remainder of the way, turning it in the direction that it entered in order to remove the shavings from the hole. If an auger bit is allowed to bore completely through a board, it will split the board as it comes out.

- **Forstner bit:** The Forstner bit is used to bore holes that must extend nearly all the way through a piece of wood, as it does not split the other side. It is also used to clean out the rough bottom of a hole made by an auger bit and to bore a large hole where a small one has been previously drilled. It cuts end grain and knots effectively, as well as holes in thin stock. The average set of Forstner bits ranges from $\frac{1}{4}$ to 1 inch in diameter.

- **Expansion bit:** This is an auger-type bit. Because it has adjustable cutting blades, it takes the place of several large auger bits. Usually, two interchangeable cutting blades are available. The smaller one cuts holes ranging from $\frac{7}{8}$ to $1\frac{1}{2}$ inches in diameter, and the larger one cuts holes ranging from $1\frac{1}{2}$ to 3 inches in diameter.

- **Screwdriver bit:** This specialized bit has a screwdriver blade on one end and a square shank that fits a brace or a breast drill on the other end. It is used for driving screws. Care must be taken to select the bit with the blade tip that will fill the slot of the screw.

- **Countersink bit:** The countersink bit has a conical cutting head and a square shank. It is to be used in a brace or a breast drill to form the top of the pilot hole for a screw. This bit enables the flathead of a screw to be flush with the surface of the wood. The rose type suitable for both wood and soft metals is ordinarily used.

Chisels

Chisels are simple tools with a single blade that is used for the careful removal of small areas of wood, often from otherwise inaccessible places.

Wood chisels are used for accurate cutting and for fitting and shaping as required in making wood joints. They are also used for surface decorating. The chisel consists of a single beveled steel blade fitted with a wooden handle. Chisels are divided into two types according to the way in which the handle is attached.

- **Tang chisel:** The upper end of a tang chisel blade is shaped into a tapering point that is driven into the wooden handle. A ring, called a *ferrule,* is fitted around the lower end of the handle to prevent the wood in the handle from splitting. Because of its design and light construction, the tang chisel will not withstand heavy blows.

- **Socket chisel:** The upper part of a socket chisel blade is shaped like a hollow cone. The handle of the tool is fitted into it. The construction is heavy so that the chisel will withstand the blow of a mallet when heavy work is being done. Chisel handles used for heavy or medium work are usually tipped with leather to prevent the handle from splitting under the blows of the mallet. The handle should fit well so that the chisel does not come out and cause an accident.

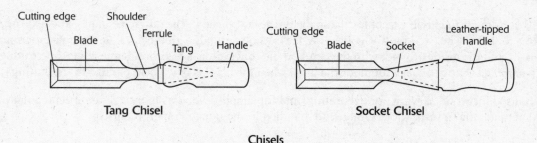

Chisels

Chisel Blades

Chisel blades are made in different weights and thicknesses and are shaped appropriately for the type of work to be done. Some are designed specifically for a certain type of job. They range in width from $\frac{1}{8}$ inch to 2 inches. The width of the chisel should be smaller than the width of the cut to be made. Most chisel blades fall into one of the three general types:

- **Paring:** The paring chisel blade is the thinnest and longest and is usually beveled. It is used for fine smoothing rather than for heavy work.
- **Firmer:** The firmer chisel blade is thicker than the paring chisel blade. It is used for heavier work that requires a stronger blade.
- **Framing:** The framing chisel blades are for heavy work. They are for socket chisels, which can be tapped with a mallet.

How to Use the Chisel

When using a chisel, the wood must be held securely in a vise. The cuts must be planed, taking into consideration the following.

Cutting against the grain of the wood tends to split the wood and make the tool more difficult to control. To obtain a cut that is well controlled and smooth, cut with the grain of the wood. When making heavy cuts in which wood is to be removed, the work must be planed so that if the wood splits, it will split in only the portion that is to be removed. You can contain the split with a *stop cut,* which is made by tapping the chisel vertically into the wood at the point where the cut should stop. In making this vertical cut, it should be remembered that when the beveled edge goes vertically into the wood, it will leave a straight cut on the flat side of the blade and an angular cut on the beveled side. Therefore, the bevel should always face the area to be removed.

Holding the chisel with the bevel down gives a lifting or gouging action; holding the bevel up or away from the surface gives a planing action. For smoothing cuts, the chisel should be held with the left hand close to the cutting edge so as to guide the chisel accurately. The right hand furnishes the power to make the cut. If the smoothing or planing stroke is done in a sideways manner, the shearing action will give a smoother cut. In smoothing an outside curve with a chisel, the chisel is held with the bevel up, and a series of short strokes is used.

Chisel Safety

Safety precautions are important to observe when using a chisel. Its shape and sharpness and the way in which it is used make it a dangerous tool.

- Always keep both hands in back of the cutting edge.
- Always cut away from the body.

- Do not carry a chisel in a clothing pocket.
- Clamp the wood firmly so that it does not move.
- Place the chisel on the workbench in a way that will prevent it from rolling off the bench onto someone's foot.

Gouges

These tools are similar to chisels except for the shape of the cutting end. The different shapes (sweeps) vary from a wide arc to a V-shape. The two kinds of gouges are the outside ground, with the bevel on the convex surface, or outside the blade; and the inside ground, with the bevel on the concave surface, or inside the blade. Some gouges are made with an offset shank to make room for the hand when the bevel is being held parallel to the cutting surface.

Gouges are used for wood carving, for decorating, and for shaping wood as in modeling. Special gouges are made to be used with a lathe to turn wood. Gouges are handled in the same manner as chisels.

Pliers

Pliers are used to hold materials, to grasp objects that are difficult to reach with the fingers, to bend wire, and to accomplish various tasks pertaining to specific crafts.

Pliers are made in a variety of shapes and sizes. The size of pliers is determined by the overall length, which ranges from 5 to 10 inches. The better ones are made of drop-forged steel to withstand hard use. The slip joint on the pliers permits a wider opening of the jaws, which are serrated for gripping.

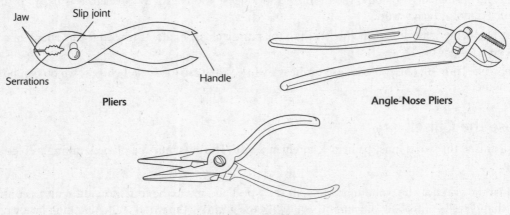

Jaw   Slip joint

Serrations   Handle

Pliers

Angle-Nose Pliers

Long-Nose/Needle-Nose Pliers

Some pliers are side-cutting. The jaws of side-cutting pliers do not open as far as those with slip joints. These pliers have two sharp edges between the nose and the joint. They are designed to cut and strip wire. Side-cutting pliers also come in various shapes and sizes.

When using side-cutting pliers, keep the wire being cut as near the joint as possible, increasing the leverage and preventing misalignment of the jaws. Select the appropriate-size pliers for cutting a specific weight of wire. If force is required to cut wire, either the wire is too heavy for the pliers or the cutters are dull.

Wrenches

Wrenches are used to tighten or loosen nuts and bolts. Many wrenches have been designed to serve various purposes. They can be described as either fixed-end or adjustable.

Fixed-End Wrenches

As the name implies, fixed-end wrenches are not adjustable. Instead, they are made in various sizes that can be purchased in sets. These fixed-end wrenches are designed with open ends and with closed (box) ends. The three main types of fixed-end wrenches are shown in the following figure.

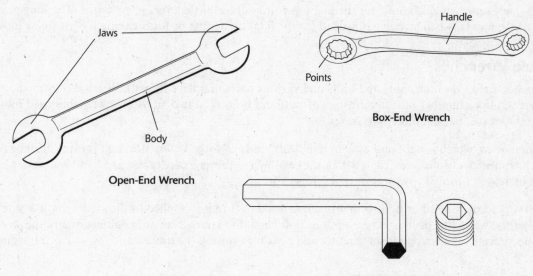

Jaws

Handle

Points

Body

Box-End Wrench

Open-End Wrench

Allen Wrench and Setscrew

- **Open-end wrenches:** These tools are forged from chrome vanadium steel and are heat treated. They usually have a double end with each end angled 10° to 23° to the body of the wrench. These angles enable the user to work more effectively in close quarters. The jaws may also be offset to facilitate turning a nut that is recessed. The size of the opening between the jaws is the size shown on the wrench. A double-end wrench with $\frac{1}{2}$-inch and $\frac{9}{16}$-inch openings is called a $\frac{1}{2}$-by-$\frac{9}{16}$ wrench. The size is usually stamped on the side of the wrench. As the size increases, the length and weight increase to provide greater leverage and strength.

  It is important for a wrench to fit squarely on the nut or bolt head. If it is too loose, the wrench will slip and round the corners. After each turn of the nut, the wrench should be turned over with the angle of its opening in reverse. If a nut is difficult to turn, a very small amount of penetrating oil should be applied and allowed to run into the threads of the bolt.

- **Box-end wrenches:** Box-end wrenches are made to surround or box in a nut or bolt head. They usually have a double end with either 6 or 12 points arranged within the circle. They are available in the same sizes as open-end wrenches. The circular ends on some of the wrenches are set at an angle to provide clearance for the user's hand. Such wrenches are available with a ratchet that eliminates the need to remove the wrench from the nut to start a new stroke.

  Compared with the open-end wrench, the box-end wrench has some advantages and at least one disadvantage.

  The advantages

  - With 12 points within the circle, the wrench can be used with a 15° swing of the handle, making it suitable for working in close quarters.

  - The thin sides of the circular end allow the wrench to be used in places where the thick jaws of the open-end wrench will not fit.

  - The box end does not slip off the nut.

  The disadvantage is that the box end must be lifted off the nut at the end of each stroke and placed back onto the nut in a different position for the next stroke. This disadvantage does not apply to the ratchet box wrench.

A combination wrench, with one end the open type and the other end the box type, is made in different sizes, offsets, and angles. The advantage of this wrench is that a tight nut can be broken loose more easily with the box end and removed more quickly with the open end.

- **Allen wrenches:** The Allen wrench is a special bar of tool steel that is usually six-sided and L-shaped. Both ends fit into hollow setscrews. The steel bars come in a set sized to fit most setscrews. The short portion of the L-shape serves as the handle for turning screws rapidly, as little leverage is needed. The long portion is used as the handle when leverage is needed for the final tightening or for breaking a tight screw loose.

Adjustable Wrenches

These wrenches are used to turn nuts and bolts and various parts that have threads. Because they are adjustable, the same wrench fits a number of different sizes of nuts and bolts. The two adjustable wrenches used most frequently are the crescent and monkey wrenches.

The *crescent wrench,* which is light and easy to handle, is made of forged alloy steel and is often chrome plated. This wrench comes in various sizes, each with a range of adjustable jaw capacities. The handle is somewhat longer as the sizes increase to provide the necessary leverage.

The wrench is placed on a nut or bolt so that the force used to turn it is applied to the stationary jaw side of the wrench. After the wrench is positioned on a nut or bolt head, the knurled screw is tightened until the wrench fits securely. This prevents the wrench from slipping and possibly injuring the user's hand, as well as damaging the nut or bolt.

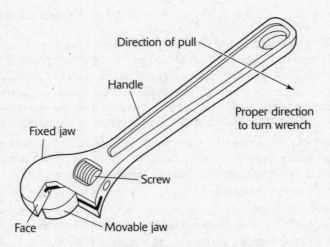

Crescent or Single Open-End Wrench

Pipe wrenches are used to turn soft iron pipes and rounded fittings. A pipe wrench functions in the same way as the crescent wrench; the turning force is applied on the fixed jaw. The care and safety precautions are also the same as those for the crescent wrench.

Screwdrivers

A joint or fixture held with screws is more secure and durable than one held with nails; furthermore, it can be taken apart and reassembled. For the insertion of screws, many types of screwdrivers are available. Some are designed for highly specialized jobs; however, in this section only the most frequently used screwdrivers will be discussed.

Types of Screwdrivers

The *standard screwdriver* has a round or square steel blade anchored firmly in a hardwood or plastic handle. For heavy-duty work, an integral-handle screwdriver is standard; its blade, which forms an integral part of the handle's surface, is locked in place by rivets. The tip of a standard screwdriver is flat and it is made of steel. The standard screwdriver is sized according to its blade lengths, ranging from $1\frac{1}{4}$ to 12 inches with tips ranging from $\frac{1}{8}$ to $\frac{3}{8}$ inch. It is very important that the screwdriver tip fits securely into the screw slot and that the width of the tip equals the length of the screw slot.

The *Phillips screwdriver* is available with blades of various lengths. The blade tips, which are shaped like a cross to fit the Phillips screw, are made in four sizes.

Screwdriver Tip Sizes	Phillips Screw Sizes
1	4 and smaller
2	5 through 9
3	10 through 16
4	18 and larger

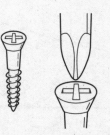

Phillips Screw and Screwdriver

While standard and Phillips head are the two main types of screwdrivers, variations exist:

- **Clutch-head screwdriver:** This screwdriver is made to fit the recessed head of the clutch-bit screw, more commonly called the butterfly or figure-8 screw. It comes in several sizes to fit the various sizes of screws.
- **Offset screwdriver:** The offset screwdriver is used to reach screws located in tight corners inaccessible to other screwdrivers. It is made in a variety of sizes and tip widths.
- **Ratchet screwdriver:** With the ratchet screwdriver, screws can be driven and removed more rapidly than with a standard screwdriver. The ratchet arrangement makes it possible to drive in one direction and release in the other. This screwdriver can be adjusted to turn to the right or to the left and can be locked so it works like a standard screwdriver. Some screwdrivers of this type have a chuck into which various sizes of blades may be inserted.

In addition, screwdriver bits (blades) are made to fit into the chuck of other tools such as the breast drill and socket wrench. The use of such tools reduces the work and time required to drive screws. Care must be taken to select the bit with a tip that fits the screws to be driven.

Using Screwdrivers

First, select the screwdriver with the largest tip that will properly fit into the screw slot. Hold the screwdriver in the palm of one hand with the forefinger extending down the handle toward the ferrule. With the other hand, steady the tip of the blade in the head of the screw. Apply downward pressure to the handle of the screwdriver and at the same time turn the screw clockwise (to the right). If the screw is difficult to drive or if it is going into hardwood, drill a pilot hole. If the screw is still difficult to drive, apply soft soap to the threads of the screw. For additional leverage, use a wrench, placing it either at the flared tip or near the handle of the screwdriver with a square blade.

When driving brass screws, do not force them, as they are soft and easily damaged. If such a screw becomes difficult to turn before it is seated, remove the screw and enlarge the pilot hole. Finally, if a screw is difficult to remove, tighten it slightly; then loosen it. Use this back-and-forth motion until the screw can be removed.

Saws

The saws used in woodworking are the crosscut, ripsaw, backsaw, miter, keyhole, compass, plumber's, and coping. Although these saws share certain similarities, each one has a specific use.

The cutting edge of a saw is a line of sharp teeth. Because these teeth are set with one to the right and one to the left, alternately, they act as two rows of cutting instruments, running close together in parallel grooves. With the cut made wider than the thickness of the saw, the saw does not bind as it is pushed through the wood. This cut or groove is known as the *kerf*. The kerf width that is necessary depends largely upon the type of lumber to be cut. Green or soft lumber requires a wider kerf than hard or dry lumber. A coarse saw is better for doing fast work and for cutting green (undried) wood; a fine saw does smoother, more accurate cutting on seasoned lumber. The teeth of woodworking saws are designed to cut as the saw is being pushed away from the operator. Saws are sized by the number of tooth points to the inch. There is always one more point per inch than there are teeth per inch. Three common types of saws are depicted in the following illustration.

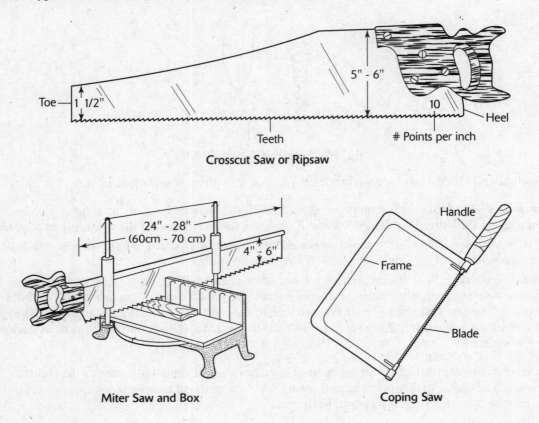

Crosscut Saw or Ripsaw

Miter Saw and Box

Coping Saw

Crosscut Saw

The teeth of a crosscut saw are designed to cut across the grain of the wood. The cutting edge of each tooth is on the side; the sharp point is on the outside of each tooth and the bevel is on the inside. For general use, a good size of crosscut saw is 8 to 10 points per inch. The number stamped near the handle indicates the number of points per inch. The blade of a crosscut saw is tapered in width and is 18 to 20 inches long.

To use a saw, grasp the handle with the index finger extended toward the point, the other fingers curled around the grip, and the thumb pointed in the direction opposite to the fingers. The extended index finger tends to give better accuracy in sawing.

Start the cut by placing the saw on the wood so that the heel of the saw rests with the inside edge touching the line to be sawed. Use the thumb of the opposite hand to guide the blade and the fingers and palm to hold the lumber. Pull the saw, exerting no pressure but allowing the weight of the saw to rest on the lumber. In this manner, a small groove is made in which the saw can be run.

Cut the wood by holding the saw perpendicular to the lumber at about a 45° angle and pushing it forward with just enough pressure to make a cut. During this pushing motion, guide the saw with the forefinger of the hand on the handle and with the thumb of the other hand. Do not force the saw, as this may cause it to bend or to jump out of the groove and scar the face of the lumber.

Continue the backward (pull) and forward (push) motions, exerting pressure only on the push (cutting) stroke. Just before the cut is completed, support the part that may fall until all of the fibers are cut. This precaution prevents the edge from splitting when the last strokes are made.

Other Types of Saws

The crosscut saw is the most common type of saw. Other varieties include

- **Ripsaw:** The parts of a ripsaw are the same as those of a crosscut saw. The teeth, however, are designed to cut with the grain of the wood. They are sharpened straight across the front edge, making the cutting edge function like two rows of chisels cutting into the wood. A good size for a ripsaw is 5 to 7 points per inch. It is used in the same manner as the crosscut saw except that the blade is held at a 60° angle to the lumber.

- **Backsaw:** The teeth of a backsaw are similar to those of a crosscut except that they are smaller and finer, with about 14 teeth per inch. On average, the blade is about 12 inches in length. The blade is thin; however, it is stiffened with a heavy metal back. The construction of the backsaw makes it more suitable than the crosscut saw for cutting pieces that must fit together exactly, such as joints. The backsaw, which cuts either with or across the grain, is used in the same manner as the crosscut saw and ripsaw.

- **Hacksaw:** The hacksaw is a saw that supports a fine-tooth blade in tension between its two frame members. The frame of the saw is similar to an arch with a grip on one end of the frame. This frame design allows the blade to slide easily through the material being cut, while also supporting the blade on both ends. Typically, hacksaws are used to cut various types of metals; they can, however, be used to cut a wide array of other materials, including plastics and composites.

- **Miter saw:** The miter saw looks like a hacksaw, except that it is longer than a hacksaw. A miter box issued with the miter saw makes it possible to cut lumber accurately at almost any angle. It is especially useful in cutting lumber for joints. A device on the commercial miter box is set for cutting the desired angle. A small wooden miter box can be designed for cutting certain angles used frequently.

- **Keyhole saw:** The keyhole saw is made for small jobs, such as cutting keyholes and fitting locks in doors. It is narrow enough to enter a ¼-inch hole. It cuts a wide kerf so that the blade may turn in making curved cuts. It frequently comes nested with a compass saw and a plumber's saw with a common, easily removable pistol-grip handle.

- **Coping saw:** The coping saw is a versatile saw for cutting thin wood and plastic. It consists of a steel frame, handle, and replaceable blade. The blade can be inserted with the teeth pointing away from or toward the handle. With the teeth pointing away from the handle, the saw can be used in the same way as a ripsaw or crosscut saw. With the teeth pointing toward the handle, the saw can be used in the same way as a jeweler's saw.

Maintenance of Handsaws

Here are a few things to keep in mind when using a saw or putting it away:

- Do not bend or kink the blade of a handsaw, as such distortions prevent the blade from sliding through the kerf. Applying pressure to force a jammed handsaw through the wood causes the blade to bend, usually resulting in a kinked blade. Laying a handsaw on an uneven surface and placing other tools on top of it will bend the blade.

- Do not saw through a metal object in the wood with a saw designed to cut only wood; either remove the object or cut it with a plumber's saw.

- When a saw is not in use, oil and store it properly to prevent it from becoming rusty and bent. A rusty saw will bend easily in a cut.

- Do not use a saw to twist off waste pieces of wood, as this action distorts the blade. Break off such pieces with the hand or a mallet.

- When sawing, do not let the blade strike the floor. If necessary, either raise the work being sawed or use short strokes.

- Keep saws sharpened. Because the sharpening process requires a great deal of skill, have your saws sharpened professionally.

- Label the saws, especially the ripsaw and the crosscut saw, to prevent misuse.

Files

Files are used for shaping and for smoothing materials in many trades. In occupational therapy, they are used for smoothing metal, plastic, and wood. Because filing wood leaves a rather rough surface, it should be done sparingly unless the primary goal is therapy. There are supposed to be more than 3,000 types of files, each made for a specific purpose. The following illustration gives some examples.

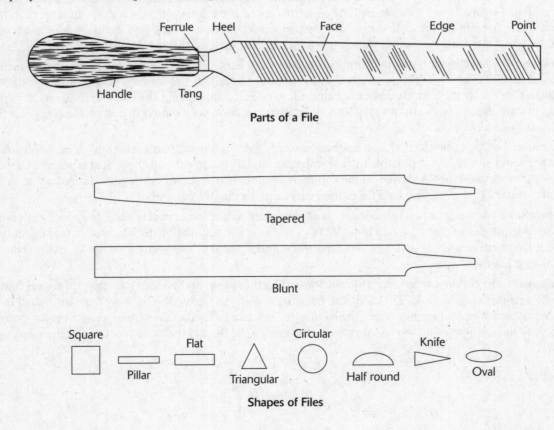

Parts of a File

Tapered

Blunt

Shapes of Files

Planes

Planes are used to smooth boards; to remove relatively small amounts of wood from the surface or edge of a board, thereby obtaining the desired thickness or width; or to true or square a board. Generally, planes are classified as either bench planes or block planes. Although planes are similar in general construction, method of operation, and care, they vary in size, shape of blade, and other details, as each one is designed for a specific job. Three common types of planes are shown below.

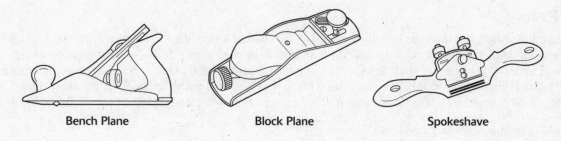

Bench Plane   Block Plane   Spokeshave

Bench Plane

As its name implies, a bench plane is designed for use while the work is held on a workbench. It is used primarily for shaving and smoothing with the grain of the wood. For this purpose, the bevel of the cutting edge of the blade is turned down.

Types of bench planes include

- **Jointer plane:** This largest bench plane is 18 to 24 inches long with blades $2\frac{3}{8}$ to $2\frac{5}{8}$ inches wide. Because of its length, it rides across small hollows or depressions in the work without cutting. This jointer plane is, therefore, used to true edges or surfaces of boards.

- **Jack plane:** The jack plane is similar to the jointer. It is $11\frac{1}{2}$ to 15 inches long with blades $1\frac{3}{4}$ to $2\frac{3}{8}$ inches wide. It can be used for the same type of work as the jointer plane, provided the lumber is not too wide. Furthermore, when only one plane is to be purchased, the jack plane is a good choice in that its size is between the sizes of the jointer plane and the smoothing plane.

- **Junior jack plane:** The junior jack plane is smaller than the jack plane. It is 10 to $11\frac{1}{2}$ inches long with blades about $1\frac{3}{4}$ inches wide. Because it is smaller and lighter than the jack plane, it is easier to handle.

- **Smoothing plane:** The smallest bench plane is the smoothing plane, which is $5\frac{1}{2}$ to 10 inches long with blades $1\frac{1}{4}$ to $2\frac{3}{8}$ inches wide. Unlike the other bench planes, it is not used to true a board but rather to smooth rough surfaces. For this reason, the cutting edge of the blade is shaped like that of the block plane.

To use a bench plane, follow these steps:

1. Securely clamp the piece of wood to be planed.
2. Grasp the plane with the left hand on the knob and the right hand on the handle.
3. Position and keep the body well over the work to facilitate pressure control.
4. Keep the board even while planing by bearing down firmly on the knob when starting the stroke, bearing evenly on both knob and handle in the middle of the stroke, and lightening the pressure on the knob and bearing down on the handle at the end of the stroke.
5. On the return stroke, raise the cutting edge of the plane so that it will not drag on the wood.

When using a bench plane, keep the following in mind:

- For rough cuts, angle the plane approximately 30°; for smooth cuts, angle it about 10° to 15°.
- When planing sides and edges, work from the outside toward the middle and, as much as possible, with the grain of the wood.

- If the grain is torn or roughened by the plane, reverse the direction in which the plane is being pushed. A common cause of this difficulty is a plane adjusted to take too deep a cut; the shaving should be thin and should come up and through the mouth to be deflected by the cap iron.
- To avoid splits in the wood, bevel the edges of excess (waste) stock; then work toward the bevel.
- To keep the edges true while planing, hold a block of wood against the side of the work and under part of the plane.

Block Plane

The block plane is smaller than the bench plane. It is 4 to 8 inches long with a blade ranging from 1 to $1\frac{5}{8}$ inches wide. It is designed to smooth across the end grain and to make close joints. It is also used for smoothing many other small areas. Although it is made somewhat differently from a bench plane, it is adjusted in the same manner. The blade is shaped like that of the smoothing plane, but it is used with the bevel up instead of down. Also, the blade is held in place by a lever lock instead of a cap iron. Following are guidelines for using the block plane:

- Hold the plane with only one hand.
- To smooth cross-grained wood, adjust the plane to take light, not deep, cuts; make the strokes short and at an angle.
- Always plane cross-grained wood toward the center of the board to prevent the blade from running over the edge and splitting off a corner of the wood. Slightly beveling the waste portion of the stock also helps prevent a split.

Related Tools

The following tools are variations on the two basic types of planes:

- **Spokeshave:** The spokeshave is a greatly modified plane used for smoothing and shaping convex and concave surfaces of wood. It has a short bottom that makes it adaptable for shaping. The blade is held in place with a screw and a clamp. The adjustments for the spokeshave are similar to those of a plane. Before starting the planing process, the work is clamped firmly in a vise. The spokeshave is grasped by the handle with the thumbs near the center of the tool. The cut is then made either by pushing or by pulling the tool. It is best to cut with, rather than against, the grain of the wood.
- **Cabinet scraper:** The cabinet scraper, made of a metal frame with two handles, holds a blade that can be adjusted to the desired depth by means of the thumbscrew. This blade produces fine, thin, even shavings as it is pushed with the grain, using long, even strokes. A cabinet scraper removes irregularities left in the wood by the plane. It also works well in the final dressings of burls or woods with irregular grain.
- **Hand scraper:** The hand scraper is a rectangular piece of steel. The sharp edge of this piece of steel, rather than an actual blade, is used to remove mill marks and scratches before the sanding process is started. The scraper is held firmly in both hands and is angled toward the wood about 30° in the direction that it is being pushed or pulled. Before steel is stored, it must be covered with a light coat of oil to prevent rust.

Clamps and Vises

Tools such as C-clamps, hand screws, bar clamps, miter clamps, and vises are very important in holding pieces to be shaped and in assembling the finished parts of a project. Knowledge of these tools and skill in their use make the work easier and help to produce a better product.

Clamps

Clamps are holding devices made of two parts that are squeezed together, usually with screws. These clamps are not fixed to a bench or worktable. Clamps most commonly used in woodworking are described below.

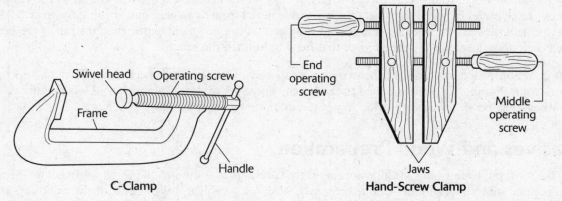

C-Clamp

Hand-Screw Clamp

- **C-clamp:** This clamp is shaped like the letter "C." Its shape makes it suitable for clamping small pieces of wood, for applying pressure at points inaccessible to other clamps, and for holding work onto the bench. The C-clamp consists of a steel frame, threaded to receive an operating screw with a swivel head. Small pieces of soft wood or heavy leather should be placed between the clamp and the wood.
- **Hand-screw clamp:** This clamp consists of two hard maple jaws with two operating screws. Each jaw has two metal inserts into which the screws are threaded. Although this clamp was designed to hold flat wood blocks together, the jaws may be adjusted to hold a wide variety of irregularly shaped objects.
- **Bar clamp:** This steel clamp is available with opening sizes ranging from 2 to 6 feet. Several clamps are ordinarily used at one time to hold stock too wide to be spanned by other clamping devices, such as wide pieces being glued together for a tabletop.
- **Miter (corner) clamp:** This clamp makes it easy to miter corners such as those of picture frames. Miter clamps open to 3 inches, thus accommodating most sizes of molding. Using four clamps, one for each corner of the frame, decreases the time required for the gluing process.

Vises

Vises are holding devices made to fasten to a workbench and to secure objects by means of two jaws that open and close as a screw is turned. The most common woodworking vise is the bench vise; however, the machinist's vise is often used in woodworking.

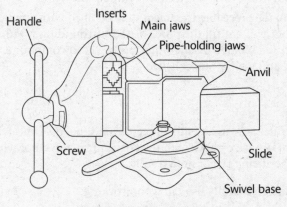

Machinist's Bench Vise

The woodworker's bench vise holds lumber to be worked. It is attached to the bench so that the top edges of the vise are flush with the top of the bench. The movable jaws may be adjusted entirely by turning the handle; in some vises, they may be more rapidly adjusted by setting the handle, pushing the movable jaw to approximately the correct position, and then firming it against the work by turning the handle. These vises vary in size and weight and usually open from 9 to 12 inches. Material to be worked on is held between the jaws of the vise. It is wise to use small pieces of wood to protect the worked material from damage. Lumber too large to be held in the vise may be held between the vise dog (the part of the vise that can be pulled higher than the top of the bench) and the bench dog (the metal, T-shaped piece that fits into holes in the bench).

The less-commonly used machinist's bench vise is a heavy-duty, versatile, large steel vise with rough jaws to prevent work from slipping. The vise is bolted to the bench, where it swivels and stands about 9 inches above the bench. Work must be protected with wood to prevent marking by the rough jaws.

Abrasives and Wood Preparation

One of the most important steps in woodworking is the careful preparation of the wood for finishing. Most of the sanding and smoothing should be done before the work is assembled. It is this part of the work that brings out the beauty of the wood and produces the fine, smooth surface so admired in good woodworking. Too often, woodworkers, especially amateurs, take shortcuts in repairing the wood. This practice frequently results in a disappointing piece of work rather than in one to be admired.

Preparation of Wood

In preparing wood for finishing, you must carefully examine it to determine the nature of the defects. Some of the defects commonly found in wood and the methods of correction are explained below.

- **Mill marks** may be evident in a wavy unevenness across the surface of the lumber caused by the planer or jointer, marks from the saw blade, or circular marks from the disc sander. If they are deep, removal may be started with a belt sander. To finish the job, or to remove the mill marks if they are not deep, use a cabinet scraper or sandpaper of the proper grade.

- **Scratches** along the grain are less noticeable than those across the grain. The method used to remove the scratches depends upon their extent and depth. If they are deep, sanding may be started with a belt sander and finished with hand sanding. Light scratches may be removed with only hand sanding. To prevent wavy areas in the surface of the wood, the scratches and the area around them must both be sanded.

- **Dents that have only crushed the wood and not broken its surface** can often be raised by wetting the affected area with a few drops of water. If this trick does not raise the dents, steam may be more effective. Steaming may be accomplished by placing a few drops of water on the area and touching the dents with a hot instrument. Also, holding a steam iron over the area may bring up the dents.

- **Dents that do not respond to the preceding treatment** may be filled with a material that will adhere to the wood and take stain well but will not fill the pores of the surrounding wood nor shrink when it becomes dry. Materials that can be used include plastic water putty, wood compound paste, plastic wood, a glue-and-sawdust mixture, and melted stick shellac.

Sanding

After dents have been raised or filled, the unassembled pieces are sanded. Although sanding tends to be a tedious process, selecting the best type of abrasive paper with the correct grit and employing the best working methods can speed the process without sacrificing the desired results.

Three types of abrasive papers are commonly used in woodworking:

- **Flint paper:** Grayish-tan in color, this paper is used most frequently because it is the least expensive. It is less durable than other papers, as it dulls rather rapidly.

- **Garnet paper:** Reddish in color, this paper is more expensive than flint paper and becomes dull less rapidly. It cuts not only longer but also faster than flint paper. It is especially good for sanding plastic.
- **Aluminum oxide paper:** Dark gray (almost black) in color, this paper can be used either wet or dry. It is used wet only on varnished and lacquered surfaces.

All three types of abrasive papers are available with different sizes of grits, ranging from very fine to very coarse. Flint and garnet papers are usually marked very fine, fine, medium, or coarse rather than with a number. Selecting the best paper for the job is a matter of judgment sharpened by experience. The rougher the flaws in the wood, the coarser the paper must be to remove them. Fine paper is used to remove the scratches left by the coarse paper.

Sandpaper is ordinarily purchased in sheets that are 9 by 11 inches in size. For ease of handling and for economy, it can be torn into several pieces. The smooth side of the paper should first be worked over the rounded edge of the bench to limber the paper and to prevent cracking when it is torn or wrapped around the sandblock.

Most sanding should be done with the sandpaper wrapped around a sandblock. The block can be made of scrap wood. It should be a size comfortable to hold and should also fit the pieces of sandpaper. A good size is about ¾ by 2½ by 4 inches. A cushioning substance such as cork, rubber, felt, or leather should be glued to the bottom of the block. This cushion prolongs the life of the sandpaper and makes the sanding smoother.

Different types of surfaces require different sanding techniques:

- **Flat surfaces** are always sanded with the grain of the wood, never across it or with a circular motion.
- **End grain** should be sanded in one direction rather than with a back-and-forth motion.
- **Corners or a curve** should be sanded in one direction (not back and forth) and with the grain of the wood.
- **Concave surfaces and the edges** of holes are sanded with the sandpaper wrapped around a dowel or broom handle. The dowel should be padded before the sandpaper is wrapped around it.
- **Edges may be rounded** or **rounded edges** may be sanded by holding the paper in the palm of the hand while sanding.

An extra-smooth finish may be obtained by sponging the wood with water after sanding to raise the small wood fiber. After the wood has dried, the raised fibers are smoothed off by using extra-fine sandpaper held in the hand. For an extra-fine surface, repeat this sponging process several times.

After the work has been assembled and sanded the final time, any glue that has not been removed with the sandpaper should be removed with a knife. Just before the finish is applied, the sanded piece is cleaned of dust and sandpaper residue, using either a clean brush with fairly stiff bristles or a clean cloth dampened slightly with turpentine.

Steel Wool

Steel wool is another form of abrasive used in woodworking. It is used for rubbing down wood between coats of finish. It is frequently used with a lubricant, such as linseed oil, to prevent scratching.

Final Polishing

Pumice and rottenstone are both fine powders used with an oil in the final polishing of shellac, varnish, and lacquer finishes.

- **Pumice** is a spongy, light, porous volcanic rock ground to different degrees of fineness for the polishing of wood finishes, ivory, marble, and fine metals. Pumice stone is available in several types and colors; the type most commonly used in woodworking is grayish in color. FF and FFF indicate the degree of coarseness. Pumice is mixed with fine motor oil, paraffin oil, linseed oil, or lemon oil to form a paste, and then it is rubbed on the final coat of shellac, varnish, or lacquer to make the surface highly polished and smooth.
- **Rottenstone** is limestone decomposed to a powder. Dark brown and finer than pumice, it is used in the same way as pumice to produce a higher polish.

Joints and Gluing

The strength, durability, and worth of a piece of furniture or equipment depend a great deal upon the suitability of joints used, the workmanship employed in making the joints, and the types of glues and fasteners used to reinforce the joints.

Types of Joints

A piece of furniture or equipment usually includes one or more types of joints. Fundamental to wise planning is a knowledge of joint designs and their specific purposes.

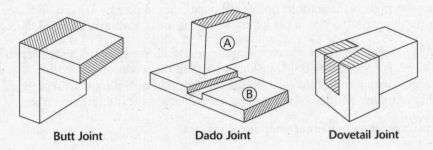

Butt Joint   Dado Joint   Dovetail Joint

Here are the most common types of joints:

- **Butt joint:** This commonly used joint is simple to make; however, care must be taken to ensure that the ends and surfaces where the two pieces meet are as square as possible. The butt joint does not look as nice as other joints; furthermore, it is not as strong as others. Its strength can be increased by applying glue and reinforcing with dowels, nails, screws, or corrugated fasteners.

- **Dado joint:** The dado joint is useful in making items with shelves and drawers. It is also used in the construction of doors and windows. One piece of wood fits snugly into a recess cut into another piece.

- **Dovetail joint:** The dovetail joint is one of the strongest joints. However, in order to get the maximum holding power of this type of joint, it should be glued. In better furniture, both old and new, this joint appears in a series to give strength and to improve appearance.

- **Lap joints:** The several types of lap joints serve specific purposes. Lap joints tend to be stronger than many of the other joints because of their shape and the extent of the area to which glue can be applied.

- **Miter joint:** The miter joint is one of the more commonly used joints. It is useful in making such items as picture frames, in which symmetry is desirable and view of the end grain is undesirable. Miter joints are usually made at a 45° angle, which can be cut with an accurate miter box or measured with a try square, combination square, or T-bevel.

- **Mortise-and-tenon joint:** In this joint the tenon forms one half, and the mortise the other half. Because this joint is one of the strongest and most attractive, it is used extensively in tables, chairs, desks, window sashes, and other articles in which both strength and attractiveness are important.

- **Rabbet joint:** The rabbet joint is similar to the dado joint, except that the pieces are joined at the ends. This joint is used extensively in making such woodworking projects as drawers, window and door frames, bookshelves, and furniture. Both pieces must be squared. The joint is marked, cut, chiseled, and reinforced in the same manner as the dado joint. If the joint is made with the grain, it can be cut with a power saw or a rabbet plane.

- **Tongue-and-groove joint:** This joint is similar to the mortise-and-tenon joint; however, both the mortise and the tenon are continuous. The tongue-and-groove joint is usually machine made. Lumber for flooring can be purchased already tongued and grooved.

Joint Reinforcements

Only a few joints are so strong that no reinforcement is required. Selecting a particular reinforcement depends upon the strength needed and the appearance desired.

Common reinforcements include

- **Spline:** A spline is a thin piece of wood that fits into a groove made in both parts of a joint. Because it is glued into place, it strengthens the joint. Splines are often used to reinforce miter joints or to join two long boards. The spline can be hidden if the groove for the spline is made with the circular saw in such a way that the cut does not run the full length of the board.

- **Dowels:** Almost any type of joint can be strengthened with dowels. A dowels is a round piece of wood, usually birch or maple, that comes in 36-inch lengths, ranging from ¼ to 1 inch in diameter. Dowels grooved to hold additional glue are also available. To insert a dowel, you must drill holes, measured carefully, through each piece to be joined. Use a depth gauge to ensure accuracy in drilling the holes the correct depth, and either a doweling jig or try square to ensure that you drill the holes at a 90° angle to the edge of the board.

- **Screws:** A joint held with glue and screws is solid and durable; even a butt or miter joint reinforced in this manner is very stable.

- **Nails:** Nails are used to hold joints in rough work. If the nails are driven at an angle (called *toenailing*), they have greater holding power. The addition of glue greatly strengthens a nailed joint.

- **Corrugated fasteners:** Because appearance is not important in rough temporary constructions, corrugated fasteners may be used to hold miter and butt joints together. Glue may or may not be used, depending upon the purpose of the construction and the degree of stability required.

Gluing

Gluing is said to be the oldest, neatest, strongest, and most durable method of fastening wood joints together. Glue is ordinarily used in combination with various types of fasteners to provide added strength. Most glues (with the exception of casein; see the following paragraph and table) should not be used as a filler of space created by a poorly fitted joint.

Selection of the most suitable glue depends not only upon the design of a particular object but also upon how and where the object is to be used. Casein and plastic glues are more resistant to water and dampness; hot animal glue and plastic glue are stronger than others. (*Casein* is a byproduct of the curd of soured milk after removal of the fat, and is put on the market in the form of a dry powder. The powder is mixed with borax that has been dissolved in very little hot water in order for form the final glue.) Some glues set in a short time; others do not. The newer types of glues come ready to use; others must be mixed. The following table contains the most commonly used types of glues and their general characteristics.

Glue Types				
Type	**Drying Time**	**Strength**	**Shop Uses**	**Water Resistance**
Animal	Sets rapidly	Very strong	Joint work, not exposed to water	Low
Cold liquid animal	Varies with type	Medium	Repair work	Low
Casein, powdered	4–5 hours	Good for oily woods	For semiwater-resistant joint work and as filler	Good
Plastic	4–5 hours, clamping necessary	Very strong	Joint work	Very high
Epoxy	Hardens overnight	Strong, resists heat	Wood, masonry, metal, china, glass	Waterproof
Resorcinol glue	8–10 hours, clamping necessary	Strong at any temperature	Outdoor furniture, boats, etc.	100% waterproof
Powdered resin	Clamping necessary	Strong if joint fits well	Not good for poor joints or oily surfaces	Good
Contact cement	Bonds on contact when dry	Light duty	Leather, large surfaces such as wall paneling	High
White glue	Sets in 20–30 minutes with moderate pressure	Moderate	Paper, fabric, canvas, felt, and cork to wood	Moderate

A glued joint must be put under pressure until the glue becomes set. The joint can be held with nails, screws, or clamps. Various types of clamps are available for holding glued work under pressure. When clamps are not available in the appropriate type or in an adequate number for a particular piece, an improvised method may be used. The method to be used must be planned and set up before the glue is applied. If clamps are to be used, the clamps and protective blocks must be in place before the glue is applied, especially when using a fast-drying glue.

Lumber

Many kinds of lumber are used in woodworking. Each one has certain qualities that make it more or less adaptable for specific types of work. The appearance of a finished product is greatly dependent upon selection of the most appropriate lumber in the correct size, grade, and finish.

Categories of Wood

The two main categories of wood are hardwood and softwood. These terms are somewhat misleading, as they have nothing to do with the hardness or softness of the wood.

- **Hardwoods:** The hardwoods are cut from deciduous (broad-leaf) trees. Both maple and basswood are considered hardwoods even though maple is hard and basswood is soft. The more common hardwoods include maple, basswood, birch, oak, yellow poplar, chestnut, mahogany, cherry, walnut, ash, and elm.
- **Softwoods:** Conifers (trees with needle-shaped leaves) furnish the type of lumber classified as softwood. Georgia yellow pine is heavy and hard, and northern white pine is light and soft; yet both are considered softwoods. Yellow pine, Douglas fir, western pine, hemlock, white pine, redwood, cedar, cypress, and spruce are some of the most common softwoods.

Purchasing Lumber

Specific terms, abbreviations, and numerals are used by wood dealers to describe wood qualities, grades, and measurements. Because lumber dealers have not converted their measurements to the metric system, measurements are normally expressed in feet and inches.

Grades of Wood

Lumber is graded by the number of flaws it contains. In relation to flaws, the following terminology is used: A *blemish* is a small knot in the wood that mars the appearance but does not alter the soundness of the wood. A *defect* mars the soundness of the wood. A *knot* of more than $1\frac{1}{4}$ inches in diameter is considered a defect.

The two types of lumber generally available are *select* and *common*. Select lumber, as the name indicates, is the better of the two. It is subdivided into grades:

- Grade A is practically free from defects.
- Grade B may have minor defects or blemishes.
- Grade C contains more defects or blemishes.
- Grade D contains still more defects or blemishes.

Common lumber is not as free from imperfections as select lumber, but it is adequate for some purposes and is less expensive. It is subdivided as follows:

- No. 1 Common is sound, even though it may have small knots.
- No. 2 Common has large, coarse defects.

- No. 3 Common contains a greater number of defects.
- No. 4 Common contains still more defects.
- No. 5 Common is considered poor lumber and is unusable for shop work.

Measurement of Lumber

The price of lumber is based on the cost per board foot. A board foot is 1 inch thick, 12 inches wide, and 1 foot long. The measurements are given in the following order: thickness, width, and length. Thickness and width are given in inches; length is given in feet. To determine how many board feet are in, for example, four pieces of lumber with measurements 2 inches by 6 inches by 5 feet, multiply $2 \times \frac{6}{12} \times 5 \times 4 = 20$ board feet.

The measurements discussed above are used for rough lumber. Planing not only smoothes the surface but also decreases the size of the piece. A board sold as 1 inch thick is actually $\frac{13}{16}$ of an inch thick. When lumber is requested, this variation must be taken into consideration.

Plywood is made in sheets 4 by 8 feet. The request for plywood must indicate whether the plywood is to be *clear* (without knots) on both sides or on just one side.

Power Tools

Some woodworking and plastic operations can be accomplished more easily, quickly, and accurately with power tools. Some of the more common power tools are discussed in this section.

Bandsaw

The bandsaw consists of metal band with teeth that is tracked over two or three rubber-tired pulley wheels. Although it can be used to cut a variety of materials including wood, it cannot perform as many different operations as the circular saw.

Cutting should be done only when the saw is running at full speed. The stock is fed into the blade with light pressure from one hand; the other hand helps guide the work. Both hands must be kept well away from the blade. The blade must be the appropriate width for the size of the circle to be cut. The more narrow the blade, the smaller the circle that may be cut. Attempting to cut too small a circle can pinch or break the blade. In some designs, several cuts can be made to the edge of the curve to break it into smaller parts and release the pinch on the blade. A change in the sound of the saw often indicates when the blade is being pinched.

A square corner may be cut by boring a hole in the square corner and cutting the stock sawed away. Although stock is usually fed into the band saw manually, it is possible to use a *fence* for straight cuts or a miter gauge for miter cuts.

Several pieces of lumber can be sawed at the same time. One way to keep all the pieces in proper alignment is to drive flails or brads into the waste parts through all the pieces. Care must be taken, however, to avoid sawing through the nails.

Sawing at an angle is accomplished by tilting the table of the saw to the desired angle as indicated on the gauge under the table.

Jigsaw

The jigsaw is regarded by some as an auxiliary to the bandsaw. It can be used for such sawing operations as curved outlines or pierced work that cannot be performed with a bandsaw. The jigsaw blade moves rapidly up and down through a $\frac{1}{8}$ to $\frac{3}{4}$-inch stroke; it saws on the downward part of the stroke. The jigsaw can be either a hand-held or bench type.

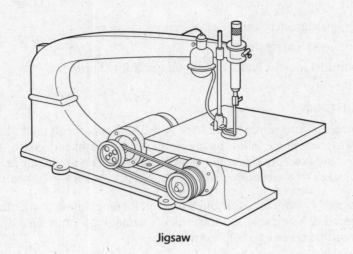

Jigsaw

Table or Circular Saw

The table saw is considered by some to be the most useful power tool. A motor-driven circular saw blade is adjusted by a hand wheel until it projects through a slot in the top of the flat cast-iron table a little farther than the thickness of the board to be sawed. The fence is set as far from the blade as the length of the lumber to be cut; the wood is fed into the saw by holding it against this guide. It is possible to perform various operations, such as grooving and mitering, by adjusting the saw or by using different blades. To be safe, use a saw guard.

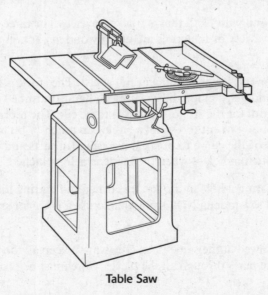

Table Saw

The saw is sized according to the maximum diameter of the saw blade used with the machine, such as a 7-, 8-, or 10-inch blade.

Three types of circular saw blades are used for all ordinary work: the *rip blade,* the *crosscut blade,* and the *combination blade.* The combination blade, which has both crosscut and ripsaw teeth, can be used for both ripping and crosscutting. For general shop work, this blade is used the most frequently.

Sanders

Two types of power sanders are most commonly used:

- **Disk sander:** A disk sander is a sandpaper-covered metal disk that is rotated rapidly by a motor. An adjustable table fastened to the sander can be tilted to hold the stock at an angle for beveling. The disk can also be attached to an electric drill for hand use.
- **Belt sander:** The belt sander is used to sand flat as well as curved surfaces. Sanding is done by pressing the work against an abrasive belt. Types of belt sanders include the vertical, the horizontal, and the combination of disk and belt sander. Also available is a sander that can be used in either the vertical or the horizontal position, or as a portable hand tool.

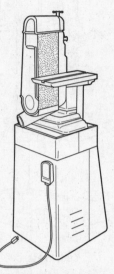

Vertical Belt Sander

Portable Belt Sander

Drill Press

A drill press consists of a vertical column set in a bench or floor base, with a motor on the upper end of the column to drive the drill. Both the column and drill are moved down to the work by means of either a hand-operated or foot-operated lever. The press is equipped with a depth-gauge mechanism. The table can be raised, lowered, or tilted 45° to both sides.

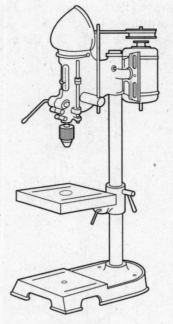

Drill Press

Jointer

The jointer is essentially an electric planer. It differs from an electric planer, however, in that it is designed to plane the *edges* of wood so that they can be joined together. The planer is designed to smooth the surfaces of wood. The size of a jointer is determined by the maximum width of the stock that can be passed through it, such as a 6-inch width.

Lathe

The wood-turning lathe, invented centuries before other machines, rotates a piece of wood on a horizontal axis to allow it to be shaped with a hand tool. This machine is unique in that the art and skill of hand-tool work must be combined with the mechanical movement of the machine. The lathe is sized by the distance between the headstock and the lathe bed. A 6-inch lathe will turn a 12-inch bowl.

Portable Router

A portable router consists of a high-speed motor mounted to a base that is fitted with two handles and a guide for cutting both straight and curved edges. It is held in the hands and guided over the stock. The depth of the cut can be controlled by adjusting the depth gauge. The portable router is used for veining, shaping, and other purposes:

- **Veining:** To *vein* and *flute* means to cut shallow grooves. Veined lines are narrow; flutes are somewhat larger. These grooves are used to decorate a wood surface.
- **Shaping:** Shaping work may be done with special bits that have a round shank below the cutting edges.
- **Miscellaneous work:** Small holes, mortises, grooves, dadoes, and rabbets may be easily and quickly made with a router.

Working with Concrete

One of the strongest building mediums is concrete. Concrete is a mixture of cement, sand, gravel, and water, combined in specific proportions. Mixing them produces a chemical reaction that changes these separate materials into a uniform compound. Concrete is ideal for building driveways and runways or for small jobs such as constructing steps or anchoring fence posts.

For big jobs, it is normal to have the concrete delivered by a specialized truck. The truck is equipped with an apparatus that continually mixes the ingredients so they are ready to use.

To determine how much concrete you need, measure the length times the width times the thickness that you intend to pour. After you know how much you need, you can either order it by the truckload, or if it is a small amount, you can prepare it yourself.

Concrete is prepared by mixing cement with sand, gravel, and water in a container, such as a trough or a wheelbarrow. Premixed concrete only requires you to add water. Using a shovel, work the mixture thoroughly until the proper consistency is reached. If it is too dry, it will not float in the frame, and pieces or chunks will show. If it is too wet, it will not adhere properly, nor will it dry well.

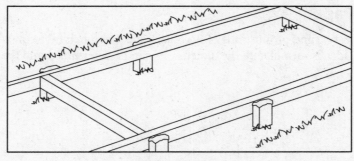

Building a Form

Concrete is normally poured into a form that you can create with scrap wood. The form can be straight or curved. Normally, if you're pouring a walk or driveway, you will want to pour about 4 inches of concrete, and thus you should dig down at least 6 inches and fill the bottom 2 inches with sand or gravel. Pack down the filler with a concrete block or special tamping tool. Pour the concrete on top of the filler.

As you pour the concrete, continue to smooth it down with a trowel. Then, using a long, flat board, run it over the surface in a back-and-forth sawing motion to ensure that everything is level. This process is called *screeding*. Then, using a tool called a *darby,* give a final smoothing to make sure there are no unsightly bumps, ridges, or open areas along the frame.

After the concrete has dried, you should apply a concrete sealer. It is helpful to cover the concrete with a plastic tarp to let it dry slowly and make sure all of the water has evaporated.

To join bricks or cement blocks, you would use concrete of the same consistency as you would to pour a sidewalk. Because this job is smaller and you're not pouring the cement, use a mason's trowel to apply (*butter*) concrete to the bricks. Then fit the blocks in the appropriate pattern, and, using a jointer, finish the joints between the bricks.

Keep in mind that well-mixed and cured concrete reaches most of its strength in about a month.

To clean an existing concrete walk or driveway, use a stiff brush and a mixture of muriatic acid (5%) and water. Make sure to wear protective clothing, gloves, and eye protection. After scrubbing, flush the acid wash with a trisodium phosphate solution and then use your garden hose to wash it clean. Again, use a sealer to preserve the finish.

Design, Planning, and Layout

Design

The three elements of good design are usefulness, durability, and proportions pleasing to the eye.

For a piece to be useful, it must fulfill the purpose for which it is intended. The size depends in part upon the use to which it will be put and where it will be used. Somewhat standard heights exist for chairs, tables, coffee tables, lamps, and similar projects. These standard measurements should be used unless a good reason makes deviation logical. A table designed to fit into a small space in the kitchen should be made the standard table height so that it will fit with chairs and other furniture. An invaluable source for standard measurements of many everyday items is a large mail-order catalog.

Durability of a project is achieved by using suitable materials and observing proper construction techniques.

Proportion is the size relationship of the parts to the whole object. A good proportion relationship is 2 to 3; a table that is 2 units wide and 3 units long is in proportion. Deviations from this basic rule, however, can be interesting and pleasing.

Putting Ideas on Paper

When planning the general style and proportions of an object, it is often helpful to make a number of small sketches. After the general idea is formulated, the dimensions can be determined and the pieces drawn to scale.

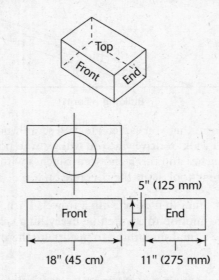

Arrangement of a Three-View Drawing

In the drawings, an object may be shown from several views. The front-view drawing is usually sketched on the lower part of the paper with the side view to one side of it. If a top view is necessary, it is customarily drawn above the front view. These drawings are usually made to scale with various types of lines used to convey specific meanings.

Step-by-Step Planning

Proper planning is worthwhile in time saved and in the quality of the finished product. Each joint must be planned. The operations must be carried out in the proper sequence, and the proper tools must be used for each operation.

Layout

Laying out the pattern for your building material is the important first step. Errors made in measuring are almost impossible to correct later.

1. Examine the lumber for cracks, knots, or any other flaws. Plan the layout of the pattern so that these flaws will not be incorporated into (or be visible in) the completed project.

2. Ensure that the lumber is of the required thickness.

3. Lay out the pattern to avoid waste of lumber.

4. Use a square for marking lines so that the cuts will be square with the edge.

5. Check the measurements before starting the sawing process.

Auto and Shop Information Practice Questions

1. The _____ means that each cycle is made up of four strokes.

    A. four-stroke cycle
    B. quad four
    C. rotary cycle
    D. None of the above.

2. The engine block cylinders are closed at the top by a

    A. piston.
    B. air filter.
    C. cylinder head.
    D. All of the above.

3. Car engines generally use

    A. four, six, or eight cylinders.
    B. diesel fuel.
    C. glow plugs.
    D. manual transmissions.

4. Higher-performance engines usually call for higher-octane fuel because they

    A. operate with higher compression.
    B. require more oxygen.
    C. burn fuel faster.
    D. None of the above.

5. There are many technical terms that relate to engine performance: _____, torque, bore, stroke, and displacement are just a few.

    A. Newton-meters
    B. kilopascals
    C. horsepower
    D. amperes

6. The strokes of the combustion process occur in a specific sequence and are called the _____ stroke, _____ stroke, _____ stroke, and _____ stroke.

    A. exhaust, compression, intake, power
    B. compression, intake, power, exhaust
    C. power, intake, compression, exhaust
    D. intake, compression, power, exhaust

7. Most automatic transmissions have a final drive gear called the _____ gear.

    A. passing
    B. overdrive
    C. reverse
    D. neutral

8. In a combustion engine, the _____ aids in creating a seal between the cylinder wall and the piston.

    A. crank shaft
    B. piston rings
    C. manifold
    D. bearings

9. With a manual transmission, the _____ connects and disconnects the engine crankshaft to the transmission.

    A. clutch assembly
    B. flex plate
    C. bell housing
    D. All of the above.

10. The drivetrain transfers power from the _____ to the _____.

    A. engine, transmission
    B. tires, pavement
    C. tires, transmission
    D. engine, driving wheels

11. A _____ brake system matches a front brake hydraulic circuit on one side with a rear brake hydraulic circuit on the other side.

    A. diagonally split
    B. disc/drum
    C. front and rear split
    D. None of the above.

12. A _____ front suspension is a combination strut and shock absorber mounted inside a coil spring.

    A. torsion bar
    B. coil spring
    C. MacPherson strut
    D. All of the above.

13. The brake linings contact the drum or rotor and through friction convert the _____ to _____.

    A. motion energy, stopping power
    B. vehicle's speed, rested power
    C. motion energy, heat energy
    D. heat energy, stopping distance

14. _____ hold the vehicle up while _____ work to control or dampen the action of the spring.

    A. Springs, shocks
    B. Tires, struts
    C. Shocks, springs
    D. Struts, dampers

15. _____ are used in currently produced vehicles.

    A. Torsion bars
    B. Leaf springs
    C. Coil springs
    D. All of the above.

16. While sharpening a chisel, you should dip it in cold water frequently. This action is called

    A. steeling.
    B. bluing.
    C. tempering.
    D. washing.

17. When clamping large pieces of wood stock together, you would normally use a

    A. vise.
    B. bar clamp.
    C. C-clamp.
    D. miter clamp.

18. To round over an edge of a wooden table, you would use a

    A. router.
    B. electric drill.
    C. electric plane.
    D. miter box.

19. To pour a curved walk for concrete, you should

    A. build a form from wood.
    B. cut the surrounding grass to fit the shape.
    C. pour the concrete and shape it with a trowel.
    D. mark the boundaries with string.

20. The final smoothing of a concrete driveway should be done with a

    A. trowel.
    B. 2 × 4 board.
    C. darby.
    D. rake.

21. The term "hardwood" refers to

    A. the wood's capability to withstand drilling.
    B. the type of tree from which the wood comes.
    C. the wood's tensile strength.
    D. whether or not the wood can be used for woodworking.

22. Hammers are most commonly classified by the

    A. width of the head.
    B. material used to make the head.
    C. weight of the head.
    D. length of the shaft.

23. A miter clamp is used to

    A. hold together long pieces of wood.
    B. hold together the edges of a picture frame.
    C. steady wood when sawing.
    D. hold plastic tubing.

24. To affix a sheet of veneer to a plywood countertop, you would use

    A. epoxy.
    B. white glue.
    C. contact cement.
    D. finishing nails.

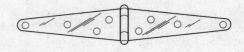

25. The illustration above is an example of a

    A. butt hinge.
    B. T-hinge.
    C. spring hinge.
    D. strap hinge.

Answers and Explanations for Practice Questions

1. **A.** The four cycles of the internal combustion engine are intake, compression, power, and exhaust.

2. **C.** The engine block is where the crankshaft, connecting rods, and pistons are located. The engine block is sealed by a cylinder head gasket and cylinder head.

3. **A.** The most common engines used in today's vehicles are 4 (inline), 6 (inline and V), and 8 (V) cylinders. Other configurations are used as well. Examples are the Honda inline 3 cylinders, Audi inline 5 cylinders, and Chrysler and Ford V10. Some manufacturers use an inline 8 and V12 and V16 engines.

4. **A.** Higher-performance engines generally use cylinders with higher compression ratios and are more prone to detonation, and therefore require higher-octane fuel. The octane rating of gasoline refers to the mixture's capability to resist detonation.

5. **C.** Horsepower is a unit of power that measures the rate at which a mechanical device performs work.

6. **D.** The following takes place in the internal combustion four-cycle ignition-fired engine. Intake: Air and fuel are introduced into the cylinder (intake valve open). Compression: Air and fuel are compressed with both valves (intake and exhaust) closed. Power: The spark plug fires and the piston is forced into the downward stroke with both valves closed. Exhaust: The piston now moves upward from the burn that has taken place in the previous cycle. The exhaust valve is open for emissions. Diesel engines do not use a spark plug; they use 20 to 1 or more compression ratio to heat the air mixture in the cylinder. The diesel engine sprays fuel into the cylinder with the correct timing (cycle) and burns the mixture.

7. **B.** Most manufacturers use overdrive for better fuel economy. The overdrive gear is like fourth or fifth gear on a standard transmission. When the vehicle is at the correct speed and rpm, overdrive is applied by the computer that controls solenoids in the transmission. This gives the driveline a 1:1 ratio.

8. **B.** Piston rings surround the pistons and seal them against the cylinder walls. Because no piston can fit tightly enough in the cylinder bore, the rings are used to help provide a seal to keep the air-fuel mixture and burnt gases in the combustion chambers.

9. **A.** The clutch plate is a thin steel disc connected to the transmission input shaft by a hub. The disc is covered with material that is similar to the brake linings. The clutch assembly consists of parts that allow the clutch, a thin composite disc attached to the engine output, to come into contact with the clutch plate, a steel plate attached to output of the transmission.

10. **D.** The engine produces power that is transferred through the transmission (transfer case power) to the wheels. This transfer from the transmission is accomplished with the help of the drive shaft and/or CV axles.

11. **A.** Many front-wheel drive vehicles with disc and drum brakes use the diagonally split brake system. This system connects the right front caliper and the left rear wheel cylinder through one chamber of the master cylinder. The left front caliper and right rear wheel cylinder will be connected the same way.

12. **C.** The MacPherson strut unit consists of a shock absorber, coil spring, upper pivot plate, bearing, and lower metal rim that sometimes uses a rubber insert. The upper plate assembly usually has three studs that attach the unit to the vehicle's body. The lower end is usually attached to a hub knuckle.

13. **C.** The brake system uses friction material to slow or stop the vehicle when the brake pedal is depressed. Brake pads/shoes are forced into contact with the brake rotor/drums that slow the rotation of the wheels.

14. **A.** Springs take the weight of the frame and body and work to level and stabilize the vehicle. Shocks control bounce and some of the body roll of a vehicle.

15. **D.** Manufacturers use different types of springs on today's cars and trucks. Their construction, shapes, sizes, rates, and capacities vary. Types include leaf springs, coil springs, air springs, torsion bars, and electromagnetic springs. Their main job is to stabilize the vehicle while keeping a specific ride height.

16. **C.** Dipping hot steel into water is a way to temper the metal, maintaining its strength, which may be lost from the heat that builds up during the grinding process.

17. **B.** A bar clamp is a steel clamp with openings as wide as 6 feet or more, ideal for large projects.

18. **A.** You would use a round-over bit in a router. Or, if you wanted to create a decorative edge on the tabletop, you have hundreds of bit designs you could use in the router to create almost any style you want.

19. **A.** The proper way to pour any walk or curved area is to build a form from wood so that the concrete will flow into that form in the shape you desire. After the concrete has cured, you should remove the form; the shape will remain.

20. **C.** A darby is a long, smooth board with a handle used specifically for smoothing concrete.

21. **B.** Hardwoods and softwoods have nothing to do with the hardness or softness of the wood. The terms refer to the types of trees from which the wood comes.

22. **C.** Hammers are sized by the weight of their head. The most common head weights are 12, 16, and 20 ounces. For general use, the best option is to use the 16-ounce head.

23. **B.** A miter clamp is designed to hold together corners of molding as well as picture frames.

24. **C.** Contact cement is perfect for attaching surfaces. The contact cement is applied to both sides of the pieces to be joined—in this case, the plywood top and the underside of the veneer. When both sides are dry and tacky, the veneer is carefully laid on top of the plywood surface. After the two sides have touched, they cannot be moved or adjusted. To remove any air bubbles between surfaces, use a roller to push them out.

25. **D.** The strap hinge is usually used on garage and cellar doors, gates, and even toolboxes.

Mathematics Knowledge

The Mathematics Knowledge section of the ASVAB tests your knowledge of major concepts and principles taught in high school math. While you will, of course, need to perform some mathematical computations in the course of solving these problems, the emphasis is not on computation. Instead, the emphasis is on mathematical procedures and ideas.

The following section contains a summary of the math you need to know to be able to answer the questions on the test. The material has been written as a continuation of the material discussed in the Arithmetic Reasoning section, so if you are not familiar with that material, it is a good idea to review it now. In addition to the examples throughout, at the end of this section is a series of questions that review the material and give you a lot of practice for the test itself.

> The ASVAB contains 25 Mathematics Knowledge questions. You will have 24 minutes to answer these questions.

Number Theory

Factors

Whole numbers are the set of numbers 0, 1, 2, 3, 4, 5, and so on. This section looks at some of the properties of whole numbers, and then those of the set of numbers called the *integers*, the positive and negative numbers and zero.

To begin, a *factor* of a given whole number is any whole number that you can use in multiplication that results in the given whole number. For example, consider the whole number 24. Both 6 and 4 are factors of 24 because $6 \times 4 = 24$. Further, both 2 and 12 are factors of 24, because $2 \times 12 = 24$. Technically, both 1 and 24 are also factors of 24 because $1 \times 24 = 24$.

To determine whether a particular number is a factor of a given whole number, simply divide the number into the given whole number. If you have no remainder, then the number is a factor.

---

1. Is 8 a factor of 72?

To determine if 8 is a factor of 72, divide 8 into 72. Because it goes in evenly (9 times), 8 is a factor of 72.

---

2. If 13 is a factor of 91, determine another factor other than 1 and 91.

You are told that 13 is a factor of 91, so you know that if you divide 13 into 91 it will go in evenly. If you perform this division, you get $13\overline{)91}$ with quotient 7.

Thus, $13 \times 7 = 91$, so 7 is another factor of 91.

Common Factors

A number that is a factor of each of two different whole numbers is called a *common factor,* or a *common divisor,* of those numbers. As the following examples show, two given whole numbers may have no common factors (other than, of course, 1) or they may have one or more. If two numbers have several common factors, the largest one is called the *greatest common factor.*

> Find all of the common factors and the greatest common factor of 36 and 48.

The factors of 36 are 1, 2, 3, 4, 6, 9, 12, 18, and 36.

The factors of 48 are 1, 2, 3, 4, 6, 8, 12, 16, 24, and 48.

The common factors of 36 and 48 are 1, 2, 3, 4, 6, and 12.

The greatest common factor is 12.

Prime Numbers

Obviously, every number has at least two factors—the number itself and 1. Some other numbers have additional factors. For example, the number 14 not only has 1 and 14 as factors, but also 2 and 7, because $2 \times 7 = 14$.

Numbers that have no additional factors other than themselves and 1 are known as *prime numbers*. An example of a prime number is 13. While 1 and 13 divide evenly into 13, no other whole numbers divide evenly into 13.

By definition, the smallest prime number is 2. The number 1 is not a prime number. The first 10 prime numbers are

$$2, 3, 5, 7, 11, 13, 17, 19, 23, 29$$

To determine if a number is prime or not, you need to find out if any whole numbers (other than the number itself and 1) divide evenly into the number.

> **1.** Which of the following numbers are prime: 33, 37, 39, 42, 43?

33 is not prime because $33 = 3 \times 11$.

37 is prime; it has no factors other than 1 and 37.

39 is not prime because $39 = 3 \times 13$.

42 is not prime because $42 = 2 \times 21$, or 6×7, and so on.

43 is prime; it has no factors other than 1 and 43.

A number that is not prime is called a *composite number*. Any composite number can be *prime factored*—that is, can be written as a product of prime numbers in one, and only one, way. For example, 35 is a composite number, and can be prime-factored as 5×7. The number 12 is also composite. Note that 2×6 is a factorization of 12, but is not the prime factorization because 6 is not prime. The prime factorization of 12 would be $2 \times 2 \times 3$. The quickest way to prime-factor a number is to break up the number as a product of two smaller numbers, and then break those two numbers up, until you are left with only prime numbers. The example below illustrates this process.

> **2.** Prime-factor the number 150.

By inspection, you can see that 150 can be factored as 15×10. This is not the prime factorization, however, as neither 15 nor 10 is prime. The number 15, however, can be further broken down as $15 = 3 \times 5$, and both 3 and 5 are prime. The number 10 can be further broken down as $10 = 2 \times 5$, and both 2 and 5 are prime. Therefore, the number 150 can be prime-factored as $3 \times 5 \times 2 \times 5$. When prime-factoring numbers, it is standard to rearrange the factors so that the numbers are in increasing order. Therefore, the prime factorization of 150 can best be expressed as $2 \times 3 \times 5 \times 5$.

Multiples

A *multiple* of a given whole number is a number that results from the multiplication of the given whole number by another whole-number factor. For example, the multiples of 7 are 7, 14, 21, 28, 35, 42, 49, and so on, because $7 = 7 \times 1$, $14 = 7 \times 2$, $21 = 7 \times 3$, and so on.

A *common multiple* of two numbers is a number that is a multiple of both numbers. For example, 32 is a common multiple of both 8 and 16 because it is a multiple of both 8 and 16. Should you ever need to find a common multiple of two numbers, one quick way is to multiply the two numbers together. For example, a common multiple of 4 and 10 would be $4 \times 10 = 40$. Note, however, that 40 is not the smallest common multiple of 4 and 10 because 20 is also a common multiple.

The smallest common multiple of two numbers is called the *least common multiple,* abbreviated *LCM.* A quick way to find the LCM of two numbers is to write out the first several multiples of each number, and then find the smallest multiple that they have in common. The examples that follow show this process.

---

1. Find the first eight multiples of 11.

To answer this question, you simply need to compute 11×1, 11×2, 11×3, and so on. The first eight multiples would be 11, 22, 33, 44, 55, 66, 77, and 88.

---

2. Find the least common multiple of 3 and 8.

The first several multiples of 3 are 3, 6, 9, 12, 15, 18, 21, 24, and 27.

The first several multiples of 8 are 8, 16, 24, 32.

The LCM is 24 (in this case, the LCM is the same as the product of 3 and 8).

Exponents

As you saw previously, the numbers that you use in multiplication are called factors. Whenever the same factor is repeated more than once, you can use a special shorthand, called *exponential notation,* to simplify the expression. In this notation, the repeated factor (called the *base*) is written only once, and above and to the right of this number is written another number called the *exponent* or *power,* which indicates the number of times the base is repeated.

For example, instead of writing 7×7, you can write 7^2. This expression is read "7 to the second power," or more simply, "7 squared," and represents the fact that the 7 is multiplied by itself. In the same way, $5 \times 5 \times 5 \times 5$ can be written as 5^4, which is read "5 to the fourth power," or simply "5 to the fourth."

Recall that earlier you saw how to prime-factor the number 150 and obtain $2 \times 3 \times 5 \times 5$. It is more common (and a bit simpler) to write this prime factorization using exponential notation as $2 \times 3 \times 5^2$.

---

1. What is the value of 3^5?

Based on the definition above, 3^5 represents $3 \times 3 \times 3 \times 3 \times 3 = 243$.

---

2. Simplify the expression $a \times a \times a \times a \times b \times b \times b \times b \times b \times b \times b$ by using exponential notation.

Because you have four factors of *a* and seven factors of *b,* the expression is equal to $a^4 \times b^7$.

---

3. Prime-factor the number 72, and write the prime factorization using exponential notation.

Begin by prime factoring the number 72. One way to prime-factor it is as follows:

$$72 = 2 \times 36 = 2 \times 6 \times 6 = 2 \times 2 \times 3 \times 2 \times 3 = 2 \times 2 \times 2 \times 3 \times 3$$

Then, writing this using exponents, you get $2^3 \times 3^2$.

Square Roots

The *square root* of a given number is the number whose square is equal to the given number. For example, the square root of 25 is the number which, when multiplied by itself, yields 25. This number would be 5 because $5 \times 5 = 25$. The square root of 25 is denoted by the symbol $\sqrt{25}$.

The square roots of most numbers turn out to be messy, infinite, nonrepeating decimal numbers. For example, $\sqrt{2}$ is equal to 1.414213562 . . . to nine decimal places. When such numbers appear on the test, you will be able to leave them in what is known as *radical form*. That is, if the answer to a problem is $\sqrt{2}$, you can express the answer as $\sqrt{2}$, without worrying about its value.

There are, however, certain numbers that have nice whole-number square roots. Such numbers are called *perfect squares*. You should certainly be familiar with the square roots of the first ten or so perfect squares. You can see them in the following table.

Perfect Square	Square Root
1	$\sqrt{1} = 1$
4	$\sqrt{4} = 2$
9	$\sqrt{9} = 3$
16	$\sqrt{16} = 4$
25	$\sqrt{25} = 5$
36	$\sqrt{36} = 6$
49	$\sqrt{49} = 7$
64	$\sqrt{64} = 8$
81	$\sqrt{81} = 9$
100	$\sqrt{100} = 10$

From time to time, the test may ask you to find the cube root of a number. The cube root is similar to the square root. For example, the cube root of 8 is the number that, when multiplied by itself three times, is equal to 8. The cube root of 8 would be 2, because $2 \times 2 \times 2 = 8$. Cube roots also have a special notation. The cube root of 8 is written as $\sqrt[3]{8}$. Therefore, $\sqrt[3]{8} = 2$.

Just as perfect squares have whole-number square roots, perfect cubes have whole-number cube roots. You don't really have to learn many of these, as they become large very quickly, but it is helpful to know the cube roots of the first five perfect cubes. The following table gives the values for these numbers.

Perfect Cube	Cube Root
1	$\sqrt[3]{1} = 1$
8	$\sqrt[3]{8} = 2$
27	$\sqrt[3]{27} = 3$
64	$\sqrt[3]{64} = 4$
125	$\sqrt[3]{125} = 5$

> **1.** What is the value of $\sqrt{81} \times \sqrt{36}$?

Because $\sqrt{81} = 9$ and $\sqrt{36} = 6$, $\sqrt{81} \times \sqrt{36} = 9 \times 6 = 54$.

> **2.** What is the value of $12\sqrt{49}$?

To begin, you must know that $12\sqrt{49}$ is shorthand for $12 \times \sqrt{49}$. Then, because $\sqrt{49} = 7$, $12\sqrt{49} = 12 \times 7 = 84$.

The Order of Operations

When a numerical expression contains more than one mathematical operation, the order in which you perform the operations can affect the answer. For example, consider the simple expression $2 + 3 \times 5$. If you perform the addition first, the expression becomes $5 \times 5 = 25$. On the other hand, if you perform the multiplication first, the expression becomes $2 + 15 = 17$. To eliminate this ambiguity, mathematicians have established a specific order in which to perform the operations. This procedure is called the *order of operations,* and is stated below:

1. Perform all operations in parentheses or any other grouping symbol.
2. Evaluate all exponents and roots.
3. Perform all multiplications and divisions in the order they appear in the expression, from left to right.
4. Perform all additions and subtractions in the order they appear in the expression, from left to right.

Note, then, that the order of operations consists of four steps. A common acronym to help you remember these steps is PEMDAS—parentheses, exponents, multiplication and division, addition and subtraction. If you choose to memorize this acronym, be careful. The expression PEMDAS may make it appear as if the order of operations has six steps, but actually it has only four. In the third step, all multiplications and divisions are performed in the order they appear. In the fourth step, all additions and subtractions are performed in the order they appear. The examples that follow will help make this clear.

> **1.** Evaluate the expression $18 - 6 \div 3 \times 7 + 4$.

Resist the temptation to begin by subtracting 6 from 18. Because this expression contains no parentheses and no roots, begin by starting on the left and performing all multiplications and divisions in the order they occur. This means that the division must be performed first. Because $6 \div 3 = 2$, you obtain

$$18 - 6 \div 3 \times 7 + 4 = 18 - 2 \times 7 + 4$$
$$18 - 2 \times 7 + 4 = 18 - 14 + 4$$
$$18 - 14 + 4 = 4 + 4 = 8$$

> **2.** Evaluate $14 - 2(1 + 5)$.

To begin, you must perform the operation in parentheses. The expression becomes $14 - 2(6)$. Now, remember that a number written next to another number in parentheses, such as $2(6)$, is a way of indicating multiplication. Because multiplication comes before subtraction in the order of operations, you multiply $2(6)$ to get 12. Finally, $14 - 12 = 2$.

> **3.** Evaluate $5^3 - 3(8 - 2)^2$.

The first operation to perform is the one in parentheses, which gives you $5^3 - 3(6)^2$.

Next, evaluate the two exponents: $125 - 3(36)$. You now multiply, and then finish by subtracting: $125 - 108 = 17$.

Operations with Integers

When you include the negatives of the whole numbers along with the whole numbers, you obtain the set of numbers called the *integers*. Integers are the set of positive and negative whole numbers that extend forever on either side of 0, including 0:

$$\ldots -4, -3, -2, -1, 0, 1, 2, 3, 4, \ldots$$

The dots to the left and right indicate that the numbers continue forever in both directions.

Up to this point in the chapter, when adding, subtracting, multiplying, and dividing, you have worked with positive numbers. However, on the ASVAB, you are just as likely to have to compute with negative numbers as positive numbers. Therefore, this chapter looks at how to perform mathematical operations on positive *and* negative numbers—that is, how to perform mathematical operations on *signed* numbers.

Adding Positive and Negative Numbers

You have two circumstances to consider when adding positive and negative numbers. The first circumstance is adding two signed numbers that both have the same sign; the second is adding numbers with different signs.

If the numbers that you are adding have the same sign, simply add the numbers in the usual way. The sum will then have the same sign as the numbers you have added. For example

$(+4) + (+7) = +11$

$(-5) + (-9) = -14$

In the second problem above, because the signs of the two numbers you are adding are the same, simply add them $(5 + 9 = 14)$. The result is negative, however, because both numbers are negative. It may help to think of positive numbers as representing a gain, and negative numbers as representing a loss. In this case, $(-5) + (-9)$ represents a loss of 5 followed by a loss 9, which, of course, is a loss of 14.

Now, what if you have to add two numbers with different signs? Again, the rule is simple. Begin by ignoring the signs, and subtract the two numbers—the smaller from the larger. The sign of the answer is the same as the sign of the number with the larger size, again, ignoring signs.

For example, to compute $(+9) + (-5)$, begin by computing $9 - 5 = 4$. Then, because 9 is bigger than 5, the answer is positive, or +4. You can think of the problem in this way: A gain of 9 followed by a loss of 5 is equivalent to a gain of 4.

On the other hand, to compute $(-9) + (+5)$, begin in the same way, by computing $9 - 5 = 4$. This time, however, the "larger" number is negative, so the answer is –4. In other words, a loss of 9 followed by a gain of 5 is equivalent to a loss of 4.

> $(+6) + (-8) + (+12) + (-4) =$

You can evaluate this expression in two ways. One way is to simply perform the additions in order from left to right. To begin, $(+6) + (-8) = -2$. Then, $(-2) + (+12) = +10$. Finally, $(+10) + (-4) = +6$.

The other way to solve the problem—which may be a bit quicker—is to add the positive numbers, then add the negative numbers, and then combine the result. In this case, $(+6) + (+12) = +18$, $(-8) + (-4) = -12$, and, finally $(+18) + (-12) = +6$.

Subtracting Positive and Negative Numbers

The easiest way to perform subtraction on two signed numbers is to change the problem to an equivalent addition problem—that is, an addition problem with the same answer. To do this, simply change the sign of the second number and add instead of subtract. For example, suppose you need to compute $(+7) - (-2)$. This problem will have the same solution as the addition problem $(+7) + (+2)$, and is therefore equal to $+9$. Take a look at the samples below to help clarify the procedure:

To evaluate $(-7) - (+2)$, make the problem into an equivalent addition problem by changing the sign of the second number. Therefore, $(-7) - (+2) = (-7) + (-2) = -9$.

In the same way, you see that $(-7) - (-2) = (-7) + (+2) = -5$.

> Find the value of $(-7) - (+4) - (-3) + (-1)$.

Begin by rewriting the problem with all subtractions expressed as additions:

$$(-7) - (+4) - (-3) + (-1) = (-7) + (-4) + (+3) + (-1)$$

Now, just add the four numbers in the usual way:

$$(-7) + (-4) + (+3) + (-1) = (-11) + (+3) + (-1) = -8 + (-1) = -9$$

Multiplying and Dividing Positive and Negative Numbers

An easy way to multiply (or divide) signed numbers is to begin by ignoring the signs, and multiply (or divide) in the usual way. Then, to determine the sign of the answer, count up the number of negative signs in the original problem. If the problem contained an even number of negative signs, the answer will be positive; if it contained an odd number of negative signs, the answer will be negative. Thus, $(-2) \times (+3) = -6$, because there is one negative sign in the original problem. However, $(-2) \times (-3) = +6$, because there are two negative signs in the original problem.

What about the problem $(-4) \times (-2) \times (-1) \times (+3)$? First of all, ignoring the signs and multiplying the four numbers, you get 24. Now, because the problem contains a total of three negative signs, the answer must be negative. Therefore, the answer is -24.

Division works in exactly the same way. For example, $(-24) \div (+6) = -4$, but $(-24) \div (-6) = +4$.

> 1. Find the value of $\dfrac{(-6)(+10)}{(-2)(-5)}$.

The easiest way to proceed with this problem is to evaluate the number on top and the number on the bottom separately, and then divide them. Now, because $(-6)(+10) = -60$, and $(-2)(-5) = +10$, you have

$$\frac{(-6)(+10)}{(-2)(-5)} = \frac{-60}{+10} = -6$$

> 2. Find the value of $(+5)(-2)(+4) - 6(-3)$.

The multiplications in this problem must be performed before the subtractions. Because $(+5)(-2)(+4) = -40$, and $6(-3) = -18$, you have

$$(+5)(-2)(+4) - 6(-3) = -40 - (-18) = -40 + 18 = -22$$

Negative Numbers and Exponents

Be careful when evaluating negative numbers raised to powers. For example, if you are asked to find the value of $(-2)^8$, the answer will be positive because you are technically multiplying eight -2s. On the other hand, for a similar reason, the value of $(-2)^9$ will be negative.

Also, you must be careful to distinguish between an expression like $(-3)^2$ and one like -3^2. The expression $(-3)^2$ means -3×-3 and is equal to $+9$. On the other hand, -3^2 means $-(3^2)$, which is equal to -9. According to the order of operations, you evaluate using the exponent before doing subtraction.

---

1. Evaluate $-2^4 - (-2)^2$.

Evaluating the exponents first, you get $-2^4 - (-2)^2 = -16 - (4) = -16 - 4 = -20$.

---

2. Find the value of $\dfrac{(-3)^3 + (-2)(-6)}{-5^2 + (-19)(-1)}$.

Again, determine the values of the top and bottom separately and then divide. To begin, $(-3)^3 = -27$, and $(-2)(-6) = +12$, so the value on the top is $-27 + 12 = -15$. On the bottom, you have $-25 + 19 = -6$. Therefore:

$$\frac{(-3)^3 + (-2)(-6)}{-5^2 + (-19)(-1)} = \frac{-15}{-6} = \frac{15}{6} = 2.5$$

Operations with Fractions

The Arithmetic Reasoning section of this book covers how to write a fraction as a decimal and vice versa. One thing that it doesn't cover is how to perform arithmetic operations on fractions. This section reviews these operations.

Equivalent Fractions

You probably remember learning a procedure called *reducing* or *simplifying* fractions. Simplifying a fraction refers to rewriting it in an equivalent form, with smaller numbers. As an easy example, consider the fraction $\frac{5}{10}$. You can simplify this fraction by dividing the top and bottom numbers by the number 5. When you perform this division, you get $\frac{5}{10} = \frac{5 \div 5}{10 \div 5} = \frac{1}{2}$. Thus, $\frac{5}{10}$ and $\frac{1}{2}$ have the same value, but $\frac{1}{2}$ is in simpler form.

In general, to simplify a fraction, you need to find a number that will divide evenly into both the top and bottom numbers, and then perform this division. Sometimes, after you divide by one number, you may notice another number you can further divide by.

For example, suppose you wish to simplify $\frac{12}{18}$. The first thing you may notice is that the top and bottom can be divided by 2. Dividing by 2, you get the fraction $\frac{6}{9}$. Now, this fraction can be further divided by 3, and if you do this division, you get the fraction $\frac{2}{3}$. Because there are no other numbers (except 1, of course) that can divide evenly into the top and bottom, you have reduced the fraction to *lowest terms*.

If a problem on the test has a fractional answer, you should always reduce the answer to lowest terms.

Just as you can reduce a fraction to lower terms by dividing the top and bottom by the same number, you can raise a fraction to *higher terms* by multiplying the top and bottom by the same number. Consider the fraction $\frac{3}{4}$. If you multiply the top and bottom by 2, you get $\frac{6}{8}$. If you instead multiply the top and bottom by 5, you get $\frac{15}{20}$. The fractions $\frac{6}{8}$ and $\frac{15}{20}$ are two different ways to write $\frac{3}{4}$ in higher terms. As you can see in the next section, it is often necessary to raise fractions to higher terms to be able to add and subtract them.

> **1.** Express the fraction $\frac{12}{15}$ in lowest terms.

The number 3 can be divided evenly into both the top and bottom numbers. Performing this division, you get $\frac{12}{15} = \frac{12 \div 3}{15 \div 3} = \frac{4}{5}$, which is in lowest terms.

> **2.** Rewrite the fraction $\frac{2}{3}$ as an equivalent fraction with a denominator of 21.

To change the denominator of 3 to 21, you need to multiply by 7. Because you need to perform the same operation to the numerator as well, you would get $\frac{2}{3} = \frac{2 \times 7}{3 \times 7} = \frac{14}{21}$.

Adding and Subtracting Fractions

The number on the top of a fraction is called the *numerator* and the number on the bottom of a fraction is called the *denominator*. If two fractions have the same denominator, they are said to have *common denominators*.

Adding or subtracting two fractions with common denominators is easy. Simply add or subtract the numerators and retain the common denominator. For example

$$\frac{2}{9} + \frac{5}{9} = \frac{7}{9} \text{ and } \frac{7}{8} - \frac{5}{8} = \frac{2}{8} = \frac{1}{4}$$

Note that, in the subtraction problem, you get a fraction that can be simplified, and you perform the simplification before finishing.

If you need to add or subtract two fractions that do not have the same denominator, begin by raising them to higher terms so that they do have a common denominator. The first step in this process is determining a common denominator for the two fractions.

For example, suppose that you are asked to add $\frac{3}{4} + \frac{1}{3}$. You need to find a common denominator for 4 and 3. There are actually an infinite number of common denominators for 4 and 3. Some of them would be 24, 36, and 48. While you can work with any of these denominators, it is easiest to work with the smallest one, which in this case is 12. This number is the *least common denominator* of 4 and 3, and it is actually the same number as the least common multiple (discussed earlier). Thus, you can find the least common denominator by using the same process as you use to find the least common multiple.

After you know the least common denominator (LCD), simply multiply the top and bottom of each fraction by the appropriate number to raise the denominators to the LCD. In this case

$$\frac{3}{4} + \frac{1}{3} = \frac{3}{3} \times \frac{3}{4} + \frac{4}{4} \times \frac{1}{3} = \frac{9}{12} + \frac{4}{12} = \frac{13}{12}$$

Note that the answer, $\frac{13}{12}$, is an improper fraction. You can also write any improper fraction as a mixed number by dividing the denominator into the numerator and writing the remainder as the numerator of a fraction with the original denominator. In this case, 12 goes into 13 one time, with a remainder of 1, so $\frac{13}{12} = 1\frac{1}{12}$, which is another way to write the answer to the question.

Note that you can also reverse the process of making a mixed number into an improper fraction. So, for example, the mixed number $2\frac{1}{5}$ can be written as an improper fraction. The denominator is the same—5—and the numerator is the denominator times the whole number plus the numerator—$5 \times 2 + 1 = 11$. Therefore, $2\frac{1}{5} = \frac{11}{5}$. Often, when performing operations on mixed numbers, it is helpful to write them as improper fractions. The upcoming examples illustrate this.

> Add $2\frac{3}{5} + 3\frac{1}{7}$.

You can solve this equation in two ways. You can write both mixed numbers as improper fractions and add, but it is quicker to add the whole-number part ($2 + 3 = 5$) and the fractional part:

$$\frac{3}{5} + \frac{1}{7} = \frac{21}{35} + \frac{5}{35} = \frac{26}{35}$$

The answer is $5\frac{26}{35}$.

Multiplying and Dividing Fractions

Multiplying fractions is actually a bit easier than adding or subtracting them. When multiplying, you don't need to worry about common denominators—just multiply the numerators, and then multiply the denominators, and then simplify if possible. For example:

$$\frac{2}{3} \times \frac{4}{5} = \frac{2 \times 4}{3 \times 5} = \frac{8}{15}$$

That's all you need to do!

To understand the procedure for dividing fractions, you need to know one definition. The *reciprocal* of a number is the number that is obtained by switching the numerator and the denominator. For example, the reciprocal of $\frac{3}{8}$ is $\frac{8}{3}$. To find the reciprocal of a whole number, such as 7, visualize the 7 as the fraction $\frac{7}{1}$. The reciprocal, then, is $\frac{1}{7}$.

The easiest way to divide two fractions is to change the division sign to a multiplication sign and then change the second fraction to its reciprocal and multiply. For example

$$\frac{4}{5} \div \frac{3}{4} = \frac{4}{5} \times \frac{4}{3} = \frac{16}{15} = 1\frac{1}{15}$$

> 1. What is the value of $2\frac{2}{3} \times 1\frac{4}{5}$?

Before you can multiply these mixed numbers, you need to write them as improper fractions:

$$2\frac{2}{3} \times 1\frac{4}{5} = \frac{8}{3} \times \frac{9}{5} = \frac{72}{15} = 4\frac{12}{15} = 4\frac{4}{5}$$

> 2. Evaluate $2\frac{2}{5} \div 6$.

Begin by writing the problem as $\frac{12}{5} \div \frac{6}{1}$. Then

$$\frac{12}{5} \div \frac{6}{1} = \frac{12}{5} \times \frac{1}{6} = \frac{12}{30} = \frac{2}{5}$$

Algebraic Operations and Equations

Numerical Evaluation

Algebra is a generalization of arithmetic. In arithmetic, you learn how to perform mathematical operations (such as addition, subtraction, multiplication, and division) on different types of numbers, such as whole numbers, decimals, percentages, and fractions. Algebra extends these concepts by considering how to perform mathematical operations on symbols standing for numbers, and how to use these techniques to solve a variety of practical word problems.

In algebra, numbers that have a definite value are called *constants*. For example, the numbers $17, -3, \frac{2}{3}, \sqrt{41}$, 5.123, and 12% are constants. Symbols standing for numbers are called *variables* because, until it is further specified, they can take on any value. For example, in the expression $3x + 13y + 29$, the numbers 3, 13, and 29 are constants, and the symbols x and y are variables. As the examples that follow show, after you know the values of all variables in an expression, you can find the value of the expression.

---

1. If $a = 4$ and $b = -3$, find the value of the expression $a^3 - b$.

When evaluating numerical expressions, it is crucial to remember the order of operations and to pay careful attention to plus and minus signs. Begin by substituting the values of a and b into the given expression, and then carefully evaluate them as in the previous section:

$$a^3 - b = (4)^3 - (-3) = 64 + 3 = 67$$

---

2. The formula for the perimeter of a rectangle is $p = 2l + 2w$, where l represents the length of the rectangle and w represents the width. What is the perimeter of a rectangle with length 21 and width 15?

$$p = 2l + 2w = 2(21) + 2(15) = 42 + 30 = 72$$

Solving Equations

An *equation* is simply a mathematical expression that contains an equal sign. For example, $10 = 4 + 6$ is an equation, and is always true. On the other hand, $10 = 5 + 4$ is also an equation, only this time, it is always false.

An equation that contains a variable, such as $2x + 1 = 7$, may or may not be true depending upon the value of x. *Solving an equation* refers to the process of finding the value of the unknown that makes both sides of the equation equal. Note that the number 3 makes both sides of $2x + 1 = 7$ equal. You therefore say that 3 *solves* the equation, or that 3 is the *solution* of the equation.

Some equations, like the one above, are easy to solve by just looking at them. Others are so complicated that you need to follow an organized series of steps to solve them. This section examines how to do this.

The principle for solving equations is, essentially, to rewrite the equation in simpler and simpler form (without, of course, changing the solution) until the solution becomes obvious. The simplest equation of all is an equation of the form $x = a$, where x is the variable and a is some number. Whenever you are given an equation that is more complicated than $x = a$, the idea is to change the equation so that it eventually looks like $x = a$.

Now, what can you do to "change" an equation? The answer is simple: Almost anything you want as long as you do the same thing on both sides of the equal sign. To start, you can add or subtract the same number to or from both sides, multiply both sides by the same number, or divide both sides by the same number (as long as that number isn't 0). The following examples demonstrate this procedure with some simple equations; after this, you will look at some that are more complicated.

The Distributive Property lets you multiply a sum by multiplying each addend separately and then adding the products. For example: $6(3x - 5) = 6 \times 3x - 6 \times 5 = 18x - 30$. (Each term in the parentheses is multiplied by the 6 on the outside.) Another example: $2x(3w - 4y + 7) = (2x) \times (3w) - (2x)(4y) + (2x)(7) = 6xw - 8xy + 14x$.

---

1. Solve for x in the following equation: $x + 7 = 20$.

Remember that the easiest-possible type of equation is one in the form $x = a$. The equation that you have isn't quite like that; it has a +7 on the left-hand side that you would like to get rid of. Now, how can you get rid of it? Easy—you just subtract 7 from both sides.

$$x + 7 = 20$$
$$\underline{-7 \quad -7}$$
$$x = 13$$

So, the solution to this equation is $x = 13$.

---

2. Solve for t in the following equation: $4t - 3 = 9$.

In this equation, you have a few things on the left-hand side that you need to get rid of. First of all, undo the subtraction of 3 by adding 3 to both sides:

$$4t - 3 = \ 9$$
$$\underline{+3 \quad +3}$$
$$4t = 12$$

Now, you need to undo the multiplication by 4; you can undo it by dividing both sides by 4:

$$\frac{4t}{4} = \frac{12}{4}, \text{ or } t = 3$$

Note that you can check your answer to any equation by substituting the answer back into the equation and making certain that it makes both sides equal. For example, you know that you performed the above problem correctly because

$$4(3) - 3 = 9$$
$$12 - 3 = 9$$
$$9 = 9$$

---

3. Solve for p in the following equation: $15p = 3p + 24$.

This problem puts you in a situation that you have yet to encounter. The variable p appears on both sides of the equation, but you want it only on one side. To get this equation into the form you want, subtract $3p$ from both sides:

$$15p = \ 3p + 24$$
$$\underline{-3p \quad -3p}$$
$$12p = \ 24$$

Now you have an equation that looks better. If you divide both sides of $12p = 24$ by 12, you end up with the answer $p = 2$.

---

4. Solve for q in the following equation: $5q - 64 = -2(3q - 1)$.

$$
\begin{array}{lll}
5q - 64 = -6q + \ 2 & & \\
\underline{+64 \qquad +64} & & \text{Add 64 to both sides.} \\
5q \quad\ \ = -6q + 66 & & \\
\underline{+6q \qquad\quad +6q} & & \text{Add } 6q \text{ to both sides.} \\
\dfrac{11q}{11} \ = \ \dfrac{66}{11} & & \text{Divide both sides by 11.} \\
\quad\ q = 6 & &
\end{array}
$$

Solving Word Problems

Many problems that deal with practical applications of mathematics are expressed in words. To solve such problems, it is necessary to translate the words into an equation that you can solve. The following table lists some common words and the mathematical symbols that they represent:

Words	Mathematical Representation
a equals 9, a is 9, a is the same as 9	$a = 9$
a plus 9, the sum of a and 9, a added to 9, a increased by 9, a more than 9	$a + 9$
9 less than a, a minus 9, a decreased by 9, the difference of a and 9, a less 9	$a - 9$
9 times a, the product of 9 and a, 9 multiplied by a	$9a$ (or $9 \times a$)
The quotient of a and 9, a divided by 9, 9 divided into a	$\dfrac{a}{9}$
$\dfrac{1}{2}$ of a	$\dfrac{1}{2} \times a$ or $\dfrac{a}{2}$
50% of a	$50\% \times a$

When you have to solve a word problem, begin by translating the words into an equation, and then solve the equation to find the solution.

> **1.** If 5 increased by 3 times a number is 20, what is the number?

Call the number x.

The problem statement tells you that $5 + 3x = 20$.

Subtract 5 from both sides to get $3x = 15$.

Divide by 3 to get $x = 5$.

Thus, the number is 5.

> **2.** Brian needs $54 more to buy new hockey gloves. If the gloves cost $115, how much money does he already have to spend on the gloves?

In this problem, let m represent the amount of money that Brian has to spend on the gloves. Then, you have an easy equation: $m + 54 = 115$. If you subtract 54 from both sides, you get $m = 61$. Brian already has $61 to spend on the gloves.

Multiplication with Exponents

Consider the problem $x^3 \times x^5$. If you think about it, you will realize that, if you compute $x^3 \times x^5$, you end up with eight xs multiplied together, and that, therefore, $x^3 \times x^5 = x^8$. This indicates the general rule for multiplication of numbers with exponents: $x^m \times x^n = x^{m+n}$. In other words, to multiply two numbers with exponents, simply add the exponents and keep the common base.

You can extend this result to enable you to perform other types of multiplication. For example, if you need to multiply $x(x + 3)$, you can use the distributive property to obtain

$x(x + 3) = x^2 + 3x$

Now, how would you multiply something like $(x + 2)(x + 5)$? Basically, you need to take each of the terms in the first expression—that is, the x and the 2—and distribute them to both of the terms in the second expression. Doing this, you end up with

$(x + 2)(x + 5) = x(x + 5) + 2(x + 5) = x^2 + 5x + 2x + 10 = x^2 + 7x + 10$

199

> **1.** Multiply $2x(x^2 - 3x)$.

Begin by distributing as you did previously:

$$2x(x^2 - 3x) = 2x(x^2) - 2x(3x)$$

Now, perform the multiplication:

$$2x(x^2) - 2x(3x) = 2x^3 - 6x^2$$

> **2.** Multiply $(2x + 7)(3x - 4)$.

As above, begin by distributing the $2x$ and the 7 to the other terms:

$$(2x + 7)(3x - 4) = 2x(3x) - 2x(4) + 7(3x) - 7(4)$$

Now, perform the multiplications and combine terms where possible:

$$2x(3x) - 2x(4) + 7(3x) - 7(4) = 6x^2 - 8x + 21x - 28 = 6x^2 + 13x - 28$$

Factoring

Earlier in this chapter, you learned about factoring whole numbers; for example, you can factor 35 as $35 = 5 \times 7$. As you can see, the word *factoring* refers to taking a mathematical quantity and breaking it down into a product of other quantities.

You can factor certain algebraic expressions, too. Earlier in this review section, you saw how to perform two types of multiplication. In the first, you used the distributive property to perform multiplications such as $x(x + 3) = x^2 + 3x$. To use the correct vocabulary, the x at the front of this expression is a *monomial* (one term), whereas the expression $x + 3$ is a *binomial* (two terms). Thus, you use the distributive property to help you multiply a monomial by a binomial. You also saw how to multiply two binomials together—for example, $(2x + 7)(3x - 4) = 6x^2 + 13x - 28$.

The process of taking the results of these multiplications and breaking them back down into their component factors is factoring. It is not difficult to factor, but it often requires a bit of trial and error.

For example, if the exam asks you to multiply the expression $2x(x - 7)$, you would get $2x^2 - 14x$. If, on the other hand, you were given $2x^2 - 14x$ and asked to factor it, you would basically need to undo the distribution process, and return the expression back to what it originally was.

To do this, begin by looking at the expression $2x^2 - 14x$, and try to find the largest common monomial factor—that is, the largest monomial that divides into both $2x^2$ and $14x$ evenly. In this problem, the largest common factor is $2x$. You then place the $2x$ outside a set of parentheses. Finish by dividing the $2x$ into each of the two terms $2x^2$ and $14x$, and write the resulting terms inside the parentheses. You end up with $2x(x - 7)$, and you have successfully factored the expression.

> **1.** Factor $2a^2b - 8ab$.

The largest common monomial factor in this expression is $2ab$. If you divide $2a^2b$ by $2ab$, you get a. If you divide $8ab$ by $2ab$, you get 4. Thus, putting the $2ab$ outside of the parentheses, and the a and 4 on the inside, you get $2ab(a - 4)$.

Note that it is easy to check whether you have factored correctly or not by multiplying the expression out and seeing if you get the original expression back.

It is also possible to factor certain *trinomial* (three-term) expressions into two binomials. Consider a simple example. If you were asked to multiply $(x + 2)(x + 3)$, you would get $x^2 + 5x + 6$. Now, what if you were given the expression $x^2 + 5x + 6$ and asked to factor it back down into the two binomials it came from?

To begin, make two sets of parentheses, and note that you can position xs in the first position of each set, because the two first-most terms in the binomials multiply to give the x^2 in $x^2 + 5x + 6$. Therefore, to begin

$$x^2 + 5x + 6 = (x \quad)(x \quad)$$

Next, because both signs in $x^2 + 5x + 6$ are positive, you can position plus signs within the parentheses:

$$x^2 + 5x + 6 = (x +)(x +)$$

Now, what are the two last entries? Well, you know that whatever you put in these spots must multiply out to 6, so the possibilities would be 1 and 6 or 2 and 3. The correct entries, however, must add up to 5 to get the correct middle term. Thus, it must be 2 and 3, and you get $x^2 + 5x + 6 = (x + 2)(x + 3)$. You can check the answer by multiplying:

$$(x + 2)(x + 3) = x^2 + 3x + 2x + 6 = x^2 + 5x + 6$$

As you can see, factoring a trinomial into two binomials requires a bit of trial and error. The examples below give you a bit more practice with this process.

---

2. Factor $x^2 - 8x + 12$.

Begin as before, by making two sets of parentheses and entering first terms of x in each:

$$x^2 - 8x + 12 = (x \quad)(x \quad)$$

Now, the two last entries must multiply out to +12, but add to –8, so that you get the correct middle term. Proceed by trial and error, and it won't take you long to determine the two numbers that work are –2 and –6, and the factorization is $x^2 - 8x + 12 = (x - 2)(x - 6)$.

---

3. Factor $x^2 - 49$.

This one may look a bit tricky, but actually it is rather easy. Begin, as before, by writing $x^2 - 49 = (x \quad)(x \quad)$. Now, the two last entries must multiply to 49 and add up to 0, so that the middle term is essentially 0. This will work with +7 and –7. Thus, $x^2 - 49 = (x + 7)(x - 7)$.

Simplifying Algebraic Expressions

Earlier in this chapter you learned about simplifying fractions. If, for example, the answer to a problem turns out to be $\frac{15}{20}$, you should simplify it to $\frac{3}{4}$. In the same way, you can simplify certain algebraic expressions as well. Consider this algebraic fraction:

$$\frac{x^2 - 16}{3x + 12}$$

To simplify this expression, begin by factoring the expressions on the top and on the bottom:

$$\frac{x^2 - 16}{3x + 12} = \frac{(x + 4)(x - 4)}{3(x + 4)}$$

Now, the common factor of $x + 4$ can be divided out from the top and bottom, giving you a simplified fraction of $\frac{x - 4}{3}$.

You can perform mathematical operations on algebraic fractions in much the same way you perform them on fractions that contain only numbers. Consider this example:

Add $\dfrac{x+1}{4x+6} + \dfrac{x+2}{4x+6}$.

Because these two fractions have the same denominator, they can be added in the usual way:

$$\frac{x+1}{4x+6} + \frac{x+2}{4x+6} = \frac{x+1+x+2}{4x+6} = \frac{2x+3}{4x+6}$$

Now, finish by factoring the expression on the bottom and dividing out:

$$\frac{x+1}{4x+6} + \frac{x+2}{4x+6} = \frac{x+1+x+2}{4x+6} = \frac{2x+3}{4x+6} = \frac{2x+3}{2(2x+3)} = \frac{1}{2}$$

1. $\dfrac{x^2-7x+6}{x^2-1} \times \dfrac{x+1}{x-6}$

Begin by factoring as much as possible, then multiply and cancel:

$$\frac{x^2-7x+6}{x^2-1} \times \frac{x+1}{x-6} = \frac{(x-6)(x-1)}{(x-1)(x+1)} \times \frac{x+1}{x-6} = \frac{(x-6)(x-1)(x+1)}{(x-1)(x+1)(x-6)} = 1$$

2. $\dfrac{a^2-b^2}{5} \div \dfrac{a^2+ab}{5a-5}$

Begin by changing the problem to a multiplication problem by reciprocating the second fraction. Then factor and cancel:

$$\frac{a^2-b^2}{5} \div \frac{a^2+ab}{5a-5} = \frac{a^2-b^2}{5} \times \frac{5a-5}{a^2+ab} = \frac{(a+b)(a-b)5(a-1)}{5a(a+b)} = \frac{(a-b)(a-1)}{a}$$

Geometry and Measurement

Chapter 3, about the Arithmetic Reasoning section of the ASVAB, looks at some geometric properties of squares and rectangles. On the Mathematics Knowledge section, you are responsible for some additional facts from geometry, which the following section covers.

Angle Measurement

You measure angles in degrees, which you indicate by the symbol °. By definition, the amount of rotation needed to go completely around a circle one time is 360°.

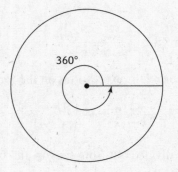

You can measure every angle by determining what fraction of a complete rotation around a circle it represents. For example, an angle that represents $\frac{1}{4}$ of a rotation around a circle would have a measurement of $\frac{1}{4}$ of $360° = 90°$. The diagram below depicts a 90° angle. $\overline{AB}$ and $\overline{AC}$ are the sides of the angle, and point A is the vertex. Angles that measure 90° are called *right angles*.

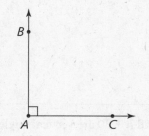

Angles that measure less than 90° are called *acute* angles, and angles that measure more than 90° but less than 180° are called *obtuse angles*. The diagram below depicts an acute angle of 60° as well as an obtuse angle of 120°.

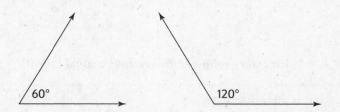

Note that an angle that has the size of $\frac{1}{2}$ of a revolution around the circle has a measure of 180°. In other words, a *straight line* can be thought of as an angle of 180°.

Two angles whose measures add up to 90° are called *complementary angles*, and two angles whose measures add up to 180° are called *supplementary angles*. In the diagram below, angles 1 and 2 are complementary, and angles 3 and 4 are supplementary. As the diagram shows, whenever a straight angle is partitioned into two angles, the angles are supplementary.

Another important fact about angles relates to vertical angles. As the diagram below shows, when two lines intersect, four angles are formed. In this situation, the angles that are across from each other are called *vertical angles*. All vertical angles are equal, so $a° = b°$, and $c° = d°$.

1. In the diagram below, what is the value of *a*?

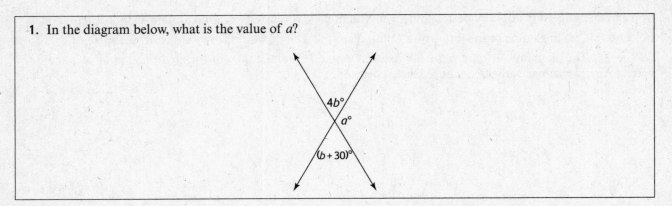

Begin by noting that the angles labeled 4*b* and *b* + 30 are vertical angles, and therefore have the same measure. In this case, you can set the two angles equal and solve the resulting equation for *b*.

$$4b = b + 30$$
$$\underline{3b = 30}$$
$$b = 10$$

If *b* = 10, then 4*b* = 40.

Because the angle labeled *a*° is supplementary to this angle, *a* must be equal to 140°.

2. In the diagram below, what is the value of *x*?

Begin by noting that the angle labeled *y* is supplementary to the angle labeled 150°, and is therefore equal to 30°. Next, note that the angle labeled *x* is complementary to that 30° angle, and is therefore equal to 60°.

Properties of Triangles

A *triangle* is a geometric figure that has three straight sides. One of the most important facts about a triangle is that, regardless of its shape, the sum of the measures of the three angles it contains is always 180°. If you know the measures of two of the angles of a triangle, you can determine the measure of the third angle by adding up the two angles you are given, and subtracting from 180.

Some triangles have special properties that you should know. To begin, an *isosceles triangle* is a triangle that has two sides of the same length. In an isosceles triangle, the two angles opposite the equal sides have the same measurement. For example, in the figure below, $AB = BC$, and therefore the two angles opposite these sides, labeled $x°$, have the same measure.

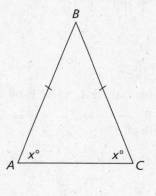

$$AB = BC$$

A triangle that has all three sides the same length is called an *equilateral triangle*. In an equilateral triangle, all three angles also have the same measure. Because the sum of the three angles must be 180°, each angle in an equilateral triangle must measure 180° ÷ 3 = 60°. Therefore, in the equilateral triangle that follows, all three angles are 60°.

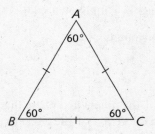

Another extremely important triangle property relates to what are known as *right triangles*—that is, triangles containing a right angle. In such triangles, the side opposite the right angle is called the *hypotenuse,* and is the longest side of the triangle. The other two sides of the triangle are called its *legs.* Therefore, in the right triangle below, the side labeled c is the hypotenuse, and sides a and b are the legs.

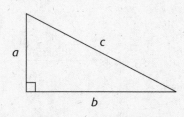

The three sides of a right triangle are related by a formula known as the *Pythagorean theorem.* The Pythagorean theorem states that the square of the hypotenuse is equal to the sum of the squares of the legs of the triangle, or, using the notation in the diagram above

Pythagorean Theorem
$$a^2 + b^2 = c^2$$

The importance of this result is that it enables you, if you're given the lengths of two of the sides of a right triangle, to find the length of the third side.

1. In triangle XYZ, angle X is twice as big as angle Y, and angle Z is equal to angle Y. What is the measure of angle X?

Because the measure of angle X is twice as big as angle Y, you can say that the measure of angle X is equal to $2Y$. Because it must be true that $X + Y + Z = 180$, you can write

$$2Y + Y + Y = 180$$
$$4Y = 180$$
$$Y = 45$$

If the measure of angle Y is 45°, the measure of angle X, which is twice as big, must be 90°.

2. In the triangle below, what is the length of a?

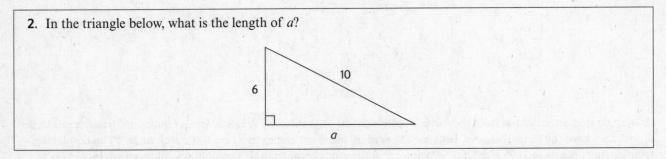

The triangle is a right triangle, so you can use the Pythagorean theorem to find the length of the missing side. Note that the hypotenuse is 10, one of the legs is 6, and you are looking for the length of the other leg. Therefore

$$a^2 + 6^2 = 10^2, \text{ or } a^2 + 36 = 100, \text{ so } a^2 = 64, \text{ and } a = 8.$$

Properties of Circles

A circle is a closed figure, consisting of all of the points in a plane that are the same distance from a fixed point—the *center* of the circle. A line segment from the center of the circle to any point on the circle is a *radius* of the circle. A line segment from one point on a circle, through the center of the circle, and to another point on the circle, is a *diameter* of the circle. As you can see in the diagram that follows, the length of a diameter of a circle is always twice the length of a radius of the circle.

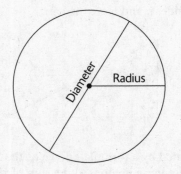

Perimeter and Area

The Arithmetic Reasoning chapter reviews the formulas for finding the perimeter and the area of rectangles and squares. To find the perimeter of a triangle, simply add together the lengths of the three sides. The area of a triangle is given by the formula

$$\text{Area} = \frac{1}{2}bh,$$

where b represents the length of the base of the triangle and h represents the height of the triangle.

The *height of a triangle* is the length of a line segment drawn from a *vertex* (corner) of the triangle to the base so that it hits the base at a right angle.

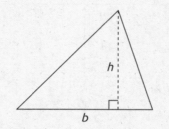

Concerning circles, formulas exist for the perimeter (which is more commonly known as the *circumference*) and the area. These formulas are based on the length of the radius, and include the symbol π, which represents a number that is approximately equal to 3.14.

The circumference of a circle is given by the formula $C = 2\pi r$, where r is the radius of the circle. The area of the circle is given by the formula $A = \pi r^2$. Unless you are told otherwise, when answering problems involving the circumference or the area of a circle, you can leave the answer in terms of π, as in the following problem.

---

1. What is the circumference of a circle whose area is 36π?

The area of a circle is πr^2, so you have $\pi r^2 = 36\pi$. This means that $r^2 = 36$, so $r = 6$.

Now, the circumference of a circle is $2\pi r$, so the circumference in this case would be $2\pi(6) = 12\pi$.

---

2. What is the area of the shaded part of the rectangle below?

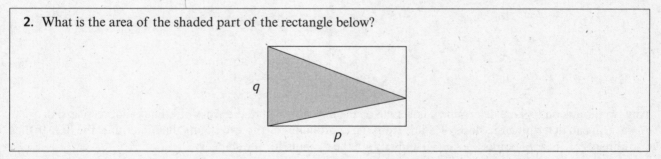

The shaded area is a triangle, so you can use the formula $A = \frac{1}{2}bh$ to find its area. The width of the rectangle, labeled q, is also the base of the triangle. You can also see that the length of the rectangle, labeled p, is equal to the height of the triangle. Therefore, the area of the shaded region is $\frac{1}{2}pq$.

Coordinates and Slope

You can locate points in a plane by means of a reference system called the *coordinate system.* Two number lines are drawn at right angles to each other, and the point where the lines cross is considered to have the value 0 for both lines. Then, positive and negative numbers are positioned on the lines in the usual way:

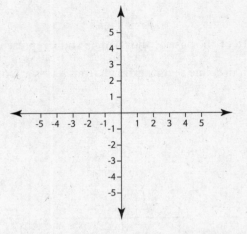

The horizontal line is called the *x-axis,* and the points on this axis are called *x-intercepts.* The vertical line is called the *y-axis,* and the points on this axis are called *y-coordinates.* Points on the plane are identified by first writing a number that represents where they lie in reference to the *x*-axis, and then writing a number that expresses where they lie in reference to the *y*-axis. You call these numbers the *coordinates of the point.* You can see the coordinates of a variety of points in the diagram below:

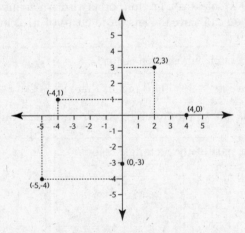

Any two points on a plane determine a line. One of the important characteristics of a line is its steepness, or *slope.* You can determine the slope of a line from the coordinates of the two points that determine the line. If the coordinates of the two points are (x_1, y_1) and (x_2, y_2), the formula for the slope is:

$$\frac{y_2 - y_1}{x_2 - x_1}$$

In other words, to find the slope of a line, find two points on the line and divide the difference of the *y*-coordinates by the difference of the *x*-coordinates, keeping the order of subtraction the same.

> Find the slope of the line that goes through the points (9, 5) and (3, –2).

The slope of the line can be computed as

$$\frac{y_2 - y_1}{x_2 - x_1} = \frac{5 - (-2)}{9 - 3} = \frac{5 + 2}{6} = \frac{7}{6}$$

Mathematics Knowledge Practice Questions

1. Find the value of $4^3 \times 3^2$.

   A. 343
   B. 576
   C. 16,807
   D. 248,832

2. Find the value of $(2 \times 3)^2$.

   A. 10
   B. 12
   C. 25
   D. 36

3. What is the greatest common factor of 42 and 28?

   A. 6
   B. 7
   C. 14
   D. 21

4. Prime-factor the number 48, and write the prime factorization using exponential notation.

   A. $2^4 \times 3$
   B. $2^3 \times 3^2$
   C. $2^5 \times 3$
   D. 6×8

5. Evaluate $18 - 3(5 - 2)$.

   A. 0
   B. 1
   C. 9
   D. 45

In problems 6 through 8, perform the indicated operations.

6. $(+8) - (+2) - (-7) =$

   A. −1
   B. 3
   C. 13
   D. 17

7. $(-1)^{100}(-2)^3 =$

   A. −800
   B. −8
   C. 8
   D. 800

8. $\dfrac{(+12)(-4)}{(-2)(-8)} =$

   A. −3
   B. $-1\frac{1}{2}$
   C. $1\frac{1}{2}$
   D. 3

9. $\dfrac{8}{9} - \dfrac{1}{3} =$

   A. $\dfrac{5}{9}$
   B. $\dfrac{2}{3}$
   C. $\dfrac{7}{9}$
   D. $\dfrac{7}{6}$

10. $4\frac{1}{4} \times 3\frac{2}{3} =$

   A. $7\frac{1}{6}$
   B. $12\frac{1}{6}$
   C. $15\frac{7}{12}$
   D. $15\frac{11}{12}$

11. $\dfrac{4}{5} \div \dfrac{7}{10} =$

   A. $\dfrac{14}{25}$
   B. $\dfrac{7}{8}$
   C. $1\frac{1}{7}$
   D. $1\frac{1}{5}$

12. Find the value of $-3a + 4b$ if $a = -2$ and $b = -3$.

   A. −30
   B. −18
   C. −6
   D. 18

In problems 13 and 14, solve for the variable indicated.

13. $\frac{x}{4} = -9$

    A. -36

    B. $-\frac{1}{9}$

    C. $-\frac{1}{36}$

    D. 13

14. $2(a - 3) = 14 - 3a$

    A. -8

    B. $\frac{17}{5}$

    C. 4

    D. 8

15. A piece of wood that is 27 inches long is cut into two pieces, such that one piece is twice as long as the other. Find the length of the shorter piece.

    A. 6 inches

    B. 9 inches

    C. 12 inches

    D. 18 inches

16. If the sum of three consecutive integers is 57, find the smallest of the integers.

    A. 17

    B. 18

    C. 19

    D. 20

17. If a number is added to twice the same number, and the result is equal to 8 less than five times the number, what is the number?

    A. 4

    B. 6

    C. 8

    D. 12

18. Multiply $(3x - 7)(4x + 2)$.

    A. $12x^2 + 22x - 14$

    B. $12x^2 - 22x - 14$

    C. $12x^2 + 34x + 14$

    D. $12x^2 - 22x + 14$

19. Factor $6x^4y^3 - 3x^3y^5$.

    A. $3x^3y^3 (2x - y^2)$

    B. $6x^3y^3 (x - y^2)$

    C. $3x^4y^5 (2x - y^2)$

    D. $3x^4y^3 (2 - y^2)$

20. Factor $x^2 - 2x - 35$.

    A. $(x + 7)(x - 5)$

    B. $(x + 35)(x - 1)$

    C. $(x - 35)(x + 1)$

    D. $(x - 7)(x + 5)$

21. $\dfrac{x}{3x+15} \div \dfrac{x^2}{x^2-25} =$

    A. $\dfrac{x}{3x+15} \div \dfrac{x^3}{3(x+5)^2(x-5)}$

    B. $\dfrac{3(x-5)}{x}$

    C. $\dfrac{3x}{x+5}$

    D. $\dfrac{x-5}{3x}$

22. In the diagram below, $x =$

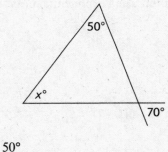

    A. $50°$

    B. $60°$

    C. $65°$

    D. $70°$

23. An airplane flies 50 miles due north, and then turns and flies 120 miles due east. How far has the plane flown from its starting point?

    A. 70 miles

    B. 130 miles

    C. 145 miles

    D. 170 miles

24. What is the slope of the line that goes through the points (8, –2) and (–4, 4)?

   A. –2

   B. $-\dfrac{1}{2}$

   C. $\dfrac{1}{2}$

   D. 2

25. In the figure below, the circle fits exactly inside the square. If the circumference of the circle is 10π, what is the area of the square?

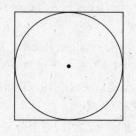

   A. 5

   B. 10

   C. 20

   D. 100

Answers and Explanations for Practice Questions

1. **B.** $4^3 \times 3^2 = (4 \times 4 \times 4) \times (3 \times 3) = 64 \times 9 = 576$

2. **D.** $(2 \times 3)^2 = 6^2 = 36$

3. **C.** The factors of 42 are 1, 2, 3, 6, 7, 14, 21, and 42. The factors of 28 are 1, 2, 4, 7, 14, and 28. The greatest common factor, therefore, is 14.

4. **A.** $48 = 6 \times 8 = 2 \times 2 \times 2 \times 2 \times 3 = 2^4 \times 3$

5. **C.** $18 - 3(5 - 2) = 18 - 3(3) = 18 - 9 = 9$

6. **C.** $(+8) - (+2) - (-7) = (+8) + (-2) + (+7) = +13$

7. **B.** $(-1)^{100}(-2)^3 = (+1)(-8) = -8$

8. **A.** $\dfrac{(+12)(-4)}{(-2)(-8)} = \dfrac{-48}{+16} = -3$

9. **A.** $\dfrac{8}{9} - \dfrac{1}{3} = \dfrac{8}{9} - \dfrac{3}{9} = \dfrac{5}{9}$

10. **C.** $4\dfrac{1}{4} \times 3\dfrac{2}{3} = \dfrac{17}{4} \times \dfrac{11}{3} = \dfrac{187}{12} = 15\dfrac{7}{12}$

11. **C.** $\dfrac{4}{5} \div \dfrac{7}{10} = \dfrac{4}{5} \times \dfrac{10}{7} = \dfrac{40}{35} = 1\dfrac{5}{35} = 1\dfrac{1}{7}$

12. **C.** $-3a + 4b = -3(-2) + 4(-3) = +6 - 12 = -6$

13. **A.** $\frac{x}{4} = -9$. Multiplying both sides by 4 gives $x = -36$.

14. **C.** $2(a - 3) = 14 - 3a$. Distribute to get $2a - 6 = 14 - 3a$. Add $+6$ and $+3a$ to get $5a = 20$. Thus, $a = 4$.

15. **B.** Let S = the length of the shorter piece. Then, the longer piece is of length $2S$, and $S + 2S = 27$, or $3S = 27$, so $S = 9$.

16. **B.** Let N = the smallest integer. Then, $N + 1$ is the middle integer, and $N + 2$ is the largest. $N + (N + 1) + (N + 2) = 57$ or $3N + 3 = 57$, so $3N = 54$ or $N = 18$.

17. **A.** Let N equal the number. Then $N + 2N = 5N - 8$ or $3N = 5N - 8$. Subtract $5N$ to get $-2N = -8$. Divide by -2 to get $N = 4$.

18. **B.** $(3x - 7)(4x + 2) = 12x^2 + 6x - 28x - 14 = 12x^2 - 22x - 14$

19. **A.** The factorization begins with the greatest common factor, the largest value that divides into each term. In this example, that greatest common factor is $3x^3y^3$. Once the greatest common factor is identified, the distributive property is incorporated into it: $6x^4y^3 - 3x^3y^5 = 3x^3y^3(2x - y^2)$. To check this, distribute that $3x^3y^3$ into each term in the parentheses. You will end up with $6x^4y^3 - 3x^3y^5$. (Remember to check that the terms in the parentheses have no common factor. That is how you will know that you have completed the factoring process.)

20. **D.** When you factor a trinomial, (three terms), with a leading coefficient, (the number multiplying the highest power of x), the two numbers in the parentheses must add up to the coefficient of x, (-2), and must also multiply to the constant, (-35). The two numbers that both add up to -2 and multiply to -35 are -7 and $+2$.

21. **D.** $\frac{x}{3x + 15} \div \frac{x^2}{x^2 - 25} = \frac{x}{3x + 15} \times \frac{x^2 - 25}{x^2} =$

$\frac{x}{3(x + 5)} \times \frac{(x - 5)(x + 5)}{x^2} = \frac{x - 5}{3x}$

22. **B.** The unlabeled angle of the triangle has the same measure as the angle labeled $70°$. Thus, the triangle has angles of $70°$ and $50°$. The missing angle must be $60°$ so that the three angles add up to $180°$.

23. **B.** The airplane is flying the two legs of a right triangle, and the distance from the starting point is equal to the hypotenuse of the triangle. By the Pythagorean theorem, $50^2 + 120^2 = d^2$, or $2,500 + 14,400 = d^2$. Thus, $d^2 = 16,900$, or $d = 130$.

24. **B.** $\frac{y_2 - y_1}{x_2 - x_1} \div \frac{-2 - (4)}{8 - (-4)} = \frac{-6}{12} = -\frac{1}{2}$

25. **D.** The circumference of the circle is $2\pi r = 10\pi$, so the radius of the circle is 5. Then, the diameter of the circle is 10. Because the side of the square is equal to the diameter of the circle, the area of the square is $10^2 = 100$.

Mechanical Comprehension

A thorough knowledge of the mechanical world is necessary to successfully complete numerous everyday tasks. From understanding how engines operate, to using tools to build and repair existing structures, to providing support against various external forces, grasping a few general principles provides a solid base that you can use while you gain more specific understanding. This section presents various physical concepts ranging from application of forces and properties of materials to fluid dynamics and compound machines.

The ASVAB includes 25 Mechanical Comprehension questions. You will have 19 minutes to answer these questions.

Properties of Materials

You encounter many different types of materials on a daily basis. Almost all of these are better suited for specific uses than for others. For example, wood and metal are more appropriate when you need a rigid, sturdy structure (as with a bookcase, sturdy door, or large crate to transport heavy objects). You would use cardboard and plastic for smaller containers designed to hold lighter material. This section explores in detail the differences between various materials that determine their usefulness in various situations.

Weight, Density, and Strength

Consider first the weight of a given material. You can consider the *weight* of the material as a measure of how much force is needed to move (or support) a given amount of this material. At first thought, most people would say that iron is heavy while paper is light. This statement by itself is false, and needs to be more specific. You can see this immediately by considering that it is possible to have 5 pounds of iron on one table and 10 pounds of paper on an adjacent table.

The missing detail that you must also consider is density. *Density* is defined as the ratio of the mass (or weight) of an object to the volume that it occupies. In other words, if two objects take up the same amount of space (if they have the same volume), the one that weighs more has a higher density.

It is important, however, to make sure that you don't confuse the weight of a material and the density of a material with the *strength* of a material. While, for the most part, a material that is heavier will also be stronger, sometimes it is not. The strength of a material can best be considered as its capability to maintain its shape even as external forces on the material increase. Creating materials that are lightweight (have a lower density) but that are also high strength is an important challenge in many fields, including transportation (for example, in the building of airplanes).

Expansion and Contraction

Materials *expand* (take up more volume) and *contract* (take up less volume) when exposed to a change in temperature. As a general rule, a substance expands with heat and contracts with cold. This general rule applies to solids, liquids, and gases. Different solids, as well as different liquids, will expand and contract at varying rates. In other words, one solid may expand noticeably more when exposed to a specific temperature change than another solid. Gases, on the other hand, exhibit a more uniform expansion rate; ie., most gases will expand by the same amount when exposed to a similar change in temperature.

For example, the following materials are listed, from left to right, in order of decreasing expansion under a similar temperature change. The materials at the beginning of the list will expand and contract more than those near the end of the list.

lead—aluminum—brass—copper—concrete—glass

Water is an interesting exception to the general rule about temperature-related expansion and contraction. Recall that water boils at 100°C and freezes at 0°C. When the temperature of water drops anywhere in the range between 4°C and 100°C, its volume decreases (the water contracts). However, when the temperature of water drops anywhere in the range between 4°C and 0°C, its volume increases (the water expands). A direct consequence of this phenomenon is that water achieves its greatest density at 4°C.

Absorption

Absorption refers to the capability of the material to pick up and retain a liquid that it comes in contact with. For example, sponges and paper towels are very good at picking up and retaining liquid. Thus they are considered to be very good at absorbing the liquids with which they come in contact.

Some materials do not absorb liquid well at all. One example is the coating used on the hulls of boats. Other materials can absorb a large quantity of liquid but require a considerable amount of time to do so. Wood (such as a fallen tree or a non-treated piece of lumber) is an example.

Center of Gravity

An object's center of gravity is important in determining structural support, among other things. The simplest definition for the *center of gravity* is that it is the point on the object at which the object can be balanced. In other words, it is the point at which gravity exerts the same force on either side of the balance point so that the object does not fall.

Consider the following diagram, which shows an object and its center of gravity. The object is considered to be uniform. Following the diagram are several thoughts and examples to explain the process that you use to find the center of gravity.

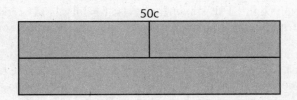

The first step is to define a rigid, uniform body. A body is *rigid* if it is solid and does not alter its shape easily despite pressure from external forces. A body is *uniform* if its volume and density are constant from one end of the body to the other. A meter stick is an example of a uniform body. Any automobile that you see on the road is an example of a non-uniform body.

The center of gravity for a uniform body is its *geometric center*. A meter stick is 100 centimeters in length. Therefore, the center of gravity for the meter stick is the point marked 50 centimeters, which is midway between the two ends of the meter stick. If you have a piece of treated lumber (such as a 5- or 6-foot-long 2-by-4), the center of gravity is midway between the two ends of the piece of lumber (a long piece of lumber is like an enlarged version of the meter stick). For non-uniform bodies, determining the location of the center of gravity requires a bit more analysis. To understand the process fully, it is best to build up to it by considering several examples.

Consider two golf balls that, for all intents and purposes, are identical to each other. Now place these golf balls on a table some distance apart—use 80 centimeters for this example. The center of gravity between the two golf balls is on the line that connects the centers of the two golf balls and is the same distance from each golf ball. In other words, the center of gravity is directly between the two golf balls and 40 centimeters away from either golf ball. This type of example works for any two identical objects.

Now think about having two objects that are not identical. Consider placing an object that weighs 10 pounds 3 meters away from an object that weighs 20 pounds. The center of gravity is no longer midway between the two objects, and will be closer to the object that is heavier (with two objects of different weights, the center of gravity is always closer to the heavier object). Use the following diagram to help determine and understand the location for the center of gravity between these two objects.

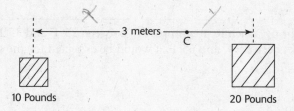

The object on the left weighs 10 pounds and the object on the right weighs 20 pounds. The distance between the two objects is 3 meters. Notice that this distance is measured from the centers of the objects and is not the distance from the right-hand side of the 10-pound object to the left-hand side of the 20-pound object. The center of gravity is located at the point marked "C" and is 2 meters from the 10-pound object and 1 meter from the 20-pound object.

Justification is when the ratio of the weights of the two objects must equal the inverse ratio of the respective distances of the center of gravity from the two objects. In other words, let x be the distance between the 10-pound object and the center of gravity. Let y be the distance between the 20-pound object and the center of gravity. The following equation must be true:

$$\frac{20}{10} = \frac{x}{y}$$

This equation can be written as

$$20 \times y = 10 \times x$$

You also know that $x + y$ must be equal to 3 because the distance between the two objects is 3 meters. Combining these two pieces of information, you can figure out that x must be equal to 2 meters and y must be equal to 1 meter. This can be done by rearranging the equation $x + y = 3$ to $x = 3 - y$. Substitute $3 - y$ for x in the equation $20 \times y = 10 \times x$ to yield

$$20 \times y = 10 \times (3 - y)$$
$$20y = 30 - 10y$$
$$20y + 10y = 30$$
$$30y = 30$$
$$y = \frac{30}{30}$$
$$y = 1$$

Now consider a non-uniform body. The center of gravity is *not* simply the point at which there is an equal weight of material on either side. This idea can be understood from the previous example, in which there was 10 pounds of material on one side of the center of gravity and 20 pounds of material on the other. Problems that require determining the precise location of the center of gravity for non-uniform bodies are beyond the scope of the ASVAB, but a general understanding of the principles mentioned here will be helpful in theoretical questions regarding this matter.

> 1. If the volume of an object is increased while its weight remains the same, then the density of the object
>
>   A. increases.
>   B. decreases.
>   C. remains the same.
>   D. cannot be determined.

The answer is **B**. Recall that density is equal to mass (weight) divided by volume. By keeping the weight unchanged and increasing the volume, you are effectively increasing the denominator of a fraction. This causes the value of the fraction to decrease.

> **2.** From the beginning of spring, when temperatures are between 25°F and 35°F, until the end of spring when temperatures are between 55°F and 65°F, it would be expected for the segments of a bridge to
>
>   **A.** expand.
>   **B.** contract.
>   **C.** remain the same size.
>   **D.** cannot be determined.

The answer is **A.** Remember that, generally, objects expand when heated and contract when cooled. Generally, the average temperature increases from the beginning of spring to the end of spring.

> **3.** Two identical basketballs are placed 50 centimeters apart. How far from the first basketball is the center of gravity?
>
>   **A.** 15 centimeters
>   **B.** 20 centimeters
>   **C.** 25 centimeters
>   **D.** 30 centimeters

The answer is **C.** Recall that the center of gravity between two identical objects is midway between the objects.

> **4.** There are two crates of supplies in a room. Some of the supplies from the first crate are moved into the second crate. What happens to the center of gravity between the two crates?
>
>   **A.** Nothing, it remains where it was originally.
>   **B.** It moves closer to the first crate.
>   **C.** It moves closer to the second crate.
>   **D.** Cannot be determined.

The answer, again, is **C.** This is a slightly trickier question. Recall that the center of gravity is located closer to the heavier object. By moving supplies from the first crate to the second crate, the second crate becomes heavier than it was originally, while the first crate becomes lighter than it was originally. As a result, the center of gravity moves closer to the second crate.

Structural Support

Structural support combines the concepts of strength, density, expansion, and center of gravity. The general idea is to take a given amount of material and use it to provide effective support for a large weight.

For a first example, consider the structural support that a tall building requires. A sturdy foundation must be used that can support the weight of the building and all the furniture and people that will eventually occupy the building. Also, a solid skeletal structure must be built that will be capable of separating and supporting the individual floors, walls, and other building components. Finally, the building must be constructed in such a way that it can withstand the forces associated with the various winds that will be blowing against the building.

Now consider bridges. They must be capable of supporting the constant flow of traffic across the top of the bridge. If the bridge crosses a large body of water, the supports must capable of withstanding the pressures that the water exerts.

On a smaller scale, consider the average table. It has four legs that are placed, for the most part, one at each of the four corners (if the table is round, the legs are spaced evenly around the perimeter of the table). The legs are placed in this way for two reasons. First, the center of gravity for the table is its geometric center, so the legs must be placed such that they share the load of gravity equally (if all four legs were placed along the same side of the table, it would not stand). The other reason is so that the weight of the table plus whatever is placed on it will be shared fairly evenly by the legs.

Consider a square table with four legs placed at the corners as described earlier. The center of gravity for the top of the table will be in the center of the table, an equal distance away from each leg. As a result, each leg will support the same amount of weight. Now, imagine that you place a heavy box in the exact center of the table. Each leg of the table will still support the same amount of weight because the center of gravity is still the same distance from each leg. However, if you place the box closer to one leg in particular (call this leg A), then that leg will support a larger weight than any of the three remaining legs because the center of gravity has been moved so that it is closest to leg A. This is the same basic theory that is used, on a much larger and more intricate scale, in the construction of buildings and bridges.

The other point to remember is that materials (solids especially) expand and contract when exposed to a change in temperature. Any structure must be capable of withstanding the internal forces that accompany such structural changes.

---

1. When determining the wind force on the side of a building, the most important characteristic of the building to consider is its

   A. height.
   B. width.
   C. area.
   D. foundation.

The correct answer is **C**. Remember that the force from the wind becomes greater as the area of the building increases. Thus, while the height and width are important, it is their product (the area) that is of primary concern.

---

2. A large number of circular pieces of wood, each of a different size (radius), need to be stacked. It would be best to stack them

   A. with the larger radius toward the bottom.
   B. with the larger radius toward the top.
   C. in the order they are found.
   D. Does not matter.

The correct answer is **A**. The wood pieces on the bottom need to support more weight than the wood pieces on top. By placing a smaller piece atop a larger piece, the entire smaller piece receives support, which would not be the case if the larger piece were placed atop the smaller piece.

---

3. A bridge is being built on the hottest day of the year. The surface that vehicles will drive on consists of several concrete slabs with a small space between each slab. Compared with building the bridge on a much colder day, the spaces should be

   A. separated more.
   B. separated less.
   C. separated exactly the same.
   D. cannot be determined.

The correct answer is **B**. Remember that materials expand when they are heated. Thus, there should be very little space between the slabs on the hot day, so that when the temperature falls the slabs won't be overly far apart.

4. Consider the following four configurations for two supports, a rigid uniform beam, and various loads. Which configuration is the most stable?

A.

B.

C.

D.

The correct answer is **B.** Convince yourself that this is true by comparing the positions of the supports relative to the center of gravity for the board as well as the position of the added load relative to the supports.

Fluid Dynamics

There are a few differences between the ways that a solid behaves and the ways that a fluid behaves. Some of the more general differences are outlined in this section. First, however, you need to understand a few terms.

The first one is *viscosity,* which is the relative difficulty with which a fluid will flow. Engine oil has a low viscosity because it flows easily. Molasses has a high viscosity because it flows slowly. If the two liquids were allowed to flow down an incline, the oil would reach the bottom of the incline first. The second term is *compressibility*. Compressibility is one of the two main characteristics of liquids that lead to hydraulics; the other characteristic is the way that liquids transfer a force from one region to another. In a closed container filled with liquid, the pressure of the liquid will be the same at all points that are at the same height.

In the diagram above, the pressure at point *A* is the same as the pressure at point *B*. Notice first that the liquid is open to the atmosphere at points *A* and *B* and that the remainder of the container is closed. Also notice that neither the shape nor the height of the rest of the container has any bearing on the fact that the pressure is the same at points *A* and *B*. Remember that *pressure* is defined as the force per unit area. In other words, because the area at point *B* is larger than the area at point *A*, a small force exerted at point *A* produces a larger force at point *B*. This is a simple definition for the process of hydraulics. The ratio of the force applied at point *A* to the force exerted at point *B* is equal to the ratio of the area at point *A* to the area at point *B*.

Remember two main ideas about hydraulics:

- It is very difficult to compress a liquid.
- The pressure (not the exerted force) remains the same throughout a liquid.

The reason that specific liquids are chosen to use in hydraulic mechanisms is that they flow easily and are more resistant to being compressed.

1. A force is applied at one end of a hydraulic jack. The area at the other end of the jack is five times the area where the force is applied. How much larger is the exerted force than the applied force?

   A. twice as large
   B. one-fifth as large
   C. five times as large
   D. half as large

The correct answer is **C**. Remember that the ratio of the applied force to the exerted force is the same as the ratio of the areas. Also remember that the force is greater where the area is greater.

2. Choose the best answer. A hydraulic jack works because

   A. liquids are incompressible.
   B. liquids maintain the same pressure in a closed system.
   C. both **A** and **B**.
   D. none of the above.

The correct answer is **C**. These two facts are key concepts in hydraulics.

Mechanical Motion

Any discussion of motion requires consideration of several concepts. To understand these concepts, it is best to develop them from basic ideas. You can combine these ideas to understand more complicated situations.

First, consider the difference between speed and velocity. *Speed* is the total distance traveled divided by the total time required to travel that distance. *Velocity* is the total *displacement* divided by the time in which this displacement occurs. Consider the following example.

A racetrack is shaped in an oval and has a total length of 1 mile. Now consider that a car drives around this track 10 times and does so in exactly 6 minutes. The total distance traveled is 10 miles. The speed is found using the following equation:

$$\text{speed} = \frac{10 \text{ miles}}{6 \text{ minutes}} = \frac{100 \text{ miles}}{60 \text{ minutes}} = \frac{100 \text{ miles}}{\text{hour}}$$

Thus, the speed of the car is 100 miles per hour. However, the velocity of the car is zero! Why is this true? Because after the car has gone around the track ten times, it returns to where it started. Thus, its *displacement* is zero. Remember that displacement is the distance between the starting point and the finishing point, regardless of the path traveled between the two points.

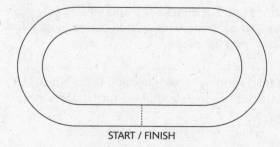

START / FINISH

The acceleration of an object is defined as the change in the speed (or velocity) of the object divided by the amount of time required for that change to take place. In other words, consider a man who is walking at a speed of 3 feet every second. Now consider that his speed changes to 4 feet every second. He is said to have accelerated his speed (he is traveling faster than before). Had he slowed to a speed of 2 feet every second, he would have decelerated (slowed down).

These ideas can be applied to machines. Instead of thinking about a car going around a track, think of a machine that is doing work. If the machine begins to do the work faster, then the machine has accelerated the rate at which it is doing work. In other words, the machine has increased the speed with which it is doing the work. Similarly, if the machine begins to do the work more slowly, then the machine has decelerated the rate at which it is doing work. The machine has decreased the speed with which it is doing the work.

Friction is a related concept. The two types of friction are referred to as static friction and kinetic friction. *Static friction* tends to keep things from moving. When you push against an object on the floor that does not move because it is so heavy, static friction between the object and the floor is what keeps the object from moving. *Kinetic friction* tends to slow moving objects. Kinetic friction is the reason an object sliding across the floor will eventually come to rest.

Consider now any type of engine that has moving parts. These parts interact with one another as well as with stationary parts of the engine. These moving parts produce kinetic friction, which tends to slow the speed of the engine. In this case, the friction is referred to as *internal friction* because the interaction of the moving parts of the engine tends to decrease the speed with which the engine can operate.

When approaching a steep hill in a car, you must depress the accelerator further to maintain the same speed up the hill that the car had been traveling on level ground. Which of the following statements is true?

A. The engine is doing the same amount of work.
B. The engine is doing more work.
C. The engine is doing less work.
D. Cannot be determined.

The answer is **B**. This question is a bit trickier than most. Even though the speed of the car has not changed, the speed of the engine has. The engine has increased its speed to compensate for the extra work needed to go up the hill.

Centrifuges

A *centrifuge* is a machine designed to spin very rapidly in order to separate a liquid from a solid or to separate particles from a suspension. A container holding the mixture is placed in the centrifuge and then accelerated to a high rate of rotation very quickly. After spinning for an amount of time, the solid forms on the inner portion of the container that is farthest from the center of the centrifuge.

To understand why this happens, consider a car traveling straight on a level road. The car comes to a moderately sharp left-hand turn. As the car goes around the turn, the passengers lean toward the right side of the car. Are the people being pushed to the right?

No—the car is turning to the left and the passengers are merely trying to continue in a straight line.

The same thing happens in the centrifuge. The container is spinning rapidly while the liquid and solid within the container are trying to continue in a straight line. This motion causes the solid within the container to collect on the portion of the container farthest from the center.

A vehicle driving down the road approaches a right-hand turn. Which side of the vehicle should the passengers brace against if they are going to round the turn quickly?

A. the left side
B. the right side
C. either side
D. the roof

The answer is **A**. In trying to continue in a straight line, the passengers will end up leaning toward the left side of the vehicle.

Simple Machines

Simple machines are used by nearly everyone in some form or another on a daily basis. This section specifically addresses how and why these machines are helpful. Also, this section examines the concept of mechanical advantage for some of the machines discussed. *Mechanical advantage* is a measure of the degree to which a specific job is made easier by a simple machine.

Lever

The first simple machine to be considered is a lever (sometimes referred to as a lever arm). A *lever* is a rigid object (such as a board, rod, pipe, or bar) that pivots about a single point. A crowbar is a good example of a lever. The force applied at one end of the lever is magnified at the other end of the lever.

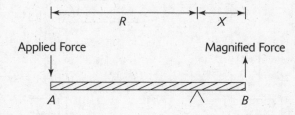

In the illustration, the applied force occurs at point A and a magnified force is produced at point B. Notice that the point of applied force is farther away from the pivot point than the point of magnified force—this physical arrangement will always be necessary for a lever to work. The mechanical advantage is the ratio of the distance R (from the applied force to the pivot point) to the distance X (from the pivot point to the magnified force). In other words, if the distance R is three times the distance X, then the mechanical advantage for this lever is

$$\text{mechanical advantage} = \frac{R}{X} = 3$$

Inclined Plane

Another example of a simple machine is the *inclined plane*. An inclined plane is nothing more than a flat surface that is used to move a heavy object from one height to another. A frequent application of an inclined plane is to move a heavy crate from a lower point to a higher point (when loading a truck, for instance).

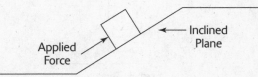

The concept of mechanical advantage does not apply directly to an inclined plane because the applied force is not magnified by the inclined plane. Notice that the most efficient way to use the inclined plane is to make the applied force parallel to the inclined plane. In other words, you want to push the crate up the plane, not into the plane.

Screw

Another example of a simple machine that does not magnify the applied force is a *screw*. You use a screw to hold two objects together.

Consider, for example, using a screw to fasten a nameplate to a wooden door. You insert the screw into the door until the nameplate is flush against the door and the head of the screw is flush against the nameplate. The main characteristic of the screw that holds the nameplate to the door is the threads. The threads act much like the barb on a fishing hook. Once you insert the screw into the door, you cannot simply pull it back out.

Pulley

One of the more intricate simple machines is the *pulley*. Pulleys are useful in that there are many diverse ways in which to combine them, depending on the task at hand. You can use a single pulley in conjunction with a rope to lift a heavy object above the ground.

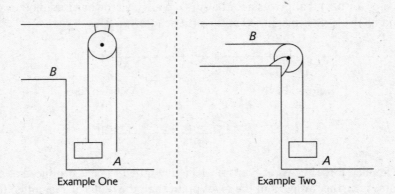

Example One   Example Two

Notice that you can arrange the pulley system so that you can raise the object from point *A* to point *B* in several different ways. In Example One, the person operating the pulley is at point *A* lifting the object to someone else at point *B*. In Example Two, however, the person is already at point *B* and uses the pulley to lift the heavy object to point *B*. In both of these examples, though, the applied force is equal to the exerted force.

Now consider a slight variation of Example One. In the example below, the mechanical advantage is 2.

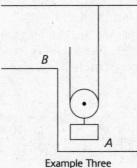

Example Three

Why is this true? Look back to Example One. In this case, the person lifting the load is pulling down on the rope and gravity is pulling down on the load. The rope supporting the pulley is actually supporting twice the weight of the load! In Example Three, however, the person is pulling up on the rope, gravity is pulling down on the load, and the point where the rope is secured acts as another upward force.

As an additional point of interest, notice that in Example Three the pulley is moving, while in Examples One and Two the pulley is stationary. For any pulley system to have a mechanical advantage greater than 1, at least one pulley must be movable. In other words, it is impossible to construct a pulley system in which all the pulleys are fixed (don't move) that has a mechanical advantage greater than 1.

As a result, the person doing the lifting needs to exert only half of the force required in Example One. However, the person must pull twice as much rope. In other words, if the person in Example Three wants to lift the load 10 feet, then 20 feet of rope must be pulled through the pulley. Recalling that work is equal to force × distance, we see that the amount of work performed has remained the same.

Two more thoughts about pulley systems should be mentioned. First, it is possible to create systems with many movable pulleys that have mechanical advantages of 2, 3, or even higher. The following diagram shows a pulley system that has a mechanical advantage of 3.

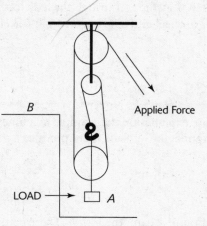

Remember, though, that to lift the crate 5 feet, 15 feet of rope must be pulled through the pulley system (the person lifting the crate is exerting less force but is still doing the same amount of work).

The final thought is that the mechanical advantages that this section discusses are theoretical. In other words, the actual mechanical advantage will be slightly less, mainly because of friction in the pulleys and from the rope through the pulleys.

A system of pulleys is designed to lift heavy objects. This system has a total of three pulleys. What is the mechanical advantage of the system?

A. 1
B. 2
C. 3
D. Cannot be determined

The correct answer is **D.** If all the pulleys are fixed, the mechanical advantage will be 1. The configuration of the pulleys must be known in order to determine the mechanical advantage.

Wedge

Another simple machine that is used frequently is a wedge. A *wedge,* which is a double inclined plane, is designed to split apart a single object or separate two objects from one another. Using a crowbar is one method to separate two objects (two boards that have been nailed together, for example). A wedge accomplishes the same thing but works a bit differently.

The following diagram shows an example of a wedge.

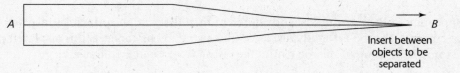

At end *A*, the rods are not connected. This end is used as the handle for the wedge. At end *B*, the rods are connected and are very thin. This end is inserted between the two objects to be separated, and the handles are pulled apart. This simple machine will be more effective if the length of the wedge is long compared with the size of the objects to be separated.

Wheel and Axle

The last simple machine that this section discusses is the wheel and axle. For this simple machine, the force is applied by turning the wheel, and is then transferred through the axle to the point where the force is to be exerted. One of the most common examples of a wheel and axle is a steering wheel for a car or boat. Another example is an outdoor water faucet.

Compound Machines

Compound machines require a bit more explanation than simple machines. Compound machines normally consist of moving parts and multiple components. Some of them produce a mechanical advantage, just as some simple machines do.

Cam and Piston

Consider a *cam* and a specific application of a cam, the *piston*. These compound machines are used to change linear motion into circular motion, and vice versa. First, consider a cam, in which a rotating rod is used to change circular motion to linear motion.

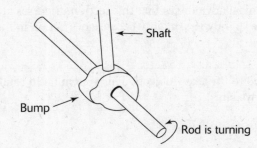

The rod turns, and as it turns so does the attached ring. Notice that the ring has a bump on it, and as this bump passes beneath the shaft, it causes the shaft to move up and down. The circular motion of the rod creates linear motion in the shaft.

There are many applications converting circular motion to linear motion in the mechanical world today. One such example is an oil pump. A more common example, however, is a piston.

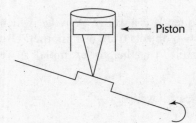

Although the appearance of the piston is slightly different than the cam, the principles involved are exactly the same. In this case, part of the rod is slightly displaced and a second bar connects this displaced portion of the rod to the actual piston. The turning of the rod causes the piston to move up and down.

Gears

Now consider how a system of *gears* works. Consider the simple example, consisting of only two gears, in the following diagram.

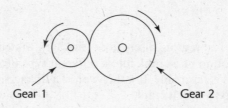

Gear 1   Gear 2

The smaller gear is designed to have 5 teeth, while the larger gear is designed to have 20 teeth. This means that for every rotation of the larger gear, the smaller gear has gone through four rotations. This system of gears can be used to increase or decrease the speed of circular motion. Also notice that if the smaller gear is turning counterclockwise, then the larger gear must be turning clockwise. The mechanical advantage for such a system of gears is simply the ratio of number of teeth for the gears, as in the following equation:

$$\text{mechanical advantage} = \frac{20}{5} = 4$$

If you want both components to rotate in the same direction, then you can use a system of four gears, as in the illustration below.

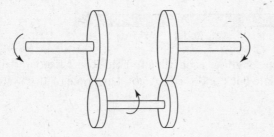

In going from the first rod to the intermediate rod, the direction of rotation changes. Then, in going from the intermediate rod to the final rod, the direction of rotation changes again, returning to what it was originally. A common application of this type of gear system is in an automobile transmission.

Crank and Winch

Another compound machine is the crank. A *crank* consists of a rod of varying radius with a rope (or chain, or other connecting device) that wraps around the smaller radius portion of the rod and connects to the weight that is being lifted (or otherwise moved).

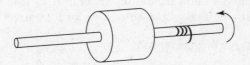

The mechanical advantage for this type of compound machine is simply the ratio of the larger radius portion of the rod to the smaller radius portion. You can also call this type of device a *winch*.

Linkages

The next compound machine requires a bit more discussion—linkages. Stated as simply as possible, *linkages* are capable of converting the rotating motion of a crank into a different type of rotating motion, oscillatory motion, or reciprocating motion. This process is reversible. In other words, a linkage is also capable of taking any of the three types of motion and using them to turn a crank.

The simplest type of a linkage is the four-bar variety, shown below.

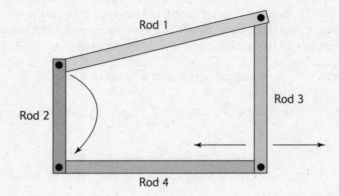

By making the four bars the appropriate length, it is possible to hold Rod 1 fixed and allow Rod 2 to rotate in full circular motion. Rod 3, then, will oscillate back and forth. A good example of this system in use is an automobile windshield wiper.

Belts and Chains

The last two compound machines this section covers are *belts* and *chains*. Belts and chains serve the same purpose: changing rotational motion of one speed to rotational motion of another speed. The principle is similar to a system of gears, except that the rotating elements are not in contact with one another. Belts are used in automobile motors, while chains are used on bicycles. Motorcycles can be either belt-driven or chain-driven.

Scoring Well on Mechanical Comprehension

Doing well on any test requires more than simply understanding the material. For a test such as the ASVAB, you have a distinct advantage in that you know the exact format of the test before the test begins. In this section, you can find some suggestions to help maximize your performance on the exam.

You can also apply the most important suggestion to the other sections: *Do not spend too much time on any one question.* After you read the question, if you know the answer, then simply select the answer and move on. If, however, you are unsure of the answer, then determine if there are any answers you can rule out. Cross out any answers you know are wrong. At this point, if you know the answer, select it. If you are still unsure of the answer, then move on to another question. Sometimes it takes a few moments for the correct answer to pop into your head.

Here is some advice for particular types of questions:

- **For properties-of-materials questions,** you need to understand how liquids and solids respond to outside stimuli, most specifically, forces and temperature. Be familiar with the way that mass, volume, and density are related. Finally, be able to understand what types of material are best suited for specific applications.

- **For structural-support questions,** try to visualize whether the configuration in question is well-balanced. In other words, will it be able to have external forces applied to it without falling over, or otherwise changing its orientation?

- **For fluid-dynamics questions,** determine whether a high-viscosity or low-viscosity fluid would be more appropriate. Be certain to understand that a fluid maintains equal pressure throughout (as long as the height remains the same), while an applied force can be magnified by increasing the area over which it acts.

- **For mechanical-motion questions,** be sure to understand the concepts of position, speed, velocity, and acceleration. Know how to apply these concepts to both linear motion and circular motion. Also, be aware that friction is present in all mechanical systems. Understand the consequences of friction for each situation that you are considering.

- **For both simple- and compound-machine questions,** be able to visualize a diagram of the machine. Be completely aware of which parts have to remain stationary as well as which parts are mobile. Be familiar with the mechanical advantage for the various machines, and understand that to gain in one area means to lose in another. In linear motion, you gain force but you lose distance. In circular motion, you gain torque but you lose speed.

Mechanical Comprehension Practice Questions

1. How much power is developed by a machine that performs 300 joules of work in 10 seconds?

    A. 30 W
    B. 2,500 W
    C. 240 W
    D. 260 W

2. A workman wants to move a TV along a ramp 12 ft long and 3 ft high. The TV weighs 350 pounds. How much force will it take to move the TV along the ramp? (Neglect friction.)

    A. 29.16 pounds
    B. 87.5 pounds
    C. 116.66 pounds
    D. 1050 pounds

3. What type of compound machine is shown in the following diagram?

    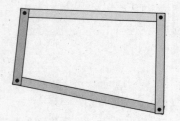

    A. piston
    B. linkages
    C. cam
    D. crank

4. An unevenly shaped object will have its center of gravity

    A. such that the weight is equal on both sides.
    B. such that the density is equal on both sides.
    C. such that the torque is equal on both sides.
    D. none of the above.

5. A crank is a useful compound machine that

    A. increases torque.
    B. decreases friction.
    C. increases speed.
    D. none of these.

6. An object is in free-fall near the surface of the Earth. What is the velocity before impact if it takes 5 seconds to hit the ground? Assume g to be 10 m/s^2.

    A. 5 m/s
    B. 2 m/s
    C. 50 m/s
    D. 125 m/s^2

7. A system consists of two pulleys, both of which are fixed. What is the mechanical advantage for the system?

    A. 1
    B. 2
    C. 3
    D. cannot be determined

8. All of the following are simple machines except

    A. the pulley.
    B. the cam.
    C. the screw.
    D. the wheel and axle.

9. While traveling from one point to another, a poorly secured load in the back of a truck hits the left wall of the truck in a curve. Which way did the truck turn?

    A. left
    B. right
    C. need to know the speed of the truck
    D. cannot be determined regardless of truck speed

10. Which of the following statements is true?

    A. The average speed can never be less than the average velocity.
    B. The average speed can never equal the average velocity.
    C. The average speed always equals the average velocity.
    D. The average speed may or may not equal the average velocity.

11. A force of 50 pounds is applied to a hydraulic jack. If the area where the force is exerted is five times the area where the force is applied, what is the maximum load that the jack can lift?

    A. 100 pounds
    B. 200 pounds
    C. 300 pounds
    D. none of these

12. A hydraulic system works best with a fluid that is

    A. highly viscous.
    B. moderately viscous.
    C. not highly viscous.
    D. does not depend on fluid viscosity.

13. On a cold day in the winter, compared to a hot day in the summer, solids and liquids will generally

    A. expand.
    B. contract.
    C. retain the same volume.
    D. cannot be determined.

14. Which substance has the highest density?

    A. lead
    B. wood
    C. water
    D. paper

15. In general, a load is best supported by a structure when it is placed as close as possible to that structure's

    A. center of gravity.
    B. geometric center.
    C. both of these.
    D. neither of these.

Answers and Explanations for Practice Questions

1. **A.** The solution requires direct substitution into the equation $P = W/t$.

2. **B.** In order to determine the mechanical advantage of an incline plane, use the following formula:

$$\frac{\text{length of ramp}}{\text{height of ramp}} = \frac{\text{weight of object}}{\text{force}}$$

$$\frac{12}{3} = \frac{350}{f}$$
$$4f = 350$$
$$f = 87.5 \text{ pounds}$$

3. **B.** Remember that the most common type of linkage is the four-bar variety, which is shown in the diagram.

4. **D.** Finding the center of gravity for an irregularly shaped object is beyond the scope of the ASVAB, but you should know that the center of gravity is not necessarily the point at which the weight is equal on both sides. Density (**B**) and torque (**C**) are unrelated.

5. **A.** A crank produces circular motion, so your two properties of interest are torque and speed. A crank increases torque at the sacrifice of speed (number of rotations).

6. **C.** The answer is obtained by direct substitution into one of the equations of kinematics: $v = vo + gt$. Because the object falls from rest, vo is equal to 0 m/s and the equation is reduced to $v = gt$.

7. **A.** Remember that for a system of pulleys to create a mechanical advantage greater than 1, at least one of the pulleys must be mobile. Because both pulleys are fixed, there is no mechanical advantage.

8. **B.** A cam is a compound machine.

9. **B.** Remember that the load will try to continue in a straight line. As the truck moves to the right, the load will hit the left side.

10. **D.** Velocity is displacement divided by time and may never be greater than speed. It may be equal to speed if the motion is in a straight line.

11. **D.** To find the exerted force, multiply the applied force by the ratio of the areas. In other words, exerted force = $50 \times 5 = 250$ pounds.

12. **C.** It is desirable to use a fluid that can flow through the system readily, without much internal friction to retard the flow.

13. **B.** Remember that both solids and liquids generally expand when heated and contract when cooled.

14. **A.** Higher density means that there is a greater weight in a given volume. A container filled with lead will be much heavier than the same container when it is filled with any of the other three substances.

15. **A.** While the center of gravity can be near the geometric center, it does not have to be.

Electronics Information

Electricity is an essential part of a modern technological society. Electricity is used to power and control everything from simple devices like electric lights to sophisticated electronics like computers. The Electronics Information test measures your knowledge of electrical theory, components, systems, and test equipment. The sections that follow cover the key elements of electricity that you will need to know to do well on this part of the ASVAB.

The ASVAB contains 20 Electronics Information questions. You will have 9 minutes to answer these questions.

Basics of Electricity

The two kinds of electric charges are *positive* and *negative*. In ordinary matter, the positive charges are *protons* and the negative charges are *electrons*. Relatively heavy protons are found in the dense core (nucleus) of an atom, while the much lighter electrons are in a cloud surrounding the nucleus.

Electric charges create an *electric field* around themselves, and this field exerts a force on other charges. Like charges repel each other, while opposite charges attract. Charges in motion create a *magnetic field* that exerts a force on other moving charges. If the magnetic field varies with time, it creates an electric field through *electromagnetic induction*. Time-varying electric fields also produce magnetic fields.

Electric and magnetic fields are both forms of energy. When charges are accelerated, they create changing electric and magnetic fields that can travel through space far from any charges that created them. Because time-varying electric and magnetic fields can create one another, the fields exist even where there are no charges. This traveling electric and magnetic disturbance is called an *electromagnetic* (EM) wave. The electric and magnetic fields vary with time so that they repeat many times each second. That rate is known as the *frequency* and is measured in hertz (Hz).

Light, radio waves, and X-rays are examples of EM waves. Electromagnetic waves can travel through a variety of media, depending on their frequency. Visible light can travel through air, glass, or water, while X-rays can penetrate those and many other materials. On the other hand, radio waves do not travel through water or metals. Unlike sound or water waves, EM waves do not require a medium to propagate; all EM waves can travel through a vacuum. All EM waves travel through the vacuum at the same speed, the speed of light, about 300,000 kilometers (or 186,000 miles) per second.

Most applications of electricity involve *electric current:* the movement of charges in a conductor. Current is denoted by I and measured in amperes or amps. By convention, the direction of current is defined as the direction of the flow of positive charge. Generally, the conductor is a metal, which means that the charges in motion are electrons. Only the electrons (negative charges) are free to move in a metal. So the direction of current flow is opposite the flow of electrons.

Some materials are better conductors than others. Most metals are excellent conductors, with silver and copper being the best. Materials such as silicon and germanium are called *semiconductors* because they do not have free electrons, but it is relatively easy for electrons to become free to conduct electricity. Impurities are often added to silicon to change its electrical properties to make devices such as transistors and diodes, as discussed below. Finally, there are materials, *insulators,* that are very poor conductors. Insulators include most plastics, glass, wood, and ceramics.

When electric current flows for any period of time, it must flow in a complete circuit; charge cannot accumulate in any one place. In the following simple circuit, electric current flows from the battery to the light and back to the battery or, more generally, from the *source* to the *load* and back to the source. If the circuit is not complete, so electrons cannot flow back to the source, it is called an *open circuit*. If an unintended path closes the circuit so that it does not flow through the load, it is a *short circuit*.

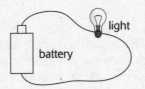

The electrons will not flow in the circuit unless they are pushed. The force pushing them is provided by the battery as a source of voltage, usually denoted by *V.* The voltage can be compared to pressure pushing water through a pipe. In this analogy, the electric current is the flowing water. The light bulb resists the flow of current. In general, any component that affects the flow of current is an *impedance.* A particular kind of impedance is *resistance,* in which electrical energy is converted to heat, as in the light bulb. Inductors and capacitors, described in the section "Electrical Components, Units, and Symbols," are also impedances, but do not dissipate energy.

The questions below illustrate how this content may appear on the ASVAB.

---

1. In a metal conductor, charges flow

   A.   in the same direction as the current.
   B.   in the opposite direction from the current.
   C.   in both directions.
   D.   in either direction, depending on the metal.

The answer is **B.** The moving charges in a metal are electrons, so they flow in the opposite direction from the direction of current flow.

---

2. A short circuit is

   A.   the shortest path for current flow.
   B.   a circuit with short wires.
   C.   an accidental path for current that bypasses the load.
   D.   a path for current that is shorter than the one through the load.

The answer is **C.** In a short circuit, the current flows through an unintended path instead of through the load.

---

3. Poor conductors of electricity are known as

   A.   metals.
   B.   insulators.
   C.   semiconductors.
   D.   electrons.

The answer is **B.** Insulators are the poorest conductors.

---

4. Which of the following is an electromagnetic wave?

   A.   light
   B.   radio
   C.   X-rays
   D.   all of the above

The answer is **D.** Light, radio, and X-rays are all electromagnetic waves.

5. All electromagnetic waves can travel through

   A. a vacuum.
   B. water.
   C. metals.
   D. electrical conductors.

The answer is **A.** Any EM wave travels through a vacuum. Radio waves cannot penetrate water or metals. Metals are electrical conductors, so **D** is also wrong.

Electric Power Generation

Electricity is typically generated from fuels, either fossil or nuclear, that are used to heat water in a boiler that turns a turbine, which then turns an electric generator (see the following figure). Certain renewable methods, such as wind or hydroelectric generation, do not require the consumption of fuels. Instead, natural forces provide the motion directly to the generator. For instance, in a hydroelectric plant, water flows through a turbine to turn the generator.

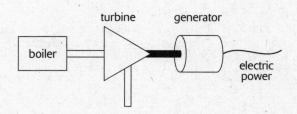

Most electricity generation is in the form of alternating current (AC), discussed in the section "AC and DC Power," later in this chapter. The voltage of the generator's output is increased to hundreds of thousands of volts for transmission over large distances on the *power grid,* and then stepped back down to lower voltage near the users. Voltage is stepped down and power is distributed at electrical substations. Transformers on power poles or underground bring the voltage down to levels used in homes and offices. Large motors in manufacturing plants often use power delivered at higher voltages.

The questions below illustrate how this content may appear on the ASVAB.

1. Electricity is generated by

   A. fossil fuels.
   B. nuclear materials.
   C. renewable sources.
   D. all of the above.

The answer is **D.** All three methods are used, although fossil fuels are the most common.

2. Voltage from the generator is

   A. sent directly to the users.
   B. stepped up for transmission.
   C. stepped down for transmission.
   D. decreased for transmission, and then increased for users.

The answer is **B.** Voltage from the generator is increased (stepped up) for transmission.

Electrical Components, Units, and Symbols

Electrical components are represented by special symbols. For example, the circuit in the "Basics of Electricity" section would be drawn as follows:

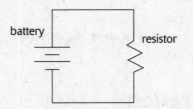

The figure below is a partial list of electrical components and their symbols.

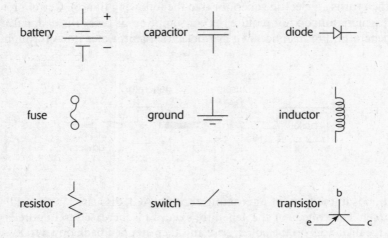

The following list describes the functions and composition of the components in the figure above.

- **Battery:** A source of voltage to push current through a circuit. The longer horizontal lines indicate the positive terminal, as shown in the figure. External current flows from the positive to the negative terminal. Batteries consist of cells in which a chemical reaction provides the energy to the electrons in the conductors (*electrodes*) that are immersed in the chemicals (*electrolytes*) in the cell. Batteries wear out when the electrolytes are consumed.
- **Capacitor:** A component that accumulates charge, storing electrical energy in an electric field. The letter C denotes *capacitance*, which is measured in farads. Two metal plates or curved surfaces close together that are separated by an insulator make up a capacitor.
- **Diode:** A semiconductor component that allows current to flow only in one direction, defined by the arrow in the previous figure. Diodes are used to convert AC current to DC (see "AC and DC Power," later in this chapter).
- **Fuse:** A circuit element that allows the flow of current below a certain value, but opens the circuit when the current exceeds this value. Fuses are used to protect circuits from damage by excessive electric current. Fuses consist of a strip or coil of metal with a low melting temperature. When too much current flows through the metal, it melts and opens the circuit.
- **Ground:** A common voltage reference level defined by the container of the electric circuit (chassis ground) or by the Earth (Earth ground).
- **Inductor:** A device that opposes changes in the flow of current, storing electrical energy in a magnetic field. The letter *L* denotes *inductance*, which is measured in henries. Inductors usually consist of a coil of wire, sometimes wrapped around a piece of iron (*iron core*) or an insulating shell (*air core*).
- **Resistor:** A component that opposes the flow of current, transforming electrical energy to heat. The letter *R* denotes *resistance*, which is measured in ohms.

- **Switch:** A device that interrupts or allows the flow of current in a circuit.
- **Transistor:** A component that controls the flow of current between the *emitter (e)* and *collector (c)* by the voltage applied to the *base (b)*. Transistors are the essential element in an electrical amplifier. A small amount of current can be used to change the voltage applied to the base, resulting in a large change in the current flowing between the emitter and collector.

The following table is a summary of units used in electronics.

Quantity	Unit Name	Unit Symbol
voltage	volt	V
current	ampere	A
frequency	hertz	Hz
resistance	ohm	Ω
inductance	henry	H
capacitance	farad	F
charge	coulomb	C
power	watt	W
energy	joule	J

Many electrical quantities are very small or large. To avoid writing many 0s before or after the decimal point for very small or large numbers, prefixes are used for powers of 10. The following table provides the decimal and scientific notation equivalents of common prefixes.

Decimal	Scientific Notation	Prefix	Abbreviation
0.000000000001	10^{-12}	pico	p
0.000000001	10^{-9}	nano	n
0.000001	10^{-6}	micro	μ
0.001	10^{-3}	milli	m
1,000	10^{3}	kilo	k
1,000,000	10^{6}	mega	M
1,000,000,000	10^{9}	giga	G

Electrical components are frequently connected using *solder,* a metal alloy of tin and copper or silver with a low melting temperature that joins wires mechanically and electrically. Electrical solder usually includes a rosin core, called a *flux,* to clean the oxidation from the wires being joined. Some solder, such as the kind used for plumbing, contains acid flux. Acid-core solder should not be used for electric circuits because it will eventually corrode the wires. A joint that has been soldered and allowed to cool correctly has a smooth, shiny appearance. A joint that appears dull and rough is called a *cold solder joint.*

The questions below illustrate how your knowledge of electrical components may be tested on the ASVAB.

---

1. Electric current is measured in

    A.   volts.
    B.   amps.
    C.   watts.
    D.   farads.

The answer is **B.** Electric current is measured in amps (or amperes).

2. One thousand ohms could be written as

    A. 1 MΩ.
    B. 1 kΩ.
    C. 1 mΩ.
    D. 1,000 kΩ.

The answer is **B.** The prefix *k* denotes 1,000, and the symbol Ω denotes the unit ohms.

3. Solder for electric circuits usually consists of

    A. acid flux and a tin-lead alloy.
    B. rosin flux and an acid core.
    C. a tin-lead alloy and a rosin core.
    D. oxidation and a rosin core.

The answer is **C.** Electrical solder is made of a tin-lead alloy and usually contains a rosin core.

4. Properly soldered joints appear

    A. shiny and rough.
    B. shiny and smooth.
    C. dull and smooth.
    D. dull and rough.

The answer is **B.** Joints that have been soldered correctly are shiny and smooth.

AC and DC Power

Electric current can be constant (*direct current,* DC) or oscillating (*alternating current,* AC). Batteries are sources of DC current. Power outlets are generally sources of AC. Alternating current is delivered by making the voltage vary with time, as shown in the following figure (a solid curve). The voltage waveform repeats many times each second, usually at either 50 or 60 Hz.

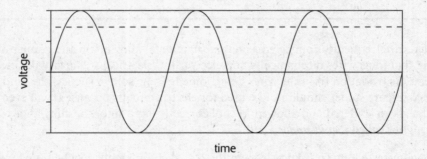

In the United States and Canada, the voltage of AC outlets is about 115 V at 60 Hz. Most European countries use 220 to 240 V and 50 Hz. The voltage quoted is the *root-mean-square* (rms) value, drawn as a dashed line in the figure. For AC power, the rms is typically about 70% of the peak voltage. For instance, 115 V AC power has a peak voltage of about 163 V.

One hot and one neutral terminal deliver the power in home or office electrical outlets. Three-prong outlets also have a separate ground terminal, which is connected to the neutral terminal at the service entrance (circuit breakers or fuses). Polarized electrical plugs have flat prongs of different widths: The narrow one is hot, the wide one is neutral. In a three-prong plug, the ground connector has a U-shaped cross section.

Home and office power for lights and small appliances is generally delivered at 115 V in a *single phase,* meaning that the voltage at the hot terminal oscillates with time as shown in the previous figure. Current flows between the hot and neutral terminals. Higher voltages are often delivered in the form of *three-phase power,* which requires three hot terminals. Each terminal has the same oscillatory voltage, but with phases separated by 120 degrees. Current flows between each phase and the other two terminals. Three-phase power is often used for heavy machinery with large motors.

The main advantage of AC power is that its voltage can be easily changed using a transformer. It usually consists of two inductors, the primary and the secondary, wrapped around an iron core, as shown in the figure below. The side of the transformer nearest the voltage source is the primary inductor. The two inductors have a different number of loops or turns. The ratio of primary to secondary voltage is equal to the ratio of the number of turns. For instance, a transformer with 500 turns on the primary and 100 turns on the secondary will transform 115 V to 23 V. This is a *step-down* transformer because the voltage on the secondary inductor is lower than on the primary inductor. If the secondary voltage is higher, it is a *step-up* transformer.

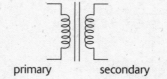

primary   secondary

Electric generators normally produce AC power because they use rotating coils in magnetic fields, which result in time-varying voltage. If DC power is required, a *rectifier* is used to convert AC power to DC power. Diodes are usually the key element of a rectifier because they allow current to flow only in one direction. It is also possible to transform DC power into AC power by using a solid-state device called an *inverter.*

The questions below illustrate how your knowledge of AC and DC power may be tested on the ASVAB.

---

1. Homes and offices are normally served by

   A. three-phase power.
   B. two hot terminals and one neutral.
   C. single-phase power.
   D. three hot terminals and one ground.

The answer is **C.** Outlets in homes and offices use single-phase power, which requires one hot terminal and one neutral. Sometimes they also include one ground terminal.

---

2. A transformer with 250 turns on the primary coil and 1,000 turns on the secondary is connected to a 230 V source. The voltage on the secondary is about

   A. 57 V.
   B. 115 V.
   C. 230 V.
   D. 920 V.

The answer is **D.** The secondary voltage is equal to the primary voltage times the ratio of the number of turns in the secondary to the primary: $230 \times (1{,}000/250) = 920$ V.

---

3. A device that transforms AC current to DC is a(n)

   A. inverter.
   B. converter.
   C. rectifier.
   D. transformer.

The answer is **C.** AC to DC converters are rectifiers. Inverters convert DC to AC and transformers change the voltage and current of AC power.

Ohm's Law

Consider the circuit shown in the following figure. The current flows from the positive terminal of the battery, through the resistor, and back to the negative terminal. The current can follow only one path, so it is the same everywhere in the circuit. The voltage, current, and resistance are related by *Ohm's law,* which states that the voltage is equal to the current × the resistance: V = IR. Using algebra, you can change the equation so that if you know any two of these values, you can calculate the third: $I = \frac{V}{R}$ and $R = \frac{V}{I}$.

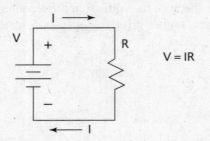

The questions below illustrate how Ohm's law may appear on the ASVAB.

1. A 5-ohm resistor is connected across a 10-V battery. What is the current flowing through the resistor?

   A. 2 A
   B. 5 A
   C. 10 A
   D. 50 A

The answer is **A.** According to Ohm's law, the current is the voltage divided by the resistance: I= V/R = 10/5 = 2 A.

2. A circuit requires that 3 A flow through a 30-ohm resistor. How much voltage is required across the resistor?

   A. 3 V
   B. 10 V
   C. 30 V
   D. 90 V

The answer is **D.** The voltage is the current times the resistance: V = IR = (3)(30) = 90 V.

You can apply Ohm's law to more complicated circuits. Electrical components can be connected in *series* or in *parallel.* When components are in series, the same current flows through both of them; when they are in parallel, the current divides between them. The following figure illustrates these two modes with resistors.

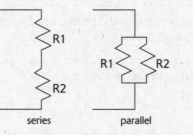

Resistors in series have an equivalent resistance to the sum of their individual resistances: R = R_1 + R_2. Resistors in parallel combine in a somewhat more complicated way: $\frac{1}{R} = \frac{1}{R_1} + \frac{1}{R_2}$.

The questions that follow illustrate how this content may appear on the ASVAB.

---

3. A 10-ohm resistor is wired in series with a 40-ohm resistor. The composite resistance is

  A. 8 ohms.
  B. 30 ohms.
  C. 40 ohms.
  D. 50 ohms.

The answer is **D.** Series resistors are summed: 10 + 40 = 50. Answer **A** would have been correct if the resistors had been in parallel.

---

4. Two 10-ohm resistors are wired in parallel. A single resistor can be substituted for these two without changing the behavior of the circuit. What is the value of the replacement resistor?

  A. 5 ohms
  B. 10 ohms
  C. 20 ohms
  D. 100 ohms

The answer is **A.** The correct answer is found by applying the parallel resistance equation:

$$\frac{1}{R} = \frac{1}{R_1} + \frac{1}{R_2}$$
$$= \frac{1}{10} + \frac{1}{10}$$
$$= \frac{2}{10}$$
$$= \frac{1}{5}$$
$$R = 5 \text{ ohms}$$

Joule's Law

When current flows through a resistor, it converts electrical energy into heat. The power dissipated in a resistor, R, is the product of the current through the resistor, I, and the voltage across the resistor, V: P = IV. Ohm's law can be used to substitute for the voltage in Joule's law to obtain a form only in terms of current and resistance: $P = I^2R$. For AC power, rms (root mean square) values for voltage and current are used in the formulas.

Many appliances, such as toasters, space heaters, electric stoves, and hair dryers, use resistive heating. The heating element in these appliances is usually a long metal wire with a high resistance. Incandescent light bulbs also work by resistive heating. The filament in a light bulb has a high resistance and heats to a high temperature so that it radiates light.

The questions below illustrate how this content may appear on the ASVAB.

---

1. A toaster draws 10 A from a 115 V outlet. How much power does it use?

  A. 1.15 W
  B. 11.5 W
  C. 115 W
  D. 1,150 W

The answer is **D.** To find the power, multiply the current times the voltage: 10 × 115 = 1,150 W.

---

2. A hair dryer with a 15-ohm resistive element draws 10 A of current. How much power does it consume?

    A.   1,500 W

    B.   150 W

    C.   15 W

    D.   10 W

The answer is **A.** $P = I^2R = (10)^2(15) = 1,500$ W.

Wires, Cables, and Traces

The simplest connection between electrical components is made with simple wires. They can be either *solid* or *stranded.* A solid wire consists of a single piece of metal wire, while a stranded wire is composed of many thinner solid wires twisted together to form a single conductor. Stranded wires offer increased flexibility and are more resistant to breaking than solid wires. Single conductors can be bare or *insulated,* for example, covered by a thin layer of plastic that does not conduct electricity. Insulated wires are used to avoid unintended connections when conductors need to be close together.

Some connections require more elaborate conductors. Single conductors are subject to noise from other parts of the circuit or the environment. Noise can be minimized by positioning a signal wire very near its return path, as in a *twisted pair,* where two insulated conductors are twisted around each other. For example, Category 5 Ethernet computer networking cables consist of four twisted pairs held together in an insulating jacket.

Coaxial cables (coax cables) provide even better isolation from noise. The cross section of a coax cable is shown in the following figure. It consists of a solid or stranded center conductor, surrounded by an insulator (the *dielectric*) and a braided outer conductor (the *shield*). In addition to enhanced noise immunity, coax cables can carry high-frequency signals without distortion.

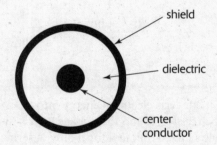

Electrical components are frequently mounted on printed circuit boards. These boards are made of an insulating material and coated with a conductor, usually copper. Most of the copper is etched away by acid, leaving a pattern of conducting strips on the insulator that will connect the components that are installed on it. The conducting strips are called *traces.*

The following questions illustrate how this content may appear on the ASVAB.

---

1. Compared to solid wires, stranded wires are

    A.   better conductors.

    B.   stronger.

    C.   more flexible.

    D.   thicker.

The answer is **C.** Stranding makes conductors more flexible. They are not necessarily stronger, thicker, or better conductors.

2. Category 5 Ethernet cable consists of

A. a single wire.
B. four twisted pairs.
C. one conductor.
D. a coax cable.

The answer is **B.** Category 5 networking cables are made up of four twisted conductor pairs.

3. Coax cables are used to obtain

A. better noise immunity.
B. more flexibility.
C. distortion-free high-frequency signals.
D. A and C.

The answer is **D.** Coax cables offer better noise immunity than ordinary wires and can carry high-frequency signals with minimal distortion. They are generally less flexible than single conductors or twisted pairs.

4. Traces on printed circuits are

A. conductors.
B. insulators.
C. dielectrics.
D. components.

The answer is **A.** Traces are the conductors on circuit boards. They connect the components on circuit boards.

Electric Motors

Electrical energy can be converted to mechanical energy by an electric motor. Motors are used in a wide variety of appliances, ranging from refrigerators and hair dryers to VCRs and windshield wipers. A typical car has about a dozen electric motors. It would be hard to imagine a modern industrial society without electric motors.

A typical motor consists of one or more coils of wire and a permanent magnet. In some motors, an electromagnet is substituted for the permanent magnet. When electric current is passed through the coil, it produces a magnetic field. The attractive force between the magnet and the coil causes the motor to turn. The current in the coil is reversed when the coil passes the magnet so the force reverses direction to repel the coil. If DC current is used to power the motor, a device is required to reverse the direction of the current flow twice each revolution of the motor. With AC current, the direction of the current itself reverses so no steps have to be taken to change the direction of the force.

The two kinds of AC motors are *synchronous* and *induction*. A synchronous motor follows the oscillations of the AC current; it turns at the frequency of the AC. While that can be an advantage, more often it is a limitation because motors need to be able to turn at different speeds for different situations. This limitation is overcome by induction motors, in which the coils surround a conductor rather than a magnet. Electromagnetic induction causes a current to flow in the conductor as the magnetic field created by the coils varies. In this kind of motor, it is not necessary to have a permanent magnet or rotating coil.

Industrial applications usually use three-phase motors, either synchronous or induction, to avoid some of the limitations of single-phase motors. Three-phase motors are more efficient and capable of delivering higher power.

The questions below illustrate how this content may appear on the ASVAB.

---

1. All electric motors work by using

   A. electric attraction.
   B. magnetic attraction.
   C. the force between static charges.
   D. electromagnetic induction.

The answer is **B.** Electric motors use magnetic forces. Electrostatic attraction is not used in motors. Some use electromagnetic induction, but not all, so **D** is incorrect.

---

2. Synchronous motors

   A. have the highest torque.
   B. can turn at any speed.
   C. turn at the frequency of the AC current.
   D. can be either AC or DC.

The answer is **C.** Synchronous motors turn at the frequency of the AC current, so they cannot be DC. Their torque is not necessarily higher or lower than that of other kinds of motors.

Analog and Digital Devices

Electronic devices can be *analog* or *digital.* In analog devices, voltages vary continuously. In digital devices, voltages can take on only discrete values. Most signals are analog, but digital devices sample analog signals to make them easier to store and manipulate. Numbers are represented as series of ones and zeros, called *binary* numbers. Each binary digit (one or zero) is called a *bit;* a string of eight bits is a *byte.* Digital information is usually converted to analog form for people to use; human interfaces are analog.

Many analog electronics have digital counterparts. For instance, a CD player is the digital replacement for a cassette tape player. Music is stored in analog form on an audiotape, while the same information is stored in digital form on a music CD. A CD player converts the digitally stored information to analog voltages that become analog audio signals.

Computers manipulate and store information in binary form. Once the information is ready to be presented to the user, the computer converts the information to analog form. Pictures stored as digital data are converted analog electrical signals that a monitor displays. Likewise, digitally stored sounds become analog voltages that drive speakers.

The following questions illustrate how this content may appear on the ASVAB.

---

1. Digital devices use

   A. analog data.
   B. binary numbers.
   C. continuous signals.
   D. audio signals.

The answer is **B.** Information is represented as binary numbers in digital devices. Analog data is continuous and audio signals can be digital or analog.

2. How many bits are in each byte?

    A. 2
    B. 4
    C. 8
    D. 10

The answer is **C**. Each byte consists of 8 bits.

Vacuum Tubes

Complex electronic devices such as amplifiers require components that control the flow of electric current, essentially electronic switches. Before the advent of semiconductor devices, vacuum tubes filled this function. They consist of an enclosure, usually glass, from which the air has been removed. A metal electrode (*cathode*) inside the tube emits electrons that another electrode (*anode*) collects. The cathode is heated to boil off the electrons. An electric field between cathode and anode can be used to push the electrons toward the anode. One or more electrodes between the cathode and the anode are used to control the flow of electrons.

The simplest tube is a diode. When a negative voltage is applied to the cathode, electrons flow toward the anode. If the voltage is reversed, electrons do not flow from anode to cathode because only the cathode is heated. A triode has a third electrode (the *grid*) that controls the flow of electrons from cathode to anode by repelling or attracting the electrons from the cathode. If a voltage is applied to the grid to repel the electrons, the current flow to the anode stops. The semiconductor replacement for a triode is a transistor.

Almost all vacuum tubes have been replaced by semiconductor devices; semiconductors are smaller and consume less power. Because they consume less power, they also dissipate less heat, which makes it possible to put them closer together as they require less cooling. Tubes are still used in some devices—older guitar amps, for example—and a few other selected applications that semiconductors cannot handle because of the voltage or current requirements.

The following questions illustrate how this content may appear on the ASVAB.

1. A vacuum tube is filled with

    A. helium.
    B. no gas.
    C. oxygen.
    D. air.

The answer is **B**. All the gases are removed from a vacuum tube.

2. Vacuum tubes are rarely used because they

    A. use too much power.
    B. take up too much space.
    C. are too hard to cool.
    D. all of the above.

The answer is **D**. Tubes use more power, take up more space, and produce more heat than semiconductors.

Semiconductors

Certain materials, *semiconductors,* can be either fairly good conductors or insulators, depending on some external control. The external control might be a voltage applied to the material or a light shining on it. For instance, a transistor's conductivity between collector and emitter depends on how much voltage is applied to the base. Similarly, light shining on a photodiode changes its electrical properties. Silicon, germanium, selenium, and gallium arsenide are commonly used semiconductors.

Semiconductors are essential to the manufacture of miniaturized electronic components such as integrated circuits, described in the "Integrated Circuits" section. The first application of semiconductors to electronics came about with the invention of the transistor in 1947. Since that time, semiconductors have replaced vacuum tubes in an increasing number of applications. Diodes and transistors are the two most common semiconductor devices.

The questions below illustrate how this content may appear on the ASVAB.

---

1. Semiconductors are

   A. good insulators.
   B. good conductors.
   C. somewhere between conductors and insulators.
   D. A or B, depending on external control.

The answer is **D.** The conductivity of semiconductors depends on external conditions. They can act like insulators or conductors.

---

2. Semiconductors are used to make

   A. vacuum tubes.
   B. transistors.
   C. lamps.
   D. batteries.

The answer is **B.** Transistors are made of semiconductor materials.

Integrated Circuits

The need for a higher density of components than a circuit board could accommodate led to the development of *integrated circuits* (ICs) in 1958, informally known as *chips.* A silicon wafer is covered with an insulating layer that is patterned with conducting paths and components, much like a printed circuit but on a much smaller scale. The process of patterning and etching is called *photolithography.* Photolithography is currently capable of putting about 2 billion transistors on a single chip.

A great variety of components can be made with photolithography on silicon, including resistors, capacitors, inductors, diodes, and transistors. This capability makes it possible to create almost any electronic function on a chip. Chips can be used in place of circuit boards with larger components, a development that has caused a dramatic miniaturization of modern electronics.

Integrated circuits are used in many electronic devices, ranging from cars and telephones to refrigerators and toasters. A *microprocessor* is a particular kind of chip that is at the heart of personal computers and other sophisticated electronics. Microprocessors consist of a large number of transistors and other components, and are designed to perform arithmetic operations.

Computers also contain memory chips to store data for the microprocessor. Random access memory (RAM) is usually dynamic, meaning that it must continuously be refreshed and is erased when power is no longer applied to the chip. The processor can write data to, or read data from, RAM. On the other hand, read-only memory (ROM) retains information stored even without power, but the data in ROM is written when the chip is made, and can be read only by the processor.

The following questions illustrate how this content may appear on the ASVAB.

---

1. Integrated circuits are usually made mostly of

- **A.** copper.
- **B.** silicon.
- **C.** germanium.
- **D.** gold.

The answer is **B.** Silicon is the most common material for wafers used to make ICs.

---

2. The chip that executes the arithmetic operations in a personal computer is a

- **A.** diode.
- **B.** RAM.
- **C.** ROM.
- **D.** microprocessor.

The answer is **D.** Microprocessors perform the calculations in computers. RAM and ROM are memory chips, and a diode is a component.

---

3. Microprocessors are found in

- **A.** telephones.
- **B.** cars.
- **C.** refrigerators.
- **D.** all of the above.

The answer is **D.** Microprocessors are found in almost every kind of appliance.

Radio and Television

Electromagnetic waves are used to communicate because they travel over long distances almost instantaneously. The first practical use of EM waves for communication was radio. The simplest way to send signals with radio is to use *amplitude modulation* (AM), which means that the signal is used to modulate the strength of the EM wave. In its most primitive form, the signal is an on-off code like Morse code and the EM wave is simply turned on and off to send a signal. More complicated signals, such as voice and music, can be sent by continuously increasing and decreasing the intensity of the EM wave to follow the signal. This change in the intensity of the EM wave is illustrated in the following figure.

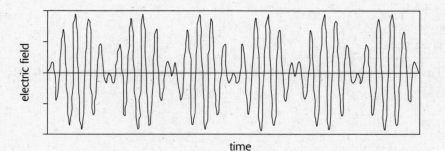

The name of the basic EM wave is the *carrier,* while the signal is the modulation. Typically, commercial AM radio is broadcast with a carrier at about 1 MHz frequency. The carrier frequency is the one that the station gives when it identifies itself. The rate of modulation (frequency) is about 5 kHz, only a fraction of the audio band, which extends to about 20 kHz.

A more sophisticated transmission method is *frequency modulation* (FM). Instead of changing the intensity of the EM wave, FM changes the frequency of the wave to carry the signal, as shown in the following figure. Note that the amplitude remains constant and the changing frequency of the wave contains the signal. In commercial FM radio, the carrier is modulated up to about 15 kHz, giving better audio fidelity than AM radio.

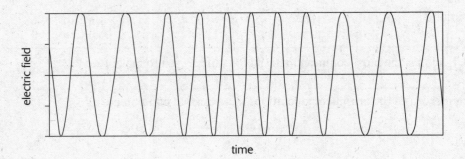

Broadcast radio and television signals use this method. The frequency for commercial FM radio is between 88 MHz and 108 MHz, with channels spaced at 200 kHz. Each of the broadcast TV channels 2 through 13 (VHF) is 6 MHz wide, between 54 MHz and 216 MHz. A gap between channels 6 and 7 is reserved for the FM radio band and other uses. The higher (UHF) channels begin at 470 MHz (channel 14) and extend almost to 900 MHz. Many other users (maritime, aeronautical, police, fire, and other emergency services) also use various frequencies between 10 kHz and 1 GHz.

Other communications applications such as cellular telephones and other wireless technologies use these same methods. Cellular telephone service is between 1 GHz and 2 GHz. Further improvements in modulation methods and the introduction of digital methods have created more reliable service.

The questions below illustrate how this content may appear on the ASVAB.

---

1. Which typically broadcasts at a lower frequency?

   A. television
   B. AM radio
   C. FM radio
   D. FM radio and television

The answer is **B.** Commercial AM radio uses about 1 MHz, about 100 times lower than FM and television.

---

2. Compared to commercial television and FM radio, the frequency of cellular telephone service is

   A. similar.
   B. 10 times lower.
   C. 10 times higher.
   D. 100 times higher.

The answer is **C.** The 1 GHz used for cellular service is about 10 times higher than the 100 MHz used for FM and television.

3. A radio station identifies itself as being at "93.7 on your FM dial." This means that

   A.   the carrier is at 93.7 MHz.
   B.   the carrier is at 93.7 kHz.
   C.   the modulation is at 93.7 MHz.
   D.   the modulation is at 93.7 kHz.

The answer is **A.** The carrier frequency is part of the station's identification, not the modulation rate. The commercial FM broadcast band is between 88 and 108 MHz, so 93.7 MHz could be an FM radio frequency, but 93.7 kHz could not.

Electronic Test Equipment

Troubleshooting and characterization of electric circuits requires the use of specialized equipment to measure the values of current and voltage at various locations in the circuit. The simplest and most commonly used instrument is the *digital multimeter* (DMM), shown in the following figure. Test leads are wires connected to the terminals of the meter and used to probe the circuit. The dial in the center allows the user to select different scales or parameters to measure (voltage, current). Usually, the user must also choose between AC and DC. The digital display shows the parameter selected, with some averaging so that the display does not change faster than the user can read it. For AC values, the voltage or current displayed is the rms value.

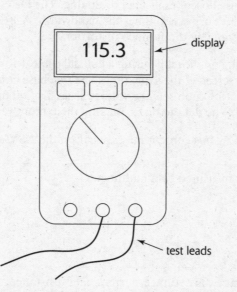

The analog equivalent is a *volt-ohm meter* (VOM). The term *multimeter* refers to analog and digital versions. A basic multimeter can measure the voltage or current across the test leads. The multimeter normally contains a battery to enable it to measure resistance by applying a known voltage across the test leads, measuring the resulting current, and using Ohm's law to find the resistance.

Another commonly used instrument is the *oscilloscope,* shown in the figure that follows. This device is most useful when measuring voltages that are not constant with time, such as AC voltages. The oscilloscope is also widely used in characterizing complex circuits such as radio and television receivers.

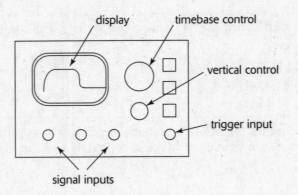

Oscilloscopes display a graph of the voltage as a function of time. In other words, a line on the display shows how the voltage varies with time, with voltage plotted in the vertical direction and time in the horizontal direction. The plot is made by sweeping an electron beam in a cathode ray tube (CRT) across a screen coated with a phosphor, much like a television set. Some oscilloscopes also use liquid crystal displays instead of CRTs.

A trigger signal begins the sweep at the left of the screen. In an analog oscilloscope, the signal voltage is amplified and applied to horizontal plates inside the CRT to deflect the beam vertically, tracing out a curve of the voltage plotted against time. Digital oscilloscopes digitize the voltage signal and store it in RAM. A microprocessor controls analog electronics that drive the display.

Almost all applications use digital oscilloscopes instead of analog. The fastest such devices have bandwidths of several GHz and digital sampling rates of several times the bandwidth. A 1 GHz bandwidth means that the oscilloscope can display up to a 1 GHz signal without much distortion.

The signal is usually connected to the oscilloscope using a coaxial cable. Most oscilloscopes can accept more than one signal and display them on the screen at the same time. The timebase control knob sets the horizontal scale of the display, while the vertical control knob sets the voltage scale. Digital oscilloscopes can display stored signals alongside new signals and can write data to disks, making them more versatile than analog models.

The following questions illustrate how this content may appear on the ASVAB.

1. Which of the following is not measured by a multimeter?

    A. voltage
    B. current
    C. inductance
    D. resistance

The answer is **C.** Multimeters measure only voltage, current, and resistance.

2. An oscilloscope displays

    A. voltage as a function of time.
    B. current as a function of time.
    C. resistance as a function of current.
    D. current as a function of voltage.

The answer is **A.** Oscilloscopes plot voltage as a function of time.

3. The fastest oscilloscopes can display signals up to

A. a few kHz.
B. 1 MHz.
C. a few MHz.
D. a few GHz.

The answer is **D**. Modern digital oscilloscopes have a bandwidth of several GHz.

Compact Discs and Digital Video Discs

Compact discs (CDs) and *digital video discs* (DVDs) are storage media for music, data, and video. The information on these discs is stored as digital data in microscopic pits in a piece of thin plastic 12 centimeters in diameter. A laser shining on the disc is reflected differently from the pits than from the rest of the plastic, resulting in either a high or low voltage: a digital signal. CD and DVD writers, or burners, use a laser to make the pits in a recordable disc to store data, including music, video, or other kinds of information.

Audio CDs can hold more than an hour of music, about 700 megabytes (MB) of data. Compact discs are used for the long-term storage of information. DVDs can store about ten times as much data because of several improvements in the technology, including smaller pits. The video data is compressed so that a DVD can hold an entire feature-length movie. A single-sided DVD can hold about 4 gigabytes (GB), corresponding to a 2-hour movie. Multilayer and double-sided DVDs offer even higher capacities. The video information on commercial DVDs is stored in an encrypted form so that the DVDs cannot easily be copied.

The question below illustrates how this content may appear on the ASVAB.

Compact discs can store

A. 100 MB.
B. 700 KB.
C. 700 MB.
D. 4 GB.

The answer is **C**. CDs can store up to about 700 MB of data.

Electronics Information Practice Questions

1. The best conductors of electricity are

    A. glass and ceramics.
    B. metals.
    C. semiconductors.
    D. plastics.

2. The carriers of electric current in metal conductors are

    A. protons.
    B. ions.
    C. electrons.
    D. electrons and protons.

3. For transmission over long distances, electric power is

    A. stepped up to higher voltage.
    B. stepped down to lower voltage.
    C. stepped up to higher current.
    D. converted to DC.

4. Which of the following electrical components dissipates electricity as heat?

    A. inductor
    B. capacitor
    C. diode
    D. resistor

5. AC electric power in the United States is delivered at

    A. 50 Hz.
    B. 60 Hz.
    C. 50 kHz.
    D. 60 kHz.

6. 15 kΩ is the same as

    A. 150 Ω.
    B. 1,500 Ω.
    C. 15,000 Ω.
    D. 150,000 Ω.

7. The figure below represents

    A. two resistors in series.
    B. two resistors in parallel.
    C. two inductors in series.
    D. two inductors in parallel.

8. 240 pF is an amount of

    A. energy.
    B. frequency.
    C. current.
    D. capacitance.

9. The speed of electromagnetic waves in a vacuum is

    A. the same for all frequencies.
    B. higher for higher frequencies.
    C. lower for higher frequencies.
    D. higher for stronger waves.

10. Two 30 Ω resistors are connected in parallel. The equivalent resistance is

    A. 60 Ω.
    B. 30 Ω.
    C. 15 Ω.
    D. 10 Ω.

11. In the figure below, the battery supplies 10 V, the resistor is 100 Ω, and the inductor is 10 mH. What is the current in this circuit?

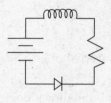

  A.   10 A
  B.   1 A
  C.   100 mA
  D.   0 A

12. Two amps flow through a 30 Ω resistor. How much power is dissipated in the resistor?

  A.   30 W
  B.   60 W
  C.   120 W
  D.   240 W

13. Cellular telephones operate

  A.   between 1 and 2 GHz.
  B.   between 100 MHz and 1 GHz.
  C.   near 10 MHz.
  D.   below 1 MHz.

14. FM stands for

  A.   fast modulation.
  B.   frequency mixing.
  C.   frequency modulation.
  D.   fast mixing.

15. Commercial television broadcast frequencies are

  A.   higher than commercial AM radio.
  B.   lower than commercial AM radio.
  C.   about the same as commercial AM radio.
  D.   higher than cellular telephone.

16. Digital multimeters generally measure

  A.   current and resistance.
  B.   resistance and voltage.
  C.   capacitance and resistance.
  D.   current, voltage, and resistance.

17. An oscilloscope displays a plot of

  A.   current vs. voltage.
  B.   voltage vs. time.
  C.   resistance vs. current.
  D.   inductance vs. capacitance.

18. Integrated circuits are made using

  A.   photolithography.
  B.   printed circuits.
  C.   coax cables.
  D.   vacuum tubes.

19. Vacuum tubes are used in

  A.   most electronics.
  B.   televisions and other displays.
  C.   radios.
  D.   no modern electronics.

20. Electric motors work by using

  A.   electric attraction and repulsion.
  B.   DC current only.
  C.   magnetic attraction and repulsion.
  D.   resistive heating.

Answers and Explanations for Practice Questions

1. **B.** Metals are good electrical conductors. Glass, ceramics, and plastics are insulators. Semiconductors are much poorer conductors than metals.

2. **C.** Only electrons carry electric current in metals.

3. **A.** Power is stepped up to a higher voltage for transmission. It is not converted to DC. Stepping the power to higher current is equivalent to stepping down to lower voltage.

4. **D.** Resistors convert electrical energy to heat. Ideal inductors, capacitors, and diodes do not.

5. **B.** AC power has a frequency of 60 Hz in the U.S.

6. **C.** The prefix "k" means 1,000, so 15 kΩ is 15,000 Ω.

7. **B.** The symbols represent resistors, and they are connected in parallel.

8. **D.** The symbol "F" stands for farad, a unit of capacitance. The prefix "p" means 10^{-12}.

9. **A.** All EM waves have the same speed in a vacuum, about 300,000 km/sec.

10. **C.** Resistors in parallel are combined according to this formula:

$$\frac{1}{R} = \frac{1}{R_1} + \frac{1}{R_2}$$
$$= \frac{1}{30} + \frac{1}{30}$$
$$= \frac{2}{30}$$
$$R = 15\ \Omega$$

11. **D.** The diode in this circuit prevents current from flowing from the positive to the negative terminals of the battery, so no current can flow.

12. **C.** Calculate the power using Joule's law, $P = I^2R = (2)^2(30) = 120$ W.

13. **A.** Cellular frequencies are between 1 and 2 GHz, much higher than the numbers given in the other answers.

14. **C.** FM means frequency modulation.

15. **A.** Commercial FM radio frequencies are at about 100 MHz, about 100 times higher than AM radio and 10 times lower than cellular telephones.

16. **D.** Digital multimeters measure voltage and current, and have a battery to measure resistance by applying Ohm's law.

17. **B.** An oscilloscope trace sweeps with time horizontally and plots voltage vertically.

18. **A.** Photolithography is the manufacturing method used to make integrated circuits. Printed circuits are much larger, and coax cables are used to connect electronic devices. Vacuum tubes are not used in ICs.

19. **B.** Vacuum tubes are still used in CRT displays for televisions and computers. Semiconductors have replaced tubes in most appliances, including radios.

20. **C.** Motors turn because of magnetic forces. There is no electrostatic force in motors. They can use AC or DC current. Resistors are not usually a part of a motor.

Assembling Objects

Past versions of the ASVAB test included two sections that have been dropped: Coding and Numerical Operations. Assembling Objects was added to the computerized version of the exam, and eventually became part of the pencil-and-paper test. The Assembling Objects test is given in the Enlistment Testing Program but *not* the Student Testing Program. For some people, this section will seem fairly easy. For others—almost impossible. However, when you finish this chapter, you should have very little trouble with these types of questions.

Keep in mind that the ASVAB test is not a pass-fail test; instead, it's designed to measure your aptitudes in a variety of different areas. If you do well on one portion of the ASVAB, and not as well on another portion, it merely signals your strengths and weaknesses. A left-handed batter, for instance, would not bat right-handed in a game—unless he was a switch-hitter. You play to your strength. Thus, doing poorly on the verbal portions of this exam might indicate that you're not really cut out to be a company clerk in the Army. Weak mechanical skills would probably steer you away from the base motor pool.

So it is with the Assembling Objects part of this test. It is supposed to measure your spatial aptitude and your ability to understand and process information about form, direction, and path. For some, this comes easy. For others, it's a complete mystery, although this section will try to demystify it for you.

> On the computer version of the ASVAB, you will have 12 minutes to answer 16 questions, and on the paper-and-pencil version of the Enlistment test you will have 15 minutes to answer 25 questions.

The Questions

The Assembling Objects portion of the ASVAB contains two types of questions. One type of question is very similar to solving a jigsaw puzzle. The other type of question is a matter of making appropriate connections given a diagram and instructions.

Puzzles

We begin by discussing the questions resembling the pieces of a puzzle. As with a jigsaw puzzle, you will be given the pieces of a small puzzle. Unlike a jigsaw puzzle, it is your job to determine what the final configuration will be.

Example 1 below is similar to one of the test questions:

Example 1

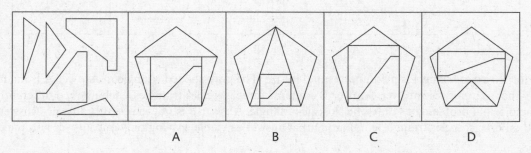

A   B   C   D

In the first box of the problem, on the left, are the pieces of the puzzle. The four answers are the assembled puzzle pieces. But only one of the answers is the correct configuration that goes with the provided puzzle pieces.

The first step to solving this type of problem is to eliminate any answers that are obviously wrong. In the given problem, there are five puzzle pieces. Examine each of the answers that you are given and eliminate any of the answers that have more, or fewer, puzzle pieces than your puzzle has. In this way we can eliminate Answer B, which has seven puzzle pieces, and Answer D, which has eight puzzle pieces.

With the choices narrowed down to two possibilities, it is important to note the differences and similarities in the two answers that are left. Answer A has two right triangles and a larger isosceles triangle, whereas Answer C has two scalene triangles and a smaller isosceles triangle. There are differences in the two irregular polygons that might also be clues, but if the correct answer can be determined using the simpler shapes, there is no reason to work with the more complex shapes. The puzzle pieces we are given have three triangles, with two of them being scalene and one being isosceles. This eliminates Answer A, so the correct answer must be C.

Another method of determining the possible correct answer is to look at the shape of the different puzzle pieces and number the pieces that are a specific shape. Two of the pieces are irregular hexagons. Those two pieces might be numbered 1 and 2, and all pieces like them would be numbered similarly, as shown in the following figure:

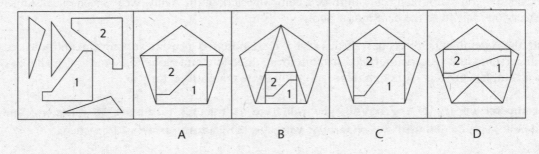

If the answer isn't already clear, then examining the remaining three puzzle pieces might make it clear. The three remaining triangles are approximately the same size. Only Answer C has three triangles that are approximately the same size. Sometimes it is necessary to continue to label the pieces with similar shapes until incorrect answers become obvious and are eliminated.

Another technique is to focus on one unique-shaped piece, and determine which of the answers contain a piece of that shape and size. In the example below, the isosceles triangle is shaded. Isosceles triangles in each of the answers are also shaded:

Remember: The correct answer choice will always have the same-size pieces as those shown in the far-left box.

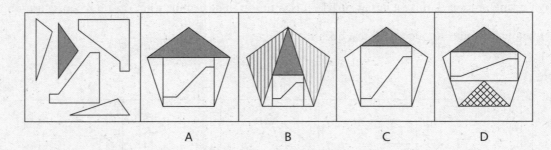

Note that the isosceles triangle is medium to small in size. The gray-shaded triangle in Answer A is much larger, eliminating that as a possible answer. Answer B contains three isosceles triangles, each marked differently. Because the original problem has only one isosceles triangle, Answer B is not the correct answer. Answer D also has more than one isosceles triangle, eliminating that answer as viable, leaving only one answer left, the correct answer, C.

In Example 2, each of the solutions has four puzzle pieces, making it impossible to base your elimination of choices solely on the number of pieces.

Example 2

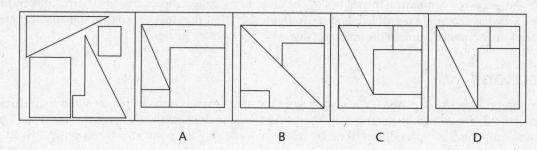

In this problem it is helpful to note the shapes of the puzzle pieces. The problem has two rectangles, a triangle, and one irregular pentagon. Answers B and C do not have a triangle in them, eliminating them as answers. Examining the irregular pentagon, and comparing it to the pentagon in answers A and D, it soon becomes obvious that the pentagon in Answer D is identical to the original problem, making this the correct answer.

Some of the problems in the test may include circles as well as polygons. Look at Example 3:

Example 3

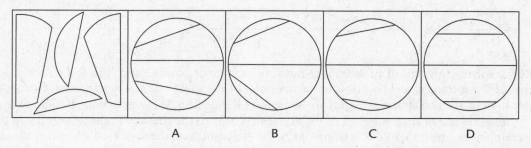

In this puzzle the circle has been cut in half, and each half is cut into two additional pieces. To determine the correct answer it is important to look at the shape of the pieces. Note that there are two larger central pieces, and two smaller end pieces. The larger pieces are roughly the same size, and the two long sides are both at an angle to one another. In Answer D, the sides of the larger pieces are roughly parallel, which is markedly different from the original problem, eliminating that as a possible answer. Answer B has a very steep angle, especially in the larger bottom piece. None of the pieces in the original problem have the same shape or angle, which eliminates Answer B as a possible answer as well. Looking at the final two answers, the clue lies in the size of the two end pieces. In Answer C they are mere slivers, but in Answer A they appear roughly the correct size and shape as the original, making Answer A the correct answer.

Sometimes the edges of the pieces are full of curves and wavy lines, instead of the more ordered and rigid edges in the examples we have thus far examined. See Example 4, which follows:

Example 4

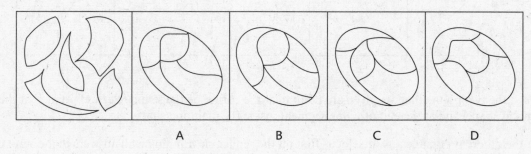

In a problem like this it might help to line up the pieces so that the edges form the basic shape of an oval. Numbering the pieces, or comparing the shapes of the largest or smallest pieces, can also help. Look at the correct answer as well as the original problem and try to figure out what the clues are that would enable you to pick out the correct answer and eliminate the incorrect answers. The correct answer is C.

Connections

The connection problems on the ASVAB ask you to put together two pieces given points *a* and *b* that are marked on two geometric figures, and a line segment *ab* that will be used to connect the two points. This type of problem is similar to assembling a complex object like a bicycle or a desk using the nonverbal directions provided. Here is Example 1:

Example 1

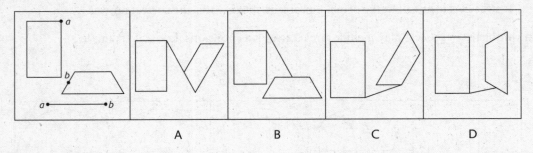

A   B   C   D

The first step in solving this type of problem is to note the location of points *a* and *b*. In this example, point *a* is on the corner of the rectangle, and point *b* is at the midpoint of the short side of the trapezoid. Once you have noted the location of the two endpoints, each of the answers should also be examined. In all four answers the corner of the rectangle is one of the endpoints of the line segment. Thus the true key to the answer lies in the position of the endpoint on the trapezoid. On trapezoid A, the endpoint is on the vertex, which makes this an incorrect answer. The same is true of Answer C. Answer B has an endpoint at the midpoint of one of the sides, but it is not the midpoint of the short side of the trapezoid. This makes Answer D the correct answer.

> **Remember: The key to finding the correct answer in an ASVAB connection problem is to find the location of the points, and then find the answer choice in which the location matches.**

Some of the geometric figures also have a line segment already embedded in the object, making the problem slightly more complicated; see Example 2:

Example 2

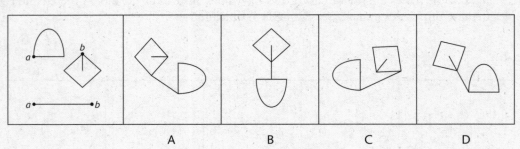

A   B   C   D

In Example 2, the two points that are given are point *a,* at the corner of the semicircle, and point *b,* at the corner of the diamond shape, and at the end of a line segment inside the diamond shape.

Looking at the different possible answers, focus first on the semicircle. Eliminate all answers that do not connect the corner of the semicircle. This eliminates Answer B, which goes to the midpoint of the straight side of the semicircle. The next thing to look at is the corner of the diamond shape. Note that the line must extend from the corner that touches the interior line segment. Answers A and C do not come from the corner containing that line segment, and can be eliminated, leaving only one correct answer, D.

Some of the problems include seemingly familiar shapes that resemble letters of the alphabet or other recognizable shapes. It is important to focus on the points that are being connected and how they are connected, rather than thinking too much about how familiar the object is.

Example 3

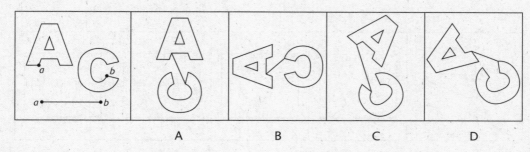

In this example, the two points that will be connected include the inner and lower vertex of the letter A, and the inner vertex of the letter C. See if you can determine why Answer C is the correct answer.

Final Word

Now that these problems are demystified, here are a few more practice problems. Remember the various techniques for solving them. You can number the parts and shade the similar pieces that are alike. Solving the connection problems is easier if you circle the connections and compare them to the original. Keep in mind that the key to success in all of the parts of the ASVAB is to continuously practice and review the material in both the text and review questions and solutions throughout the rest of this book.

Assembling Objects Practice Questions

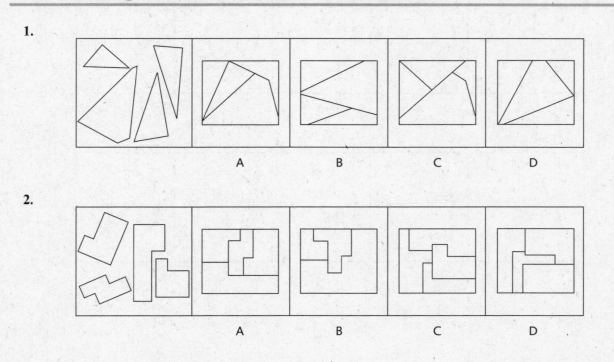

3.

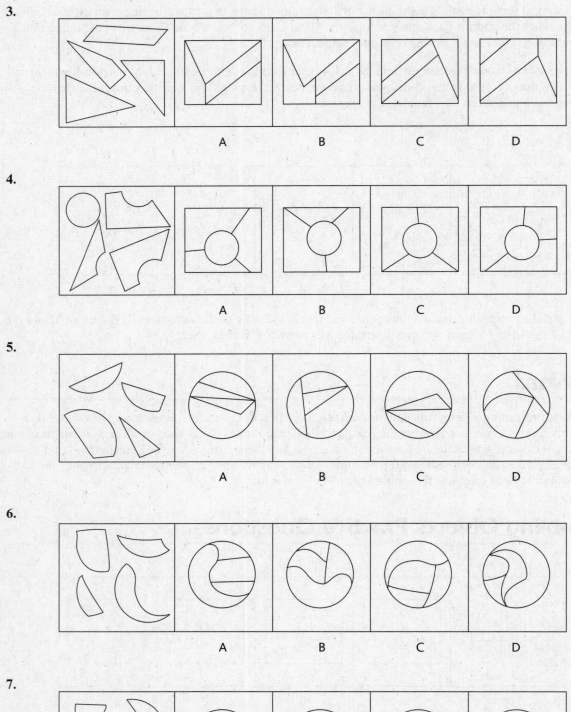

4.

5.

6.

7.

8.

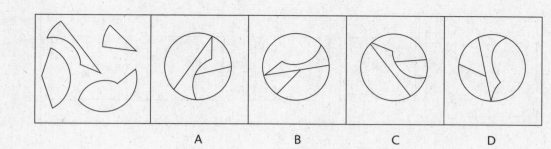

A   B   C   D

9.

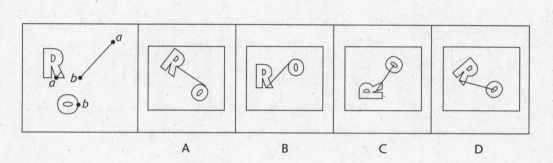

A   B   C   D

10.

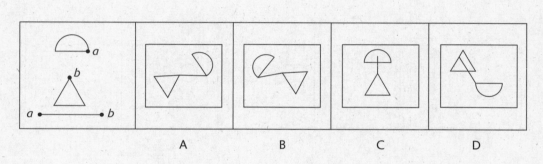

A   B   C   D

11.

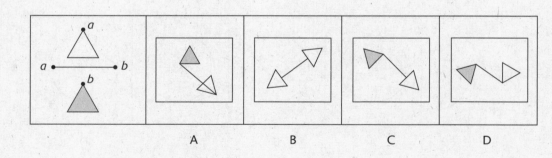

A   B   C   D

12.

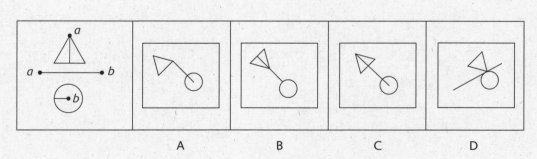

A   B   C   D

13.

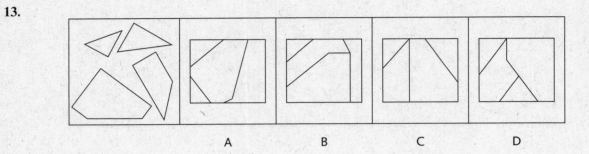

A   B   C   D

14.

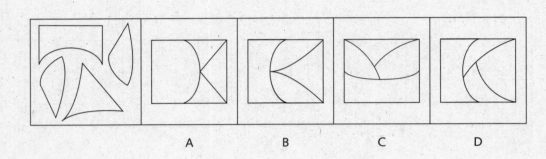

A   B   C   D

15.

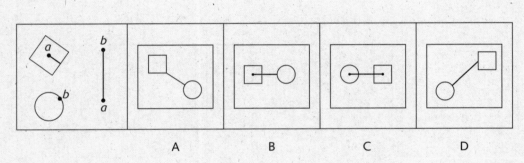

A   B   C   D

16.

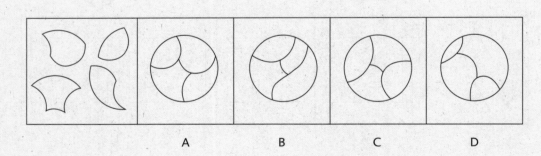

A   B   C   D

Answers to Practice Questions

1. **D.** puzzle
2. **A.** puzzle
3. **A.** puzzle
4. **C.** puzzle
5. **B.** circles
6. **C.** circles
7. **B.** circles
8. **B.** circles
9. **B.** joining
10. **A.** joining
11. **D.** joining
12. **C.** joining
13. **C.** puzzle
14. **B.** puzzle
15. **B.** joining
16. **A.** circles

PART III

FOUR FULL-LENGTH PRACTICE TESTS

ASVAB Practice Test I

Answer Sheet for Practice Test I

(Remove this sheet and use it to mark your answers.)

General Science

1 Ⓐ Ⓑ Ⓒ Ⓓ
2 Ⓐ Ⓑ Ⓒ Ⓓ
3 Ⓐ Ⓑ Ⓒ Ⓓ
4 Ⓐ Ⓑ Ⓒ Ⓓ
5 Ⓐ Ⓑ Ⓒ Ⓓ
6 Ⓐ Ⓑ Ⓒ Ⓓ
7 Ⓐ Ⓑ Ⓒ Ⓓ
8 Ⓐ Ⓑ Ⓒ Ⓓ
9 Ⓐ Ⓑ Ⓒ Ⓓ
10 Ⓐ Ⓑ Ⓒ Ⓓ
11 Ⓐ Ⓑ Ⓒ Ⓓ
12 Ⓐ Ⓑ Ⓒ Ⓓ
13 Ⓐ Ⓑ Ⓒ Ⓓ
14 Ⓐ Ⓑ Ⓒ Ⓓ
15 Ⓐ Ⓑ Ⓒ Ⓓ

16 Ⓐ Ⓑ Ⓒ Ⓓ
17 Ⓐ Ⓑ Ⓒ Ⓓ
18 Ⓐ Ⓑ Ⓒ Ⓓ
19 Ⓐ Ⓑ Ⓒ Ⓓ
20 Ⓐ Ⓑ Ⓒ Ⓓ
21 Ⓐ Ⓑ Ⓒ Ⓓ
22 Ⓐ Ⓑ Ⓒ Ⓓ
23 Ⓐ Ⓑ Ⓒ Ⓓ
24 Ⓐ Ⓑ Ⓒ Ⓓ
25 Ⓐ Ⓑ Ⓒ Ⓓ

Arithmetic Reasoning

1 Ⓐ Ⓑ Ⓒ Ⓓ
2 Ⓐ Ⓑ Ⓒ Ⓓ
3 Ⓐ Ⓑ Ⓒ Ⓓ
4 Ⓐ Ⓑ Ⓒ Ⓓ
5 Ⓐ Ⓑ Ⓒ Ⓓ
6 Ⓐ Ⓑ Ⓒ Ⓓ
7 Ⓐ Ⓑ Ⓒ Ⓓ
8 Ⓐ Ⓑ Ⓒ Ⓓ
9 Ⓐ Ⓑ Ⓒ Ⓓ
10 Ⓐ Ⓑ Ⓒ Ⓓ
11 Ⓐ Ⓑ Ⓒ Ⓓ
12 Ⓐ Ⓑ Ⓒ Ⓓ
13 Ⓐ Ⓑ Ⓒ Ⓓ
14 Ⓐ Ⓑ Ⓒ Ⓓ
15 Ⓐ Ⓑ Ⓒ Ⓓ

16 Ⓐ Ⓑ Ⓒ Ⓓ
17 Ⓐ Ⓑ Ⓒ Ⓓ
18 Ⓐ Ⓑ Ⓒ Ⓓ
19 Ⓐ Ⓑ Ⓒ Ⓓ
20 Ⓐ Ⓑ Ⓒ Ⓓ
21 Ⓐ Ⓑ Ⓒ Ⓓ
22 Ⓐ Ⓑ Ⓒ Ⓓ
23 Ⓐ Ⓑ Ⓒ Ⓓ
24 Ⓐ Ⓑ Ⓒ Ⓓ
25 Ⓐ Ⓑ Ⓒ Ⓓ
26 Ⓐ Ⓑ Ⓒ Ⓓ
27 Ⓐ Ⓑ Ⓒ Ⓓ
28 Ⓐ Ⓑ Ⓒ Ⓓ
29 Ⓐ Ⓑ Ⓒ Ⓓ
30 Ⓐ Ⓑ Ⓒ Ⓓ

Word Knowledge

1 Ⓐ Ⓑ Ⓒ Ⓓ
2 Ⓐ Ⓑ Ⓒ Ⓓ
3 Ⓐ Ⓑ Ⓒ Ⓓ
4 Ⓐ Ⓑ Ⓒ Ⓓ
5 Ⓐ Ⓑ Ⓒ Ⓓ
6 Ⓐ Ⓑ Ⓒ Ⓓ
7 Ⓐ Ⓑ Ⓒ Ⓓ
8 Ⓐ Ⓑ Ⓒ Ⓓ
9 Ⓐ Ⓑ Ⓒ Ⓓ
10 Ⓐ Ⓑ Ⓒ Ⓓ
11 Ⓐ Ⓑ Ⓒ Ⓓ
12 Ⓐ Ⓑ Ⓒ Ⓓ
13 Ⓐ Ⓑ Ⓒ Ⓓ
14 Ⓐ Ⓑ Ⓒ Ⓓ
15 Ⓐ Ⓑ Ⓒ Ⓓ
16 Ⓐ Ⓑ Ⓒ Ⓓ
17 Ⓐ Ⓑ Ⓒ Ⓓ
18 Ⓐ Ⓑ Ⓒ Ⓓ
19 Ⓐ Ⓑ Ⓒ Ⓓ
20 Ⓐ Ⓑ Ⓒ Ⓓ

21 Ⓐ Ⓑ Ⓒ Ⓓ
22 Ⓐ Ⓑ Ⓒ Ⓓ
23 Ⓐ Ⓑ Ⓒ Ⓓ
24 Ⓐ Ⓑ Ⓒ Ⓓ
25 Ⓐ Ⓑ Ⓒ Ⓓ
26 Ⓐ Ⓑ Ⓒ Ⓓ
27 Ⓐ Ⓑ Ⓒ Ⓓ
28 Ⓐ Ⓑ Ⓒ Ⓓ
29 Ⓐ Ⓑ Ⓒ Ⓓ
30 Ⓐ Ⓑ Ⓒ Ⓓ
31 Ⓐ Ⓑ Ⓒ Ⓓ
32 Ⓐ Ⓑ Ⓒ Ⓓ
33 Ⓐ Ⓑ Ⓒ Ⓓ
34 Ⓐ Ⓑ Ⓒ Ⓓ
35 Ⓐ Ⓑ Ⓒ Ⓓ

Paragraph Comprehension

1 Ⓐ Ⓑ Ⓒ Ⓓ
2 Ⓐ Ⓑ Ⓒ Ⓓ
3 Ⓐ Ⓑ Ⓒ Ⓓ
4 Ⓐ Ⓑ Ⓒ Ⓓ
5 Ⓐ Ⓑ Ⓒ Ⓓ
6 Ⓐ Ⓑ Ⓒ Ⓓ
7 Ⓐ Ⓑ Ⓒ Ⓓ
8 Ⓐ Ⓑ Ⓒ Ⓓ
9 Ⓐ Ⓑ Ⓒ Ⓓ
10 Ⓐ Ⓑ Ⓒ Ⓓ
11 Ⓐ Ⓑ Ⓒ Ⓓ
12 Ⓐ Ⓑ Ⓒ Ⓓ
13 Ⓐ Ⓑ Ⓒ Ⓓ
14 Ⓐ Ⓑ Ⓒ Ⓓ
15 Ⓐ Ⓑ Ⓒ Ⓓ

Auto and Shop Information

1 Ⓐ Ⓑ Ⓒ Ⓓ
2 Ⓐ Ⓑ Ⓒ Ⓓ
3 Ⓐ Ⓑ Ⓒ Ⓓ
4 Ⓐ Ⓑ Ⓒ Ⓓ
5 Ⓐ Ⓑ Ⓒ Ⓓ
6 Ⓐ Ⓑ Ⓒ Ⓓ
7 Ⓐ Ⓑ Ⓒ Ⓓ
8 Ⓐ Ⓑ Ⓒ Ⓓ
9 Ⓐ Ⓑ Ⓒ Ⓓ
10 Ⓐ Ⓑ Ⓒ Ⓓ
11 Ⓐ Ⓑ Ⓒ Ⓓ
12 Ⓐ Ⓑ Ⓒ Ⓓ
13 Ⓐ Ⓑ Ⓒ Ⓓ
14 Ⓐ Ⓑ Ⓒ Ⓓ
15 Ⓐ Ⓑ Ⓒ Ⓓ

16 Ⓐ Ⓑ Ⓒ Ⓓ
17 Ⓐ Ⓑ Ⓒ Ⓓ
18 Ⓐ Ⓑ Ⓒ Ⓓ
19 Ⓐ Ⓑ Ⓒ Ⓓ
20 Ⓐ Ⓑ Ⓒ Ⓓ
21 Ⓐ Ⓑ Ⓒ Ⓓ
22 Ⓐ Ⓑ Ⓒ Ⓓ
23 Ⓐ Ⓑ Ⓒ Ⓓ
24 Ⓐ Ⓑ Ⓒ Ⓓ
25 Ⓐ Ⓑ Ⓒ Ⓓ

Mathematics Knowledge

1 Ⓐ Ⓑ Ⓒ Ⓓ
2 Ⓐ Ⓑ Ⓒ Ⓓ
3 Ⓐ Ⓑ Ⓒ Ⓓ
4 Ⓐ Ⓑ Ⓒ Ⓓ
5 Ⓐ Ⓑ Ⓒ Ⓓ
6 Ⓐ Ⓑ Ⓒ Ⓓ
7 Ⓐ Ⓑ Ⓒ Ⓓ
8 Ⓐ Ⓑ Ⓒ Ⓓ
9 Ⓐ Ⓑ Ⓒ Ⓓ
10 Ⓐ Ⓑ Ⓒ Ⓓ
11 Ⓐ Ⓑ Ⓒ Ⓓ
12 Ⓐ Ⓑ Ⓒ Ⓓ
13 Ⓐ Ⓑ Ⓒ Ⓓ
14 Ⓐ Ⓑ Ⓒ Ⓓ
15 Ⓐ Ⓑ Ⓒ Ⓓ

16 Ⓐ Ⓑ Ⓒ Ⓓ
17 Ⓐ Ⓑ Ⓒ Ⓓ
18 Ⓐ Ⓑ Ⓒ Ⓓ
19 Ⓐ Ⓑ Ⓒ Ⓓ
20 Ⓐ Ⓑ Ⓒ Ⓓ
21 Ⓐ Ⓑ Ⓒ Ⓓ
22 Ⓐ Ⓑ Ⓒ Ⓓ
23 Ⓐ Ⓑ Ⓒ Ⓓ
24 Ⓐ Ⓑ Ⓒ Ⓓ
25 Ⓐ Ⓑ Ⓒ Ⓓ

Mechanical Comprehension

1 Ⓐ Ⓑ Ⓒ Ⓓ
2 Ⓐ Ⓑ Ⓒ Ⓓ
3 Ⓐ Ⓑ Ⓒ Ⓓ
4 Ⓐ Ⓑ Ⓒ Ⓓ
5 Ⓐ Ⓑ Ⓒ Ⓓ
6 Ⓐ Ⓑ Ⓒ Ⓓ
7 Ⓐ Ⓑ Ⓒ Ⓓ
8 Ⓐ Ⓑ Ⓒ Ⓓ
9 Ⓐ Ⓑ Ⓒ Ⓓ
10 Ⓐ Ⓑ Ⓒ Ⓓ
11 Ⓐ Ⓑ Ⓒ Ⓓ
12 Ⓐ Ⓑ Ⓒ Ⓓ
13 Ⓐ Ⓑ Ⓒ Ⓓ
14 Ⓐ Ⓑ Ⓒ Ⓓ
15 Ⓐ Ⓑ Ⓒ Ⓓ

16 Ⓐ Ⓑ Ⓒ Ⓓ
17 Ⓐ Ⓑ Ⓒ Ⓓ
18 Ⓐ Ⓑ Ⓒ Ⓓ
19 Ⓐ Ⓑ Ⓒ Ⓓ
20 Ⓐ Ⓑ Ⓒ Ⓓ
21 Ⓐ Ⓑ Ⓒ Ⓓ
22 Ⓐ Ⓑ Ⓒ Ⓓ
23 Ⓐ Ⓑ Ⓒ Ⓓ
24 Ⓐ Ⓑ Ⓒ Ⓓ
25 Ⓐ Ⓑ Ⓒ Ⓓ

Electronics Information

1 Ⓐ Ⓑ Ⓒ Ⓓ
2 Ⓐ Ⓑ Ⓒ Ⓓ
3 Ⓐ Ⓑ Ⓒ Ⓓ
4 Ⓐ Ⓑ Ⓒ Ⓓ
5 Ⓐ Ⓑ Ⓒ Ⓓ
6 Ⓐ Ⓑ Ⓒ Ⓓ
7 Ⓐ Ⓑ Ⓒ Ⓓ
8 Ⓐ Ⓑ Ⓒ Ⓓ
9 Ⓐ Ⓑ Ⓒ Ⓓ
10 Ⓐ Ⓑ Ⓒ Ⓓ
11 Ⓐ Ⓑ Ⓒ Ⓓ
12 Ⓐ Ⓑ Ⓒ Ⓓ
13 Ⓐ Ⓑ Ⓒ Ⓓ
14 Ⓐ Ⓑ Ⓒ Ⓓ
15 Ⓐ Ⓑ Ⓒ Ⓓ
16 Ⓐ Ⓑ Ⓒ Ⓓ
17 Ⓐ Ⓑ Ⓒ Ⓓ
18 Ⓐ Ⓑ Ⓒ Ⓓ
19 Ⓐ Ⓑ Ⓒ Ⓓ
20 Ⓐ Ⓑ Ⓒ Ⓓ

Assembling Objects

1 Ⓐ Ⓑ Ⓒ Ⓓ
2 Ⓐ Ⓑ Ⓒ Ⓓ
3 Ⓐ Ⓑ Ⓒ Ⓓ
4 Ⓐ Ⓑ Ⓒ Ⓓ
5 Ⓐ Ⓑ Ⓒ Ⓓ
6 Ⓐ Ⓑ Ⓒ Ⓓ
7 Ⓐ Ⓑ Ⓒ Ⓓ
8 Ⓐ Ⓑ Ⓒ Ⓓ
9 Ⓐ Ⓑ Ⓒ Ⓓ
10 Ⓐ Ⓑ Ⓒ Ⓓ
11 Ⓐ Ⓑ Ⓒ Ⓓ
12 Ⓐ Ⓑ Ⓒ Ⓓ
13 Ⓐ Ⓑ Ⓒ Ⓓ
14 Ⓐ Ⓑ Ⓒ Ⓓ
15 Ⓐ Ⓑ Ⓒ Ⓓ
16 Ⓐ Ⓑ Ⓒ Ⓓ

CUT HERE

General Science

Time: 11 minutes

25 questions

Directions: The following questions will test your knowledge of general science principles. Read the question and select the choice that best answers the question. Indicate that letter on your answer sheet.

1. The building blocks of sugars, and the substances used by plants in photosynthesis, are

   A. oxygen and nitrogen.
   B. oxygen and carbon dioxide.
   C. water and carbon dioxide.
   D. water and oxygen.

2. Members of a group that can interbreed and produce fertile offspring are in the same

   A. kingdom.
   B. phylum.
   C. family.
   D. species.

3. The normal body temperature of a person is

   A. 37° Fahrenheit.
   B. 37° centigrade.
   C. 98° Celsius.
   D. 98° centigrade.

4. A liter is about the same as

   A. a quart.
   B. a gallon.
   C. a pint.
   D. a half-gallon.

5. When heat is added to water, the added energy

   A. raises the electrons to a higher energy level.
   B. makes the molecules move faster.
   C. splits the molecules apart.
   D. increases the number of electrons in the molecules.

6. Look at the graph below of someone's blood sugar after he or she had been injected with a substance. Which of the following statements is true?

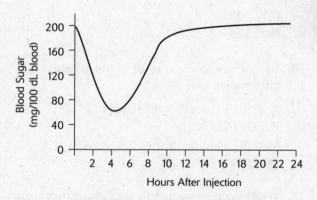

   A. The person's blood sugar level fell faster than it rose.
   B. The person had just eaten a big meal.
   C. The person was injected with glucagon, which converts glycogen to glucose.
   D. The person was a diabetic.

7. Using the drawing of the arm below, which of the following statements is true?

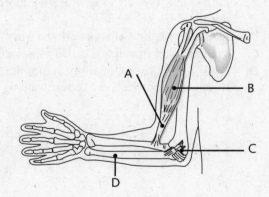

   A. A is a ligament, and C is a tendon.
   B. A is the biceps muscle, and C is a tendon.
   C. C is a ligament, and A is a tendon.
   D. A and C are both tendons.

GO ON TO THE NEXT PAGE

8. There are 2.54 cm in 1 in, 10 mm in 1 cm, 12 in in 1 ft, and 3 ft in 1 yd. Approximately how many millimeters are in a yard?

    A. 30
    B. 300
    C. 390
    D. 900

9. The expression 35 parts per million (35 ppm) is the same as

    A. 0.035%.
    B. 0.35%.
    C. 3.5%.
    D. 35%.

10. In which organelle is most of the hereditary information found?

    A. in the endoplasmic reticulum
    B. in the nucleus
    C. in vacuoles
    D. in the ribosome

11. Which sequence correctly lists the relative sizes from smallest to largest?

    A. solar system, galaxy, universe
    B. galaxy, universe, solar system
    C. galaxy, solar system, universe
    D. solar system, universe, galaxy

12. Which of the following statements about diffusion is FALSE?

    A. Diffusion is very effective over very short distances.
    B. Diffusion requires energy to do its work.
    C. The diffusion of water is called osmosis.
    D. Diffusion is the movement of molecules from a greater to a lesser concentration.

13. Based on the geologic diagram below, which of the following statements is NOT true?

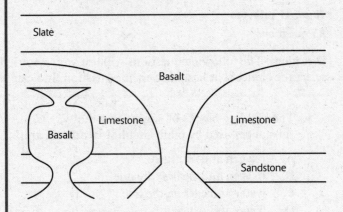

    A. The slate layer is older than the basaltic intrusion.
    B. The limestone is not the oldest layer portrayed.
    C. Basalt is an igneous rock.
    D. The sandstone layer is older than the basalt.

14. Which of the following is the result of the angle of tilt that the Earth has on its axis?

    A. day and night
    B. summer and winter
    C. continental drift
    D. different stars visible in Northern and Southern hemispheres

15. On a hike through the woods, a student discovers a multicellular organism that is growing on a tree. Upon closer analysis, the student notes that the organism is causing breakdown in the portion of the tree to which it is attached. This organism is most likely a member of which of the following groups?

    A. Plantae
    B. Fungi
    C. Protista
    D. Eubacteria

16. When air masses meet, why does warm air rise over cooler air and consequently cause rain?

    A. Warm air is less dense than cooler air.
    B. Warm air is denser than cooler air.
    C. Cooler air can hold less water vapor than warmer air.
    D. Cooler air is very volatile.

17. The process of dividing one cell nucleus into two nuclei is called

    A. mitosis.
    B. meiosis.
    C. cytokinesis.
    D. cell division.

18. Sodium ions have a charge of +1. This is because

    A. they have one more proton than electron.
    B. they have one more neutron than electron.
    C. they have one more electron than neutron.
    D. they have one more proton than neutron.

19. Which of the following statements is TRUE?

    A. Electrons are negatively charged and are found in the nucleus of an atom.
    B. Electrons are negatively charged and are found outside the nucleus.
    C. Neutrons are positively charged and are found in the nucleus.
    D. Protons are positively charged and are found outside the nucleus.

20. What is the oxidation state of oxygen in H_2O?

    A. +1
    B. +2
    C. –1
    D. –2

21. Humans have 46 chromosomes in each of their cells. How many are in their gametes?

    A. 2
    B. 23
    C. 46
    D. 92

22. A gas has a volume of 0.25 liter at a pressure of 1 atmosphere. If the volume increases to 0.50 liter, and the temperature remains constant, the new pressure will be

    A. 0.25 atmosphere.
    B. 0.5 atmosphere.
    C. 1 atmosphere.
    D. 2 atmospheres.

23. What are the total number of hydrogen atoms represented in the following formula: $C_6H_{10}(OH)_6$?

    A. 6
    B. 16
    C. 22
    D. 60

24. If red flowers were crossed with white flowers and all the resulting flowers were pink, what percentage of a cross between two pinks would be pink?

    A. 0%
    B. 25%
    C. 50%
    D. 100%

25. Vaccines work well because they prepare one's

    A. T-helper cells.
    B. T-killer cells.
    C. antibodies.
    D. memory cells.

Arithmetic Reasoning

Time: 36 minutes

30 questions

Directions: Each of the following questions will test your knowledge about basic arithmetic. Read the question and select the choice that best answers the question. Indicate that letter on your answer sheet.

1. A bread recipe calls for $3\frac{1}{4}$ cups of flour. If you only have $2\frac{1}{8}$ cups, how much more flour is needed?

   A. $1\frac{1}{8}$

   B. $1\frac{1}{4}$

   C. $1\frac{3}{8}$

   D. $1\frac{3}{4}$

2. How many omelets can be made from 2 dozen eggs if an omelet contains 3 eggs?

   A. 1
   B. 3
   C. 6
   D. 8

3. Two runners finished a race in 80 seconds, another runner finished in 72 seconds, and the final runner finished in 68 seconds. The average of these times is

   A. 73 seconds.
   B. 74 seconds.
   C. 75 seconds.
   D. 76 seconds.

4. If 400 people can be seated in 8 subway cars, how many people can be seated in 5 subway cars?

   A. 200
   B. 250
   C. 300
   D. 350

5. An employee earns $8.25 an hour. In 30 hours, what earnings has the employee made?

   A. $240.00
   B. $247.50
   C. $250.00
   D. $255.75

6. There are 72 freshmen in the band. If freshmen make up $\frac{1}{3}$ of the entire band, the total number of students in the band is

   A. 24.
   B. 72.
   C. 144.
   D. 216.

7. Dana receives $30 for her birthday and $15 for cleaning the garage. If she spends $16 on a CD, how much money does she have left?

   A. $29
   B. $27
   C. $14
   D. $1

8. A television is on sale for 20% off. If the sale price is $800, what was the original price?

   A. $160
   B. $640
   C. $960
   D. $1,000

9. Staci earns $9.50 an hour plus 3% commission on all sales made. If her total sales during a 30-hour work week were $500, how much did she earn?

   A. $15
   B. $250
   C. $285
   D. $300

10. The area of one circle is four times as large as a smaller circle with a radius of 3 in. The radius of the larger circle is

    A. 12 in.
    B. 9 in.
    C. 8 in.
    D. 6 in.

11. You use a $20 bill to buy a magazine for $3.95. What change do you get back?

   A. $16.05
   B. $16.95
   C. $17.05
   D. $17.95

12. Standing by a pole, a boy $3\frac{1}{2}$-ft tall casts a 6-ft shadow. The pole casts a 24-ft shadow. How tall is the pole?

   A. 14 ft
   B. 18 ft
   C. 28 ft
   D. 41 ft

13. Rae earns $8.40 an hour plus an overtime rate equal to $1\frac{1}{2}$ times her regular pay for each hour worked beyond 40 hours. What are her total earnings for a 45-hour workweek?

   A. $336
   B. $370
   C. $399
   D. $567

14. A sweater originally priced at $40 is on sale for $30. What percent has the sweater been discounted?

   A. 25%
   B. 33%
   C. 70%
   D. 75%

15. A cardboard box has a length of 3 ft, a width of $2\frac{1}{2}$ ft, and a depth of 2 ft. If the length and depth are doubled, by what percent does the volume of the box increase?

   A. 200%
   B. 300%
   C. 400%
   D. 600%

16. Mr. Triber earns a weekly salary of $300 plus 10% commission on all sales. If he sold $8,350 last week, what were his total earnings?

   A. $835
   B. $865
   C. $1,135
   D. $1,835

17. Jamie collects 300 stamps the first week, 420 stamps the second week, and 180 stamps the third week. He can trade the stamps for collector coins. If 25 stamps earn him 1 coin, how many coins can Jamie collect?

   A. 36
   B. 50
   C. 900
   D. 925

18. On a map, 1 cm represents 4 miles. A distance of 10 miles would be how far on the map?

   A. $1\frac{3}{4}$ cm
   B. 2 cm
   C. $2\frac{1}{2}$ cm
   D. 4 cm

19. Davis donates $\frac{4}{13}$ of his paycheck to his favorite charity. If he donates $26.80, what is the amount of his paycheck?

   A. $8.25
   B. $82.50
   C. $87.10
   D. $348.40

20. Rachel ran $\frac{1}{2}$ mile in 4 minutes. At this rate, how many miles can she run in 15 minutes?

   A. $1\frac{7}{8}$
   B. 4
   C. 30
   D. 60

21. Tiling costs $2.89 per square foot. What is the cost to tile a kitchen the dimensions of which are 4 yd by 5 yd?

   A. $57.80
   B. $173.40
   C. $289.00
   D. $520.20

GO ON TO THE NEXT PAGE

22. One-eighth of a bookstore's magazines are sold on a Friday. If $\frac{1}{4}$ of the remaining magazines are sold the next day, what fractional part of the magazines remains at the end of the second day?

    A. $\frac{1}{32}$

    B. $\frac{1}{8}$

    C. $\frac{7}{32}$

    D. $\frac{21}{32}$

23. Roxanne deposited $300 into a savings account earning $5\frac{1}{4}\%$ annually. What is her balance after one year?

    A. $15.75
    B. $315
    C. $315.25
    D. $315.75

24. One phone plan charges a $20 monthly fee and $0.08 per minute on every phone call made. Another phone plan charges a $12 monthly fee and $0.12 per minute for each call. After how many minutes would the cost be the same for both plans?

    A. 60 minutes
    B. 90 minutes
    C. 120 minutes
    D. 200 minutes

25. The length of a rectangle is three times its width. If the perimeter of the rectangle is 48, what is its area?

    A. 108
    B. 96
    C. 54
    D. 48

26. A machine can produce 8,000 widgets in 3 hours. How many widgets are produced in 1 day?

    A. 96,000
    B. 64,000
    C. 32,000
    D. 8,000

27. Sam buys three candy bars for 45 cents each and two packs of gum for 79 cents each. What is the total cost of this purchase?

    A. $1.24
    B. $2.93
    C. $6.20
    D. $6.24

28. Devin throws a football $7\frac{1}{3}$ yd. Carl throws it $2\frac{1}{2}$ times farther. How much farther did Carl's throw travel than Devin's?

    A. $2\frac{1}{2}$ yd

    B. $7\frac{1}{3}$ yd

    C. 11 yd

    D. $18\frac{1}{3}$ yd

29. This morning, Taryn drove 13 miles to the library and then returned home. In the afternoon, she drove 9 miles to the movies and returned home. How much farther did Taryn travel in the morning?

    A. 4 miles
    B. 6 miles
    C. 8 miles
    D. 9 miles

30. Heidi tallied the different car colors in the parking lot and summarized her results in a pie chart (see below). There are 260 cars in the lot. How many cars are either red or black?

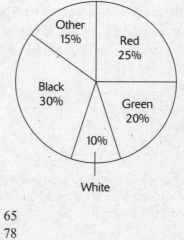

    A. 65
    B. 78
    C. 130
    D. 143

Word Knowledge

Time: 11 minutes

35 questions

Directions: This portion of the exam will test your knowledge of the meaning of words. Each question has an underlined word. Decide which of the four choices most nearly means the same as the underlined word; then indicate that letter on your answer sheet.

1. Adversity most nearly means

   A. help.
   B. hardship.
   C. love.
   D. ease.

2. Caustic most nearly means

   A. smooth.
   B. corrosive.
   C. soft.
   D. heavy.

3. They tried not to mar the furniture.

   A. spoil
   B. move
   C. overturn
   D. sell

4. Zest most nearly means

   A. enjoyment.
   B. sadness.
   C. stealth.
   D. annoyance.

5. Several of the people in the audience began to sway.

   A. tumble head-over-heels
   B. move back and forth
   C. laugh
   D. jump around

6. Enigma most nearly means

   A. pleasure.
   B. discomfort.
   C. celebration.
   D. mystery.

7. Punctual most nearly means

   A. missing.
   B. prompt.
   C. late.
   D. quick.

8. Loiter most nearly means

   A. dawdle.
   B. dive.
   C. enlarge.
   D. lose.

9. Fortunately they had an auxiliary light.

   A. bright
   B. helping
   C. halogen
   D. welcoming

10. You could tell that the carpenter was deft with his tools.

    A. angry
    B. foreign
    C. skillful
    D. careless

11. Meander most nearly means

    A. skip.
    B. scold.
    C. wander.
    D. want.

12. Parsimony most nearly means

    A. generosity.
    B. stinginess.
    C. willingness.
    D. payment.

GO ON TO THE NEXT PAGE

13. The crop was extremely <u>prolific</u> this year.

    A. wasted
    B. barren
    C. necessary
    D. fruitful

14. <u>Pithy</u> most nearly means

    A. full.
    B. concise.
    C. enlarged.
    D. incomplete.

15. The movie seemed <u>bizarre</u> to the crowd.

    A. exciting
    B. slow
    C. scary
    D. strange

16. The gathering was a <u>tribute</u> to the policemen.

    A. show of respect
    B. protest
    C. dinner
    D. payment

17. The man was accused of <u>slandering</u> his opponent.

    A. hitting gently
    B. speaking untruth
    C. pleasing
    D. tricking

18. <u>Somber</u> most nearly means

    A. straight.
    B. tipsy.
    C. elevated.
    D. grave.

19. The mansions indicated the town's <u>affluence</u>.

    A. decline
    B. growth
    C. silence
    D. wealth

20. <u>Docile</u> most nearly means

    A. sweet.
    B. easily led.
    C. soft.
    D. heavy.

21. <u>Hale</u> most nearly means

    A. wet.
    B. healthy.
    C. snowy.
    D. ill.

22. The old man became <u>reclusive</u>.

    A. annoyed
    B. solitary
    C. queasy
    D. obstinate

23. His work was of the highest <u>caliber</u>.

    A. price
    B. quality
    C. respect
    D. size

24. <u>Infinite</u> most nearly means

    A. endless.
    B. original.
    C. marked.
    D. happy.

25. <u>Opulent</u> most nearly means

    A. golden.
    B. wealthy.
    C. slim.
    D. empty.

26. <u>Trite</u> most nearly means

    A. pleasurable.
    B. ordinary.
    C. magnificent.
    D. tawdry.

27. <u>Vital</u> most nearly means

    A. healthy.
    B. essential.
    C. wasted.
    D. needless.

28. My mother gave me a present as an <u>incentive</u>.

  A. surprise
  B. motivator
  C. punishment
  D. accident

29. The workers began to <u>raze</u> the old building.

  A. burn
  B. sell
  C. repair
  D. demolish

30. <u>Scurry</u> most nearly means

  A. tumble.
  B. stroll.
  C. clean.
  D. scamper.

31. <u>Prudent</u> most nearly means

  A. toothy.
  B. wise.
  C. careless.
  D. willing.

32. <u>Ardent</u> most nearly means

  A. passionate.
  B. starchy.
  C. ignorant.
  D. final.

33. <u>Bland</u> most nearly means

  A. gourmet.
  B. tasteless.
  C. landlocked.
  D. homey.

34. <u>Solicit</u> as much advice as possible before your trip.

  A. worry about
  B. take
  C. ask for
  D. scorn

35. In the <u>interim</u>, I used my brother's car.

  A. winter
  B. meantime
  C. morning
  D. first stage

Paragraph Comprehension

Time: 13 minutes
15 questions

Directions: This is a test of reading comprehension. Read each paragraph and then select the choice below that best answers that question. Indicate that letter on your answer sheet.

1. Tsunamis are large ocean waves caused by earthquakes or underwater landslides. The word *tsunami* is a Japanese word meaning "harbor wave" because of the destructive effects that these waves have had on coastal Japanese communities.

   What is the best title for this selection?

   A. What Is a Tsunami?
   B. Japanese Natural Disasters
   C. Japanese Words and Their Meanings
   D. Effects of a Tsunami

2. Pyromaniacs are very rarely the setters of most criminal fires. Most people who set fires do so for insurance fraud, although others often set fires for revenge and terrorism. Very few people actually start fires because they receive strong psychological gratification from the act.

   A *pyromaniac* could best be defined as

   A. a person who never sets fires.
   B. a person who is afraid of fire.
   C. a person who sets fires and receives strong psychological gratification from the act.
   D. a person who sets fires to obtain revenge.

3. *Panther* refers to two different types of animals—the leopard and the concolour. *Concolours* are called by many other names: cougar, puma, mountain lion, and panther are just a few. In fact, the panther has more dictionary names than any other known predator.

   Which of the following is *not* mentioned as another name for the concolour?

   A. cougar
   B. mountain lion
   C. bobcat
   D. panther

Questions 4 and 5 relate to the following passage.

   Thomas Alva Edison is one of the most well-known inventors in history. He is most famous for inventions like the phonograph, the motion picture camera, and the light bulb. However, even Edison failed in a few attempts at invention, namely in trying to develop a better way to mine iron ore during the late 1880s and early 1890s. He was tenacious in his attempts to find a method that worked, but he eventually gave up after having lost all the money he had invested in iron-ore mining projects.

4. In this context, the word *tenacious* means

   A. angry.
   B. persistent.
   C. lazy.
   D. happy.

5. This passage is mainly about

   A. Edison's successful inventions.
   B. the light bulb.
   C. iron-ore mining.
   D. Edison's invention attempt in iron-ore mining.

6. In Alaska, there are long periods of darkness in certain regions because much of the state is located so far north of the Arctic Circle. Thus, those regions above the Arctic Circle experience unending daylight in certain summer months and unending darkness in some winter months.

   It can be inferred from the above passage that

   A. all regions of Alaska experience unending dark in winter.
   B. all regions of Alaska experience unending daylight in summer.
   C. regions south of the Arctic Circle experience alternating dark and daylight in the winter and summer months.
   D. regions south of the Arctic Circle have unending daylight in summer.

7. In an age that stresses the importance of water conservation, there are many plants that require less water than other more traditionally grown plants. In order to optimize their water usage efficiency, experts recommend watering such plants during the cooler times of the day.

One may conclude from the above statements that water-efficient plants should be watered

A. at 12:00 noon, when the sun is at its hottest.
B. at 6:00 a.m., when the sun has just risen.
C. at 10:00 a.m., when the day is warming up.
D. at 3:00 p.m., before the sun goes down.

8. Water is needed to sustain us as human beings. In fact, two-thirds of the human body is comprised of water. Because our bodies are so water dependent, we must drink water every day.

In this context, the word *comprised* means

A. consists of.
B. less than.
C. full of.
D. demands.

9. Obesity has become a national epidemic. Recent studies have shown that obesity is more serious than previously thought. In fact, obesity is harder on the health than cigarette smoking. Since 27% of Americans are currently obese, and 61% are overweight, this weight problem is exacting a huge cost from the medical community.

The percentage of Americans who are currently overweight is

A. 27%.
B. 52%.
C. 73%.
D. 61%.

10. Weight loss experts recommend lowered calorie intake and regular exercise to get rid of excess weight. However, lowering calories too much or exercising too strenuously can be detrimental to good health. Caloric intake should never go lower than 1,200 calories per day, and exercise should consist of at least 30 minutes 4 to 5 times per week to achieve healthy weight loss.

The best title for this selection is

A. How to Achieve Healthy Weight Loss and Avoid Injury.
B. Warning About Too Much Exercise.
C. Weight Loss Woes.
D. Caloric Recommendations for Weight Loss.

Questions 11 and 12 relate to the following passage.

Recently, cellular phone use has become a nationwide epidemic. A new study confirms that this epidemic might not be such a positive one. The study found that drivers who talk on their cellular phones while driving perform 30% worse on the road than drunk drivers do. Many have proposed using a hands-free cellular phone to solve this problem of dangerous driving. However, researchers discovered that even hands-free cellular phones distract drivers.

11. The author probably believes that

A. cellular phone use is not dangerous while driving.
B. hands-free cellular phones are safe for drivers to use.
C. cellular phones of any kind should never be used while driving.
D. cellular phones are a safe alternative to drunk driving.

12. This paragraph is mainly about

A. drunk driving.
B. hands-free cellular phones.
C. the dangers of driving with cellular phones.
D. the safe alternative provided by hands-free cellular phones.

GO ON TO THE NEXT PAGE

Questions 13, 14, and 15 relate to the following passage.

Although carjacking has become more common in the past 10 years, there are preventive measures that drivers can take. First, never walk alone to your car at night. Second, always drive with the windows rolled up and the doors locked. Lastly, drive on well-lit and often-traveled roads.

13. The best title for this selection is

    A.   Preventing Carjacking.
    B.   Carjacking Becoming More Common.
    C.   Driving Safety.
    D.   Night Driving Safety.

14. Which of the following is not mentioned as a preventive measure against carjacking?

    A.   driving on well-lit roads
    B.   carrying pepper spray
    C.   driving with windows rolled up
    D.   never walking to your car alone at night

15. The author probably believes that

    A.   it is almost impossible to avoid carjacking.
    B.   carjacking cannot be avoided at night.
    C.   carjacking never happens during the day.
    D.   carjacking can often be avoided by employing simple preventive measures.

Auto and Shop Information

Time: 11 minutes

25 questions

Directions: There are two parts to this test. The first will test your basic knowledge of automobiles. The second will test your knowledge of basic shop practices and the use of tools. Read each question carefully and select the choice that best answers the question. Indicate that letter on your answer sheet.

1. A technician is performing a cylinder leakage test on an engine. The technician sees air bubbles in the radiator with the cap off. What is the most likely cause?

   A. cracked cylinder head
   B. bad intake valve
   C. bad exhaust valve
   D. bad piston rings

2. Looking at a brake system with the drum off, the secondary brake shoe location is

   A. the front shoe (closest to the front).
   B. the rear shoe (closest to the rear).
   C. not important.
   D. only required for disc/drum systems.

3. If a thermostat in a vehicle's engine is stuck in the open position, the engine will

   A. overheat.
   B. not heat up to a proper temperature.
   C. wind up with a blown head gasket.
   D. use too much antifreeze.

4. In order for electricity to jump across the gap of a spark plug, a _____ increases the voltage to about 10,000 volts.

   A. distributor.
   B. rotor.
   C. coil.
   D. battery.

5. Looking at the figure below, technician A says Figure A indicates an improperly installed brake lining, while technician B says Figure B indicates worn brake pads. Who is right?

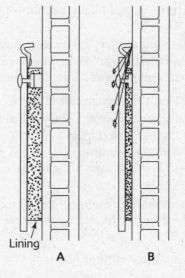

Lining   A   B

   A. technician A only
   B. technician B only
   C. both technician A and technician B
   D. neither technician A or technician B

6. A vehicle with front disc brakes and rear drum brakes has wheel cylinders on

   A. the front wheels only.
   B. all four wheels.
   C. the rear wheels only.
   D. one front wheel and one rear wheel.

7. Which of the following components is not part of the secondary of an ignition system?

   A. spark plug wires
   B. rotor
   C. distributor cap
   D. pick-up coil

GO ON TO THE NEXT PAGE

8. Which of the following is not one of the three main pollutants exhausted from a gas-powered vehicle's engine?

   A. carbon monoxide (CO)
   B. methane (CH_4)
   C. hydrocarbons (HC)
   D. nitrogen oxides (NOX)

9. In a computer-controlled ignition system, the ignition module

   A. changes ignition timing.
   B. controls the amount of secondary voltage.
   C. controls the magnetic pickup.
   D. turns on and off the primary current.

10. A starting system includes components such as the starter motor, solenoid, and/or relay. What do these components have in common?

    A. They are mechanically controlled.
    B. They are parallel to each other.
    C. They use the principles of electromagnetism.
    D. They operate on A/C current.

11. In an automotive electrical series circuit, what will be the effect of adding an additional resistance?

    A. increased current flow
    B. increased voltage
    C. reduced current flow
    D. no affect on current flow

12. Which of the following requires an extractor for removal?

    A. pistons
    B. bushings
    C. broken bolts
    D. All of the above.

13. A tap is used to

    A. cut internal threads.
    B. cut external threads.
    C. center-punch before drilling.
    D. detect vibration.

14. A veining bit is used with a

    A. hand drill.
    B. drill press.
    C. router.
    D. electric saw.

15. Lumber from trees with needles is referred to as

    A. softwood.
    B. hardwood.
    C. refined wood.
    D. common wood.

16. The illustration below is an example of a

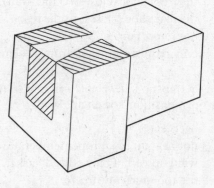

    A. bevel joint.
    B. notch joint.
    C. lap joint.
    D. dovetail joint.

17. A pipe wrench would usually be used by a

    A. plumber.
    B. carpenter.
    C. woodworker.
    D. auto-body repairperson.

18. The illustration below is an example of

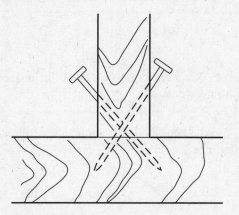

- **A.** clamping.
- **B.** lap joints.
- **C.** doweling.
- **D.** toenailing.

19. A lathe is normally used to make

- **A.** walls.
- **B.** cabinet doors.
- **C.** chair legs.
- **D.** a bookshelf.

20. The screw head illustrated below is a

- **A.** drywall screw.
- **B.** Phillips head screw.
- **C.** roundhead screw.
- **D.** flathead screw.

21. To mix concrete, you should mix

- **A.** cement, stones, and sand.
- **B.** cement, water, gravel, and sand.
- **C.** cement and sand.
- **D.** cement, dirt, and water.

22. To use a bit in a hand drill,

- **A.** insert the lip into the flute.
- **B.** insert the auger into the base.
- **C.** insert the tang into the chuck.
- **D.** insert the spur into the chuck.

23. What is a countersink?

- **A.** type of drill bit
- **B.** type of file
- **C.** type of inlay material
- **D.** type of bench plane

24. A contour gauge measures

- **A.** the length of an object.
- **B.** the width of an object.
- **C.** the diameter of an object.
- **D.** and forms an outline of an object.

25. To stop a board from chipping on the end as you plane, you can

- **A.** nail a piece of wood to the end of the board as an extension of the board.
- **B.** cut off the end after planing.
- **C.** glue the chipped pieces back after finishing.
- **D.** insert a nail into the end of the board to hold it together.

Mathematics Knowledge

Time: 24 minutes

25 questions

Directions: This section will test your knowledge of basic mathematics. Read each question carefully and select the choice that best answers the question. Indicate that letter on your answer sheet.

1. If $a = \frac{5}{2}$ then $\frac{1}{a} =$
   - A. 2.
   - B. 5.
   - C. $\frac{2}{5}$.
   - D. $\frac{5}{2}$.

2. 12 is 15% of what number?
   - A. 0.0125
   - B. 1.8
   - C. 18
   - D. 80

3. Evaluate $3x + 7$ when $x = -3$.
   - A. −2
   - B. 10
   - C. 16
   - D. 30

4. Find the length of the diagonal of a square the area of which is 36.
   - A. 6
   - B. $6\sqrt{2}$
   - C. 9
   - D. $9\sqrt{2}$

5. If $a + b = 6$, what is the value of $3a + 3b$?
   - A. 9
   - B. 12
   - C. 18
   - D. 24

6. Find the length of the radius in the following figure.

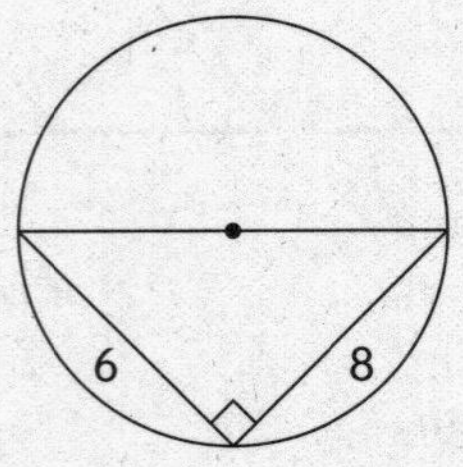

   - A. 3
   - B. 4
   - C. 5
   - D. 10

7. $(3 - 1) \times 7 - (12 \div 2) =$
   - A. 1
   - B. −2
   - C. 4
   - D. 8

8. The greatest common factor of 24 and 36 is
   - A. 6.
   - B. 12.
   - C. 36.
   - D. 72.

9. Solve for m: $3m - 12 = -6$
   - A. −6
   - B. 0
   - C. 2
   - D. 6

10. If $7p + 5q = -3$, find q when $p = 1$.
    - A. −1
    - B. −2
    - C. $-\frac{8}{7}$
    - D. $-\frac{2}{7}$

11. The slope of the line shown is

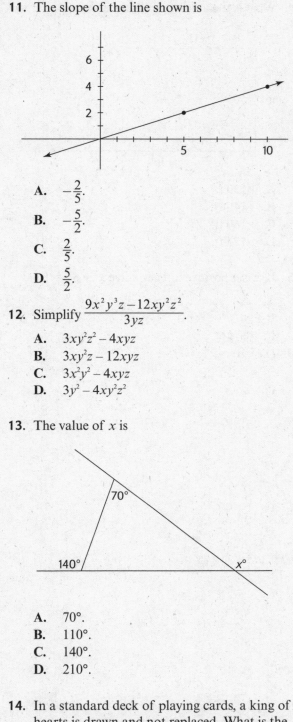

A. $-\dfrac{2}{5}$.

B. $-\dfrac{5}{2}$.

C. $\dfrac{2}{5}$.

D. $\dfrac{5}{2}$.

12. Simplify $\dfrac{9x^2y^3z - 12xy^2z^2}{3yz}$.

A. $3xy^2z^2 - 4xyz$

B. $3xy^2z - 12xyz$

C. $3x^2y^2 - 4xyz$

D. $3y^2 - 4xy^2z^2$

13. The value of x is

A. $70°$.

B. $110°$.

C. $140°$.

D. $210°$.

14. In a standard deck of playing cards, a king of hearts is drawn and not replaced. What is the probability of drawing another king from the deck?

A. $\dfrac{1}{4}$

B. $\dfrac{1}{13}$

C. $\dfrac{1}{17}$

D. $\dfrac{3}{52}$

15. How many minutes are there in 1 week?

A. 10,080

B. 1,440

C. 420

D. 168

16. If $2^{b+3} = \dfrac{1}{8}$, $b =$

A. -6.

B. -3.

C. 0.

D. 2.

17. The angles of a triangle are in the ratio 3:4:5. What is the measure of the smallest angle?

A. $15°$

B. $30°$

C. $45°$

D. $75°$

18. $(2x^3 - 3x + 1) - (x^2 - 3x - 2) =$

A. $2x^3 - x^2 + 3$

B. $2x^3 - x^2 - 6x - 1$

C. $x^3 - 6x + 1$

D. $x^2 + 3$

19. If the area of a square is 400, what is the length of its side?

A. 20

B. 40

C. 100

D. 200

20. Seven more than 3 times a number is equal to 70. Find the number.

A. 10

B. 17

C. 21

D. 30

21. Which expression represents the volume of a cylinder the height of which is equivalent to the length of the radius?

A. πr^2

B. πr^3

C. $(\pi r)^2$

D. $(\pi r)^3$

GO ON TO THE NEXT PAGE

22. How many distinct prime factors are there in 120?

    A. 2

    B. 3

    C. 4

    D. 5

23. What percent of $\frac{3}{4}$ is $\frac{1}{8}$?

    A. $9\frac{3}{8}\%$

    B. 12%

    C. $16\frac{2}{3}\%$

    D. 25%

24. What is the area of the figure shown?

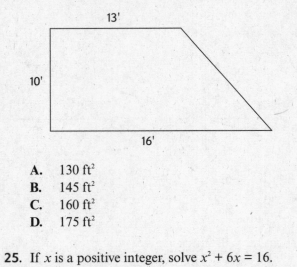

    A. 130 ft^2

    B. 145 ft^2

    C. 160 ft^2

    D. 175 ft^2

25. If x is a positive integer, solve $x^2 + 6x = 16$.

    A. 2

    B. 4

    C. 8

    D. 10

STOP

Mechanical Comprehension

Time: 19 minutes

25 questions

Directions: This section will test your knowledge of mechanical principles. Read each question carefully and then select the choice that best answers the question. Indicate that letter on your answer sheet.

1. A stone is tied to the end of a string and swings in a circular motion. If the speed of the stone is tripled, the centripetal force of the stone will become

   A. 3 times as great.
   B. $\frac{1}{3}$ as much.
   C. 9 times as great.
   D. $\frac{1}{9}$ as much.

2. Which of the following units measures the weight of a body?

   A. calorie
   B. newton
   C. kilogram
   D. kg · m/s

3. The joule is a unit of

   A. work only.
   B. kinetic energy only.
   C. potential energy only.
   D. heat, kinetic energy, and potential energy.

4. Two objects with different weights are dropped at the same moment from the top of the Leaning Tower of Pisa.

   A. Both objects hit the ground at the same time.
   B. The heavier object hits the ground first.
   C. The heavier object hits the ground last.
   D. The arrival time at the ground depends on the density of each object.

5. The quantity 2 m/s² is a measure of

   A. speed.
   B. acceleration.
   C. velocity.
   D. metric volume.

6. For a car moving around a circular track at a constant speed, the acceleration is

   A. away from the center of the circle.
   B. toward the center of the circle.
   C. in the direction of motion.
   D. opposite to the direction of motion.

7. A ball thrown vertically upward has an initial potential energy of 100 J and an initial kinetic energy of 700 J. At the top of the trajectory its energy in joules is

   A. 100.
   B. 700.
   C. 800.
   D. 1,000.

8. A simple pendulum has a frequency of oscillation f. In order to double f, the length of the pendulum should be

   A. increased by a factor of 2.
   B. decreased by a factor of 2.
   C. increased by a factor of 4.
   D. decreased by a factor of 4.

9. The velocity of a baseball 4 seconds after it is thrown vertically upward with a speed of 32.1 m/s is

   A. –7.2 m/s.
   B. 71.2 m/s.
   C. 7.20 m/s.
   D. 14.6 m/s.

10. Two masses fall 3 meters to the ground. If friction is neglected, when they reach the ground

    A. both masses have the same speed.
    B. both masses have the same energy.
    C. both masses have the same momentum.
    D. the heavier mass has a higher speed.

GO ON TO THE NEXT PAGE

11. Which of the following is considered a simple machine?

    A. gears
    B. linkage
    C. bicycle
    D. lever

12. The torque required to loosen a nut that holds a wheel on a car has a magnitude of 56 newton-meters. If a 0.35-meter lug wrench is used to loosen the nut when the angle of the wrench is 56°, the force that must be exerted at the end of the wrench is

    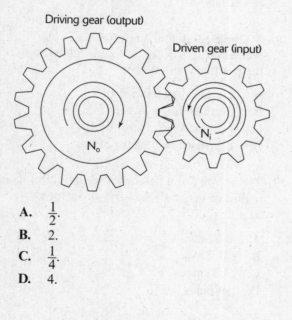

    A. 200 N.
    B. 286 N.
    C. 143 N.
    D. 100 N.

13. In the spur gear arrangement shown in the figure below, the ratio of the number of teeth on the output gear (N_o) to the number of teeth on the input gear (N_i) is 2. The speed ratio of the input to output gear is

    Driving gear (output)

    Driven gear (input)

    N_o

    N_i

    A. $\frac{1}{2}$.
    B. 2.
    C. $\frac{1}{4}$.
    D. 4.

14. The gain in kinetic energy if a 400-kilogram satellite moves from a distance of 3×10^6 meters above the surface of the Earth to a point 1.50×10^6 meters above the surface is _____ J. The mass of the Earth is 5.98×10^{24} kilograms and the radius of the Earth is 6.37×10^6 meters.

    A. -1.7×10^9
    B. 3.25×10^9
    C. 1.7×10^9
    D. -3.25×10^9

15. The speed of a baseball with a momentum of $5.8 \ kg \cdot m/s$ and a mass of 0.145 kg is

    A. 0.841 m/s.
    B. 1.19 m/s.
    C. 36.0 m/s.
    D. 40.0 m/s.

16. A 0.24-kilogram glider moving with a velocity of 0.6 m/s collides with and sticks to a 0.26-kilogram glider moving with a velocity of 0.2 m/s. The final velocity v of the two gliders is

    A. 0.392 m/s.
    B. 0.184 m/s.
    C. 0.092 m/s.
    D. −0.092 m/s.

17. A massless, horizontal, rigid rod of length $3d$ is pivoted at a fixed point W, and two forces each of magnitude F are applied vertically upward as shown in the figure. In order to achieve rod equilibrium, a third vertical force of magnitude F is to be applied at which of the labeled points?

    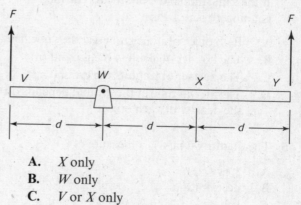

    A. X only
    B. W only
    C. V or X only
    D. X or Y only

18. Two balls of different masses are thrown vertically up from the same point and at the same time. The two balls will experience the same change in

   A. velocity.
   B. acceleration.
   C. momentum.
   D. kinetic energy.

19. An arrow is shot vertically up. As the arrow approaches its maximum altitude, the amount of work done against gravity

   A. increases.
   B. decreases.
   C. increases and then decreases.
   D. remains the same.

20. In the lever shown below, a force is exerted on the left side to lift the mass on the right. Assuming the lever is ideal, which of the following is the same on both sides?

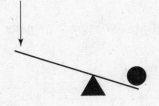

   A. force
   B. momentum
   C. velocity
   D. work

21. Which of the following units is equivalent to the joule?

   A. $kg \cdot m/s$
   B. $kg \cdot m/s^2$
   C. kg/s^2
   D. $kg \cdot m^2/s^2$

22. A 15-gram bullet is fired into a 3-kilogram block of plastic suspended from the ceiling by a string. As a result of the impact, the block with the bullet swings 12 centimeters above its original level. The velocity of the bullet as it strikes the block is nearly

   A. 3.08 m/s.
   B. 30.8 m/s.
   C. 308 m/s.
   D. 3,080 m/s.

23. An astronaut lands on Mars. Which of the following is true?

   A. Mass increases but weight decreases.
   B. Mass remains the same but weight decreases.
   C. Mass decreases but weight remains the same.
   D. Both mass and weight decrease.

24. Ignoring air resistance, the acceleration of a person sliding down an inclined plane with a constant coefficient of kinetic friction

   A. is constant.
   B. increases with time.
   C. decreases with time.
   D. depends on the mass and shape of the person.

25. A bicycle collides head-on with a large truck moving at the same speed. Following the collision, the bicycle and the truck stick together. Which of the two had the greatest net change in momentum?

   A. the bicycle
   B. the truck
   C. both had equal change
   D. None of the above.

Electronics Information

Time: 9 minutes

20 questions

Directions: The following portion of the exam will test your knowledge of electronics, electrical, and radio information. Read each question carefully and select the choice that best answers the question. Indicate that letter on your answer sheet.

1. Which of the following symbols represents a diode?

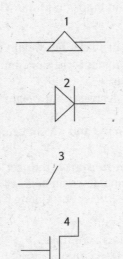

   A. 1
   B. 2
   C. 3
   D. 4

2. Electronic current is measured in

   A. farads.
   B. volts.
   C. amperes.
   D. ohms.

3. The total resistance for this circuit if all resistors are 200 ohms is

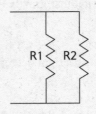

   A. 100 ohms.
   B. 200 ohms.
   C. 150 ohms.
   D. 400 ohms.

4. For the lamp to be turned on in the following circuit

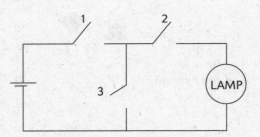

   A. switch 1 only should be closed.
   B. switch 2 only should be closed.
   C. switches 1 and 2 only should be closed.
   D. all the switches must be closed.

5. A voltmeter is a device used for measuring

   A. electrical current.
   B. electrical charge.
   C. energy.
   D. difference in voltage.

6. Leather gloves must be used when

   A. working with low-power transistors.
   B. working with live high-voltage devices.
   C. testing low-power DC circuits.
   D. designing a low-power circuit.

7. The frequency of this signal is

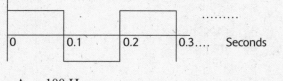

   A. 100 Hz.
   B. 10 Hz.
   C. 5 Hz.
   D. 1 Hz.

8. An AM radio signal is

   A. amplitude modulated.
   B. frequency modulated.
   C. phase modulated.
   D. DC modulated.

9. The reading of the ammeter in this circuit is

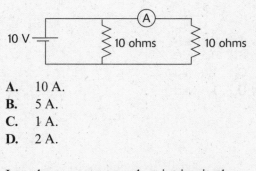

   A. 10 A.
   B. 5 A.
   C. 1 A.
   D. 2 A.

10. In order to protect an electric circuit, the following component can be used:

   A. a fuse.
   B. a capacitor.
   C. an inductor.
   D. an ammeter.

11. Which of these symbols represents a bipolar junction transistor (BJT)?

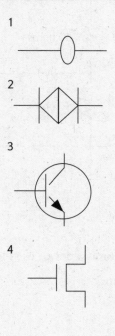

   A. 1
   B. 2
   C. 3
   D. 4

12. A signal is transmitted wirelessly by carrying it on

   A. a square wave.
   B. a DC signal.
   C. a triangular wave.
   D. a high-frequency sinusoidal wave.

13. The signal $s(t) = 10 \sin(120\pi t)$ has the following amplitude and frequency, respectively:

   A. 5 V and 120 Hz.
   B. 10 V and 60 Hz.
   C. 10 V and 120 Hz.
   D. 5 V and 60 Hz.

GO ON TO THE NEXT PAGE

14. The reading of the voltmeter in this circuit is

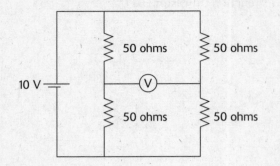

    A. 5 V

    B. 10 V

    C. 0 V

    D. 2.5 V

15. An ohmmeter is a device used to measure

    A. resistance.

    B. voltage.

    C. power.

    D. current.

16. A certain signal is carried on a radio signal by using which one of the following electronic components?

    A. resistor

    B. mixer

    C. capacitor

    D. on-off switch

17. In a diode (PN Junction), the current flows

    A. from anode to cathode.

    B. from cathode to anode.

    C. in both directions.

    D. when voltage is below threshold.

18. A component of a parts list has the following specifications: "10 mH." The component specified is a

    A. capacitor.

    B. transistor.

    C. coil.

    D. resistor.

19. Electronic devices are grounded to

    A. reduce the cost.

    B. protect the user.

    C. reduce the power dissipation.

    D. enhance performance.

20. The power dissipated in the resistors in the following circuit is

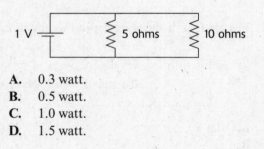

    A. 0.3 watt.

    B. 0.5 watt.

    C. 1.0 watt.

    D. 1.5 watt.

Assembling Objects

Time: 9 minutes

16 questions

Directions: In the Assembling Objects portion of the ASVAB there are two types of questions. One type is very similar to solving a jigsaw puzzle. The other is a matter of making appropriate connections given a diagram and instructions. In each of the questions, the first drawing is the problem, and the remaining four drawings offer possible solutions. Look at each of the four illustrations, and then select the choice that best solves that particular problem. Indicate that letter on your answer sheet.

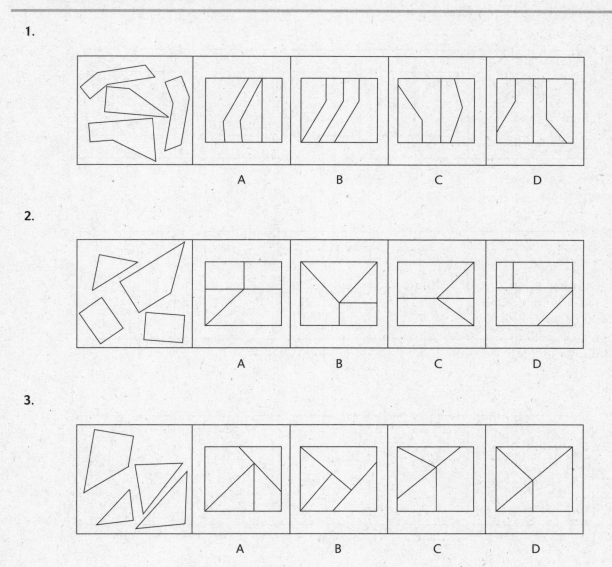

1.

    A   B   C   D

2.

    A   B   C   D

3.

    A   B   C   D

GO ON TO THE NEXT PAGE

Practice Test 1

4.

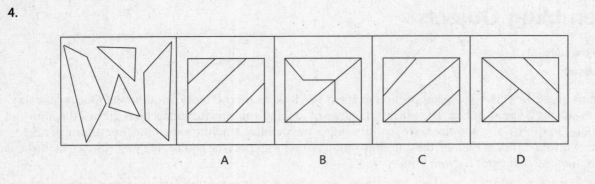

A   B   C   D

5.

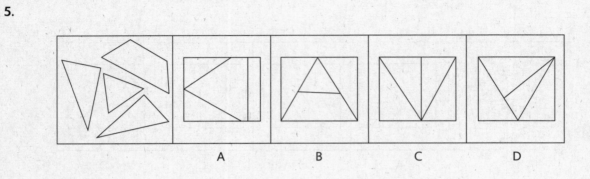

A   B   C   D

6.

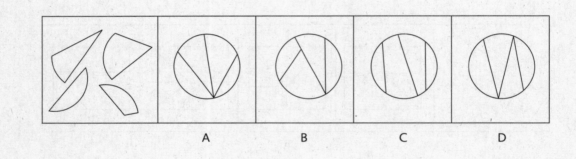

A   B   C   D

7.

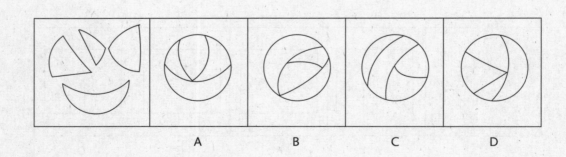

A   B   C   D

8.

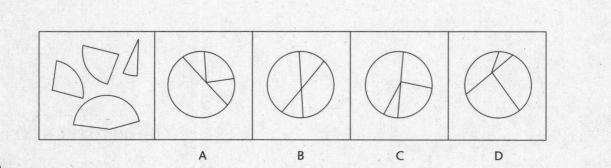

A   B   C   D

9.

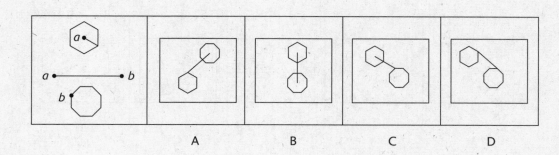

A B C D

10.

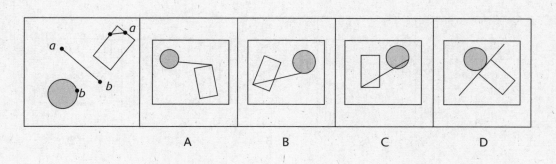

A B C D

11.

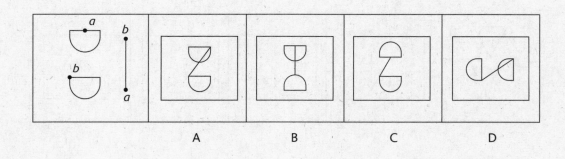

A B C D

12.

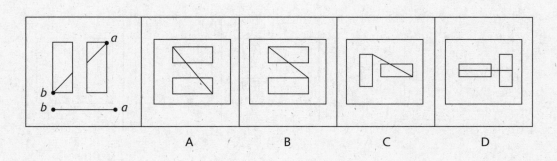

A B C D

GO ON TO THE NEXT PAGE

13.

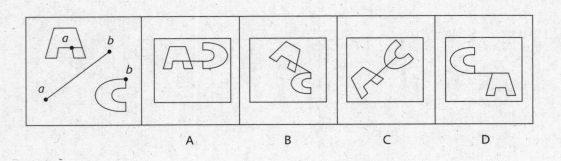

       A   B   C   D

14.

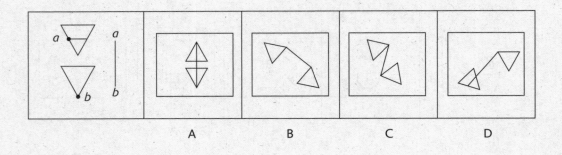

       A   B   C   D

15.

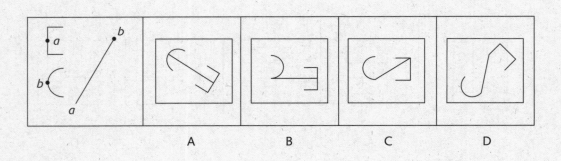

       A   B   C   D

16.

       A   B   C   D

Answer Key for Practice Test I

General Science

1. C	10. B	19. B
2. D	11. A	20. D
3. B	12. B	21. B
4. A	13. A	22. B
5. B	14. B	23. B
6. A	15. B	24. C
7. C	16. C	25. D
8. D	17. A	
9. B	18. A	

Arithmetic Reasoning

1. A	11. A	21. D
2. D	12. A	22. D
3. C	13. C	23. D
4. B	14. A	24. D
5. B	15. B	25. A
6. D	16. C	26. B
7. A	17. A	27. B
8. D	18. C	28. C
9. D	19. C	29. C
10. D	20. A	30. D

Word Knowledge

1. B	13. D	25. B
2. B	14. B	26. B
3. A	15. D	27. B
4. A	16. A	28. B
5. B	17. B	29. D
6. D	18. D	30. D
7. B	19. D	31. B
8. A	20. B	32. A
9. B	21. B	33. B
10. C	22. B	34. C
11. C	23. B	35. B
12. B	24. A	

Paragraph Comprehension

1. A	6. C	11. C
2. C	7. B	12. C
3. C	8. A	13. A
4. B	9. D	14. B
5. D	10. A	15. D

Auto and Shop Information

1. A	10. C	19. C
2. B	11. C	20. B
3. B	12. C	21. B
4. C	13. A	22. C
5. B	14. C	23. A
6. C	15. A	24. D
7. D	16. D	25. A
8. B	17. A	
9. D	18. D	

Mathematics Knowledge

1. C	10. B	19. A
2. D	11. C	20. C
3. A	12. C	21. B
4. B	13. B	22. B
5. C	14. C	23. C
6. C	15. A	24. B
7. D	16. A	25. A
8. B	17. C	
9. C	18. A	

Mechanical Comprehension

1. C	10. A	19. D
2. B	11. D	20. D
3. D	12. B	21. D
4. A	13. B	22. C
5. B	14. B	23. B
6. B	15. D	24. A
7. C	16. A	25. C
8. D	17. C	
9. A	18. A	

Electronics Information

1. B	8. A	15. A
2. C	9. C	16. B
3. A	10. A	17. A
4. C	11. C	18. C
5. D	12. D	19. B
6. B	13. B	20. A
7. C	14. C	

Assembling Objects

1. B	7. D	13. B
2. A	8. C	14. B
3. D	9. C	15. D
4. C	10. B	16. A
5. B	11. C	
6. B	12. A	

Practice Test I Answers and Explanations

General Science

1. **C.** In photosynthesis, water is split, oxygen is given off as a waste product, and hydrogen is combined with carbon dioxide to form sugars.

2. **D.** Only members of the same species meet in the wild and mate to produce fertile offspring.

3. **B.** Celsius and centigrade are the same thing. Water boils at 100° centigrade, 100° Celsius, or 212° Fahrenheit.

4. **A.** A liter is slightly larger than a quart. There are about 33 ounces in a liter, while a quart has 32 ounces.

5. **B.** Adding heat to water gives the molecules more kinetic energy, resulting in faster motion. It does not change the energy level of electrons or the number of electrons in the molecules.

6. **A.** The slope of the line is a measure of the rate. Anyone who is injected with insulin has the same type of response.

7. **C.** Ligaments connect bone to bone, and tendons connect bone to muscle.

8. **D.** A yard is slightly less than a meter. Because there are 1,000 millimeters in a meter, there should be slightly less in a yard.

9. **B.** Parts per million can be converted to parts per hundred by dividing by 10,000 or setting up a proportion. 35 ppm = 0.0035 parts per hundred. Any number can be expressed as a percent by multiplying that number by 100%. So, $0.0035 \times 100\% = 0.35\%$.

10. **B.** The hereditary material is DNA and is found in the nucleus in most cells.

11. **A.** Our sun and eight planets make up a small speck in the Milky Way galaxy. The Milky Way galaxy is one of billions in the universe.

12. **B.** Diffusion is the movement of molecules of liquid from a greater to a lesser concentration. The diffusion of water is osmosis, and no energy is required as these molecules move down a concentration gradient.

13. **A.** According to the Law of Superposition, all other factors being accounted for, the most recent (youngest) geologic layers are on the top. Because the slate layer is closest to the surface, it is the youngest.

14. **B.** Day and night are the results of the rotation of the earth. Continental drift is often offered as evidence of plate tectonics. While the variable star field may be affected by planetary tilt, the position of the observer relative to the star field is also a major factor. The seasons, Choice B, are the result of the directness of the sun's rays hitting Earth's surface. The primary factor controlling directness of the rays of the sun is planetary tilt.

15. **B.** The breakdown on the tree would seem to indicate that the organism is using extracellular digestion, releasing enzymes into its environment to break down organic matter for its own nutrition. Combined with the observation that the organism is multicellular, this would place the organism in the Kingdom Fungi.

16. **C.** Choice A is a true statement but it does not explain rain, only the motion of the fronts. The motion of the warmer air over cooler air is due to differing densities, but it is the drop in temperature due to increased elevation and contact with cooler air (among other things) that causes the rain. As air cools, its capacity to hold water vapor decreases. As the saturation point is reached, excess water vapor condenses on particles in the air and eventually can fall as rain.

17. **A.** Mitosis is nuclear division, cytokinesis is cell division, and meiosis is used for sex cell production.

18. **A.** Protons have a positive charge and electrons have a negative charge.

19. **B.** Both protons and neutrons exist in the nucleus, while electrons orbit the nucleus.

20. **D.** The oxidation state of hydrogen (H) is always +1. Two hydrogen atoms would result in a +2 charge. Because there is only one atom of oxygen in H_2O, oxygen would have to have a –2 charge to balance the positive hydrogen atoms.

21. **B.** Gametes (eggs and sperm) need to have half the normal chromosome number, so that when they combine the correct number appears in the new cell.

22. **B.** As you decrease the volume, the pressure will increase proportionally, and if you increase the volume, then the pressure will decrease proportionally.

23. **B.** The subscript applies to each of the atoms within the parentheses.

24. **C.** In this case of incomplete dominance, each pink flower has one gene for red and one for white. When they combine randomly, one-fourth will be white, one-fourth red, and half pink.

25. **D.** Memory cells help us mount quicker responses to antigens we have previously encountered.

Arithmetic Reasoning

1. **A.** $3\frac{1}{4} - 2\frac{1}{8} = \frac{13}{4} - \frac{17}{8} = \frac{26}{8} - \frac{17}{8} = \frac{9}{8} = 1\frac{1}{8}$ more cups of flour.

2. **D.** There are 24 eggs in 2 dozen eggs. If 3 eggs are in an omelet, then $24 \div 3$, or 8 omelets, can be made.

3. **C.** Because two runners finished in 80 seconds, the average of 80, 80, 72, and 68 must be found. This average is $\frac{80 + 80 + 72 + 68}{4} = \frac{300}{4} = 75$ seconds.

4. **B.** If 400 people fit in 8 subway cars, then $400 \div 8$, or 50, people fit in 1 subway car. Therefore, 50×5, or 250, people fit in 5 subway cars.

5. **B.** The earnings for 30 hours are $\$8.25 \times 30 = \$247.50$.

6. **D.** Let n represent the number of students in the band. Then $\frac{1}{3}n = 72$, so $n = 72 \times 3 = 216$.

7. **A.** Add the amount of money received and subtract the amount spent: $\$30 + \$15 - \$16 = \$29$.

8. **D.** If an item is discounted 20%, the sale price is 80% of the original price. Let p represent the original price. Then $\$800 = 80\% \times p$ and $p = \frac{800}{80\%} = \frac{800}{.80} = \$1,000$.

9. **D.** For a 30-hour week with $500 in sales, total earnings are $(30 \times \$9.50) + (3\% \times \$500) = \$285 + \$15 = \$300$.

10. **D.** The area of the circle with a radius of 3 in is $\pi r^2 = \pi \times r^2 = 9\pi$. The area of the larger circle is $4 \times 9\pi = 36\pi$. Therefore, $r^2 = 36$, so $r = \sqrt{36} = 6$. The radius of the larger circle is 6 in.

11. **A.** $\$20 - \$3.95 = \$16.05$.

12. **A.** Using the ratio $\frac{\text{height}}{\text{shadow}}$, the proportion $\frac{3\frac{1}{2}}{6} = \frac{x}{24}$ models this situation, where x represents the height of the pole. Cross multiply. $3\frac{1}{2} \times 24 = 6x$, so $84 = 6x$, and $x = \frac{84}{6} = 14$ ft.

13. **C.** The overtime rate is $\$8.40 \times 1.5 = \$12.60$. Five hours of overtime were completed, so the total earnings are $(\$8.40 \times 40) + (\$12.60 \times 5) = \$336 + \$63 = \$399$.

14. **A.** The amount of discount is $\$40 - \$30 = \$10$. The percent of discount is the amount of discount divided by the original price. $\frac{10}{40} = \frac{1}{4} = 25\%$.

15. **B.** The volume of the original box is $3 \times 2\frac{1}{2} \times 2 = 15$. The volume of the box with the length and depth doubled is $6 \times 2\frac{1}{2} \times 4 = 60$. The amount of change in volume is $60 - 15 = 45$. The percent change is the amount of change in volume divided by the original volume: $\frac{45}{15} = 3 = 300\%$.

16. **C.** The amount of commission is $10\% \times \$8,350 = \$835$. Total earnings are $\$300 + \$835$ commission $= \$1,135$.

17. **A.** The total number of stamps collected is $300 + 420 + 180 = 900$. The number of coins that can be collected is $\frac{900}{25} = 36$.

18. **C.** The proportion $\frac{1 \text{ cm}}{4 \text{ miles}} = \frac{x \text{ cm}}{10 \text{ miles}}$ models this situation. Cross multiply. $1 \times 10 = 4x$, so $10 = 4x$ and $x = \frac{10}{4} = 2\frac{1}{2}$.

19. **C.** Let p represent the amount of the paycheck. $\frac{4}{13}p = \$26.80$, so $p = \$26.80 \times \frac{13}{4} = \$87.10$.

20. **A.** The proportion $\frac{\frac{1}{2} \text{ mile}}{4 \text{ minutes}} = \frac{x \text{ miles}}{15 \text{ minutes}}$ models this situation. Cross multiply. $\frac{1}{2} \times 15 = 4x$, so $\frac{15}{2} = 4x$ and $x = \frac{15}{2} \times \frac{1}{4} = \frac{15}{8} = 1\frac{7}{8}$ miles.

21. **D.** There are 3 ft in a yard, so a kitchen 4 yd by 5 yd is equivalent to (4×3) ft by (5×3) ft, or 12 ft by 15 ft. The area of the kitchen is $12 \times 15 = 180$ sq ft. The cost to tile is $\$2.89 \times 180 = \$520.20$.

22. **D.** At the end of the first day, there are $1 - \frac{1}{8} = \frac{7}{8}$ of the magazines remaining. $\frac{7}{8} \times \frac{1}{4} = \frac{7}{32}$ sold the next day. So at the end of the second day, there are $\frac{7}{8} - \frac{7}{32} = \frac{28}{32} - \frac{7}{32} = \frac{21}{32}$ of the magazines remaining.

23. **D.** Interest earned in one year is $300 \times 5\frac{1}{4}\% = \$15.75$. The total amount of the account after one year is $300 + \$15.75 = \$315.75$.

24. **D.** Let m represent the per-minute-charge of the phone calls. The monthly charge for the first plan is $20 + 0.08m$. The monthly charge for the second plan is $12 + 0.12m$. When the monthly charges are the same, $20 + 0.08m = 12 + 0.12m$.

    $20 + 0.08m - 0.08m = 12 + 0.12m - 0.08m$

    $20 = 12 + 0.04m$

    $20 - 12 = 12 + 0.04m - 12$

    $8 = 0.04m$

    $\frac{8}{0.04} = \frac{800}{4} = 200$ minutes

25. **A.** The perimeter of a rectangle is $l + w + l + w = 48$. Because $l = 3w$, the perimeter is $3w + w + 3w + w = 48$ so $8w = 48$ and $w = 6$. Therefore, the length is 3×6 or 18 and the area of the rectangle is $l \times w = 18 \times 6 = 108$.

26. **B.** If a machine produces 8,000 widgets in 3 hours, it produces $\frac{8,000}{3}$ widgets in 1 hour. There are 24 hours in a day, so, $\frac{8,000}{3} \times 24 = 8,000 \times 8 = 64,000$ widgets are produced in 1 day.

27. **B.** The total cost of the purchase is $(3 \times \$0.45) + (2 + \$0.79) = \$1.35 + \$1.58 = \$2.93$.

28. **C.** Carl's throw went $7\frac{1}{3} \times 2\frac{1}{2} = \frac{22}{3} \times \frac{5}{2} = \frac{110}{6} = 18\frac{1}{3}$ yd. The difference between the two throws is $18\frac{1}{3} - 7\frac{1}{3} = 11$ yd.

29. **C.** The total distance traveled in the morning was $13 \times 2 = 26$ miles. The total distance traveled in the afternoon was $9 \times 2 = 18$ miles. The difference between the two distances is $26 - 18 = 8$ miles.

30. **D.** The percentage of cars that are either red or black are $25\% + 30\% = 55\%$. The total cars that are either red or black is $260 \times 55\% = 143$.

Word Knowledge

1. **B.** *Hardship,* which means a difficult time or experience.

2. **B.** *Corrosive,* which means harsh or stinging.

3. **A.** *Spoil,* which means ruin or destroy.

4. **A.** *Enjoyment.* Zest means enthusiasm or delight.

5. **B.** *Move back and forth.* In this sentence, *sway* means to lean or incline.

6. **D.** *Mystery.* Enigma refers to a puzzle or problem, as *mystery* also suggests.

7. **B.** *Prompt,* which means precise or immediate.

8. **A.** *Dawdle,* which means to loaf or waste time.

9. **B.** *Helping.* Here, auxiliary means supplementary.

10. **C.** *Skillful.* In this sentence, deft means adept or proficient.

11. **C.** *Wander,* which can mean to ramble or roam.

12. **B.** *Stinginess.* Stingy means miserly, closefisted, or selfish.

13. **D.** *Fruitful.* In this sentence, prolific means abundant or plentiful.

14. **B.** *Concise,* which means brief, to the point, or condensed.

15. **D.** *Strange.* Bizarre can mean odd, weird, or unusual.

16. **A.** *Show of respect.* Tribute means acclaim or recognition.

17. **B.** *Speaking untruth.* Slander can mean to vilify or to denigrate.

18. **D.** *Grave,* which can mean dismal or gloomy.

19. **D.** *Wealth.* Affluence means riches or abundance.

20. **B.** *Easily led.* Docile can mean submissive, compliant, or tame.

21. **B.** *Healthy.* Hale can mean hardy or fit, as in good health.

22. **B.** *Solitary.* Reclusive means reserved or aloof.

23. **B.** *Quality.* Caliber means nature or essence.

24. **A.** *Endless,* which can mean limitless or unbounded.

25. **B.** *Wealthy,* which can mean rich or prosperous.

26. **B.** *Ordinary.* Trite can mean commonplace, stale, or stereotyped.

27. **B.** *Essential,* meaning important or necessary.

28. **B.** *Motivator.* Incentive means driving force or impetus.

29. **D.** *Demolish,* which means to destroy, damage, or wreck.

30. **D.** *Scamper,* which means to hasten or hustle.

31. **B.** *Wise.* Prudent can mean sensible or cautious.

32. **A.** *Passionate,* which can mean excitable or eager.

33. **B.** *Tasteless,* which can mean dull or uninteresting.

34. **C.** *Ask for.* Solicit means to beg or to implore.

35. **B.** *Meantime.* Interim means time between events or interval.

Paragraph Comprehension

1. **A.** This selection explains what a tsunami is. It does not focus on any other Japanese words, natural disasters, or the effects of a tsunami.

2. **C.** The first sentence discusses the fact that pyromaniacs rarely start criminal fires. The last sentence explains what a pyromaniac is.

3. **C.** The bobcat is the only name not listed in the paragraph as another name for the concolour.

4. **B.** Because the selection states that Edison did not give up easily, you can assume that *tenacious* is a synonym for *persistent*.

5. **D.** The third sentence states that Edison had a few failed inventions, and the rest of the selection elaborates on the iron-ore mining invention attempt.

6. **C.** The selection states that regions north of the Arctic Circle experience unending periods of daylight and dark. However, regions below the Arctic Circle are not included in this analysis of daylight and dark.

7. **B.** The selection states that such plants should be watered during the cooler parts of the day. 6:00 a.m. is the coolest time of day listed.

8. **A.** This choice is the only one that makes sense in the context of the first and last sentences. That is why our bodies are "water dependent," as the sentence states.

9. **D.** The answer is stated in the fourth sentence of the selection.

10. **A.** The entire selection focuses on proper steps to ensure healthy weight loss. Too much weight loss, by severely limiting calories and/or exercising in a manner that can cause physical damage, would be unhealthy weight loss. It would deprive the body of needed calories while, at the same time, causing physical damage.

11. **C.** The article discusses the dangers of driving with any type of cellular phone; thus, it can be inferred that this is the best answer.

12. **C.** The article focuses on the dangerous nature of cellular phone usage while driving.

13. **A.** The first sentence of the paragraph states that there are many preventive measures drivers can take to avoid carjacking. The supporting sentences in the paragraph give specific ways to prevent carjacking.

14. **B.** Carrying pepper spray is not mentioned in the paragraph as a preventive measure against carjacking.

15. **D.** The author of the selection gives three practical ways to avoid carjacking. None of the other choices are statements made by the author. Thus, you may assume that carjacking can often be avoided by following the preventive measures given in the selection.

Auto and Shop Information

1. **A.** The high pressures developed in the combustion chamber can reach the coolant through the crack in the head and show up as air bubbles in the radiator as the coolant is circulated.

2. **B.** The self-energizing effect of this type of brake system requires that the longer lined secondary shoe be in the rear part of that wheel's brake system.

3. **B.** The idea of a thermostat is to be in a closed position until a proper engine temperature is reached.

4. **C.** A coil is an electrical component of an engine that produces upward of 10,000 volts. This voltage then travels down the spark plug wire, through the spark plug, and jumps the small gap on the tip of the plug, producing a spark.

5. **B.** The scraping metal clip is used to audibly indicate a worn brake pad condition to the driver.

6. **C.** The front wheels have calipers that combine the function of a wheel cylinder and can also be an attaching component for the brake pads.

7. **D.** The pick-up coil is part of the primary control circuit.

8. **B.** Hydrocarbons, nitrogen oxides, and carbon monoxides are the three main pollutants emitted from a gas-powered vehicle's engine. Methane, however, is the main component found in the Earth's natural gas, and is not one of a vehicle's three main pollutants.

9. **D.** The ignition module turns on and off the primary current based on a signal it gets from the computer.

10. **C.** All three components use an electromagnetic field to perform work. In the motor, the electromagnetic field is used to turn the armature. In the solenoid, it is used to move a plunger, and in the relay it is used to move a set of contacts.

11. **C.** A relationship exists between voltage, current flow, and resistance in a series circuit. If resistance is increased, current flow is reduced. If resistance is reduced, current flow will increase.

12. **C.** Extractors are used on bolts and screws that are typically broken off flush or below the surface.

13. **A.** A tap is a hard tool used for cutting internal threads.

14. **C.** A veining bit is used in a router to cut fine lines in material, often for decorative purposes.

15. **A.** Softwood is a type of lumber that comes specifically from trees known as conifers, or evergreens, both of which bear needles rather than leaves.

16. **D.** This is an example of a dovetail joint. It can be cut by hand or with a dovetail jig and an electric jigsaw.

17. **A.** The large jaws and heavier weight of a pipe wrench are ideal for loosening and tightening large nuts and bolts that are usually encountered by plumbers. While it is possible for other workers to use a pipe wrench, the question uses the word "usually," suggesting that one type of person would be more likely than the others to use the wrench.

18. **D.** The use of toenailing lends greater strength and holding power to joints. It is used often in framing and other rough construction projects.

19. **C.** A lathe is used for "turning" and cutting grooves and other decorative lines in spindle legs for chairs and tables. It is also used for turning wooden bowls.

20. **B.** The Phillips head screw has a cross-shaped opening and is usually easier to start than a standard flat head screw because the screwdriver will be more secure in the grooves. You need a Phillips head screwdriver to insert these screws.

21. **B.** Concrete is a mixture of cement, water, gravel, and sand. If you are using premixed cement, you only need to add water.

22. **C.** The tang is the end of the drill that is inserted into the chuck and tightened. The tang may be square for slower hand drills, and round for high-speed electric drills.

23. **A.** A countersink is a drill bit with a cone-shaped cutting head, used to expand the top of a screw hole. This allows the head of the screw to lie flush with the material into which it is screwed.

24. **D.** A contour gauge is used to measure and form an outline of an object. The gauge presses against the object, assumes its shape with dozens of little steel pins, and then is transferred to whatever you are cutting — wood, glass, metal, tile, and so on.

25. **A.** If you nail an extension piece of wood to the end of the board you are cutting, the plane will continue along from one board to the next without chipping the end of the first board.

Mathematics Knowledge

1. **C.** Substitute $\frac{5}{2}$ for a, giving you $\frac{1}{a} = \frac{1}{\frac{5}{2}} = 1 \div \frac{5}{2} = 1 \times \frac{2}{5} = \frac{2}{5}$.

2. **D.** Let n represent the number. If 12 is 15% of n, then $12 = 0.15n$. Divide both sides by 0.15. Therefore, $n = 80$.

3. **A.** Substitute –3 for x. Then $3(-3) + 7 = -9 + 7 = -2$.

4. **B.** The area of a square is s^2 where s is a side of the square. If $s^2 = 36$, then $s = 6$. The diagonal of a square forms two right triangles; d is the hypotenuse and the two legs are 6 units long.

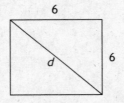

Using the Pythagorean theorem, $d^2 = 6^2 + 6^2 = 36 + 36 = 72$. Therefore, $d = \sqrt{72} = 6\sqrt{2}$.

5. **C.** $3a + 3b = 3(a + b)$. Since $a + b = 6$, $3a + 3b = 3(6) = 18$.

6. **C.** The hypotenuse of the triangle is the diameter, d, of the circle. By the Pythagorean theorem, $d^2 = 6^2 + 8^2 = 36 + 64 = 100$. So $d = \sqrt{100} = 10$, and the radius is $\frac{10}{2} = 5$.

7. **D.** Following the correct order of operations produces
$(3 - 1) \times 7 - 12 \div 2 = 2 \times 7 - (12 \div 2) = 14 - 6 = 8$.

8. **B.** Factors of 24 are $2 \times 2 \times 2 \times 3$. Factors of 36 are $2 \times 2 \times 3 \times 3$. The greatest common factor is $2 \times 2 \times 3 = 12$.

9. **C.** $3m - 12 = -6$
$3m - 12 + 12 = -6 + 12$
$\qquad 3m = 6$

Dividing both sides by 3 results in $m = 2$.

10. **B.** Substitute 1 for p and solve for q. $7(1) + 5q = -3 \rightarrow 7 + 5q = -3 \rightarrow 7 + 5q - 7 = -3 - 7 \rightarrow 5q = -10$. Dividing both sides by 5 results in $q = -2$.

11. **C.** Slope is found by identifying two points on the line and finding the $\frac{\text{change in } y}{\text{change in } x}$. The points $(0,0)$ and $(5,2)$ form the slope $\frac{2-0}{5-0} = \frac{2}{5}$.

12. **C.** $\dfrac{9x^2y^3z - 12xy^2z^2}{3yz} = \dfrac{9x^2y^3z}{3yz} - \dfrac{12xy^2z^2}{3yz} = 3x^2y^2 - 4xyz$

13. **B.**

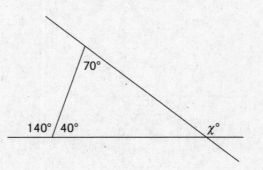

The angle adjacent to the 140° angle is 40° because supplementary angles add to 180°. The angles of a triangle add to 180°, so the angle adjacent to $\angle x$ is 180° – 70° – 40° = 70°. $\angle x$ and 70° are supplementary, so $\angle x$ = 180° – 70° = 110°.

14. **C.** Probability is $\dfrac{\text{number of expected outcomes}}{\text{number of possible outcomes}}$. Because one king was drawn and not replaced, three kings remain in the deck of 51 cards. So the probability of drawing another king is $\dfrac{3}{51} = \dfrac{1}{17}$.

15. **A.** There are 60 minutes in 1 hour, 24 hours in 1 day, and 7 days in 1 week. So

$$1 \text{ week} = \frac{7 \text{ days}}{1 \text{ week}} \times \frac{24 \text{ hours}}{1 \text{ day}} \times \frac{60 \text{ minutes}}{1 \text{ hour}} = 7 \times 24 \times 60 = 10{,}080 \text{ minutes.}$$

16. **A.** $\dfrac{1}{8} = \dfrac{1}{2^3} = 2^{-3}$, so $2^{b+3} = 2^{-3}$ and $b + 3 = -3$. Therefore, $b + 3 - 3 = -3 - 3 = -6$.

17. **C.** Angles in a triangle add to 180°. So $3x + 4x + 5x = 180°$ and $12x = 180°$. Dividing both sides by 12 results in $x = 15°$. The smallest angle is represented by $3x = 3(15°) = 45°$.

18. **A.** Subtraction can be changed to addition by changing the signs in the entire term being subtracted. $(2x^3 - 3x + 1) - (x^2 - 3x - 2) = (2x^3 - 3x + 1) + (-x^2 + 3x + 2)$. Combine like terms: $2x^3 - x^2 - 3x + 3x + 1 + 2 = 2x^3 - x^2 + 3$.

19. **A.** The area of a square is s^2, where s is a side of the square. If $s^2 = 400$, then $s = \sqrt{400} = 20$.

20. **C.** Translate to a mathematical expression and solve. $3x + 7 = 70$, so $3x + 7 - 7 = 70 - 7$ and $3x = 63$. Divide both sides by 3. Therefore, $x = 21$.

21. **B.** The volume of a cylinder is given by the formula $V = \pi r^2 h$, where r is the radius of the circular base and h is the height. Because $h = r$, $V = \pi r^2 r = \pi r^3$.

22. **B.** Prime factors of 120 are $2 \times 2 \times 2 \times 3 \times 5$. Distinct factors are 2, 3, and 5. Therefore, there are three distinct prime factors.

23. **C.** Let p represent the unknown percent. $p \times \dfrac{3}{4} = \dfrac{1}{8}$. Solve for p by multiplying both sides by the reciprocal of $\dfrac{3}{4}$. $p \times \dfrac{3}{4} \times \dfrac{4}{3} = \dfrac{1}{8} \times \dfrac{4}{3} = \dfrac{4}{24} = \dfrac{1}{6}$. As a percent, $\dfrac{1}{6}$ is $16\dfrac{2}{3}\%$.

24. **B.** Divide the figure into a rectangle and triangle as shown.

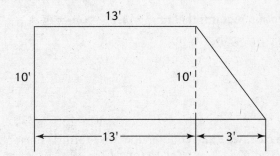

The area of the figure equals the area of the rectangle plus the area of the triangle.

The rectangle's area = length × width or $10 \times 13 = 130 \text{ ft}^2$; the triangle's area = $\dfrac{1}{2}$ base × height or $\dfrac{1}{2} \times 3 \times 10 = 15 \text{ ft}^2$. Together, the area is $130 + 15 = 145 \text{ ft}^2$.

25. **A.** Set the equation equal to 0 and factor. $x^2 + 6x - 16 = 0$ and $(x + 8)(x - 2) = 0$. Then, either $x + 8 = 0$ or $x - 2 = 0$, so $x = -8$ or $x = 2$. Since x is positive, $x = 2$.

Mechanical Comprehension

1. **C.** The centripetal force of the stone is proportional to the square of the velocity.

2. **B.** The weight of a body is a force, and newton is the unit of force.

3. **D.** The joule is the unit of work, kinetic energy, potential energy, and heat.

4. **A.** The travel time depends on the height above ground and the acceleration of gravity, both of which are the same for both objects.

5. **B.** The quantity 2 m/s^2 can be thought of as 2 m/s per second; that is, speed per unit time, or acceleration.

6. **B.** From Newton's second law of motion, the centripetal force, or the inward force necessary to maintain uniform circular motion, is the product of mass and centripetal acceleration.

7. **C.** At the top of the trajectory the ball stops and all the kinetic energy has already been converted to potential energy. Thus, the total energy is the sum of 100 and 700, or 800 J.

8. **D.** Because the frequency of oscillation is inversely proportional to the square root of the length of the pendulum, the length has to be decreased by a factor of 4 for the frequency to be doubled.

9. **A.** The final velocity is the initial velocity minus 4 × the acceleration of gravity (9.8 m/s) or −7.14 (about −7.2) m/s.

10. **A.** The acceleration of objects in free-fall is independent of mass, resulting in the same speed at the end of a fall. The momentum and energy are proportional to the mass.

11. **D.** A lever is a rigid object that pivots on a single point and is considered a simple machine.

12. **B.** Because the torque $T = Fd \cos \theta$ where F is the force, d is the arm, and θ is the angle between the force and arm, then you can solve for F to obtain 286 N.

13. **B.** The speed ratio of input to output gears equals the mechanical advantage, which is the ratio N_o/N_i, or 2.

14. **B.** $K + \dfrac{(6.67 \times 10^{-11})(400)(5.98 \times 10^{24})}{(6.37 \times 10^6 + 3 \times 10^6)} = \dfrac{(6.67 \times 10^{-11})(400)(5.98 \times 10^{24})}{(6.37 \times 10^6 + 1.5 \times 10^6)}$ or K = +3.25 × 10^9 J.

15. **D.** Because the momentum P equals the mass m × the velocity v, it follows that $v = P/m = 40.0$ m/s.

16. **A.** Conservation of momentum requires that $m_1v_1 + m_2V_2 = (m_1 + m_2)v_{1,2}$.

    $0.24(0.6) + 0.26(0.2) = (0.24 + 0.26)v_{1,2}$

    $0.144 + 0.052 = 0.50 \, v_{1,2}$

    $\dfrac{0.196}{0.50} = v_{1,2}$

    Hence $v = 0.392$ m/s.

17. **C.** For rod equilibrium the clockwise and counterclockwise torques must be equal, i.e., (F at V + F at V)(d) = (F at Y) ($2d$) or (F at V) (d) = (F at Y) ($2d$) − (F at X)(d), which means that the third force can only be applied upward at V or downward at X.

18. **A.** Acceleration will be constant for both balls. Momentum and energy are dependent on mass and will therefore be different. Only the change in velocity will be the same for both balls.

19. **D.** The work done does not depend on time or path of travel because the deceleration of the arrow is constant.

20. **D.** The work done by the force is the same as the work done on the load in an ideal simple machine.

21. **D.** The joule is a unit of work that is force × distance. The force is mass × acceleration, which has the units of kg · m/s^2. Hence, kg · m^2/s^2 is the product of the units of force and distance.

22. C. Letting the masses of the bullet and block be m and M, their initial velocities be u and U, and their combined velocity be V, then the conversion from kinetic to potential energy requires that $\frac{1}{2}(m+M)V^2 = (m+M)gh$, where h is the increment in height (12 centimeters). This leads to $V = 1.533$ m/s. The conservation of momentum requires that $mu + MU = (m + M)V$ where $U = 0$. Hence, solving for u, you obtain 308.258, or about 308 m/s.

23. B. Mass cannot change because of changes in the gravitational acceleration, but weight changes—and in this case decreases — because the gravitational acceleration is lower.

24. A. The acceleration is the ratio of the force and the mass. The mass remains the same while the net force is set by the mass, acceleration of gravity, slope of the inclined plane, and the coefficient of kinetic friction, which are all constant. Thus the acceleration remains the same.

25. C. Since momentum is conserved, any momentum gained by one is lost by the other, and therefore both had equal change.

Electronics Information

1. **B.** Symbol 2 represents a diode. A diode is like one-way valve that allows electric current to flow in one direction but generally does not allow it to flow in the opposite direction.

2. **C.** Electronic current is measured in amperes. Capacitance is measured in farads. Voltage is measured in volts. Resistors are measured in ohms.

3. **A.** Total resistance for parallel resistors is $\dfrac{1}{\frac{1}{200} + \frac{1}{200}} = 100$ ohms.

4. **C.** Switches 1 and 2 only should be closed. Switch 3 must be opened; otherwise, it will cause a short circuit.

5. **D.** A voltmeter is a device used to measure the difference in voltage. An ammeter is used to measure electrical current. Electrical charge or energy cannot be measured by a voltmeter.

6. **B.** Leather gloves withstand high voltage.

7. **C.** Frequency of a wave is given as $\dfrac{1}{\text{wave period}} = \dfrac{1}{0.2} = 5$ Hz.

8. **A.** An AM-modulated signal is an amplitude-modulated signal. FM signals are frequency-modulated signals. PSK signals are phase-modulated signals. DC cannot be used for modulation.

9. **C.** The ammeter in the circuit reads the value of the current flowing in the resistor. The current flowing is calculated as $\dfrac{V}{R} = \dfrac{10}{10} = 1$ A.

10. **A.** In order to protect an electric circuit, a fuse can be used. Once the current is higher than the fuse rating, the fuse will break, preventing the flow of current.

11. **C.** Symbol 3 represents a bipolar junction transistor (BJT). The three terminals of a transistor are typically used as the input, output and the common terminal of both input and output.

12. **D.** A signal is transmitted wirelessly by being carried on a high-frequency sinusoidal wave called a carrier signal.

13. **B.** The signal $s(t)$ can be written in the form $s(t) = \text{amplitude} \times \sin(2\pi f t)$, so that the amplitude is 10 V and the frequency is 60 Hz.

14. **C.** Because all of the resistors are equal in value, then the currents in both branches of the circuit are equal. This makes the voltage difference between the leads of the voltmeter equal to zero.

15. **A.** An ohmmeter is a device used to measure resistance. A voltmeter is used to measure a voltage difference. A wattmeter is used to measure power, and an ammeter is used to measure current.

16. **B.** Signals are carried on other high frequency signals by frequency mixers.

17. **A.** A diode permits the flow of the current in one direction only: from the anode to the cathode, when the voltage applied is greater than the threshold level.

18. **C.** A coil inductance is measured in henries. Capacitance is measured in farads. Transistors have numbers to identify them. Resistance is measured in ohms.

19. **B.** Electronic devices are grounded to protect the user from an electric shock.

20. **A.** Power dissipated in the circuit can be calculated as $\dfrac{V^2}{R1} + \dfrac{V^2}{R2} = \dfrac{1}{5} + \dfrac{1}{10} = 0.3$ watt.

Assembling Objects

For answers, see the answer key, earlier in this section.

Answer Sheet for Practice Test II

(Remove this sheet and use it to mark your answers.)

CUT HERE

General Science

1 Ⓐ Ⓑ Ⓒ Ⓓ	16 Ⓐ Ⓑ Ⓒ Ⓓ	
2 Ⓐ Ⓑ Ⓒ Ⓓ	17 Ⓐ Ⓑ Ⓒ Ⓓ	
3 Ⓐ Ⓑ Ⓒ Ⓓ	18 Ⓐ Ⓑ Ⓒ Ⓓ	
4 Ⓐ Ⓑ Ⓒ Ⓓ	19 Ⓐ Ⓑ Ⓒ Ⓓ	
5 Ⓐ Ⓑ Ⓒ Ⓓ	20 Ⓐ Ⓑ Ⓒ Ⓓ	
6 Ⓐ Ⓑ Ⓒ Ⓓ	21 Ⓐ Ⓑ Ⓒ Ⓓ	
7 Ⓐ Ⓑ Ⓒ Ⓓ	22 Ⓐ Ⓑ Ⓒ Ⓓ	
8 Ⓐ Ⓑ Ⓒ Ⓓ	23 Ⓐ Ⓑ Ⓒ Ⓓ	
9 Ⓐ Ⓑ Ⓒ Ⓓ	24 Ⓐ Ⓑ Ⓒ Ⓓ	
10 Ⓐ Ⓑ Ⓒ Ⓓ	25 Ⓐ Ⓑ Ⓒ Ⓓ	
11 Ⓐ Ⓑ Ⓒ Ⓓ		
12 Ⓐ Ⓑ Ⓒ Ⓓ		
13 Ⓐ Ⓑ Ⓒ Ⓓ		
14 Ⓐ Ⓑ Ⓒ Ⓓ		
15 Ⓐ Ⓑ Ⓒ Ⓓ		

Arithmetic Reasoning

1 Ⓐ Ⓑ Ⓒ Ⓓ	16 Ⓐ Ⓑ Ⓒ Ⓓ
2 Ⓐ Ⓑ Ⓒ Ⓓ	17 Ⓐ Ⓑ Ⓒ Ⓓ
3 Ⓐ Ⓑ Ⓒ Ⓓ	18 Ⓐ Ⓑ Ⓒ Ⓓ
4 Ⓐ Ⓑ Ⓒ Ⓓ	19 Ⓐ Ⓑ Ⓒ Ⓓ
5 Ⓐ Ⓑ Ⓒ Ⓓ	20 Ⓐ Ⓑ Ⓒ Ⓓ
6 Ⓐ Ⓑ Ⓒ Ⓓ	21 Ⓐ Ⓑ Ⓒ Ⓓ
7 Ⓐ Ⓑ Ⓒ Ⓓ	22 Ⓐ Ⓑ Ⓒ Ⓓ
8 Ⓐ Ⓑ Ⓒ Ⓓ	23 Ⓐ Ⓑ Ⓒ Ⓓ
9 Ⓐ Ⓑ Ⓒ Ⓓ	24 Ⓐ Ⓑ Ⓒ Ⓓ
10 Ⓐ Ⓑ Ⓒ Ⓓ	25 Ⓐ Ⓑ Ⓒ Ⓓ
11 Ⓐ Ⓑ Ⓒ Ⓓ	26 Ⓐ Ⓑ Ⓒ Ⓓ
12 Ⓐ Ⓑ Ⓒ Ⓓ	27 Ⓐ Ⓑ Ⓒ Ⓓ
13 Ⓐ Ⓑ Ⓒ Ⓓ	28 Ⓐ Ⓑ Ⓒ Ⓓ
14 Ⓐ Ⓑ Ⓒ Ⓓ	29 Ⓐ Ⓑ Ⓒ Ⓓ
15 Ⓐ Ⓑ Ⓒ Ⓓ	30 Ⓐ Ⓑ Ⓒ Ⓓ

Word Knowledge

1 Ⓐ Ⓑ Ⓒ Ⓓ	21 Ⓐ Ⓑ Ⓒ Ⓓ
2 Ⓐ Ⓑ Ⓒ Ⓓ	22 Ⓐ Ⓑ Ⓒ Ⓓ
3 Ⓐ Ⓑ Ⓒ Ⓓ	23 Ⓐ Ⓑ Ⓒ Ⓓ
4 Ⓐ Ⓑ Ⓒ Ⓓ	24 Ⓐ Ⓑ Ⓒ Ⓓ
5 Ⓐ Ⓑ Ⓒ Ⓓ	25 Ⓐ Ⓑ Ⓒ Ⓓ
6 Ⓐ Ⓑ Ⓒ Ⓓ	26 Ⓐ Ⓑ Ⓒ Ⓓ
7 Ⓐ Ⓑ Ⓒ Ⓓ	27 Ⓐ Ⓑ Ⓒ Ⓓ
8 Ⓐ Ⓑ Ⓒ Ⓓ	28 Ⓐ Ⓑ Ⓒ Ⓓ
9 Ⓐ Ⓑ Ⓒ Ⓓ	29 Ⓐ Ⓑ Ⓒ Ⓓ
10 Ⓐ Ⓑ Ⓒ Ⓓ	30 Ⓐ Ⓑ Ⓒ Ⓓ
11 Ⓐ Ⓑ Ⓒ Ⓓ	31 Ⓐ Ⓑ Ⓒ Ⓓ
12 Ⓐ Ⓑ Ⓒ Ⓓ	32 Ⓐ Ⓑ Ⓒ Ⓓ
13 Ⓐ Ⓑ Ⓒ Ⓓ	33 Ⓐ Ⓑ Ⓒ Ⓓ
14 Ⓐ Ⓑ Ⓒ Ⓓ	34 Ⓐ Ⓑ Ⓒ Ⓓ
15 Ⓐ Ⓑ Ⓒ Ⓓ	35 Ⓐ Ⓑ Ⓒ Ⓓ
16 Ⓐ Ⓑ Ⓒ Ⓓ	
17 Ⓐ Ⓑ Ⓒ Ⓓ	
18 Ⓐ Ⓑ Ⓒ Ⓓ	
19 Ⓐ Ⓑ Ⓒ Ⓓ	
20 Ⓐ Ⓑ Ⓒ Ⓓ	

Paragraph Comprehension

1 Ⓐ Ⓑ Ⓒ Ⓓ
2 Ⓐ Ⓑ Ⓒ Ⓓ
3 Ⓐ Ⓑ Ⓒ Ⓓ
4 Ⓐ Ⓑ Ⓒ Ⓓ
5 Ⓐ Ⓑ Ⓒ Ⓓ
6 Ⓐ Ⓑ Ⓒ Ⓓ
7 Ⓐ Ⓑ Ⓒ Ⓓ
8 Ⓐ Ⓑ Ⓒ Ⓓ
9 Ⓐ Ⓑ Ⓒ Ⓓ
10 Ⓐ Ⓑ Ⓒ Ⓓ
11 Ⓐ Ⓑ Ⓒ Ⓓ
12 Ⓐ Ⓑ Ⓒ Ⓓ
13 Ⓐ Ⓑ Ⓒ Ⓓ
14 Ⓐ Ⓑ Ⓒ Ⓓ
15 Ⓐ Ⓑ Ⓒ Ⓓ

Auto and Shop Information

1 Ⓐ Ⓑ Ⓒ Ⓓ	16 Ⓐ Ⓑ Ⓒ Ⓓ
2 Ⓐ Ⓑ Ⓒ Ⓓ	17 Ⓐ Ⓑ Ⓒ Ⓓ
3 Ⓐ Ⓑ Ⓒ Ⓓ	18 Ⓐ Ⓑ Ⓒ Ⓓ
4 Ⓐ Ⓑ Ⓒ Ⓓ	19 Ⓐ Ⓑ Ⓒ Ⓓ
5 Ⓐ Ⓑ Ⓒ Ⓓ	20 Ⓐ Ⓑ Ⓒ Ⓓ
6 Ⓐ Ⓑ Ⓒ Ⓓ	21 Ⓐ Ⓑ Ⓒ Ⓓ
7 Ⓐ Ⓑ Ⓒ Ⓓ	22 Ⓐ Ⓑ Ⓒ Ⓓ
8 Ⓐ Ⓑ Ⓒ Ⓓ	23 Ⓐ Ⓑ Ⓒ Ⓓ
9 Ⓐ Ⓑ Ⓒ Ⓓ	24 Ⓐ Ⓑ Ⓒ Ⓓ
10 Ⓐ Ⓑ Ⓒ Ⓓ	25 Ⓐ Ⓑ Ⓒ Ⓓ
11 Ⓐ Ⓑ Ⓒ Ⓓ	
12 Ⓐ Ⓑ Ⓒ Ⓓ	
13 Ⓐ Ⓑ Ⓒ Ⓓ	
14 Ⓐ Ⓑ Ⓒ Ⓓ	
15 Ⓐ Ⓑ Ⓒ Ⓓ	

Mathematics Knowledge

1 Ⓐ Ⓑ Ⓒ Ⓓ	16 Ⓐ Ⓑ Ⓒ Ⓓ
2 Ⓐ Ⓑ Ⓒ Ⓓ	17 Ⓐ Ⓑ Ⓒ Ⓓ
3 Ⓐ Ⓑ Ⓒ Ⓓ	18 Ⓐ Ⓑ Ⓒ Ⓓ
4 Ⓐ Ⓑ Ⓒ Ⓓ	19 Ⓐ Ⓑ Ⓒ Ⓓ
5 Ⓐ Ⓑ Ⓒ Ⓓ	20 Ⓐ Ⓑ Ⓒ Ⓓ
6 Ⓐ Ⓑ Ⓒ Ⓓ	21 Ⓐ Ⓑ Ⓒ Ⓓ
7 Ⓐ Ⓑ Ⓒ Ⓓ	22 Ⓐ Ⓑ Ⓒ Ⓓ
8 Ⓐ Ⓑ Ⓒ Ⓓ	23 Ⓐ Ⓑ Ⓒ Ⓓ
9 Ⓐ Ⓑ Ⓒ Ⓓ	24 Ⓐ Ⓑ Ⓒ Ⓓ
10 Ⓐ Ⓑ Ⓒ Ⓓ	25 Ⓐ Ⓑ Ⓒ Ⓓ
11 Ⓐ Ⓑ Ⓒ Ⓓ	
12 Ⓐ Ⓑ Ⓒ Ⓓ	
13 Ⓐ Ⓑ Ⓒ Ⓓ	
14 Ⓐ Ⓑ Ⓒ Ⓓ	
15 Ⓐ Ⓑ Ⓒ Ⓓ	

Mechanical Comprehension

1 Ⓐ Ⓑ Ⓒ Ⓓ	16 Ⓐ Ⓑ Ⓒ Ⓓ
2 Ⓐ Ⓑ Ⓒ Ⓓ	17 Ⓐ Ⓑ Ⓒ Ⓓ
3 Ⓐ Ⓑ Ⓒ Ⓓ	18 Ⓐ Ⓑ Ⓒ Ⓓ
4 Ⓐ Ⓑ Ⓒ Ⓓ	19 Ⓐ Ⓑ Ⓒ Ⓓ
5 Ⓐ Ⓑ Ⓒ Ⓓ	20 Ⓐ Ⓑ Ⓒ Ⓓ
6 Ⓐ Ⓑ Ⓒ Ⓓ	21 Ⓐ Ⓑ Ⓒ Ⓓ
7 Ⓐ Ⓑ Ⓒ Ⓓ	22 Ⓐ Ⓑ Ⓒ Ⓓ
8 Ⓐ Ⓑ Ⓒ Ⓓ	23 Ⓐ Ⓑ Ⓒ Ⓓ
9 Ⓐ Ⓑ Ⓒ Ⓓ	24 Ⓐ Ⓑ Ⓒ Ⓓ
10 Ⓐ Ⓑ Ⓒ Ⓓ	25 Ⓐ Ⓑ Ⓒ Ⓓ
11 Ⓐ Ⓑ Ⓒ Ⓓ	
12 Ⓐ Ⓑ Ⓒ Ⓓ	
13 Ⓐ Ⓑ Ⓒ Ⓓ	
14 Ⓐ Ⓑ Ⓒ Ⓓ	
15 Ⓐ Ⓑ Ⓒ Ⓓ	

Electronics Information

1 Ⓐ Ⓑ Ⓒ Ⓓ
2 Ⓐ Ⓑ Ⓒ Ⓓ
3 Ⓐ Ⓑ Ⓒ Ⓓ
4 Ⓐ Ⓑ Ⓒ Ⓓ
5 Ⓐ Ⓑ Ⓒ Ⓓ
6 Ⓐ Ⓑ Ⓒ Ⓓ
7 Ⓐ Ⓑ Ⓒ Ⓓ
8 Ⓐ Ⓑ Ⓒ Ⓓ
9 Ⓐ Ⓑ Ⓒ Ⓓ
10 Ⓐ Ⓑ Ⓒ Ⓓ
11 Ⓐ Ⓑ Ⓒ Ⓓ
12 Ⓐ Ⓑ Ⓒ Ⓓ
13 Ⓐ Ⓑ Ⓒ Ⓓ
14 Ⓐ Ⓑ Ⓒ Ⓓ
15 Ⓐ Ⓑ Ⓒ Ⓓ
16 Ⓐ Ⓑ Ⓒ Ⓓ
17 Ⓐ Ⓑ Ⓒ Ⓓ
18 Ⓐ Ⓑ Ⓒ Ⓓ
19 Ⓐ Ⓑ Ⓒ Ⓓ
20 Ⓐ Ⓑ Ⓒ Ⓓ

Assembling Objects

1 Ⓐ Ⓑ Ⓒ Ⓓ
2 Ⓐ Ⓑ Ⓒ Ⓓ
3 Ⓐ Ⓑ Ⓒ Ⓓ
4 Ⓐ Ⓑ Ⓒ Ⓓ
5 Ⓐ Ⓑ Ⓒ Ⓓ
6 Ⓐ Ⓑ Ⓒ Ⓓ
7 Ⓐ Ⓑ Ⓒ Ⓓ
8 Ⓐ Ⓑ Ⓒ Ⓓ
9 Ⓐ Ⓑ Ⓒ Ⓓ
10 Ⓐ Ⓑ Ⓒ Ⓓ
11 Ⓐ Ⓑ Ⓒ Ⓓ
12 Ⓐ Ⓑ Ⓒ Ⓓ
13 Ⓐ Ⓑ Ⓒ Ⓓ
14 Ⓐ Ⓑ Ⓒ Ⓓ
15 Ⓐ Ⓑ Ⓒ Ⓓ
16 Ⓐ Ⓑ Ⓒ Ⓓ

CUT HERE

General Science

Time: 11 minutes

25 questions

Directions: The following questions will test your knowledge of general science principles. Read the question and select the choice that best answers the question. Indicate that letter on your answer sheet.

1. Increasing which of the following factors would not help a plant photosynthesize faster?

   A. oxygen
   B. carbon dioxide
   C. light intensity
   D. water

2. A man with O-type blood and a woman with AB-type blood could have which type of children?

   A. O
   B. AB
   C. A or B
   D. all of the above

3. Ammonia can be produced from nitrogen and hydrogen, according to the unbalanced equation: $N_2 (g) + H_2 (g) \rightarrow NH_3 (g)$.

   After balancing the equation, the coefficient before ammonia should be

   A. 1.
   B. 2.
   C. 3.
   D. 4.

4. Given the reaction $2\ CO\ (g) + O_2\ (g) \rightarrow 2\ CO_2\ (g)$, when there is an increase in pressure to the system you would expect

   A. an increase in the amount of carbon dioxide.
   B. an increase in the amount of carbon monoxide and oxygen.
   C. a decrease in the amount of carbon dioxide.
   D. no change in the system.

5. Summers are warmer than winters in the Northern Hemisphere because the Earth

   A. is closer to the sun in the summer.
   B. is inclined on its axis toward the sun in the summer.
   C. slows in its orbit in the summer.
   D. speeds up in its orbit in the winter.

6. Consider the chemical structure below. Which of the following statements is true?

   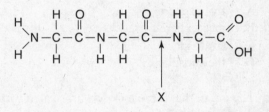

   A. It represents an amino acid and X points to a disulfide bridge.
   B. It represents two amino acids and X points to a peptide bond.
   C. It represents three amino acids and X points to a disulfide bridge.
   D. It represents three amino acids and X points to a peptide bond.

7. When blood leaves the heart and enters the pulmonary artery, it

   A. has just left the right atrium.
   B. is heading to the lungs.
   C. has just left the left atrium.
   D. is heading to the aorta.

8. A snake is an example of a

   A. mammal.
   B. reptile.
   C. amphibian.
   D. rodent.

GO ON TO THE NEXT PAGE

Practice Test II

9. Jack has 100 milliliters of a 12 molar solution of sulfuric acid. How much of it should he put into a graduated cylinder to make 20 milliliters of a 1.2 molar solution?

   A. 1
   B. 2
   C. 10
   D. 12

10. The transformation of a solid directly into a gas is called

   A. vaporization.
   B. ionization.
   C. sublimation.
   D. polarization.

11. In which layer of the atmosphere does sea level exist?

   A. troposphere
   B. mesosphere
   C. stratosphere
   D. thermosphere

12. The organ that is most closely associated with the digestion of proteins is the

   A. stomach.
   B. liver.
   C. small intestine.
   D. large intestine.

13. Based on the dynamics of the river portrayed in the figure below, what are the most likely changes in river flow over 500 years?

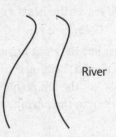

River

   A. The bends in the river will diminish and the river will straighten.
   B. The bends in the river will increase and the river will bend more.
   C. The river will flow faster as it matures.
   D. It is not possible to deduce the changes in the river in 500 years.

14. The further a planet is from the sun, the longer it takes to complete an orbital revolution. The closest planet, Mercury, has an orbital period of almost 88 days. Jupiter has an orbital period of about 12 Earth-years. Based on this information, what is your best guess as to the length of the orbital period of Neptune?

   A. 200 days
   B. 5 years
   C. 10 years
   D. 165 years

15. The vast dust bowls of the American Midwest during the Great Depression of the 1930s were the result of a combination of factors leading to massive erosion. Which of the following could be argued as the most instrumental in creating wastelands?

   A. high winds
   B. lack of ground cover
   C. flat topography
   D. periodic thunderstorms

16. Which of the following gases is least common in the atmosphere?

   A. methane
   B. oxygen
   C. argon
   D. nitrogen

17. Which of the following organisms is NOT an invertebrate?

   A. sponge
   B. jellyfish
   C. snail
   D. fish

18. If a solution has a hydronium ion concentration of 0.1 mole/liter, what would be its pH?

   A. 0.1
   B. 0.2
   C. 1.0
   D. 2.0

19. The correct structural formula for ethyne is

   A. $H - C = C - H$.
   B. $H - C = C = H$.
   C. $H - C \equiv C - H$.
   D. $H = C = C = H$.

20. What is a vaccine made out of?

   A.   a substance that will destroy viruses
   B.   medicine to keep bacteria from reproducing
   C.   a weakened dose of a virus
   D.   a weakened dose of bacteria

21. If you were looking for DNA in a cell, you would find it in the

   A.   endoplasmic reticulum.
   B.   nucleus.
   C.   vacuole.
   D.   plasma membrane.

22. What is the oxidation number of lead (Pb) in PbF_2?

   A.   −1
   B.   −2
   C.   +1
   D.   +2

23. As you move down a column on the left side of the periodic table, which of the following statements is true?

   A.   The radius of the ion becomes smaller.
   B.   The electronegativity decreases.
   C.   The electrons are held more tightly.
   D.   The number of neutrons remains the same.

24. The male part of a flower is referred to as the

   A.   ovary.
   B.   pistil.
   C.   sepal.
   D.   stamen.

25. The central nervous system in humans is made up of

   A.   the brain and the spinal cord.
   B.   the brain and the muscles.
   C.   the brain and the heart.
   D.   the brain and the lungs.

Practice Test II

STOP

Arithmetic Reasoning

Time: 36 minutes

30 questions

Directions: Each of the following questions will test your knowledge about basic arithmetic. Read the question and select the choice that best answers the question. Indicate that letter on your answer sheet.

1. Mattie walked 45 yd north, 36 yd west, and 41 yd south. Jacob walked 16 yd north, 49 yd west, and 33 yd south. How much farther did Mattie walk than Jacob?

   A. 20 yd
   B. 22 yd
   C. 24 yd
   D. 28 yd

2. A cylinder whose height is 8 inches has a volume of 128π cm³. If its radius is doubled and its height is cut in half, the volume of the resulting cylinder is

   A. 64π cm³.
   B. 128π cm³.
   C. 256π cm³.
   D. 512π cm³.

3. The sum of 2 ft $2\frac{1}{2}$ in, 4 ft $3\frac{3}{8}$ in, and 3 ft $9\frac{3}{4}$ in is

   A. 9 ft $\frac{7}{8}$ in.
   B. 9 ft $9\frac{5}{8}$ in.
   C. 10 ft $\frac{5}{8}$ in.
   D. 10 ft $3\frac{5}{8}$ in.

4. Doug earns 15% commission on all sales over $5,000. Last month, his sales totaled $12,500. What were Doug's earnings?

   A. $750
   B. $1,125
   C. $1,875
   D. $2,625

5. Fencing costs $4.75 per foot. Posts cost $12.50 each. How much will it cost to fence a garden if 10 posts and 34 ft of fencing are needed?

   A. $472.50
   B. $336.50
   C. $315.50
   D. $286.50

6. How much change would you get back from a $20.00 bill if you purchased eight CD covers costing $1.59 each?

   A. $7.28
   B. $10.41
   C. $12.00
   D. $18.41

7. The scale on a map shows 500 miles for every $\frac{1}{4}$ inch. If two cities are 6 inches apart on the map, what is the actual distance they are apart?

   A. 125 miles
   B. 750 miles
   C. 2,000 miles
   D. 12,000 miles

8. A 10-ft rope is to be cut into equal segments measuring 8 inches each. The total number of segments is

   A. 1.
   B. 8.
   C. 15.
   D. 40.

9. Rayanne can read 1 page in 2 minutes. If a book has 80 pages, how long will it take her to read?

   A. 160 minutes
   B. 120 minutes
   C. 80 minutes
   D. 40 minutes

10. Three boxes are needed to hold 18 reams of paper. How many boxes are needed for 90 reams?

    A. 5
    B. 6
    C. 9
    D. 15

11. The area of the figure below is

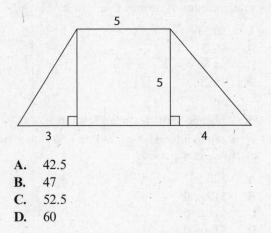

    A. 42.5
    B. 47
    C. 52.5
    D. 60

12. Cards normally sell for $3.00 each. How much was saved if five cards were purchased on sale for two for $5.00?

    A. $2.50
    B. $5.00
    C. $12.50
    D. $15.00

13. One gallon of paint covers 400 sq ft. How many gallons are needed to cover 2,225 sq ft?

    A. 5 gallons
    B. 6 gallons
    C. 7 gallons
    D. 8 gallons

14. A restaurant bill without tax and tip comes to $38.40. If a 15% tip is included after a 6% tax is added to the amount, how much is the tip?

    A. $6.11
    B. $5.76
    C. $5.15
    D. $2.30

15. The figure below contains five equal squares. If the area is 405, what is the perimeter?

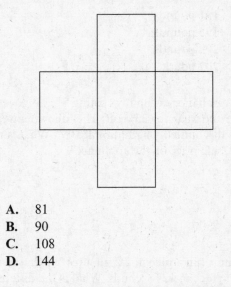

    A. 81
    B. 90
    C. 108
    D. 144

16. Find the length of x in the following figure.

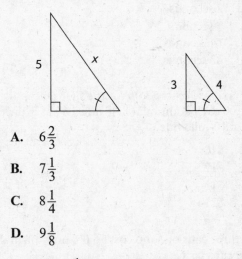

    A. $6\frac{2}{3}$

    B. $7\frac{1}{3}$

    C. $8\frac{1}{4}$

    D. $9\frac{1}{8}$

17. Joann eats $\frac{1}{4}$ of a peach pie and divides the remainder of the pie among her four friends. What fraction of the pie does each of her friends receive?

    A. $\frac{1}{3}$

    B. $\frac{7}{12}$

    C. $\frac{3}{16}$

    D. $\frac{1}{8}$

GO ON TO THE NEXT PAGE

Practice Test II

18. Max weighs 209 pounds. If he loses 2 pounds per week, how much will he weigh in 7 weeks?

    A. 191 pounds
    B. 195 pounds
    C. 202 pounds
    D. 207 pounds

19. An appliance originally costing $1,000 goes on sale one week for 25% off. The following week, it is discounted an additional 10%. What is the new sale price of the appliance?

    A. $650
    B. $675
    C. $750
    D. $900

20. Dennis ran a race in 2.2 minutes. Kayla ran the same race in 124 seconds. What is the difference between these two times?

    A. 2 seconds
    B. 8 seconds
    C. 14 seconds
    D. 22 seconds

21. A taxi ride costs $3.00 for the first mile and $1.00 each additional half mile. What is the cost of a 10-mile ride?

    A. $10
    B. $12
    C. $13
    D. $21

22. If three cans of soup cost $5.00, how much do ten cans cost?

    A. $15.00
    B. $16.45
    C. $16.67
    D. $17.33

23. Kyle ran 3 miles in $17\frac{1}{2}$ minutes on Saturday, $4\frac{1}{2}$ miles in 22 minutes on Sunday, and 2 miles in 9 minutes on Monday. What was Kyle's average rate of speed while running?

    A. 1.6 minutes per mile
    B. 5.1 minutes per mile
    C. 16.2 minutes per mile
    D. 17.8 minutes per mile

24. You have 40 nickels and 12 dimes. What is the total amount of money that you have?

    A. $0.52
    B. $3.20
    C. $4.60
    D. $5.20

25. A savings account earns $2\frac{1}{4}\%$ interest each year. How much interest is earned on a $1,000 deposit after a 5-year period?

    A. $22.50
    B. $100.00
    C. $112.50
    D. $150.00

26. Vanda types 6 pages in 8 minutes. She needs to type 36 pages. If she continues at the same rate of 6 pages in 8 minutes, how many minutes will it take her to type 36 pages?

    A. 16 minutes
    B. 20 minutes
    C. 27 minutes
    D. 32 minutes

27. Stanley types 35 words per minute. If it takes him a half-hour to type a document, how many words are in it?

    A. 900
    B. 1,050
    C. 1,500
    D. 2,100

28. Sandy bought $4\frac{1}{2}$ pounds of apples and six kiwi fruits. Brandon bought $3\frac{1}{4}$ pounds of apples and nine kiwi fruits. If apples cost $1.39 per pound and kiwis are two for $1.00, how much more money did Sandy spend than Brandon?

    A. $0.24
    B. $0.94
    C. $1.54
    D. $2.32

29. Bryan agrees to pay back a $50,000 loan over a 10-year period. He must also pay 8% annual simple interest. If he pays back the same amount each of those 10 years, how much does he pay back per year?

   A. $41.67
   B. $500.00
   C. $900.00
   D. $9,000.00

30. In a nut mixture, there are $1\frac{1}{8}$ pounds of almonds, $2\frac{3}{4}$ pounds of cashews, and $3\frac{1}{3}$ pounds of peanuts. The total weight of the mixture is

   A. $6\frac{1}{3}$ pounds.
   B. $6\frac{23}{24}$ pounds.
   C. $7\frac{5}{24}$ pounds.
   D. $7\frac{7}{12}$ pounds.

Practice Test II

Word Knowledge

Time: 11 minutes
35 questions

Directions: This portion of the exam will test your knowledge of the meaning of words. Each question has an underlined word. Decide which of the four choices most nearly means the same as the underlined word; then indicate that letter on your answer sheet.

1. <u>Innovation</u> most nearly means

   A. a myriad.
   B. a threat.
   C. an antique.
   D. a new idea.

2. She would not <u>divulge</u> who told her.

   A. care for
   B. leave
   C. reveal
   D. hurt

3. The child did not <u>heed</u> her mother's advice.

   A. pay attention to
   B. learn from
   C. ignore
   D. solicit

4. <u>Foil</u> most nearly means

   A. pass time.
   B. prevent.
   C. jump.
   D. assist.

5. <u>Startle</u> most nearly means

   A. climb.
   B. surprise.
   C. reject.
   D. sparkle.

6. <u>Stupefy</u> most nearly means

   A. stretch.
   B. repress.
   C. astonish.
   D. agonize.

7. She was upset by the <u>blemish</u> on her record.

   A. grade
   B. writing
   C. defect
   D. message

8. She cared only about her child's <u>proximity</u> to her.

   A. obedience
   B. behavior
   C. grades
   D. nearness

9. They were all involved in the <u>clash</u>.

   A. conflict
   B. party
   C. dance
   D. singing

10. <u>Wry</u> most nearly means

    A. seeded.
    B. twisted.
    C. on-target.
    D. holistic.

11. <u>Verdant</u> most nearly means

    A. green.
    B. late.
    C. mountainous.
    D. true.

12. The crowd began to <u>jeer</u> when Alvin got up to speak.

    A. laugh
    B. scoff
    C. cry
    D. whistle

13. Strident most nearly means

   A. harsh.
   B. running.
   C. walking.
   D. soft.

14. Shear most nearly means

   A. cut.
   B. clear.
   C. empty.
   D. violate.

15. They would always relish their time in Vermont.

   A. feel sorrow at
   B. enjoy
   C. forget
   D. talk about

16. She was dressed in a crimson sweater.

   A. reddish
   B. yellow
   C. moth-eaten
   D. torn

17. Obsolete most nearly means

   A. original.
   B. out of use.
   C. new.
   D. beginning.

18. Facet most nearly means

   A. a waterfall.
   B. a side.
   C. a trophy.
   D. a quest.

19. Extol most nearly means

   A. slander.
   B. remove.
   C. withdraw.
   D. praise.

20. Exodus most nearly means

   A. bundle.
   B. departure.
   C. religion.
   D. season.

21. He rubbed his arms vigorously.

   A. painfully
   B. energetically
   C. slowly
   D. quietly

22. Emily was a familiar figure in town.

   A. lonesome
   B. well-known
   C. welcome
   D. unusual

23. Detriment most nearly means

   A. sludge.
   B. pleasure.
   C. damage.
   D. decision.

24. Glutton most nearly means

   A. gourmet.
   B. flavor.
   C. overeater.
   D. sheepskin.

25. They could not refute his testimony.

   A. care for
   B. disprove
   C. return to
   D. ignore

26. Luster most nearly means

   A. intelligence.
   B. dullness.
   C. cleanliness.
   D. brilliance.

GO ON TO THE NEXT PAGE

Practice Test II

27. Lucrative most nearly means

    A. barren.
    B. majestic.
    C. profitable.
    D. probable.

28. They wanted to go on a leisurely ride along the water.

    A. quick
    B. cautious
    C. sight-seeing
    D. unhurried

29. Accord most nearly means

    A. bicycle.
    B. agreement.
    C. threat.
    D. sideline.

30. He showed her the excerpt in the notebook.

    A. drawing
    B. extract
    C. poem
    D. signature

31. The coach could not diagnose the team's scoring problem.

    A. diminish
    B. analyze
    C. talk about
    D. grant

32. Innate most nearly means

    A. stalwart.
    B. inborn.
    C. favorite.
    D. primary.

33. Maxim most nearly means

    A. an enlargement.
    B. an endorsement.
    C. a saying.
    D. a faculty.

34. Hyperbole most nearly means

    A. exaggeration.
    B. a joke.
    C. withdrawal.
    D. excitement.

35. The oil began to seep through the surface of the earth.

    A. fall
    B. ooze
    C. rain
    D. stretch

Paragraph Comprehension

Time: 13 minutes

15 questions

Directions: This is a test of reading comprehension. Read each paragraph and then select the choice below that best answers that question. Indicate that letter on your answer sheet.

1. The business executive's presentation was incoherent. His slurred words and mumbling made his speech very difficult to understand.

   In this context, the word *incoherent* means

   A. brilliant.
   B. successful.
   C. illogical.
   D. understandable.

2. Many plants that appear pretty are actually invasive and harmful to the environment in which they grow. Such plants establish themselves in new areas and eventually displace plants that grow naturally in the region. Eventually, many plant species become displaced and then endangered.

   The best title for this selection is

   A. Endangered Species.
   B. Beautiful Plants Can Be Dangerous to the Environment.
   C. Displaced Species.
   D. The Plant World.

3. There are many easy ways to conserve water in the home. One way to use less water is to take shorter showers. Another method of conserving water is to make sure there are no leaky faucets or running toilets in the home. These are only a few ways to conserve water. There are many other quick-and-easy tricks everyone can learn in order to help conserve environmental resources and lower the water bill.

   Which of the following is not mentioned as a method of conserving water?

   A. checking for leaky faucets
   B. taking shorter showers
   C. using dishwashers
   D. checking for running toilets

4. Regular weight lifting has been shown to improve muscle mass in people of all ages. Even 90-year-old participants in weight-lifting studies benefited by supplementing their muscle mass.

   It can be inferred from the above passage that

   A. ninety-year-old participants show the most improvements in muscle mass in weight-lifting studies.
   B. younger people would not benefit from weight lifting.
   C. weight lifting ten times a year would produce benefits for all ages.
   D. you can begin regular weight lifting at any age and see benefits.

5. Comets have been known of since antiquity, unlike many of the planets and other small bodies in space. In fact, Chinese records dating as far back as 240 B.C.E. mention Halley's comet in particular. The famous Bayeux Tapestry, which portrays the Norman Conquest in 1066, also shows the image of Halley's comet.

   The best title for this passage is

   A. Halley's Comet.
   B. Ancient Knowledge of Comets.
   C. Art and Comets.
   D. Comets and Planets.

GO ON TO THE NEXT PAGE

6. Alexander Fleming's discovery of penicillin in the 1920s happened in part because of his disorganized lab. While straightening up his lab one day, he noticed an unidentified type of mold growing in his petri dishes. All around this particular mold, staph bacteria had been killed. Fleming noted that this eradication of staph bacteria by a mold was highly unusual. Thus began his work on penicillin, for which he won the Nobel Prize in 1945.

It can be inferred from the above passage that Fleming's discovery of penicillin was partly due to

A. his long search for it.
B. his years of work with mold of all types.
C. his disorganized lab.
D. his belief that such a wonder drug existed.

7. Recent sociological studies report that violence among adolescents is linked to television watching. Researchers found that teens who watch more than one hour of television per day are at increased risk for being involved in assaults, fights, and other violent criminal behaviors later in life.

The author probably believes that

A. television exposure should be strictly limited for teens.
B. teens should watch only nonviolent programming.
C. teens can watch as much television as they would like.
D. teens can watch more than one hour of television per day as long as they watch nonviolent programs.

8. Newly developed, cheap, plastic solar cells could be the answer to more effective use of solar energy. Such cells offer many advantages over current solar cells. The first advantage is the small size of these plastic solar cells that would replace the bulky solar cells being used at this time. Also, such plastic solar cells are very easily manufactured. Perhaps the most convincing argument for implementing these new plastic solar cells is that they are very inexpensive to make.

Which of the following is not mentioned as a reason for using plastic solar cells?

A. They are cheap.
B. They are very energy efficient.
C. They are small.
D. They are easy to make.

9. Early, controversial studies of chimpanzees and language showed that these animals can understand the basics of language on the 2½-year-old level of children. Recent studies have shown that other chimpanzees, such as the bonobo or pygmy, are more humanlike and adept in language and communication than the earlier chimpanzees that were studied.

The best title for this selection is

A. Recent Studies of Chimpanzees and Language Skills.
B. Language Levels of Various Chimps.
C. The Pygmy Chimp.
D. The Evolution of Chimpanzees and Language Skills.

10. In the winter of 1999, many central and northeastern states received less snow in winter than the average. Scientists have proposed several reasons for the situation. One possible factor is global warming; however, scientists still know very little about this phenomenon. Another credible reason for less snowfall is La Niña, which causes unusually cold ocean temperatures in the Equatorial Pacific. The result of a strong La Niña is greatly increased snowfall in the northwest and less snowfall in the central and northeastern United States. Thus, it may appear that there is less snow in a given year.

It may be inferred from the selection that

A. many environmental factors influence average annual snowfall.
B. La Niña determines annual snowfall averages.
C. global warming affects annual snowfall averages.
D. annual snowfall averages always stay constant.

Questions 11 and 12 relate to the following passage.

Recent sociological studies indicate several key factors in determining a person's risk of being mugged. One factor is the particular neighborhood in which a person lives and works. If the home or workplace is on a street in a suburban area or in the inner city, risk increases significantly. Also, weekdays present a higher risk for mugging than weekends. Finally, a person who walks alone either during the day or at night is more likely to be targeted for mugging.

11. According to the selection, a person is most likely to be mugged if

    A. he or she lives in a rural area.
    B. he or she is in a small group of people.
    C. he or she goes shopping during the week.
    D. he or she takes the bus to work.

12. The most appropriate title for this selection is

    A. Risk Factors for Mugging.
    B. How to Prevent Mugging.
    C. Recent Studies on Mugging.
    D. Popularity of Mugging in the Suburbs.

Questions 13 to 15 relate to the following passage.

If you are thirsty, most likely you are already dehydrated. Most people underrate the importance of drinking water all day long. They wait until their throats are parched or they eat meals before they drink any fluids—and they usually don't choose water. Because the human body is about two-thirds water, drinking water is essential to maintaining good health. Just a few of the benefits of staying hydrated are better memory throughout the day, increased energy, and less tiredness.

13. In this context, *parched* means

    A. sore.
    B. wet.
    C. dry.
    D. hydrated.

14. It can be inferred from this selection that most people are

    A. rarely ever dehydrated.
    B. dehydrated quite often without knowing it.
    C. dehydrated despite drinking large quantities of water.
    D. often hospitalized for severe dehydration.

15. The best title for this selection is

    A. The Benefits of Drinking Water.
    B. Dehydration and the Importance of Drinking Water.
    C. Better Memory with Water.
    D. How to Stay Hydrated.

Practice Test II

Auto and Shop Information

Time: 11 minutes

25 questions

Directions: There are two parts to this test. The first will test your basic knowledge of automobiles. The second will test your knowledge of basic shop practices and the use of tools. Read each question carefully and select the choice that best answers the question. Indicate that letter on your answer sheet.

1. When replacing a battery, what is the first step of a replacement procedure?

   A. Clean the battery area.
   B. Remove any hold-down device.
   C. Disconnect the ground cable.
   D. Disconnect the positive cable.

2. Which is the most likely cause of a vibration after a U-joint is replaced on a two-piece drive shaft?

   A. The U-joint is not lubricated.
   B. The drive shaft is out of phase.
   C. A snap ring is not seated.
   D. The pinion seal let go.

3. Engine oil is used to _____ various parts of the engine.

   A. cool
   B. lubricate
   C. seal
   D. all of the above

4. In the illustration below, a bar is being removed. What is the purpose of this bar?

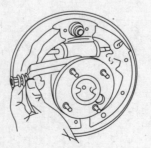

   A. to force the shoes against the drum when the parking brakes are applied
   B. to prevent the shoes from going too far into the wheel cylinder
   C. to center the shoes
   D. to allow the shoes to return after a brake application

5. Looking at the following figure, technician A says this figure shows the setup for the drives on a front-wheel drive car. Technician B says this setup shows a two-piece drive in phase. Who is right?

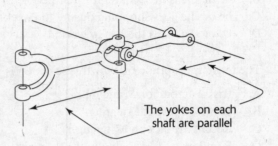

The yokes on each shaft are parallel

   A. Technician A only
   B. Technician B only
   C. both technicians A and B
   D. neither technician A nor B

6. The part "X" shown below is used for what purpose?

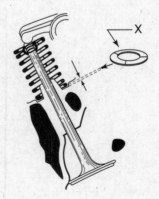

   A. to seal the valve guide
   B. to rotate the valve spring
   C. to correct spring height
   D. to adjust valve clearance

7. A torque converter in an automatic transmission is used to

   A.   shift the transmission through different gears.
   B.   transfer engine torque from the engine to the transmission.
   C.   convert torque direction from forward to reverse.
   D.   reduce engine torque to the transmission.

8. Most cylinder heads contain all of the following EXCEPT

   A.   intake valves.
   B.   camshafts.
   C.   exhaust valves.
   D.   EGR valves.

9. The primary purpose of a vacuum check valve on a power brake booster is to

   A.   balance vacuum with atmosphere pressure.
   B.   provide power assist in the event of engine failure.
   C.   prevent excess vacuum from entering booster.
   D.   reduce vacuum flow.

10. The function of a brake drum or rotor is to act as

   A.   a friction element.
   B.   a heat sink.
   C.   a heat extinguisher.
   D.   all of the above.

11. Which of the following statements about carburetor systems is NOT true?

   A.   A dashpot is used during rapid deceleration to speed the closing of the throttle.
   B.   An accelerator pump is needed to supply fuel rapidly during sudden acceleration.
   C.   A power valve is a vacuum-operated metering rod.
   D.   Metering rods are actuated mechanically or by vacuum.

12. Which of the following measurements CANNOT be performed with a DVOM?

   A.   open circuit voltage
   B.   voltage drop
   C.   resistance
   D.   resistance on a live circuit

13. When an ammeter is directly connected to the negative and positive of a vehicle's battery, the result will be

   A.   slow discharge of the battery.
   B.   an indication of the battery's amperage.
   C.   usually a burned-out meter.
   D.   an accurate reading.

14. To make a wide groove in a board with a table saw, what type of blade would you use?

   A.   miter
   B.   cross-cut
   C.   rip
   D.   dado

15. Concrete is a mixture of all of the following EXCEPT

   A.   cement.
   B.   sand.
   C.   water.
   D.   soil.

16. The following type of nut is called a

   A.   butterfly nut.
   B.   wing nut.
   C.   clip nut.
   D.   screw bolt.

17. You are most likely to find a dovetail joint

   A.   on the back of a mirror.
   B.   on the back of a drawer.
   C.   on floorboards.
   D.   on metal appliances.

18. A cold chisel is used to cut

   A.   metal.
   B.   plywood.
   C.   hardwood.
   D.   glass.

GO ON TO THE NEXT PAGE

19. The following is an illustration of a(n)

   A. hex screw.
   B. Allen wrench.
   C. corner joiner.
   D. square screw hook.

20. The tool illustrated below is used to

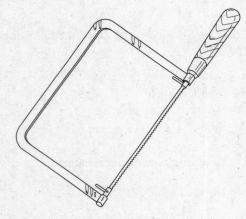

   A. cut through soft metals or nails.
   B. cut thin wood or plastic.
   C. cut Sheetrock.
   D. cut holes in wood for door locks.

21. For heavy-duty construction work, such as sectioning large framing timber, you would probably choose a

   A. circular saw.
   B. saber saw.
   C. reciprocating saw.
   D. chain saw.

22. The strongest bond for a wood joint would be

   A. carpenter's glue.
   B. corrugated fasteners.
   C. tack nails.
   D. grooved dowels and glue.

23. Which of the following is used for finishing a piece of wood?

   A. belt sander
   B. palm sander
   C. disk sander
   D. no. 40 sandpaper

24. What is a kerf?

   A. an unused portion of wood that has been sawed
   B. the width of a saw's cut
   C. the angle of the saw's teeth
   D. the number of teeth on a saw

25. A nail set is used to

   A. align nails in a straight line.
   B. drive nail heads below the surface of the wood.
   C. remove old nails.
   D. flatten the heads of finishing nails for decorative purposes.

Mathematics Knowledge

Time: 24 minutes

25 questions

Directions: This section will test your knowledge of basic mathematics. Read each question carefully and select the choice that best answers the question. Indicate that letter on your answer sheet.

1. Multiply $(2x + 1)(2x + 1)$.

   A. $2x^2 + 1$
   B. $4x^2 + 1$
   C. $4x^2 + 2x + 1$
   D. $4x^2 + 4x + 1$

2. $\frac{5}{16} + \frac{9}{24} =$

   A. $\frac{11}{16}$
   B. $\frac{14}{40}$
   C. $\frac{7}{20}$
   D. $\frac{14}{48}$

3. The sum of $\sqrt{50} + 3\sqrt{72}$ is

   A. $4 + \sqrt{122}$.
   B. $4\sqrt{122}$.
   C. $7\sqrt{2}$.
   D. $23\sqrt{2}$.

4. Simplify $5(a - 2) - (4a - 6)$.

   A. $a - 4$
   B. $a - 8$
   C. $a - 10$
   D. $a + 4$

5. What is the diameter of a circle whose circumference is equivalent to its area?

   A. 2
   B. 3
   C. 4
   D. 6

6. The cube of 8 is

   A. 2.
   B. 24.
   C. 512.
   D. 8,000.

7. Find the area of a triangle whose base is 3 in less than its height.

   A. $\frac{1}{2}h^2 - 3h$
   B. $\frac{1}{2}h^2 - \frac{3}{2}h$
   C. $\frac{1}{2}h^2 - \frac{3}{2}$
   D. $\frac{1}{2}h^2 - 3$

8. Evaluate $3r^3 - 2s^2 + t$ if $r = -1$, $s = -2$, and $t = -3$.

   A. 2
   B. 4
   C. -8
   D. -14

9. The product of two numbers is 117. If one of the numbers is 9, what is the other?

   A. 11
   B. 13
   C. 15
   D. 17

10. Simplify $\left(\frac{a^{-3}b^2}{2ab^{-1}} \right)^{-3}$.

    A. $\frac{2a^6}{b}$
    B. $\frac{8a^{12}}{b^9}$
    C. $\frac{a^8}{8b^3}$
    D. $\frac{a^{12}}{8b^9}$

11. There are five more boys in the kindergarten class than girls. If there are 27 children altogether, how many are boys?

    A. 10
    B. 11
    C. 16
    D. 22

GO ON TO THE NEXT PAGE

Practice Test II

331

12. The area of the shaded region is

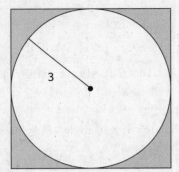

3

  A. $9 - 3\pi$.
  B. $36 - 3\pi^2$.
  C. $36 - 9\pi$.
  D. $81 - 9\pi$.

13. The product of the square of x and 3 less than x is

  A. $\sqrt{x}(x - 3)$.
  B. $\sqrt{x}(3 - x)$.
  C. $x^2(x - 3)$.
  D. $x^2(3 - x)$.

14. The cube root of 512 is

  A. 8.
  B. 56.
  C. $170\frac{2}{3}$.
  D. 1,536.

15. What is the probability of rolling a sum of 9 using two dice?

  A. $\frac{1}{4}$
  B. $\frac{1}{9}$
  C. $\frac{5}{12}$
  D. $\frac{7}{36}$

16. If the diameter of a circle is increased by 100%, the area is increased by

  A. 50%.
  B. 100%.
  C. 300%.
  D. 400%.

17. Which mathematical statement best represents the following statement?

   Six less than a number is four.

  A. $6 = n - 4$
  B. $6 < n + 4$
  C. $6 - n = 4$
  D. $n - 6 = 4$

18. Factor $2a^2 - 4ab + ab - 2b^2$.

  A. $(a + 2b)(2a - b)$
  B. $(a - 2b)(2a + b)$
  C. $(2a - b)(a + 2b)$
  D. $(2a + b)(a - b)$

19. If $\frac{m}{n} = \frac{3}{5}$ and $n = 20$, what is the value of $m + n$?

  A. 2
  B. 8
  C. 32
  D. $\frac{9}{25}$

20. Floor tiling costs $13.50 per square yard. What would it cost to tile a room 15 ft long by 18 ft wide?

  A. $20
  B. $405
  C. $1,350
  D. $3,645

21. A rope is made by linking beads that are $\frac{1}{2}$ inch in diameter. How many feet long is a rope made from 60 beads?

  A. $2\frac{1}{2}$ ft
  B. 10 ft
  C. 30 ft
  D. 120 ft

22. If $2y + 6 = 3y - 2$, then $y =$

  A. -2.
  B. 2.
  C. 4.
  D. 8.

23. $-3(-4-5) - 2(-6) =$

   A.   0
   B.   −5
   C.   15
   D.   39

24. Which of the following expressions represents the cost of five books and three magazines if books cost twice as much as magazines?

   A. $8b$
   B. $8m$
   C. $11b$
   D. $13m$

25. Squares *ADEC, BCFG,* and *ABHI* are shown. If the area of *ADEC* is 81 and the area of *BCFG* is 144, what is the perimeter of triangle *ABC*?

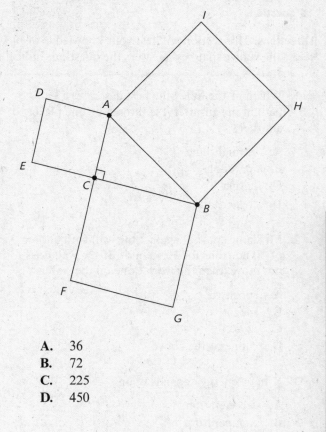

   A.   36
   B.   72
   C.   225
   D.   450

STOP

Mechanical Comprehension

Time: 19 minutes

25 questions

Directions: This section will test your knowledge of mechanical principles. Read each question carefully and then select the choice that best answers the question. Indicate that letter on your answer sheet.

1. Which of the following best describes a ball's path in the air after it is thrown by one player to another?

   A. straight line
   B. parabola
   C. circle
   D. hyperbola

2. Mr. James pushes against the wall with a force of 30 newtons for 30 seconds. If the wall does not move, then the work done on the wall is

   A. positive.
   B. negative.
   C. zero.
   D. none of the above.

3. Kinetic energy depends upon

   A. acceleration.
   B. temperature.
   C. position.
   D. velocity.

4. Potential energy depends upon

   A. temperature.
   B. position.
   C. velocity.
   D. motion.

5. In the absence of any force, a moving object will

   A. continue to move in a circular path.
   B. immediately stop.
   C. slow down and eventually stop.
   D. move in a straight line at a constant speed.

6. If the acceleration of an object is zero, then

   A. the net force on the object is zero.
   B. there are no forces acting on the object.
   C. the object is at rest.
   D. the applied force is larger than zero.

7. A ball is thrown horizontally from the top of a building. At the same time, another ball is dropped from the same height. Which ball will hit the ground first?

   A. the ball thrown horizontally
   B. the ball dropped from rest
   C. depends on the height of the building
   D. both will hit the ground at the same time

8. The force of kinetic friction is always directed opposite to

   A. the applied force.
   B. the direction of motion.
   C. the direction of gravity.
   D. the normal force.

9. If a mass at the end of a simple pendulum with a small amplitude of motion is increased by a factor of 2, other things remaining constant,

   A. its period will double.
   B. its frequency will increase by a factor of 2.
   C. the period will increase by a factor of 2.
   D. the frequency remains the same.

10. For an object with simple harmonic motion, simultaneously its

    A. displacement is maximum when its acceleration is maximum.
    B. velocity is maximum when its displacement is maximum.
    C. kinetic energy is maximum when its displacement is maximum.
    D. velocity is maximum and its acceleration is maximum.

11. A 50-centimeter-long metal rod expands 2 millimeters when heated in an oven. How much would a 75-centimeter-long rod of the same material expand in the same oven?

    A. 1 millimeter
    B. 2 millimeters
    C. 3 millimeters
    D. 4 millimeters

12. A skater is spinning with a constant angular momentum. If she pulls her arms in toward her body, her angular momentum will

    A. double.
    B. increase.
    C. decrease.
    D. remain constant.

13. The average acceleration of a runner who changes her speed from 3.60 to 4.24 m/s in a time of 5.6 seconds is

    A. 0.700 m/s^2.
    B. 0.114 m/s^2.
    C. 0.580 m/s^2.
    D. 0.230 m/s^2.

14. A ball is thrown vertically upward with a speed of 14.5 m/s from the top of a 50-meter-tall building. The ball will reach the ground after a time of

    A. 1.48 seconds.
    B. 2.96 seconds.
    C. 3.00 seconds.
    D. 5.00 seconds.

15. A 4-kilogram ball moving at a speed of 2 m/s collides head-on with another ball of 2-kilogram mass and 4 m/s speed. If the two balls stick together, their joint speed after the inelastic collision is

    A. 0 m/s.
    B. 1 m/s.
    C. 2 m/s.
    D. 4 m/s.

16. The input force required to lift a 200-newton load W in the pulley arrangement shown in the figure is

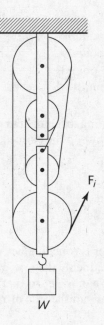

    A. 40 newtons.
    B. 50 newtons.
    C. 800 newtons.
    D. 1,000 newtons.

17. A force of 20 newtons is applied for 10 seconds to an object that has an initial momentum of 300 kilograms · m/s. The final momentum of the object is

    A. 150 kilograms · m/s.
    B. 200 kilograms · m/s.
    C. 300 kilograms · m/s.
    D. 500 kilograms · m/s.

18. An object is thrown with a horizontal velocity of 10 m/s from the edge of a building that is 12.5 meters above ground level. If the air resistance is negligible, the time, t, that it takes the object to reach the ground and the distance, d, from the building where it strikes the ground, are most nearly

    A. 3 s, 100 m, respectively.
    B. 1.6 s, 16 m, respectively.
    C. 3.2 s, 32 m, respectively.
    D. 1.6 s, 32 m, respectively.

GO ON TO THE NEXT PAGE

Practice Test II

19. Neglecting friction, if a ramp measures 9 ft in length and 3 ft in height, how much force does it take to move a box weighing 400 pounds along the ramp?

    A. 14.81 pounds
    B. 44.44 pounds
    C. 133.33 pounds
    D. 140 pounds

20. A car is driving around a curve on a level road. The force holding the car on the curve is

    A. friction.
    B. gravity.
    C. tension.
    D. magnetic.

21. An ice skater is touching her waist while spinning. Suddenly the music changes and she extends her hands out so that her fingers are twice as far from the axis of rotation. Her spin rate

    A. increases significantly.
    B. decreases significantly.
    C. increases slightly.
    D. decreases slightly.

22. A net force of 40 newtons on an object results in an acceleration of 8 m/s². The mass of the object is

    A. 0.2 kilograms.
    B. 2 kilograms.
    C. 5 kilograms.
    D. 320 kilograms.

23. The unit kg·m²/s² is equivalent to

    A. a newton.
    B. horsepower.
    C. a watt.
    D. a joule.

24. A 15-newton force that is parallel to the plane is used to push a 2-kilogram mass up a 30° frictionless inclined plane. The acceleration of the mass is nearly

    A. 0.32 m/s².
    B. 3.2 m/s².
    C. 0.16 m/s².
    D. 2.6 m/s².

25. A 20-kilogram box is raised to a height of 75 meters in 2 minutes. The power required is

    A. 12.25 watts.
    B. 122.5 watts.
    C. 750 watts.
    D. 1,500 watts.

Electronics Information

Time: 9 minutes

20 questions

Directions: The following portion of the exam will test your knowledge of electronics, electrical, and radio information. Read each question carefully and select the choice that best answers the question. Indicate that letter on your answer sheet.

1. An ammeter is a device used for measuring

   A. electrical current.
   B. electrical charge.
   C. energy.
   D. difference in voltage.

2. For the lamp to be turned on in the following circuit

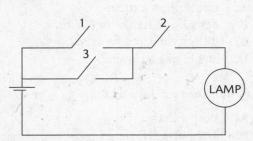

   A. switch 1 or switch 2 should be closed.
   B. switch 2 only should be closed.
   C. switches 1 or 3 and switch 2 should be closed.
   D. all the switches should be opened.

3. Which of the following symbols represents a transistor?

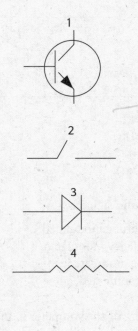

   A. 1
   B. 2
   C. 3
   D. 4

4. The total resistance for the circuit below is

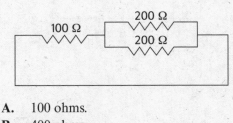

   A. 100 ohms.
   B. 400 ohms.
   C. 50 ohms.
   D. 200 ohms.

GO ON TO THE NEXT PAGE

Practice Test II

5. Inductance is measured in

   A. farads.
   B. volts.
   C. amperes.
   D. henries.

6. The following signal is expressed as

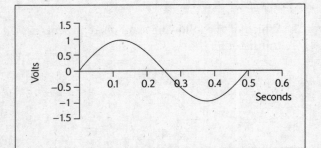

   A. sin (πt).
   B. 5 sin (πt).
   C. sin (4πt).
   D. sin (2πt).

7. An FM radio signal is

   A. amplitude modulated.
   B. frequency modulated.
   C. phase modulated.
   D. DC modulated.

8. The reading of the voltmeter in this circuit is

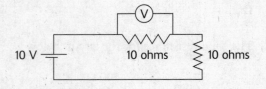

   A. 10 V.
   B. 5 V.
   C. 1 V.
   D. 2 V.

9. Capacitors are used in transistor circuits to

   A. separate AC signals from DC bias.
   B. rectify currents.
   C. invert signals.
   D. reduce cost.

10. The reading of the ammeter in this circuit is

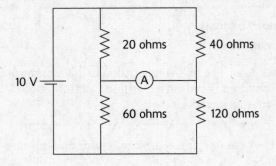

   A. 5 V.
   B. 0 A.
   C. 0 V.
   D. 2.5 A.

11. Modulation is used when

   A. measuring a current.
   B. designing a transistor circuit.
   C. transmitting a radio signal.
   D. amplifying a current.

12. A transistor can be used to

   A. store a charge.
   B. generate a DC signal.
   C. generate a triangular wave.
   D. amplify a current.

13. The total power dissipated in the resistors in the following circuit is

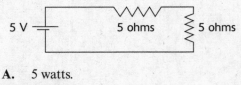

   A. 5 watts.
   B. 6 watts.
   C. 10 watts.
   D. 2.5 watts.

14. Electric transformers use the following component to transform the level of voltage:

   A. resistor.
   B. coil.
   C. power.
   D. current.

15. A component of a parts list has the following specifications: "10 Ω." The component specified is a

    A. capacitor.
    B. transistor.
    C. coil.
    D. resistor.

16. A diode can be used to

    A. rectify a signal.
    B. store a charge.
    C. amplify a current.
    D. induce an electromagnetic field.

17. Frequency mixers are used to

    A. mix electrical charges.
    B. amplify audio signals.
    C. carry audio signals on RF signals.
    D. rectify RF signals.

18. Shapes of electrical signals can be monitored by

    A. a voltmeter.
    B. an oscilloscope.
    C. an ammeter.
    D. an ohmmeter.

19. As a safety design requirement, electronic devices must be

    A. low in cost.
    B. low in weight.
    C. grounded.
    D. digitally designed.

20. The total capacitance of this circuit is

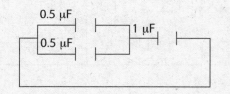

    A. 0.5 μF.
    B. 1 μF.
    C. 2 μF.
    D. 3 μF.

STOP

Assembling Objects

Time: 9 minutes

16 questions

Directions: In the Assembling Objects portion of the ASVAB there are two types of questions. One type is very similar to solving a jigsaw puzzle. The other is a matter of making appropriate connections given a diagram and instructions. In each of the questions, the first drawing is the problem, and the remaining four drawings offer possible solutions. Look at each of the four illustrations, and then select the choice that best solves that particular problem. Indicate that letter on your answer sheet.

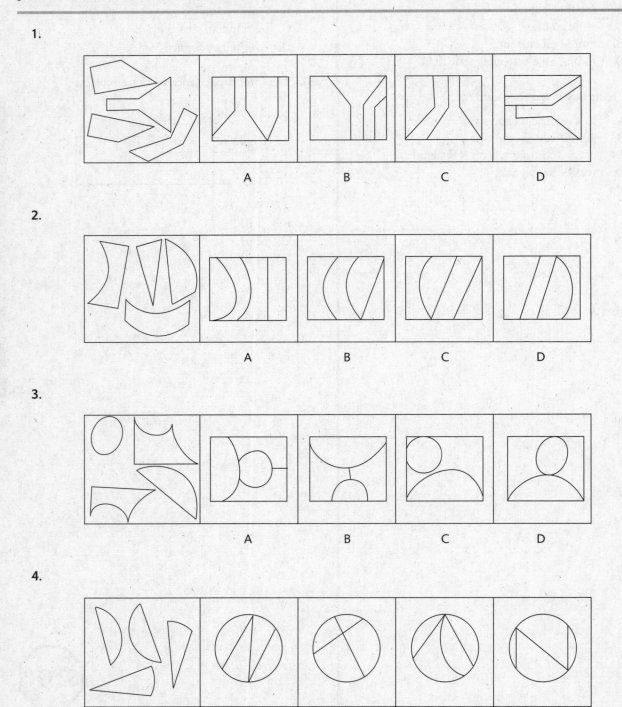

1.

    A   B   C   D

2.

    A   B   C   D

3.

    A   B   C   D

4.

    A   B   C   D

5.

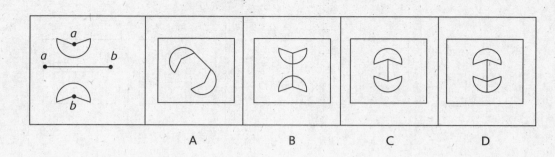

6.

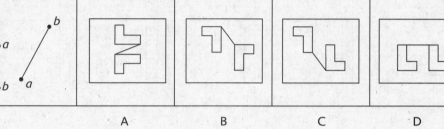

7.

8.

GO ON TO THE NEXT PAGE

9.

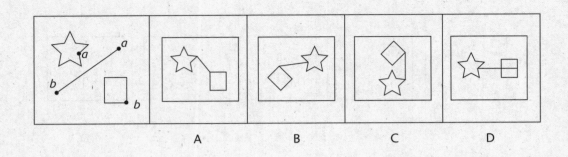

A   B   C   D

10.

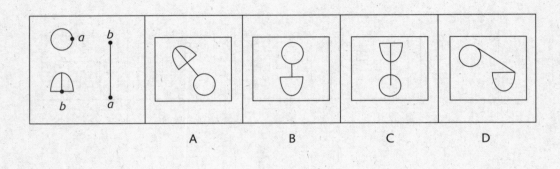

A   B   C   D

11.

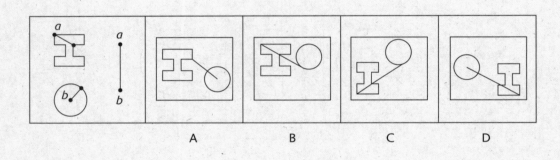

A   B   C   D

12.

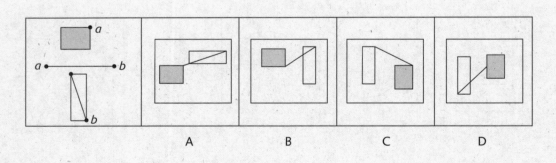

A   B   C   D

13.

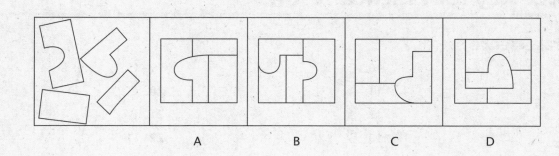

A   B   C   D

14.

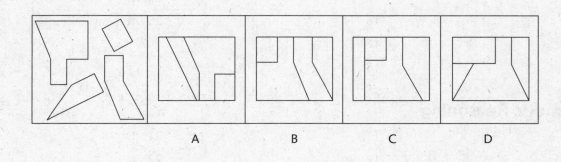

A   B   C   D

15.

A   B   C   D

16.

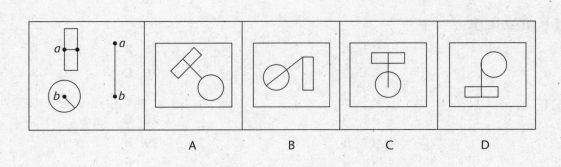

A   B   C   D

Answer Key for Practice Test II

General Science

1. A	10. C	19. C
2. C	11. A	20. C
3. B	12. A	21. B
4. A	13. B	22. D
5. B	14. D	23. B
6. D	15. B	24. D
7. B	16. A	25. A
8. B	17. D	
9. B	18. C	

Arithmetic Reasoning

1. C	11. A	21. D
2. C	12. A	22. C
3. D	13. B	23. B
4. B	14. A	24. B
5. D	15. C	25. C
6. A	16. A	26. C
7. D	17. C	27. B
8. C	18. B	28. A
9. A	19. B	29. D
10. D	20. B	30. C

Word Knowledge

1. D	13. A	25. B
2. C	14. A	26. D
3. A	15. B	27. C
4. B	16. A	28. D
5. B	17. B	29. B
6. C	18. B	30. B
7. C	19. D	31. B
8. D	20. B	32. B
9. A	21. B	33. C
10. B	22. B	34. A
11. A	23. C	35. B
12. B	24. C	

Paragraph Comprehension

1. C	6. C	11. C
2. B	7. A	12. A
3. C	8. B	13. C
4. D	9. D	14. B
5. B	10. A	15. B

Auto and Shop Information

1. C	10. D	19. B
2. B	11. A	20. B
3. D	12. D	21. C
4. A	13. C	22. D
5. B	14. D	23. B
6. C	15. D	24. B
7. B	16. B	25. B
8. D	17. B	
9. B	18. A	

Mathematics Knowledge

1. D	10. B	19. C
2. A	11. C	20. B
3. D	12. C	21. A
4. A	13. C	22. D
5. C	14. A	23. D
6. C	15. B	24. D
7. B	16. C	25. A
8. D	17. D	
9. B	18. B	

Mechanical Comprehension

1. B	10. A	19. C
2. C	11. C	20. A
3. D	12. D	21. D
4. B	13. B	22. C
5. D	14. D	23. D
6. A	15. A	24. D
7. D	16. A	25. B
8. B	17. D	
9. D	18. B	

Electronics Information

1. A	8. B	15. D
2. C	9. A	16. A
3. A	10. B	17. C
4. D	11. C	18. B
5. D	12. D	19. C
6. C	13. D	20. A
7. B	14. B	

Assembling Objects

1. C	7. A	13. A
2. B	8. C	14. B
3. D	9. B	15. B
4. A	10. A	16. C
5. C	11. D	
6. B	12. A	

ASVAB Practice Test II Answers and Explanations

General Science

1. **A.** Oxygen slows down the rate because most plants will use it in photorespiration, which is caused by the plants' enzymes picking up oxygen rather than carbon dioxide.

2. **C.** Both A and B are dominant to O; O is a lack of the A or B protein (antigen).

3. **B.** The balanced equation is $N_2(g) + 3H_2(g) \rightarrow 2NH_3(g)$.

4. **A.** To relieve the stress on the system, fewer moles will exist. This is an application of LeChatlier's principle. Because there is more pressure, the reaction is pushed toward the right because there are less total moles of gas on the product side of the reaction. In other words, both reactants are gases (a total of 3 moles) while only one gaseous product (a total of 2 moles) exists.

5. **B.** The inclination of the Earth's axis causes seasons. The Earth is closer to the sun during winter in the Northern Hemisphere. Though the Earth's orbital speed changes slightly over the course of the year, it is not the cause of seasonal variation.

6. **D.** Three amino acids are joined by a peptide bond.

7. **B.** Arteries carry blood away from the heart.

8. **B.** Even though some snakes are able to spend time in water, snakes, by definition, are reptiles.

9. **B.** You should apply the equation $V_1M_1 = V_2M_2$, where V = volume and M = molarity.

   Solving, $V_1 = \dfrac{V_2M_2}{M_1}$.

   $$V_1 = \frac{(20) \times (1.2)}{(12)}$$
   $$= \frac{24}{12}$$
   $$= 2 \text{ ml}$$

10. **C.** Typically, when solids transform with added heat, they melt to become liquids. As more heat is added, liquids then evaporate to become gases. When a solid skips the liquid phase and directly transforms to a gas (as happens with dry ice), this process is known as sublimation.

11. **A.** The troposphere is the lowest level of the atmosphere, the level that we live in, and where weather occurs.

12. **A.** The only function for the stomach is protein digestion, while the small intestine digests all food types.

13. **B.** As the river matures, more erosion and deposition of sediments will effectively increase the meanders in the river. Choice C is incorrect because river speed is determined by water volume and net elevation change. While volume may increase over time, as rivers mature, dramatic changes in elevation are often eroded away.

14. **D.** Because the orbit of Neptune is further than Jupiter, the orbital period would also be longer. The only choice larger than 12 years (Jupiter's orbital period) is 165 years.

15. **B.** While the other choices are definitely major agents of erosion, ground cover is the single best way to combat erosion. Vegetation helps maintain topsoil through high winds and heavy rains.

16. **A.** The three most common gases in the atmosphere are nitrogen (78%), oxygen (21%), and argon (0.9%). All other gases combined make up the remaining 0.1%.

17. **D.** Fish are vertebrates (they have backbones). The other organisms listed (sponge, jellyfish, snail) are all invertebrates (they do not have backbones).

18. **C.** pH is defined as the negative log of the hydrogen ion concentration.

19. **C.** Knowing that carbon has four bonds and hydrogen has only one bond leaves C as the only choice.

20. **C.** Vaccines are weakened doses of a virus. They are meant to stimulate the immune system to make antibodies without actually getting the individual sick.

21. **B.** DNA is stored in the nucleus.

22. **D.** Lead (Pb) is a metal and will have a positive oxidation number. Fluorine is the most electronegative, and has an oxidation number of −1.

23. **B.** The most electronegative elements, those that will attract electrons the most readily, are on the top right.

24. **D.** The stamen is made up of the anther, which makes pollen, and the filament, which holds up the anther. The pistil is the homologous female structure.

25. **A.** The brain and the spinal cord constitute the central nervous system.

Arithmetic Reasoning

1. **C.** Mattie walked 45 + 36 + 41 = 122 yd. Jacob walked 16 + 49 + 33 = 98 yd. The difference between these two distances is 122 – 98 = 24 yd.

2. **C.** The volume of a cylinder is $\pi r^2 h$. In the original cylinder, $\pi r^2 h = 128\pi$ so $r^2 = \dfrac{128\pi}{8\pi} = 16$ and the radius, r, equals $\sqrt{16} = 4$. In the new cylinder, the radius is doubled to 8 and the height is cut in half to 4. The resulting volume is $\pi \times 8^2 \times 4 = 256\pi$ cm³.

3. **D.** First add the number of feet together and then add the number of inches.

   2 ft + 4 ft + 3 ft = 9 ft

   $2\frac{1}{2}$ in $+ 3\frac{3}{8}$ in $+ 9\frac{3}{4}$ in $= \dfrac{5}{2} + \dfrac{27}{8} + \dfrac{39}{4} = \dfrac{20}{8} + \dfrac{27}{8} + \dfrac{78}{8} = \dfrac{125}{8} = 15\frac{5}{8}$ in

   $15\frac{5}{8}$ in = 1 ft $3\frac{5}{8}$ in, so altogether 9 ft + 1 ft $3\frac{5}{8}$ in = 10 ft $3\frac{5}{8}$ in.

4. **B.** The amount of commissions over $5,000 is $12,500 – $5,000 = $7,500. Earnings are $7,500 × 15% = $1,125.

5. **D.** The total cost for the posts and fencing is (10 × $12.50) + (34 × $4.75) = $125.00 + $161.50 = $286.50.

6. **A.** The cost of the eight CD covers is 8 × $1.59 = $12.72. The change received back is $20.00 – $12.72 = $7.28.

7. **D.** The proportion $\dfrac{500 \text{ miles}}{\frac{1}{4}\text{ inch}} = \dfrac{x \text{ miles}}{6 \text{ inches}}$ can be used to find the actual distance. Cross multiply. $500 \times 6 = \frac{1}{4}x$, so $3{,}000 \times 6 = \frac{1}{4}x$ and $x = 3{,}000 \times 4 = 12{,}000$ miles.

8. **C.** The total number of inches in a 10-ft rope is 10 × 12 = 120 in. The number of 8-in segments that can be cut is $\dfrac{120}{8} = 15$.

9. **A.** If 1 page can be read in 2 minutes, then 80 pages can be read in 80 × 2 or 160 minutes.

10. **D.** The proportion $\dfrac{3 \text{ boxes}}{18 \text{ reams}} = \dfrac{x \text{ boxes}}{90 \text{ reams}}$ can be used to find the number of boxes. Cross multiply. $3 \times 90 = 18x$, so $270 = 18x$ and $x = \dfrac{270}{18} = 15$ boxes.

11. **A.** Add the areas of the two triangles and the square to find the total area. The area of the square is $5^2 = 25$. Both triangles have a height of 5. The area of one triangle is $\frac{1}{2}bh = \frac{1}{2} \cdot 3 \cdot 5 = \dfrac{15}{2} = 7.5$. The area of the other triangle is $\frac{1}{2}bh = \frac{1}{2} \cdot 4 \cdot 5 = \dfrac{20}{2} = 10$. The total area is 25 + 7.5 + 10 = 42.5.

12. **A.** Five cards at $3.00 each cost 5 × $3.00 = $15.00. If cards are two for $5.00, the cost per card is $\dfrac{\$5.00}{2} = \$2.50$, so five cards would cost $2.50 × 5 = $12.50. The amount saved is $15.00 – $12.50 = $2.50.

13. **B.** If 1 gallon covers 400 sq ft, then $\dfrac{2{,}225}{400} = 5.5625$, or 6 whole gallons are needed to cover 2,225 sq ft.

14. **A.** The tax on the bill is $38.40 × 6% = $2.30. The amount, including tax, is $38.40 + $2.30 = $40.70. The tip is $40.70 × 15% = $6.11.

15. **C.** The area of one square is $\dfrac{405}{5} = 81$. So the length of each side is $\sqrt{81} = 9$. The total number of sides in the figure is 12, so the perimeter is 9 × 12 = 108.

16. **A.** The proportion $\dfrac{5}{3} = \dfrac{x}{4}$ can be used to find x. Cross multiply. $5 \times 4 = 3x$ so $20 = 3x$ and $x = \dfrac{20}{3} = 6\frac{2}{3}$.

17. **C.** After eating $\frac{1}{4}$ of a pie, what remains is $1 - \frac{1}{4} = \frac{3}{4}$. If four friends share the remainder, then each receives $\dfrac{3}{4} \div 4 = \dfrac{3}{4} \times \dfrac{1}{4} = \dfrac{3}{16}$.

18. **B.** If Max loses 2 pounds each week, then after 7 weeks, Max will have lost $7 \times 2 = 14$ pounds. His weight after 7 weeks is $209 - 14 = 195$ pounds.

19. **B.** The discounted amount after the first week is $\$1,000 \times 25\% = \$250$, so the sale price is $\$1,000 - \$250 = \$750$. The discounted amount after the second week is $\$750 \times 10\% = \$75$, so the sale price is $\$750 - \$75 = \$675$.

20. **B.** Convert 2.2 minutes to seconds. $2.2 \times 60 = 132$ seconds. The difference in the two times is $132 - 124 = 8$ seconds.

21. **D.** In a 10-mile trip, after the first mile, there are 9 additional miles. If each additional half mile is $1, then an additional mile is $2. The cost of the trip is $3 for the first mile + ($2 × 9) for the additional miles. $3 + $18 = $21.

22. **C.** The proportion $\dfrac{\$5.00}{3 \text{ cans}} = \dfrac{\$x}{10 \text{ cans}}$ can be used to find the cost of ten cans. Cross multiply. $5 \times 10 = 3x$, so $50 = 3x$ and $x = \dfrac{50}{3} = \$16.67$.

23. **B.** The average is the total time divided by the total miles run. The total time is $17.5 + 22 + 9 = 48.5$ minutes. The total number of miles run is $3 + 4.5 + 2 = 9.5$. The average is $\dfrac{48.5}{9.5} = 5.1$ minutes per mile.

24. **B.** The total amount of money is $(40 \times \$0.05) + (12 \times \$0.10) = \$2.00 + \$1.20 = \$3.20$.

25. **C.** Interest = principal × rate × time. Interest $= \$1,000 \times 2\frac{1}{4}\% \times 5 = \$1,000 \times 0.0225 \times 5 = \$112.50$.

26. **C.** The ratio of pages per minute is $\dfrac{6 \text{ pages}}{8 \text{ minutes}}$. Setting up a proportion, two equal fractions, with pages over minutes becomes $\dfrac{6}{8} = \dfrac{p}{36}$. Solve a proportion by multiplying the values along each diagonal and setting those products equal: $8p = 6 \times 36$ or $8p = 216$. Then, dividing each side of this equation by 8, you find that $p = 27$. It will, therefore, take 27 minutes for Vanda to type 36 pages.

27. **B.** There are 30 minutes in a half-hour. $30 \times 35 = 1,050$ words.

28. **A.** The cost of Sandy's purchase is $\left(4\frac{1}{2} \times \$1.39\right) + (6 \times \$0.50) = \$9.26$. The cost of Brandon's purchase is $\left(3\frac{1}{4} \times \$1.39\right) + (9 \times \$0.50) = \$9.02$. Sandy spent $\$9.26 - \$9.02 = \$0.24$ more.

29. **D.** Bryan will pay back the $50,000 along with the interest. The interest is found by multiplying the amount of money Bryan borrows by the interest rate as a decimal times the amount of time in years: $\$50,000 \times .08 \times 10 = \$40,000$. He will, therefore, owe $\$50,000 + \$40,000 = \$90,000$. If he pays this back in 10 equal installments, each year he will have to pay $\$90,000 \div 10 = \$9,000$.

30. **C.** $1\frac{1}{8} + 2\frac{3}{4} + 3\frac{1}{3} = \frac{9}{8} + \frac{11}{4} + \frac{10}{3} =$
    $\frac{27}{24} + \frac{66}{24} + \frac{80}{24} = \frac{173}{24} = 7\frac{5}{24}$ pounds.

Word Knowledge

1. **D.** *A new idea.* <u>Innovation</u> involves making changes or offering new methods.

2. **C.** *Reveal.* <u>Divulge</u> means disclose or make known.

3. **A.** *Pay attention to.* <u>Heed</u> means listen, mind, or obey.

4. **B.** *Prevent.* <u>Foil</u> means hinder, thwart, or frustrate.

5. **B.** *Surprise.* <u>Startle</u> means disturb or frighten.

6. **C.** *Astonish.* <u>Stupefy</u> means astound or bewilder.

7. **C.** *Defect.* <u>Blemish</u> means flaw or imperfection.

8. **D.** *Nearness.* <u>Proximity</u> means closeness.

9. **A.** *Conflict.* <u>Clash</u> means hostility or strife.

10. **B.** *Twisted.* <u>Wry</u> means distorted, crooked, or bent.

11. **A.** *Green.* <u>Verdant</u> means flourishing, thriving, or covered with plants.

12. **B.** *Scoff.* <u>Jeer</u> means mock or ridicule.

13. **A.** *Harsh.* <u>Strident</u> means shrill, blaring, or loud.

14. **A.** *Cut.* <u>Shear</u> means to clip or to prune.

15. **B.** *Enjoy.* <u>Relish</u> means appreciate or value.

16. **A.** *Reddish.* <u>Crimson</u> means cherry or scarlet, both of which refer to red.

17. **B.** *Out of use.* <u>Obsolete</u> means outmoded, ancient, or extinct.

18. **B.** *A side.* <u>Facet</u> means phase or aspect.

19. **D.** *Praise.* <u>Extol</u> means exalt or glorify.

20. **B.** *Departure.* <u>Exodus</u> means leaving or exit.

21. **B.** *Energetically.* <u>Vigorously</u> means strenuously or actively.

22. **B.** *Well-known.* <u>Familiar</u> means recognized or famous.

23. **C.** *Damage.* <u>Detriment</u> means harm or injury.

24. **C.** *Overeater.* <u>Glutton</u> means greedy person or hog.

25. **B.** *Disprove.* <u>Refute</u> means undermine or deny.

26. **D.** *Brilliance.* <u>Luster</u> means brightness or radiance.

27. **C.** *Profitable.* <u>Lucrative</u> means money-making or gainful.

28. **D.** *Unhurried.* <u>Leisurely</u> means casual, tranquil, or sedate.

29. **B.** *Agreement.* <u>Accord</u> means peace, conformity, or unanimity.

30. **B.** *Extract.* <u>Excerpt</u> means piece, section, or portion.

31. **B.** *Analyze.* <u>Diagnose</u> means investigate, study, or look into.

32. **B.** *Inborn.* <u>Innate</u> means intrinsic or native.

33. **C.** *A saying.* <u>Maxim</u> means adage or proverb.

34. **A.** *Exaggeration.* <u>Hyperbole</u> means overstatement or embellishment.

35. **B.** *Ooze.* <u>Seep</u> means leak or trickle.

Paragraph Comprehension

1. **C.** The second sentence states that the speaker's slurred words and mumbling made the speech very difficult to understand. Thus, the speech would be illogical.

2. **B.** The first sentence in the paragraph states that beautiful plants are often dangerous to their environments.

3. **C.** Using dishwashers is not mentioned as a way to conserve water.

4. **D.** The first sentence states that people of all ages can benefit from regular weight lifting. Furthermore, the selection cites the example of 90-year-old participants who saw improvements in muscle mass. Thus, it can be inferred that you can start lifting weights at any age and see improvements.

5. **B.** The paragraph discusses historical references to comets since antiquity.

6. **C.** The first sentence implies that the discovery of penicillin was mainly due to the disorganization of Fleming's lab.

7. **A.** Because watching more than one hour a day of television increases the risk for violent behavior later in life, it is safe to conclude that the author believes that children should watch less than one hour of television per day.

8. **B.** Energy efficiency is not mentioned in the selection. The other three choices are.

9. **D.** The article suggests that chimpanzees are now viewed in a different and more positive light concerning their capability to use language and to communicate.

10. **A.** At least two possible reasons—La Niña and global warming—are given as factors in decreased average annual snowfall. Thus, you must reason that there may be other factors that work together to influence average annual snowfall.

11. **C.** Weekdays present the highest risk for muggings, according to the selection.

12. **A.** The article states the major risk factors for being a victim of mugging.

13. **C.** The article discusses dehydration and the fact that most people do not feel the need to drink water until their throat signals them that they need to drink something. Thus, the only logical answer is C.

14. **B.** The first sentence of the selection states that being thirsty is a sign of dehydration.

15. **B.** The selection discusses both dehydration and the benefits of drinking water.

Auto and Shop Information

1. **C.** If you accidentally come in contact with the frame or body with your wrench, no current will flow because the wrench will also be at the negative potential. However, if the positive cable is removed first while accidentally touching the frame or body with the wrench, sparks can occur.

2. **B.** A multiple-piece drive shaft requires that the yokes on the same shaft be parallel to each other when reassembling. The technician probably neglected this.

3. **D.** All of the above. Oil takes on many tasks in an engine, all of which include cooling the cylinder, lubricating the parts, and sealing each component of the engine.

4. **A.** This component, through the action of a park cable and a lever attached to the brake shoe, forces the shoes against the brake drum.

5. **B.** Some vehicles have a multiple drive shaft system that requires the end yokes to be in phase.

6. **C.** This shim is used to correct installed valve spring height to maintain a proper spring tension after a valve's face and seat have been grounded.

7. **B.** The torque converter automatically engages and disengages power from the engine to the transmission. At idle, there is not enough fluid flow for power transfer. Increased engine speed increases the fluid flow to transmit engine power through the torque converter assembly to the transmission.

8. **D.** Most EGR valves are located in the intake or between the intake and exhaust manifolds. Several cylinder heads have overhead camshafts.

9. **B.** A vacuum check valve is a one-way valve that prevents vacuum from escaping from the booster. This allows for a few boosted brake applications in the event the engine cannot provide any vacuum.

10. **D.** A brake system works on the principle of friction, which develops heat in the process of braking. The drum absorbs and dissipates the heat developed.

11. **A.** The dashpot is used during rapid deceleration to retard the closing of the throttle to prevent a possible stalling due to an overly rich air/fuel mixture.

12. **D.** A live circuit can damage the meter when in the ohms setting.

13. **C.** Most ammeters, unless they are inductive types, are only protected to 10 amps. A battery is typically rated over 450 amps.

14. **D.** A dado head blade is actually a series of blades packed together to make wide grooves. By adjusting the number of blades (or dividers between the blades) on the saw spindle, you can adjust the width of the dado cut.

15. **D.** Specific combinations of cement, sand, and water are used in order to produce a concrete mixture for the job it will be performing.

16. **B.** This is called a wing nut, and is typically used in scenarios that require low torque and can be hand-tightened by an individual.

17. **B.** Dovetails are often used to make drawers for higher-quality furniture.

18. **A.** Unlike a wood chisel, a cold chisel is made of forged steel and is heat tempered in order to be able to withstand the shock of cutting metal.

19. **B.** The Allen wrench is normally six-sided and L-shaped and is used to tighten set-screws.

20. **B.** This is a coping saw, used to cut thin wood or plastic. The blade can be adjusted to different angles in order to cut irregular shapes.

21. **C.** The reciprocating saw is a tool designed for contractors for use in heavy-duty remodeling. The circular saw is good for cutting smaller lumber like two-by-fours, the saber saw or jigsaw is used for fine lines or cutting contours, and the chain saw is used primarily for pruning or delimbing trees.

22. **D.** The grooved dowel plus glue is the strongest joint. Glue alone would not last because the glue can dry out and crack. The fasteners and nails are weak connectors.

23. **B.** The palm sander vibrates rapidly and is used to give a piece of furniture a smooth finish. The belt and disk sanders are rougher on the wood, and can accidentally cut grooves if the user is not careful. No. 40 sandpaper is very coarse. The higher the number, the finer the grit—no. 400 would be used for fine finishing.

24. **B.** The cut or groove made by the saw's blade is called the kerf. It is important to know that measurement when cutting different types of wood in order to prevent the saw from binding, or getting stuck in the wood as it is being cut. It is also important to know the kerf size when cutting true sizes because you will lose part of the wood to the saw's blade, and therefore you must allow for that loss.

25. **B.** In order to have a smooth finish, the nail set is used to hammer the nail below the surface of the wood. Then the hole is filled with putty or wood filler, sanded, and painted or stained.

Mathematics Knowledge

1. **D.** Using the distributive property, $(2x + 1)(2x + 1) = 4x^2 + 2x + 2x + 1 = 4x^2 + 4x + 1$.

2. **A.** The least common multiple of the divisors 16 and 24 is 48.
$\frac{5}{16} + \frac{9}{24} = \frac{15}{48} + \frac{18}{48} = \frac{33}{48} = \frac{11}{16}$

3. **D.** Simplifying $\sqrt{50} + 3\sqrt{72}$ yields $\sqrt{25 \cdot 2} + 3\sqrt{36 \cdot 2}$, which yields $5\sqrt{2} + 18\sqrt{2} = 23\sqrt{2}$.

4. **A.** $5(a - 2) - (4a - 6) = 5a - 10 - 4a + 6 = a - 4$.

5. **C.** The circumference of a circle is given by the formula $C = 2\pi r$, and the area of a circle is given by $A = \pi r^2$. If the circumference is equal to the area, then $2\pi r = \pi r^2$. Solving for r, $\frac{2\pi r}{\pi r} = \frac{\pi r^2}{\pi r}$ and $2 = r$. The diameter is $2r$, or 4.

6. **C.** The cube of 8 is $8^3 = 8 \times 8 \times 8 = 512$.

7. **B.** The area of a triangle is $A = \frac{1}{2}bh$. If the base is 3 in less than the height, then $b = h - 3$. Substituting this value for b gives $A = \frac{1}{2}(h - 3)h = \frac{1}{2}h^2 - \frac{3}{2}h$.

8. **D.** Substituting the given values for r, s, and t into $3r^3 - 2s^2 + t$ gives $3(-1)^3 - 2(-2)^2 + (-3) = 3(-1) - 2(4) - 3 = -3 - 8 - 3 = -14$.

9. **B.** Let x be the unknown number. Then $9x = 117$ and $x = \frac{117}{9} = 13$.

10. **B.** $\left(\frac{a^{-3}b^2}{2ab^{-1}}\right)^{-3} = \frac{a^9 b^{-6}}{2^{-3}a^{-3}b^3} = 2^3 a^{9-(-3)}b^{-6-3} = 8a^{12}b^{-9} = \frac{8a^{12}}{b^9}$.

11. **C.** Let b represent the number of boys in the class and g represent the number of girls. Then $b + g = 27$. If $b = g + 5$, then $(g + 5) + g = 27$. $2g + 5 = 27$ and $2g = 22$ so $g = 11$. Therefore, the number of boys is $27 - 11$, or 16.

12. **C.**

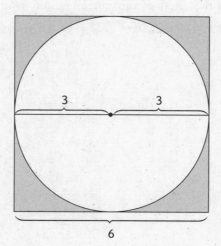

The area of the shaded region equals the area of the square minus the area of the circle. Because the radius of the circle is 3, the square has a side length of 6. The area of the square is 6^2 or 36. The area of the circle is $\pi r^2 = \pi \times 3^2 = 9\pi$. The shaded region, therefore, is $36 - 9\pi$.

13. **C.** The square of x is x^2. Three less than x is $x - 3$. Their product is $x^2(x - 3)$.

14. **A.** The cube root of 512 is $\sqrt[3]{512} = \sqrt[3]{8 \times 8 \times 8} = 8$.

15. B. There are four possible ways to roll a 9 using two dice: 3 and 6, 4 and 5, 5 and 4, 6 and 3. The total number of possible outcomes when rolling two dice is 6^2 or 36. Therefore, the probability of rolling a 9 is $\frac{4}{36} = \frac{1}{9}$.

16. C. Let's say the diameter of a circle is 4. Increasing it by 100% means increase the 4 by itself, bring the diameter to 8. A circle with a diameter of 4 has a radius of 2. The area of a circle is found by the formula: $A = \pi r^2$. So the area of the original circle is $A = \pi r^2 = \pi(2^2) = 4\pi$. The radius of the new circle will be 4. Hence, the area of that circle will be $A = \pi r^2 = \pi(4^2) = 16\pi$. Increasing 4π to 16π is increasing it by 12π. That is 3 times 4π. Three times is 300%.

17. D. Six less a number is shown by $n - 6$. So "six less than a number is four" is represented by $n - 6 = 4$.

18. B. Group the first two terms and the last two terms together: $(2a^2 - 4ab) + (ab - 2b^2)$. Factoring out common terms from each group gives $2a(a - 2b) + b(a - 2b)$. Common to both terms is $(a - 2b)$. Factoring this out results in $(a - 2b)(2a + b)$.

19. C. First, we need to find the value of m, knowing that $n = 20$. Solving the proportion $\frac{m}{n} = \frac{3}{5} = \frac{m}{20}$, we find that $5m = 3 \times 20$. So $5m = 60$. Dividing both sides by 5, the result is $m = 12$. Thus $m + n = 12 + 20 = 32$.

20. B. The area of a room 15 ft wide by 18 ft long is $15 \times 18 = 270$ sq ft. Because there are 3 ft in a yard, there are 3×3 or 9 ft in a square yard. Convert 270 sq ft to square yards. $\frac{270}{9} = 30$ square yards. Because the cost is $13.50 per square yard, the total cost is 13.50×30, or $405.

21. A. 60 beads $\times$ 1/2 in = 30 in. Converting this to feet gives 30 inches $\times \frac{1 \text{ foot}}{12 \text{ inches}} = \frac{30}{12} = 2\frac{1}{2}$ ft.

22. D. Subtract $2y$ from both sides. $2y + 6 - 2y = 3y - 2 - 2y$, so $6 = y - 2$. Adding 2 to both sides gives $y = 8$.

23. D. Using the correct order of operations, $-3(-4 - 5) - 2(-6) = -3(-9) - 2(-6) = 27 - (-12) = 27 + 12 = 39$.

24. D. If books are twice as much as magazines, then $b = 2m$. Five books + three magazines = $5b + 3m$. Substituting $2m$ for b gives $5(2m) + 3m = 10m + 3m = 13m$.

25. A. Because the area of $ADEC$ is 81, $AC = \sqrt{81} = 9$. Because the area of $BCFG$ is 144, $BC = \sqrt{144} = 12$. Use the Pythagorean theorem to find the length of the remaining side AB.

$AB^2 = 9^2 + 12^2$ so $AB^2 = 81 + 144 = 225$ and $AB = \sqrt{225} = 15$. Therefore, the perimeter of the triangle = 9 + 12 + 15 = 36.

Mechanical Comprehension

1. **B.** Neglecting friction with air, the velocity vector of the ball has a horizontal component that remains constant and a vertical component that suffers deceleration due to the force of gravity. Because distance is speed times time, the path gradually curves downward due to gravity.

2. **C.** Work is force × distance. That is zero in this example.

3. **D.** Kinetic energy is half the product of the mass and the square of the velocity.

4. **B.** Potential energy is proportional to the weight of the object and its elevation above the ground reference.

5. **D.** This is clearly stated in Newton's first law.

6. **A.** Because acceleration is the net force divided by the mass, the net force must be zero because the mass is not infinite.

7. **D.** The horizontal component of the velocity of the first ball has no effect on the vertical travel, and initially both balls have zero vertical velocity.

8. **B.** Friction tries to slow down the motion.

9. **D.** If the acceleration of gravity is constant, the period and, hence, the frequency is determined solely by the length of the connecting cord or rod.

10. **A.** Because the direction of the vibrating body is reversed at the end point of its motion, its velocity must be zero when its displacement is a maximum. It is then accelerated toward the center by the restoring force until it reaches its maximum speed at the center of oscillation, i.e., when its displacement is zero. Because the restoring force is maximum at the end point, its acceleration at that moment is also a maximum by Newton's second law of motion.

11. **C.** The heat of expansion of a metal is related to the coefficient of expansion, with each metal having its own unique coefficient. The coefficient of expansion of the metal in the question can be calculated by dividing the increase in length by the original length: Changing the 2 millimeters to centimeters yields 0.2 cm. In formula form: 0.2 cm/50.0 cm = 0.004

    The coefficient of expansion is 0.004. Substituting the coefficient of expansion and the new length will yield: x/75.0 cm = 0.004

    Solving for x produces 0.3 cm or 3 millimeters.

12. **D.** The total angular momentum is equal to the product of the body's angular velocity and the moment of inertia. Pulling the arms toward the body increases the first by a certain ratio and decreases the second by the same ratio, thus keeping the angular momentum the same.

13. **B.** Acceleration is defined as the change in velocity over time. In formula form, it is represented as:
    $a = \dfrac{dv}{dt}$, where a is the acceleration, dv is the change in velocity, and dt is the change in time. Substituting in the equation yields:

    $dv = 4.24 - 3.60 = 0.64$ m/s

    $a = \dfrac{0.64 \text{ m/s}}{5.6 \text{ sec}}$

    $a = 0.114$ m/s^2

14. **D.** Using the expressions $s = v_o t + \frac{1}{2}at^2$ and $vf = v_o + at$, we set the time of travel as the sum of t_1 to travel the distance s_1 from the top of the building to the maximum height and t_2, s_2 as the corresponding values from the maximum height to the ground. Substituting numbers, we obtain $t_1 = 1.48$ seconds, $s_1 = 10.72$ m and $t_2 = 3.52$, $s_2 = 50$ meters, so the total time = 1.48 + 3.52 = 5 seconds.

15. **A.** Because this is an inelastic collision, momentum is conserved. Hence 4(2) – 2(4) = (4 + 2)v, in other words, $v = 0$ m/s.

16. **A.** Because five strands support the movable load, the required force is $\frac{200}{5} = 40$ newtons.

17. **D.** The final momentum equals $300 + 20 \times 10 = 500$ kg $\cdot$ m/s.

18. **B.** Projectile motion results from the combination of the horizontal and vertical motions, each acting independently of the other. Two formulas are needed to solve this problem. Let's start with the time it takes the object to strike the ground. We know the distance, *s*, of the object is 12.5 meters above the ground and that falling objects are affected by gravity, *g*, which will accelerate them at the rate of 9.8 m/s^2. Using the following formula takes into account that the object's initial velocity in the vertical direction is zero.

$$s = v_o t + \frac{1}{2} g t^2$$

Substituting into the equation yields

$$12.5 \text{ m} = (0)t + \frac{1}{2}(9.8)t^2$$

$$12.5 \text{ m} = \frac{1}{2}(9.8)t^2$$

$$12.5 \text{ m} = 4.9 t^2$$

$$\frac{12.5}{4.9} = t^2$$

$$2.55 = t^2$$

$$t = 1.59 \text{ s or } 1.6 \text{ s}$$

Now that we know how long the projectile is in the air, the distance it travels can be calculated from the horizontal distance formula: $d_x = v_x t$, where d_x is the distance in the horizontal or *x* direction, v_x is the velocity in the horizontal or *x* direction, and *t* is the time the projectile is in the air. Substituting in the equation yields

$$d_x = (10 \text{ m/s})(1.6 \text{ s})$$

$$d_x = 16 \text{ m}$$

19. **C.** In order to determine the mechanical advance of an inclined plane, use the following formula:

$$\frac{\text{length of ramp}}{\text{height of ramp}} = \frac{\text{weight of object}}{\text{force}}$$

$$\frac{9}{3} = \frac{400}{f}$$

$$3f = 400$$

$$f = 133.33 \text{ pounds}$$

20. **A.** When cars drive on a curved road, whether it's a race track or the local street, they have a tendency to travel in a straight line that is tangent to or at a right angle to the direction of travel. It is the friction between the tires of the car and the surface of the road that keeps the car traveling around the curve.

21. **D.** The spin rate (or angular velocity) is inversely proportional to the distance from the axis of rotation. So as the skater stretches her hands, the distance from her hands to the axis of rotation increases and the spin rate decreases slightly.

22. **C.** Newton's second Law of Motion relates the force of an object to its mass and the acceleration of that mass: $F = ma$. Substituting into the equation and solving for *m* yields

$$F = ma$$

$$40 \text{ N} = m \ (8 \text{ m/s}^2)$$

$$\frac{40 \text{ N}}{8 \text{ m/s}^2} = m$$

$$5 \text{ kg} = m$$

23. D. This unit is equivalent to the unit of force × distance, which is the unit of work or the joule.

24. D. Remember that gravity exerts a force on all masses, therefore a 2 kg mass has a force of 19.6 N acting on it by virtue of Newton's second Law of Motion, $F = ma$. In this instance $F = (2 \text{ kg}) (9.8 \text{ m/s}^2) = 19.6$ N. But because the mass is on a 30 degree incline, the force will be affected by the angle. This is taken into consideration by including the sin of the angle: $F = (\sin 30°)(2)(9.8) = 9.8$ N. Therefore the net force acting on the box is 15 N – 9.8 N = 5.2 N. This difference in the force is what will accelerate the mass up the ramp. Substituting back into $F = ma$ yields:

5.2 N = (2 kg) a. Solving for a produces 2.6 m/s².

25. B. Power is defined as the amount of work done in a unit of time, or $P = \dfrac{W}{t}$. Work is defined as the amount of force exerted over a distance, or $W = F \times d$. The first thing that needs to be done is to change the mass in kg to a force in Newtons: $F = ma$.

$F = (20 \text{ kg}) (9.8 \text{ m/s}^2)$

$F = 196$ N

Substituting this force into the equation for work yields

$W = (196 \text{ N}) (75 \text{ m}) = 14,700$ N·m.

Substituting this work into the power equation and converting 2 minutes to 120 seconds yields

$P = \dfrac{(14,700 \text{ N·m})}{120 \text{ sec}}$

$P = 122.5$ watts

Electronics Information

1. **A.** An ammeter measures electrical current. A voltmeter is used to measure a voltage difference. Electrical charge or energy cannot be measured by an ammeter.

2. **C.** For the lamp to be on, switches 1 or 3 must be closed, and switch 2 must also be closed to allow the current to flow in the circuit.

3. **A.** Symbol 1 represents a transistor.

4. **D.** The total resistance in the circuit can be calculated as follows:

$$100 + \frac{1}{\frac{1}{200} + \frac{1}{200}} = 200 \ \Omega$$

5. **D.** Inductance is measured in henries. Capacitance is measured in farads. Voltage difference is measured in volts. Electrical current is measured in amperes.

6. **C.** The shown signal can be written in the form: Amplitude $\times \sin(2\pi ft)$. From the figure, the amplitude is 1 V and the frequency is 1/period = 2 Hz, so the signal is $\sin(4\pi t)$.

7. **B.** An FM radio signal is a frequency-modulated signal. An AM radio signal is an amplitude-modulated signal. PSK signals are phase-modulated signals. DC cannot be used for modulation.

8. **B.** The voltmeter reads the voltage across the resistor. Because both resistors are equal, then the battery voltage will be equally divided between the two resistors, so that the reading of the voltmeter will be 5 V.

9. **A.** Capacitors are used to separate AC signals from the DC bias of the bipolar junction transistor.

10. **B.** The reading of the ammeter will be 0 A. This means that there is no current flowing into the ammeter. This is because the ratio of the 20-ohm resistor to the 60-ohm resistor is equal to the ratio of the 40-ohm resistor to the 120-ohm resistor. This causes the voltage at both ammeter leads to be equal. As a result, no current will flow.

11. **C.** Modulation is used when transmitting a radio signal. It involves carrying a certain signal on a high frequency.

12. **D.** A transistor can be used to amplify a current. The input current is the base current and the output current is the collector current. The amplification ratio is called Beta, β.

13. **D.** The power dissipated in the circuit can be calculated as $P = I^2R = \left(\frac{5}{5+5}\right)^2 (5+5) = 2.5$ watts.

14. **B.** Electric transformers use coils to transform the level of voltage. The value of the induced voltage depends on the number of turns of the coil.

15. **D.** Resistors are measured in ohms. Capacitance is measured in farads. Transistors have numbers to identify them. Inductance of a coil is measured in henries.

16. **A.** A diode can be used to rectify a signal. This is because it allows the current to pass in one direction only. As a result, the positive part of the signal passes and the negative part is blocked.

17. **C.** Frequency mixers are used to carry certain signals (like audio signals) on a high-frequency carrier for wireless transmission.

18. **B.** Shapes of electrical signals can be watched on an oscilloscope. Other instruments will measure a certain parameter, but will not show the shape of the signal with respect to time.

19. **C.** Electronic devices must be grounded to avoid electrical shock.

20. **A.** Total capacitance of the circuit is calculated as follows:

$$\frac{1}{\frac{1}{(.5 \ \mu F + .5 \ \mu F)} + \frac{1}{1 \ \mu F}} = .5 \ \mu F$$

Assembling Objects

The answers for the Assembling Objects questions can be found in the answer key, earlier in this section.

Answer Sheet for Practice Test III

(Remove this sheet and use it to mark your answers.)

General Science

1 (A) (B) (C) (D)	16 (A) (B) (C) (D)
2 (A) (B) (C) (D)	17 (A) (B) (C) (D)
3 (A) (B) (C) (D)	18 (A) (B) (C) (D)
4 (A) (B) (C) (D)	19 (A) (B) (C) (D)
5 (A) (B) (C) (D)	20 (A) (B) (C) (D)
6 (A) (B) (C) (D)	21 (A) (B) (C) (D)
7 (A) (B) (C) (D)	22 (A) (B) (C) (D)
8 (A) (B) (C) (D)	23 (A) (B) (C) (D)
9 (A) (B) (C) (D)	24 (A) (B) (C) (D)
10 (A) (B) (C) (D)	25 (A) (B) (C) (D)
11 (A) (B) (C) (D)	
12 (A) (B) (C) (D)	
13 (A) (B) (C) (D)	
14 (A) (B) (C) (D)	
15 (A) (B) (C) (D)	

Arithmetic Reasoning

1 (A) (B) (C) (D)	16 (A) (B) (C) (D)
2 (A) (B) (C) (D)	17 (A) (B) (C) (D)
3 (A) (B) (C) (D)	18 (A) (B) (C) (D)
4 (A) (B) (C) (D)	19 (A) (B) (C) (D)
5 (A) (B) (C) (D)	20 (A) (B) (C) (D)
6 (A) (B) (C) (D)	21 (A) (B) (C) (D)
7 (A) (B) (C) (D)	22 (A) (B) (C) (D)
8 (A) (B) (C) (D)	23 (A) (B) (C) (D)
9 (A) (B) (C) (D)	24 (A) (B) (C) (D)
10 (A) (B) (C) (D)	25 (A) (B) (C) (D)
11 (A) (B) (C) (D)	26 (A) (B) (C) (D)
12 (A) (B) (C) (D)	27 (A) (B) (C) (D)
13 (A) (B) (C) (D)	28 (A) (B) (C) (D)
14 (A) (B) (C) (D)	29 (A) (B) (C) (D)
15 (A) (B) (C) (D)	30 (A) (B) (C) (D)

Word Knowledge

1 (A) (B) (C) (D)	21 (A) (B) (C) (D)
2 (A) (B) (C) (D)	22 (A) (B) (C) (D)
3 (A) (B) (C) (D)	23 (A) (B) (C) (D)
4 (A) (B) (C) (D)	24 (A) (B) (C) (D)
5 (A) (B) (C) (D)	25 (A) (B) (C) (D)
6 (A) (B) (C) (D)	26 (A) (B) (C) (D)
7 (A) (B) (C) (D)	27 (A) (B) (C) (D)
8 (A) (B) (C) (D)	28 (A) (B) (C) (D)
9 (A) (B) (C) (D)	29 (A) (B) (C) (D)
10 (A) (B) (C) (D)	30 (A) (B) (C) (D)
11 (A) (B) (C) (D)	31 (A) (B) (C) (D)
12 (A) (B) (C) (D)	32 (A) (B) (C) (D)
13 (A) (B) (C) (D)	33 (A) (B) (C) (D)
14 (A) (B) (C) (D)	34 (A) (B) (C) (D)
15 (A) (B) (C) (D)	35 (A) (B) (C) (D)
16 (A) (B) (C) (D)	
17 (A) (B) (C) (D)	
18 (A) (B) (C) (D)	
19 (A) (B) (C) (D)	
20 (A) (B) (C) (D)	

Paragraph Comprehension

1 (A) (B) (C) (D)
2 (A) (B) (C) (D)
3 (A) (B) (C) (D)
4 (A) (B) (C) (D)
5 (A) (B) (C) (D)
6 (A) (B) (C) (D)
7 (A) (B) (C) (D)
8 (A) (B) (C) (D)
9 (A) (B) (C) (D)
10 (A) (B) (C) (D)
11 (A) (B) (C) (D)
12 (A) (B) (C) (D)
13 (A) (B) (C) (D)
14 (A) (B) (C) (D)
15 (A) (B) (C) (D)

CUT HERE

Auto and Shop Information

1 Ⓐ Ⓑ Ⓒ Ⓓ
2 Ⓐ Ⓑ Ⓒ Ⓓ
3 Ⓐ Ⓑ Ⓒ Ⓓ
4 Ⓐ Ⓑ Ⓒ Ⓓ
5 Ⓐ Ⓑ Ⓒ Ⓓ
6 Ⓐ Ⓑ Ⓒ Ⓓ
7 Ⓐ Ⓑ Ⓒ Ⓓ
8 Ⓐ Ⓑ Ⓒ Ⓓ
9 Ⓐ Ⓑ Ⓒ Ⓓ
10 Ⓐ Ⓑ Ⓒ Ⓓ
11 Ⓐ Ⓑ Ⓒ Ⓓ
12 Ⓐ Ⓑ Ⓒ Ⓓ
13 Ⓐ Ⓑ Ⓒ Ⓓ
14 Ⓐ Ⓑ Ⓒ Ⓓ
15 Ⓐ Ⓑ Ⓒ Ⓓ

16 Ⓐ Ⓑ Ⓒ Ⓓ
17 Ⓐ Ⓑ Ⓒ Ⓓ
18 Ⓐ Ⓑ Ⓒ Ⓓ
19 Ⓐ Ⓑ Ⓒ Ⓓ
20 Ⓐ Ⓑ Ⓒ Ⓓ
21 Ⓐ Ⓑ Ⓒ Ⓓ
22 Ⓐ Ⓑ Ⓒ Ⓓ
23 Ⓐ Ⓑ Ⓒ Ⓓ
24 Ⓐ Ⓑ Ⓒ Ⓓ
25 Ⓐ Ⓑ Ⓒ Ⓓ

Mathematics Knowledge

1 Ⓐ Ⓑ Ⓒ Ⓓ
2 Ⓐ Ⓑ Ⓒ Ⓓ
3 Ⓐ Ⓑ Ⓒ Ⓓ
4 Ⓐ Ⓑ Ⓒ Ⓓ
5 Ⓐ Ⓑ Ⓒ Ⓓ
6 Ⓐ Ⓑ Ⓒ Ⓓ
7 Ⓐ Ⓑ Ⓒ Ⓓ
8 Ⓐ Ⓑ Ⓒ Ⓓ
9 Ⓐ Ⓑ Ⓒ Ⓓ
10 Ⓐ Ⓑ Ⓒ Ⓓ
11 Ⓐ Ⓑ Ⓒ Ⓓ
12 Ⓐ Ⓑ Ⓒ Ⓓ
13 Ⓐ Ⓑ Ⓒ Ⓓ
14 Ⓐ Ⓑ Ⓒ Ⓓ
15 Ⓐ Ⓑ Ⓒ Ⓓ

16 Ⓐ Ⓑ Ⓒ Ⓓ
17 Ⓐ Ⓑ Ⓒ Ⓓ
18 Ⓐ Ⓑ Ⓒ Ⓓ
19 Ⓐ Ⓑ Ⓒ Ⓓ
20 Ⓐ Ⓑ Ⓒ Ⓓ
21 Ⓐ Ⓑ Ⓒ Ⓓ
22 Ⓐ Ⓑ Ⓒ Ⓓ
23 Ⓐ Ⓑ Ⓒ Ⓓ
24 Ⓐ Ⓑ Ⓒ Ⓓ
25 Ⓐ Ⓑ Ⓒ Ⓓ

Mechanical Comprehension

1 Ⓐ Ⓑ Ⓒ Ⓓ
2 Ⓐ Ⓑ Ⓒ Ⓓ
3 Ⓐ Ⓑ Ⓒ Ⓓ
4 Ⓐ Ⓑ Ⓒ Ⓓ
5 Ⓐ Ⓑ Ⓒ Ⓓ
6 Ⓐ Ⓑ Ⓒ Ⓓ
7 Ⓐ Ⓑ Ⓒ Ⓓ
8 Ⓐ Ⓑ Ⓒ Ⓓ
9 Ⓐ Ⓑ Ⓒ Ⓓ
10 Ⓐ Ⓑ Ⓒ Ⓓ
11 Ⓐ Ⓑ Ⓒ Ⓓ
12 Ⓐ Ⓑ Ⓒ Ⓓ
13 Ⓐ Ⓑ Ⓒ Ⓓ
14 Ⓐ Ⓑ Ⓒ Ⓓ
15 Ⓐ Ⓑ Ⓒ Ⓓ

16 Ⓐ Ⓑ Ⓒ Ⓓ
17 Ⓐ Ⓑ Ⓒ Ⓓ
18 Ⓐ Ⓑ Ⓒ Ⓓ
19 Ⓐ Ⓑ Ⓒ Ⓓ
20 Ⓐ Ⓑ Ⓒ Ⓓ
21 Ⓐ Ⓑ Ⓒ Ⓓ
22 Ⓐ Ⓑ Ⓒ Ⓓ
23 Ⓐ Ⓑ Ⓒ Ⓓ
24 Ⓐ Ⓑ Ⓒ Ⓓ
25 Ⓐ Ⓑ Ⓒ Ⓓ

Electronics Information

1 Ⓐ Ⓑ Ⓒ Ⓓ
2 Ⓐ Ⓑ Ⓒ Ⓓ
3 Ⓐ Ⓑ Ⓒ Ⓓ
4 Ⓐ Ⓑ Ⓒ Ⓓ
5 Ⓐ Ⓑ Ⓒ Ⓓ
6 Ⓐ Ⓑ Ⓒ Ⓓ
7 Ⓐ Ⓑ Ⓒ Ⓓ
8 Ⓐ Ⓑ Ⓒ Ⓓ
9 Ⓐ Ⓑ Ⓒ Ⓓ
10 Ⓐ Ⓑ Ⓒ Ⓓ
11 Ⓐ Ⓑ Ⓒ Ⓓ
12 Ⓐ Ⓑ Ⓒ Ⓓ
13 Ⓐ Ⓑ Ⓒ Ⓓ
14 Ⓐ Ⓑ Ⓒ Ⓓ
15 Ⓐ Ⓑ Ⓒ Ⓓ
16 Ⓐ Ⓑ Ⓒ Ⓓ
17 Ⓐ Ⓑ Ⓒ Ⓓ
18 Ⓐ Ⓑ Ⓒ Ⓓ
19 Ⓐ Ⓑ Ⓒ Ⓓ
20 Ⓐ Ⓑ Ⓒ Ⓓ

Assembling Objects

1 Ⓐ Ⓑ Ⓒ Ⓓ
2 Ⓐ Ⓑ Ⓒ Ⓓ
3 Ⓐ Ⓑ Ⓒ Ⓓ
4 Ⓐ Ⓑ Ⓒ Ⓓ
5 Ⓐ Ⓑ Ⓒ Ⓓ
6 Ⓐ Ⓑ Ⓒ Ⓓ
7 Ⓐ Ⓑ Ⓒ Ⓓ
8 Ⓐ Ⓑ Ⓒ Ⓓ
9 Ⓐ Ⓑ Ⓒ Ⓓ
10 Ⓐ Ⓑ Ⓒ Ⓓ
11 Ⓐ Ⓑ Ⓒ Ⓓ
12 Ⓐ Ⓑ Ⓒ Ⓓ
13 Ⓐ Ⓑ Ⓒ Ⓓ
14 Ⓐ Ⓑ Ⓒ Ⓓ
15 Ⓐ Ⓑ Ⓒ Ⓓ
16 Ⓐ Ⓑ Ⓒ Ⓓ

CUT HERE

General Science

Time: 11 minutes
25 questions

Directions: The following questions will test your knowledge of general science principles. Read the question and select the choice that best answers the question. Indicate that letter on your answer sheet.

1. The oldest fossils are those of bacteria. They existed as far back as

   A.   35 thousand years ago.
   B.   35 million years ago.
   C.   350 million years ago.
   D.   3.5 billion years ago.

2. To answer this question, refer to the diagram below.

   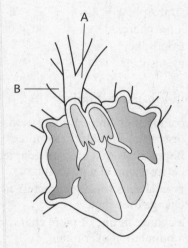

   When blood is leaving the left ventricle, it is

   A.   oxygenated and moving to structure A.
   B.   not oxygenated and moving to structure A.
   C.   oxygenated and moving to structure B.
   D.   not oxygenated and moving to structure B.

3. In the Haber process, ammonia is produced according to the following equation:
   $N_2 (g) + 3H_2 (g) \rightarrow 2NH_3 (g)$

   How many moles of hydrogen gas are needed to react with 1 mole of nitrogen?

   A.   1
   B.   3
   C.   6
   D.   22.4

4. Given the reaction: $2CO (g) + O_2 (g) \rightarrow 2CO_2 (g)$, how many liters of oxygen are required to react with the carbon monoxide to make carbon dioxide at STP?

   A.   1
   B.   2
   C.   22.4
   D. 6.02×10^{23}

5. Which organ produces the hormones that control the secondary sex characteristics in a female?

   A.   uterus
   B.   ovaries
   C.   oviduct
   D.   cervix

6. An example of a marine animal with radial symmetry would be a

   A.   flounder.
   B.   jellyfish.
   C.   squid.
   D.   tuna fish.

7. Water moves up a stem because of

   A.   the cohesion of water molecules.
   B.   the adhesion of water molecules.
   C.   the transpiration of water molecules.
   D.   All of the above.

8. The phase in which molecules move the fastest is

   A.   liquid.
   B.   solid.
   C.   gas.
   D.   plasma.

GO ON TO THE NEXT PAGE

9. Mixing carbon and oxygen together to make carbon dioxide is a

    A. chemical reaction.
    B. physical reaction.
    C. liquid reaction.
    D. None of the above.

10. The gravitational attraction of the moon on the Earth results in a high tide

    A. every 24 hours.
    B. on the side of the Earth facing the moon.
    C. on the sides 90° to the moon.
    D. on the side facing the moon and on the opposite side.

11. A spring ocean tide results in the greatest difference between high tide and low tide. At which two moon phases do spring tides occur on Earth?

    A. new and full moon
    B. 1st and 3rd quarter
    C. waxing and waning gibbous
    D. waxing and waning crescent

12. Consider the following drawing of the interior of a human.

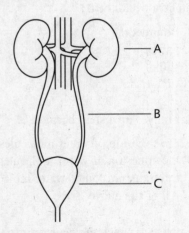

    Which of the following statements is true?

    A. A is the kidney, B is the urethra, and C is the bladder.
    B. A is the bladder, B is the ureter, and C is the kidney.
    C. A is the kidney, B is the ureter, and C is the bladder.
    D. A is the bladder, B is the urethra, and C is the kidney.

13. Which of the following options could represent fossil evidence of the existence of an earlier human life form?

    A. footprints found in slate
    B. dinosaur bones
    C. pottery shards
    D. a carbonized imprint of a fish skeleton

14. Which layer of the Earth's structure is the most dense?

    A. crust
    B. mantle
    C. outer core
    D. inner core

15. Oxygen is most abundant in which atmospheric layer?

    A. stratosphere
    B. ionosphere
    C. troposphere
    D. mesosphere

16. Evolution can be defined as

    A. competition among populations of organisms for natural resources.
    B. populations that are best adapted to their environment at a given time.
    C. populations whose characteristics do not change over time.
    D. a change in one or more characteristics of a population over time.

17. Blood is approximately

    A. 20% cells and 80% plasma.
    B. 30% cells and 70% plasma.
    C. 45% cells and 55% plasma.
    D. 30% plasma and 70% cells.

18. A gas sample has a volume of 50 milliliters at 20° Celsius. What will the new volume be at 100° Celsius if the pressure stays the same?

    A. 1 milliliter
    B. 63 milliliters
    C. 4,980 milliliters
    D. .004 milliliters

19. Which of the following is the best heat conductor?

    A. metalloid
    B. plastic
    C. metal
    D. wood

20. During which month is the Earth closest to the sun?

    A. March
    B. June
    C. September
    D. December

21. Organelles that are considered "powerhouses of the cell" are

    A. mitochondria.
    B. vacuoles.
    C. peroxisomes.
    D. ribosomes.

22. As the volume of a gas increases, the pressure

    A. increases.
    B. decreases.
    C. remains the same.
    D. remains the same if it is a gas.

23. The number of _____ determines the atomic number of a substance.

    A. protons
    B. neutrons
    C. protons and electrons
    D. protons and neutrons

24. Red-green colorblindness is a sex-linked trait in humans. If a girl is born colorblind, which of the following statements is true?

    A. Her father is colorblind.
    B. Her mother is colorblind.
    C. Her mother is a carrier for the mutant gene.
    D. All of the above could be true.

25. The HIV virus infects which type of cells?

    A. cytotoxic T cells
    B. helper T cells
    C. phagocytes
    D. monocytes

STOP

Arithmetic Reasoning

Time: 36 minutes

30 questions

Directions: Each of the following questions will test your knowledge about basic arithmetic. Read the question and select the choice that best answers the question. Indicate that letter on your answer sheet.

1. Jack lives $6\frac{1}{2}$ miles from the library. If he walks $\frac{1}{3}$ of the way and takes a break, what is the remaining distance to the library?

   A. $5\frac{5}{6}$ miles

   B. 4 miles

   C. $4\frac{1}{3}$ miles

   D. $2\frac{1}{6}$ miles

2. Amelia casts a shadow 5 ft long. Her father, who is 6 ft tall, casts a shadow 8 ft long. How tall is Amelia?

   A. 6 ft 8 in

   B. 4 ft 10 in

   C. 4 ft 6 in

   D. 3 ft 9 in

3. John spent 30 minutes vacuuming, 12 minutes dusting, and 37 minutes washing dishes. How many minutes did John spend on these chores?

   A. 34

   B. 79

   C. 100

   D. 124

4. A recipe calls for 3 cups of wheat and white flour combined. If $\frac{3}{8}$ of this is wheat flour, how many cups of white flour are needed?

   A. $1\frac{1}{8}$

   B. $1\frac{7}{8}$

   C. $2\frac{3}{8}$

   D. $2\frac{5}{8}$

5. Jared rents three videos for $8.00. What would the cost of two video rentals be?

   A. $1.33

   B. $5.00

   C. $5.33

   D. $6.00

6. Rockford is 439 miles from Springville and 638 miles from Davenport. How much closer is Rockford to Springville than Rockford to Davenport?

   A. 199 miles

   B. 201 miles

   C. 439 miles

   D. 1,077 miles

7. A winter coat is on sale for $150. If the original price was $200, what percent has the coat been discounted?

   A. 50%

   B. 40%

   C. 33%

   D. 25%

8. A square garden is to be built inside a circular area. Each corner of the square touches the circle. If the radius of the circle is 2, how much greater is the area of the circle than the area of the square?

   A. $4 - 4\pi$

   B. $4 - 8\pi$

   C. $4\pi - 4$

   D. $4\pi - 8$

9. A blueprint has a scale of 3 ft per $\frac{1}{2}$ in. If a bathroom on the blueprint is $1\frac{1}{2}$ in × 2 in, what are its actual dimensions?

   A. $4\frac{1}{2}$ ft by 6 ft

   B. 6 ft by $7\frac{1}{2}$ ft

   C. $7\frac{1}{2}$ ft by 9 ft

   D. 9 ft by 12 ft

10. A barrel holds 60 gallons of water. If a crack in the barrel causes $\frac{1}{2}$ gallon to leak out each day, how many gallons of water remain after 2 weeks?

    A. 30
    B. 53
    C. $56\frac{1}{2}$
    D. 59

11. The basketball game starts at 8:00 p.m. If it is now 5:30 p.m., how much time is left before the game starts?

    A. 1 hour, 30 minutes
    B. 2 hours, 30 minutes
    C. 3 hours, 30 minutes
    D. 4 hours, 30 minutes

12. How many blocks 6 in × 4 in × 4 in can fit in a box 8 ft × 6 ft × 4 ft?

    A. 2
    B. 48
    C. 576
    D. 3,456

13. Janice buys a quart of milk and two dozen eggs. If milk costs $1.39 and eggs are $1.28 a dozen, how much change will Janice get back if she pays with a $10.00 bill?

    A. $3.95
    B. $5.94
    C. $6.05
    D. $7.33

14. There are 800 employees at a company. If 60% drive to work and 40% take the train, how many employees arrive at work by car?

    A. 240
    B. 480
    C. 540
    D. 600

15. Min read three hardcover mysteries and four soft-cover mysteries. She read three times as many nonfiction books as she did mysteries. How many nonfiction books did Min read?

    A. 9
    B. 12
    C. 18
    D. 21

16. The volume of a cube is 343 cm³. The surface area of the cube is

    A. 7 cm².
    B. 49 cm².
    C. 294 cm².
    D. 2,401 cm².

17. Melodi eats $\frac{3}{8}$ of a pizza and divides the rest between her two friends. What percentage of the pizza do her friends each receive?

    A. 62.50%
    B. 37.50%
    C. 31.25%
    D. 18.75%

18. Kim's favorite movie is 144 minutes long. Justin's favorite movie is 127 minutes long. How much longer is Kim's favorite movie?

    A. 17 minutes
    B. 23 minutes
    C. 36 minutes
    D. 44 minutes

19. Roger collects bottle caps. Each cap can be traded for 5 cents. If Roger receives $40.50, how many bottle caps did he trade?

    A. 810
    B. 405
    C. 200
    D. 8

GO ON TO THE NEXT PAGE

20. A batch of cookies requires 2 cups of milk and 4 eggs. If you have 9 cups of milk and 9 eggs, how many complete batches of cookies can be made?

    A. 9
    B. 6
    C. 4
    D. 2

21. Find the value of x in the following figure:

    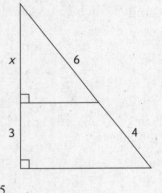

    A. 4.5
    B. 4.8
    C. 5
    D. 5.2

22. A piece of wood measuring 16.5 in long is cut into 2.75-in pieces. How many smaller pieces of wood are there?

    A. 3
    B. 5
    C. 6
    D. 8

23. Shanella has 17 quarters, 33 dimes, and 8 pennies. The total amount of money she has is

    A. $7.63.
    B. $7.95.
    C. $5.80.
    D. $15.55.

24. While dining out, Chad spent $25.00. If the bill totaled $21.00 before the tip was added, approximately what percent tip did Chad leave?

    A. 16%
    B. 19%
    C. 21%
    D. 25%

25. A right triangle has an area of 24 ft^2. If one leg is 3 times as long as the other, what is the length of the longest side?

    A. 12.6
    B. 12
    C. 8.4
    D. 6.3

26. Interest earned on an account at the end of one year totals $100. If the interest rate is $7\frac{1}{4}$%, what is the principal amount?

    A. $725
    B. $1,333
    C. $1,379
    D. $1,428

27. Yan can read 2 pages in 3 minutes. At this rate, how long will it take him to read a 360-page book?

    A. 30 minutes
    B. 2 hours
    C. 6 hours
    D. 9 hours

28. Tanya's bowling scores this week were 112, 156, 179, and 165. Last week, her average score was 140. How many points did her average improve?

    A. 18
    B. 13
    C. 11
    D. 8

29. Felix buys three books for $8.95 each. How much does he owe if he uses a $12.73 credit toward his purchase?

    A. $39.58
    B. $26.85
    C. $21.68
    D. $14.12

30. The value of 18 quarters, 6 dimes, and 24 nickels is

    A. $5.34.
    B. $6.30.
    C. $18.84.
    D. $24.24.

Word Knowledge

Time: 11 minutes

35 questions

Directions: This portion of the exam will test your knowledge of the meaning of words. Each question has an underlined word. Decide which of the four choices most nearly means the same as the underlined word; then indicate that letter on your answer sheet.

1. There was not enough room to <u>display</u> everything.

    A. sell
    B. exhibit
    C. store
    D. worry about

2. <u>Superficial</u> most nearly means

    A. deep.
    B. cursory.
    C. quality.
    D. intensive.

3. Please <u>cease</u> your complaining.

    A. stop
    B. forget
    C. change
    D. continue

4. He was <u>prevented</u> from boarding the ship.

    A. assisted
    B. encouraged
    C. hindered
    D. called

5. <u>Uniform</u> most nearly means

    A. unchanging.
    B. decreasing.
    C. increasing.
    D. forming.

6. <u>Conveyed</u> most nearly means

    A. talked about.
    B. carried.
    C. forgot.
    D. spotted.

7. <u>Impose</u> most nearly means

    A. protect.
    B. halt.
    C. require.
    D. border.

8. They tried to ignore the <u>hazard</u> in the alley.

    A. water
    B. hole
    C. danger
    D. odors

9. <u>Vacant</u> most nearly means

    A. empty.
    B. full.
    C. dependable.
    D. relaxed.

10. He enjoyed the <u>camaraderie</u> of the other soldiers.

    A. singing
    B. friendship
    C. playfulness
    D. yelling

11. She thought that the sweater was <u>irritating.</u>

    A. tight
    B. loose
    C. annoying
    D. sloppy

12. <u>Abandon</u> most nearly means

    A. affect.
    B. placate.
    C. enjoin.
    D. relinquish.

GO ON TO THE NEXT PAGE

13. Triumph most nearly means

    A. delegation.
    B. victory.
    C. enjoyment.
    D. wistfulness.

14. Taboo most nearly means

    A. painted.
    B. off limits.
    C. skinny.
    D. on target.

15. Prior most nearly means

    A. earlier.
    B. humorous.
    C. latest.
    D. matured.

16. Require most nearly means

    A. extricate.
    B. be silent.
    C. need.
    D. hope.

17. Appropriate most nearly means

    A. incorrect.
    B. sufficient.
    C. purchased.
    D. quarantined.

18. He was able to specify what he wanted.

    A. cite
    B. order
    C. forget
    D. take heed

19. Intermittent most nearly means

    A. constant.
    B. at irregular intervals.
    C. warm.
    D. between buildings.

20. He was able to sift through the residue.

    A. odor
    B. remainder
    C. garden
    D. residence

21. The two lawyers could not concur about the result.

    A. satisfy
    B. plead
    C. argue
    D. agree

22. Implore most nearly means

    A. explode.
    B. set on fire.
    C. beg.
    D. find.

23. Fortunately, the teacher was always convivial.

    A. inquisitive
    B. punctual
    C. absent
    D. pleasant

24. Impeccable most nearly means

    A. penniless.
    B. flawless.
    C. degrading.
    D. bored.

25. <u>Quandary</u> most nearly means

    A. foil.
    B. definition.
    C. predicament.
    D. trust.

26. They searched for a <u>resolution</u> to the problem between them.

    A. payoff
    B. decision
    C. exclusion
    D. relationship

27. <u>Obnoxious</u> most nearly means

    A. smelly.
    B. unpleasant.
    C. hurtful.
    D. plentiful.

28. <u>Encroach</u> most nearly means

    A. intrude.
    B. depart.
    C. prosecute.
    D. slither.

29. <u>Divergent</u> most nearly means

    A. stubborn.
    B. despicable.
    C. drawn apart.
    D. not desirable.

30. <u>Duplicity</u> most nearly means

    A. double.
    B. official.
    C. deceit.
    D. anger.

31. The man used an <u>alias</u> to join the club.

    A. strange look
    B. another name
    C. smiling face
    D. frown

32. <u>Sparse</u> most nearly means

    A. complete.
    B. meager.
    C. empty.
    D. enormous.

33. <u>Diminutive</u> most nearly means

    A. loud.
    B. small.
    C. revived.
    D. magnified.

34. <u>Exhort</u> most nearly means

    A. call to task.
    B. urge strongly.
    C. falter.
    D. yell at.

35. She was able to <u>suppress</u> the noise.

    A. tune out
    B. enhance
    C. hold up
    D. stifle

Paragraph Comprehension

Time: 13 minutes

15 questions

Directions: This is a test of reading comprehension. Read each paragraph and then select the choice below that best answers that question. Indicate that letter on your answer sheet.

1. More American children are obese than ever before. Experts blame increased television watching, easy access to junk food, less outdoor exercise, and unhealthy school lunches as possible culprits.

   In this context, the word *culprits* means

   A. causes.
   B. burglars.
   C. outcomes.
   D. criminals.

2. A new study suggests that one in four Americans does not get enough sleep. Sleep experts recommend 8 hours of sleep per night, and most Americans report an average of 6.9 hours of sleep on weeknights and 7.5 hours of sleep on weekends.

   The average American sleeps

   A. 8 hours on weekend nights.
   B. 9 hours on weekend nights.
   C. 6.5 hours on weeknights.
   D. 7.5 hours on weekend nights.

3. According to a recent study, sports cause the most accidental injuries for children. Sports-related injuries increase with age, and adolescence is the peak time period for such injuries to occur.

   The best title for this selection is

   A. Adolescents and Sports.
   B. Most Childhood Accidental Injuries Caused by Sports.
   C. Sports Are Harmful to Children.
   D. Sports and Your Child.

4. The phenomenon of planetary alignment only occurs once every several hundred years. Such an alignment occurs when all of the planets line up on the right side of the sun within 90° of each other or closer. This positioning of the planets is visible to the naked eye. A true planetary alignment occurred in May 2002. Before that, such an alignment had not occurred since April 1128.

   The following fact is NOT mentioned in the selection:

   A. Planetary alignments are visible to the naked eye.
   B. Planetary alignments cause planets to line up on the left side of the sun.
   C. Planetary alignments cause planets to line up on the right side of the sun.
   D. The last planetary alignment occurred in 2002.

5. In most cases, ferns are easy plants for the beginning gardener to grow. There are hundreds of species around the world that require only soil, a little compost, and water. After the initial planting and care for the plant, many ferns can survive outdoors on their own. They only need to be weeded and thinned occasionally.

   The best title for this selection is

   A. Outdoor Ferns.
   B. The Beginning Gardener.
   C. Ferns: The Easy-Care Plants.
   D. What You Need to Plant Ferns.

6. The Gila monster may be more than just a ghoulish looking creature that frightens people with its appearance. According to scientists, this creature might hold the key to a cure for Alzheimer's disease. Although the bite of the Gila monster can be deadly, its saliva contains a chemical that affects memory.

In this context, *ghoulish* means

A. friendly.
B. horrid.
C. silly.
D. cute.

7. Health experts claim that an aspirin a day may cut the risk of developing polyps commonly found in colon cancer. However, a full-size aspirin does not cut the risk as much as the smaller baby aspirin does.

The best title for this selection is

A. Health Benefits of Aspirin.
B. Cancer and Aspirin Dosage.
C. Aspirin May Prevent Colon Cancer.
D. Colon Cancer Prevention.

8. The debate continues among experts concerning whether organic foods are more healthy or just more expensive. Organic foods are those that are free of artificial pesticides and fertilizers and contain no herbicides.

Organic foods are

A. more healthy than regular foods.
B. ones that do not contain any pesticides.
C. inexpensive.
D. ones that contain no herbicides.

9. Scientists have recently found two stars that could possibly change the current understandings of physics and astronomy. Initially, these stars were thought to be neutron stars, which are the remnants of supernovas. However, they are smaller and cooler than neutron stars. Scientists hypothesize that these objects are indeed neutron stars but that they are just smaller and cooler than those that have been studied previously.

You may conclude from this selection that

A. the two stars are definitely neutron stars.
B. more study is needed to determine what these stars are.
C. neutron stars are usually much smaller than these stars.
D. neutron stars are usually much cooler than these stars.

10. Global warming and the greenhouse effect may not be all that human beings need to worry about. Environmentalists predict that climate change over the next 50 years will shift the current balance of ecosystems and bring new predators and prey closer together. This shift may not cause vast extinction of species, but it will most probably cause unbalanced distributions of predators and prey throughout the world. Such an altered distribution of animal species will affect humans in unpredictable ways.

The author of this selection probably feels that climate changes in the next 50 years

A. can only be beneficiary to humans.
B. will have no effect on humans.
C. may have ill effects on humans.
D. will not happen.

GO ON TO THE NEXT PAGE

Practice Test III

Questions 11 and 12 refer to the following excerpt.

Cardiologists say that a better survival rate for heart attack patients is at the touch of the patients' fingertips. Although the typical American suffering from a heart attack waits 2 hours to call 911, damage to the heart that can lead to death occurs much sooner. One doctor's answer is house calls, which would be performed in response to 911 calls. With his plan, a team of trained doctors would come to the patient's home and quickly assess the situation. This novel heart attack treatment plan would alleviate patients' worries of calling unneeded ambulances to their residence. Because more than 1.1 million Americans a year will suffer a heart attack, the American Heart Association is backing this experiment to save more lives.

11. The author of this selection probably feels that house calls to heart attack patients

   A. will be an improvement over the current system.
   B. will cause more problems than the current system does.
   C. will be alarming for suffering heart attack patients.
   D. will be too expensive to implement.

12. In this context, *alleviate* means

   A. irritate.
   B. increase.
   C. ease.
   D. strengthen.

Questions 13, 14, and 15 refer to the following selection.

A new study in the latest issue of Archives of Dermatology shows that even though doctors in casual dress might be acceptable on television sitcoms, patients in the real world want their doctors to dress formally. Instead of the often popular informal garb of blue jeans and sandals, patients want to see their physicians wearing white lab coats and name badges. Thus, even though our society as a whole is entering an age of casualness, people still want their doctors to dress professionally.

Researchers speculate that patients feel that their doctor appears more professional in formal clothes and is thus more trustworthy. Informal dress such as blue jeans and sandals might also suggest flippancy about the job being performed.

13. The best title for this selection is

   A. Doctors and Dress.
   B. Informally Dressed Society Prefers Formally Dressed Physicians.
   C. Doctors' Clothing Style Unimportant.
   D. Reasons Professionals Should Dress Professionally.

14. You might infer from the selection that informal garb

   A. is acceptable in all other professions.
   B. is preferred for certain kinds of doctors.
   C. such as scrubs for doctors is also viewed negatively.
   D. includes white lab coats and badges.

15. In this context, *flippancy* means

   A. concern.
   B. thoughtlessness.
   C. worry.
   D. anger.

Auto and Shop Information

Time: 11 minutes

25 questions

Directions: There are two parts to this test. The first will test your basic knowledge of automobiles. The second will test your knowledge of basic shop practices and the use of tools. Read each question carefully and select the choice that best answers the question. Indicate that letter on your answer sheet.

1. A car comes in with a complaint of the brakes seeming to not release after the driver steps on the brakes. Which of these could be the cause?

   A. no brake pedal, free travel
   B. a leaking wheel cylinder
   C. air in the hydraulic
   D. a bad cup in the master cylinder

2. You have just installed an engine that you rebuilt. When should you time the distributor?

   A. after road-testing the vehicle
   B. before starting the engine
   C. after the engine has warmed up
   D. while cranking the engine

3. Technician A says planetary gears are used in automatic transmissions. Technician B says planetary gears are used in manual transmissions. Who is right?

   A. technician A only
   B. technician B only
   C. both technicians A and B
   D. neither technician A nor B

4. Hydraulic systems in automatic transmissions are being discussed. Technician A says fluid is used to perform work. Technician B says fluid transfers heat. Who is correct?

   A. technician A only
   B. technician B only
   C. both technicians A and B
   D. neither technician A nor B

5. The front suspension system of a vehicle is being discussed. Technician A says that the spindle and knuckle assembly supports braking system components. Technician B says the spindle and knuckle assembly supports steering components Who is right?

   A. technician A only
   B. technician B only
   C. both technicians A and B
   D. neither technician A nor B

6. The main advantage of electronic engine controls and fuel injection is that they have made it possible to eliminate the _____.

   A. carburetor.
   B. catalytic converter.
   C. EGR valve.
   D. evaporative emissions system.

7. Hybrid electric vehicles (HEVs) allow the owner to save on gas and reduce exhaust pollutants by using

   A. higher octane fuels.
   B. expired gasoline.
   C. hydrogen fuel cells.
   D. two or more power sources.

8. In which of the strokes in a four-cycle engine is the piston going down and both valves are closed?

   A. intake
   B. compression
   C. power
   D. exhaust

GO ON TO THE NEXT PAGE

Practice Test III

9. Which of the following statements about four-wheel drive vehicles is NOT true?

   A. Front hubs must be locked during 4WD operation.
   B. Some front hub designs lock automatically.
   C. All 4WD systems require the driver to lock the hubs manually at the wheels.
   D. When unlocked in 2WD, the front wheels still turn.

10. Technician A says when a vehicle is locked in 2WD on a 4WD system, the front wheels still turn, including the front axles. Technician B says the front wheels still turn but the entire front drivetrain stops turning. Who is correct?

    A. technician A only
    B. technician B only
    C. both technicians A and B
    D. neither technician A nor B

11. Clutches are being discussed. Technician A says when the clutch pedal is depressed, the pressure plate squeezes the clutch disc onto the flywheel. Technician B says when the clutch pedal is released, the pressure plate stops squeezing the clutch disc onto the flywheel. Who is correct?

    A. technician A only
    B. technician B only
    C. both technicians A and B
    D. neither technician A nor B

12. Looking at the figure below, what is indicated on the drums?

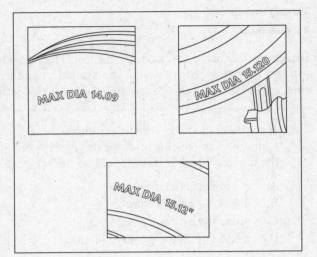

    A. diameter of the drums
    B. maximum drum to lining fit
    C. drum discard dimension
    D. none of the above

13. An accurate reading for brake rotor runout requires the use of a

    A. dial indicator.
    B. micrometer.
    C. straight edge.
    D. caliper.

14. Before cutting a piece of metal, the best way to mark the cut is by using a

    A. saw blade.
    B. chisel.
    C. scratch awl.
    D. grease pen.

15. The term "penny" is used

    A. to designate the size of a nail.
    B. to indicate the cost of screws.
    C. when installing roof flashing.
    D. as a measure of battery size.

16. What type of saw is used in a miter box?

    A. rip saw
    B. coping saw
    C. backsaw
    D. keyhole saw

17. The purpose of a push stick is to

    A. push scrap wood from a radial arm saw.
    B. guide wood through the blade of a bench saw.
    C. hold wood in the frame of a drill press.
    D. align the fence on a router table.

18. Of the following, which is the best wood for building furniture?

    A. balsa
    B. cedar
    C. spruce
    D. maple

19. The illustration below is an example of a

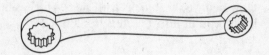

    A. pipe wrench.
    B. box-end wrench.
    C. combination wrench.
    D. open-end wrench.

20. The illustration below is an example of

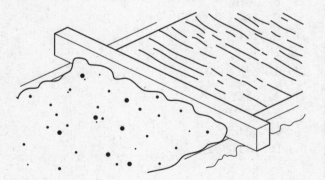

    A. flattening.
    B. screeding.
    C. turning.
    D. troweling.

21. When purchasing lumber, the price is based on the cost per

    A. yard foot.
    B. inch foot.
    C. board foot.
    D. grade foot.

22. The hinge illustrated below is often used on

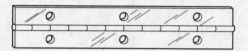

    A. closets.
    B. pianos.
    C. garage doors.
    D. outdoor gates.

23. A bolt differs from a screw in that

    A. a bolt has more threads.
    B. bolts are not tapered like screws.
    C. screws have more threads.
    D. bolts cannot hold two pieces of wood together.

24. A spline is used to

    A. support the end of a window frame.
    B. join two pieces of wood.
    C. seal the open end of a plywood sheet.
    D. test the sharpness of a wood chisel.

25. Concrete cures in about

    A. 1 day.
    B. 1 week.
    C. 1 month.
    D. 1 year.

STOP

Mathematics Knowledge

Time: 24 minutes
25 questions

Directions: This section will test your knowledge of basic mathematics. Read each question carefully and select the choice that best answers the question. Indicate that letter on your answer sheet.

1. If $w - 3 = 3 - w$, what is the value of w^2?

    A. 0
    B. 1
    C. 3
    D. 9

2. $\frac{24}{96} - \frac{8}{12} =$

    A. $\frac{1}{4}$

    B. $\frac{5}{96}$

    C. $-\frac{5}{12}$

    D. $\frac{4}{21}$

3. If $6m - 2$ is divided by 2, the result is –4. What is the value of m?

    A. –1
    B. 0
    C. 1
    D. 2

4. The diagonal of a square is 10 in. What is the area of the square?

    A. 40 in^2
    B. 50 in^2
    C. 100 in^2
    D. 150 in^2

5. A car travels 20 miles in 30 minutes. At this rate, how far will the car travel in 2 hours?

    A. 40 miles
    B. 60 miles
    C. 80 miles
    D. 100 miles

6. Simplify $\frac{15\sqrt{3}}{\sqrt{5}}$.

    A. $3\sqrt{3}$
    B. $3\sqrt{15}$
    C. $15\sqrt{15}$
    D. $75\sqrt{3}$

7. How many cubic blocks with sides 4 inches in length can fit into a crate 3 ft × 2 ft × 2 ft?

    A. 3
    B. 32
    C. 196
    D. 324

8. If $x = -3$ and $y = 2$, evaluate x^2y.

    A. –64
    B. –18
    C. 18
    D. 64

9. $0.00525 \div 0.01 =$

    A. 5.25
    B. 0.525
    C. 0.0525
    D. 0.000525

10. $\frac{3}{4} \div \frac{4}{3} =$

   A.   0

   B.   1

   C. $\frac{9}{16}$

   D. $\frac{16}{9}$

11. If the area of the circle in the figure below is 121π, find the area of the square.

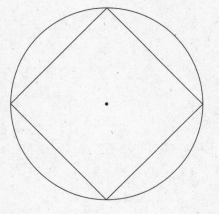

   A.   121

   B.   242

   C.   363

   D.   484

12. Simplify $(3x^2 + 2x - 5) - (2x^2 - 5) + (4x - 7)$.

   A. $x^2 + 6x - 17$

   B. $x^2 + 4x - 7$

   C. $x^2 + 6x - 2$

   D. $x^2 + 6x - 7$

13. One-fourth of the cars purchased at a dealership are luxury models. If 360 luxury models were purchased last year, how many total cars were purchased?

   A.   90

   B.   250

   C.   1,440

   D.   3,600

14. What is the measure of $\angle A$ in the figure below?

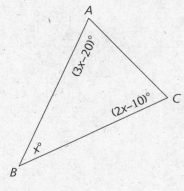

   A.   35°

   B.   60°

   C.   75°

   D.   85°

15. Find the product of $(3 - 4x)$ and $(3 + 4x)$.

   A.   9

   B. $9 + 12x - 16x^2$

   C. $9 - 16x^2$

   D. $9 + 16x^2$

16. Round $(2.5)^4$ to the nearest tenth.

   A.   10.0

   B.   25.4

   C.   39.0

   D.   39.1

Practice Test III

GO ON TO THE NEXT PAGE

17. In the figure below, the radius of the smaller circle is $\frac{1}{4}$ as long as the radius of the larger circle. What percent of the figure shown below is shaded?

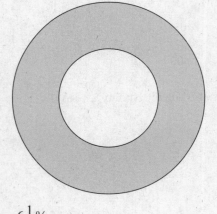

A. $6\frac{1}{4}\%$

B. 25%

C. 75%

D. $93\frac{3}{4}\%$

18. The least common multiple of 8, 12, and 20 is

A. 4.

B. 24.

C. 60.

D. 120.

19. Multiply $(5a^3bc^2)(-3a^2c)$.

A. $-15a^5bc^3$

B. $15a^5bc^3$

C. $-15a^6bc^2$

D. $2abc$

20. Simplify $\frac{x^2-25}{5-x}$.

A. $x+5$

B. $x-5$

C. $-(x+5)$

D. $5-x$

21. Given that the point $(x,1)$ lies on a line with a slope of $-\frac{3}{2}$ and a y-intercept of -2, find the value of x.

A. -2

B. -1

C. 1

D. 2

22. What is the probability of flipping three heads in a row using a fair coin?

A. $\frac{1}{2}$

B. $\frac{2}{3}$

C. $\frac{1}{8}$

D. $\frac{3}{8}$

23. If $0.08z = 6.4$, then $z =$

A. 0.8.

B. 8.

C. 80.

D. 800.

24. Find the area of a regular hexagon whose sides measure 6 cm.

A. 36

B. $9\sqrt{2}$

C. $54\sqrt{3}$

D. 108

25. The girls' basketball team won three times as many games as they lost. How many games were won if they played a total of 24 games?

A. 6

B. 8

C. 12

D. 18

Mechanical Comprehension

Time: 19 minutes

25 questions

Directions: This section will test your knowledge of mechanical principles. Read each question carefully and then select the choice that best answers the question. Indicate that letter on your answer sheet.

1. The location of the center of mass of a person

   A. is always located inside the person.
   B. is always located outside the person.
   C. is a fixed point that does not change.
   D. can change if the person moves.

2. If a baseball is thrown, then _____ follows a parabolic path.

   A. every part of the baseball
   B. only the center of mass always
   C. every part of the surface of the ball
   D. every part of the ball except the center of mass

3. If the Earth exerts a force of 400 N on a woman, then the gravitational force that the woman exerts on the Earth is

   A. zero.
   B. 400 N.
   C. much less than 400 N.
   D. much more than 400 N.

4. People driving up a mountain will find that their mass will _____ and their weight will _____.

   A. increase, decrease
   B. decrease, increase
   C. decrease, remain the same
   D. remain the same, decrease

5. A heavy object is dropped from the top of a tower. If it falls 5 meters after 1 second, how far from the top will it be 3 seconds after it was released? Ignore air resistance.

   A. 10 meters
   B. 15 meters
   C. 30 meters
   D. 45 meters

6. During an elastic collision

   A. both momentum and kinetic energy are conserved.
   B. only momentum is conserved.
   C. only kinetic energy is conserved.
   D. only kinetic and potential energies are conserved.

7. A car bumper protects a car during a collision because it

   A. decreases the impact time.
   B. increases the impact time.
   C. increases the impact force.
   D. increases the transfer of kinetic energy.

8. A student makes a graph of the force applied in the direction of motion versus the displacement. The work done by this force is associated with

   A. the slope of the graph.
   B. the area under the curve on the graph.
   C. the value of the force at a particular value of displacement.
   D. cannot be determined from the graph.

9. In simple harmonic motion, there is always a constant ratio between the displacement of the mass and its

   A. acceleration.
   B. speed.
   C. period.
   D. mass.

10. The angular velocity of the seconds hand of a clock is

    A. 0.105 rad/s.
    B. 9.53 rad/s.
    C. 6.28 rad/s.
    D. 0.159 rad/s.

GO ON TO THE NEXT PAGE

11. Two masses are resting on a beam of negligible mass, as shown below. Where should the fulcrum be positioned so that the masses will be in balance?

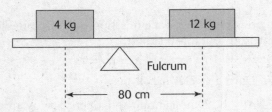

A. 20 centimeters from the 4-kilogram mass
B. 20 centimeters from the 12-kilogram mass
C. 30 centimeters from the 4-kilogram mass
D. 40 centimeters from the 12-kilogram mass

12. An object can accelerate by

A. changing the direction of its velocity but not the magnitude.
B. changing the magnitude of the velocity but not the direction.
C. changing the speed.
D. All of the above.

13. A foul ball hit vertically upward with an initial speed of 46.8 m/s will take _____ to reach the top of its trajectory.

A. 9.56 seconds
B. 5.82 seconds
C. 4.78 seconds
D. 0.21 seconds

14. Anne walks 8 meters to the right, then 24 meters to the left, and finally 48 meters to the right. If she completes this in 160 seconds, then her average velocity is

A. 0.6 m/s.
B. 0.5 m/s.
C. 0.2 m/s.
D. 0.3 m/s.

15. A wheel with a moment of inertia of $0.3 \ kg \cdot m^2$ is rotating with an initial angular velocity of 4 rad/s. The magnitude of the torque needed to increase the angular velocity to 6.5 rad/s in 4 seconds is

A. 1.50 newton · meters.
B. 3.00 newton · meters.
C. 0.188 newton · meters.
D. 0.788 newton · meters.

16. The work done on a building by a 75-kilogram wrecking ball striking at a speed of 4 m/s is

A. 300 joules.
B. 1,200 joules.
C. 600 joules.
D. none of the above.

17. A 60-N weight is lifted by the lever arrangement shown in the figure below. If the weight of the lever is negligible, the ideal mechanical advantage (F_o/F_i) and the input force F_i required to achieve equilibrium are

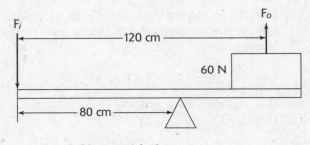

A. 3, 30, respectively.
B. 2, 30, respectively.
C. 2, 120, respectively.
D. 3, 1, respectively.

18. The velocity needed to escape the gravitational pull of a planet of 8×10^{24} kilograms and a radius of 5×10^6 meters is nearly

A. 11.2 km/s.
B. 14.6 km/s.
C. 18.7 km/s.
D. 23.4 km/s.

19. The magnitude of the force necessary to change the momentum of a particle from 10 kg m/s to 50 kg m/s in 12 seconds is

   A. 3.33 newtons.
   B. 4.16 newtons.
   C. 4.0 newtons.
   D. 720 newtons.

20. A truck goes around a sharp right-hand turn. A passenger would feel pressure moving her to the

   A. right.
   B. left.
   C. back.
   D. roof.

21. A 10-kilogram mass attached to a spring oscillates with a period of 3.14 seconds. The force constant of the spring, k, is

   A. 40.
   B. 20.
   C. 4.
   D. 2.

22. A 5-kilogram block starts downward from rest at the top of a 40-meter-long frictionless inclined plane. If the block starts at a height of 10 meters above the ground, its speed as it hits the ground is _____ m/s and the force on the block while sliding is _____.

   A. 19.6, 1.225 newtons, respectively
   B. 19.6, 12.25 newtons, respectively
   C. 14, 12.25 newtons, respectively
   D. 14, 1.225 newtons, respectively

23. The instantaneous momentum times acceleration of a body is proportional to

   A. work done.
   B. travel distance.
   C. mechanical force.
   D. output power.

24. A worker is pulling a box at a constant speed in a straight line along the floor.

   Which of the following statements is true?

   A. The forces on the box equal the force of gravity acting on the box.
   B. The forces on the box are unbalanced and in the direction of motion.
   C. The forces on the box are balanced and the net force is zero.
   D. The forces on the box exceed the frictional forces opposing motion.

25. An object is moving at a constant speed. It is safe to say that

   A. a constant force is applied to move the object.
   B. no forces are acting on the object.
   C. the object is moving on a frictionless surface.
   D. the kinetic energy of the object is constant.

Practice Test III

Electronics Information

Time: 9 minutes

20 questions

Directions: The following portion of the exam will test your knowledge of electronics, electrical, and radio information. Read each question carefully and select the choice that best answers the question. Indicate that letter on your answer sheet.

1. For the lamp to be turned on in the circuit shown below,

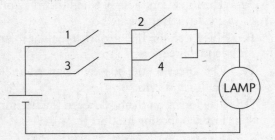

   A. switch 1 or switch 2 should be closed.
   B. switch 4 only should be closed.
   C. switches 1 and 3 should be closed.
   D. switches (1 or 3) and (2 or 4) should be closed.

2. A wattmeter is a device used for measuring

   A. electrical current.
   B. electrical voltage.
   C. electrical power.
   D. electrical charge.

3. The total resistance for the circuit shown below is

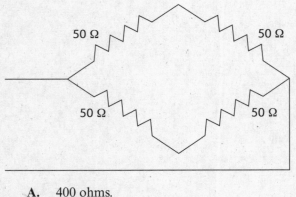

   A. 400 ohms.
   B. 100 ohms.
   C. 50 ohms.
   D. 200 ohms.

4. Which one of the symbols shown below represents a variable resistor?

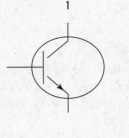

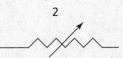

   A. 1
   B. 2
   C. 3
   D. 4

5. The square wave voltage signal shown in the following illustration has

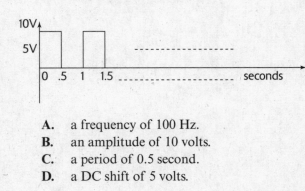

   A. a frequency of 100 Hz.
   B. an amplitude of 10 volts.
   C. a period of 0.5 second.
   D. a DC shift of 5 volts.

6. Which of the following components has a measurement unit of farads?

    A. capacitor
    B. coil
    C. resistor
    D. diode

7. The reading of the ammeter in the circuit below is

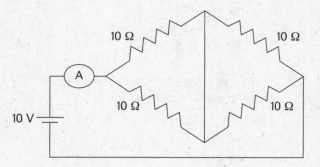

    A. 0.5 ampere.
    B. 1 ampere.
    C. 0.1 ampere.
    D. 0.25 ampere.

8. An audio signal is transmitted by

    A. storing it.
    B. multiplying it with a triangular wave.
    C. carrying it on a sinusoidal signal.
    D. filtering it.

9. If the reading of the voltmeter in the circuit shown below is 2 volts, then the value of the unknown resistor is

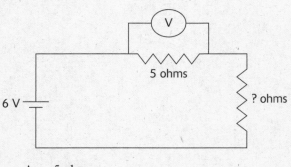

    A. 5 ohms.
    B. 10 ohms.
    C. 1 ohm.
    D. 2 ohms.

10. A diode will pass electrical current when the

    A. voltage applied is less than the threshold level.
    B. voltage applied is zero.
    C. voltage applied is greater than the threshold level.
    D. voltage difference between the anode and the cathode is zero.

11. If a transistor is connected using the common emitter configuration, then the collector current will be

    A. less than the base current.
    B. an amplification of the base current.
    C. same as the base current.
    D. a rectification of the base current.

12. As a safety requirement, electrical devices are

    A. designed to be effective.
    B. grounded.
    C. used in communications systems.
    D. placed on tables.

13. An oscillator circuit is used to

    A. amplify current.
    B. generate a DC signal.
    C. rectify current.
    D. generate a high-frequency carrier signal.

14. The total power dissipated across the resistors in the circuit shown below is

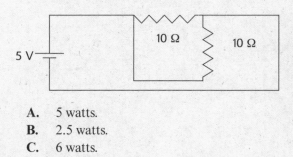

    A. 5 watts.
    B. 2.5 watts.
    C. 6 watts.
    D. 0.5 watts.

15. A capacitor can be used as a

    A. frequency filter.
    B. rectifier.
    C. transformer.
    D. current amplifier.

GO ON TO THE NEXT PAGE

16. The total capacitance of the circuit shown below is

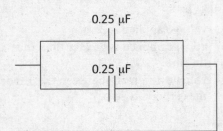

0.25 μF

0.25 μF

    A.   0.125 μF.
    B.   1 μF.
    C.   0.5 μF.
    D.   1.5 μF.

17. A square wave can be obtained from

    A.   a voltmeter.
    B.   a function generator.
    C.   an ammeter.
    D.   an ohmmeter.

18. Coils are used in electric transformers to

    A.   rectify the current.
    B.   induce a different level of voltage.
    C.   reduce the value of the current.
    D.   pass the DC signal.

19. Bipolar Junction Transistors (BJTs) can be

    A.   NP.
    B.   PN.
    C.   PNP.
    D.   PPN.

20. In order to reduce the total resistance of a circuit, resistors are connected in

    A.   series.
    B.   parallel.
    C.   series followed by parallel.
    D.   parallel followed by series.

STOP

Assembling Objects

Time: 9 minutes

16 questions

Directions: In the Assembling Objects portion of the ASVAB there are two types of questions. One type is very similar to solving a jigsaw puzzle. The other is a matter of making appropriate connections given a diagram and instructions. In each of the questions, the first drawing is the problem, and the remaining four drawings offer possible solutions. Look at each of the four illustrations, and then select the choice that best solves that particular problem. Indicate that letter on your answer sheet.

1.

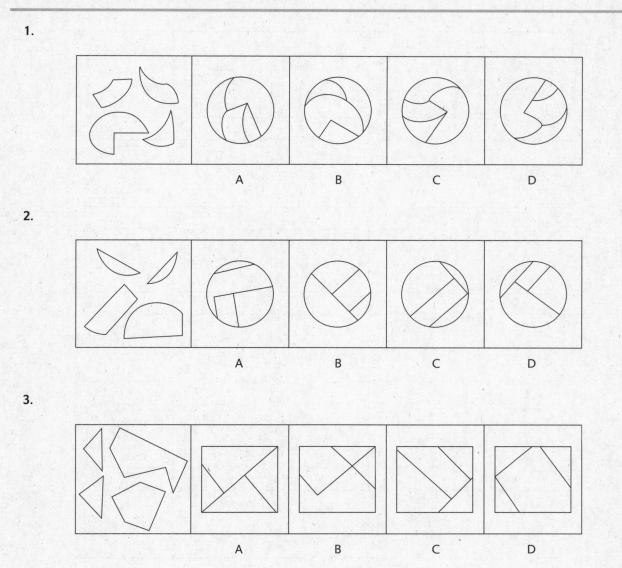

        A   B   C   D

2.

        A   B   C   D

3.

        A   B   C   D

GO ON TO THE NEXT PAGE

4.

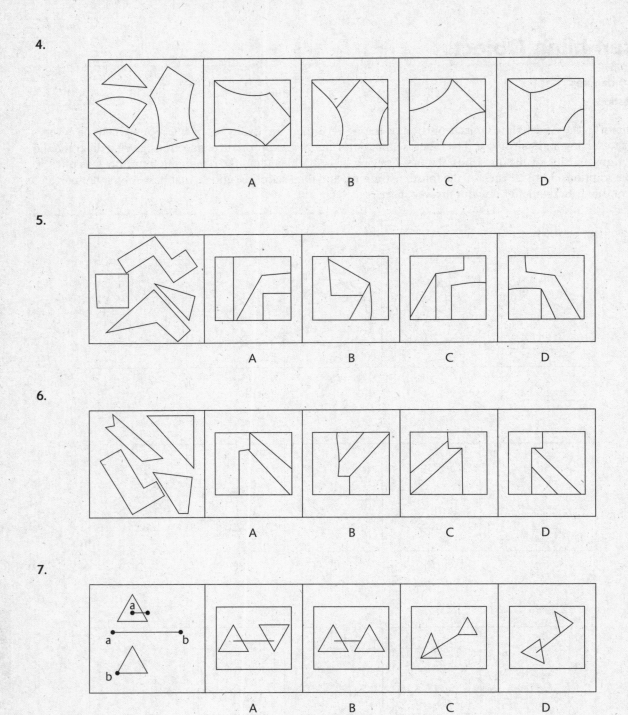

5.

6.

7.

8.

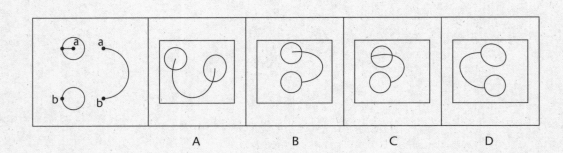

9.

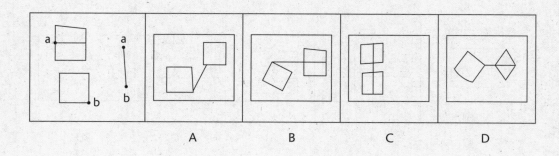

A   B   C   D

10.

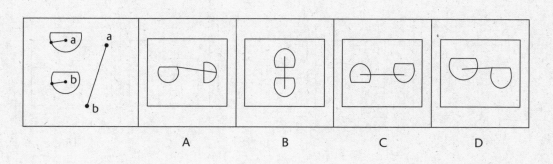

A   B   C   D

11.

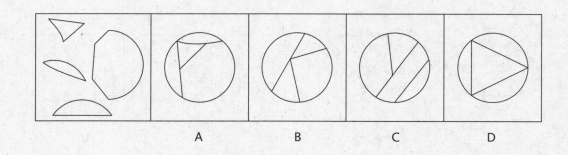

A   B   C   D

12.

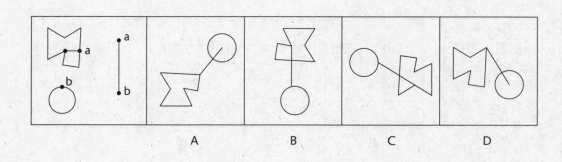

A   B   C   D

GO ON TO THE NEXT PAGE

13.

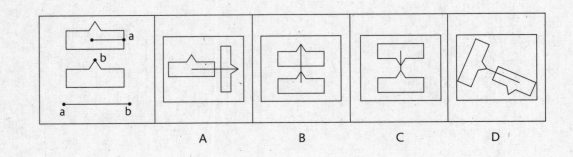

A   B   C   D

14.

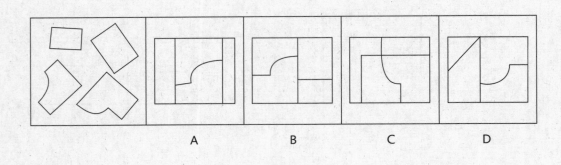

A   B   C   D

15.

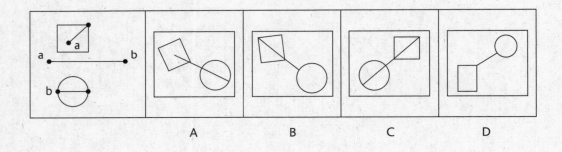

A   B   C   D

16.

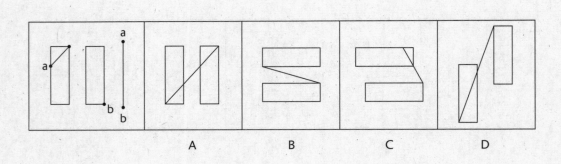

A   B   C   D

Answer Key for Practice Test III

General Science

1. D	10. D	19. C
2. C	11. A	20. D
3. B	12. C	21. A
4. C	13. C	22. B
5. B	14. D	23. A
6. B	15. C	24. D
7. D	16. D	25. B
8. D	17. C	
9. A	18. B	

Arithmetic Reasoning

1. C	11. B	21. A
2. D	12. D	22. C
3. B	13. C	23. A
4. B	14. B	24. B
5. C	15. D	25. A
6. A	16. C	26. C
7. D	17. C	27. D
8. D	18. A	28. B
9. D	19. A	29. D
10. B	20. D	30. B

Word Knowledge

1. B	13. B	25. C
2. B	14. B	26. B
3. A	15. A	27. B
4. C	16. C	28. A
5. A	17. B	29. C
6. B	18. A	30. C
7. C	19. B	31. B
8. C	20. B	32. B
9. A	21. D	33. B
10. B	22. C	34. B
11. C	23. D	35. D
12. D	24. B	

Paragraph Comprehension

1. A	6. B	11. A
2. D	7. C	12. C
3. B	8. D	13. B
4. B	9. B	14. C
5. C	10. C	15. B

Auto and Shop Information

1. A	10. B	19. B
2. B	11. D	20. B
3. A	12. C	21. C
4. C	13. A	22. B
5. C	14. C	23. B
6. A	15. A	24. B
7. D	16. C	25. C
8. C	17. B	
9. C	18. D	

Mathematics Knowledge

1. D	10. C	19. A
2. C	11. B	20. C
3. A	12. D	21. A
4. B	13. C	22. C
5. C	14. D	23. C
6. B	15. C	24. C
7. D	16. D	25. D
8. C	17. D	
9. B	18. D	

Mechanical Comprehension

1. D	10. A	19. A
2. B	11. B	20. B
3. B	12. D	21. A
4. D	13. C	22. C
5. D	14. C	23. D
6. A	15. C	24. C
7. B	16. C	25. D
8. B	17. B	
9. A	18. B	

Electronics Information

1. D	8. C	15. A
2. C	9. B	16. C
3. C	10. C	17. B
4. B	11. B	18. B
5. D	12. B	19. C
6. A	13. D	20. B
7. B	14. A	

Assembling Objects

1. C	7. D	13. D
2. C	8. B	14. B
3. B	9. B	15. A
4. C	10. C	16. C
5. C	11. A	
6. C	12. B	

Practice Test III Answers and Explanations

General Science

1. **D.** The Earth is approximately 4.5 billion years old. There has been life on Earth for much of that time.

2. **C.** The heart pumps blood from its right side to the lungs. The left ventricle pumps blood throughout the rest of the body, initially through the aorta (structure B in the diagram).

3. **B.** The coefficients are the number of moles.

4. **C.** A mole of any gas occupies 22.4 liters at STP.

5. **B.** The ovaries produce estrogen and progesterone, the hormones responsible for the secondary sex characteristics that women develop at puberty.

6. **B.** Radial symmetry is like a wheel with spokes. Of the possible answers, only a jellyfish displays radial symmetry.

7. **D.** Cohesion is the attraction of water molecules to one another. Adhesion is the attraction of water molecules to the walls of a vessel. Transpiration is the force that provides the pull of the water molecules up the stem.

8. **D.** Plasma molecules have the highest kinetic energy.

9. **A.** The two substances come together to form a new compound; hence, it's a chemical reaction.

10. **D.** Tidal bulges occur on the side of the Earth facing the moon and on the opposite side, resulting in a high tide about every 12 hours in most locations.

11. **A.** Tides are controlled by the position of the moon relative to the Earth. During the new and full moon phases, the sun is lined up with the moon, providing additional gravitational attraction, which influences the tides.

12. **C.** The kidneys produce urine that travels through the ureter to the bladder and then out the urethra.

13. **C.** Pottery may be evidence of an extinct civilization. The other three choices offer evidence of organisms that may have died off long ago.

14. **D.** The inner core has an average density of about 13 g/cm^2. The crust has an average density of about 2.5 g/cm^2, the mantle has an average density of about 4.5 g/cm^2, and the outer core has an average density of 11 g/cm^2. It is possible to deduce the answer without knowing the actual numbers, knowing that gravity pulls the densest materials closest to the center of an object's mass. Because the inner core matter is closest to the center, it must be densest.

15. **C.** The troposphere is the atmospheric layer closest to the Earth and contains 75% of all gases, oxygen included.

16. **D.** While each of the other answer choices is part of the process that Darwin said causes evolution, evolution itself, by definition, is a change in one or more characteristics of a population over time.

17. **C.** Plasma takes up slightly more space than cells. Blood plasma, by the way, is about 90% water with dissolved nutrients, waste, hormones, and proteins.

18. **B.** All calculations involving gas laws and temperature require that Celsius temperatures be converted to the Kelvin scale by adding 273. So, 20° C is 293 K, and 100° C is 373 K. The equation is then as follows:

$$\frac{T_1}{T_2} = \frac{V_1}{V_2}.$$

$$\frac{293 \text{ K}}{373 \text{ K}} = \frac{50 \text{ ml}}{V_2}.$$

Solving for V_2 by cross multiplying and dividing, we get approximately 63 ml.

19. **C.** Metal is the best heat conductor because of the capability of the electrons in the outer shells of metals to move.

20. **D.** The Earth is closest to the sun on January 1 and farthest on July 1. The reason for seasonal differences in temperature involves the tilt of the Earth, not its distance from the sun.

21. **A.** Mitochondria are used in the cell respiration of eukaryotic organisms. Cellular respiration is the process that all eukaryotic cells use to break down glucose and release its energy in the form of ATP, allowing the cell to power all other processes.

22. **B.** $\frac{V_1}{V_2} = \frac{P_1}{P_2}$, as volume and pressure are inversely proportional.

23. **A.** Both protons and neutrons have mass, but only protons determine atomic number.

24. **D.** Any sex-linked trait is carried on the X chromosome. Males have one, a copy of which they give to all their daughters. Females have two X chromosomes, and they give a copy of one of them to all their daughters. The mother could have two mutated chromosomes or just one. Women who carry a mutated gene but do not express it are said to be carriers. Any boy born to a carrier has a 50% chance of inheriting that mutated gene.

25. **B.** The HIV virus infects the helper T cells that are used to initiate many specific immune responses.

Arithmetic Reasoning

1. **C.** $\frac{1}{3}$ of $6\frac{1}{2}$ miles is $\frac{1}{3} \times 6\frac{1}{2} = \frac{1}{3} \times \frac{13}{2} = \frac{13}{6}$ miles walked. The remaining distance is

   $6\frac{1}{2} - \frac{13}{6} = \frac{13}{2} - \frac{13}{6} = \frac{39}{6} - \frac{13}{6} = \frac{26}{6} = 4\frac{1}{3}$ miles.

2. **D.** Using the ratio $\frac{\text{height}}{\text{shadow}}$, the proportion $\frac{x \text{ ft}}{5 \text{ ft}} = \frac{6 \text{ ft}}{8 \text{ ft}}$ can be used to find the unknown height. Cross

   multiply: $8x = 5 \times 6$, so $8x = 30$ and $x = \frac{30}{8} = 3\frac{3}{4}$ feet.

   Convert $\frac{3}{4}$ feet to inches: $\frac{3}{4} \times 12 = 9$ inches. Therefore, Amelia is 3 ft 9 in tall.

3. **B.** The time spent cleaning was 30 minutes + 12 minutes + 37 minutes = 79 minutes.

4. **B.** If $\frac{3}{8}$ is wheat flour, then $1 - \frac{3}{8}$ or $\frac{5}{8}$ is white flour. So $3 \times \frac{5}{8} = \frac{15}{8} = 1\frac{7}{8}$ cups of white flour are needed.

5. **C.** Using the ratio $\frac{\text{price}}{\text{video}}$, the proportion $\frac{8}{3} = \frac{x}{2}$ can be used to find the cost to rent two videos. Cross

   multiply. $8 \times 2 = 3x$ so $16 = 3x$ and $x = \frac{16}{3} = \$5.33$.

6. **A.** The difference in miles is $638 - 439 = 199$.

7. **D.** The percent discounted is the amount discounted divided by the original price. The amount discounted

   is $\$200 - \$150 = \$50$. The percent discounted is $\frac{50}{200} = 0.25 = 25\%$.

8. **D.**

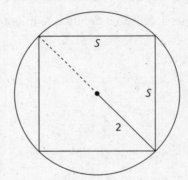

   Find the difference between the area of the circle and the area of the square. The area of the circle is
   $\pi r^2 = \pi \times 2^2 = 4\pi$. The area of the square is s^2, where s represents the length of the square. The radius is half
   the length of the square's diagonal, so the diagonal is 4. By the Pythagorean theorem, $s^2 + s^2 = 4^2$. $2s^2 = 16$
   so $s^2 = 8$. The difference in area is $4\pi - 8$.

9. **D.** If the blueprint shows $\frac{1}{2}$ in for every 3 ft, then 1 in represents 6 ft. The actual dimensions of a room

   $1\frac{1}{2}$ by 2 in would be $\left(1\frac{1}{2} \times 6\right)$ by (2×6) or 9 ft by 12 ft.

10. **B.** In 2 weeks, or 14 days, $\frac{1}{2} \times 14 = 7$ gallons leak out, leaving $60 - 7 = 53$ gallons.

11. **B.** At 5:30 p.m., there are 30 minutes to 6:00 p.m. and 2 additional hours until 8:00 p.m. for a total of 2
    hours and 30 minutes.

12. **D.** Convert the dimensions of the box from feet to inches. 8 ft × 6 ft × 4 ft is equivalent to
    $(8 \times 12 \text{ in}) \times (6 \times 12 \text{ in}) \times (4 \times 12 \text{ in}) = 96 \text{ in} \times 72 \text{ in} \times 48 \text{ in}$. The volume of the box = $96 \times 72 \times 48 = 331,776$.

    The volume of each block is $6 \times 4 \times 4 = 96$. The number of blocks that fit in the box is $\frac{331,776}{96} = 3,456$.

13. **C.** The cost for milk and 2 dozen eggs is $\$1.39 + (2 \times \$1.28) = \$3.95$. The change is $\$10.00 - \$3.95 = \$6.05$.

14. B. 60% arrive to work by car, so $800 \times 60\% = 480$.

15. D. Min read a total of $3 + 4$ or 7 mysteries. Therefore, she read 3×7 or 21 nonfiction books.

16. C. The volume of a cube is s^3, where s represents the length of an edge. Surface area is $6s^2$. If the volume = 343 cm^3, then $s = \sqrt[3]{343} = \sqrt[3]{7 \cdot 7 \cdot 7} = 7$. So the surface area is $= 294$ cm^2.

17. C. If $\frac{3}{8}$ of the pizza is eaten, then $1 - \frac{3}{8} = \frac{5}{8}$ remains. If that is divided by 2, then each receives $\frac{5}{8} \div 2 = \frac{5}{8} \times \frac{1}{2} = \frac{5}{16} = 0.3125 = 31.25\%$.

18. A. The difference is $144 - 127 = 17$ minutes.

19. A. Let c represent the number of caps traded in. Then $0.05c = 40.50$ and $c = \frac{40.50}{0.05} = 810$ caps.

20. D. With 9 cups of milk, $\frac{9}{2} = 4\frac{1}{2}$ or four full batches can be made. However, with nine eggs, only $\frac{9}{4} = 2\frac{1}{4}$ or two full batches can be made. At most, only two batches can be made with the given ingredients.

21. A. The proportion $\frac{x}{6} = \frac{x+3}{10}$ can be used to find x. Cross multiply. $10x = 6(x + 3)$ and $10x = 6x + 18$. Bring all x terms to one side by subtracting $6x$ from each side. Then $4x = 18$ and $x = \frac{18}{4} = 4.5$.

22. C. The number of smaller pieces is $\frac{16.5}{2.75} = 6$.

23. A. The total amount is $(17 \times \$0.25) + (33 \times \$0.10) + (8 \times \$0.01) = \$4.25 + \$3.30 + \$0.08 = \$7.63$.

24. B. The percent tip is the amount of tip over the total before tip. The amount of the tip is $\$25.00 - \$21.00 = \$4.00$. The percent of the tip is $\frac{4}{21} = 0.19 = 19\%$.

25. A. The area of a triangle is $\frac{1}{2}bh$. Let b represent the length of one leg. Then $h = 3b$, so the area is $\frac{1}{2}bh = \frac{1}{2} \cdot b \cdot 3b = \frac{3}{2}b^2 = 24$. Isolate b: $\frac{2}{3} \cdot \frac{3}{2}b^2 = \frac{2}{3} \cdot 24$ and $b^2 = 16$. $b = \sqrt{16} = 4$, and $h = 3 \times 4 = 12$.

The longest side of a right triangle is the hypotenuse. Using the Pythagorean theorem, leg^2 + leg^2 = hypotenuse^2, so $4^2 + 12^2 = c^2$ and $16 + 144 = c^2$. Therefore, $160 = c^2$ and $c = \sqrt{160} = 12.6$.

26. C. Interest = principal × rate. Let p represent the principal. Then $\$100 = p \times 7\frac{1}{4}\%$, so $p = \frac{\$100}{7\frac{1}{4}\%} = \frac{\$100}{0.0725} = \$1,379$.

27. D. Using the ratio $\frac{\text{pages}}{\text{minutes}}$, the proportion $\frac{2}{3} = \frac{360}{x}$ can be used to find the time. Cross multiply: $2x = 3 \times 360$, so $2x = 1,080$ and $x = \frac{1080}{2} = 540$ minutes. Convert minutes to hours: There are 60 minutes in 1 hour so $\frac{540}{60} = 9$ hours.

28. B. The average is found by adding up all the scores and dividing by the total number of scores. The average this week is $\frac{112 + 156 + 179 + 165}{4} = \frac{612}{4} = 153$. The amount of improvement is $153 - 140 = 13$.

29. D. The total cost of the purchase is $\$8.95 \times 3 = \$26.85$. With a $\$12.73$ credit, the amount owed is $\$26.85 - \$12.73 = \$14.12$.

30. B. The total is $(18 \times \$0.25) + (6 \times \$0.10) + (24 \times \$0.05) = \$4.50 + \$0.60 + \$1.20 = \$6.30$.

Word Knowledge

1. **B.** *Exhibit.* Display means to show or make visible.

2. **B.** *Cursory.* Superficial means casual or perfunctory.

3. **A.** *Stop.* Cease means to stop, halt, or end.

4. **C.** *Hindered.* Prevented means stopped, restrained, or restricted.

5. **A.** *Unchanging.* Uniform means constant or invariable.

6. **B.** *Carried.* Conveyed means transported or brought.

7. **C.** *Require.* Impose means demand or direct.

8. **C.** *Danger.* Hazard means pitfall or peril.

9. **A.** *Empty.* Vacant means uninhabited or unoccupied.

10. **B.** *Friendship.* Camaraderie means companionship or fellowship.

11. **C.** *Annoying.* Irritating means disturbing or bothersome.

12. **D.** *Relinquish.* Abandon means to yield or give up.

13. **B.** *Victory.* Triumph means success or win.

14. **B.** *Off limits.* Taboo means forbidden or prohibited.

15. **A.** *Earlier.* Prior means previously or beforehand.

16. **C.** *Need.* Require means desire or call for.

17. **B.** *Sufficient.* Appropriate means adequate or satisfactory.

18. **A.** *Cite.* Specify means designate or point out.

19. **B.** *At irregular intervals.* Intermittent means recurrent or periodic.

20. **B.** *Remainder.* Residue means leavings or remnants.

21. **D.** *Agree.* Concur means to reach an agreement or come to terms.

22. **C.** *Beg.* Implore means plead or appeal.

23. **D.** *Pleasant.* Convivial means friendly or congenial.

24. **B.** *Flawless.* Impeccable means perfect or faultless.

25. **C.** *Predicament.* Quandary means dilemma or difficulty.

26. **B.** *Decision.* Resolution means determination or conclusion.

27. **B.** *Unpleasant.* Obnoxious means offensive, repulsive, or detestable.

28. **A.** *Intrude.* Encroach means to trespass, infringe, or bother.

29. **C.** *Drawn apart.* Divergent means different, digressing, or deviating.

30. **C.** *Deceit.* Duplicity means dishonesty or deviousness.

31. **B.** *Another name.* Alias means assumed name, pseudonym, or pen name.

32. **B.** *Meager.* Sparse means insufficient, inadequate, or lacking.

33. **B.** *Small.* Diminutive means little, miniature, or tiny.

34. **B.** *Urge strongly.* Exhort means to advise or alert.

35. **D.** *Stifle.* Suppress means to restrain, repress, or check.

Paragraph Comprehension

1. **A.** This word is the only one that is logical when placed in the context of the selection. All of the listed activities are causes of increased obesity among children.

2. **D.** The last sentence of the selection states that the average night's sleep on weekends is 7.5 hours.

3. **B.** The first sentence of the selection, or topic sentence, states this.

4. **B.** The selection states that in a planetary alignment, the planets line up on the right side of the sun.

5. **C.** The whole selection focuses on how easy ferns are to care for.

6. **B.** The first sentence states that this creature frightens people.

7. **C.** Aspirin is discussed as a possible preventive medication for colon cancer.

8. **D.** The last sentence states that organic foods do not contain herbicides.

9. **B.** The selection makes it clear that scientists are puzzled by these stars, and their hypothesis is that they are neutron stars.

10. **C.** The last sentence of the selection states that such changes in climate will affect humans in "unpredictable ways." Thus, you may infer that these changes could be negative ones.

11. **A.** The overall tone of the selection is positive with regard to the move to incorporate a system of house calls for heart attack patients.

12. **C.** The selection describes a new procedure for handling heart attack patients that would ease worry concerning 911 calls.

13. **B.** The selection discusses how today's casual society still prefers physicians who dress formally, rather than casually.

14. **C.** Scrubs, like jeans and sandals, are also informal garb. Thus, you might conclude that such dress would not be acceptable to most patients.

15. **B.** Because the passage as a whole is concerned with the negative effects that doctors in informal dress have on patients, this meaning is the clear choice.

Auto and Shop Information

1. **A.** If there is no free play, chances are the compensating port is covered inside the master cylinder. This prevents fluid from returning properly, thus keeping enough pressure in the brake circuit to possibly keep the brakes slightly applied.

2. **B.** To prevent backfire or possible damage, time the ignition distributor before attempting to start this engine.

3. **A.** Automatic transmissions rely on planetary gear sets to transfer power and multiply engine torque to the drive axle.

4. **C.** Both A and B. Transmission fluid performs multiple jobs. It transmits engine torque in the torque converter and controls valve body operation. It acts as a cooling agent to transfer heat at the transmission cooler to maintain a safe operating temperature of the transmission.

5. **C.** The spindle and knuckle assembly supports components of the braking, suspension, and steering systems.

6. **A.** The electronic ignition controls work with the fuel injection system in order to directly inject fuel into each cylinder.

7. **D.** Hybrid vehicles allow the owners to use both electric motors as well as gasoline powered engines in order to power the vehicle.

8. **C.** The intake and exhaust stroke have a valve that is open. The compression stroke has both valves closed; however, the piston is going up.

9. **C.** There are two basic hub systems used with 4WD systems: systems that lock automatically and systems that require the driver to get out and turn a knob or lever at each wheel.

10. **B.** When unlocked in 2WD, both are correct only in that the wheels still turn, but only technician B is correct because the entire drivetrain stops turning, including the front axles.

11. **D.** As long as the clutch pedal is depressed, the clutch is disengaged (not squeezed). When the pedal is released, the pressure plate moves to squeeze the clutch disc between the flywheel and pressure plate.

12. **C.** Brake drums are manufactured stamped with a discard dimension. This is the allowable wear dimension, not the allowable machining dimension.

13. **A.** By installing the dial indicator in a fixed position, the rotor is turned to indicate a runout in thousandths of an inch.

14. **C.** A scratch awl will leave a clear and thin mark on whatever material you are cutting. Using a saw blade or chisel on metal will damage the blades. A grease pen may often leave side, messy marks, and can easily smear.

15. **A.** It is a measure of the size of a nail. The term "penny" is from the old English penny system and actually stands for *pound*. The letter *d* is now used instead. Thus, nails weighing 6 pounds per 1,000 are six-penny (or 6d) nails.

16. **C.** The backsaw is used in a miter box. It is used with or across the grain, and its thin blade makes it ideal for cutting pieces that have to fit together.

17. **B.** Using a push stick to guide wood through the blades of a bench (table) saw keeps your fingers away from the rotating blades.

18. **D.** Maple is the hardest wood of those on the list. It is fairly easy to work with and resists splitting.

19. **B.** This is a box-end, or closed-end, wrench. Box-end, or closed end, are typically used in order to protect the nut or bolt being extracted or or tightened from stripping, caused by slipping wrenches.

20. **B.** Screeding is the process of using a board in a sawing motion to smooth down concrete and assure that all of the spaces and air holes are filled in.

21. **C.** A board foot is approximately 1 foot by 1 foot in area.

22. **B.** This is a continuous hinge, also known as a piano hinge. It is probably not strong enough to support the other types of doors.

23. **B.** Unlike screws, bolts are not tapered and are ideal for holding heavy-duty work together. They are fastened with a square nut or wing nut.

24. **B.** A spline is a thin piece of wood that fits into a groove cut into both parts of a joint. It is glued and gives strength to the joint.

25. **C.** It takes about 30 days (a month) to cure concrete.

Mathematics Knowledge

1. **D.** Solve for w by adding w to both sides. $w - 3 + w = 3 - w + w$, so $2w - 3 = 3$. Adding 3 to both sides gives $2w = 6$. So $\frac{2w}{2} = \frac{6}{2}$ and $w = 3$. Therefore $w^2 = 3^2 = 9$.

2. **C.** The least common denominator of 96 and 12 is 96, so $\frac{24}{96} - \frac{8}{12} = \frac{24}{96} - \frac{64}{96} = \frac{-40}{96} = -\frac{5}{12}$.

3. **A.** $\frac{6m - 2}{2}$, so $3m - 1 = -4$. Solve for m by adding 1 to both sides. $3m - 1 + 1 = -4 + 1$ and $3m = -3$. Dividing both sides by 3 gives $m = -1$.

4. **B.**

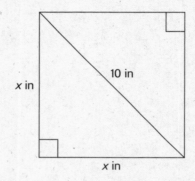

Let x represent a side of the square. The area of the square is x^2. To find the value of x^2, use the Pythagorean theorem. $x^2 + x^2 = 10^2$, so $2x^2 = 100$ and $x^2 = \frac{100}{2}$ or 50.

5. **C.** There are 120 minutes in 2 hours. Setting up a proportion yields $\frac{20 \text{ miles}}{30 \text{ minutes}} = \frac{x \text{ miles}}{120 \text{ minutes}}$. Cross multiplying results in $30x = 20 \times 120$ or $30x = 2,400$. Dividing both sides by 30 gives $x = \frac{30}{2,400} = 80$ miles.

6. **B.** $\frac{15\sqrt{3}}{\sqrt{5}} = \frac{15\sqrt{3}}{\sqrt{5}} \cdot \frac{\sqrt{5}}{\sqrt{5}} = \frac{15\sqrt{15}}{5} = 3\sqrt{15}$

7. **D.** The volume of each cube is $4 \times 4 \times 4 = 64$ in³. The volume of the crate, in inches, is $(3 \times 12) \times (2 \times 12) \times (2 \times 12) = 20,736$ in³. The number of blocks that can fit in the crate is $\frac{20,736}{64} = 324$.

8. **C.** If $x = -3$ and $y = 2$, then $x^2y = (-3)^2 (2) = sbx^2y = (-3)^2(2) = (9)(2) = 18$.

9. **B.** $0.00525 \div 0.01 = \frac{0.00525}{0.01} = 0.525$

10. **C.** $\frac{3}{4} \div \frac{4}{3} = \frac{3}{4} \times \frac{3}{4} = \frac{9}{16}$

11. **B.** The area of the circle is $\pi r^2 = 121\pi$. So $r^2 = 121$ and $r = 11$. The radius represents half the diagonal of the square, so the diagonal is 22 units long. If x represents the length of a side of the square, then x^2 is the area of the square. Using the Pythagorean theorem, $x^2 + x^2 = 22^2$ and $2x^2 = 484$. Therefore $x^2 = \frac{484}{2} = 242$.

12. **D.** $(3x^2 + 2x - 5) - (2x^2 - 5) + (4x - 7) = 3x^2 + 2x - 5 - 2x^2 + 5 + 4x - 7 = 3x^2 - 2x^2 + 2x + 4x - 5 + 5 - 7 = x^2 + 6x - 7$

13. **C.** $\frac{1}{4}$ of the total cars, t, sold are luxury. Luxury cars sold = 360, so $\frac{1}{4}t = 360$ and $t = 360 \times 4 = 1,440$ total cars sold.

14. **D.** The sum of all angles in a triangle equals 180°. So $(3x - 20)° + x° + (2x - 10)° = 180°$.

$3x + x + 2x - 20 - 10 = 180$ and $6x - 30 = 180$. Then $6x = 210$ and $x = \frac{210}{6} = 35$.

Therefore, $\angle A$ is $3(35) - 20$ or 85°.

15. C. $(3 - 4x)(3 + 4x) = 9 + 12x - 12x - 16x^2 = 9 - 16x^2$.

16. D. $(2.5)^4 = 2.5 \times 2.5 \times 2.5 \times 2.5 = 39.0625$. Rounded to the nearest tenth, it's 39.1.

17. D. Let the radius of the smaller circle = 1. Then the radius of the larger circle is 4. The shaded region is found by subtracting the area of the smaller circle from the area of the larger circle. The area of the smaller circle is $\pi(1)^2$ or π. The area of the larger circle is $\pi(4)^2$ or 16π. The shaded region is $16\pi - \pi$ or 15π. The percent of the whole figure that is shaded is $\frac{15\pi}{16\pi} = 0.9375 = 93\frac{3}{4}\%$.

18. D. Factors of 8 are $2 \times 2 \times 2$; factors of 12 are $2 \times 2 \times 3$; factors of 20 are $2 \times 2 \times 5$. The least common multiple of 8, 12, and 20 is $2 \times 2 \times 2 \times 3 \times 5$ or 120.

19. A. $(5a^3bc^2)(-3a^2c) = 5 \cdot -3 \cdot a^{3+2}bc^{2+1} = -15a^5bc^3$

20. C. $\frac{x^2 - 25}{5 - x} = \frac{(x+5)(x-5)}{5-x} = \frac{(x+5)(x-5)}{-(x-5)} = \frac{(x+5)}{-1} = -(x+5)$

21. A. The equation of a line with a slope of $-\frac{3}{2}$ and a y-intercept of -2 is $y = -\frac{3}{2}x - 2$. To find the value of x in the point $(x, 1)$, substitute 1 for y and solve the equation for x. Then $1 = -\frac{3}{2}x - 2$, which you can rewrite as $3 = -\frac{3}{2}x$. So $(3)\left(-\frac{2}{3}\right) = \left(-\frac{2}{3}\right)\left(-\frac{3}{2}x\right)$ and $x = -\frac{6}{3}$ or -2.

22. C. The probability of flipping one head is $\frac{1}{2}$. The probability of flipping three heads in a row is $\frac{1}{2} \times \frac{1}{2} \times \frac{1}{2}$ or $\frac{1}{8}$.

23. C. If $0.08z = 6.4$ then $\frac{0.08z}{0.08} = \frac{6.4}{0.08}$. Moving the decimal two places to the right in both the numerator and denominator gives $z = \frac{640}{8} = 80$.

24. C.

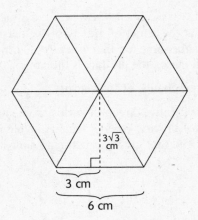

A regular hexagon is made up of six equilateral triangles. Find the area of one equilateral triangle and multiply that by 6 to find the area of the hexagon. The height, or altitude, of a triangle can be found by the Pythagorean theorem. The right triangle formed by the altitude has a hypotenuse of 6 and a shorter leg of $\frac{6}{2}$ or 3. So $3^2 + h^2 = 6^2$, so $9 + h^2 = 36$ and $h^2 = 27$. Therefore, $h = \sqrt{27} = 3\sqrt{3}$. The area of one equilateral triangle is $\frac{1}{2}bh = \frac{1}{2} \cdot 6 \cdot 3\sqrt{3} = 9\sqrt{3}$, and the area of the hexagon is $6 \times 9\sqrt{3} = 54\sqrt{3}$.

25. D. Let w represent the games won and l represent the games lost. Then $w = 3 \times l = 3l$. The total number of games played is $w + l = 24$. Substituting $3l$ in for w yields $3l + l = 24$ or $4l = 24$. The number of losses is $\frac{24}{4} = 6$, and the number of wins is $24 - 6 = 18$.

Mechanical Comprehension

1. **D.** As the person moves, his or her mass moves so that the center of mass moves also.

2. **B.** All the path analysis applies to a point mass or mass considered to be concentrated at one point, called the *center of mass*.

3. **B.** This is a consequence of Newton's third law of motion.

4. **D.** Mass is independent of gravity, while weight is proportional to the acceleration of gravity, which decreases with height or distance away from the center of the Earth.

5. **D.** The distance a mass travels in free fall is proportional to the square of the time. Because 3 seconds is 3 times more than 1 second, the distance is 9 times greater, $9 \times 5 = 45$ meters.

6. **A.** Any change in momentum or kinetic energy following a collision would mean inelastic collision.

7. **B.** Because collision involves work, or force times distance, and distance is velocity times time, the bumper offers a greater collision distance and hence greater collision time for the damage to take place.

8. **B.** Work is the product of force × distance, which is the area under the curve for the range in question.

9. **A.** This relationship is based on the motion of the mass attached to a spring. When the mass is displaced a certain distance, x, a force, F, in combination with the spring constant, k, will attempt to return the mass (and spring) to its original position. As it does so it is accelerated to that position. The more the mass is displaced, the greater the restoring force acting on it and the greater the acceleration. But because the mass has gained momentum, it moves past the original position with the restoring force slowing it down until it reaches zero velocity. At that point the mass will attempt to return to its resting position. This motion will continue indefinitely in the absence of friction.

10. **A.** Each rotation of the seconds hand amounts to 2π radians over 60 seconds. Hence, the angular velocity is $\frac{2\pi}{60}$ or 0.105.

11. **B.** The fulcrum must be placed at the center of gravity of the masses, which is the place where the product of the mass times the distance is the same for all masses. At 20 centimeters from the 12-kilogram mass (60 centimeters from the 4-kilogram mass), the product is the same: $20 \times 12 = 60 \times 4$.

12. **D.** Acceleration is the time rate of change of the velocity.

13. **C.** Let's assume that "up" is the positive direction in this problem. The instant the ball leaves the bat it is being slowed down by the force of gravity. When it reaches its highest point its velocity is zero. Knowing its initial velocity, its final velocity, and that gravity is acting to slow it down at the rate of 9.8 m/s², the formula $v_f = v_i + at$ may be used:

    0 m/s = 46.8 m/s − 9.8t

    $$\frac{9.8t}{9.8} = \frac{46.8}{9.8}$$

    $t = 4.78\ s$

14. **C.** $\dfrac{(8 - 24 + 48)}{160} = 0.2$

15. **C.** Because $\omega_f = \omega_i + \alpha t$, where ω_f and ω_i are the initial and final angular velocities respectively, we can use this formula to determine α, which is the angular acceleration. The angular acceleration is needed in the formula for torque T = Iα where I is the moment of inertia. Substituting in the first equation, $\omega_f = \omega_i + \alpha t$ yields: 6.5 = 4.0 + α (4 sec), and you obtain α = 0.625. Substituting this value into the second equation, T = Iα, yields T = 0.625 × 0.3 = 0.188 N·m.

16. **C.** The work done is equal to the kinetic energy of the ball, which is $\frac{1}{2}mv^2 = \frac{1}{2}(75)(4^2) = 600$ J.

17. **B.** For equilibrium, the clockwise and counterclockwise moments must be the same, in other words, $F_i \times 80 = F_o \times 40$ or $F_i = 30$ N and $\frac{F_o}{F_i} = \frac{60}{30} = 2$.

18. **B.** Escape velocity is actually not a velocity, but speed as there is no direction indicated. Escape velocity, v_e, is determined from the formula $v_e = \left(\frac{2GM}{r}\right)^{1/2}$

    Where G is the gravitational constant, 6.67×10^{-11} and M is the mass of the planet, and r is the radius of the planet.

    Substituting into the formula yields

    $$v_e = \frac{\left[2\left(6.67 \times 10^{-11}\right)\left(8 \times 10^{24}\right)\right]^{1/2}}{\left(5 \times 10^6\right)^{1/2}}$$

    $$v_e = \frac{\left[\left(1.334 \times 10^{-10}\right)\left(8 \times 10^{24}\right)\right]^{1/2}}{\left(5 \times 10^6\right)^{1/2}}$$

    $$v_e = \frac{\left(1.0672 \times 10^{15}\right)^{1/2}}{\left(5 \times 10^6\right)^{1/2}}$$

    $$v_e = \left(2.1344 \times 10^8\right)^{1/2}$$

    $$v_e = 14{,}609.585 \text{ m/s}$$

    At this point the answer is in m/s. The answer choices are in km/s so the above answer must be divided by 1,000 to produce 14.6 km/s.

19. **A.** The change in momentum ΔP equals the force, F, times the time increment, t. Hence, you obtain F
    $$F = \frac{40}{12} = 3.33 \text{ N}.$$

20. **B.** Due to centrifugal force, the passenger continues to move forward while the vehicle is turning to the right. As a result, she would feel herself leaning to the left side of the truck.

21. **A.** This represents an example of simple harmonic motion. The amount of time it takes for the spring to complete one complete cycle of its oscillation is called the *period* and is represented by the letter T. The following formula is used to find components of simple harmonic motion: $T = 2\pi \left[\frac{m}{k}\right]^{1/2}$ where m is the mass of the object and k is the spring constant. Substituting into the formula yields

    $3.14 = 2(3.14)\left[\frac{10}{k}\right]^{1/2}$ (the $\frac{1}{2}$ power indicates the square root)

    $$3.14 = 6.28\left[\frac{10}{k}\right]^{1/2}$$

    $$\frac{3.14}{6.28} = \frac{6.28\left[\frac{10}{k}\right]^{1/2}}{6.28}$$

    $$0.50 = \left[\frac{10}{k}\right]^{1/2}$$

    $$(0.50)^2 = \left(\left[\frac{10}{k}\right]^{1/2}\right)^2$$

    $$0.25 = \frac{10}{k}$$

    $$k = \frac{10}{0.25}$$

    $$k = 40$$

22. **C.** To answer this question, first realize the relationship $PE = KE$ exists: The 5 kg block possesses Potential Energy due to its position at the top of the 40 meter-long plane that is 10 meters above ground. In equation form: $PE = mgh$ where m is the mass, g is the force due to gravity and h is the height the object is above the ground. Substituting into the formula yields $PE = (5)\ (9.8)\ (10)$, which produces 490 joules of energy. This 490 J is set equal to KE, which is equal to $\left(\dfrac{1}{2}\right)mv^2$. Substituting in this formula yields

$$490 = \frac{1}{2}(5)v^2$$
$$490 = 2.5\ v^2$$
$$\frac{490}{2.5} = v^2$$
$$196 = v^2$$
$$v = 14 \text{ m/s}$$

In order to determine the force on the block while it is sliding, you need to know the sin of the angle of the inclined plane. Using the trigonometry function, sine equals the opposite side divided by the hypotenuse. Substituting in the formula yields

$$\sin = \frac{O}{H}$$
$$\sin = \frac{10}{40}$$
$$\sin = 0.25$$

This value is then used in the formula for Force, or $F = ma$, where m is the mass and a is the acceleration of the box due to gravity. Because the angle of the plane influences the acceleration, it needs to be included in the formula, thus: $F = \sin\ (angle)\ ma$. Substituting in the formula yields: $F = (0.25)\ (5)\ (9.8)$ producing

$$F = 12.25 \text{ N}$$

23. **D.** Because momentum is mass $\times$ velocity and acceleration is $\dfrac{\text{velocity}}{\text{time}}$, the product equals $\dfrac{(\text{mass})(\text{velocity})^2}{\text{time}}$, which is proportional to $\dfrac{\text{kinetic energy}}{\text{time}}$ or output power.

24. **C.** If there is a net force acting on the box, then there will be acceleration that contradicts the condition of constant speed.

25. **D.** Because the mass and speed of the object are constant, it is the kinetic energy that is constant.

Electronics Information

1. **D.** For the lamp to be turned on, switches (1 or 3) must be closed, and switches (2 or 4) must be closed to allow the current to flow in the circuit.

2. **C.** A wattmeter is a device used to measure electrical power. An ammeter is used to measure current. A voltmeter is used to measure a voltage difference. Electrical charge cannot be measured by a wattmeter.

3. **C.** The total resistance in the circuit can be calculated as follows:

$$\frac{1}{\frac{1}{50+50}+\frac{1}{50+50}} = 50 \ \Omega$$

4. **B.** Symbol 2 represents a variable resistor.

5. **D.** The shown signal has a DC shift of 5 volts. Its frequency is 1 Hz, and its amplitude is 5 volts.

6. **A.** Capacitance is measured in farads. Inductance is measured in henries. Resistance is measured in ohms. Diodes have identification numbers to identify them.

7. **B.** The ammeter reads the current flowing in the circuit. The current is calculated as follows:

$$I = \frac{V}{R} = \frac{10}{\frac{1}{\frac{1}{10}+\frac{1}{10}}+\frac{1}{\frac{1}{10}+\frac{1}{10}}} = 1 \ A$$

8. **C.** An audio signal is transmitted wirelessly by being carried on a high-frequency sinusoidal signal.

9. **B.** The unknown resistor value can be calculated as follows:

$$R = \frac{V}{I} = \frac{6-2}{\frac{2}{5}} = 10 \ \Omega$$

10. **C.** A diode will pass electrical current only if the voltage applied is greater than the threshold voltage.

11. **B.** The collector current in the common emitter configuration is $I_B \times \beta$, which is an amplification of the base current.

12. **B.** Electrical devices are grounded to prevent an electric shock.

13. **D.** An oscillator circuit is used to generate a high-frequency sinusoidal signal that is used as a carrier signal.

14. **A.** The power dissipated in the circuit can be calculated as follows:

$$P = \frac{V^2}{R} = \frac{5^2}{\frac{1}{\frac{1}{10}+\frac{1}{10}}} = 5 \ W$$

15. **A.** A capacitor can be used as a frequency filter. In some circuits it is used as a high-pass filter, where it allows high-frequency signals to pass and blocks lower-frequency signals. In some other circuits it is used as a low-pass filter, where it allows low-frequency signals to pass and suppresses higher-frequency signals.

16. **C.** Total capacitance of the circuit is calculated as follows:

    $0.25 \ \mu F + 0.25 \ \mu F = 0.5 \ \mu F.$

17. **B.** A square wave can be obtained from a function generator device.

18. **B.** Coils are used in electrical transformers to induce a different level of voltage.

19. **C.** Bipolar junction transistors (BJTs) can be PNP or NPN.

20. **B.** In order to reduce the total resistance of a circuit, the resistors are connected in parallel.

Assembling Objects

The answers for the Assembling Objects questions can be found in the answer key, earlier in this section.

Answer Sheet for AFQT Practice Test

(Remove this sheet and use it to mark your answers.)

CUT HERE

Arithmetic Reasoning

1 Ⓐ Ⓑ Ⓒ Ⓓ	16 Ⓐ Ⓑ Ⓒ Ⓓ
2 Ⓐ Ⓑ Ⓒ Ⓓ	17 Ⓐ Ⓑ Ⓒ Ⓓ
3 Ⓐ Ⓑ Ⓒ Ⓓ	18 Ⓐ Ⓑ Ⓒ Ⓓ
4 Ⓐ Ⓑ Ⓒ Ⓓ	19 Ⓐ Ⓑ Ⓒ Ⓓ
5 Ⓐ Ⓑ Ⓒ Ⓓ	20 Ⓐ Ⓑ Ⓒ Ⓓ
6 Ⓐ Ⓑ Ⓒ Ⓓ	21 Ⓐ Ⓑ Ⓒ Ⓓ
7 Ⓐ Ⓑ Ⓒ Ⓓ	22 Ⓐ Ⓑ Ⓒ Ⓓ
8 Ⓐ Ⓑ Ⓒ Ⓓ	23 Ⓐ Ⓑ Ⓒ Ⓓ
9 Ⓐ Ⓑ Ⓒ Ⓓ	24 Ⓐ Ⓑ Ⓒ Ⓓ
10 Ⓐ Ⓑ Ⓒ Ⓓ	25 Ⓐ Ⓑ Ⓒ Ⓓ
11 Ⓐ Ⓑ Ⓒ Ⓓ	26 Ⓐ Ⓑ Ⓒ Ⓓ
12 Ⓐ Ⓑ Ⓒ Ⓓ	27 Ⓐ Ⓑ Ⓒ Ⓓ
13 Ⓐ Ⓑ Ⓒ Ⓓ	28 Ⓐ Ⓑ Ⓒ Ⓓ
14 Ⓐ Ⓑ Ⓒ Ⓓ	29 Ⓐ Ⓑ Ⓒ Ⓓ
15 Ⓐ Ⓑ Ⓒ Ⓓ	30 Ⓐ Ⓑ Ⓒ Ⓓ

Word Knowledge

1 Ⓐ Ⓑ Ⓒ Ⓓ	21 Ⓐ Ⓑ Ⓒ Ⓓ
2 Ⓐ Ⓑ Ⓒ Ⓓ	22 Ⓐ Ⓑ Ⓒ Ⓓ
3 Ⓐ Ⓑ Ⓒ Ⓓ	23 Ⓐ Ⓑ Ⓒ Ⓓ
4 Ⓐ Ⓑ Ⓒ Ⓓ	24 Ⓐ Ⓑ Ⓒ Ⓓ
5 Ⓐ Ⓑ Ⓒ Ⓓ	25 Ⓐ Ⓑ Ⓒ Ⓓ
6 Ⓐ Ⓑ Ⓒ Ⓓ	26 Ⓐ Ⓑ Ⓒ Ⓓ
7 Ⓐ Ⓑ Ⓒ Ⓓ	27 Ⓐ Ⓑ Ⓒ Ⓓ
8 Ⓐ Ⓑ Ⓒ Ⓓ	28 Ⓐ Ⓑ Ⓒ Ⓓ
9 Ⓐ Ⓑ Ⓒ Ⓓ	29 Ⓐ Ⓑ Ⓒ Ⓓ
10 Ⓐ Ⓑ Ⓒ Ⓓ	30 Ⓐ Ⓑ Ⓒ Ⓓ
11 Ⓐ Ⓑ Ⓒ Ⓓ	31 Ⓐ Ⓑ Ⓒ Ⓓ
12 Ⓐ Ⓑ Ⓒ Ⓓ	32 Ⓐ Ⓑ Ⓒ Ⓓ
13 Ⓐ Ⓑ Ⓒ Ⓓ	33 Ⓐ Ⓑ Ⓒ Ⓓ
14 Ⓐ Ⓑ Ⓒ Ⓓ	34 Ⓐ Ⓑ Ⓒ Ⓓ
15 Ⓐ Ⓑ Ⓒ Ⓓ	35 Ⓐ Ⓑ Ⓒ Ⓓ
16 Ⓐ Ⓑ Ⓒ Ⓓ	
17 Ⓐ Ⓑ Ⓒ Ⓓ	
18 Ⓐ Ⓑ Ⓒ Ⓓ	
19 Ⓐ Ⓑ Ⓒ Ⓓ	
20 Ⓐ Ⓑ Ⓒ Ⓓ	

Paragraph Comprehension

1 Ⓐ Ⓑ Ⓒ Ⓓ
2 Ⓐ Ⓑ Ⓒ Ⓓ
3 Ⓐ Ⓑ Ⓒ Ⓓ
4 Ⓐ Ⓑ Ⓒ Ⓓ
5 Ⓐ Ⓑ Ⓒ Ⓓ
6 Ⓐ Ⓑ Ⓒ Ⓓ
7 Ⓐ Ⓑ Ⓒ Ⓓ
8 Ⓐ Ⓑ Ⓒ Ⓓ
9 Ⓐ Ⓑ Ⓒ Ⓓ
10 Ⓐ Ⓑ Ⓒ Ⓓ
11 Ⓐ Ⓑ Ⓒ Ⓓ
12 Ⓐ Ⓑ Ⓒ Ⓓ
13 Ⓐ Ⓑ Ⓒ Ⓓ
14 Ⓐ Ⓑ Ⓒ Ⓓ
15 Ⓐ Ⓑ Ⓒ Ⓓ

Mathematics Knowledge

1 Ⓐ Ⓑ Ⓒ Ⓓ	16 Ⓐ Ⓑ Ⓒ Ⓓ
2 Ⓐ Ⓑ Ⓒ Ⓓ	17 Ⓐ Ⓑ Ⓒ Ⓓ
3 Ⓐ Ⓑ Ⓒ Ⓓ	18 Ⓐ Ⓑ Ⓒ Ⓓ
4 Ⓐ Ⓑ Ⓒ Ⓓ	19 Ⓐ Ⓑ Ⓒ Ⓓ
5 Ⓐ Ⓑ Ⓒ Ⓓ	20 Ⓐ Ⓑ Ⓒ Ⓓ
6 Ⓐ Ⓑ Ⓒ Ⓓ	21 Ⓐ Ⓑ Ⓒ Ⓓ
7 Ⓐ Ⓑ Ⓒ Ⓓ	22 Ⓐ Ⓑ Ⓒ Ⓓ
8 Ⓐ Ⓑ Ⓒ Ⓓ	23 Ⓐ Ⓑ Ⓒ Ⓓ
9 Ⓐ Ⓑ Ⓒ Ⓓ	24 Ⓐ Ⓑ Ⓒ Ⓓ
10 Ⓐ Ⓑ Ⓒ Ⓓ	25 Ⓐ Ⓑ Ⓒ Ⓓ
11 Ⓐ Ⓑ Ⓒ Ⓓ	
12 Ⓐ Ⓑ Ⓒ Ⓓ	
13 Ⓐ Ⓑ Ⓒ Ⓓ	
14 Ⓐ Ⓑ Ⓒ Ⓓ	
15 Ⓐ Ⓑ Ⓒ Ⓓ	

Introduction to the AFQT Practice Test

As we discussed earlier in this book, the purpose of the AFQT is to determine your eligibility for all branches of the military.

The Armed Forces Qualifying Test (AFQT) is the most important part of the entire ASVAB exam, regardless of which version you sit for. This is the "make or break" section because it will determine whether you are accepted into the military or not. The score for this portion of the ASVAB is derived from your performance on four parts of the overall ASVAB: Word Knowledge, Paragraph Comprehension, Arithmetic Reasoning, and Mathematics Knowledge. In actuality, the two math sections are scored once, and the scores of both the Word Knowledge and the Paragraph Comprehension sections are scored twice (Arithmetic + Mathematics) + 2(Words + Paragraphs). Essentially there will be six scores that will be tallied.

Thus, it's imperative that you focus on these four tests above all. Your percentile score on this portion of the test will determine whether you are eligible or not for the Armed Forces. *If you score lower than the 30th percentile, it is unlikely that you will be accepted for military training.* If you hold a GED diploma, you must score at least 50 percent in order to be eligible.

The following AFQT Practice Test is just that—an additional test to help reinforce your understanding of the subjects and to give you even more practice on these four essential parts of the ASVAB.

Try to take this practice test under actual conditions adhering to the time limits provided for each test section. When you've completed the entire exam, use the Answer Key and the AFQT Answers and Explanations section to check your answers.

Arithmetic Reasoning

Time: 36 Minutes

30 Questions

Directions: Each of the following questions will test your knowledge about basic arithmetic. Read the question and select the choice that best answers the question. Indicate that letter on your answer sheet.

1. It took Mathew 30 minutes to run $1\frac{1}{2}$ miles to his friend's house. What was Mathew's speed?

   A. 1 mile/hour
   B. 2 miles/hour
   C. 3 miles/hour
   D. 4 miles/hour

2. A 20-ft tall tree casts a shadow that is 3 ft long. A nearby lamp post casts a shadow that is 1 ft long. How tall is the lamp post?

   A. $6\frac{2}{3}$ ft
   B. 7 ft
   C. 10 ft
   D. $10\frac{1}{3}$ ft

3. Diego spent 20 minutes having breakfast, after which he started getting ready for work: He took a 10-minute shower, got dressed in 5 minutes and spent the last 3 minutes making sure he had all his equipment. How long did it take Diego to get ready for work?

   A. 28 minutes
   B. 20 minutes
   C. 18 minutes
   D. 15 minutes

4. A cake recipe calls for 5 tablespoons of white sugar and brown sugar combined. If $\frac{7}{8}$ of this mixture is white sugar, how many tablespoons of brown sugar are needed?

   A. $\frac{5}{8}$ tablespoons
   B. $3\frac{1}{8}$ tablespoons
   C. 4 tablespoons
   D. $4\frac{3}{8}$ tablespoons

5. Minju buys 3 identical pairs of boots for $741.90. Shumin wants to buy two pairs herself. How much does she have to pay?

   A. $494.60
   B. $490.60
   C. $247.30
   D. $241.30

6. Marco is 150 miles from Josh and 253 miles from Shanice. How much farther is Marco from Shanice than from Josh?

   A. 100 miles
   B. 101 miles
   C. 102 miles
   D. 103 miles

7. Mike buys an anniversary gift for $270, on sale from $300. What percent was the discount?

   A. 5%
   B. 10%
   C. 27%
   D. 30%

8. A triangular garden is to be built inside a circular area with radius 3 ft such that the corners of the triangle all touch the circle, the legs of the triangle are equal in size, and its hypotenuse passes through the center of the circle. How much area will not be gardened?

   A. $9\pi - 9$
   B. $9 - 9\pi$
   C. $9 - \pi$
   D. π

9. A blueprint has a scale of 5 ft per every $\frac{1}{2}$ in. If the lot shown is $5\frac{1}{2}$ in × 4 in, what is its actual area?

   A. 2,200 ft²
   B. 2,000 ft²
   C. 1,998 ft²
   D. 1,900 ft²

GO ON TO THE NEXT PAGE

10. Laura fills up her 60-gallon barrel of water and in the first day drinks 2 gallons. The barrel was defective and leaked $\frac{1}{3}$ of a gallon out every day. How many gallons of water did she have left ten days after she filled it up?

    A. 20 gallons
    B. 50 gallons
    C. $55\frac{1}{3}$ gallons
    D. $54\frac{2}{3}$ gallons

11. A dance starts at 7:45 p.m. If it is now 3:20 p.m., how much time is left until the dance starts?

    A. 4 hours and 15 minutes
    B. 4 hours and 20 minutes
    C. 4 hours and 25 minutes
    D. 4 hours and 30 minutes

12. How many blocks 3 in × 2 in × 2 in fit in box that is 4 ft × 3 ft × 2 ft?

    A. 3,456
    B. 3,546
    C. 3,465
    D. 3,454

13. Sam buys two books at $3.35 each, and a cup of coffee at $2.29. How much change will he get back if he paid with a 10 dollar bill?

    A. $1
    B. $1.01
    C. $2.05
    D. $3

14. There are 900 students in a school. If 40% come to school by car, 30% walk, and 30% take the bus, how many students take the bus?

    A. 250
    B. 270
    C. 360
    D. 370

15. Skyler read ten novels and twice as many mysteries. If he reads three times as many biographies as mysteries, how many biographies does he read?

    A. 30
    B. 60
    C. 70
    D. 90

16. A box with base measuring 5 ft by 3 ft has a volume of 60 ft³. Find its surface area.

    A. 90 ft²
    B. 91 ft²
    C. 94 ft²
    D. 95 ft²

17. Fabian eats $\frac{1}{7}$ of his birthday cake and shares the rest equally among his six friends. Approximately, what percentage of the cake does each of his friends eat?

    A. 1.4%
    B. 11.5%
    C. 14.3%
    D. 14.6%

18. Luke's favorite book is 543 pages, while Melissa's book is 297 pages. How many more pages are in Luke's book than in Melissa's?

    A. 346
    B. 264
    C. 246
    D. 146

19. Lionel made $6.15 by bringing all his recycled bottles to the supermarket. If he made 5 cents per bottle, how many bottles did he have?

    A. 100
    B. 103
    C. 113
    D. 123

20. A batch of chocolate-chip cookies requires 2 cups of chocolate chips and 4 cups of flour. If you have 5 cups of chocolate chips and 10 cups of flour, how many complete batches of cookies can you make?

    A. 2 batches
    B. 3 batches
    C. 4 batches
    D. 5 batches

21. Find the value of x in the following figure:

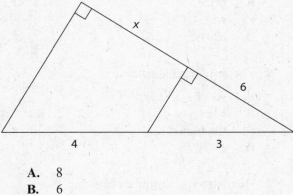

    A. 8
    B. 6
    C. 4
    D. 3

22. A 3.5 m log is cut into 0.7 m pieces. How many pieces will there be?

    A. 5
    B. 6
    C. 7
    D. 8

23. Ramsadeen has 15 quarters, 31 dimes, and 9 nickels. How much money does he have?

    A. $5.00
    B. $5.10
    C. $7.30
    D. $13.67

24. Stacy and Rob spent $54 on dinner, including the tip. If without the tip it would've cost them only $45, what percentage of the bill did they leave for the tip?

    A. 20%
    B. 22%
    C. 25%
    D. 28%

25. A right triangle has an area of 40 sq ft. If one leg is 2 ft longer than the other leg, what is size of the shorter leg?

    A. 7 ft
    B. 8 ft
    C. 10 ft
    D. 15 ft

26. If $13 in interest is earned at a $3\frac{1}{4}$% interest rate, what was the amount of the principal?

    A. $1,000
    B. $655
    C. $566
    D. $400

27. Josephina's math grades are 100, 96, 76, 88, and 55. The average of her English grades is 90. By how many points is her English average higher than her math average?

    A. 7
    B. 8
    C. 9
    D. 10

28. Christopher reads at a rate of three pages every 5 minutes. If his book is 450 pages long, how long will it take him to read it?

    A. 12 hours
    B. 12 hours and 30 minutes
    C. 15 hours
    D. 15 hours and 30 minutes

29. Sharon buys four books for $9.50 each using a $5 gift card and some of her own money. How much of her own money did she spend on the books?

    A. $30
    B. $32.55
    C. $33
    D. $35

30. Kim has 10 quarters, three times as many dimes as quarters, and half as many nickels as dimes. How much money does she have in total?

    A. $6.25
    B. $6
    C. $5.95
    D. $5.30

Word Knowledge

Time: 11 minutes

35 questions

Directions: This portion of the exam will test your knowledge of the meaning of words. Each question has an underlined word. Decide which of the four choices most nearly means the same as the underlined word; then indicate that letter on your answer sheet.

1. To <u>abet</u> means to
   A. wager.
   B. divan.
   C. assist.
   D. promote.

2. The word <u>abash</u> most nearly means
   A. smash.
   B. party.
   C. sound.
   D. embarrass.

3. <u>Ablution</u> means
   A. wash.
   B. solvent.
   C. confess.
   D. hate.

4. To <u>abrogate</u> means to
   A. dismiss.
   B. cancel.
   C. close.
   D. reveal.

5. When one is <u>vehement</u> one is
   A. placid.
   B. fierce.
   C. wrong.
   D. terse.

6. <u>Temerity</u> means
   A. timidity.
   B. boldness.
   C. timely.
   D. happiness.

7. To <u>atrophy</u> is to
   A. grow.
   B. prize.
   C. win.
   D. decay.

8. The word <u>oscillate</u> means
   A. steady.
   B. wind.
   C. fluctuate.
   D. open.

9. He tried to <u>abstain</u> from smoking.
   A. mar.
   B. refrain from.
   C. lie.
   D. link.

10. <u>Intransigent</u> means
    A. yielding.
    B. lucky.
    C. lasting.
    D. stubborn.

11. The word <u>attest</u> means to
    A. affirm.
    B. examine.
    C. utter.
    D. value.

12. To <u>allocate</u> means to
    A. complete.
    B. express.
    C. inspire.
    D. distribute.

13. <u>Abominate</u> means

    A. loathe.
    B. like.
    C. yield.
    D. smell.

14. To <u>thwart</u> is to

    A. promote.
    B. block.
    C. handle.
    D. spawn.

15. To obtain <u>parity</u> means

    A. happiness.
    B. equality.
    C. openness.
    D. wealth.

16. To <u>avert</u> means to

    A. cause.
    B. prevent.
    C. promote.
    D. loathe.

17. The animals seemed <u>torpid</u>.

    A. hot
    B. dangerous
    C. vigorous
    D. listless

18. To <u>accede</u> means

    A. agree.
    B. leave.
    C. retreat.
    D. flee.

19. To <u>obfuscate</u> means to

    A. clarify.
    B. muddle.
    C. explain.
    D. praise.

20. <u>Autonomous</u> means

    A. tied.
    B. unknown.
    C. sound.
    D. independent.

21. Their visit was <u>transitory</u>.

    A. fast
    B. loud
    C. permanent
    D. temporary

22. He seemed <u>urbane</u>.

    A. bucolic
    B. urban
    C. suave
    D. helpful

23. The word <u>balm</u> means

    A. hard.
    B. easy.
    C. calming.
    D. rising.

24. The word <u>accolade</u> most nearly means

    A. burden.
    B. award.
    C. drink.
    D. money.

25. The sky was <u>azure</u>.

    A. clean
    B. clear
    C. blue
    D. stormy

26. To <u>rue</u> is to

    A. regret.
    B. smile.
    C. cook.
    D. wander.

GO ON TO THE NEXT PAGE

27. A <u>bauble</u> is a

    A. bath.
    B. soap.
    C. trinket.
    D. package.

28. He was <u>resolute</u> about the move.

    A. firm
    B. undecided
    C. perceptive
    D. excited

29. <u>Scathing</u> most nearly means

    A. hot.
    B. bitter.
    C. better.
    D. loud.

30. To <u>berate</u> is to

    A. applaud.
    B. scold.
    C. weep.
    D. worry.

31. <u>Trepidation</u> most nearly means

    A. courage.
    B. fear.
    C. boldness.
    D. ease.

32. A <u>renegade</u> is a

    A. runner.
    B. teacher.
    C. traitor.
    D. sponsor.

33. <u>Umbrage</u> most nearly means

    A. trust.
    B. shady.
    C. shadowed.
    D. offense.

34. The word <u>civil</u> means

    A. clandestine.
    B. polite.
    C. bored.
    D. unhappy.

35. The cough was <u>chronic</u>.

    A. brief
    B. illness
    C. daily
    D. stupid

STOP

Paragraph Comprehension

Time: 13 minutes

15 Questions

Directions: This is a test of reading comprehension. Read each paragraph and then select the choice below that best answers that question. Indicate that letter on your answer sheet.

1. After a five-year journey as a naturalist aboard the *HMS Beagle,* Charles Darwin had seen signs that plant and animal species were not permanent as had long been held to be true. It was as if he had an inkling of the upheavals to come.

   In this context, the word *inkling* means

   A. contradiction.
   B. resolution.
   C. theory.
   D. feeling.

2. The federal government began subsidizing wolf extermination on federal lands in 1915, and the last known wolf den in Yellowstone was destroyed in 1923. By the 1940s, the animals were extinct in the northern Rocky Mountains—shot, trapped, or poisoned.

   The best title for this section is

   A. The Danger of Wolves in Nature.
   B. How to Kill Wolves More Effectively.
   C. Government's Role in Wolf Extermination.
   D. Nature in the Rocky Mountain Area.

3. Not long ago, newspapers and magazines reported that, by the end of the century, redheads will be extinct. Gone. Kaput. The world will be frightfully ordinary without redheads in the world of 2150.

   In this context, the word *kaput* means

   A. nonexistent.
   B. unimportant.
   C. abundant.
   D. dangerous.

4. Americans spent about $107 million on *Ginkgo biloba* supplements in 2007, according to the *Nutrition Business Journal.* They're probably hoping to enhance memory and increase mental focus, claims often made for ginkgo. The supplement is available in pills and teas and is commonly used in an effort to help prevent Alzheimer's disease and other forms of dementia.

   The following fact is not mentioned in this selection:

   A. People spend millions of dollars on ginkgo.
   B. Ginkgo is an effective medical treatment.
   C. The supplement is available in pills and teas.
   D. People are trying to prevent Alzheimer's disease.

5. To measure fuel economy for scooters in city driving conditions, the same course that was used for cars was used. Also, a steady cruising speed test to mimic the village or suburban speeds was employed.

   In this context, the word *mimic* means

   A. ignore.
   B. mock.
   C. imitate.
   D. exaggerate.

6. Gas flares and rig lights illuminate the night sky in the Savuiskoye oil field. Russia is now the world's top producer of crude oil. Some 70 percent of its reserves are found in western Siberia. Once extracted, most oil is shipped to foreign consumers.

   The best title for this section is

   A. Oil and Global Warming.
   B. Oil: A Disappearing Resource.
   C. Alternative Energy Sources.
   D. Oil Production in Russia.

GO ON TO THE NEXT PAGE

7. Mollusks' tiny eyes see little more than light and dark. Instead, the animals smell, taste, and feel their world using head-mounted sensory appendages and oral tentacles. Chemical signals help them track their food.

Appendages are

A. additional attachments.
B. internal organs.
C. severed limbs.
D. brain cells.

8. The most common causes of abdominal pain are generally the least serious, even though they can be temporarily disabling. Upper abdominal pain is often due to simple gastritis, or stomach inflammation. A common cause is the overuse of aspirin or another anti-inflammatory medication like ibuprofen.

The following fact is not mentioned in this selection:

A. A common cause of stomach pain is aspirin.
B. Gastritis can cause stomach pain.
C. The least common cause of stomach pain is cancer.
D. Ibuprofen can cause stomach discomfort.

9. If you are among the 60 percent of Americans who use a tax preparer to fill out your annual return, tens of thousands of them are vying for your business. There are many tax preparers in the market offering their services, whether they work for a franchise or independently.

In this context, the word *vying* means

A. competing.
B. lying.
C. exaggerating.
D. searching.

10. Negotiating for a new car can strike fear into the hearts of even the most rugged individuals. It's not surprising. Car dealers and manufacturers have arranged pricing in a manner designed to daze and confuse the consumer. By understanding the tricks of the trade, consumers can save hundreds of dollars.

The best title for this selection is

A. How to Sell a Car.
B. Car Sales Drop Drastically.
C. Saving Money Buying a Car.
D. Government Regulation of Car Sales.

11. The way Americans get their movies at home is changing. DVD sales are down. The walk-in movie rental outlets are being edged out. DVDs are increasingly being rented by mail through subscription plans or rented on demand from providers.

The following fact is not mentioned in this selection:

A. DVD rentals are down in stores.
B. Renting movies for home is changing.
C. Mail rentals have increased.
D. Ticket sales are down at theaters.

12. The Inca Empire was formed during the reign of Pachacutec Yupanqui, who conquered and united other Amerindian nations in the fifteenth century. The united tribes of Andean farmers called themselves the "Children of the Sun." They had a knowledge of textiles, irrigation, and building techniques to form an advanced and structured society.

The best title for this section is

A. Tourism in the Andes.
B. Origins of the Inca Empire.
C. Farming in South America.
D. Children and Sun Protection.

13. Cell phones, CD players, iPods, fast food, and mascara are some of the potentially dangerous items to use when behind the wheel of a car. The distraction they can cause can result in a car accident that harms the driver and others on the road, especially teens. Now, text messaging has been added to the activities that hamper concentration of young and old drivers alike.

In this context, the word *potentially* means

A. absolutely.
B. always.
C. possibly.
D. never.

14. Florida Caverns State Park is one of the few state parks in the U.S. with dry (air filled) caves and is the only Florida state park to offer cave tours to the public. The cave has dazzling formations of limestone stalactites, stalagmites, soda straws, flowstones, and draperies. Native Americans used the caverns for shelter for thousands of years.

The following fact is not mentioned in this selection:

A. Native Americans used caverns for shelter.
B. Caves can be dangerous.
C. The public can tour caves.
D. Stone formations are plentiful.

15. Reptile World is a working farm that provides venom for use in medicine and herpetological research worldwide. You can watch while staff milk venomous snakes to harvest their valuable venom. The snake is held behind its head, and the firmness of the grip usually brings its fangs to the fore. The snake is induced to bite through the covering on the collecting vial.

In this context, the word *induced* means

A. influenced.
B. prevented.
C. requested.
D. allowed.

423

Mathematics Knowledge

Time: 24 Minutes
25 Questions

1. If $2z + 3 = z + 1$, then the value of z^3 is
   A. −8.
   B. 8.
   C. 2.
   D. −2.

2. $\frac{3}{56} - \frac{5}{14} =$
   A. $-\frac{2}{42}$
   B. $\frac{2}{42}$
   C. $\frac{17}{56}$
   D. $-\frac{17}{56}$

3. If $10y + 6$ is divided by 2, the result is 8. What is the value of y?
   A. 1
   B. −1
   C. 2
   D. −2

4. The area of a square with a 3-inch diagonal is
   A. $\frac{9}{2}$.
   B. 6.
   C. $\sqrt{3}$.
   D. $\sqrt{6}$.

5. A motorcycle travels 15 km in 20 minutes. At this rate, how many kilometers will it travel in 2 hours?
   A. 30 km
   B. 60 km
   C. 90 km
   D. 120 km

6. Simplify completely: $\frac{3\sqrt{2}}{\sqrt{6}}$
   A. 1
   B. $3\sqrt{3}$
   C. 3
   D. $\sqrt{3}$

7. How many cubes with an edge of 6 in fit into a box with dimensions 3 ft × 4 ft × 5 ft?
   A. 60 cubes
   B. 70 cubes
   C. 400 cubes
   D. 480 cubes

8. If $a = -6$ and $b = 2$, evaluate $3a^2b^3$.
   A. −864
   B. 864
   C. 144
   D. −144

9. $1.02315 + 0.0098 =$
   A. 1.03295
   B. 0.03295
   C. 1.02295
   D. 0.02295

10. $\frac{3}{5} \div \frac{2}{5} =$
    A. $\frac{3}{2}$
    B. $\frac{2}{3}$
    C. $\frac{5}{3}$
    D. $\frac{2}{5}$

11. In the figure below, the area of the square is 100 ft². Find the area of the circle.

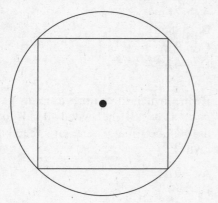

   A. $10\sqrt{2}\pi$ ft²
   B. 100π ft²
   C. 50π ft²
   D. 25π ft²

12. Simplify: $(2 - 3x) + (4x^2 - 4x + 7) - (3x - 2)$

   A. $4x^2 - 10x + 11$
   B. $4x^2 - 10x + 7$
   C. $4x^2 + 10x + 11$
   D. $4x^2 - 10x - 11$

13. In a school, one-third of the budget is used for teachers' salaries. If the total of all the teachers salaries is $6,660,000, how big, to the nearest million, is the school's budget?

   A. $2,000,000
   B. $10,000,000
   C. $13,000,000
   D. $20,000,000

14. In a triangle, m∠A = 5w + 9, m∠B = 50, and m∠C = 1 + w. Find the measure of the obtuse angle.

   A.   109
   B.   159
   C.   160
   D.   161

15. What is the product of $(1 - 7x)$ and $(3 + 5x)$?

   A. $35x^2 - 16x + 3$
   B. $-35x^2 - 16x + 3$
   C. $-35x^2 - 16x - 3$
   D. $35x^2 - 16x - 3$

16. Round $(1.7)^3$ to the nearest hundredth.

   A.   4.93
   B.   4.91
   C.   4.19
   D.   4.13

17. The radius of a larger circle is 3 times the radius of a smaller circle. How many times larger is the area of the larger circle than the area of the smaller circle?

   A.   3 times
   B.   6 times
   C.   9 times
   D.   12 times

18. The greatest common factor of 24, 18, and 12 is

   A.   6.
   B.   12.
   C.   18.
   D.   48.

19. The product of $(-2x^2y^3)$ and $(3xy^4z)$ is

   A. $6x^3y^7z$.
   B. $-6x^3y^7z$.
   C. $-6x^2y^{12}z$.
   D. $6x^2y^{12}z$.

20. Simplify completely: $\dfrac{16 - x^2}{x - 4}$

   A. $x - 4$
   B. $x + 4$
   C. $-(x + 4)$
   D. $-(x - 4)$

21. Name one point on the line $2x + 3y = -5$.

   A.   (2, 3)
   B.   (2, -5)
   C.   (2, -3)
   D.   (2, 5)

GO ON TO THE NEXT PAGE

22. When rolling a fair, six-sided die three times, what is the probability of getting an even number each time?

    A. $\frac{1}{8}$

    B. $\frac{1}{6}$

    C. $\frac{3}{6}$

    D. $\frac{3}{8}$

23. If $0.04\theta = 5$, then $\theta =$

    A. 250.
    B. 125.
    C. 100.
    D. 90.

24. Find the area of a rhombus with diagonals of 3 in and 6 in.

    A. 24 in²
    B. 18 in²
    C. 9 in²
    D. 6 in²

25. Renne invited three times as many girls to his party as boys. If he invited 40 kids to his party in total, how many more girls than boys did he invite?

    A. 3
    B. 10
    C. 20
    D. 40

Answer Key for AFQT Test

Arithmetic Reasoning

1. C		16. C	
2. A		17. C	
3. C		18. C	
4. A		19. D	
5. A		20. A	
6. D		21. A	
7. B		22. A	
8. A		23. C	
9. A		24. A	
10. D		25. B	
11. C		26. D	
12. A		27. A	
13. B		28. B	
14. B		29. C	
15. B		30. A	

Word Knowledge

1. C		19. B	
2. D		20. D	
3. A		21. D	
4. B		22. C	
5. B		23. C	
6. B		24. B	
7. D		25. C	
8. C		26. A	
9. B		27. C	
10. D		28. A	
11. A		29. B	
12. D		30. B	
13. A		31. B	
14. B		32. C	
15. B		33. D	
16. B		34. B	
17. D		35. C	
18. A			

Paragraph Comprehension

1. D
2. C
3. A
4. B
5. C
6. D
7. A
8. C

9. A
10. C
11. D
12. B
13. C
14. B
15. A

Mathematics Knowledge

1. A
2. D
3. A
4. A
5. C
6. D
7. D
8. B
9. A
10. A
11. C
12. A
13. D

14. A
15. B
16. B
17. C
18. A
19. B
20. C
21. C
22. A
23. B
24. C
25. C

AFQT Answers and Explanations

Arithmetic Reasoning

1. **C.** Because it takes a half-hour to run $1\frac{1}{2}$ miles, it will take twice as long, 1 hour, to run 3 miles.

2. **A.** Let x = the height of the lamp post. $\frac{20}{3} = \frac{x}{1} \rightarrow 20 = 3x \rightarrow x = \frac{20}{3} = 6\frac{2}{3}$.

3. **C.** $10 + 5 + 3 = 18$

4. **A.** If $\frac{7}{8}$ of the mixture is white sugar, then $\frac{1}{8}$ of the mixture is brown sugar. $\frac{1}{8} \times 5 = \frac{5}{8}$ tablespoons of brown sugar.

5. **A.** One pair of boots costs $\frac{\$741.90}{3} = \$247.30$. Two pairs of boots cost $2 \times \$247.30 = \$494.60$

6. **D.** $253 - 150 = 103$

7. **B.** The discount was $30 out of $300 or $\frac{30}{300} = \frac{10}{100} = 10\%$.

8. **A.** The area not gardened is the area inside the circle and outside the triangle, or $A_o - A_\Delta$.

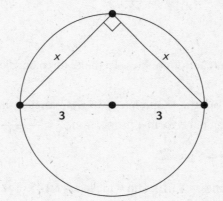

$A_o = \pi r^2 = \pi(3)2 = 9\pi$

$A_\Delta = \frac{1}{2}x^2$.

Using the Pythagorean theorem, $x^2 + x^2 = 6^2 \rightarrow 2x^2 = 36 \rightarrow x^2 = 18$. So, $A_\Delta = \frac{1}{2}x^2 = \frac{1}{2} \times 18 = 9$. The area not gardened is $A_o - A_\Delta = 9\pi - 9$.

9. **A.** The scale of 5 ft per every $\frac{1}{2}$ in is equivalent to a scale of 10 ft per inch.

So, the length of the lot, $5\frac{1}{2}$ in, is equivalent to $5\frac{1}{2}$ in $\times 10$ ft/in = 55 ft.

The width of the lot, 4 in, is equivalent to 4 in $\times$ 10 ft/in = 40 ft.

The area of the lot is length $\times$ width = 55 ft $\times$ 40 ft = 2200 ft².

10. **D.** Losing $\frac{1}{3}$ of a gallon of water every day for ten days means she lost $\frac{1}{3} \times 10 = \frac{10}{3} = 3\frac{1}{3}$ gallons. Because she also drank 2 gallons after filling the barrel, the water she had left over was 60 gallons – 2 gallons – $3\frac{1}{3}$ gallons = 58 gallons – $3\frac{1}{3}$ gallons = $54\frac{2}{3}$ gallons.

11. **C.** From 3:20 p.m. to 7:20 p.m., there are 4 hours. From 7:20 p.m. to 7:45 p.m. there are 25 minutes. Therefore, there are 4 hours and 25 minutes between 3:20 p.m. and 7:45 p.m.

12. A. 1 ft = 12 in. The dimension of the box, in inches, is 48 in × 36 in × 24 in. Assume 48 in is the length of the box, 36 in is its width, and 24 in is its height. If the blocks are placed such that the 3-in sides lie along the length of the box and the other two sides lie along the height and the width, then 48 ÷ 3 = 16 blocks fit along the length, 36 ÷ 2 = 18 blocks fit along the width, and 24 ÷ 2 = 12 blocks fit along the height. The number of blocks that fit in the box is 16 × 18 × 12 = 3,456.

13. B. Sam's total cost is $3.35 × 2 + $2.29 = $8.99. $10 – $8.99 = $1.01.

14. B. 30% of 900 is $\frac{30}{100} \times 900 = 270$

15. B. The number of mysteries Skyler read is 10 × 2 = 20. The number of biographies is 3 × 20 = 60.

16. C. The surface area of a box is the sum of the areas of all its faces, $S = 2(lw) + 2(lh) + 2(wh)$.

Before calculating this, we need to calculate the height of the box. $V_{box} = l \times w \times h \rightarrow 60 = 5 \times 3 \times h \rightarrow h = 4$.

$S = 2(5 \times 3) + 2(5 \times 4) + 2(3 \times 4) = 30 + 40 + 24 = 94 \text{ ft}^2$.

17. C. After Fabian ate $\frac{1}{7}$ of the cake, $\frac{6}{7}$ of the cake was left over, which means each of his friends ate $\frac{1}{7}$ of the cake.

$\frac{1}{7} \approx 14.3\%$

18. C. 543 – 297 = 246 pages

19. D. $\frac{\$6.15}{\$.05\,/\,\text{bottle}} = 123$ bottles

20. A. You can only make two batches of cookies. To make three batches, you would need 6 cups of chocolate chips and 12 cups of flour.

21. A. These two triangles share one angle and have two right angles, thus making them similar. Beacause they are similar, their corresponding parts form a proportion: $\frac{6}{3} = \frac{x+6}{7} \rightarrow 2 = \frac{x+6}{7} \rightarrow 14 = x + 6 \rightarrow x = 8$.

22. A. There will be $\frac{3.5\,\text{m}}{0.7\,\text{m}\,/\,\text{piece}} = 5$ pieces.

23. C. 15 quarters = $3.75, 31 dimes = $3.10, and 9 nickels = $0.45. Total = $3.75 + $3.10 + $0.45 = $7.30

24. A. The tip was $54 – $45 = $9. $\frac{\$9}{\$45} = 20\%$.

25. B. Let x = shorter leg.

$A_\Delta = \frac{1}{2}b \times h = \frac{1}{2}(x) \times (2 + x) = 40 \rightarrow x(2 + x) = 80 \rightarrow x = 8$

26. D. Let x = the principal. $0.0325x = 13 \rightarrow x = \frac{13}{0.0325} = 400$

27. A. Her math average is $\frac{100 + 96 + 76 + 88 + 55}{5} = 83$. Her English average is 90 – 83 = 7 points higher than her math average.

28. B. Using proportions, $\frac{3}{5} = \frac{450}{x} \rightarrow x = \frac{5 \times 450}{3} = 750$ minutes. $\frac{750}{60} = 12\frac{30}{60} = 12.5$ hours.

29. C. Sharon's total purchase is 4 × $9.50 = $38. She spent $38 – $5 = $33.

30. A. 10 quarters = $2.50, 30 dimes = $3, and 15 nickels = $0.75. Total = $2.50 + $3 + $0.75 = $6.25

Word Knowledge Answers

1. The correct answer is (C) *assist*. Abet means to help or support.

2. The correct answer is (D) *embarrass*. Abash means to humiliate or mortify.

3. The correct answer is (A) *wash*. Ablution means cleanse or purify.

4. The correct answer is (B) *cancel*. Abrogate means end or annul.

5. The correct answer is (B) *fierce*. Vehement means violent or passionate.

6. The correct answer is (B) *boldness*. Temerity means nerve or gall.

7. The correct answer is (D) *decay*. Atrophy means deteriorate or waste.

8. The correct answer is (C) *fluctuate*, which means to swing or vary.

9. The correct answer is (B) *refrain from*. Abstain means to avoid or stay away from.

10. The correct answer is (D) *stubborn*. Intransigent means uncompromising or obstinate.

11. The correct answer is (A) *affirm*, which means assert or verify.

12. The correct answer is (D) *distribute*. Allocate means allot or assign.

13. The correct answer is (A) *loathe*, which means hate or despise.

14. The correct answer is (B) *block*. Thwart means prevent or stop.

15. The correct answer is (B) *equality*. Parity means uniformity or similarity.

16. The correct answer is (B) *prevent*. Avert means avoid or forestall.

17. The correct answer is (D) *listless*, which means sluggish or lethargic.

18. The correct answer is (A) *agree*. Accede means assent or allow.

19. The correct answer is (B) *muddle*, which means confuse or confound.

20. The correct answer is (D) *independent*. Autonomous means self-directed or sovereign.

21. The correct answer is (D) *temporary*. Transitory means brief or passing.

22. The correct answer is (C) *suave*, which means polished or sophisticated.

23. The correct answer is (C) *comfort*. Balm means relief or solace.

24. The correct answer is (B) *award*. Accolade means honor or tribute.

25. The correct answer is (C) *blue*. Azure means navy or cobalt in color, which are shades of blue.

26. The correct answer is (A) *regret*. Rue means lament or mourn.

27. The correct answer is (C) *trinket*, which means an ornament or charm.

28. The correct answer is (A) *firm*. Resolute means determined or unyielding.

29. The correct answer is (B) *bitter*. Scathing means sarcastic or mocking.

30. The correct answer is (B) *scold*, which means reprimand or admonish.

31. The correct answer is (B) *fear*. Trepidation means anxiety or unease.

32. The correct answer is (C) *traitor*. Renegade means betrayer or defector.

33. The correct answer is (D) *offense*. Umbrage means resentment or indignation.

34. The correct answer is (B) *polite*. Civil means well-mannered or courteous.

35. The correct answer is (C) *constant*. Chronic means continual or persistent.

Paragraph Comprehension Answers

1. **D.** The context clue is "to come," which indicates the upheavals will be in the future; therefore, Darwin had a *feeling* about potential controversy.

2. **C.** The paragraph describes how the federal government subsidized the extermination of wolves.

3. **A.** The context clue is the preceding word, "Gone." That is a synonym for the German word *kaput*.

4. **B.** Nowhere in the paragraph does it state that ginkgo is actually an effective medicine; it just states that people try it.

5. **C.** The context clue is that the scooter test used the same course that the cars used; therefore, the scooter test *imitated* the car test.

6. **D.** The paragraph is specifically about the oil production in the Savuiskoye oil field in Russia and doesn't pertain to the other choices.

7. **A.** The sensory appendages are mounted on the head; therefore, they are additional attachments.

8. **C.** Cancer, as a cause of stomach pain, is never referenced in the article.

9. **A.** The context clue is that there are "tens of thousands" of tax preparers, so they are *competing* for business.

10. **C.** The paragraph stresses that consumers can "save hundreds of dollars" when purchasing a car.

11. **D.** Theater ticket sales are never referenced in the paragraph.

12. **B.** The paragraph describes when the "Inca Empire was formed."

13. **C.** The context clue is that the distractions described "can result" in a car accident, which implies that it is a possibility.

14. **B.** Florida Caverns State Park is described in the paragraph, but no mention is made of the danger of caves.

15. **A.** Holding the snake behind the head causes it to bite and release venom into the collecting vial.

Mathematics Knowledge Answers

1. **A.** $2z + 3 = z + 1 \rightarrow z = -2$, $z^3 = (-2)^3 = -8$

2. **D.** $\dfrac{3}{56} - \dfrac{5}{14} = \dfrac{3}{56} - \dfrac{20}{56} = \dfrac{-17}{56}$

3. **A.** $\dfrac{10y + 6}{2} = 8 \rightarrow 5y + 3 = 8 \rightarrow 5y = 5 \rightarrow y = 1$

4. **A.** Let x equal the length of a side of the square. By the Pythagorean theorem, $x^2 + x^2 = 3^2 \rightarrow 2x^2 = 9 \rightarrow x^2 = \dfrac{9}{2}$. The area of a square with side x is x^2, so the area of the square is $\dfrac{9}{2}$ sq in (see figure below).

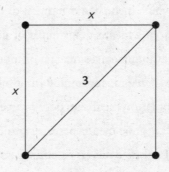

5. **C.** Because the motorcycle travels 15 km in 20 minutes, it will travel 45 km in 1 hour and 90 km in 2 hours.

6. **D.** Rationalizing the denominator, $\dfrac{3\sqrt{2}}{\sqrt{6}} \cdot \dfrac{\sqrt{6}}{\sqrt{6}} = \dfrac{3\sqrt{12}}{6} = \dfrac{6\sqrt{3}}{6} = \sqrt{3}$.

7. **D.** 1 ft = 12 in so the box dimensions, in inches, are 36 in × 48 in × 60 in. Then, 6 cubes fit along the 36-in edge, 8 cubes fit along the 48-in edge, and 10 cubes fit along the 60-in edge. $6 \times 8 \times 10 = 480$ cubes fit into the box.

8. **B.** Because $a = -6$ and $b = 2$, $3a^2b^3 = 3(-6)^2(2)^3 = 3(36)(8) = 864$

9. **A.**

$$\begin{array}{r} 1.02315 \\ + \ 0.00980 \\ \hline 1.03295 \end{array}$$

10. **A.** $\dfrac{3}{5} \div \dfrac{2}{5} = \dfrac{3}{5} \cdot \dfrac{5}{2} = \dfrac{15}{10} = \dfrac{3}{2}$

11. **C.** Let d equal the length of the diagonal of the square. Because the area of the square is 100 ft^2, the side of the square is 10 ft. By the Pythagorean theorem, $10^2 + 10^2 = d^2 \rightarrow 200 = d^2 \rightarrow d = 10\sqrt{2}$. Since the diagonal of the square is also the diameter of the circle and the radius of the circle is half of the diameter, the radius of the circle is $5\sqrt{2}$ ft. $A_o = \pi r^2 = \pi\left(5\sqrt{2}\right)^2 = 50\pi \ \text{ft}^2$.

12. **A.** $(2 - 3x) + (4x^2 - 4x + 7) - (3x - 2) = 4x^2 - 3x - 4x - 3x + 2 + 7 + 2 = 4x^2 - 10x + 11$

13. **D.** Let x equal the teachers' salaries. Then $\$6{,}660{,}000 \times 3 = \$19{,}980{,}000$, rounded to $\$20{,}000{,}000$.

14. **A.** Because the sum of the measures of the angles of a triangle is 180°, $\text{m}\angle A + \text{m}\angle B + \text{m}\angle C = (5w + 9) + (50) + (1 + w) = 6w + 60 = 180 \rightarrow 6w = 120 \rightarrow w = 20$.

    $\text{m}\angle A = 5(20) + 9 = 109°$, which must be the obtuse angle of the triangle because it measures between 90° and 180° and because a triangle can only contain one obtuse angle.

15. **B.** $(1 - 7x) \cdot (3 + 5x) = 3 + 5x - 21x - 35x^2 = 3 - 16x - 35x^2 = -35x^2 - 16x + 3$

16. **B.** $(1.7)^3 = (1.7)(1.7)(1.7) = (2.89)(1.7) = 4.913 \approx 4.91$

17. **C.** Let r = radius of smaller circle. Then $3r$ = radius of the larger circle.

    $A_{\text{smaller circle}} = \pi r^2$ and $A_{\text{larger circle}} = 9\pi r^2$

    Therefore, the area of the larger circle is 9 times the area of the smaller circle.

18. **A.** The greatest common factor of a set of numbers is the largest number that divides the numbers evenly. The greatest common factor of 24, 18, and 12 is 6.

19. **B.** The product of $(-2x^2y^3) \cdot (3xy^4z) = -6x^3y^7z$

20. **C.** $\dfrac{16 - x^2}{x - 4} = \dfrac{(4 - x)(4 + x)}{x - 4} = -(x + 4)$ because $\dfrac{4 - x}{x - 4} = -1$

21. **C.** By trial and error, $(2, 3)$ does not work because $2(3) + 3(3) \neq -5$. $(2, -3)$ works because $2(2) + 3(-3) = -5$.

22. **A.** The probability of rolling an even number is $\dfrac{3}{6}$ or $\dfrac{1}{2}$ since there are 3 even numbers on every fair, six-sided die: 2, 4, and 6. The probability of rolling an even number 3 times is $\dfrac{1}{2} \times \dfrac{1}{2} \times \dfrac{1}{2} = \dfrac{1}{8}$.

23. **B.** $0.04\theta = 5 \rightarrow \theta = \dfrac{5}{0.04} \rightarrow \theta = 125$

24. **C.** $A_{\text{rhombus}} = \dfrac{1}{2}(d_1 \times d_2) = \dfrac{1}{2}(3 \times 6) = \dfrac{1}{2}(18) = 9$

25. **C.** Let x = the number of boys; then $3x$ = the number of girls and $x + 3x = 40 \rightarrow 4x = 40 \rightarrow x = 10$. So Renne invited 10 boys and 30 girls. He invited 20 more girls than boys.

PART IV

MILITARY CAREER OPPORTUNITIES

Military Career Opportunities

According to the military, the Department of Defense recruits and trains almost 220,000 enlisted members and officers each year, making it one of the largest employers in the United States. The following material will give you some basic information about the different opportunities available to you as an enlisted person in different branches of the military. Related civilian occupations are also given. Thus, you can have an idea of not only what you can do once you've entered the military, but also how those specific jobs may be transferable when you leave the military.

Each job description is preceded by an indication of which branches of the service the job is available in, as not all branches of the service offer the same careers. For example, the Air Force offers no career for Divers (for obvious reasons). Similarly, an Aircraft Launch and Recovery Specialist will find employment only in the Navy, Marine Corps, and Coast Guard. For additional information beyond what we offer here, you can also visit the following Internet sites: www.careersintthemilitary.com and www.todaysmilitary.com/careers.

This chapter features over 90 different occupational descriptions for enlisted personnel, within the following 12 career fields:

- Human Services
- Media and Public Affairs
- Health Care
- Engineering, Science, and Technical
- Administrative
- Service
- Vehicle and Machinery Mechanic
- Electronic and Electrical Equipment Repair
- Construction Occupations
- Machine Operator and Precision Work
- Transportation and Material Handling
- Combat Specialty

Dozens of additional occupations and career paths are available for officers, but the requirements are different for officers. The ASVAB is currently for those applying for enlisted positions. If you plan to go to college, you can become an officer through ROTC training or Officer Training School. As an enlisted person, you can apply to the Officer Training Corps program to follow a career path to become an officer. But that's down the road.

How to Use This Career Opportunities Section

This section is organized to help you easily find a satisfying career or occupation. You can start by skimming this chapter, reading through the different jobs that are available. There are probably dozens that you never thought of before.

After you've done that, you can either go back to one of those 12 career areas and find a specific occupation within that area or merely read through all of those occupations that are described. As you do so, keep in mind not only the description of what a job entails, but also the physical demands that might be placed on you. If you'd like to look into your future, discover how these jobs translate into civilian jobs. You may, of course, end up choosing the military as a full-time career, and you can anticipate advancement within your career area. If, however, you stay for the initial enlistment period only, it's important to have an idea of what you can do when you get out. That's why the section on civilian opportunities is included.

Because you've purchased this book, it's safe to assume that you're studying for the exam. This section can help you make some decisions about whether the military is for you.

Enlisted Occupational Descriptions

HUMAN SERVICE OCCUPATIONS

Caseworkers and Counselors

Army

Navy

Air Force

Marine Corps

Coast Guard

As with some civilians, some military personnel can develop drug or alcohol addictions. Others may suffer from depression or other emotional problems. Caseworkers and counselors help military personnel and their families to overcome personal problems.

They work as part of a team that may include social workers, psychologists, medical officers, chaplains, personnel specialists, and commanders.

What They Do

Caseworkers and counselors in the military perform some or all of the following duties:

Interview personnel who request help or are referred by their commanders

Identify personal problems and determine the need for professional help

Counsel personnel and their families

Administer and score psychological tests

Teach classes on human relations

Keep records of counseling sessions and give reports to supervisors

Where They Work

Caseworkers and counselors usually work in offices or clinics.

Opportunities in Civilian Life

Civilian caseworkers and counselors work in rehabilitation centers, hospitals, schools, and public agencies. Their duties are similar to duties in the military. Civilian caseworkers and counselors, however, are usually required to have a college degree in social work, psychology, or counseling. They may be called group workers, human relations counselors, or drug and alcohol counselors.

Physical Requirements

Caseworkers and counselors must be able to speak clearly and distinctly in order to teach classes and work with personnel who have problems.

Religious Program Specialists

Army

Navy

Air Force

The military is composed of personnel from many religions and faiths. The military provides chaplains and religious program specialists to help meet the spiritual needs of its personnel. Religious program specialists assist chaplains with religious services, religious education programs, and related administrative duties.

What They Do

Religious program specialists in the military perform some or all of the following duties:

- Assist chaplains in planning and preparing religious programs and activities
- Assist chaplains in conducting religious services
- Prepare religious, educational, and devotional materials
- Organize charitable and public-service volunteer programs
- Maintain relations with religious communities and public-service organizations
- Perform administrative duties for chaplains, such as scheduling appointments, handling correspondence, maintaining files, and handling finances

Where They Work

Religious program specialists in the military usually work indoors. They also serve aboard ships or with land and air units in the field.

Opportunities in Civilian Life

Civilian religious program specialists help manage churches and religious schools. Their duties are similar to those performed by military religious program specialists, including planning religious programs and preparing religious educational materials. They are also called directors of religious activities.

Physical Requirements

The ability to speak clearly and distinctly is required to enter this occupation.

MEDIA AND PUBLIC AFFAIRS OCCUPATIONS

Audiovisual and Broadcast Technicians

Army
Navy
Air Force
Marine Corps
Coast Guard

Television and film productions comprise an important part of military communications. Films are used for training in many military occupations. They are also used to record military operations, ceremonies, and news events. These productions require the teamwork of many technicians. Audiovisual and broadcast technicians perform many specialized tasks, ranging from filming to script editing to operating audio recording devices.

What They Do

Audiovisual and broadcast technicians in the military perform some or all of the following duties:

- Work with writers, producers, and directors to prepare and interpret scripts
- Plan and design production scenery, graphics, and special effects
- Operate media equipment and special-effects devices, including cameras, sound recorders, and lighting
- Follow the script and instructions of film or TV directors to move a camera, zoom, pan, or adjust focus

Where They Work

Audiovisual and broadcast technicians work in studios or outdoors on location. They sometimes work from aircraft or ships. They travel and work in all climates.

Opportunities in Civilian Life

Civilian audiovisual and broadcast technicians work for film-production companies, government audiovisual studios, radio and television stations, and advertising agencies. Their duties are similar to those performed by military journalists and newswriters. They may be called motion picture camera operators, audiovisual production specialists, sound mixers, recording engineers, and broadcasting and recording technicians.

Physical Requirements

Normal color vision and the ability to speak clearly are required for some specialties in this area.

Broadcast Journalists and Newswriters

Army

Navy

Air Force

Marine Corps

Coast Guard

The military publishes newspapers and broadcasts television and radio programs for its personnel and the public. These services are an important source of general information about people and events in the military. Broadcast journalists and newswriters write and present news programs, music programs, and radio talk shows.

What They Do

Broadcast journalists and newswriters in the military perform some or all of the following duties:

- Gather information for military news programs and publications
- Write radio and TV scripts
- Develop ideas for news articles
- Arrange and conduct interviews
- Collect information for commercial media use
- Select photographs and write captions for news articles
- Write news releases, feature articles, and editorials

Where They Work

Broadcast journalists and newswriters work in broadcasting studios on land or aboard ships, or sometimes outdoors, depending upon the research needed for their articles.

Opportunities in Civilian Life

Broadcast journalists and newswriters work for newspapers, magazines, wire services, and radio and television stations. Their duties are similar to those performed by military journalists and newswriters. They may be employed as newscasters, disc jockeys, writers, directors, producers, editors, or correspondents.

Physical Requirements

Normal color vision and the passing of a voice audition are required for some specialties in this area.

Graphic Designers and Illustrators

Army

Navy

Air Force

Marine Corps

The military produces many publications, such as training manuals, newspapers, reports, and promotional materials. Graphic artwork is used in these publications and for signs, charts, posters, and TV and motion picture productions. Graphic designers and illustrators produce graphic artwork, drawings, and other visual displays.

What They Do

Graphic designers and illustrators in the military perform some or all of the following duties:

- Produce computer-generated graphics
- Draw graphs and charts to represent budgets, numbers of troops, supply levels, and office organization
- Develop ideas and design posters and signs
- Help instructors design artwork for training courses
- Draw illustrations of parts of the human body for medical training
- Draw cartoons for filmstrips and animation for films
- Make silkscreen prints
- Work with TV and film producers to design backdrops and props for film sets

Where They Work

Graphic designers and illustrators usually work in offices on land or aboard ships.

Opportunities in Civilian Life

Civilian graphic designers and illustrators work for government agencies, advertising agencies, print shops, and engineering firms. They also work for many large organizations that have their own graphics departments. Their duties are similar to those of military graphic designers and illustrators. They may be known as commercial artists or graphic artist technicians.

Interpreters and Translators

Army

Navy

Air Force

Marine Corps

Some members of the military must be able to read and understand the many languages of the world. Information from foreign-language newspapers, magazines, and radio broadcasts is important to the nation's defense. Interpreters and translators convert written or spoken foreign languages into English or other languages. They usually specialize in a particular foreign language.

What They Do

Interpreters and translators in the military perform some or all of the following duties:

Translate written and spoken foreign-language material to and from English, making sure to preserve the original meaning

Interrogate (question) prisoners of war, enemy deserters, and civilian informers in their native languages

Record foreign radio transmissions using sensitive communications equipment

Prepare written reports about the information obtained

Translate foreign documents, such as battle plans and personnel records

Translate foreign books and articles describing foreign equipment and construction techniques

Where They Work

Interpreters and translators normally work on military bases, aboard ships, or in airplanes.

Opportunities in Civilian Life

Civilian interpreters and translators work for government agencies, embassies, universities, and companies that conduct business overseas. Their work is similar to the work of military interpreters and translators.

Physical Requirements

Normal hearing and the ability to speak clearly and distinctly are usually required to enter this occupation.

Musicians

Army

Navy

Air Force

Marine Corps

Coast Guard

Music is an important part of military life. Service bands and vocal groups have a strong tradition of performing at ceremonies, parades, concerts, festivals, and dances. Musicians and singers perform in service bands, orchestras, and small groups. They perform many types of music, including marches, classics, jazz, and popular music.

What They Do

Musicians in the military perform some or all of the following duties:

Play in or lead bands, orchestras, combos, and jazz groups

Sing in choral groups or as soloists

Perform for ceremonies, parades, concerts, festivals, and dances

Rehearse and learn new music when not performing

Play brass, percussion, woodwind, or string instruments

Where They Work

Musicians play indoors in theaters, concert halls, and at dances and outdoors at parades and open-air concerts. They also travel regularly.

Opportunities in Civilian Life

Civilian musicians work for many types of employers, including professional orchestras, bands, and choral groups. They work in nightclubs, concert halls, theaters, and recording studios.

Photographic Specialists

Army

Navy

Air Force

Marine Corps

Coast Guard

The military uses photographs for many purposes, such as intelligence gathering and news reporting. The services operate photographic laboratories to develop the numerous photos taken by the military. Photographic specialists take and develop still color or black-and-white photographs.

What They Do

Photographic specialists in the military perform some or all of the following duties:

Select camera, film, and other equipment needed for photo assignments

Determine camera angles, lighting, and any special effects needed

Take still photos of people, events, military equipment, land areas, and other subjects

Develop, duplicate, or retouch film negatives, photos, or slides

Maintain photographic equipment

Where They Work

Photographic specialists work both indoors and outdoors while photographing their subjects. They may take photos from aircraft or ships. They process photographs in photographic laboratories on bases or aboard ships.

Opportunities in Civilian Life

Civilian photographic specialists work for photography studios, newspapers, magazines, advertising agencies, commercial photograph developers, and large businesses. They perform duties similar to those of military specialists. Depending on the specialty, they may be known as photojournalists, aerial or still photographers, film developers, automatic print developers, or print controllers.

Physical Requirements

Normal color vision is required to produce accurate color prints.

HEALTH CARE OCCUPATIONS

Cardiopulmonary and EEG Technicians

Army

Navy

Air Force

Military health care includes medical treatment for heart, lung, and brain disorders. Physicians need sophisticated tests to help diagnose and treat these problems. Cardiopulmonary and EEG (electroencephalograph) technicians administer a variety of diagnostic tests of the heart, lungs, blood, and brain. They operate complex electronic testing equipment.

What They Do

Cardiopulmonary and EEG technicians in the military perform some or all of the following duties:

Take patients' blood-pressure readings

Attach electrodes or microphones to patients' bodies

Help physicians revive heart attack victims

Adjust settings and operate test equipment

Monitor dials, graphs, and screens during tests

Talk to physicians to learn what tests or treatments are needed

Keep records of test results and discuss them with medical staff

Operate electrocardiographs, electroencephalographs, and other test equipment

Where They Work

Cardiopulmonary and EEG technicians usually work in hospitals and clinics. In combat situations, they may work in mobile field hospitals.

Opportunities in Civilian Life

Civilian cardiopulmonary and EEG technicians work in hospitals, clinics, and physicians' offices. Their duties are similar to those performed in the military. They may specialize in either cardiovascular (heart), pulmonary (lungs), or electroencephalographic (brain) testing.

Physical Requirements

Normal color vision is required for some specialties in order to set up and monitor equipment.

Dental Specialists

Army
Navy
Air Force
Coast Guard

Dental care is one of the health services provided to all military personnel. It is available in military dental clinics all over the world. Dental specialists assist military dentists in examining and treating patients. They also help manage dental offices.

What They Do

Dental specialists in the military perform some or all of the following duties:

Help dentists perform oral surgery

Prepare for patient examinations by selecting and arranging instruments and medications

Help dentists during examinations by preparing dental compounds and operating dental equipment

Clean patients' teeth using scaling and polishing instruments and equipment

Operate dental X-ray equipment and process X-rays of patients' teeth, gums, and jaws

Provide guidance to patients on daily care of their teeth

Perform administrative duties, such as scheduling office visits, keeping patient records, and ordering dental supplies

Where They Work

Dental specialists in the military usually work indoors in dental offices or clinics. Some specialists may be assigned to duty aboard ships.

Opportunities in Civilian Life

Civilian dental specialists work in dental offices or clinics. Their work is similar to work in the military. They typically specialize in assisting dentists to treat patients, providing clerical support (dental assistants), or cleaning teeth (dental hygienists).

Physical Requirements

Dental specialists must sometimes stand for long periods.

Medical Care Technicians

Army
Navy
Air Force
Coast Guard

The military provides medical care to all men and women in the services. Medical care technicians work with teams of physicians, nurses, and other health-care professionals to provide treatment to patients. They help give patients the care and treatment required to recover from illness or injury. They also prepare rooms, equipment, and supplies in hospitals and medical clinics.

What They Do

Medical care technicians in the military perform some or all of the following duties:

Provide bedside care in hospitals, including taking the body temperature, pulse, and respiration rate of patients

Feed, bathe, and dress patients

Prepare patients, operating rooms, equipment, and supplies for surgery

Make casts, traction devices, and splints according to physicians' instructions

Administer medication to patients under the direction of physicians and nurses

Where They Work

Medical care technicians work in hospitals and clinics on land or aboard ships. In combat situations, they may work in mobile field hospitals.

Opportunities in Civilian Life

Civilian medical care technicians work in hospitals, nursing homes, rehabilitation centers, psychiatric hospitals, or physicians' offices. They perform similar duties to those performed in the military. They may be called nurses' aides, orderlies, operating room technicians, orthopedic assistants, or practical nurses.

Physical Requirements

Some specialties in this area require sufficient strength to lift and move patients, and some require a normal skin condition to guard against infection.

Medical Laboratory Technicians

Army

Navy

Air Force

Coast Guard

Medical laboratories are an important part of the military health-care system. The staffs of medical laboratories perform clinical tests required to detect and identify diseases in patients. Medical laboratory technicians conduct tests on the tissue, blood, and body fluids of patients.

What They Do

Medical laboratory technicians in the military perform some or all of the following duties:

Use lab equipment to analyze specimens (samples) of tissue, blood, and body fluids

Examine blood and bone marrow under microscopes

Test specimens for bacteria or viruses

Draw blood from patients

Assist in collecting specimens at autopsies (medical examinations of the dead)

Record and file results of laboratory tests

Where They Work

Medical laboratory technicians work in medical centers, clinics, and hospitals on land or aboard ships.

Opportunities in Civilian Life

Civilian medical laboratory technicians usually work for privately owned laboratories, hospitals, clinics, or research institutions. They perform duties similar to those of military medical laboratory technicians.

Physical Requirements

Normal color vision is required to work with colored chemicals and dyes.

Medical Record Technicians

Army

Navy

Air Force

Coast Guard

Medical records are important for health-care delivery. To provide proper treatment, physicians need complete and accurate information about patient symptoms, test results, illnesses, and prior treatments. Medical record technicians prepare and maintain patient records, reports, and correspondence.

What They Do

Medical record technicians in the military perform some or all of the following duties:

Fill out admission and discharge records for patients entering and leaving military hospitals

Assign patients to hospital rooms

Prepare daily reports about patients admitted and discharged

Organize, file, and maintain medical records

Type reports about physical examinations, illnesses, and treatments

Maintain libraries of medical publications

Where They Work

Medical record technicians work in admissions or medical records sections of hospitals and clinics. They work in land-based facilities and aboard ships.

Opportunities in Civilian Life

Civilian medical record technicians usually work for hospitals, clinics, and government health agencies. They perform duties similar to those of military medical record technicians. However, civilian medical record technicians tend to specialize in areas such as admissions, ward, or outpatient records. Those working in admission or discharge units are called admitting or discharge clerks.

Medical Service Technicians

Army

Navy

Air Force

Coast Guard

In emergencies or in combat, physicians are not always immediately available to treat the injured or wounded. When a physician is not available, medical service technicians provide basic and emergency medical treatment. They also assist medical officers in caring for sick and injured patients.

What They Do

Medical service technicians in the military perform some or all of the following duties:

- Examine and treat emergency or battlefield patients
- Interview patients and record their medical histories
- Take patients' temperature, pulse, and blood pressure
- Prepare blood samples for laboratory analysis
- Keep health records and clinical files up to date
- Administer shots and medicines to patients

Where They Work

Medical service technicians usually work in hospitals and clinics on land or aboard ships. Medical service technicians may provide emergency medical treatment in the field.

Opportunities in Civilian Life

Civilian medical service technicians work in hospitals, clinics, nursing homes, and rehabilitation centers. They perform duties similar to those performed by medical service technicians in the military. Civilian medical service technicians are known for the type of work they do: Emergency medical technicians treat victims of accidents, fire, or heart attacks; medical assistants work for physicians and perform routine medical and clerical tasks; medication aides administer shots and medicine under the close supervision of physicians; and physician assistants perform routine examinations and treatment for physicians.

Optometric Technicians

Army

Navy

Air Force

Coast Guard

Optometry, or vision care, is one of the many health benefits available to military personnel. The military operates its own clinics to examine eyes and fit glasses or contact lenses. Optometric technicians assist optometrists in providing vision care. They work with patients and manage clinic offices.

What They Do

Optometric technicians in the military perform some or all of the following duties:

- Administer screening tests of patients' vision and record results
- Order eyeglasses and contact lenses from prescriptions
- Measure patients for eyeglass frames
- Fit eyeglasses to patients
- Make minor repairs to glasses
- Place eyedrops and ointment into patients' eyes
- Keep records in optometry offices

Where They Work

Optometric technicians normally work in optometric clinics.

Opportunities in Civilian Life

Civilian optometric technicians work in private optometry offices, clinics, and government health agencies. They perform duties similar to those performed by military optometric technicians. Optometric technicians are also called optometric assistants.

Physical Requirements

Normal color vision is required for some specialties to use optometric instruments.

Pharmacy Technicians

> Army
>
> Navy
>
> Air Force
>
> Coast Guard

Prescription drugs and medicines are important to medical treatment. Patients and physicians depend on military pharmacies to fill their prescriptions accurately. Pharmacy technicians prepare and dispense prescribed drugs and medicines under the supervision of pharmacists or physicians. They also maintain pharmacy supplies and records.

What They Do

Pharmacy technicians in the military perform some or all of the following duties:

- Read physicians' prescriptions to determine the types and amount of drugs to prepare
- Weigh and measure drugs and chemicals
- Mix ingredients to produce prescription medications
- Prepare labels for prescriptions
- Dispense medications to patients
- Keep records of drugs prescribed
- Store shipments of drugs and medications

Where They Work

Pharmacy technicians usually work in hospitals and clinics on land or aboard ships. They may also work in field hospitals.

Opportunities in Civilian Life

Civilian pharmacy technicians work in pharmacies, drugstores, hospitals, and clinics under the direction of pharmacists. They are usually known as pharmacy helpers and generally do not have responsibility for the compounding and dispensing of drugs. They perform simple tasks, such as storing supplies, cleaning equipment, and delivering prescriptions. While military pharmacy technicians generally have more job responsibilities than civilian pharmacy helpers, they do not have the qualifications needed to become civilian pharmacists. Prospective pharmacists must complete a college pharmacy degree program, pass a state board exam, and serve in a pharmacy internship.

Physical Requirements

Normal color vision is required as is the ability to speak clearly. Some specialties may involve heavy lifting.

Physical and Occupational Therapy Specialists

> Army
>
> Navy
>
> Air Force
>
> Coast Guard

Physical and occupational therapy consists of treatment and exercise for patients disabled by illness or injury. Physical and occupational therapy specialists assist in administering treatment aimed at helping disabled patients regain strength and mobility and preparing them to return to work.

What They Do

Physical and occupational therapy specialists in the military perform some or all of the following duties:

- Test and interview patients to determine their physical and mental abilities
- Assist physical and occupational therapists in planning therapy programs and exercise schedules
- Fit artificial limbs (prostheses) and train patients in their use
- Provide massages and heat treatments to patients
- Teach patients new mobility skills
- Set up and maintain therapeutic equipment such as exercise machines and whirlpools

Where They Work

Therapy specialists work in hospitals, clinics, and rehabilitation centers.

Opportunities in Civilian Life

Civilian therapy specialists work in hospitals, rehabilitation centers, nursing homes, schools, and community health centers. They perform duties similar to those of military therapy specialists. Civilian therapy specialists often specialize in treating a particular type of patient, such as children, the severely disabled, the elderly, or those who have lost arms or legs (amputees).

Physical Requirements

Therapy specialists may have to lift and support patients during exercises and treatments.

Radiologic (X-Ray) Technicians

Army
Navy
Air Force
Coast Guard

Radiology (the use of X-rays) is a health-care service provided to men and women in the military. X-ray photographs help physicians detect injuries and illnesses. Radiology is also used to treat some diseases, such as cancer. Radiologic technicians operate X-ray and related equipment used in diagnosing and treating injuries and diseases. They work as part of a medical team of physicians and specialists to provide health care to patients.

What They Do

Radiologic technicians in the military perform some or all of the following duties:

Read requests or instructions from physicians to determine each patient's X-ray needs

Position patients under radiologic equipment

Operate X-ray equipment

Adjust X-ray equipment to the correct time and power of exposure

Process X-ray pictures

Prepare and administer radioactive solutions to patients

Keep records of patient treatment

Where They Work

Radiologic technicians work in hospitals and clinics. In combat situations, they may work in mobile field hospitals. They follow strict safety procedures to minimize exposure to radiation.

Opportunities in Civilian Life

Civilian radiologic technicians work in hospitals, diagnostic clinics, and medical laboratories. They perform duties similar to those of military radiologic technicians. They may specialize in various areas of radiology and may be called X-ray technologists or nuclear medical technologists.

ENGINEERING, SCIENCE, AND TECHNICAL OCCUPATIONS

Air Traffic Controllers

Army
Navy
Air Force
Marine Corps

Every day, hundreds of military airplanes and helicopters take off and land all over the world. Their movements are closely controlled to prevent accidents. Air traffic controllers direct the movement of aircraft into and out of military airfields. They track aircraft by radar and provide voice instructions by radio.

What They Do

Air traffic controllers in the military perform some or all of the following duties:

Operate radio equipment to issue takeoff, flight, and landing instructions to pilots

Relay weather reports, airfield conditions, and safety information to pilots

Use radar equipment to track aircraft in flight

Plot airplane locations on charts and maps

Compute speed, direction, and altitude of aircraft

Maintain air traffic control records and communication logs

Where They Work

Air traffic controllers work in land-based and shipboard control centers.

Opportunities in Civilian Life

Civilian air traffic controllers work for the Federal Aviation Administration in airports and control centers around the country. They perform duties similar to those of military air traffic controllers. They may specialize in specific areas, such as aircraft arrivals, departures, ground control, or en route flights.

Physical Requirements

Normal color vision, normal hearing, and a clear speaking voice are required to enter this occupation. Controllers must pass a special physical exam.

447

Chemical Laboratory Technicians

Army

Navy

Coast Guard

Fuels and oils must be free of water and other contaminants to be safely used in aircraft or vehicles. The same is true for chemicals and other materials used by the military. Chemical laboratory technicians test fuels, oils, chemicals, and other materials for quality, purity, and durability.

What They Do

Laboratory technicians in the military perform some or all of the following duties:

- Obtain petroleum test samples from storage tanks, barges, and tankers
- Test fuels and oils for water, sediment, and other contaminants using laboratory equipment
- Analyze chemicals for strength, purity, and toxic qualities
- Perform chemical and physical tests on clothing, food, paints, and plastics
- Keep detailed laboratory records and files

Where They Work

Chemical laboratory technicians work in laboratories on military bases and aboard ships.

Opportunities in Civilian Life

Civilian chemical laboratory technicians work for petroleum refineries, chemical companies, manufacturing firms, and government agencies. They perform duties similar to those of military laboratory technicians. Civilian chemical laboratory technicians specialize in particular industries, such as petroleum, food processing, or medical drugs. They also may be called fuel and chemical laboratory technicians or laboratory testers.

Physical Requirements

Normal color vision is required to perform chemical tests. Some specialties may require moderate to heavy lifting.

Communications Equipment Operators

Army

Navy

Air Force

Marine Corps

Coast Guard

The ability to link air, sea, and ground forces through communication systems is critical in the military. Communications equipment operators enable messages to be transmitted and received.

What They Do

Communications equipment operators in the military perform some or all of the following duties:

- Transmit, receive, and log messages according to military procedures
- Encode and decode classified messages
- Operate different types of telephone switchboards
- Install, maintain, and operate communications equipment
- Monitor and respond to emergency calls

Where They Work

Communications equipment operators may work either indoors or outdoors, depending on the specialty. They may be assigned to ships, aircraft, land bases, or mobile field units.

Opportunities in Civilian Life

Civilian communications equipment operators work in airports, harbors, police stations, fire stations, telephone companies, and many businesses. They may also work aboard ships. Their duties are similar to duties assigned to military communications equipment operators, although civilian communications equipment operators do not usually work in field units. They may be called radio operators, telephone operators, radiotelephone operators, switchboard operators, or teletype operators, depending on their specialty.

Physical Requirements

Normal color vision, normal hearing, and the ability to speak clearly and distinctly are required to enter some specialties in this occupation. Operators must often sit for long periods.

Computer Programmers

> Navy
> Air Force
> Marine Corps
> Coast Guard

The military is one of the largest users of data-processing equipment in the world. Information about communications, personnel, finance, and supply is kept in its many high-speed computers. This information is important for planning and management. Computer programmers plan and prepare instructions, called programs, that command computers to solve problems and organize data.

What They Do

Computer programmers in the military perform some or all of the following duties:

> Organize and arrange computer programs into logical steps that direct computers to solve problems
>
> Determine and analyze computer systems requirements
>
> Code programs into languages that computers can read, such as COBOL and FORTRAN
>
> Design, test, and debug computer programs
>
> Review and update old programs as new information is received or changes are needed

Where They Work

Computer programmers normally work in office settings. Some work aboard ships, in missile facilities, or in space command centers.

Opportunities in Civilian Life

Civilian computer programmers work for such organizations as manufacturing firms, banks, data-processing organizations, government agencies, and private corporations. These employers handle large amounts of information that programmers help organize for convenient use. Civilian computer programmers perform duties similar to those in the military. They may also be called computer systems analysts.

Emergency Management Specialists

> Army
> Navy
> Air Force
> Marine Corps
> Coast Guard

The military prepares for emergencies or natural disasters by developing detailed warning, control, and evacuation plans. Emergency management specialists prepare emergency plans and procedures for all types of disasters, such as floods, earthquakes, hurricanes, or enemy attack.

What They Do

Emergency management specialists in the military perform some or all of the following duties:

> Assist in preparing and maintaining disaster operations plans
>
> Train military and civilian personnel on what to do in an emergency
>
> Operate and maintain nuclear, biological, and chemical detection and decontamination equipment

Where They Work

Emergency management specialists work indoors when conducting training sessions and preparing disaster plans. Sometimes they work outdoors while operating decontamination equipment and monitoring disaster training.

Opportunities in Civilian Life

Civilian emergency management specialists work for federal, state, and local governments, including law enforcement and civil defense agencies. They perform duties similar to military emergency management specialists.

Physical Requirements

Normal color vision is needed to identify chemical agents.

449

Environment Health and Safety Specialists

Army

Navy

Air Force

Marine Corps

Coast Guard

Each military base is a small community. The health and well-being of the residents and surrounding land is a major concern of the services. Keeping military workplaces and living areas sanitary helps to prevent illness. Environmental health and safety specialists inspect military facilities and food supplies for the presence of disease, germs, or other conditions hazardous to health and the environment.

What They Do

Environmental health and safety specialists in the military perform some or all of the following duties:

Monitor storage, transportation, and disposal of hazardous waste

Analyze food and water samples to ensure quality

Conduct health and safety investigations of living quarters and base facilities

Provide training in industrial hygiene, environmental health, and occupational health issues

Where They Work

Environmental health specialists work indoors while inspecting food facilities and buildings. They work outdoors while inspecting waste disposal facilities and field camps.

Opportunities in Civilian Life

Most civilian environmental health and safety specialists work for local, state, and federal government agencies. Their duties are similar to the duties of military environmental health specialists. They may be called food and drug inspectors, public health inspectors, health and safety inspectors, or industrial hygienists.

Physical Requirements

Normal color vision is required to inspect foods for quality and freshness.

Intelligence Specialists

Army

Navy

Air Force

Marine Corps

Coast Guard

Military intelligence is information needed to plan for our national defense. Knowledge of the number, location, and tactics of enemy forces and potential battle areas is needed to develop military plans. To gather information, the services rely on aerial photographs, electronic monitoring using radar and sensitive radios, and human observation. Intelligence specialists gather and study the information required to design defense plans and tactics.

What They Do

Intelligence specialists in the military perform some or all of the following duties:

Study aerial photographs of foreign ships, bases, and missile sites

Study foreign troop movements

Operate sensitive radios to intercept foreign military communications

Study land and sea areas that could become battlegrounds in times of war

Store and retrieve intelligence data using computers

Study foreign military codes

Prepare intelligence reports, maps, and charts

Where They Work

Intelligence specialists work in offices on land and aboard ships, and in tents when in the field.

Opportunities in Civilian Life

Civilian intelligence specialists generally work for federal government agencies such as the Central Intelligence Agency or the National Security Agency. Their duties are similar to those performed by military intelligence specialists. The analytical skills of intelligence specialists are also useful in other fields, such as research or business planning.

Physical Requirements

Normal color vision is required for some specialties in order to work with color-coded maps.

Meteorological Specialists

Army

Navy

Air Force

Marine Corps

Coast Guard

Weather information is important for planning military operations. Accurate weather forecasts are needed to plan troop movements, airplane flights, and ship traffic. Meteorological specialists collect information about weather and sea conditions for use by meteorologists. They make visual observations and take readings from weather equipment, radar scans, and satellite photographs.

What They Do

Meteorological specialists in the military perform some or all of the following duties:

Launch weather balloons to record wind speed and direction

Identify the types of clouds present and estimate cloud height and amount of cloud cover

Take readings of barometric pressure, temperature, humidity, and sea conditions

Operate radio equipment to receive information from satellites

Plot weather information on maps and charts

Forecast weather based on readings and observations

Where They Work

Meteorological specialists usually work in offices either on land or aboard ships. They work outdoors when making visual weather observations and launching weather balloons.

Opportunities in Civilian Life

Civilian meteorological specialists work for government agencies (such as the National Weather Service), commercial airlines, radio and television stations, and private weather-forecasting firms. They perform duties similar to those of military meteorological specialists. Civilian meteorological specialists may also be called oceanographer assistants and weather clerks.

Physical Requirements

Normal color vision is required to use color-coded maps and weather charts. Some specialties may involve heavy lifting.

Non-Destructive Testers

Navy

Air Force

Marine Corps

Coast Guard

Military equipment is often placed under heavy stress. An airplane's landing gear absorbs heavy runway impact. Submarine hulls withstand tremendous pressure in the ocean depths. In time, stress may cause structural weakening or damage. Non-destructive testers examine metal parts for stress damage. They use X-rays, ultrasonics, and other testing methods that do not damage (are non-destructive to) the parts tested.

What They Do

Non-destructive testers in the military perform some or all of the following duties:

Inspect metal parts and joints for wear and damage

Take X-rays of aircraft and ship parts

Examine X-ray film to detect cracks and flaws in metal parts and welds

Operate ultrasonic, atomic absorption, and other kinds of test equipment

Conduct oil analysis and heat damage tests to detect engine wear

Prepare inspection reports

Where They Work

Non-destructive testers work indoors in laboratories and aircraft hangars. They also work outdoors in shipyards and in the field.

Opportunities in Civilian Life

Civilian non-destructive testers work for commercial testing laboratories, airlines, aircraft maintenance companies, and industrial plants. They perform duties similar to military non-destructive testers and may be called radiographers.

Physical Requirements

Normal color vision is required to read color-coded diagrams.

Ordnance Specialists

> Army
>
> Navy
>
> Air Force
>
> Marine Corps

Ordnance is a military term for ammunition and weapons. Ordnance includes all types of ammunition, missiles, toxic chemicals, and nuclear weapons. Ammunition and weapons are hazardous materials that must be handled carefully and stored properly. Ordnance specialists transport, store, inspect, prepare, and dispose of weapons and ammunition.

What They Do

Ordnance specialists in the military perform some or all of the following duties:

> Load nuclear and conventional explosives and ammunition on aircraft, ships, and submarines
>
> Inspect mounted guns, bomb-release systems, and missile launchers to determine need for repair or destruction
>
> Assemble and load explosives such as torpedoes
>
> Defuse unexploded bombs
>
> Locate, identify, and dispose of chemical munitions

Where They Work

Ordnance specialists work both indoors and outdoors. They work in repair shops while assembling explosives and repairing weapons. They work outdoors while repairing equipment in the field and loading weapons on tanks, ships, or aircraft.

Opportunities in Civilian Life

There are no direct opportunities in civilian life for many of the military ordnance specialties. However, many occupations are indirectly related. For example, civilians work for government agencies and private industry performing ordnance research and development. Others work for police or fire departments as bomb disposal experts. Some also work as gunsmiths or work for munitions manufacturers and firearms makers. Ordnance specialists may also be called bomb disposal experts.

Physical Requirements

Ordnance specialists may have to lift and carry artillery shells and other heavy ordnance.

Radar and Sonar Operators

> Army
>
> Navy
>
> Air Force
>
> Marine Corps
>
> Coast Guard

Radar and sonar devices work by bouncing radio or sound waves off objects to determine their location and measure distance. They have many uses, such as tracking aircraft and missiles, determining positions of ships and submarines, directing artillery fire, forecasting weather, and aiding navigation. Radar and sonar operators monitor sophisticated radar and sonar equipment. They normally specialize in either radar or sonar.

What They Do

Radar and sonar operators in the military perform some or all of the following duties:

> Detect and track position, direction, and speed of aircraft, ships, submarines, and missiles
>
> Plot and record data on status charts and plotting boards
>
> Set up and operate radar equipment to direct artillery fire
>
> Monitor early-warning air-defense systems
>
> Send and receive messages using radios and electronic communication systems

Where They Work

Radar and sonar operators in the military primarily work indoors in security-controlled areas. They work in operations centers and command posts either on land or aboard aircraft, ships, or submarines. Some may work in a mobile field radar unit.

Opportunities in Civilian Life

There are no direct opportunities in civilian life for military radar and sonar operators. However, civilian workers who use radar and sonar equipment in their jobs include weather-service technicians, air traffic controllers, ship navigators, and ocean salvage specialists.

Physical Requirements

Normal color vision is required to enter this occupation.

Specialties involving flying require passing a special physical exam.

Radio Intelligence Operators

Army
Navy
Air Force
Marine Corps
Coast Guard

Knowing about the military forces of foreign governments helps our military experts plan the nation's defense. One way of learning about foreign military forces is to listen to their radio transmissions. Troop locations, battle tactics, and other secrets can be learned from listening to foreign military units sending messages to one another. Radio intelligence operators intercept, identify, and record foreign radio transmissions.

What They Do

Radio intelligence operators in the military perform some or all of the following duties:

Record radio signals coming from foreign ships, planes, and land forces

Study radio signals to understand the tactics used by foreign military forces

Tune radios to certain frequencies and adjust for clear reception

Locate the source of foreign radio signals using electronic direction-finding equipment

Translate Morse code signals into words and type them for review by superiors

Keep logs of signal interceptions

Where They Work

Radio intelligence operators may work indoors or outdoors, depending on assignment. They may also work in airplanes, ships, and land vehicles.

Opportunities in Civilian Life

Civilian radio intelligence operators work for government agencies like the National Security Agency, the Central Intelligence Agency, and the Federal Bureau of Investigation. They also work in related jobs for private electronics and communications companies. They perform duties similar to those of military radio intelligence operators and may also be called electronic intelligence operations specialists.

Physical Requirements

Radio intelligence operators may have to sit for long periods while listening to radio transmissions.

Space Operations Specialists

Navy
Air Force

Orbiting satellites and other space vehicles are used for communications, weather forecasting, and collecting intelligence data. In the future, more and more military operations will involve space systems. Space operations specialists use and repair spacecraft ground-control command equipment, including electronic systems that track spacecraft location and operation.

What They Do

Space operations specialists in the military perform some or all of the following duties:

Transmit and verify spacecraft commands using aerospace ground equipment

Monitor computers and telemetry display systems

Analyze data to determine spacecraft operational status

Repair ground and spacecraft communication equipment

Assist in preparing spacecraft commands to meet mission objectives

Operate data-handling equipment to track spacecraft

Where They Work

Space operations specialists work in space operations centers.

Opportunities in Civilian Life

Civilian space operations specialists work for the National Aeronautics and Space Administration, the National Weather Service, and private satellite communications firms. They perform duties similar to those of military space operations specialists.

Physical Requirements

Normal color vision is required to enter this occupation.

Surveying, Mapping, and Drafting Technicians

Army

Navy

Air Force

Marine Corps

Coast Guard

The military builds and repairs many airstrips, docks, barracks, roads, and other projects each year. Surveying, mapping, and drafting technicians conduct land surveys, make maps, and prepare detailed plans and drawings for construction projects. Surveys and maps are also used to locate military targets and plot troop movements.

What They Do

Surveying, mapping, and drafting technicians in the military perform some or all of the following duties:

Draw maps and charts using drafting tools such as easels, templates, and compasses

Make scale drawings of roads, airfields, buildings, and other military projects

Conduct land surveys and compute survey results

Draw diagrams for wiring and plumbing of structures

Build scale models of land areas that show hills, lakes, roads, and buildings

Piece together aerial photographs to form large photomaps

Where They Work

Surveying, mapping, and drafting technicians work both indoors and outdoors in all climates and weather conditions. Those assigned to engineering units sometimes work outdoors with survey teams. Those assigned to intelligence units may work on ships as well as on land.

Opportunities in Civilian Life

Civilian surveying, mapping, and drafting technicians work for construction, engineering, and architectural firms and government agencies such as the highway department. Their work is used for planning construction projects such as highways, airport runways, dams,

and drainage systems. Surveyors and mapmakers are also called cartographers or cartographic technicians.

Physical Requirements

Good depth perception is required to study aerial photos through stereoscopes. Normal color vision is required to work with color-coded maps and drawings.

ADMINISTRATIVE OCCUPATIONS

Administrative Support Specialists

Army

Navy

Air Force

Marine Corps

Coast Guard

The military must keep accurate information for planning and managing its operations. Paper and electronic records are kept on equipment, funds, personnel, supplies, and all other aspects of the military. Administrative support specialists record information, type reports, and maintain files to assist in the operation of military offices.

What They Do

Administrative support specialists in the military perform some or all of the following duties:

Type letters, reports, requisition (order) forms, and official orders

Proofread written material for spelling, punctuation, and grammatical errors

Organize and maintain files and publications

Order office supplies

Greet and direct office visitors

Sort and deliver mail to office workers

Schedule training and leave for unit personnel

Answer phones and provide general information

Take meeting notes

Where They Work

Administrative support specialists work in office settings, both on land and aboard ships.

Opportunities in Civilian Life

Civilian administrative support specialists work in most business, government, and legal offices. They perform duties similar to those of military administrative support specialists and are called clerk typists, secretaries, general office clerks, administrative assistants, or office managers.

Computer Systems Specialists

Army
Navy
Air Force
Marine Corps
Coast Guard

The military services use computers to store and process data on personnel, weather, finances, and many other operations. Before any information can be processed, computer systems must be set up, data entered, and computers operated. Computer systems specialists ensure information is entered, stored, processed, and retrieved in a way that meets the military services' needs.

What They Do

Computer systems specialists in the military perform some or all of the following duties:

> Identify computer user problems and coordinate to resolve them
>
> Install, configure, and monitor local and wide area networks, hardware, and software
>
> Compile, enter, and process information
>
> Provide customer and network administration services, such as passwords, electronic mail accounts, security, and troubleshooting

Where They Work

Computer systems specialists work in offices or at computer sites on military bases or aboard ships.

Opportunities in Civilian Life

Civilian computer systems specialists work for a wide variety of employers, such as banks, hospitals, retail firms, manufacturers, government agencies, and firms that design and test computer systems. They perform duties similar to those performed in the military. They may also be called network support technicians, computer operators, or data-processing technicians. Most civilian computer systems specialist positions require a four-year college degree.

Physical Requirements

Computer systems specialists may sit and key information for long periods.

Finance and Accounting Specialists

Army
Navy
Air Force
Marine Corps
Coast Guard

Millions of paychecks are issued and large amounts of materials are purchased by the services each year. To account for military spending, exact financial records of these transactions must be kept. Finance and accounting specialists organize and keep track of financial records. They also compute payrolls and other allowances, audit accounting records, and prepare payments for military personnel.

What They Do

Finance and accounting specialists in the military perform some or all of the following duties:

> Record details of financial transactions on accounting forms
>
> Audit financial records
>
> Prepare pay and travel vouchers (checks), earnings and deductions statements, bills, and financial accounts and reports
>
> Disburse cash, checks, advance pay, and bonds
>
> Organize information on past expenses to help plan budgets for future expenses

Where They Work

Finance and accounting specialists work in offices on land or aboard ships.

Opportunities in Civilian Life

Civilian finance and accounting specialists work for all types of businesses and government agencies. They perform duties similar to military finance and accounting specialists. Civilian finance and accounting specialists are also called accounting clerks, audit clerks, bookkeepers, or payroll clerks.

Special Qualifications

Depending on the specialty, entry into this occupation may require courses in mathematics, bookkeeping, or accounting.

Flight Operations Specialists

Army

Navy

Air Force

Marine Corps

Coast Guard

The services operate one of the largest fleets of aircraft in the world. Hundreds of transport, passenger, and combat airplanes and helicopters fly missions every day. Accurate flight information keeps operations safe and efficient. Flight operations specialists prepare and provide flight information for air and ground crews.

What They Do

Flight operations specialists in the military perform some or all of the following duties:

Help plan flight schedules and air crew assignments

Keep flight logs on incoming and outgoing flights

Keep air crew flying records and flight operations records

Receive and post weather information and flight plan data, such as air routes and arrival and departure times

Coordinate air crew needs, such as ground transportation

Plan aircraft equipment needs for air evacuation and dangerous cargo flights

Check military flight plans with civilian agencies

Where They Work

Flight operations specialists work indoors in flight control centers or air terminals.

Opportunities in Civilian Life

Civilian flight operations specialists work for commercial and private airlines and air transport companies. They perform duties similar to military flight operations specialists.

Physical Requirements

The ability to speak clearly and distinctly is required.

Legal Specialists and Court Reporters

Army

Navy

Air Force

Marine Corps

Coast Guard

The military has its own judicial system for prosecuting lawbreakers and handling disputes. Legal specialists and court reporters assist military lawyers and judges in the performance of legal and judicial work. They perform legal research, prepare legal documents, and record legal proceedings.

What They Do

Legal specialists and court reporters in the military perform some or all of the following duties:

Research court decisions and military regulations

Process legal claims and appeals

Interview clients and take statements

Prepare trial requests and make arrangements for courtrooms

Maintain law libraries and trial case files

Type text from stenotyped records, shorthand notes, or taped records of court proceedings

Prepare records of hearings, investigations, court-martials, and courts of inquiry

Where They Work

Legal specialists and court reporters work in military law offices and courtrooms.

Opportunities in Civilian Life

Civilian legal specialists and court reporters work for private law firms, banks, insurance companies, government agencies, and local, state, and federal courts. They perform duties similar to those of military legal specialists and court reporters. Civilian legal specialists and court reporters may also be called legal assistants, clerks, paralegal assistants, and court clerks or recorders.

Personnel Specialists

Army

Navy

Air Force

Marine Corps

Coast Guard

Personnel management helps individuals develop their military careers. It also serves the military's need to fill jobs with qualified workers. Personnel specialists collect and store information about the people in the military, such as training, job assignment, promotion, and health information. They work directly with service personnel and their families.

What They Do

Personnel specialists in the military perform some or all of the following duties:

Organize, maintain, and review personnel records

Enter and retrieve personnel information using computer terminals

Assign personnel to jobs

Prepare organizational charts, write official correspondence, and prepare reports

Provide career guidance

Assist personnel and their families who have special needs

Provide information about personnel programs and procedures to servicemen and -women

Where They Work

Personnel specialists normally work in office settings on land or aboard ships.

Opportunities in Civilian Life

Civilian personnel specialists work for all types of organizations, including industrial firms, retail establishments, and government agencies. They perform duties similar to those of military personnel clerks. However, specific jobs vary from company to company.

Postal Specialists

Army

Navy

Air Force

Marine Corps

Coast Guard

The military operates its own postal service for official military communications and messages. In addition, it delivers mail to thousands of servicemen and -women all over the world. Postal specialists process incoming and outgoing mail between military and civilian postal systems. They also sell stamps and money orders and provide services to postal customers.

What They Do

Postal specialists in the military perform some or all of the following duties:

Process mail using metering and stamp-canceling machines

Weigh packages, using scales, to determine postage due

Examine packages to ensure that they meet mailing standards

Process and sort registered, certified, and insured mail

Receive payments and issue money orders and stamps

Prepare postal reports and claims for lost or damaged mail

Where They Work

Postal specialists work in post offices and mailrooms on land or aboard ships.

Opportunities in Civilian Life

Civilian postal specialists work for the United States Postal Service and for private courier or express-mail firms. They perform many of the same duties as military postal specialists. They are usually called postal clerks.

Preventive Maintenance Analysts

Army

Navy

Air Force

Marine Corps

Coast Guard

Regular maintenance extends the time aircraft, vehicles, and machinery can be used. To make sure military equipment is well maintained, the services prepare detailed maintenance schedules. Preventive maintenance analysts promote equipment maintenance. They watch schedules and notify mechanics about upcoming maintenance needs.

What They Do

Preventive maintenance analysts in the military perform some or all of the following duties:

Review maintenance schedules and notify mechanics about the types of service needed

Compare schedules to records of maintenance work actually performed

Prepare charts and reports on maintenance activities

Calculate how many mechanics and spare parts are needed to maintain equipment

Operate computers and calculators to enter or retrieve maintenance data

Where They Work

Preventive maintenance analysts usually work in office settings.

Opportunities in Civilian Life

Civilian preventive maintenance analysts work for government agencies, airlines, and large transportation firms. They also work for firms with large numbers of machines. They perform duties similar to those of military preventive maintenance analysts.

Physical Requirements

Normal color vision is required to read and interpret maintenance charts and graphs in some specialties.

Some specialties require the ability to speak clearly.

Recruiting Specialists

Army

Navy

Air Force

Marine Corps

Coast Guard

Each year, the military services enlist approximately 200,000 young men and women. Attracting young people with the kinds of talent needed to succeed in today's military is a large task. Recruiting specialists provide information about military careers to young people, parents, schools, and local communities. They explain service employment and training opportunities, pay and benefits, and service life.

What They Do

Recruiting specialists in the military perform some or all of the following duties:

Interview civilians interested in military careers

Describe military careers to groups of high school students

Explain the purpose of the ASVAB (Armed Services Vocational Aptitude Battery) and test results to students and counselors

Participate in local job fairs and career-day programs

Talk about the military to community groups

Counsel military personnel about career opportunities and benefits

Where They Work

Recruiting specialists work in local recruiting offices, on high school campuses and in career centers, and in local communities. They may have to travel often.

Opportunities in Civilian Life

Civilian recruiting specialists work for businesses of all kinds searching for talented people to hire. Recruiters also work for colleges seeking to attract and enroll talented high school students.

Sales and Stock Specialists

> Navy
>
> Air Force
>
> Marine Corps
>
> Coast Guard

The military operates retail stores and snack bars for its personnel on bases and aboard ships in the United States and overseas. Military stores, called exchanges, sell merchandise similar to that sold in civilian stores, but at a discount. Sales and stock specialists operate retail food and merchandise stores for military personnel.

What They Do

Sales and stock specialists in the military perform some or all of the following duties:

> Operate snack bars, laundries, and dry-cleaning facilities
>
> Order and receive merchandise and food for retail sales
>
> Inspect food and merchandise for spoilage or damage
>
> Price and mark retail sales items, using markers and stamping machines
>
> Stock shelves and racks for the display of products
>
> Count merchandise and supplies during inventories
>
> Record and account for money received and prepare bank deposits

Where They Work

Sales and stock specialists work on land and aboard ships in retail stores, snack bars, and storerooms.

Opportunities in Civilian Life

Civilian sales and stock specialists work in many kinds of retail businesses, such as grocery stores and department stores. They perform duties similar to military sales and stock specialists. They may also be called sales clerks or stock clerks.

Physical Requirements

The ability to speak clearly is required. Sales and stock specialists may have to lift and carry heavy objects.

Supply and Warehousing Specialists

> Army
>
> Navy
>
> Air Force
>
> Marine Corps
>
> Coast Guard

The military maintains a large inventory of food, medicines, ammunition, spare parts, and other supplies. Keeping the military's supply system operating smoothly is an important job. The lives of combat troops in the field may depend on receiving the right supplies on time. Supply and warehousing specialists receive, store, record, and issue military supplies.

What They Do

Supply and warehousing specialists in the military perform some or all of the following duties:

> Perform inventory and financial-management procedures, including ordering, receiving, and storing supplies
>
> Locate and catalog stock
>
> Give special handling to medicine, ammunition, and other delicate supplies
>
> Select the correct stock for issue
>
> Load, unload, and move stock using equipment such as forklifts and hand trucks
>
> Keep records on incoming and outgoing stock

Where They Work

Supply and warehousing specialists work in large general supply centers, small specialized supply rooms, or ship storerooms.

Opportunities in Civilian Life

Civilian supply and warehousing specialists work for factories, parts departments in repair shops, department stores, and government warehouses and stockrooms. They perform duties similar to military supply and warehousing specialists. Civilian supply and warehousing specialists may also be called stock control clerks, parts clerks, or storekeepers.

Physical Requirements

Supply and warehousing specialists may have to lift and carry heavy boxes of ammunition and other supplies. Normal color vision is required for specialties that handle color-coded parts, supplies, and ammunition.

Training Specialists and Instructors

Navy

Air Force

Marine Corps

Coast Guard

The military trains new personnel in the job skills needed to begin their careers in the service. The military also offers advanced training and retraining to nearly all personnel. Instruction in electronics, health care, computer sciences, and aviation are just a few of the many vocational and technical areas for which the military has training programs. Training specialists and instructors teach classes and give demonstrations to provide military personnel with the knowledge needed to perform their jobs.

What They Do

Training specialists and instructors in the military perform some or all of the following duties:

- Prepare course outlines and materials to present during training
- Select training materials, such as textbooks and films
- Teach classes and give lectures in person, over closed-circuit TV, or on videotape
- Work with students individually when necessary
- Test and evaluate student progress

Where They Work

Training specialists and instructors in the military work either indoors or outdoors, depending on the type of training they provide and their specialty area.

Opportunities in Civilian Life

Civilian training specialists and instructors work for vocational and technical schools, high schools, colleges, businesses, and government agencies. Their duties are similar to those performed by military training specialists and instructors. Civilian training specialists and instructors may be called teachers, trainers, or training representatives.

Physical Requirements

Training specialists and instructors must be able to speak clearly and distinctly.

Transportation Specialists

Army

Navy

Marine Corps

Coast Guard

The military constantly moves passengers and cargo. Personnel often travel to meetings, training sessions, and new assignments. Supplies and equipment to support troops must be shipped regularly. Transportation specialists plan and assist in air, sea, and land transportation for people and cargo. Some assist passenger travel as gate agents and flight attendants.

What They Do

Transportation specialists in the military perform some or all of the following duties:

- Arrange for passenger travel via plane, bus, train, or boat
- Arrange for shipment and delivery of household goods
- Determine which vehicles to use based on freight or passenger movement requirements
- Determine transportation and shipping routes
- Prepare transportation requests and shipping documents
- Check in passengers and baggage for military transport flights
- Serve as military airplane flight attendants
- Inspect cargo for proper packing, loading, and marking

Where They Work

Transportation specialists usually work in offices. They may work outdoors when escorting passengers or processing shipments. Flight attendants work on land and in airplanes.

Opportunities in Civilian Life

Civilian transportation specialists work for airlines, shipping firms, and commercial freight lines. They perform duties similar to those of military transportation specialists. Civilian transportation specialists may also be called travel clerks, reservation clerks, or transportation agents.

SERVICE OCCUPATIONS

Firefighters

Army

Navy

Air Force

Marine Corps

Coast Guard

Military bases have their own protection services, including fire departments. Military firefighting units are responsible for protecting lives and property from fire. Firefighters put out, control, and help prevent fires in buildings, aircraft, and aboard ships.

What They Do

Firefighters in the military perform some or all of the following duties:

Operate pumps, hoses, and extinguishers

Force entry into aircraft, vehicles, and buildings in order to fight fires and rescue personnel

Drive firefighting trucks and emergency rescue vehicles

Give first aid to injured personnel

Inspect aircraft, buildings, and equipment for fire hazards

Teach fire-protection procedures

Repair firefighting equipment and fill fire extinguishers

Where They Work

Firefighters work indoors and outdoors while fighting fires. They are exposed to the smoke, heat, and flames of the fires they fight.

Opportunities in Civilian Life

Civilian firefighters work for city and county fire departments, other government agencies, and industrial firms. They perform duties similar to those performed by military firefighters, including rescue and salvage work.

Physical Requirements

Good vision without glasses and a clear speaking voice are required to enter some specialties in this occupation.

Firefighters have to climb ladders and stairs. They must also be able to lift and carry injured personnel.

Food Service Specialists

Army

Navy

Air Force

Marine Corps

Coast Guard

Every day, more than a million meals are prepared in military kitchens. Some kitchens prepare thousands of meals at one time, while others prepare food for small groups of people. Food service specialists prepare all types of food according to standard and dietetic recipes. They also order and inspect food supplies and prepare meats for cooking.

What They Do

Food service specialists in the military perform some or all of the following duties:

Order, receive, and inspect meat, fish, fruit, and vegetables

Prepare standard cuts of meat using cleavers, knives, and bandsaws

Cook steaks, chops, and roasts

Bake or fry chicken, turkey, and fish

Prepare gravies and sauces

Bake breads, cakes, pies, and pastries

Serve food in dining halls, hospitals, field kitchens, or aboard ship

Clean ovens, stoves, mixers, pots, and utensils

Where They Work

Food service specialists normally work in clean, sanitary kitchens and dining facilities. They may sometimes work in refrigerated meat lockers. Sometimes they work outdoors in tents while preparing and serving food under field conditions.

Opportunities in Civilian Life

Civilian food service specialists work in cafes, restaurants, and cafeterias. They also work in hotels, hospitals, manufacturing plants, schools, and other organizations that have their own dining facilities. Depending on specialty, food service specialists are called cooks, chefs, bakers, butchers, or meat cutters.

461

Physical Requirements

Food service specialists may have to lift and carry heavy containers of foodstuffs and large cooking utensils.

Law Enforcement and Security Specialists

Army

Navy

Air Force

Marine Corps

Coast Guard

The military services have their own law enforcement and security specialists. These specialists investigate crimes committed on military property or that involve military personnel. They also guard inmates in military correctional facilities.

What They Do

Law enforcement and security specialists in the military perform some or all of the following duties:

Investigate criminal activities and activities related to espionage, treason, and terrorism

Interview witnesses and question suspects, sometimes using polygraph machines (lie detectors)

Guard correctional facilities and conduct searches of inmates, cells, and vehicles

Perform fire and riot-control duties

Where They Work

Law enforcement and security specialists in the military work mainly indoors; they may work outdoors while conducting investigations or guarding prisoners in exercise yards.

Opportunities in Civilian Life

Civilian law enforcement and security specialists work in federal, state, and local prisons, intelligence and law enforcement agencies, and private security companies. They perform similar duties to those performed in the military. They may be called detectives, private investigators, undercover agents, corrections officers, or guards.

Physical Requirements

Normal color vision is necessary to enter some specialties in this area. Some specialties have minimum age and height requirements.

Military Police

Army

Navy

Air Force

Marine Corps

Coast Guard

The services have their own police forces for many of the same reasons that civilians do: to control traffic, prevent crime, and respond to emergencies. Military police protect lives and property on military bases by enforcing military laws and regulations.

What They Do

Military police perform some or all of the following duties:

Patrol areas on foot, by car, or by boat

Interview witnesses, victims, and suspects in the course of investigating crimes

Collect fingerprints and other evidence

Arrest and charge criminal suspects

Train and walk with police dogs

Testify in court

Guard entrances and direct traffic

Where They Work

Military police work both indoors and outdoors. They may work on foot, in cars, or in boats.

Opportunities in Civilian Life

Civilian police officers generally work for state, county, or city law enforcement agencies. Some work as security guards for industrial firms, airports, and other businesses and institutions. They perform duties similar to those of military police.

Physical Requirements

Normal color vision, hearing, and a clear speaking voice are usually required to enter this occupation. Some specialties have minimum height requirements.

VEHICLE AND MACHINERY MECHANIC OCCUPATIONS

Aircraft Mechanics

Army

Navy

Air Force

Marine Corps

Coast Guard

Military aircraft are used to fly hundreds of missions each day for transport, patrol, and flight training. They need frequent servicing to remain safe and ready to fly. Aircraft mechanics inspect, service, and repair helicopters and airplanes.

What They Do

Aircraft mechanics in the military perform some or all of the following duties:

- Service and repair helicopter, jet, and propeller aircraft engines
- Inspect and repair aircraft wings, fuselages (bodies), and tail assemblies
- Service and repair aircraft landing gear
- Repair or replace starters, lights, batteries, wiring, and other electrical parts

Where They Work

Aircraft mechanics work in aircraft hangars and machine shops located on air bases or aboard aircraft carriers.

Opportunities in Civilian Life

Civilian aircraft mechanics work for aircraft manufacturers, commercial airlines, and government agencies. They perform duties similar to those of military aircraft mechanics. They may also be called airframe or power plant mechanics.

Physical Requirements

Some specialties require moderate to heavy lifting. Normal color vision is required to work with color-coded wiring.

Automotive and Heavy Equipment Mechanics

Army

Navy

Air Force

Marine Corps

Coast Guard

Keeping automotive and heavy equipment in good working condition is vital to the success of military missions. Automotive and heavy equipment mechanics maintain and repair vehicles such as jeeps, cars, trucks, tanks, self-propelled missile launchers, and other combat vehicles. They also repair bulldozers, power shovels, and other construction equipment.

What They Do

Automotive and heavy equipment mechanics in the military perform some or all of the following duties:

- Troubleshoot problems in vehicle engines, electrical systems, steering, brakes, and suspensions
- Tune and repair engines
- Replace or repair damaged body parts, hydraulic arms or shovels, and grader blades
- Establish and follow schedules for maintaining vehicles

Where They Work

Automotive and heavy equipment mechanics usually work inside large repair garages. They work outdoors when making emergency repairs in the field.

Opportunities in Civilian Life

Civilian automotive and heavy equipment mechanics may work for service stations, auto and construction equipment dealers, farm equipment companies, and state highway agencies. They perform duties similar to those of military automotive and heavy equipment mechanics. They may also be called garage mechanics, carburetor mechanics, transmission mechanics, radiator mechanics, construction equipment mechanics, or endless track vehicle mechanics.

Physical Requirements

Automotive and heavy equipment mechanics may have to lift heavy parts and tools. They sometimes have to work in cramped positions. Normal color vision is required for some specialties to work with color-coded wiring and to read diagrams.

Divers

Army
Navy
Marine Corps
Coast Guard

Sometimes, military tasks such as ship repair, construction, and patrolling must be done under water. Divers in the military perform this work. They usually specialize either as scuba divers, who work just below the surface, or as deep-sea divers, who may work for long periods of time in depths up to 300 feet.

What They Do

Divers in the military perform some or all of the following duties:

Inspect and clean ship propellers and hulls

Patch damaged ship hulls using underwater welding equipment

Patrol the waters below ships at anchor

Salvage (recover) sunken equipment

Assist with underwater construction of piers and harbor facilities

Survey rivers, beaches, and harbors for underwater obstacles

Use explosives to clear underwater obstacles

Where They Work

Divers work underwater. However, they plan and prepare for work on land or aboard ships. Because diving is not usually a full-time job, divers often develop another job specialty in which they work.

Opportunities in Civilian Life

Civilian divers work for oil companies, salvage companies, underwater construction firms, and police or fire rescue units. They perform duties similar to those of divers in the military.

Physical Requirements

Divers must be good swimmers and physically strong.

Heating and Cooling Mechanics

Army
Navy
Air Force
Marine Corps
Coast Guard

Air-conditioning and heating equipment is used to maintain comfortable temperatures in military buildings, airplanes, and ships. Refrigeration equipment is used to keep food cold and to keep some missile fuels at subzero storage temperatures. Heating and cooling mechanics install and repair air-conditioning, refrigeration, and heating equipment.

What They Do

Heating and cooling mechanics in the military perform some or all of the following duties:

Install and repair furnaces, boilers, and air conditioners

Recharge cooling systems with refrigerant gases

Install copper tubing systems that circulate water or cooling gases

Replace compressor parts such as valves, pistons, bearings, and electrical motors on refrigeration units

Repair thermostats and electrical circuits

Where They Work

Heating and cooling mechanics may work inside repair shops. Frequently, they work wherever equipment is to be installed or repaired.

Opportunities in Civilian Life

Civilian heating and cooling mechanics work for contractors that install home furnaces and air conditioners or for firms that repair refrigerators and freezers in homes, grocery stores, factories, and warehouses. Heating and cooling mechanics in civilian life often specialize more than those in the military. They may be called heating, air-conditioning, refrigeration, or climate-control mechanics.

Physical Requirements

Heating and cooling mechanics may have to lift or move heavy equipment. They are often required to stoop, kneel, and work in cramped positions. Normal color vision is required for locating and repairing color-coded wiring.

Marine Engine Mechanics

Army

Navy

Air Force

Marine Corps

Coast Guard

The military operates many types of watercraft, ranging from small motor launches to large ships. Many of these vessels are powered by gasoline or diesel engines. Marine engine mechanics repair and maintain gasoline and diesel engines on ships, boats, and other watercraft. They also repair shipboard mechanical and electrical equipment.

What They Do

Marine engine mechanics in the military perform some or all of the following duties:

Repair and maintain shipboard gasoline and diesel engines

Locate and repair machinery parts, including valves and piping systems

Repair ship propulsion machinery

Repair and service hoisting machinery and ship elevators

Repair refrigeration and air-conditioning equipment on ships

Repair engine-related electrical systems

Where They Work

Marine engine mechanics work aboard ships, normally in the engine or power rooms. Sometimes they work in repair centers on land bases. Working conditions in engine rooms tend to be noisy and hot.

Opportunities in Civilian Life

Civilian marine engine mechanics work in many industries, including marine transportation, commercial fishing, and oil exploration and drilling. They perform duties similar to those of military marine engine mechanics.

Physical Requirements

Normal color vision is required to work with color-coded diagrams and wiring.

Powerhouse Mechanics

Army

Navy

Coast Guard

Power-generating stations (powerhouses) provide electric power for military bases, ships, and field camps. The many types of powerhouses range from small gas generators to large nuclear reactors. Powerhouse mechanics install, maintain, and repair electrical and mechanical equipment in power-generating stations.

What They Do

Powerhouse mechanics in the military perform some or all of the following duties:

Install generating equipment, such as gasoline and diesel engines, turbines, and air compressors

Repair and maintain nuclear power plants

Inspect and service pumps, generators, batteries, and cables

Tune engines using hand tools, timing lights, and combustion pressure gauges

Diagnose (troubleshoot) engine and electrical system problems

Replace damaged parts such as fuel injectors, valves, and pistons

Where They Work

Powerhouse mechanics work in equipment repair shops, power plant stations, or power-generating rooms aboard ships. Sometimes they work outdoors while repairing substation generating equipment.

Opportunities in Civilian Life

Civilian powerhouse mechanics work for a wide variety of employers, such as utility and power companies, manufacturing companies, and others that operate their own power plants. They perform duties similar to those of military powerhouse mechanics.

Physical Requirements

Powerhouse mechanics may have to lift and move heavy electrical generators or batteries. Normal color vision is required to work with color-coded wiring and cables.

ELECTRONIC AND ELECTRICAL EQUIPMENT REPAIR OCCUPATIONS

Aircraft Electricians

Army

Navy

Air Force

Marine Corps

Coast Guard

Airplanes and helicopters house complex electrical systems. Instruments, lights, weapons, ignition systems, landing gear, and many other aircraft parts are powered by electricity. Aircraft electricians maintain and repair electrical systems on airplanes and helicopters.

What They Do

Aircraft electricians in the military perform some or all of the following duties:

Troubleshoot aircraft electrical systems using test equipment

Repair or replace defective generators and electric motors

Inspect and maintain electrical systems

Replace faulty wiring

Solder electrical connections

Repair or replace instruments, such as tachometers, temperature gauges, and altimeters

Read electrical-wiring diagrams

Where They Work

Aircraft electricians usually work indoors, in aircraft hangars, airplanes, and repair shops. They may also work on aircraft parked outdoors.

Opportunities in Civilian Life

Civilian aircraft electricians work mainly for airlines and aircraft maintenance firms. They may also work

for aircraft manufacturers and other organizations that have fleets of airplanes or helicopters. Their duties are similar to those of military aircraft electricians.

Physical Requirements

Normal color vision is required to work with color-coded wiring.

Communications Equipment Repairers

Army

Navy

Air Force

Marine Corps

Coast Guard

The military relies on communication equipment to link ground, sea, and air forces. This equipment allows the military to track and direct troop, aircraft, and ship movements. Communications equipment repairers ensure that this equipment operates properly.

What They Do

Communications equipment repairers in the military perform some or all of the following duties:

Maintain, test, and repair communications equipment using frequency meters, circuit analyzers, and other electrical and electronic test equipment

Install and repair circuits and wiring using soldering irons and hand tools

Calibrate and align equipment components using scales, gauges, and other measuring instruments

String overhead-communications and electric cables between utility poles

Where They Work

Communications equipment repairers usually work in repair shops, laboratories, and outdoors, depending on the specialty.

Opportunities in Civilian Life

Civilian communications equipment repairers often work for firms that design and make communications and electronic equipment. They may also work for the federal government. They perform duties similar to those of military communications equipment repairers. They may be called radio repairers, radio mechanics, teletype repairers, or station installers and repairers, depending on their specialty.

Physical Requirements

For some specialties, normal color vision is required. Some repairers may work from ladders or on tall utility poles.

Computer Equipment Repairers

Army
Navy
Air Force
Marine Corps

The military relies on computers to support weapons systems, communications, and administration. Keeping systems "up" is crucial for all military operations. Computer equipment repairers install, test, maintain, and repair computers and related data-processing equipment.

What They Do

Computer equipment repairers in the military perform some or all of the following duties:

Install computers and other data-processing equipment

Inspect data-processing equipment for defects in wiring, circuit boards, and other parts

Test and repair data-processing equipment using electrical voltage meters, circuit analyzers, and other special testing equipment

Locate defective data-processing parts using technical guides and diagrams

Where They Work

Computer equipment repairers usually work indoors in repair shops or data-processing centers on land or aboard ships. Some specialties involve flying.

Opportunities in Civilian Life

Civilian computer equipment repairers work for computer manufacturers, repair services, and other businesses with large computer facilities. They perform duties similar to those of military computer equipment repairers. They may also be called computer service technicians.

Physical Requirements

Specialties that involve flying require passing a special physical exam. Normal color vision is required to work with color-coded wiring.

Electrical Products Repairers

Army
Navy
Marine Corps
Coast Guard

Much of the military's equipment is electrically powered. Electric motors, electric tools, and medical equipment require careful maintenance and repair. Electrical products repairers maintain and repair electrical equipment. They specialize by type of equipment.

What They Do

Electrical products repairers in the military perform some or all of the following duties:

Maintain, test, and repair electric motors in many kinds of machines, such as lathes, pumps, office machines, and kitchen appliances

Inspect and repair electrical, medical, and dental equipment

Inspect and repair electric instruments, such as voltmeters

Replace worn gaskets and seals in watertight electrical equipment

Maintain and repair portable electric tools, such as saws and drills

Maintain and repair submarine periscopes

Where They Work

Electrical products repairers usually work in repair shops on land or aboard ships.

Opportunities in Civilian Life

Civilian electrical products repairers work in many industries, including hospitals, manufacturing firms, and governmental agencies. They also work in independent repair shops. They perform duties similar to those of military electrical products repairers. They may be called electric tool repairers, electrical instrument repairers, electromedical equipment repairers, or electric motor repairers.

Physical Requirements

Normal color vision is required to work with color-coded wiring.

Electronic Instrument Repairers

> **Army**
>
> **Navy**
>
> **Air Force**
>
> **Marine Corps**
>
> **Coast Guard**

The military uses electronic instruments in many areas, including health care, weather forecasting, flight control, and combat, to name a few. Electronic instrument repairers maintain and repair electronic instruments, such as precision-measuring equipment, navigational controls, photographic equipment, and biomedical instruments. Electronic instrument repairers normally specialize by type of equipment or instrument being repaired.

What They Do

Electronic instrument repairers in the military perform some or all of the following duties:

> Test meteorological and medical instruments, navigational controls, and simulators using electronic and electrical test equipment
>
> Read technical diagrams and manuals in order to locate, isolate, and repair instrument parts
>
> Replace equipment parts such as resistors, switches, and circuit boards

Where They Work

Electronic instrument repairers usually work in repair shops and laboratories.

Opportunities in Civilian Life

Most civilian electronic instrument repairers work for manufacturing, medical research, or satellite communications firms, or commercial airlines. They may also work for government agencies, such as the Federal Aviation Administration, the National Aeronautics and Space Administration, or the National Weather Service. They perform the same kind of duties as military instrument repairers. They are called electronics mechanics, dental equipment repairers, or biomedical equipment technicians, depending on their specialty.

Physical Requirements

Normal color vision is required to work with color-coded wiring. Some specialties require a minimum age of 18 to enter.

Photographic Equipment Repairers

> **Navy**
>
> **Air Force**
>
> **Marine Corps**

The photographic equipment used by the military is composed of many sensitive mechanisms. Still cameras, video cameras, and photographic-processing equipment require regular attention to stay in working order. Photographic equipment repairers adjust and repair cameras, projectors, and photoprocessing equipment.

What They Do

Photographic equipment repairers in the military perform some or all of the following duties:

> Adjust and repair camera shutter mechanisms, focus controls, and flash units
>
> Maintain and repair aerial cameras mounted in airplanes
>
> Maintain aerial sensors that detect foreign military activities
>
> Maintain and repair motion picture cameras and sound-recording equipment
>
> Repair photoprocessing equipment such as enlargers, film processors, and printers
>
> Diagnose problems in all types of cameras

Where They Work

Photographic equipment repairers work in repair shops on land or aboard ships.

Opportunities in Civilian Life

Civilian photographic equipment repairers work for photographic laboratories, engineering firms, and government agencies. They perform duties similar to those performed in the military. Depending on the specialty, they may also be called camera repairers, motion-picture-equipment machinists, or photographic-equipment technicians.

Physical Requirements

Normal color vision is required to work with color-coded wiring.

Power Plant Electricians

Army
Navy
Air Force
Marine Corps
Coast Guard

Each military base—anywhere in the world—must provide its own electricity. Power plant electricians maintain and repair electricity-generating equipment in mobile and stationary power plants.

What They Do

Power plant electricians perform some or all of the following duties:

Maintain and repair motors, generators, switchboards, and control equipment

Maintain and repair power and lighting circuits, electrical fixtures, and other electrical equipment

Detect and locate grounds, open circuits, and short circuits in power distribution cables

Connect emergency power to the main control board from an emergency switchboard

Operate standard electrical and electronic test equipment

Read technical guides and diagrams to locate damaged parts of generators and control equipment

Where They Work

Power plant electricians work in repair shops on land, aboard ships, or wherever generating equipment needing repair is located.

Opportunities in Civilian Life

Civilian power plant electricians often work for construction companies, manufacturers, and utility companies. They perform duties similar to those of military power plant electricians.

Physical Requirements

Normal color vision is required to work with color-coded wiring.

Precision Instrument Repairers

Army
Navy
Air Force
Marine Corps

Precision instruments are measuring devices. They can be as simple as a thermometer or as complex as a gyrocompass. Precision instruments are used by the military to measure distance, pressure, altitude, underwater depth, and many other physical properties. Precision instrument repairers keep measuring devices in good working order. They calibrate (adjust) gauges and meters to ensure correct readings.

What They Do

Precision instrument repairers in the military perform some or all of the following duties:

Calibrate weather instruments, such as barometers and thermometers

Repair gyrocompasses

Adjust and repair weapon-aiming devices, such as range finders, telescopes, periscopes, and ballistic computers

Calibrate engineering instruments, such as transits, levels, telemeters, and stereoscopes

Calibrate and repair instruments used in aircraft

Repair watches, clocks, and timers

Calibrate electrical test instruments

Where They Work

Precision instrument repairers usually work in repair shops on land or aboard ships.

Opportunities in Civilian Life

Civilian precision instrument repairers work for firms that manufacture or use precision instruments, including manufacturing firms, airlines, machinery repair shops, maintenance shops, and instrument makers. Civilian precision instrument repairers perform duties similar to those of military precision instrument repairers. They may also be called instrument mechanics or calibration specialists.

Physical Requirements

Normal color vision is required to work with color-coded wiring and repair manuals.

Radar and Sonar Equipment Repairers

Army

Navy

Air Force

Marine Corps

Coast Guard

Radar and sonar equipment locates objects by bouncing radio and sound waves off them. This equipment is used to detect and track enemy ships, planes, and missiles. It is also used for ship and plane navigation and weather observation. Radar and sonar equipment repairers install, maintain, repair, and operate sonar and radar equipment.

What They Do

Radar and sonar equipment repairers perform some or all of the following duties:

Test radar systems using electronic and electrical test equipment

Monitor the operation of air traffic control, missile tracking, air defense, and other radar systems to make sure there are no problems

Repair sonar and radar components (parts), using soldering irons and other special hand and power tools

Install receivers, transmitters, and other components using technical manuals and guides

Read wiring diagrams, designs, and other drawings to locate parts and components of radar equipment

Where They Work

Radar and sonar equipment repairers work in repair shops and laboratories on land or aboard ships. Some specialties involve flying.

Opportunities in Civilian Life

Civilian radar and sonar equipment repairers work for engineering firms, the federal government, or aircraft and military hardware manufacturers. They perform duties similar to those of military radar and sonar equipment repairers. They may also be called communications technicians.

Physical Requirements

Specialties involving flying require passing a special physical exam. Normal color vision is required to work with color-coded wiring.

Ship Electricians

Navy

Coast Guard

Electrical systems supply power to operate ships and submarines. Lights, radar, weapons, laundry and cooking appliances, and machinery all need electricity. Ship electricians operate and repair electrical systems on ships. They keep electrical power plants, wiring, and machinery in working order.

What They Do

Ship electricians in the military perform some or all of the following duties:

Install wiring for lights and equipment

Troubleshoot electrical wiring and equipment using test meters

Inspect and maintain devices that distribute electricity throughout ships, such as circuits, transformers, and regulators

Monitor and maintain electrical devices connected to the ship's main engines or nuclear reactors

Repair motors and appliances

Where They Work

Ship electricians usually work indoors, aboard ships or submarines. They also work in ship repair shops on land.

Opportunities in Civilian Life

Civilian ship electricians work for shipbuilding and dry-dock firms and shipping lines. They perform duties similar to those of military ship electricians. Other civilian electricians, such as building electricians and electrical products repairers, also perform similar work. Civilian nuclear power plant electricians perform duties similar to those of ship electricians who work with nuclear plants on ships and submarines.

Weapons Maintenance Technicians

Army
Navy
Air Force
Marine Corps
Coast Guard

Combat forces use many different types of weapons, ranging from small field artillery to large ballistic missiles. Weapons may be fired from ships, planes, and ground stations. Most modern weapons have electronic components and systems that assist in locating targets, aiming weapons, and firing them. Weapons maintenance technicians maintain and repair weapons used by combat forces.

What They Do

Weapons maintenance technicians in the military perform some or all of the following duties:

- Repair and maintain artillery, naval gun systems, and infantry weapons
- Clean and lubricate gyroscopes, sights, and other electro-optical fire-control components
- Repair and maintain missile mounts, platforms, and launch mechanisms
- Test and adjust weapons firing, guidance, and launch systems

Where They Work

Weapons maintenance technicians work in workshops when testing and repairing electronic components. They may work outdoors while inspecting and repairing combat vehicles, ships, artillery, aircraft, and missile silos.

Opportunities in Civilian Life

Civilian weapons maintenance technicians work for firms that design, build, and test weapons systems for the military. They perform duties similar to those of military weapons maintenance technicians. They may also be called electronic mechanics, avionics technicians, or missile facilities repairers.

Physical Requirements

Some specialties involve moderate to heavy lifting. Normal color vision is required to read color-coded charts and diagrams.

CONSTRUCTION OCCUPATIONS

Building Electricians

Army
Navy
Air Force
Marine Corps
Coast Guard

The military relies on electricity to light hospitals, run power tools, operate computers, and much more. Building electricians install and repair electrical wiring systems in offices, repair shops, airplane hangars, and other buildings on military bases.

What They Do

Building electricians in the military perform some or all of the following duties:

- Install and wire transformers, junction boxes, and circuit breakers, using wire cutters, insulation strippers, and other hand tools
- Read blueprints, wiring plans, and repair orders to determine wiring layouts or repair needs
- Cut, bend, and string wires and conduits (pipe or tubing)
- Inspect power distribution systems, shorts in wires, and faulty equipment using test meters
- Repair and replace faulty wiring and lighting fixtures
- Install lightning rods to protect electrical systems

Where They Work

Building electricians usually work indoors while installing wiring systems. They work outdoors while installing transformers and lightning rods.

Opportunities in Civilian Life

Civilian building electricians usually work for building and electrical contracting firms. Some work as self-employed electrical contractors. They perform duties similar to those of military building electricians.

Physical Requirements

Normal color vision is required for working with color-coded wiring and circuits.

471

Construction Equipment Operators

>   Army
>
>   Navy
>
>   Air Force
>
>   Marine Corps
>
>   Coast Guard

Each year the military completes hundreds of construction projects. Tons of earth and building materials must be moved to build airfields, roads, dams, and buildings. Construction equipment operators use bulldozers, cranes, graders, and other heavy equipment in military construction.

What They Do

Construction equipment operators in the military perform some or all of the following duties:

> Drive bulldozers, road-graders, and other heavy equipment to cut and level earth for runways and roadbeds
>
> Lift and move steel and other heavy building materials using winches, cranes, and hoists
>
> Dig holes and trenches using power shovels
>
> Remove ice and snow from runways, roads, and other areas using scrapers and snow blowers
>
> Operate mixing plants to make concrete and asphalt
>
> Spread asphalt and concrete with paving machines
>
> Drill wells using drilling rigs
>
> Place and detonate explosives

Where They Work

Construction equipment operators work outdoors in all kinds of weather conditions. They often sit for long periods and are subject to loud noise and vibrations. They may work indoors while repairing equipment.

Opportunities in Civilian Life

Civilian construction equipment operators work for building contractors, state highway agencies, rock quarries, well drillers, and construction firms. Civilian construction equipment operators may also be known as operating engineers, heavy equipment operators, well drillers, or riggers.

Physical Requirements

Some specialties require normal hearing, color vision, and heavy lifting.

Construction Specialists

>   Army
>
>   Navy
>
>   Air Force
>
>   Marine Corps
>
>   Coast Guard

The military builds many temporary and permanent structures each year. Lumber, plywood, plasterboard, and concrete and masonry (bricks, stone, and concrete blocks) are the basic building materials for many of these projects. Construction specialists build and repair buildings, bridges, foundations, dams, and bunkers. They work with engineers and other building specialists as part of military construction teams.

What They Do

Construction specialists in the military perform some or all of the following duties:

> Build foundations, floor slabs, and walls with brick, cement block, mortar, or stone
>
> Erect wood framing for buildings using hand and power tools, such as hammers, saws, levels, and drills
>
> Lay roofing materials, such as asphalt, tile, and wooden shingles
>
> Install plasterboard, plaster, and paneling to form interior walls and ceilings
>
> Lay wood and ceramic tile floors and build steps, staircases, and porches
>
> Build temporary shelters for storing supplies and equipment while on training maneuvers

Where They Work

Construction specialists work indoors and outdoors on construction sites.

Opportunities in Civilian Life

Civilian construction specialists usually work for construction or remodeling contractors, government agencies, utility companies, or manufacturing firms. They perform duties similar to those of military construction specialists. They may also be called bricklayers, stonemasons, cement masons, cement finishers, carpenters, or cabinetmakers.

Physical Requirements

Construction specialists may have to lift and carry heavy building materials, such as lumber, plasterboard, and concrete. Sometimes, they climb and work from ladders and scaffolding.

Plumbers and Pipe Fitters

Army

Navy

Marine Corps

Coast Guard

Military buildings and equipment require pipe systems for water, steam, gas, and waste. Pipe systems are also needed on aircraft, missiles, and ships for hydraulic (fluid pressure) and pneumatic (air pressure) systems. Plumbers and pipe fitters install and repair plumbing and pipe systems.

What They Do

Plumbers and pipe fitters in the military perform some or all of the following duties:

Plan layouts of pipe systems using blueprints and drawings

Bend, cut, and thread pipes made of lead, copper, and plastic

Install connectors, fittings, and joints

Solder or braze pipe and tubing to join them

Install sinks, toilets, and other plumbing fixtures

Troubleshoot, test, and calibrate hydraulic and pneumatic systems

Keep accurate records of tasks completed and materials used

Where They Work

Plumbers and pipe fitters work both indoors and outdoors on land and aboard ships.

Opportunities in Civilian Life

Civilian plumbers and pipe fitters usually work for mechanical or plumbing contractors or as self-employed contractors. Some plumbers and pipe fitters work for public utilities. Civilian plumbers and pipe fitters perform duties similar to those performed in the military.

Physical Requirements

Plumbers and pipe fitters have to lift and carry heavy pipes and tubes.

MACHINE OPERATOR AND PRECISION WORK OCCUPATIONS

Compressed-Gas Technicians

Navy

Marine Corps

Compressed-gases have many uses in the military, such as breathing oxygen for jet pilots, divers, and medical patients and fuel for missiles and welding torches. Compressed-gas technicians operate and maintain the machinery used to compress or liquefy gases.

What They Do

Compressed-gas technicians in the military perform some or all of the following duties:

Operate valves to control the flow of air through machinery that compresses or liquefies gases

Remove impurities, such as carbon dioxide, from gases

Fill storage cylinders with compressed gas

Test cylinders for leaks, using pressure gauges

Operate dry ice plants

Maintain compressed-gas machinery

Where They Work

Compressed-gas technicians in the military normally work indoors in shops on bases or aboard ships. Working with air compressors may be noisy and hot.

Opportunities in Civilian Life

Civilian compressed-gas technicians work for a wide range of industrial companies and processing plants, especially distilling and chemical firms. They perform duties similar to those of military compressed-gas technicians. They may also be called oxygen plant operators, compressed-gas plant workers, or acetylene plant operators.

Physical Requirements

Normal color vision is usually required to enter this occupation.

Dental and Optical Laboratory Technicians

Army

Navy

Air Force

Coast Guard

The military provides dental and optical care as part of its comprehensive health-service program. Dental and optical laboratory technicians make and repair dental devices and eyeglasses that are provided for military personnel.

What They Do

Dental and optical laboratory technicians perform some or all of the following duties:

Make dentures, braces, and other dental or optical devices

Construct, assemble, repair, and align dental and optical devices (metal braces and retainers, eyeglass frames and lenses)

Harden and cure new dentures or lenses using high-temperature ovens or other heat-treating equipment

Grind, polish, and smooth dentures or lenses using hand or power tools

Where They Work

Dental and optical laboratory technicians normally work in dental or optical laboratories and occasionally in examination and dispensing offices.

Opportunities in Civilian Life

Civilian dental laboratory technicians normally work for small dental laboratories or large dental offices. Optical laboratory technicians work in optical laboratories or for retail opticians. They perform duties similar to those of military technicians. Civilian optical laboratory technicians may also be called opticians or ophthalmic laboratory technicians.

Physical Requirements

Normal color vision for some specialties is required to match color of artificial teeth with natural tooth color.

Machinists

Army

Navy

Air Force

Marine Corps

Coast Guard

Sometimes when engines or machines break down, the parts needed to repair them are not available. In these cases, the broken parts must be repaired or new ones made. Machinists make and repair metal parts for engines and all types of machines. They operate lathes, drill presses, grinders, and other machine shop equipment.

What They Do

Machinists in the military perform some or all of the following duties:

Study blueprints or written plans of the parts to be made

Set up and operate lathes to make parts such as shafts and gears

Cut metal stock using power hacksaws and bandsaws

Bore holes using drill presses

Shape and smooth parts using grinders

Measure work, using micrometers, calipers, and depth gauges

Where They Work

Machinists work in machine shops, which are often noisy.

Opportunities in Civilian Life

Civilian machinists work for factories and repair shops in many industries, including the electrical product, automotive, and heavy-machinery industries. They perform duties similar to those of military machinists.

Power Plant Operators

Army

Navy

Marine Corps

Coast Guard

Power plants generate electricity for ships, submarines, and military bases. The military uses many different types of power plants. Some are fueled by oil, others run on coal. Many ships and submarines are powered by nuclear power plants. Power plant operators control power generating plants on land and aboard ships and submarines. They operate boilers, turbines, nuclear reactors, and portable generators.

What They Do

Power plant operators in the military perform some or all of the following duties:

- Monitor and operate control boards to regulate power plants
- Operate and maintain diesel generating units to produce electric power
- Monitor and control nuclear reactors that produce electricity and power ships and submarines
- Operate and maintain stationary engines, such as steam engines, air compressors, and generators
- Operate and maintain auxiliary equipment, such as pumps, fans, and condensers
- Inspect equipment for malfunctions
- Operate the steam turbines that generate power for ships
- Operate and maintain auxiliary equipment, including pumps, fans, condensers, and auxiliary boilers

Where They Work

Power plant operators usually work indoors. They are subject to high temperatures, dust, and noise.

Opportunities in Civilian Life

Civilian power plant operators work for power companies, factories, schools, and hospitals. They perform duties similar to those of military power plant operators. Depending on the specialty, power plant operators may also be called boiler operators, stationary engineers, nuclear reactor operators, or diesel plant operators.

Physical Requirements

Power plant operators lift heavy parts or tools when maintaining power plants. They may also have to stoop and kneel and work in awkward positions while repairing.

Printing Specialists

Army

Navy

Air Force

Marine Corps

The military produces many printed publications each year, including newspapers, booklets, training manuals, maps, and charts. Printing specialists operate printing presses and binding machines to make finished copies of printed material.

What They Do

Printing specialists in the military perform some or all of the following duties:

- Reproduce printed matter using offset lithographic printing processes
- Prepare photographic negatives and transfer them to printing plates using copy cameras and enlargers
- Prepare layouts of artwork, photographs, and text for lithographic plates
- Produce brochures, newspapers, maps, and charts
- Bind printed material into hardback or paperback books using binding machines
- Maintain printing presses

Where They Work

Printing specialists work indoors in print shops and offices located on land or aboard ships.

Opportunities in Civilian Life

Civilian printing specialists work for commercial print shops, newspapers, insurance companies, government offices, or businesses that do their own printing. They perform duties similar to military printing specialists. They may be called offset-printing-press operators, lithograph-press operators, offset-duplicating-machine operators, lithograph photographers, or bindery workers.

Survival Equipment Specialists

Army

Navy

Air Force

Marine Corps

Coast Guard

Military personnel often undertake hazardous assignments. They depend on survival equipment (parachutes, rescue equipment) to protect their lives in case of emergencies. Survival equipment specialists inspect, maintain, and repair survival equipment such as parachutes, aircraft life-support equipment, and air-sea rescue equipment.

What They Do

Survival equipment specialists in the military perform some or all of the following duties:

Inspect parachutes for rips and tangled lines

Pack parachutes for safe operation

Repair life rafts and load them with emergency provisions

Test emergency oxygen regulators on aircraft

Stock aircraft with fire extinguishers, flares, and survival provisions

Train crews in the use of survival equipment

Repair tents, tarps, and other canvas equipment

Where They Work

Survival equipment specialists in the military work in repair shops on land or aboard ships.

Opportunities in Civilian Life

Civilian survival equipment specialists work for commercial airlines, parachute rigging and supply companies, survival equipment manufacturing firms, and some government agencies. They perform duties similar to those of military survival equipment specialists. Those who specialize in parachutes are called parachute riggers.

Physical Requirements

Normal color vision is required to work with color-coded wiring and repair charts.

Water and Sewage Treatment Plant Operators

Army

Navy

Air Force

Marine Corps

Coast Guard

Military bases operate their own water treatment plants when public facilities cannot be used. These plants provide drinking water and safely dispose of sewage. Water and sewage treatment plant operators maintain the systems that purify water and treat sewage.

What They Do

Water and sewage treatment plant operators in the military perform some or all of the following duties:

Operate pumps to transfer water from reservoirs and storage tanks to treatment plants

Add chemicals and operate machinery that purifies water for drinking or cleans it for safe disposal

Test water for chlorine content, acidity, oxygen demand, and impurities

Regulate the flow of drinking water to meet demand

Clean and maintain water treatment machinery

Keep records of chemical treatments, water pressure, and maintenance

Where They Work

Water and sewage treatment plant operators work indoors and outdoors. They may be exposed to strong odors.

Opportunities in Civilian Life

Civilian water and sewage treatment plant operators work for municipal public works and industrial plants. Their work is similar to that of military water and sewage treatment plant operators. Civilian plant operators usually specialize as water treatment plant operators, waterworks pump station operators, or wastewater treatment plant operators.

Physical Requirements

Normal color vision is needed to examine water for acidity and impurities.

Welders and Metal Workers

Army
Navy
Air Force
Marine Corps
Coast Guard

Sheet metal is used as a building material in many military construction projects. Ships, tanks, and aircraft are made of heavy metal armor. Welders and metal workers make and install sheet metal products, such as roofs, air ducts, gutters, and vents. They also make custom parts to repair the structural parts of ships, submarines, landing craft, buildings, and equipment.

What They Do

Welders and metal workers in the military perform some or all of the following duties:

Weld, braze, or solder metal parts together

Repair automotive and ship parts using welding equipment

Measure work with calipers, micrometers, and rulers

Where They Work

Welders and metal workers work indoors in metal-working shops and aircraft hangars. They also work outdoors at construction sites, on ships, and in the field.

Opportunities in Civilian Life

Civilian welders and metal workers may work for metal repair shops, auto repair shops, construction companies, pipeline companies, aircraft manufacturing plants, shipyards, and marine servicing companies. They perform duties similar to those of military welders and metal workers.

Physical Requirements

Welders and metal workers may have to lift heavy metal parts and work in crouching or kneeling positions. Good color vision is required for locating and marking reference points, setting and adjusting welding equipment, and matching paints.

TRANSPORTATION AND MATERIAL-HANDLING OCCUPATIONS

Air Crew Members

Army
Navy
Air Force
Marine Corps
Coast Guard

The military uses aircraft of all types and sizes to conduct combat and intelligence missions, rescue personnel, transport troops and equipment, and perform long-range bombing missions. Air crew members operate equipment on board aircraft during operations. They normally specialize by type of aircraft, such as bomber, intelligence, transport, or search and rescue.

What They Do

Air crew members in the military perform some or all of the following duties:

Operate aircraft communication and radar equipment

Operate and maintain aircraft defensive gunnery systems

Operate helicopter hoists to lift equipment and personnel from land and sea

Operate and maintain aircraft in-flight refueling systems

Where They Work

Air crew members work inside all sizes and types of aircraft based on land or aboard ships. They fly in all types of weather and in both hot and cold climates.

Opportunities in Civilian Life

There are no direct civilian equivalents to military air crew members. However, some of the skills gained in the military could be useful in civilian government and private agencies that provide emergency medical services. Also, weight and load computation skills are useful for civilian air transport operations.

Physical Requirements

Air crew members must be in excellent physical condition and pass a special physical exam in order to qualify for flight duty. They must be mentally sound and have normal hearing.

Aircraft Launch and Recovery Specialists

> **Navy**
>
> **Marine Corps**
>
> **Coast Guard**

The military operates thousands of aircraft that take off and land on aircraft carriers all over the world. The successful launch and recovery of aircraft is important to the completion of air missions and the safety of flight crews. Aircraft launch and recovery specialists operate and maintain catapults, arresting gear, and other equipment used in aircraft carrier takeoff and landing operations.

What They Do

Aircraft launch and recovery specialists in the military perform some or all of the following duties:

- Operate consoles to control launch and recovery equipment, including catapults and arresting gear
- Operate elevators to transfer aircraft between flight and storage decks
- Install and maintain visual landing aids
- Test and adjust launch and recovery equipment using electric and mechanical test equipment and hand tools
- Install airfield crash barriers and barricades
- Direct aircraft launch and recovery operations using hand or light signals
- Maintain logs of airplane launches, recoveries, and equipment maintenance

Where They Work

Aircraft launch and recovery specialists work outdoors aboard ships while operating and maintaining launch and recovery equipment or holding visual landing aids for incoming aircraft. They are exposed to noise and fumes from jet and helicopter engines.

Opportunities in Civilian Life

There are no direct opportunities in civilian life for military aircraft launch and recovery specialists. However, many of the skills learned are relevant to jobs performed by ground crews at civilian airports.

Physical Requirements

Normal color vision is required to work with color-coded parts and the wiring of launch and recovery equipment.

Cargo Specialists

> **Army**
>
> **Navy**
>
> **Air Force**
>
> **Coast Guard**

The military delivers supplies, weapons, equipment, and mail to United States forces in many parts of the world. Military cargo travels by ship, truck, or airplane. It must be handled carefully to ensure safe arrival at the correct destination. Cargo specialists load and unload military supplies and material using equipment such as forklifts and cranes. They also plan and organize loading schedules.

What They Do

Cargo specialists in the military perform some or all of the following duties:

- Load supplies into trucks, transport planes, and railroad cars using forklifts
- Load equipment such as jeeps, trucks, and weapons aboard ships, using dockyard cranes
- Pack and crate boxes of supplies for shipping
- Inspect cargo for damage
- Plan and inspect loads for balance and safety
- Check cargo against invoices to make sure the amount and destination of material are correct

Where They Work

Cargo specialists work outdoors on loading docks and indoors in warehouses.

Opportunities in Civilian Life

Civilian cargo specialists work for trucking firms, air cargo companies, and shipping lines. They perform duties similar to those of military cargo specialists. Depending on specialty, they may also be called industrial truck operators, stevedores, longshoremen, material handlers, or cargo checkers.

Physical Requirements

Cargo specialists must lift and carry heavy cargo.

Flight Engineers

Navy
Air Force
Marine Corps
Coast Guard

The military operates thousands of airplanes and helicopters. Pilots and air crew members rely upon trained personnel to keep aircraft ready to fly. Flight engineers inspect airplanes and helicopters before, during, and after flights to ensure safe and efficient operations. They also serve as crew members aboard military aircraft.

What They Do

Flight engineers in the military perform some or all of the following duties:

Inspect aircraft before and after flights, following pre- and postflight checklists

Plan and monitor the loading of passengers, cargo, and fuel

Assist pilots in engine start-up and shut-down

Compute aircraft load weights and fuel distribution

Compute fuel consumption using airspeed data, charts, and calculators

Monitor engine instruments and adjust engine controls following pilot orders

Check fuel, pressure, electrical, and other aircraft systems during flight

Inform pilot of aircraft performance problems and recommend corrective action

Opportunities in Civilian Life

Civilian flight engineers work for passenger and cargo airline companies. They perform the same duties as in the military.

Physical Requirements

Flight engineers, like pilots and navigators, have to be mentally alert and physically sound to perform their job. They must be in top physical shape and pass a special physical exam to qualify for flight duty.

Petroleum Supply Specialists

Army
Navy
Air Force
Marine Corps
Coast Guard

Ships, airplanes, trucks, tanks, and other military vehicles require large amounts of fuel and lubricants. These and other petroleum products require special storage and handling. Petroleum supply specialists store and ship petroleum products, such as oil, fuel, compressed gas, and lubricants.

What They Do

Petroleum supply specialists in the military perform some or all of the following duties:

Connect hoses and valves and operate pumps to load petroleum products into tanker trucks, airplanes, ships, and railroad cars

Test oils and fuels for pollutants

Repair pipeline systems, hoses, valves, and pumps

Check the volume and temperature of petroleum and gases in tankers, barges, and storage tanks

Prepare storage and shipping records

Store and move packaged petroleum products using forklifts

Where They Work

Petroleum supply specialists work outdoors in all types of weather while filling storage tanks and refueling airplanes, ships, and tankers.

Opportunities in Civilian Life

Civilian petroleum supply specialists work for oil refineries, pipeline companies, and tanker truck and ship lines. They may also refuel airplanes at large airports. They perform many of the same duties as military petroleum supply specialists.

Physical Requirements

Petroleum supply specialists may have to perform moderate to heavy lifting.

Quartermasters and Boat Operators

>   Army
>   Navy
>   Marine Corps
>   Coast Guard

The military operates many small boats for amphibious troop landings, harbor patrols, and transportation over short distances. Quartermasters and boat operators navigate and pilot many types of small watercraft, including tugboats, PT boats, gunboats, and barges.

What They Do

Quartermasters and boat operators in the military perform some or all of the following duties:

> Direct the course and speed of boats
>
> Consult maps, charts, weather reports, and navigation equipment
>
> Pilot tugboats when towing and docking barges and large ships
>
> Operate amphibious craft during troop landings
>
> Maintain boats and deck equipment
>
> Operate ship-to-shore radios
>
> Keep ship logs

Where They Work

Quartermasters and boat operators work aboard all types of boats and in all types of weather conditions. When not piloting boats, they may work on or below deck repairing boats and equipment or overseeing cargo storage. When ashore, they may work in offices that make nautical maps or in harbor management offices. Some boats are operated in combat situations.

Opportunities in Civilian Life

Civilian quartermasters and boat operators may work for shipping and cruise lines, piloting tugboats, ferries, and other small vessels. They perform duties similar to those of military quartermasters and boat operators. Depending upon specialty, they may also be called tugboat captains, motorboat operators, navigators, or pilots.

Physical Requirements

Quartermasters and boat operators may have to stand for several hours at a time. They must be able to speak clearly. Some specialties require normal depth perception and hearing.

Seamen

>   Army
>   Navy
>   Air Force
>   Coast Guard

All ships must have teams of individuals with "jack-of-all-trades" skills who make things run smoothly above deck. Seamen perform many duties to help operate and maintain military ships, boats, and submarines.

What They Do

Seamen in the military perform some or all of the following duties:

> Operate hoists, cranes, and winches to load cargo or set gangplanks
>
> Operate and maintain on-deck equipment and ship rigging
>
> Supervise firefighting and damage-control exercises
>
> Handle lines to secure vessels to wharves or other ships
>
> Stand watch for security, navigation, or communications
>
> Supervise crews painting and maintaining decks and sides of ships

Physical Requirements

Seamen may have to climb ships' rigging and perform work at heights. Their work often involves moderate to heavy lifting.

Where They Work

Seamen and deckhands work aboard all types of ships and submarines. On ships, they often work outdoors on deck while servicing shipboard equipment.

Opportunities in Civilian Life

Civilian seamen work primarily for shipping companies, sometimes called the Merchant Marine. They also work for cruise ship lines. They perform many duties similar to those of military seamen. They are called able seamen, deckhands, or boatswains.

Vehicle Drivers

Army
Navy
Marine Corps
Coast Guard

The military uses numerous vehicles to transport its troops, equipment, and supplies. Together, the services own and operate about 50,000 heavy trucks and buses. Vehicle drivers operate all types of heavy military vehicles. They drive fuel or water tank trucks, semi-tractor trailers, heavy troop transports, and passenger buses.

What They Do

Vehicle drivers in the military perform some or all of the following duties:

Read travel instructions to determine travel routes, arrival dates, and types of cargo

Make sure vehicles are loaded properly

Check oil, fuel and other fluid levels, and tire pressure

Drive vehicles over all types of roads, traveling alone or in convoys

Keep records of mileage driven and fuel and oil used

Wash vehicles and perform routine maintenance and repairs

Opportunities in Civilian Life

Civilian vehicle drivers work for trucking companies, moving companies, bus companies, and businesses with their own delivery fleets. They perform duties similar to those of military vehicle drivers. They may specialize as tractor-trailer truck drivers, tank truck drivers, heavy truck drivers, or bus drivers.

Physical Requirements

Normal color vision is required to read road maps.

COMBAT SPECIALTY OCCUPATIONS

Artillery Crew Members

Army
Navy
Marine Corps
Coast Guard

Artillery includes weapons that fire large shells or missiles. The military uses artillery to support infantry and tank units in combat. Artillery is also used to protect land and sea forces from air attack. Artillery crew members position, direct, and fire artillery guns, cannons, howitzers, missiles, and rockets to destroy enemy positions and aircraft. They normally specialize by type of artillery.

What They Do

Artillery crew members in the military perform some or all of the following duties:

Determine target location using computers or manual calculations

Set up and load artillery weapons

Prepare ammunition, fuses, and powder for firing

Fire artillery weapons according to instructions from artillery officers

Clean and maintain artillery weapons

Drive trucks and self-propelled artillery

Where They Work

Artillery crew members work outdoors when on land maneuvers. Some work in sheltered fire-control stations. At sea, they mainly work below deck.

Opportunities in Civilian Life

Although the job of artillery crew member has no equivalent in civilian life, the close teamwork, discipline, and leadership experiences it provides are helpful in many civilian jobs.

Physical Requirements

Artillery crew members must have physical stamina to perform strenuous activities for long periods without rest. They are also required to have normal color vision to identify color-coded ammunition and to read maps and charts.

Combat Engineers

Army

Navy

Marine Corps

Combat situations often require rapid travel across difficult terrain and swift-flowing rivers. A combination of combat ability and building skill is necessary to carry out field construction for fighting forces.

What They Do

Combat engineers perform some or all of the following duties:

- Construct trails, roads, and field fortifications, such as shelters, bunkers, and gun emplacements
- Erect floating or prefabricated bridges
- Lay and clear minefields and booby traps
- Place and detonate explosives, as needed
- Erect camouflage and other protective barriers for artillery and troop positions
- Load, unload, and move supplies and equipment, using planes, helicopters, trucks, and amphibious vehicles
- Construct airfields and perform ground traffic-control duties
- Participate in combat operations as infantrymen

Where They Work

Because combat engineers must be prepared to support operations anywhere in the world, they work and train for long hours under all kinds of weather conditions and in all climates. Combat engineers work, eat, and sleep outdoors during training exercises and in real combat situations. Most of the time, combat engineers are assigned to military bases.

Opportunities in Civilian Life

Although the job of combat engineer has no direct equivalent in civilian life, experience as a combat engineer is related to occupations in several civilian fields including the logging, mining, construction, shipping, and landscaping industries. Civilians in these jobs are called forestry aides, loggers, blasters, and construction workers.

Physical Requirements

Combat engineers must meet very demanding physical requirements. They need agility and balance and must be able to perform strenuous physical activities over long periods of time. Combat engineers lift and move heavy objects. Some specialties require good swimming abilities.

Infantrymen

Army

Marine Corps

The infantry is the main land combat force of the military. In peacetime, the infantry's role is to stay ready to defend our country. In combat, the role of the infantry is to capture or destroy enemy ground forces and repel enemy attacks. Infantrymen operate weapons and equipment to engage and destroy enemy ground forces.

What They Do

Infantrymen perform some or all of the following duties:

- Operate, clean, and store automatic weapons, such as rifles and machine guns
- Parachute from troop transport airplanes while carrying weapons and supplies
- Fire armor-piercing missiles from hand-held antitank missile launchers
- Carry out scouting missions to spot enemy troop movements and gun locations
- Operate two-way radios and signal equipment to relay battle orders
- Drive vehicles mounted with machine guns or small missiles
- Perform hand-to-hand combat drills that involve martial arts tactics
- Set firing angles and fire mortar shells at targets
- Dig foxholes, trenches, and bunkers for protection against attacks

Physical Requirements

The infantry has very demanding physical requirements. Infantrymen must perform strenuous physical activities, such as marching while carrying equipment, digging foxholes, and climbing over obstacles. Infantrymen need good hearing and clear speech to use two-way radios, and good night vision and depth perception to see targets and signals.

Where They Work

Because infantrymen must be prepared to go anywhere in the world they are needed, they work and train in all climates and weather conditions. During training exercises, as in real combat, infantrymen work, eat, and sleep outdoors. Most of the time, however, infantrymen work on military bases.

Opportunities in Civilian Life

Although the job of infantrymen has no equivalent in civilian life, the close teamwork, discipline, and leadership experiences it provides are helpful in many civilian jobs.

Special Operations Forces

Army

Navy

Air Force

Marine Corps

When the military has difficult and dangerous missions to perform, they call upon special operations teams. These elite combat forces stay in a constant state of readiness to strike anywhere in the world on a moment's notice. Special operations forces team members conduct offensive raids, demolitions, intelligence, search and rescue, and other missions from aboard aircraft, helicopters, ships, or submarines. Because of the wide variety of missions, special operations forces team members are trained swimmers, parachutists, and survival experts, in addition to being combat trained.

What They Do

Special operations team members in the military perform some or all of the following duties:

Go behind enemy lines to recruit, train, and equip friendly forces for guerrilla raids

Carry out demolition raids against enemy military targets, such as bridges, railroads, and fuel depots

Clear mine fields, both underwater and on land

Conduct missions to gather intelligence information on enemy military forces

Conduct offensive raids or invasions of enemy territories

Destroy enemy ships in coastal areas, using underwater explosives

Where They Work

Because special operations teams must be prepared to go anywhere in the world they are needed, team members train and work in all climates, weather conditions, and settings. They may dive from submarines or small underwater craft. Special forces team members may also be exposed to harsh temperatures, often without protection, during missions in enemy-controlled areas. Most of the time, however, they work and train on military bases or ships and submarines.

Opportunities in Civilian Life

Although the job of special operations team member has no equivalent in civilian life, training in explosives, bomb disposal, scuba diving, and swimming may be helpful in such civilian jobs as blaster, police bomb disposal specialist, diver, or swimming instructor. The discipline and dependability of special operations forces are assets in many civilian occupations.

Physical Requirements

The special operations forces have very demanding physical requirements. Good eyesight, night vision, and physical conditioning are required to reach mission objectives by parachute, overland, or under water. Also required is excellent hand-eye coordination to detonate or deactivate explosives. In most instances, special operations team members are required to be qualified divers, parachutists, and endurance runners.

Tank Crew Members

Army

Marine Corps

In peacetime, the role of tank and armor units is to stay ready to defend our country anywhere in the world. In combat, their role is to operate tanks and amphibious assault vehicles to engage and destroy the enemy. Tanks also conduct scouting missions and support infantry units during combat. Tank crew members work as a team to operate armored equipment and fire weapons to destroy enemy positions. Tank crew members normally specialize by type of armor, such as tanks or amphibious assault vehicles.

What They Do

Tank crew members in the military perform some or all of the following duties:

- Drive tanks or amphibious assault vehicles in combat formations over roadways, rough terrain, and in heavy surf
- Operate target-sighting equipment to aim guns
- Load and fire guns
- Operate two-way radios and signaling equipment to receive and relay battle orders
- Gather and report information about the terrain, enemy strength, and target location
- Perform preventive maintenance on tanks, guns, and equipment
- Read maps, compasses, and battle plans

Where They Work

Tank crew members, like other combat troops, work in all climates and weather conditions. During training exercises, as in real combat conditions, tank crew members work, eat, and sleep outdoors and in tanks.

Opportunities in Civilian Life

Although the job of tank crew member has no equivalent in civilian life, the close teamwork, discipline, and leadership experiences it provides are helpful in many civilian jobs.

Physical Requirements

Tank crew members must be in good physical condition and have exceptional stamina. They must be able to work inside the confined area of a tank for long periods of time. Good vision and normal color vision are required in order to read maps, drive vehicles around obstacles, and locate targets.

Wiley Publishing, Inc.
End-User License Agreement

READ THIS. You should carefully read these terms and conditions before opening the software packet(s) included with this book "Book." This is a license agreement "Agreement" between you and Wiley Publishing, Inc. "WPI." By opening the accompanying software packet(s), you acknowledge that you have read and accept the following terms and conditions. If you do not agree and do not want to be bound by such terms and conditions, promptly return the Book and the unopened software packet(s) to the place you obtained them for a full refund.

1. **License Grant.** WPI grants to you (either an individual or entity) a nonexclusive license to use one copy of the enclosed software program(s) (collectively, the "Software") solely for your own personal or business purposes on a single computer (whether a standard computer or a workstation component of a multi-user network). The Software is in use on a computer when it is loaded into temporary memory (RAM) or installed into permanent memory (hard disk, CD-ROM, or other storage device). WPI reserves all rights not expressly granted herein.

2. **Ownership.** WPI is the owner of all right, title, and interest, including copyright, in and to the compilation of the Software recorded on the physical packet included with this Book "Software Media". Copyright to the individual programs recorded on the Software Media is owned by the author or other authorized copyright owner of each program. Ownership of the Software and all proprietary rights relating thereto remain with WPI and its licensers.

3. **Restrictions on Use and Transfer.**

   (a) You may only (i) make one copy of the Software for backup or archival purposes, or (ii) transfer the Software to a single hard disk, provided that you keep the original for backup or archival purposes. You may not (i) rent or lease the Software, (ii) copy or reproduce the Software through a LAN or other network system or through any computer subscriber system or bulletin-board system, or (iii) modify, adapt, or create derivative works based on the Software.

   (b) You may not reverse engineer, decompile, or disassemble the Software. You may transfer the Software and user documentation on a permanent basis, provided that the transferee agrees to accept the terms and conditions of this Agreement and you retain no copies. If the Software is an update or has been updated, any transfer must include the most recent update and all prior versions.

4. **Restrictions on Use of Individual Programs.** You must follow the individual requirements and restrictions detailed for each individual program on the Software Media. These limitations are also contained in the individual license agreements recorded on the Software Media. These limitations may include a requirement that after using the program for a specified period of time, the user must pay a registration fee or discontinue use. By opening the Software packet(s), you agree to abide by the licenses and restrictions for these individual programs that are detailed on the Software Media. None of the material on this Software Media or listed in this Book may ever be redistributed, in original or modified form, for commercial purposes.

5. **Limited Warranty.**

   (a) WPI warrants that the Software and Software Media are free from defects in materials and workmanship under normal use for a period of sixty (60) days from the date of purchase of this Book. If WPI receives notification within the warranty period of defects in materials or workmanship, WPI will replace the defective Software Media.

   (b) WPI AND THE AUTHOR(S) OF THE BOOK DISCLAIM ALL OTHER WARRANTIES, EXPRESS OR IMPLIED, INCLUDING WITHOUT LIMITATION IMPLIED WARRANTIES OF MERCHANTABILITY AND FITNESS FOR A PARTICULAR PURPOSE, WITH RESPECT TO THE SOFTWARE, THE PROGRAMS, THE SOURCE CODE CONTAINED THEREIN, AND/OR THE TECHNIQUES DESCRIBED IN THIS BOOK. WPI DOES NOT WARRANT THAT THE FUNCTIONS CONTAINED IN THE SOFTWARE WILL MEET YOUR REQUIREMENTS OR THAT THE OPERATION OF THE SOFTWARE WILL BE ERROR FREE.

   (c) This limited warranty gives you specific legal rights, and you may have other rights that vary from jurisdiction to jurisdiction.